THE LAW'S ULTIMATE FRONTIER: TOWARDS AN ECOLOGICAL JURISPRUDENCE

Private international law can be seen as a repository of normative ideas about the foreign, and more metaphorically, about our cultural other (the alien) and our (social) relationship to our own outside (nature). Its methods compose a baroque assemblage of highly elaborate legal concepts, theories, doctrines, definitions and tools, that are often understood on an exclusively technical register as part of a rationalist project of legal ordering, purportedly devoid of any political significance. Yet a shadowy, 'minor jurisprudence' of pluralistic entanglement (composed of 'rattachements' or in Latour's terms, 'ligatures') invites us to explore an alternative ecology in jurisprudential but also aesthetic, ontological, ethical and political-economic terms. Law in this perspective is not disembedded, but belongs to the world.

Volume 14 in the series Hart Monographs in Transnational and International Law

Hart Monographs in Transnational and International Law

Series Editor: Craig Scott, Professor of Law, Osgoode Hall Law School of York University, Toronto

The objective of this series is to publish high-quality scholarship in public international law and private international law, as well as work that adopts "transnational law" as its thematic, theoretical or doctrinal focus. The series strives to be a leading venue for work of the following sort:

* critical reappraisals of foundational concepts and core doctrinal principles of both public and private international law, and their operation in practice, including insights drawn from general legal theory;
* analysis and development of conceptions of 'transnational law', including in relation to the role of unofficial law and informal processes in transnational regulation and in relation to theories and studies of 'governance' in transnational spheres; and
* empirical studies of the emergence, evolution and transformation of international and/or transnational legal orders, including accounts and explanations of how law is constructed within different communities of interpretation and practice.

In relation to the first of these categories, the series especially welcomes monographs that explore the interactions between the ever-integrating fields of public and private international law. Of special interest are explorations of the extent to which these interactions are structured by higher-order principles and policies, on the one hand, and by politics and the exercise of various forms of power, on the other hand.

The series is open to work not only by law scholars but also by scholars from cognate disciplines.

Recent titles in this series

Transnational Terrorism and State Accountability: A New Theory of Prevention
Vincent-Joël Proulx

Transconstitutionalism
Marcelo Neves translated by Kevin Mundy

The Institutional Problem in Modern International Law
Richard Collins

Liability for Transboundary Pollution at the Intersection of Public and Private International Law
Guillaume Laganière

Faith in Courts: Human Rights Advocacy and the Transnational Regulation of Religion
Lisa Harms

The Law's Ultimate Frontier: Towards an Ecological Jurisprudence: A Global Horizon in Private International Law
Horatia Muir Watt

The Law's Ultimate Frontier: Towards an Ecological Jurisprudence

A Global Horizon in Private International Law

Horatia Muir Watt

•HART•
OXFORD • LONDON • NEW YORK • NEW DELHI • SYDNEY

HART PUBLISHING

Bloomsbury Publishing Plc

Kemp House, Chawley Park, Cumnor Hill, Oxford, OX2 9PH, UK

1385 Broadway, New York, NY 10018, USA

29 Earlsfort Terrace, Dublin 2, Ireland

First published in Great Britain 2023

A catalogue record for this book is available from the British Library.

A catalogue record for this book is available from the Library of Congress.

ISBN: HB: 978-1-50994-010-3
ePDF: 978-1-50994-012-7
ePub: 978-1-50994-011-0

Typeset by Compuscript Ltd, Shannon

Preface

**to Karen Knop and to Bruno Latour, both of whom died so near to the day this book finally went to press (October 2022) and whose work has been a source of profound intellectual inspiration*

How has law (our Western modern *nomos*) shaped our relationship to what we perceive to be our natural world? If we accept that the concept of 'nature' has a profoundly ideological dimension – so that, as Bruno Latour has pointed out, the adjective 'natural' does not always point to the same nature, and indeed 'has changed camps', – our future depends upon a radical shift in perspective. No amount of recycling, green engineering or even 'environmental law' (however desirable *per se*) will suffice unless we rethink the (our) 'second' nature as a social problem. This book questions the role that legality has played or continues to play in the alienation of our modern cultural world from the needs of all other forms of life that coinhabit our planet. While the imprint of law on our *epistemê* or schemes of intelligibility of reality, on our mental categories and foundational myths, has been explored by excellent historians, it is harder to find a reflection on what a specifically ecological jurisprudence might look like today, in the shadow of planetary disaster. To undertake such an enterprise is all the more daunting that it is likely to push law to its ultimate limits – at least beyond those of our (largely Roman) legal tradition. This is where, among the many expressions of our normative universe, the discipline known as the conflict of laws will come into play as a heuristic within a wider debate on the shape of legality at its own last frontier.

Formally, then, this is a study of a sub-discipline within the law, also known as private international law. Under most accounts, the latter is dedicated to the juridical regulation of crossborder interactions between non-state actors. However, the content of this book is probably unrecognisable as such by many lawyers working inside this particular field. More specifically, in its attempts to use the conflict of laws to shed light on the ways in which law affects our understanding of our surrounding world, it contains relatively little reference to positive 'sources' or more standard doctrinal scholarship on environmental issues in transnational private relationships. On the contrary, it aims to renew classical approaches in the belief that this apparently modest brand of legality contains many notions which resonate powerfully among the various contemporary strands of anthropological, political, historical or feminist theory that are currently grappling with the homogenisation of lifeforms on our earth, cultural and biological extinction, or individual and societal dissociation. Reciprocally, from its specific location at the very outposts of law, the contention here is that the conflict of laws has much to offer in terms of the less visible underside of the contemporary 'turns' – variously understood as global, technological, digital, neoliberal or ontological – that all involve changing perceptions of alterity.

This whole endeavour has involved a large amount of amateur interdisciplinary borrowing – a form of intensive *bricolage* (resonating with the doctrinal concepts of 'adaptation', 'incorporation' and *dépeçage* among the legal technologies of the conflict of laws). I am immensely indebted to all those who, from the perspective of many other fields of knowledge, have kindly agreed to explain, change and comment on concepts, theories and ideas imported from elsewhere and used in unorthodox ways.

In this respect, I am very grateful to the *Institut Universitaire de France* for having provided me with the means, in the past two years (and despite the pandemic!) to have run the 'Globinar' seminar series at Sciences Po, Paris (along with my accomplices Helena Alviar, Gunter Frankenberg, Jorge Esquirol and the supporting team of wonderful doctoral students: Lucia, Agatha, Megan, Sandrine, Omar, Nicolas, Teodora and Alexia), and thereby to test and enrich various intuitions through discussions with researchers from all around the globe. As a result, the current edition of the Globinar (renamed 'Recitals', post-pandemic) now encompasses a wider interdisciplinary project devoted to the promotion of the Political Humanities, under aegis of Sciences Po colleagues Helena Alviar (again) and Astrid von Busekist, Ariel Colomonos, Frédéric Gros and Frédérique Leichter-Flack, to whom I express similar gratitude. Particular thanks are also due to Teodora Groza and Elena Divry for having accepted to serve as sounding boards for the initial stages of the book, to Jorge Esquirol, Ruth Sefton-Green, Astrid von Busekist and Jacco Bomhoff for their judicious re-reading and comments. A warm acknowledgement is due to Robert Wai for his invitation to present some very early thoughts at Osgoode Hall Law School: a discussion that led very directly to this book. Thereafter, Hans Lindahl and Ralf Michaels have shared generous observations in the context of research seminars in Tilburg and Hamburg, where I was invited to present parts of this book. Craig Scott's attentive re-reading as director of this series in which this book takes its place has been invaluable – and added much value. Finally, this book would not have seen the day without the invaluable assistance, advice and intellectual input of Felipe Gomes de Almeida Albuquerque.

Some of the guest panellists we have been privileged to hear at the Globinar are also the authors of work that has been crucial in putting together the elements of the argument herein (although of course they are not to blame for the final result!). Among these publications, some are so important – they might be described as the 'but-fors' of this book (echoing concepts of causation in climate change at stake in the discussion below) – that they are cited very often, and frequently by sole reference to the title of a particular work or article. These include PG Monateri's extraordinary *Dominus Mundi* (2018); Aldo Schiavone's *Ius. L'invenzione del diritto in Occidente* (2005); Lauren Benton's *A Search for Sovereignty* (2010); Poul Kjaer's *The Law of Political Economy* (2020); Karen Knop* and Annelise Riles' 'Space, Time, and Historical Injustice: A Feminist Conflict-of-Laws Approach to the Comfort Women Agreement'(2017); Martti Koskenniemi's 'Rethinking the Prehistory of International law' B Kingsbury and B Straumann (eds), *The Roman Foundations of the Law of Nations* (2010); Ralph Michaels' 'Law and Recognition: Towards a Relational

Concept of law' (2019); Alain Pottage's introduction, 'The fabrication of persons and things', in Pottage and Munday, *Law, Anthropology and the Constitution of the Social* (2004); and Shaun McVeigh's *Jurisprudence of jurisdiction* (2007). Many thanks too to Richard Janda, for having shared his as-yet-unpublished work in progress on *Panarchy* (cited below as 'forthcoming').

In addition, beyond the legal field *largo sensu*, particular hommage is due to Corinne Pelluchon's *Pour Comprendre Levinas* (2020), Silviano Santiago 's *The Space in-between: Essays on Latin American Culture* (2002); Philippe Descola's *Par delà Nature et Culture* (2005), Eduardo Viveiros de Castro, *The Relative Native_ Essays on Indigenous Conceptual Worlds* (HAU, 2016) and with Deborah Danowski, *The Ends of the World* (Polity Press, 2017). And of course, last but most, Bruno Latour's* monumental *Enquête sur les modes d'existence* (2012).

Paris, May 2022

Contents

Introduction: Inklings

THIS BOOK ATTEMPTS to focus on a (faint) horizon[1] that might be called 'ecological jurisprudence'.[2] It is an invitation, in the context of the 'global turn' in law,[3] to explore the ways in which modern legality shapes our[4] relationship to alterity, understood as all the other (cultural) lifeworlds and (biological) forms of life that – often imperceptibly – co-inhabit our earth alongside ourselves, and upon which we depend for our own survival.[5] It is also a search for the inklings of an alternative view of the law[6] – an inquiry as it

[1] The aptly ecological metaphor of the horizon is a reference to the phenomenological philosophy of Emmanuel Levinas. Therein, our horizon is 'split' insofar as it is constituted by alterity. The latter is the central thread that weaves through this book. In *Pour Comprendre Levinas* (Paris, Seuil, 2020), Corinne Pelluchon observes (p 37) that in contemporary philosophy, the notion of horizon has replaced the traditional concept of truth. We return to this point more specifically below, in Part III.

[2] As the idea of 'jurisprudence' suggests, this book has a theoretical dimension, but it does not engage with the classical analytical legal theory conventionally associated with the term. While the latter may arguably retain some rich potential to think about law in contemporary (or, as will be seen below, 'post-monist') terms (as developed for instance by Neil Walker, *Intimations of Global Law* (Cambridge, Cambridge University Press 2015)), this book draws on alternative jurisprudential strands (as in the critique of international law by S McVeigh (ed), *Jurisprudence of Jurisdiction* (New York, Routledge, 2007); or as in the idea of law's 'residues', P Goodrich, *Law in the Courts of Love. Literature and Other Minor Jurisprudences* (Routledge, 2013); or again, the pluriversal 'jurisprudence of the border' of W Mignolo, *Local Histories/Global Designs: Coloniality, Subaltern Knowledges, and Border Thinking* (Princeton NJ, Princeton University Press, 2000).

[3] M Xifaras, 'The Global Turn in Legal Theory' (2016) XXIX *Canadian Journal of Law & Jurisprudence* 215–43. As will become apparent below, the 'private' dimension of contemporary globalisation explains the significance of the private international forms of legality in the context described here. The 'era of the 'post'' (Xifaras' expression) will be understood below to be 'post-monist'.

[4] 'Our' here refers to the largely dominant, globalised understanding of law associated according to context with modernity (B Latour, *Enquête sur les modes d'existence. Une anthropologie des modernes* (Paris, La Découverte, 2012)), naturalism (P Descola, *Par delà nature et culture* (Paris, Gallimard, 2005), humanity (as opposed to other species or the 'natural' world), coloniality (as distinct from colonialism: see Mignolo, *Local Histories/Global Designs*), the West (or the Global North), 'white mythology' (J Derrida, 'La mythologie blanche', *Marges de la philosophie* (Paris, 1972)), neoliberal capitalism (and the production of *homo economicus et juridicus*). See too, more recently, for a critique of modernity along similar lines, the political-ecological approach of P Charbonnier, *Abondance et liberté. Une histoire environnementale des idées politiques* (Paris, La Découverte, 2022). These various categories will be spelt out progressively below, as will their relationship with further categories such as enlightenment thought.

[5] The expressions 'lifeworld' and 'form of life' will be used, in unorthodox but increasingly widespread fashion as synonyms throughout this book. Moreover, each will be understood as having both a cultural (including legal) and natural (meaning biological) dimension. The former (*Lebenswelt*) refers to the world 'as lived' phenomenologically, that is prior to reflective representation or analysis, as in Husserl's *Crisis of European Sciences* (1936), to which we return below 131. The latter (*Lebensform*) is associated with language games in Wittgenstein's *Philosophical Investigations* (on which see further below 30).

[6] This exercise has been attempted, in various ways, by F Ost *La nature hors la loi: l'écologie à l'épreuve du droit* (Paris, La Découverte, 2002); F Capra & U Mattei, *The Ecology of Law. Toward a Legal System in Tune with Nature and Community* (San Francisco CA, Berrett-Kohler Publishers, 2015; M-A Hermitte, 'Artificialisation de la nature et droit(s) du vivant' in P Descola (ed), *Les Natures en question*

were into law's 'second nature'.[7] Such an endeavor involves a perilous exercise in interdisciplinarity,[8] so as to follow various moves outside the legal field that take us beyond the confines of our 'naturalist' cosmological vision[9] – that is, the epistemological, ontological, aesthetic and ethical schemes, consciousness, world view or *episteme* that underlie Western,[10] late-modern, forms of life and modes

(coédition Odile Jacob/Collège de France, 2018) 257–84. We await the forthcoming work of Richard Janda on the possible forms of law in a future 'Panarchy' beyond extinction (see within this work, 'The Withering Away of the State', and further ideas for 'A New Constitution') of which we have had a sample in his presentation for the 'Globinar' (Sciencespo/blog/pilagg), session of 21 April 2022. And co-written by the same author on the specific question of the conflict of laws and nature (or non-human laws), see R Janda and R Lehun, 'The Conflict of Human and Nonhuman Laws' in I Braverman (ed) *Animals, Biopolitics, Law: Lively Legalities* (Abingdon, Routledge, 2017) 175. More recently still, on the concept of 'earthly legalities', see A Pottage, 'Why Nature Has No Rights', forthcoming in A Alvarez-Nakagawa & C Douzinas (eds) *Non-Human Rights. Critical Perspectives* (Cheltenham, Elgar, 2023).

[7] The reference to the first and second natures (in law and politics), is to Hobbes' *Leviathan*, ch XIV (see below 145). It is taken up by Latour in his *Enquête*. Law's 'nature' suggests both the constant reference to nature ('natural law' and 'the state of nature') in theoretical discourses about the law, and the ruse of modern 'naturalism', consisting in 'naturalising' modernity's schemes of thought, including in respect of the law (that is, creating the illusion of their non artificiality or non-artifactuality: on this ruse, see Descola, *Par delà nature et culture* 349). Law's 'second nature' evokes, ironically, the belief in its ontological status as a given, but also the idea that there may be a further legal ecology to be discovered. On 'second nature' as a 'civilising' process of self-control that separated nature and culture, see H Mazurel *L'inconscient ou l'oubli de l'histoire, Profondeurs, métamorphoses et révolutions de la vie affective* (Paris, La Découverte, 2021) 313. The critique of the severance between nature and culture within the 'ontological turn' in French anthropology echoes the feminist challenge to scientific theories of gender (see E Fox Keller, *The Mirage of a Space Between Nature and Nurture* (Durham NC, Duke University Press, 2011).

[8] The epistemological difficulties are considerable. As will be seen below, the division of disciplines – and our modes of thinking – among hard/social sciences/humanities is precisely a central part of the problem. Two outstanding scholars have been able to bring together private international law (or the law of jurisdiction) and various aspects of climate science, see M Valverde, *Chronotopes of Law: Jurisdiction, Scale and Governance* (Abingdon, Routledge, 2015); S Jasanoff, *Designs on Nature: Science and Democracy in Europe and the United States* (Princeton NJ, Princeton Univ Press, 2010). Interdisciplinarity is not of course a magic wand (Valverde, *Chronotopes of Law* 69, 77). In what follows below, the 'borrowing' from disciplines outside the law is necessarily amateur and involves a large amount of randomness and cherry-picking. In no way does the author claim to 'be' a philosopher, an anthropologist, a climate scientist, a historian, etc.

[9] In the vocabulary of the 'ontological turn' in French anthropological critique of modernity (that is, contemporary Western practices and thought processes), 'naturalism' is a scheme ingrained in the mental categories of modernity, that links humankind to the physical substance of its worldly surroundings, but excludes the non-human by reason of its absence of mind (Descartes) or soul (as in the sixteenth-century Valladolid controversy in respect of the indigenous inhabitants of the new world : see Descola, *Par delà nature et culture* 114 et seq). It refers to the new order instituted by ontological and epistemological revolutions that accompanied the Westphalian, secular, international settlement in the seventeenth century, along with the emergence of Hobbes' sovereign Leviathan (before that of the Hegelian state) and the beginnings of the colonial imperialism that culminated in the late nineteenth century with the institution of modern public international law. We shall return to these elements throughout this book. This new order in turn prepared the terrain for the rise of the market and then of neoliberal economics as a secular religion, that would secrete and extend its *nomos* to the world within and beyond the modern state.

[10] 'Western' is a highly indeterminate concept of which the contours and signification change constantly over time and according to context (see P-G Monateri, *Comparative Legal Methods, Elgar Advanced Introductions* (Cheltenham, Edward Elgar, 2021) 40 et seq). As Monateri points out, generally, the moving divide between the 'West' and the 'Rest', meaning the (oriental, exotic or corrupted) East, or the (underdeveloped, premodern, indigenous) South, reflects a self-understanding of the West as a space of freedom – as opposed to empire (Byzantine, seen from Rome), monarchies (old Europe, seen from the United States), populism (dictatorships of the global South, seen from Northern Europe) etc. Often this same divide is associated with the equally floating notion of 'culture' as a supposedly epistemological category (on which more below). Here, the use of 'Western' to characterise the 'we' from the perspective of whom this book is

of thought.[11] At stake, at this ultimate frontier of the latter, is the survival of legality as a 'mode of existence'. In exploring the ways in which we[12] relate to alterity on the terms of the law, the project of this book is to outline a (somewhat unusual) perspective of 'planetary responsibility' adapted to the challenges of the Anthropocene. The Anthropocene, understood as an irrevocable turning point in the geology, biosphere and ecosystems of the earth,[13] enjoins humanity to 'come to terms with Gaia'.[14]

written, refers to the modern mindset or *episteme* that took root in Europe towards the seventeenth century (often equated in international law to the Westphalian legal order) and which continues to assert its sway today (in science, the 'humanities', politics, law, etc). As such it is part of the various concepts that express the deep shaping of our (individual and collective) intellectual and emotional attitudes (see below).

[11] 'Late modernity' can be understood as signifying a 'naturalist' cosmological vision, but also the liberal political settlement that allowed or condoned, variously, the colonial regime or our faith in (neoliberal) economics as science. As will be further developed in this book, all these moves involved distanciation (of autonomous human subjects from their natural surroundings) and hierarchy (subjection of Nature to the free will of humankind). Whether the 'culprit' is humanity, modernity or capital is a debate that will be picked up at various points in this book. Ideas, including those that we inherit and interiorise collectively through law, are essential. Nevertheless, these alone are not enough to change power processes: this is the basic insight both of Michel Foucault's genealogical approach to modern thought, and to Bruno Latour's in sciences and technology studies, with significant implications for the study of law.

[12] As to who 'we' are in the text, see nn 10 and 11 above. 'Western' and 'late-modern' are both referents. For those whose horizons already include resistance to this dominant posture (in the form of indigenous, sacred, feminist, environmentalist nomos) this may assume too little about what is already present in 'law' (see for example, among the prolific work of feminist-environmentalist V Shiva, *Ecofeminism* (New Delhi, Kali for Women, and Zed Books, UK, 1993). But the project in this book has an important excavatory dimension, which requires a slow wading-through before reaching its more elevating dimensions present in Part II and the second chapter of Part III.

[13] *Anthropoceneas* (*anthropos* = 'human being', *kainos* = 'new, recent') is a term ascribed to Nobel prize-winner Paul Krutzen in 2000, to designate the geological epoch following after the present interglacial Holocene. On the state of the debate among geologists and stratigraphers as to the very definition and possible dating of the Anthropocene, see in particular C Bonneuil and J-B Fressoz, *L'événement Anthropocène* (Paris, ed du Seuil, 2013) 18; C Hamilton, C Bonneuil and F Gemenne (eds), *The Anthropocene and the Global Environmental Crisis. Rethinking Modernity in a new epoch* (Abingdon, Routledge Environmental Humanities, 2015). On the ways to approach climate science and controversies over issues such as global warming, we defer here, like Dipesh Chakrabarty, to 'the scientific consensus around the proposition that the present crisis of climate change is man-made' (see 'The Climate of History: Four Theses' (2009) 35(2) *Critical Inquiry* 197–22) the human having acquired 'geological agency' (see again, Bonneuil and Fressoz, *L'événement Anthropocène*). But beyond such debates, as Bonneuil and Fressoz observe, the concept has become a rallying point for climate and earth scientists, historians, philosophers, and citizens in a quest to rethink our age as witness to the irrevocable imprint of human life on the earth (*terra incognita*), that is, its geological resources, biosphere and ecosystems and the prospect of extinction of *homo sapiens* (for the effects of such a prospect on law, see Janda, 'Panarchy'). On the anthropocene itself as a juridical artefact, see A Pottage, *Globinar*, Sciences po, May 2022.

[14] As Bruno Latour reminds us (in *Face à Gaia*, 77), Gaia (an ecological concept or 'hypothesis' attributed to the earth scientist James Lovelock, in *The Revenge of Gaia, Why the Earth is Fighting Back and How We Can Still Save Humanity*) is neither reassuring, maternal, nor rational, nor a unitary, organic divinity, nor indeed a giant thermostat, but the sum of multiple, unpredictable, awe-inspiring retroactions of the earth system, causing fearful irruptions of deep eco-bio-chemical processes into our lives. Gaia is not the globe, nor mother-earth, nor indeed Nature as we have imagined it since the seventeenth century as a mirror of our human subjectivity, but an anthropological, political, philosophical and economic event, an irruption in our lives of the unforeseen effects of human action (see too Bonneuil and Fressoz, *L'événement Anthropocène* 58). On the dark and paradoxical side of Gaia, developed by Lovelock in collaboration with Royal Dutch Shell, see L Aronowsky, 'Gas guzzling Gaia; or, a prehistory of climate change denialism' (2021) 47 *Critical Inquiry* 306–27, 327, and below 245–247.

This bio-political[15] injunction is to live in intelligence with the limited resources of the earth and the diverse modes of existence of its inhabitants and, by the same token, to reverse our destructive forgetfulness of the world we inhabit. It also signifies that the accelerated conflation of geological time and human history is not 'merely' a geophysical change; it is also a profoundly political[16] and indeed legal event (perhaps even a juridical artefact[17]), as shown by increasingly frequent and urgent calls for 'environmental justice' (a half-century at least after such calls were already vocal enough to be heard). In this respect, the observers of the 'earth system'[18] foresee that we are at the threshold of a new era of extreme violence for both humanity and non-human life forms, a looming apocalyptic struggle for the *nomos* of the earth.[19] How then to acknowledge, in legal terms, nature's 'splendid alterity'[20] before the

[15] This is not necessarily the habitual use of the concept we owe to Michel Foucault, in *Naissance de la biopolitique* (Cours au Collège de France 1978–79), ed M Senellart (Paris, Gallimard-Seuil, coll ' Hautes Études', 2004). 'Biopolitics' has become a central concept in contemporary political theory, particularly through its use by the 'Italian school' in respect of the exercise of sovereignty over the body or 'bare life' (to which we shall return later in the book). In Foucault's own work, the expression referred to the rise of a new 'object' for the liberal art of government: the 'population', in its biological existence and attendant issues of health, demography and hygiene (see F Gros, D Lorenzini, A Revel, A Sforzini, 'Introduction', (2013) 4 (52) *Raisons politiques* 5).

[16] Perhaps the most important question for understanding the political economy of the 'global turn': see Chakrabarty, 'The Climate of History: Four Theses', asking (p 197) 'if … globalization and global warming are born of overlapping processes, the question is, How do we bring them together in our understanding of the world?'

[17] Meaning that it is coproduced by law: see Jasanoff, *Designs on Nature*; on law as artefact, Pottage, *Globinar*. See too, P Fitzpatrick, 'Marxism and Legal Pluralism' (1983) 46 *Australian Journal of Law & Society* ('Modern law depends on science and cannot enter some of science's realms. But science itself depends operatively and integrally on law. Law and science are mutually supportive and interdependent, yet the maintenance of their effectuality in this requires them to be significantly independent of and opposed to each other'). On the epistemology of science from a social scientific and 'humanities' perspective, see S Jasanoff, *Can Sciences Make Sense of Life?* (Cambridge, Polity, New Human Frontiers Series, 2018) (and on co production more generally Jasanoff, *Designs on Nature*).

[18] The term 'earth system' is preferable to those of 'environment' (suggesting a non-political outside), or ecological 'crisis' (assuming a horizon of normality to which we can aspire to return) or 'sustainable development' (implying an irenic future and a highly contested concept of progress) or (associated) 'externalities' (meaning that the problem of humanity's imprint upon the biosphere can be distanced, calculated in economic terms, and is somewhere outside of ourselves).

[19] P-G Monateri, *Dominus Mundi, Political Sublime and the World Order* (Oxford, Hart, 2018) esp p 1 et seq (as announced by Carl Schmitt's terrifying political theology: *The nomos of the Earth in the International law of the Jus Publicum Europaeum* (New York, Telos Press, 2006) 354: 'our times will witness the last round of the terrible struggle for a law of the planet, and the winner will become the master of the world. The winner will take possession of the whole globe – land, air and sea – dividing and assigning it according to his will and pleasure. But the sea, vast and void, will not last in the new order.' Schmitt himself links his theory to the theology of the Revelation (21:1): 'Then I saw a new heaven and a new earth, for the first heaven and the first earth had passed away, and there was no longer any sea'. *Cf* the passage, contained in Seneca's *Medea*, written more than fourteen hundred years before Colón set out into the unknown: 'There will come an age in the far-off years when Ocean shall unloose the bonds of things, when the whole broad earth shall be revealed …' (www.theoi.com/Text/SenecaMedea.html). On Monateri's resounding critique of Schmittian political theology, see below, Part II. On the literal and a-contextual use of texts such as Schmitt's, that was evidently not intended as a statement about ecological extinction, see below).

[20] 'La mise à sac irréfléchie des ressources de la planète et la destruction de sa diversité biotique reposent sur l'oubli de cette croyance des premiers âges de la modernité que la splendide altérité de la nature est nécessaire à la manifestation des spécificités de l'humanité' (Descola, *Par delà nature et culture* 675).

winner of the last round becomes master of the planet and the sea, vast and void, disappears?[21]

A very preliminary trace (the barest of inklings) of the contention that runs through this book is the unconsciously ecological imagery that has become something of a trope within the discipline of the conflict of laws. The latter has been depicted as a 'quaking quagmire' in a 'dismal swamp', meaning that it is unhelpfully complicated, often incomprehensible to lay readers and moreover unscientific and jargonic.[22] In what follows below, the swamp will appear as a complex ecosystem that occurs in many shapes across the continents of the world,[23] a site of indeterminate perimeter, of (often uncanny) alterity and shadowy exchanges, inhabited by visible and invisible forms of life in spectral, fairylike, residual and in-between forms.[24] The proposal here is to reframe this metaphor as an alternative vision of legality, whether within the current scope of the conflict of laws or beyond, at the uncertain frontiers of modern law itself, via 'hybridisms, strategic appropriations and re-readings',[25] as mooted in the field of literary critique under the banner of 'tropical cartesianism'.

I. NATURE AS ALTERITY IN LEGAL FORM

The axial argument here is that the ways in which we treat our biological and physical surroundings are indissociable from our legal approach towards alterity.[26] The assumption moreover is that our legal approach to difference, and indeed to what we perceive to be our 'environment', is entwined in turn with our cultural (social, political, psychological, epistemological) attitudes in respect of the foreign, the alien, the uncanny or the strange. The underlying intuition takes its cue from Philippe Descola's proposal that the most productive prism through which to understand 'cultural diversity' – that is, the diverse ways in which human communities make sense of the world – is through their distinctive schemes of 'identification and relation'.[27] This suggests

[21] Monateri, *Dominus Mundi*.

[22] These expressions are attributed (by S Reed and HF Goodrich, 'Forward. Directive or Dialectic?' (1953) 6 *Vanderbilt Law Review* 441 to Dean William Prosser: 'The realm of conflict of laws is a dismal swamp filled with quaking quagmires and inhabited by learned but eccentric professors who theorize about mysterious matters in a strange and incomprehensible jargon.' See for a canonical example of the use of the trope, RJ Nordstrom, 'Ohio's Borrowing Statute of Limitations – A Quaking Quagmire in a Dismal Swamp', 16 *Ohio St LJ* 183 (1955) and very recently, in the controversy over the methodology used by the authors of the Third Restatement of the conflict of laws in the United States, by L Brilmayer: https://tlblog.org/a-theory-less-restatement-for-conflict-of-laws/.

[23] www.nationalgeographic.org/encyclopedia/swamp/.

[24] On spectres, shadows, residues, and in-between ontologies, see progressively below.

[25] F Coelho, 'Improvisations of a Tropical Cartesianism' (2011) 7(1) *Critical Studies in Improvisation: Brazilian Improvisations*. On the tropical understanding of the 'in-between' and its relevance for law, see below, Part II.

[26] On the idea that the singularity of each 'legal culture' is linked to the play of similarity and difference, see L Friedman, *A History of American Law*, 4th edn (Oxford, Oxford University Press, 2019) 326; on the location of the pair difference/sameness in the 'slippery concept of culture', see Monateri, *Comparative Legal Methods*, 50.

[27] Philippe Descola proposes to understand the world's various ontologies through the ways in which they conjugate two grand schemes he labels 'identification' and 'relationality'. The resulting models (naturalism, animism, totemism, analogism) operate the interface between self and non-self, each in coherence

that modern law's treatment of the foreign – the ways in which alterity takes on a legal form – may be a promising place from which to join up with efforts undertaken within other fields to identify and reverse the various processes that legitimate humanity's 'ontological privilege' over nature.[28]

In a very broad approximation, there are several types of attitudes towards difference, and of which there are two extremes. On the one hand, hospitality, inclusion and openness; on the other, rejection, indifference or instrumentalisation. In the middle, there are multiple shades of nuance: tolerance can be more or less patronising,[29] while the exoticisation contained in orientalism may correspond to complex fantasies of domination.[30] The point here is that each has its own aesthetic signature in juridical form,[31] rests on a particular legal ethos,[32] and fits moreover into law's own political economy.[33] Each plays out in analogous ways in respect of the alien other, unfamiliar cultural belief systems, non-human species or the earth's inanimate resources.[34] Moreover, our legal approach to alterity, and indeed to what we perceive to be our 'environment', is entwined in turn with our cultural (social, political, psychological, epistemological) attitudes in respect of the foreign, the alien, the uncanny or the strange.

Contemporary political-ecological critique, expressed in multiple disciplinary idioms – anthropology and ethics, but also political economy, psychoanalysis,

with a certain understanding of the ecology in which such mediation takes place. The resulting grammar reveals a series of paired structural opposites. Descola writes, *Par delà nature et culture* 685, that such a prism helps us to 'mieux comprendre les principes grâce auxquels les humains schématisent de façon si diverse leur expérience des choses, accueillent avec plus ou moins de libéralité des non-humains dans leurs collectifs et actualisent ou non dans des systèmes d'interactions concrètes les relations qu'ils discernent entre les existants'. The relevance of this for the conflict of laws is that its methodologies can be seen as instantiations of a similar syntax in legal terms. In this respect, they offer – in various combinations between the two poles of identification and relationality – diverse ways of thinking about law's own relationship to alterity in the legal world. This point also echoes ideas of relationality to be found in the work of Levinas, as seen below in Part III.

[28] Again, Descola, *Par delà nature et culture* 306. Such processes have both a powerful intellectual sway and dire social and ecological consequences.

[29] Arguably, tolerance fits in here. But tolerance is borderline in this respect, as will be seen below. See I Stengers, *Pour en finir avec la tolérance, Cosmopolitiques VII* (Paris, La Découverte, Les empêcheurs de penser en rond, et Le Plessis-Robinson, 1997) 1.

[30] C Castoriadis, *De l'Institution imaginaire de la société* (Paris, Le Seuil, 1975); on legal orientalism and the effects of exoticisation, see T Ruskola, *Legal Orientalism. China, the United States, and Modern Law* (Boston MA, Harvard University Press, 2013); on the largely sexual fantasies projected in French colonisation of Algeria on the muslim family, with direct consequences for the status of persons and land in private international law, see J Surkis, *Sex, Law and Sovereignty in French Algeria, 1830–1930* (Ithaca NY, Cornell Univ Press, 2019); see again, T Ruskola, 'Raping Like a State' (2010) 57 *University of California Law Review* 1477. The reference to 'orientalism' in the above works is to cultural historian Edward W. Saïd's famous study of Western representations of the 'Orient' (*Orientalism*, Penguin Classics, 2003).

[31] On aesthetics as signature and law as an emblematic form of the latter, see G Agamben, *The Signature of All Things: On Method*, trans L di Santo, K Attell (Princeton NJ, Zone Books, 2009); also below, 133.

[32] On law's ethical dimension, see below Part III.

[33] On which see P Kjaer (ed), *The Law of Political Economy: Transformation in the Function of Law* (Cambridge, Cambridge University Press, 2020), and below 219.

[34] On the solidarity or parallelism between our relationship to cultural alterity and our attitudes to nature, see N Belaïdi, 'Gérer la diversité culturelle pour gérer la diversité biologique. Droits des peuples autochtones et souveraineté des Etats sur la biodiversité', in *Le protocole de Nagoya en dialogue. Biodiversité et sociétés* (Paris, Ed Museum national d'histoire naturelle et IRD, 2020).

genealogy, art or aesthetics – is directed at the 'infernal cycle' by virtue of which part of humanity (usually understood as 'society' or 'culture'[35]) claims an ontological sovereignty over alterity (whether in animal or inanimate form) and indeed, in respect of the other part of itself (differentiated in ethnic or economic terms).[36] These strands all also subscribe to a reparative project that seeks correlatively to redraw, rethink, reverse or re-enact our position towards otherness. Similarly, the critical project[37] developed below concerns the agency of law in the commodification of alterity, with all its deleterious effects for our natural surroundings. It touches on the politics, economics, ethics and aesthetics of legal thought as it gave form to a 'jurisdictional jurisprudence'[38] through ideas such as sovereignty, statehood, personhood, the distinction between public and private spheres, and more.

However, this book also explores the possibility of an alternative, ecological *nomos*,[39] drawing on alternative insights provided, diversely, by indigenous

[35] Here, 'society' and 'culture' refer to the human as opposed to the animal or inanimate 'natural' world. Both are concepts frequently associated with the law (legal culture; law as culture; law and society; *ubi ius ibi societas…*) including, prominently, in comparative legal studies. However, both are too indeterminate to provide a valid epistemological model in law (as observed by G Samuel, *Epistemology and Method in Law* (Aldershot, Ashgate, 2003) 50). From an anthropological perspective, see P Descola, *Les formes du visible* (Paris, Seuil, 2021) 11, describing culture as resulting from the relative coincidence of worlds of meanings and causations produced by humans through sets of ontological filters through which they make sense of their surroundings. The concept of 'society' is dismissed as a poor rendition of the assemblage of humans, animals, plants and spirits of which the stuff of our lives and interactions are made (ibid, p.1; *cf* B Latour, *Reassembling the Social* (Oxford, Oxford University Press, 2005) 1).

[36] C Lévi-Strauss, *Anthropologie structurelle II* (Paris, Plon, 1973) 53: 'on a commencé par couper l'homme de la nature et par là le constituer en règne souverain … en s'arrogeant le droit de séparer radicalement l'humanité de l'animalité, en accordant à l'une ce qu'il retirait à l'autre, (l'homme occidental) ouvrait un cycle maudit, et que la même frontière, constamment reculée, servirait à écarter des hommes d'autres hommes'. The role of law in the replication of these interlocking forms of severance and alienation, as observed by Lévi-Strauss, is a theme that runs throughout this book.

[37] At this stage, it may be useful to include a very brief threshold clarification on the focus of critique within this project. The critical mode here is 'external' (in the sense that it is not analytical or doctrinal and does not attempt to produce consistency within the bounds of law's own epistemology, out of its own contradictions or paradoxes). For example, the forms of schizophrenia that surface in the discipline's methodological devices (described in Part I below) are taken as the symptoms of a deeper duality; there is no attempt to demonstrate that one is more logical, rational or coherent than another. Moreover, the book draws on 'genealogical' critique (largely associated with the work of Michel Foucault) insofar as it 'de-naturalises', showing that the vision of the world that our legal consciousness (often subconscious) takes to be 'natural' (and just and desirable) is actually socially constructed (this is close but not identical to social (such as Marxist) critique, that aims rather to unveil what ideology hides). Our naturalised vision provides signification or meaning, that is, explanations and justifications for what would otherwise be inexplicable or intolerable: this is the world of meaning ('epistemè' or 'schema') 'that we construct and that shapes and channels what we say and do (on law as *nomos*, see below Part II, 131). In this context, our legal institutions and categories are the creatures of power (understood political action) and not the reflection of an inexorable social, historical or biological reality. These ideas are present in legal consciousness studies and critical legal studies (to which we shall return below, in Part III).

[38] McVeigh, *Jurisprudence of Jurisdiction.*

[39] The concept of *nomos* will appear in this book both in connection with Carl Schmitt's *The Nomos of the Earth in the International Law of Jus Publicum Europaeum* (Der Nomos der Erde im Völkerrecht des Jus Publicum Europaeum) in discussion below on sovereignty and the exception, not excluding its unintended ecological implications (see below 135) and as used by Robert Cover to signify law's role in fashioning our normative universe, in 'Foreword: *Nomos* and Narrative' (1983) 87(4) *Harv. LR* (see below 131).

cosmologies and legalities, phenomenology, feminist eco-aesthetics, and the (apparently oxymoronic) anthropology of nature. These will serve to revisit various assumptions embedded in our late-modern tunnel vision of the world and its severely constrained legal horizon, in favour of a more hospitable, responsive or responsible attitude towards alterity. In this respect, one of the underlying arguments of this book, with reference to the work of Donald Winnicott, is that 'breakdown' – our terrifying anthropocenic future – has precisely already occurred in the histories and collective psyches of many of the peoples inhabiting our earth.[40] Non-modern collectives, past and contemporary enslaved and displaced populations residing in 'sacrifice zones', can already be considered to have survived, as remnants,[41] the threat of (colonial) extinction, while the amnesia of modernity in respect of its own violent history has left a split hauntology. Hence, as will be seen below, the fruitfulness of looking towards the patterns of legality – indigenous cosmologies that dwell in the 'in-between',[42] post-Holocaust eco-phenomenology[43] – that unfold through excavation in the mode of this 'futur antérieur'.[44]

II. NATURE, LEGALITY AND NATURAL LAW

Legal scholarship is rarely, or insufficiently, present on this interdisciplinary scene in any of the above respects.[45] While the idea of responsibility is of course central to legal thought and practice, the use of idioms imported from other disciplines to renew, describe or support its terms is unusual,[46] as is the reverse intellectual move to use law as a model for shaping thought in other fields.[47] These gaps are paradoxical.

[40] D Winnicott, 'Fear of Breakdown' (written in 1963), in DW Winnicott, C Winnicott, R Shepherd, M Davis, *Psycho-Analytic Explorations* (London, Routledge, 1989). To the extent that it implies the fear of extinction, this ultimate form of breakdown may already have taken place in the histories of many peoples and species, particularly as a result of the widespread devastation wrought by successive eras of capitalism (a question to which we shall return below).

[41] C Gonzalez, A Mutua, 'Mapping Racial Capitalism: Implications for Law' (2022 forthcoming) *Journal of Law & Political Economy*.

[42] See below Part III.

[43] See below 271.

[44] The science fictional idea of the 'futur antérieur' is Philip K Dick's ('Ubik'). In art, it refers to a 'retrocipative' temporality of aesthetic modernity (questioning how the future was envisaged in the past).

[45] For exceptions, see the work of Capra & Mattei, Janda, above n 6. This is obviously not to underestimate the importance of all the critical legal scholarship (pertaining for instance to law's political economy, neoliberal legality, the genealogy of international law, or the dark sides of development) of which this book will make full use below. For recent (Western) scholarship combining law and anthropology of nature in a critical vein, see for example, S Vanuxem, 'Du droit de déambuler. Le paysage comme lieu de passages' 19 *Les Cahiers de l'Ecole de Blois,* 'Le droit au paysage' 10–19. For a wide sampling of non-Western reflection on Indigenous epistemologies and law, see B Reiter (ed), *Constructing the Pluriverse, The Geopolitics of Knowledge* (Durham NC, Duke Univ Press, 2018).

[46] Lawyers do not usually reason in terms of 'jurimorphs'. In Bruno Latour's iconoclastic terms, we might also say that the critique developed in this book aims to extirpate 'Double Click' (or the serpent of knowledge) from the legal field (see *Enquête*, 79 et seq).

[47] For notable exceptions in the form of a demonstration of the utility of such a move, see O Leclerc, R Encinas de Munagorri, S Hennette-Vauchez, CM Herrera, *L'analyse juridique de (x). Le droit parmi les sciences sociales* (Paris, Kimé, 2016).

Indeed, in the light of the deep and complex intertwining of law and nature as a central feature of modern Western thought, a specifically legal perspective with which to view humanity's fraught and frequently destructive relationship to other forms of life is more than due. The history of modern, secularised law[48] is in large part an entangled account of natural justice, human nature, evolutionary biology[49] or indeed bodies politic,[50] supported by an intense and quite extraordinary transferring of metaphors between the natural and social sciences, or between metaphysics and the arts.[51] In particular, in what we now understand to be the sphere of the international (or *inter gentes*), the '*Jus Naturae Et Gentium*'[52] depicted an international order with its own 'natural' law. Underlying this imagery is both the medieval idea that earthly embodiments of legality are the reflection of transcendent principles that govern the cosmos, while conversely, under the metaphysical legacy of ancient Greece, the laws of the city provide the model for the latter.

Evidencing the tensions, paradoxes, contradictions and polemics surrounding the 'law of nature'[53] is the astounding variety of often contradictory conceptions of

[48] VP Fitzpatrick, *The Mythology of Modern Law* (London, Routledge, Chapman & Hall, 1992) 28: 'The essence of the relationship between law and modernity is found in the alleged displacement of the irrational by the rational, the mythical by the scientific, the sacred by the secular'.

[49] On the borrowing of biological evolutionary theories by functionalist approaches in comparative law, see Monateri, *Comparative Legal Methods* 11.

[50] Playing on metaphor, feminist analysis of body politics is a highly significant part of new understandings of the ecology. For an approach that links such politics more specifically to international law, see M Drakopoulou, 'Of the founding of law's jurisdiction and the politics of sexual difference', in S McVeigh (ed), *Jurisprudence of Jurisdiction* (Abingdon, Routledge, 2007) 33.

[51] See B Latour, S Schaffer, P Gagliardi (ed), *A Book of the Body Politic. Connecting Biology, Politics and Social Theory, San Giorgio Dialogue* (Venice, Fondazione Cini, 2017). Because of the omnipresence of references to Hobbes' *Leviathan* in the course of this book, it is interesting at this stage to refer to his version of the metaphor of body politic, according to which (political) art imitates 'that Rational and most excellent work of Nature, man. For by Art is created that great Leviathan called a Commonwealth, or a State which is but an artificial Man; though of greater stature and strength than the Natural, for whose protection and defence it was intended; and in which the Sovereignty is an Artificial Soul, as giving life and motion to the whole body; the Magistrates and other officers of Judicature and Execution, artificial joints.' (Ibid, 28.)

[52] The invention of the term 'international' law is credited to Jeremy Bentham: see M Janis, 'Jeremy Bentham and the Fashioning of 'International Law' (2014) 78 (2) *American Journal of International Law* 405–18. In Bentham's epistemological world, the 'international' is a fictional concept insofar as it requires to be named in language in order to be real (on Bentham's 'Real and Fictitious Entities', see P Schofield, *Utility and Democracy: The Political Thought of Jeremy Bentham* (Oxford, 2006); online edn, Oxford Academic, 1 Sept 2007, https://doi.org/10.1093/acprof:oso/9780198208563.003.0001, accessed 8 Oct 2022; A Colomonos, 'The aesthetics of knowledge', Seminar *Recitals*, Sciences po Paris, 6 October 2022). The natural law of nations was displaced only at the end of the eighteenth century by international (or *inter gentes*) law (public and private). The genealogy is complex however: see M Koskenniemi, 'International law and Raison d'Etat : Rethinking the Prehistory of International law', in B Kingsbury and B Straumann (eds), *The Roman Foundations of the Law of Nations. Alberic Gentili and the Justice of Empire* (Oxford, Oxford University Press, 2010) 297. See too on early modern political thought and its imbrication with the international, P Schroder, *Trust in Early Modern International Political Thought, 1598–1713* (Cambridge, Cambridge University Press, 2017) (ch 3 '*Jus Naturae Et Gentium* – The Limits of a Juridical Order').

[53] For an overview of natural law theories in the enlightenment, T Hochstrasser, *Natural Law Theories in the Early Enlightenment* (Cambridge, Cambridge University Press, 2000); on the extreme complexity of the definition of nature and natural law in modern thought from an international law perspective (most relevant here as expressive of a world vision), see Koskenniemi, 'International law and Raison d'Etat' 305.

our natural surroundings that undergird the idea of 'natural law' (divine or human, religious or secular, cosmological or scientific, sublime or orderly).[54] Paradoxically, therefore, in view of the centrality of natural law to legal, philosophical and political thought, this extraordinary multiplicity of conflicting and overlapping legal doctrines, discourses and representations lead in the end to doubt that the content of law's nature is in any way important. Today, it is argued that the significance of natural law lies above all in its 'modes of veridiction' or access to reality,[55] structurally akin to those of contemporary modes of governmentality (such as benchmarking, nudging …) located outside the law.[56] Given the salience of the latter in the construction of environmental policies, there is all the more reason to turn our attention to jurisdiction and its jurisprudence. The inherent pliability of legal understandings of nature explains moreover why natural law came with a baggage of distinctively religious controversies (the speculative theological doctrines of Vitoria or Suarez in papal Spain, versus the post-Reformation Protestantism of Grotius in the struggle for Dutch independence, or of Gentili in support of the neo-civilising mission of English expansion overseas[57]) and an extraordinary dissonance among the geopolitical projects that have mobilised law's nature in diverse historical contexts (the regulation of warfare, the justification or contestation of conquest, the pacification of human communities).

Such indetermination affecting nature as a core discursive category in law[58] extends to the concrete expressions of natural law (natural rights, Roman law principles, common or customary practice), its scope (domestic, or beyond jurisdiction; affair of states or individuals), its status (within the law, or mere morality, religion, or various non-legal norms of conduct), its modes of ascertainment (inscrutable, or knowable through social norms or common practices), its figures (state of nature, natural rights, Pachamama, Gaia), and its subjects (the inclusion or not of the animal world, of the conquered indigenous inhabitants of the New World, of non-living and invisible entities). To this confused scene of the relation between law

[54] Equally changing is nature's relationship to reason, theological or secular; local or universal. In a contribution to the book (B Kingsbury and B Straumann (eds)), just cited, Martti Koskenniemi shows that by the end of the eighteenth century, the natural law tradition had taken no less than three different directions : natural rights (Locke, Montesquieu), positivism (Hume), social science and economics. ('International law and Raison d'Etat : Rethinking the Prehistory of International law', ibid, 297). We shall return to this last point below 91.

[55] Each 'mode of existence', including law (perhaps emblematically), has its own protocol of veridiction: see Latour, *Enquête*, 59 et seq.

[56] See V Forray, 'Le nouveau droit naturel', Faculty Seminar, Sciences po, October 2021 (on file with the author). He points out that nudging, behavioural economics, benchmarking and other forms of ruling by numbers claim both a privileged view of the essence of things (or social life) and equally to be located outside the law (and in many cases beyond its reach).

[57] Koskenniemi, 'International law and Raison d'Etat'.

[58] This radical indetermination of nature as a core discursive category in law has led to an uneasy commerce with the natural and social sciences, theology and ethics (and their constant exchange of metaphors), the opposing philosophical obediences of appeals to natural law (Spanish Scholastics, German Protestant humanism, French Enlightenment), natural law's claim or rejection of a classical heritage (that of the Stoics, or the *corpus iuris civilis* …) and the ensuing vast array of specifically legal doctrines that rest on a specific understanding of the essence of things (naturalism versus positivism, historicity versus immanence, *ius naturae* and *ius gentium*).

and nature, can be added further twists. Thus, past or contemporary accounts of the 'reason of state',[59] justifications of modern empire, or indeed current neoliberal ideas of world ordering, show up deeper structural links between the aesthetics of the sublime in nature and the awe and arcana of sovereignty,[60] or between fantasies of wilderness[61] and savagery and the civilising mission, or between 'natural' states of underdevelopment and the need for global capital investment.

A further consideration that justifies paying a particular attention to legality in the shaping of our relationship to our natural surroundings is precisely its central place in the genealogy of our contemporary worldviews.[62] As we shall see in further depth below, the great modern bifurcation – the separation of the autonomous subject from its natural surroundings, of mind from body, persons from things – was largely shaped through the Roman-Christian legal heritage of the European polities that populated the new Westphalian legal order of the seventeenth century,[63]

[59] T Poole, *Reason of State, Law, Prerogative and Empire* (Cambridge, Cambridge University Press, 2015). The classical *ius gentium* and the early modern law of nations was long identified with natural law in the context of the justification (and moderation) of imperial expansion. The genealogy of the modern state reveals the equally fraught relationship with nature. It points to the links between the aesthetics of nature and the politics of geographical imagination : see C Tang, *The Geographic Imagination of Modernity. Geography, Literature, and Philosophy in German Romanticism* (Stanford CA, Stanford University Press, 2008), noting that the emergence of the modern geographic imagination coincided with the rise of a 'momentous' idea in political thought, namely, the idea of nation, in the early nineteenth century, when geographic imagination was occupied with the development of European peoples toward nation-statehood.

[60] There is a sublime dimension to our 'distanced' awareness of our actual physical powerlessness in the face of nature's might: A Carlson, 'Environmental Aesthetics', *Stanford Encyclopedia of Philosophy*, https://plato.stanford.edu/entries/environmental-aesthetics/. Indeed, as Carlson writes, climate change is also a mathematically sublime idea or object. As bodies we cannot see it in its wholeness. Our knowledge of it is based on modelling by super-computers, and it can only be 'seen' by the non-human eye.

[61] D Danowski & E Viveiros de Castro, *Ends of the World* (Oxford, John Wiley, 2017) 24 surmise that the mythic theme ('mytheme', in structuralist parlance) of the Garden of Eden persists today in the concept of wilderness (on this point see the recent, glorious satire in the Washington Post: www.washingtonpost.com/opinions/2022/09/15/patagonia-give-away-billionaire-satire/). It was at the end of the eighteenth century – partly under the influence of Western imaginaries of notions such as the 'sublime' and 'the last frontier' that 'wilderness' (as opposed, say, to savagery) came to be associated with positive affects akin to the sacred and aroused by the nostalgic contemplation of a magnificent natural, uncorrupted world superior to the human (to which we return below, Part II). The fantasy is that of *horti conclusi* (enclosed gardens) that bear witness to a virgin past imagined as untouched since the dawn of time. While the blind predatory action of Western (and now geopolitically wider) capitalism and neocolonialism is undeniable, this fantasy passes over the omnipresence of technology (in the human and supposedly separate natural worlds): on the further question of whether it is desirable to 'go backwards', see below 314.

[62] Legality is highly significant among the 'many figures of Gaia' (ethical, scientific, economic, political etc), that were hidden and amalgamated under the modern notion of *Nature* (B Latour, *Face à Gaia, Huit conférences sur le Nouveau Régime Climatique* (Paris, La Découverte, 2015); *Facing Gaia*, Gifford lectures, Edinburgh, 2013, p 77).

[63] The term 'Westphalian' refers to the Peace of Westphalia that ended 30 years of endo-European, endo-Christian religious wars, by treaty of 1648. Because it was recognised that the government of each territory was sovereign to determine the religion of its subjects, the term Westphalian has come to signify the simultaneous emergence of statehood, secular political sovereignty, and territoriality, a nexus inscribed moreover in the international legal order and coincidental with modernity's grid-like division of the earth's surface. Significantly, the publication of Hobbes' *Leviathan* in 1651 gave shape to sovereignty in political thought, so that Westphalia is sometimes identified too with the first inklings of liberal democracy. Of course, the various processes that led to the emergence of any one of these axes were far more complex and progressive than the choice of this emblematic date might suggest. In particular, international law took on its modern form in the nineteenth century (in 1765, Blackstone still 'deduced' the law of nations from

subordinating the world to the free will of its new, secular, masters.[64] Thereafter, the Atlantic revolutions and the advent of the Enlightenment did not prevent late capitalist modernity from further universalising humanity's ontological privilege,[65] pursuing the severance of the ecology from the economy, marginalising other interstitial forms of life, enclosing the commons, transforming hospitality into exclusion – and all with more than a little help from the law.[66] The contemporary challenge for the latter is the need for a renewed jurisprudence at the very last frontier of modern legality, that is, before the end of human time.[67] Such a project must be capacious enough to accommodate a different, non-bifurcated relationship of humanity in respect of 'nature's radical alterity'.[68]

natural reason) and the modern nation-state appeared still later (not before the early twentieth century, at the time of its decline: see H Brunkhorst, *Critical Theory of Legal Revolutions: Evolutionary Perspectives* (London, Bloomsbury 2014), while the very meaning of sovereignty and territory was long uncertain and indeed variable over the long centuries of Western colonialism (L Benton, *A Search for Sovereignty. Law and Geography in European Empires, 1400–1900* (Cambridge, Cambridge University Press, 2010); thus, the writings of Pufendorf on the constitution of the Holy Roman Empire and the 'Present State of Germany', pointed to the inadequacy of Bodin's definition of sovereignty and observed the existence of 'a system of States'). Religious tolerance itself has significantly changed its meaning. On Westphalia as the moment of a political repression or refoulement of the ineffable part of law in the Roman-civilist legal tradition, see P-G Monateri, *Geopolitica del diritto: genesi, governo e dissoluzione dei corpi politici* (Rome/Bari, Laterza & Figli, 2013).

[64] See T Poole, *Reason of State. Law, Prerogative and Empire* (Cambridge, Cambridge University Press, 2015).

[65] A recent philosophical study of the contribution to the Enlightenment to the question of the ecology suggests that it is not the ideas of the *Lumières* but the forgetfulness of their signification, or the lack of reinterpretation of their emancipatory content in a transforming political economy that is at stake (C Pelluchon, *Les Lumières à l'Age du Vivant* (Paris, Seuil, 2021)). On the Atlantic revolutions and their 'ratchet' effect, see Brunkhorst, *Critical Theory of Legal Revolutions.*

[66] On the splitting of the *oikos*, see Latour, *Enquête*, 441 et seq. On capitalism's paradoxical inability to sustain the resources of nature on which it feeds, source of 'boundary struggles' at the core of law's political economy, see N Fraser and R Jaeggi, *Capitalism. A Conversation in Critical Theory* (Cambridge, Polity, 2018). Legality has done much to entrench the neoliberal common sense, and in particular to subtract global economic governance from political processes. As Paddy Ireland remarks, power is the great absentee of neoliberal thought (P Ireland, 'Financialization and Corporate Governance' Corporate Governance and Globalisation Colloquium, September 2008, https://ssrn.com/abstract=2068478). Society is understood as being predominantly structured by economic interests, while the invisible hand of the economy is the true driving-force of societal evolution. The law (not politics) gives form to this economic constitution by allowing markets to self-regulate. Public regulatory policies are only required in the unfortunate case of 'market failures' when the laws of the economy go awry. Law is the ultimate arbitrator, then, of the (ever-expanding) threshold between the economy and various other spheres potentially subject to political deliberation, moral rights, privacy or common good. Although there is nothing inevitable about these distinctions themselves, nor anything natural about where the lines are drawn, they are difficult to dislodge and indeed hotly defended by vested interests whenever challenged.

[67] This might be termed a 'new natural law' or a *jus publicum telluris:* B Latour, *Facing Gaia: Eight Lectures on the New Climatic Regime* (Cambridge, Polity Press, 2017) (see also, B Latour 'Facing Gaia: Six lectures on the political theology of nature', *The Gifford Lectures on Natural Religion* (Edinburgh, 2013). The implied reference is to the notion of *ius publicum europaeum*, the natural law of nations promoted by the (conventionally ascribed) father of the law of nations, Hugo Grotius (or de Groot), *De jure belli ac pacis* (1625) and moreover a twist on Carl Schmitt's famous use of the *nomos* of the *jus publicum Europaeum.* An alternative term, 'earthly legality', is proposed by A Pottage, 'Why nature has no rights', forthcoming in A Alvarez-Nakagawa & C Douzinas (eds), *Non-Human Rights. Critical Perspectives* (Cheltenham, Elgar, 2023).

[68] Again an expression of Descola, *Par delà nature et culture.*

III. LAW, BIOS AND BARE LIFE

One particular strand of interaction between law and biological life surfaces in contemporary political theory, with particular relevance for understanding our relationship to the foreign other. Taking its cue from Michel Foucault's 'biopolitics', of which the focus is the management of bodies as an object of power,[69] a brand of political-philosophical thought known as 'Italian theory' has shed the spotlight on the relationship between law, sovereignty and 'bare life',[70] or 'life before the law'.[71] It is largely a reflection upon the meaning – or the senselessness – of our political and ethical lives in late modernity and particularly our existence in a state of indetermination or threshold[72] of indifference between ontology and ethics, law and fact.[73] Being is disappearing, leaving a residue, a concept with clear geological, ecological and political implications[74] – bare existence as such. The latter is an embodied vestige of the haunting figure of the archaic Roman *homo sacer*[75] – sacrificed, banished, homeless, wandering, or encamped – that is all too familiar today in the form of the foreign vagrant or migrant. This genealogy is significant in the light of the importance that will be given in this book to Roman law in the shaping of Western metaphysics.[76]

[69] See above 9.

[70] On bare life, see again Agamben, *Homo Sacer : Sovereign Power and Bare Life*, *Meridian : Crossing Aesthetics* (Palo Alto CA, Stanford University Press, 1998); for further 'Italian theory' on the body as used in this book, see R Esposito, *Persons and Things: From the Body's Point of View (Theory Redux)* (Cambridge, Polity Press, 2015) (extending the biological metaphor through the idea of the 'self-immunity' of law, for a presentation of which see T Campbell, 'Bios, Immunity, Life: The Thought of Roberto Esposito' (2006) 36(2) *Diacritics* 2–22; from the perspective of law, see Monateri, *Dominus Mundi*, whose account of which will be central in the study of private international legal aspects of sovereignty below 159 et seq. On Foucauldian biopolitics as revitalised in Italian theory, see M Hardt & A Negri, *Empire* (Cambridge MA, Harvard University Press, 2000). On a related, quite extraordinary project to write 'a theory of the flesh' from a similar perspective, see E Santner, *The Royal Remains – the people's two bodies and the endgames of sovereignty* (Chicago, Chicago University Press, 2011); K Goodman (ed), *The Weight of All Flesh: On the Subject-Matter of Political Economy* (New York, Oxford University Press, 2016); and for a further 'twist', see F Ludeña Romandini, *A comunidade dos espectros. I. Antropotecnia,* (Florianopolis, Cultura e Barbarie, 2014).

[71] C Douzinas, 'Postmodern Jurisprudence: The Law of Text in the Texts of Law', in McVeigh (ed), *Jurisprudence of Jurisdiction.*

[72] The 'threshold' is a key concept throughout this book (see below Part II in connection with a jurisprudence of the border and Part III in connection with the law of hospitality).

[73] Agamben, *Homo Sacer* 1184: 'the residual pure effectiveness of hypostasis'. Our thanks to Richard Janda (Globinar, Paris, May 2022) for the following point: 'This "residual pure effectiveness" of hypostasis – of substance as opposed to existence – is what connects it, for Agamben, to bare existence or survival. My, perhaps accentuated, reading here is that as being (let's switch to *Dasein*, since Agamben is trying to update and reorient Heidegger) confronts extinction and as the state (our *Dominus Mundi*) becomes inoperative, a new ontology arises. My way of thinking this is that at the threshold of extinction, the very possibility of being becomes an entirely ethical question' (on this ethical dimension, see below Part III), on residue as the 'royal remains' or the 'hauntological' remnants of *Dominus Mundi* in our political economy, see Monateri, *Dominus Mundi*.

[74] On racial capitalism see Gonzalez and Mutua, 'Mapping Racial Capitalism': on geological analogy of the sedimentation of residues, see Janda, 'Panarchy'.

[75] Agamben, *Homo Sacer*.

[76] On the discovery of 'man' (meaning humanity as composed of individuals endowed with agency and subjectivity) – and appropriately here, the link with extinction see M Foucault, *Les Mots et Les Choses. Une archéologie des sciences humaines* (Paris, Gallimard, 1990) (trans: *The Order of Things: An Archaeology of the Human Sciences* (London, Vintage, 1994): '[A]s the archaeology of our thought easily

Moreover, coinciding with the centrality of our phenomenological, gendered, racialised and political bodies in contemporary eco-feminist thought,[77] bare life has singular resonance for ecological jurisprudence in that it opens the question of a possibly new legal ontology and ethics arising as the horizon of extinction emerges in the Anthropocene.[78] In our search to give legal form to new ecological modes of subjective and collective existence, it points to the idea, associated with the (already mentioned) psychoanalytical work of Donald Winnicott[79] concerning the fear of breakdown. We are reminded on the one hand that modern Western legality emerged in the secular order crafted to put an end to the bloody endo-European religious wars of the seventeenth century,[80] and that in its later modern international legal form, it endorsed colonial capitalism and its devastation of the human and ecological worlds on the European outside. This included the massive enslavement of racialised populations and the near-extinction of indigenous lifeworlds, followed closely by the further replication[81] of endo-European racial and religious terror in the form of the Holocaust.

IV. GLOBALISATION: A VERY SHORT STORY

The importance of denials of past trauma in our grand historical narrative[82] provides the context for the 'shadow' avatar of the conflict of laws that will weave through this book. For the time being, the important point here is that the universalised consensus of late Western modernity – our 'old settlement', to which we return immediately below – is haunted[83] and disrupted by the wandering shades of *homo sacer*. In other

shows, man is an invention of recent date. And one perhaps nearing its end. If those arrangements were to disappear as they appeared … as the ground of classical thought did at the end of the eighteenth century, then one can certainly wager that man would be erased, like a face drawn in sand at the edge of the sea'.

[77] See D Haraway, *Simians, Cyborgs, and Women: The Reinvention of Nature* (Abingdon, Routledge, 2015; first published 1991) presenting the cyborg as a material/semiotic figure that implodes the dichotomies of nature/technology, human/nonhuman, male/female (see 'A Manifesto for Cyborgs: Science, Technology, and Socialist Feminism in the 1980s' (1985) 80 *Socialist Review* 65–108.

[78] See A Tsing, *The Mushroom at the End of the World. On the Possibility of Life in Capitalist Ruins* (Princeton NJ, Princeton University Press, 2015).

[79] Winnicott, *Fear of breakdown.*

[80] For genealogical accounts of sovereignty and statehood that remind us of this original violence from which emerged the Westphalian order, see Monateri, *Dominus Mundi*; Poole, *Reason of State.*

[81] The idea of 'replication' here suggests that humanity cannot extract itself from the rut in which it has placed itself (and others): see more generally on the nexus between social history and the collective psyche; H Mazurel, *L'inconscient ou l'oubli de l'histoire – Profondeurs, métamorphoses et révolutions de la vie affective* (Paris, La Découverte, 2021).

[82] On the mutual denial or ignorance of modern Western history and our collective subconscious see Mazurel, *L'inconscient ou l'oubli de l'histoire*; for a psychoanalytical approach to Western colonial history and ontology, F Fanon, *Peau noire, masques blancs* (Paris, Le Seuil, 1952), C Castoriadis, *De l'institution imaginaire de la société* (Paris, Le Seuil, 1975); from the perspective of international law in particular see A Anghie, *Imperialism, Sovereignty and International Law* (Cambridge, Cambridge University Press, 2005), reminding us that the West is amnesiac in respect of its own history.

[83] Hauntology (or *hantologie*) is a neologism invented by Derrida that combines '*ontologie*' (the science of being, *être*) with haunting (the spectral, ghostly). It is linguistically a 'paronomasia', a paronym that is not a synonym. See J Derrida, *Specters of Marx: The State of the Debt, the Work of Mourning and the New International* (London, Routledge, 1994); 'Spectres de Marx' (ed Galilée, 1993) 31 writing, in substance, that hauntology is a 'catégorie … irréductible, et d'abord à tout ce qu'elle rend possible, l'ontologie,

words, while the global turn (in law and elsewhere) is usually associated with the conceit that accelerated interconnectedness will smooth out the roughness of our collective lives, this smooth surface is constantly troubled[84] by all the life forms and lifeworlds (despised or discarded as archaic, primitive, enchanted or hyperbolic[85]) that struggle to survive, albeit as 'remnants', 'residues' or radical alterity.[86]

V. THE 'OLD SETTLEMENT' AND THE LEGAL *SUMMA DIVISIO*

The old settlement or unwritten constitution of the Moderns[87] rests on the forms of political, philosophical, social and scientific thought (and their separation) that undergird the accelerating degradation of the biosphere, the ensuing, unbearable disparities of human existence, and the devastation of other cultural life worlds and non-human life forms. As suggested above, it rests on a series of radical severances – variously identified in different disciplinary idioms with (European or Western) modernity, naturalism, individualism, or capitalism (colonial and global) – that run through our collective and individual lives and shape our vision of otherness. The great divides between nature and culture, the West and the rest, inside and outside, mind and body, self and others, are in Alain Pottage's words, 'profoundly juridical'.[88] Indeed, while law is mostly absent from the preoccupations of the earth sciences,[89] it is important to understand not only that law is an ontological form

la théologie, l'onto-théologie positive ou négative … C'est une ontologie, l'ontologie de l'être du non-être et du non-être de l'être, de quelque chose ou quelqu'un qui « n'est pas là », comme tout fantôme digne de ce nom' (ibid). 'Il n'y a pas de Dasein du spectre mais il n'y a pas de Dasein sans l'inquiétante étrangeté, sans l'étrange familiarité (Unheimlichkeit) de quelque spectre' (ibid). 'Il n'y a pas d'ontologie, donc, sans hantologie.' See for the helpful explanations by S Pecastaing, *Poe et Baudelaire : pour une hantologie du texte*, 2014, https://tel.archives-ouvertes.fr/tel-00997440. On the relevance of hauntology for global governance and sovereignty, see ibid p 202 and below 193 et seq.

[84] The reference to the trouble (in the form of denial and the return of the repressed) affecting our body (politic) is to Judith Butler's *Gender Trouble: Feminism and the Subversion of Identity* (London, Taylor and Francis, 1999), and to Eric Santner's theory of the *soma* in *The Royal Remains*. On the legal dimensions of this disruption of the smooth homogeneous surface of the neoliberal legal order, see Monateri, *Geopolitica del diritto*.

[85] The adjective 'hyperbolic' is often used to disqualify multiple non-modern trains or schools of thought, including those inspired by indigenous cosmologies, Latour, or Levinas (all of which are part of the project that unfolds below).

[86] According to Bruno Latour, Gaia represents 'the (ancient) Other that is truly other', a form of radical alterity (*Enquête* p 33). We shall return below (Part III) to the question of law and the radical other. However, we can flag an objection at this point to the effect that Latour himself pays insufficient attention to residues, or 'beings without trace' (argued by L de Sutter, 'Plasma! Notes on Latour's metaphysics of Law', in K McGee (ed), *Latour and the Passage of Law* (Edinburgh, Edinburgh University Press, 2015) 197 et seq). We return to inclusion and residue below, Part III.

[87] See B Latour, *Politics of Nature* (Cambridge MA, Harvard University Press, 2004) (targeting the division of labour between science and politics). The 'new settlement' based on ontological pluralism emerges in the third part of his *Enquête*.

[88] 'Introduction: the fabrication of persons and things', in A Pottage and M Mundy, *Law, Anthropology and the Constitution of the Social* (Cambridge, Cambridge University Press, 2004). On bodies, their dualism and phenomenological embodiment, see more below 221.

[89] Except, once again, in the form of policy proposals for regulation or international treaties, as will be seen below. COP 26 is taking place in Glasgow as I write. These moves are undeniably important, but to reduce legality to these forms is a persistent 'category error', as we shall see.

that 'invaded modernity'[90] but that, as a consequence of this invasion, law has been both generative and emblematic of the obstacles that prevent us from acknowledging the entanglement of all the life forms, familiar and foreign, cultural and natural, that are present on the planet.[91]

If the modern *nomos* of the earth[92] came to represent a series of radical severances between humankind and the surrounding world of living and non-living things, a grand temporal and ontological separation between nature and society,[93] such divisions were the long silent labour of Roman-Christian legality. In this respect, modernity's language was that of Roman law.[94] The initial distinction between persons and things instated by the *Corpus Iuris Civilis*[95] in the observance of the laws of nature (further split in moving patterns between a semiotics of the cosmos or the revelation of reason, itself either human or divine[96]) became

[90] Schiavone, *Ius. L'invenzione del diritto in Occidente* (Turin, Einaudi, 2005) 13.

[91] For an argument along similar lines in respect of the role of the 'normal state', see S Bandopadhyay, *All Is Well: Catastrophe and the Making of the Normal State* (New York, Oxford Academic, 2022); online edn, 17 Feb 2022. The argument of this book is that the emergence of a struggle in the eighteenth century to master God, nature (and each other) inaugurated modern meanings of risk, normalcy, power, and responsibility. This history of disaster management reveals underlying knowledge structures and political economies that 'smuggle the unspoken costs of modernity inside the rationalized representation of past catastrophes and future risks'.

[92] On law as *nomos*, meaning the normative universe we inhabit, see R Cover, 'Foreword: Nomos and Narrative' (1983) 87(4) *Harv LR*.

[93] See Bonneuil and Fressoz, *L'événement Anthropocène* 41. We owe the structuralist division of nature/culture to Levi-Strauss, 'The Structural Study of Myth', *Structural Anthropology* (New York, Basic Books, 1963) 225. Critique of this 'great bifurcation' is, as will be seen, widespread. The question in the present book is how it has been deployed, including its ramifications in the legal field, and conversely, how law may have enabled some of its implications (for instance, in its treatment of family or gender) and not the validity of this distinction per se. That the relevance of the division itself is largely a question of scale is apparent in Engels' observation that humanity's difference in respect of other species lies in its ability to make its own history. And the moment mankind entered human history, its estrangement from nature began. 'Man alone has succeeded in impressing his stamp on nature, not only by shifting the plant and animal world from one place to another, but also by so altering the aspect and climate of his dwelling place, and even the plants and animals themselves, that the consequences of his activity can disappear only with the general extinction of the terrestrial globe': 'Dialectics of Nature' (in K Marx and F Engels, *Collected Works*, Vol 52 (New York, International Publishers, 1987) 329–30). Accepting that humanity, in forging its own history as it has done, has left its deleterious imprint on the planet is in no way an apology for the implications of the nature/culture divide on other levels. At this point, in anticipation of the project outlined in this book, on the contribution of indigenous cosmologies to an 'ecological jurisprudence', see E Viveiros de Castro, *The Relative Native* 239–40 This author's work flags the contribution of indigenous cosmologies to an 'ecological jurisprudence' and will be further referenced below.

[94] Significantly for what follows below in Part III, the language of Roman legality was also that of mathematical calculus: see Schiavone, *Ius*, 31.

[95] See Esposito, *Persons and Things*, arguing that the body fell between these supposedly exhaustive categories. On the history of the *Corpus iuris civilis*, the great code and anthology established on the initiative of Emperor Justinian in the sixth century AD, see Schiavone, *Ius*, 18 et seq. The matrix is of course the Platonic ontological dualism of *nomos* and *physis*, but while both *nomos* and *physis* were laws, there was no such thing as 'natural law' in classical Greek thought. The law of nature was modelled by Aristotle on the law of the city (even if the representation was the reverse: see Descola, *Par delà nature et culture* 128).

[96] One might add to these moving pairs, a further distinction in the perception of life itself as biographical or biological. On this further duality, see Fassin, *La vie, Mode d'Emploi critique* (Paris, ed du Seuil, 2018).

an unbreachable chasm when diffracted through medieval theology. This initial *summa divisio* between persons and things spawned further binary (and hierarchical) oppositions in metaphysics between head and body,[97] mind and matter (*res cogitans, res extensa*),[98] subject and object,[99] human and animal,[100] self and other,[101] inside and outside[102] … The chronological linearity of time itself[103] was a legal invention, a discovery of the mediaeval common lawyers incidental to the bodily duality of the mediaeval kings, physical and sublime.[104] The *oikos* was split into two distinct spheres, with an earlier (Byzantine) pastoral ecology increasingly cleaved away from what was to become the science of economics.[105]

[97] The complex interaction of the medieval metaphors of the head and body and the two bodies of the king, along with the various influences of Byzantine Christology, are explored by E Kantorowicz, *The King's Two Bodies: A Study in Medieval Political Theology* (Princeton NJ, Princeton University Press, 1957). The dualities mentioned in the text are prolonged in further divisions between whole and part, cognition and emotion, aesthetics and science, public and private etc. Such divisions, all of which are significant for law in various ways, are all equally elusive.

[98] The reference is to the emergence of the Cartesian subject. Descartes divided the universe between *res cogitans*, thinking substances, and *res extensa*, the mechanical world (however, this division did not take place in a vacuum : see Descola, *Par delà nature et culture* 310, on the role of prior distinctions between animals and humans as sole possessors of language and thereby capable of introspection and generalisation). The distinction is also scrutinised by Bruno Latour in his enquiry into the 'beings of technique' (*Enquête* 211 et seq). See too the distinction, in the context of the earth sciences between 'ego' and 'geological' perspectives.

[99] Each of these categories contains further splits and hierarchies. Objects are animate or inanimate, natural or technological, etc. One of the great divisions constructed by law is that of the civilised subject and the 'other': on the work of legal comparison in this respect, see P-G Monateri, 'Black Gaius. A Quest for the Multicultural Origins of the Western Legal Tradition' (2000) 51(3) *Hastings Law Journal* 479 ss; D Maldonado Bonilla, *Legal Barbarians* (Cambridge, Cambridge University Press, 2021).

[100] On the process of Western civilisation and the construction of social hierarchies, as from early modernity, through degrees of separation of personhood from the (animal) body, N Elias, *La Civilisation des Mœurs* (Paris, Pocket, 2003).

[101] Much of the progression of psychoanalysis in the twentieth century (particularly in the work of Jung and Winnicott) has been linked to perceptions of split between self and (m)other, self and environment, and ultimately, within self itself (false self, extended self, identification with the social *persona* …).

[102] While the divide between inside/outside has been the target of critique from multiple political and social (inclusion/exclusion), economic (externalities) or legal (foreign/national) perspectives, the most significant challenge is Gaia's warning that there is 'no outside', that is, no longer any possibility of escaping the earth's 'critical zone' that sustains life within its fragile membrane (on the critical zone, B Latour, *Ou suis-je?* (Paris, La Découverte, 2021).

[103] On the multiple topologies of time (including chronometrical time and 'chronosophies' as ways of apprehending the invisible, unknowable future), their various ontologies (natural time, historical time …) and aesthetics (cycles, linearity, individual stories), their relationship to diverse literary and conceptual forms (chronicle or narrative; social epoch or geological era), see the study of the order of times by K Pomian, *L'ordre du temps* (Paris, Gallimard, 1984). The book argues that standardised time as ordered and measured out by political, scientific and religious authority has untold psychic and somatic effects on social and individual consciousness.

[104] It was Kantorowicz (*The King's Two Bodies*) who pointed out the decisive contribution of the jurists (common lawyers) to the invention of linear temporality, through the invention of the sublime body of the king (or Crown) so as to ensure the continuity of the reign despite the death of the physical royal body.

[105] Arguably, the initial crack appeared long before modernity: see D Leshem, *The Origins of Neoliberalism. Modelling the Economy from Jesus to Foucault* (New York, Columbia University Press, 2016).

Within the law itself, further nested patterns of severance reappeared as between law and fact, *sein* and *sollen*, with significant consequences for modernity's perception of reality – and the prerogative of legal jurisdiction to arbitrate this divide.[106] Indeed, Roman law instituted a very specific relationship of deliberate non-relation between legality and the real world.[107] A similar move took place when the modern discovery of perspective[108] and its legal correlate, 'jurisdictional thinking',[109] transformed inhabited place, concrete itineraries and geographical discontinuities into abstract and empty space,[110] a world map divided into territorial (including maritime) units and thereby deprived of its 'natural entities' – including its human inhabitants and their cultures.[111] This consolidated an aesthetic perception of the outside world as scenery, a backdrop against which progress took the form of a further divorce between nature and culture. Mankind, once created by God, transcended the physical world and became the earthly master of creation through access to reason, while the modern sovereign took on a new, secular shape.[112] From *lex animata* to legal artefact.[113]

[106] Facts act in this context as law's 'epistemic filters' (T Murphy, 'Legal fabrications and the case of "cultural property"', in A Pottage and M Mundy, *Law, Anthropology and the Constitution of the Social*, (Cambridge, Cambridge University Press, 2004). 'Indeed, the difference between law and fact is not a difference of fact but one of law, and this is what defines the essence of the institution, and what makes fictions so revelatory of the artificiality of the institution' (Y Thomas, '*Fictio legis*: L'empire de la fiction romaine et ses limites médiévales' (1995) 21 *Droits* 17.

[107] The meaning of legal fictionality is often misunderstood. On the work of Roman legal fictions, which (as distinct from presumptions) deliberately did/do not correspond to empirical reality, see Y Thomas, 'Les artifices de la vérité en droit commun médiéval' (2005) juillet-septembre *L'Homme* [online] 175–76, http://journals.openedition.org/lhomme/29519; DOI : 10.4000/lhomme.29519. However, later Christian doctrine took the Roman fiction of legal personality to be purely descriptive (see A Pottage 'Introduction: the fabrication of persons and things', in Pottage and Mundy, *Law, Anthropology and the Constitution of the Social* 1, spec p 9), thereby blurring its specific mode of veridiction. Law's regime of truth is not the same as that of science, law being no more concerned with scientific truth than science with legal reality. On the centrality of the enigma that accompanied the irruption of science in the seventeenth century, questioning the relationship between truth and reality, see Latour, *Enquiry* 80 et seq.

[108] On the discovery of perspective and its consequences for the understanding of sovereignty, J Bartelson, *Sovereignty as Symbolic Form. Critical Issues in Global Politics* (Abingdon, Routledge, 2014).

[109] See McVeigh, *Jurisprudence of Jurisdiction.*

[110] L Benton, *Law and Colonial Cultures, Legal Regimes in World History 1400–1900*, spec p 210 et seq ('Constructing Sovereignty'); L Benton, L Ford, *Rage for Order. The British Empire and the Origins of International Law 1800–1850* (Cambridge MA, Harvard University Press, 2017).

[111] Aristotle's 'natural entities' were beings (including humans, as part of Nature) that contained the principle of their own movement and repose, each with a particular form of life and structural relationship with the others, contained within a complete whole (Nature) according to a specific order and under its laws (see Descola, *Par delà nature et culture* 127). Such beings faded from (modern) sight once mankind transcended the physical world and the universe became abstract space. Furthermore, as Dipesh Chakrabarty argues, distinctively modern (European) concepts such as disenchanted space, secular time, and sovereignty inform Western social sciences and are treated as universal. The irony is then that in this vision, it is the rest of the world that is seen as incomplete or lacking (*Provincializing Europe: Postcolonial Thought and Historical Difference* (Princeton NJ, Princeton University Press, 2007).

[112] Here we find the 'first' and 'second' natures: see Hobbes' *Leviathan*, ch XIV, 'Of The First And Second Naturall Lawes, And Of Contracts: The Right Of Nature, which Writers commonly call Jus Naturale, is the Liberty each man hath, to use his own power, as he will himselfe, for the preservation of his own Nature; that is to say, of his own Life; and consequently, of doing any thing, which in his own Judgement, and Reason, hee shall conceive to be the aptest means thereunto'.

[113] The process of secularisation of sovereignty was not necessarily deployed as narrated in Schmittian political theology. See, reinterpreting the rise of the Leviathan and the emergence of the modern body

The French Enlightenment proceeded thereafter to secularise nature,[114] and the nineteenth century – not so incidentally[115] – witnessed the congealing of the European imperial nation-state[116] and the invention of modern international law,[117] widening the rift between science and humanities and sealing the grand discordance between nature and society. The rest was the work of the political economy, of which the paradoxical genealogy takes us back to the very heart of the natural law of nations.[118] The exclusivism of (domestic) private property and the (international) enclosure of territories led to a dilution of all accountability of *homo economicus* to the natural world. The latter fell from its status as divine reason to that of disposable resource at the service of the capitalocene,[119] with its vast colonial conquest of lands inhabited by primitive peoples in need of 'civilisation', and the ensuing devastation of what we persist in seeing as our (natural or cultural) 'environment', as if it was outside of, and distant from, ourselves.

Unquestionably, law was constantly at work in these deep processes of bifurcation, through its insistence on objectivity, rationality, closure and order; its representation of a bodiless subject; its particular narratives of sovereignty; its mapping of a divided, placeless, territorial world; its ontological and methodological monism; its imaginaries of nationhood (both romantic and warlike; heroic and imperialistic); its assertion of axiological universalism (and its unstable definition of the values to be defended and promoted). At this stage, then, it might well be asked whether law is irremediably bound up with our 'old settlement'. Various clarifications as to law's own 'nature' are in order therefore at this stage.

politic as a dark reversal of the previous world order, see Monateri, *Dominus Mundi*. On the contemporary science and technology/anthropology approach to law as artefact, see Pottage, 'Introduction'.

[114] On the simultaneous romanticisation and aestheticization of (sublime, wild) natural landscape, see Descola, *Par delà nature et culture* 111. On the contemporaneous Germanic anti-Enlightenment movement opposing the universalism of the French Enlightenment produced culture as a central Germanic value, see ibid 142. On Enlightenment thought and the error consisting in its condemnation per se, see Pelluchon, *Les Lumières*.

[115] Nature (with a capital N) and State are the twin constructions of legal modernity. See Bonneuil and Fressoz, *L'événement Anthropocène* 41, documenting the parallel representations of world history (Michelet) and geology (Lyell). Further still, on the intimate (biopolitical) relationship between life and sovereignty, see G Agamben, *The Kingdom and the Glory: For a Theological Genealogy of Economy and Government,* transL Chiesa with M Mandarini (Palo Alto, CA, Stanford University Press, 2011).

[116] As in the analysis of the late emergence of the nation-state by Brunkhorst, *Critical Theory of Legal Revolutions*.

[117] On this chronology, along with the genealogy and the politics of public international law, see M Koskenniemi, *The Politics of International Law* (Oxford, Hart, 2011).

[118] See Koskenniemi 'International law and *Raison d'Etat*'.

[119] The 'capitalocene' can be understood as the political economy of the anthropocene (see for the term, JW Moore, 'The Capitalocene, Part I: On the Nature and Origins of Our Ecological Crisis' (2017) 44(3) *The Journal of Peasant Studies* 594–630, emphasising that the notion isn't about blame, but about identifying the system that has devastated life on this planet). On capitalism's inability to sustain the natural resources on which it feeds and depends, see the Marxist analysis developed in the current context of crisis by Fraser and Jaeggi, *Capitalism*.

VI. CAVEATS: LAW AND *NOMOS*; *LEX* AND *IUS*

Widely identified with 'regulation', legality has undeniably gestured in the direction of greater care for the earth system.[120] It has provided the groundwork for diplomatic agreements on climate change, began to assemble a new field of 'environmental law'[121] or loosened its traditional categories so as to make place for a more ecological judicial politics.[122] This is no doubt why the recurring issue of the 'judicialisation' of social controversies (the spectre of a '*gouvernement des juges*') has become so topical once again. Court rooms begin to echo with calls for planetary responsibility from private multinational or state actors, while boardrooms elaborate schemes of social and environmental corporate responsibility that purport, in the chaos of the transition to clean energy called for by local public opinion or the international community, both to circumvent hard law[123] and attract the attention of increasingly 'green' finance. However, quite clearly, none of this is enough, to judge by the increasing and accelerated degradation of the biosphere. The same is true of invocations of the rule of law to prevent the abuse of private power, or of human rights to ensure equal access to a cleaner environment. While important in many ways, these do not arm us to resist the uncanny or otherworldly actions of the 'market' or the economic 'system' – a contemporary form of sublime forces, invisible to the naked eye and above all, beyond control.[124]

A first caveat concerns the target of critique as set out above. It is important to be clear from the outset that law (or any component of it, such as 'international law', 'criminal law' or 'human rights law') and its institutions are intrinsically neither

[120] Regulation includes national and European legislation, for instance on climate-related issues (such as de-carbonisation measures) or biodiversity (regulations of the use of pesticides on crops), judicial moves (of which some are quite spectacular : see for a comparative overview on the various waves of climate–related litigation, in which states have been enjoined to repair or implement new measures, M Torre-Schwab, 'La justice rappelle les Etats à leurs obligations' (2021) Oct/Dec *La Recherche* 26) and also of course treaty-making. Moreover, interesting advances are perceptible in the appearance of a concept such as 'ecocide' that could potentially provide new foundations for legal action in domestic and international criminal and human rights law (see D Zierler, *The Invention of Ecocide: Agent Orange, Vietnam, and the Scientists Who Changed the Way We Think About the Environment* (Atlanta GA, University of Georgia Press, 2011).

[121] As seen above, part of the problem may lie in the very term 'environment', as it suggests that we are severed from our outside surroundings.

[122] This is one way of seeing the concessions made by modern legal systems to new categories of material, non-human subjects (other than virtual corporate bodies), such as rivers, mountains or Nature itself, in the form of rights (see Descola *Par delà nature et culture* 336 on this challenge to naturalism). On the limits of rights as an appropriate technology for breaking epistemological frames (to which we shall return below), see R Kapour, *Gender, Alterity and Human Rights* (Cheltenham, Elgar, 2018).

[123] See R Shamir, 'Capitalism, Governance, and Authority: The Case of Corporate Social Responsibility' (2010) 6 *Annual Review of Law and Social Science* 531–53.

[124] On such forces in political theory, see Monateri, *Dominus Mundi*. Forces such as markets have purported autonomy, warped metaphors, and unfathomable modes of algorithmic calculation in the form of decision-making. The above remark is in no way to be understood as an anathema against technology itself nor indeed mathematical calculus. One of Bruno Latour's contributions is precisely on this point: the problem does not lie in technology (from which human life has always been indissociable) nor calculation (as the usual art of accountancy) but the (exorbitant) role they are called upon to play outside their own particular social function. Neither markets nor algorithms can accomplish what we expect from law.

good nor bad (nor favourable or unfavourable to ecological causes). As a secular mode of governance they are neither progressive or regressive per se, any more than a concept such as the rule of law, or indeed Enlightenment legal thought, is inevitably emancipatory or, conversely, the auxiliary of Western colonialism.[125] At the same time, this is not to say that legality is merely a toy in the hands of powerful forces – such as the economy – and that it does not command its own, equally potent and unpredictable, effects on our vision of reality, as seen above, or indeed in particular concrete contexts. All depends upon how it is put to work in a far broader matrix.[126] Nevertheless – and this is the fundamental aporia – this broader frame is shaped, reflexively, by the beliefs, visions and narratives that law gathers up like moss as it rolls on along its own trajectory.

Law has its own ontology (*ius*), or again, as critical legal scholarship would have it, lays down its own background rules (*lex*)[127] against which the slightest move produces unforeseen consequences (or 'legal irritants').[128] In this respect, law has inherent duality: it is both form-giving and world-making, language and meaning, closure and emancipation, stabilising and disruptive, technique and policy, secular and transcendent.[129] The important point at this stage is that law is not in itself the 'culprit', any more than other modes of existence such as religion, politics, or technology[130] (or indeed modernity, or Enlightenment thought[131]) are to be blamed for similar distortions induced by deliberate instrumentalisation or by unconscious category errors.

In respect of the latter, a further caveat is necessary. Latour's *Enquiry on modes of existence* draws attention to what looks (from an anthropological perspective) like a confusing dualism affecting legality ('Law I' and 'Law II').[132] Law's two natures

[125] A helpful perspective that rises deliberately above or beyond the purely domestic or municipal legal scene is that of 'legal revolution'. All revolutions are legal revolutions, writes Hauke Brunkhorst (*Critical Theory of Legal Revolutions*). His hypothesis is that every revolution is driven by the need for justice, and always acquires something that survives later reversals. Changes in the direction of justice are never stable, but there is nevertheless some kind of 'ratchet effect' every time that seems to leave a faint but indelible trace. The line we develop here is that law is ontologically dual. As a language, legality always contains its own nested alternatives, and its institutions and categories, unpredictable and potential reversals. Private international law is particularly illustrative of this duality, both by reason of its own peculiar history, its relationship with its public counterpart, and the deliberate indeterminacy of its central categories.

[126] Whether scheme, consciousness, epistemè or world view. See Pelluchon, *Les Lumières à l'âge du vivant*, 98, and see below, Part III. This matrix is broader and deeper than the 'background rules' that critical legal studies recall when analysing the effects of a given legal institution.

[127] This canon of critical legal studies on this point can be found in D Kennedy, *The Rise and Fall of Classical Legal Thought* (Beard Books, 2006); R Hale, 'Coercion and Distribution in a Supposedly Noncoercive State' (1923) 38 *Political Science Quarterly* 470 republished in *The Canon of American Legal Thought* (Princeton NJ, Princeton University Press, 2007).

[128] G Teubner, 'Legal Irritants : Good Faith in British Law' (1998) 61 *Modern Law Review* 1.

[129] See Pottage, 'Introduction'.

[130] The same can be said of other modes of existence and their distinctive artefacts, whether scientific, artistic, theological, economic, technological or political; these are all reflections of deeper lifeworlds that are driven by them in turn. Bruno Latour makes this point in respect of modernity, as does Corinne Pelluchon in respect of Enlightenment thought.

[131] On this point, in respect of the Enlightenment (and the possibility of overcoming its anthropomorphism), see C Pelluchon, *Les Lumières à l'âge du vivant* (Paris, ed Seuil, 2021).

[132] This point about category errors within the law, building on Latour's *Enquête* and its distinction between LAW and POL, is forcefully developed in K McGee, *Latour and the Passage of Law* (Edinburgh, Edinburgh University Press, 2016).

are in reality familiar to lawyers and legal historians, at least in the classical Roman tradition (*ius* and *lex, Recht* and *Gesetz*, *droit* and *loi*):[133] *ius* (or *droit*) refers to a specifically legal ontology whereas *lex* (various substantive policies 'enacted' in legislation, *lois*, or treaties, or encapsulated in judicial decisions) is essentially politics (or policy). Nevertheless, a reiterative mistake (a 'category error') in legal theory, that is frequently carried over into law's own internal 'theory of sources', is to mistake such sources for law itself. All too frequently, to the question 'what is law?', the answer is a descriptive enumeration of possible sites of law production (legislation, case law, custom, etc) and not a reflection on the mode of existence that could qualify as singularly legal (*jus*, or Law II). Law thereby loses its distinctiveness in relation to politics. And when it is thus reduced to some sort of combination of general prescriptions and individual judicial rulings, a confused discussion arises as to whether these are or are not political. Very obviously, they are! Whatever form in which they are purported to emerge and however apparently distanced from deliberate normative choices – whether as divine or secular reason incarnate; vernacular practice from time immemorial; the voice of judicial oracles or that of the sovereign people – they are not in any way synonymous with legality.

With respect to Law I, as seen above, there exists a widespread common sense to the effect that new legal norms in various forms – again, topically, an international convention on biodiversity or global warming, or the judicial consecration of a human or constitutional right to a healthy environment – would be enough to prevent the reproduction of the self-destructive bind into which humanity has roped itself by ignoring the urgent demands (whether ecological, social, economic or political) of the world on which its very survival depends. This is precisely because, as we have seen, law in the context of contemporary political ecology is usually perceived as coextensive with 'environmental regulation', or judicial remedies for ecological harm or state inaction on climate change, or the attribution of rights to non-human entities. This is not to say that instituting new legal norms or novel legal subjects is not important; indeed, we shall see below how various legal technologies can indeed make the difference.[134] However, this book does not engage on these terrains with recent (and rapid) evolutions in positive law (*lex*, or Law I), on which there are already many volumes of excellent literature.[135]

[133] On the specific epistemology of *jus*, see Schiavone, *Ius*. In terms of semantics Richard Janda (*Panarchy*, forthcoming, p 65) suggests in this respect that 'insofar as law is the residue of what is laid down but also the threshold of what might be determined, perhaps it contains linguistic possibilities unavailable (as clearly) in other languages. The conceptual distinction between "Law" and "Right" in English brings into view the crucial question of law's relation to what is right and/or rightful, not only in the sense of having a lawful or legitimate claim but also being just, equitable, fitting. Yet this distinction appears to be subsumed, if not set aside, in the very term "law", which refers both to the idea of law and to specific, legislated rule, statute, ordinance, or regulation … If in Latin each specific law (*lex*) is part of the general sense of law (*ius*) and thus referred to the idea of justice, in German and French, such laws appear to bear the burden or at least the trace of (being) right (*droit, Recht*).'

[134] Pottage, 'Introduction'. Such moves may also serve, conversely, to support a neoliberal or naturalist perspective: see below 285.

[135] See for interesting examples among many, including a framing in legal-theoretical terms: J Rochfeld, M Cornu and F Orsi (eds), *Dictionnaire des biens communs* (Paris, PUF, 2017), Quadrige; L Neyret, 'Construire la responsabilité écologique', in A Supiot and M Delmas-Marty (eds) *Prendre la responsabilité au sérieux* (Paris, Presses Universitaires de France, 2015) 121–22; K Birrell and J Dehm, 'International law

It aims instead at a more theoretical reflection on the ways in which *jus* determines our perception of the world we inhabit. In such a context, law will be understood as *nomos* or, in Robert Cover's famous words, 'a normative universe', an imagined reality we inhabit, a narrative and an aesthetic.[136] Legality – whether or not identified with the laws of nature – necessarily engages a certain world view, or cosmological vision, that constructs both the self and our representation of the other, 'outside or in the margins of the legal world: an "other" that is imagined as body, nature, animality, and violence or as a minor iteration of the true legal subject'.[137] Modernity's figure of nature, of which the originary emptiness provided the philosophical grounding for both property (Locke) and sovereignty (Hobbes), is an abstract space, devoid of (indigenous) inhabitants and their (invisible) cultures.[138] This means that an 'engagement with the world at ground level' – in other words, leaving behind the abstract perspective of modern thought – implies a 'concern for life-in-the-law', an attention 'to life-in-the-law as it expresses itself in its multiplicity'.

Legality thus defined will serve then as a prism through which to observe, and perhaps reverse, our current deleterious relationship with the planet. Such a prism will support or complement the more usual recourse on this topic to ethics, theology, anthropology, climate science, the political economy or 'deep' ecology, showing thereby that our choices, attitudes, representations hold together as a holistic and historic bloc.[139] It means that the largely neoliberal vision that we later-moderns have interiorised (that is, made natural-seeming to ourselves) and globalised (that is, imposed upon others), whose game we play even when we are unaware of doing so (this is the meaning of hegemony) has co-opted our legal responses along with all the rest. Importantly, the ontological privileges embodied in our legal worldview frame our relationship in similar ways in respect of nature and culture, humans and non-humans alike. It is not enough therefore to change the law (in the sense of introducing new norms), or assert its rule (whether or not we believe it serves the ideals of democracy and fairness[140]), if there is no further, radical transformation of attitudes and practices that run far deeper. This is where we come back to the question of alterity, and the choice of the disciplinary lenses through which to rethink law's relationship to difference.

VII. PRIVATE INTERNATIONAL LAW AND ITS DOUBLE SCENOGRAPHY

The project pursued in this book is to design an 'ecological jurisprudence' through the specific lenses of the branch of the law known either as 'private international

and the humanities in the Anthropocene', in S Chalmers and S Pahuja (eds), *Routledge Handbook of International Law and the Humanities* (London, Routledge, 2021) 411.

[136] Cover, 'Foreword: Nomos and Narrative'.

[137] P Legrand, 'Negative Comparative Law and its Theses' (2021) 16(2) *Journal of Contemporary Law* 647.

[138] See below 143 et seq.

[139] Fraser and Jaeggi, *Capitalism*, 202.

[140] On the ambivalence of the rule of law see below, 143 et seq.

law' or (mostly in the anglophone world) 'the conflict of laws'.[141] In this context, this discipline is envisaged as a repository of ideas about foreignness as embodied in legal terms, and underwritten by a certain relationship to difference.[142] Although the politics and epistemologies present in its long history are unstable and contested, as will be seen below, under any of its versions, alterity can be nevertheless be understood as its central feature: the conflict of laws bears the burden of navigating, importing, interpreting, mediating, translating, adjusting and indeed

[141] In continental legal systems, the term 'conflict of laws' usually refers to one sub-part of the broader discipline of private international law – that is, the principles that guide the determination of the (national or municipal) law governing a legal dispute, as opposed to the related but more procedural rules of jurisdiction and enforcement of foreign judgments. We owe the (contested) nomenclature of both 'private' and 'international' to the combined contributions of Jeremy Bentham (for the 'inter-national' as opposed to the law of nations) and Joseph Story's *Commentaries on the Conflict of Laws, Foreign and Domestic* (1834), stating that 'this branch of public law may fitly be denominated private international law, since it is chiefly seen and felt in its application to the common business of private persons' (10); compare, for authentication of this claim, F Juenger, *Selected Essays on the Conflict of Laws* (Leiden, Brill, 2001) 28; A Watson, *Joseph Story and the Comity of Errors: A Case Study in Conflict of Laws* (Atlanta, University of Georgia Press, 1992). Paradoxically, continental jurists tend to use this term, while common lawyers prefer to stay with the (older) 'conflict of laws' (Ulrich Huber, *De Conflictu Legum Diversarum in Diversis Imperiis*, 1689). Its 'private' nature is, as seen in Story's account above, a recent characterisation, and means that it deals (purportedly) only in issues that are governed by private law (a claim that still has force in continental European legal systems, where the public/private distinction is considered as significant, as we shall see below, Part I). Each state has its own set of private international law rules, but because this is potentially troublesome for the cross-border movement of judgements, various international institutions (such as the Hague Conference of Private international law) engage in the diplomatic elaboration of uniform rules. Arguably, at least, it may seem that the 'best' response to cross border conflicts of laws is to legislate 'transnational' rules. Indeed, the recourse to 'Transnational law' as framed by Philip Jessup (under that title, Yale University Press, 1956) has influential proponents today (see P Zumbansen (ed), *The Oxford Handbook of Transnational Law* (Oxford University Press, reflowable e-book). Whatever the virtues of this latter trend, the time-worn vocabulary of private international law may explain at least in part why the whole discipline seems so parochial to global legal theory, as Neil Walker observes (in *Intimations of Global Law* (Cambridge, Cambridge University Press, 2015)). Perhaps it would be better to spell out conflicts as de-centred, reflexive coordination of global legal interactions, with an Escher-like interconnection between 'public' and 'private', 'national' and 'international'. For alternative nomenclatures, see H Muir Watt, 'Discours sur les méthodes du droit international privé: pour un droit de l'inter-altérité', in *Les livres de poche de l'Académie de droit international de La Haye* (Brill/Nijhoff, 2019); D Boden, '"Erga-": Contribution sémantique et lexicale à une étude unifiée des relations entre ordres juridiques' (2021) *Revue critique de droit international privé* 5. The most important point however is that of the 'politics of naming', as observed by Upendra Bax in a reflection on 'the basic question: what is "private" about private international law?' He writes: 'The politics of naming is, of course, not innocent, though opinions may vary concerning the orders of complicity. The production of legal field that we name, by way of comity among scholars and practitioners, as 'private international law', of course, entails the most profound ways of imagining the intersection between national sovereignties, rights, and justice in an era of unprecedented global capital and human mobility' ('Mass torts, multinational enterprise liability and private international law', *Collected Courses of the Hague Academy of International Law* (Leiden, Brill, 1999) 297–426, 307).

[142] It is not an account of positive private international law in any particular national system. For my own co-authored presentation, see B Bureau and H Muir Watt, *Droit international privé,* 5th edn (Paris, Press Univ France, 2021). For a comparative approach based on case law, see H Muir Watt et al, *Global Private International Law* (Cheltenham, Elgar, 2018) ; *Droit international privé et Tournant global* (Paris, ed Pédone, 2021). For a study of the conflict of laws as a relationship towards cultural alterity, see 'Discours sur les méthodes'. For the most part in this book, the references to modes of legal reasoning within the conflict of laws concern the specific part of the discipline that is devoted to the determination of the applicable law ('conflicts of laws' in the strict sense, as seen above), rather than to 'jurisdiction' (or 'conflicts of jurisdiction' as will be seen below).

sometimes rejecting exogenous forms of law. It rests moreover on peculiar types of frontier-knowledge and boundary-work, required for travelling through and passing in-between the borders of countries, languages, categories, cultures and cosmologies. Compared with other areas of legality that might serve for a similar exercise (whether comparative legal studies, international law, legal anthropology or legal history) the terrain is likely to be unfamiliar for some readers, while for others the introduction of jurisprudence and interdisciplinarity into a field widely considered as essentially technical may seem unlikely.[143] A usual but largely reductionist account points to a triad of apparently simple legal issues: what court (or forum) decides a case? Which law(s) should apply? When to recognise and/or enforce a foreign judgment? Each of these raises in turn a myriad of systemic sub-questions: what sort of fora are involved here?[144] What is meant by 'law(s)'?[145] What exactly is being recognised or enforced?[146]

Yet undoubtedly, beneath (or because of?) this 'technocratic' surface,[147] the field has a very singular aura about it. Famously and reiteratively described, as seen above, as a 'dismal swamp' and a 'quaking quagmire',[148] it has also lent itself to the following observation by critical legal scholar of international law, Upendra Baxi: 'the sphere, or the legal field (to invoke Pierre Bourdieu), named as "private international law" or "conflict of laws", is among the most fascinating arenas of intersection of the legal conduct and imagination … Almost nothing in the tradition of legal studies is as exciting as the pursuit of anachronistic mediaeval subtleties that private international law brings by way of *embarrassment de riches* to the community of its reflexive

[143] Lawyers on the outside of the discipline are rarely interested in the arcana of private international law (and indeed, as a general matter, common law schools in the United States, United Kingdom and Canada do not make it a mandatory subject of study, resulting in a largely uninformed academy and profession). Conversely, private international lawyers are rarely preoccupied with jurisprudence ('theory' in this context). On this disciplinary isolation, to which we shall return more specifically later in this book, see JR Paul, 'The Isolation of Private International Law' (1988) 7 *Wis Int'l LJ* 149.

[144] The 'forum' is often (but not always) a metaphor for a state jurisdictional system. Additionally, what kind of rules/discretionary powers are involved and to what extent is the public international law of jurisdiction involved in the content of the latter? Does 'a case' signify a dispute or a singular issue? Is there a threshold of the 'international' that triggers these questions?

[145] Law may mean a national 'legal system', but it can also signify a singular rule (or case law). Moreover, as will be seen below, the great challenge of the current 'global turn' is to determine the legal status of non-state law (whether infra-state, indigenous, religious or 'private' norms). A vertiginous issue known as *renvoi* is whether 'law' includes the private international law rules that accompany or circumscribe the scope of the substantive principles of a given legal 'system' (the latter concept being usually understood as including such rules of scope).

[146] Recognition is usually understood as the legal operation by which effect is given to a situation created abroad, but the latter may be rights and obligations (debt; custody), a legal status (parenthood; gender), or a factual relationship (unofficial partnerships). One of the hottest political debates today in Europe is the extent to which human rights law (notably, the right to privacy as in Art 8 European Convention on Human Rights) includes the right to the cross-border permanence of a family status (say, same-sex marriage; motherhood of a child born of a foreign surrogate, etc) despite the formal illegality of all the latter under the law of the state of the forum.

[147] See A Riles, 'A New Agenda for the Cultural Study of Law: Taking on the Technicalities' (2005). 53 *Buffalo LR* 973. Interestingly, the author's uses the discipline of the conflict of laws to make a forceful ethnographic point about the artefactual processes of creating legal knowledge.

[148] As already indicated above, the ecological dimension of this worn metaphor will be taken seriously, particularly in Part II of this book below.

practitioners …'.[149] A brief, preliminary presentation will be provided in Part I below for those whose curiosity is sufficiently aroused by such an (ironic) promise of intellectual excitement to delve into this book from outside the discipline. The immediate point here, as a matter of introduction, is to underline its value as heuristic[150] within the broader project pursued here. This value is linked to what might be described as the dual scenography of the conflict of laws.[151]

On the one hand, it is located at the very heart of modern legal thought.[152] It was already in central place within the political economy of the investiture struggles of the Middle Ages that arguably marked the origins of our modern state form.[153] It gave flesh thereafter to the great fictions of modernity such as the 'autonomy' of the subject, and clothed the sovereign exception or reason of state in the eminently legal form of *ordre public*. Today, in the thick of the global turn, it is at the heart of contemporary notions and discourses of governance, where it maintains the schism between the public and the private, and continues to arbitrate existential oppositions between law on the one hand and fact, politics, society, and nature on the other. In this sense, the conflict of laws is the very embodiment of the 'jurisprudence of jurisdiction', constantly drawing lines, congealing dichotomies, creating attachments, sorting the familiar from the foreign – an emblematic arbitrator of boundary struggles.[154] Produced by the geospatial turn (in law as in modern thought), the jurisdictional frontier is, as Shaun McVeigh points out, the metaphysical point at which each of the legal parts are related and put into circulation.[155] What is of further, prime importance here is that jurisdiction is an idiom that produces a form of life, a 'morphology of the modern subject'.[156] At the outpost of state or the confines of empire, it has also provided, over a long period of modern history, various sets of tools and devices, fictions and institutions, that have served the 'great bifurcation' described above, inducing the extraterritorial, groundless (*hors sol*) expansion of the economy and the correlative depletion of the world's natural resources.[157] At this point, however, cracks appear from time to time, as if Gaia was waiting beneath law's

[149] U Baxi, 'Mass torts, multinational enterprise liability and private international law', *Collected Courses of the Hague Academy of International Law* (Leiden, Brill, 1999) 305.

[150] A heuristic can be defined as an aid (in the form of a mental shortcut) to learning, discovery or problem-solving.

[151] On law's dual scenography, see Goodrich, *Law in the Courts of Love*.

[152] On this theme, see Monateri, *Dominus Mundi*: thus, the philosophical, linguistic and emblematically legal enigma of the inscription, *Dominus Mundi Sum et Autem Maris*, in the margins of the *Corpus iuris* located the conflict of laws at the symbolic core of the tensions between divine and terrestrial kingdoms and between earthly and unearthly sovereigns.

[153] Kjaer, *The Law of Political Economy*.

[154] The semantics of jurisdiction are complex. According to context, 'jurisdiction' may mean a particular court or national court system, or a given country or sovereign space, or the reach of sovereign power to prescribe, adjudicate or enforce (as in public international law). The concept of 'jurisdictional jurisprudence' (McVeigh, *Jurisprudence of Jurisdiction*) will be used to designate a particular mode of legal thought that includes all of these.

[155] McVeigh, *Jurisprudence of Jurisdiction* 14.

[156] Ibid, 15. On the various ways in which comparative law is (albeit rarely) also used liminally in domestic cases to shape the (foreign) subject (as 'legal barbarian'), see Maldonado Bonilla, *Legal Barbarians*.

[157] Law's role in this de-grounding (or disembedding) of the economy will be developed further below (in Part III). It is a point that has been made forcefully by several private international lawyers (such as R Wai, 'Transnational Liftoff and Juridical Touchdown: The Regulatory Function of Private International Law in an Era of Globalization' (2002) 40 *Columbia Journal of Transnational Law* 209; K Pistor, *Code of Capital: How the Law Creates Wealth and Inequality* (Princeton NJ, Princeton University Press, 2020).

conventional categories like a giant 'legal irritant', ready to break through existing legal frames in highly unpredictable ways.[158]

On the other hand, the long history of the discipline unveils fragile intimations[159] of an alternative mode of existence, that may serve as an intellectual model or style[160] with which to reduce (if not reverse) the marks of naturalism on legal thought. This is the cue for the entry of its 'minor jurisprudence',[161] composed of the most humble[162] but durable of legal world visions.[163] As will become further apparent, private international law's mundane 'technocratic' labour as described above, allocating and distributing at the confines of various categories and belief systems, conceals another, hidden, ontology of the frontier, in which the latter is not a wall but a place of passing,[164] not an exclusion but an in-between space,[165] not severance but ligature. Its unusual continuity with a Roman legal legacy (one indeed that predates the high Middle Ages and the emergence of modern thought[166]) is enlightening when we explore law's complex epistemology in pursuit of alternative categories and modes of reasoning. Private international law discipline is an emblematic illustration of legality's mode of existence as 'an ecology of ligatures'.[167]

[158] The expression is once again Gunter Teubner's ('Legal Irritants').

[159] The expression is Neil Walker's, *The Intimations of global law* (Oxford, Oxford University Press, 2015).

[160] On the idea of private international law as intellectual style, see K Knop, A Riles, 'Space, Time and Historical Injustice: A Feminist Conflict-of-Laws Approach to the "Comfort Women" Agreement' (2017) 102 *Cornell Law Rev* 853: 'in the mode of an interdisciplinary experiment, we deploy the conflicts technique of sequencing spatio-temporal horizons as a more specified and hopeful approach to a feminist future'.

[161] Again, Goodrich, *Law in the Courts of Love.*

[162] It is literally residual in that even in civilian 'inquisitorial or non-adversarial judicial systems, it is not (or only rarely) invoked by the court of its own motion.

[163] That 'cultures' (legal or not) are composed of multiple and contradictory world visions is nothing new. An illuminating observation can be found in W Stoczkowski, *Anthropologies rédemptrices: le monde selon Lévi-Strauss* (Paris, ed Hermann, 2008) 19 (discussing the relationship between individual idiosyncratic thought – here, that of Levi-Strauss, and wider, collective cosmologies): 'la cosmologie reste … une création collective, élaborée à partir de représentations partagées antérieures, ce qui l'inscrit dans une trame faite de plusieurs visions du monde, plus ou moins répandues, qui s'opposent et se complètent dans notre tradition culturelle. C'est donc cette dimension collective que je tenterai de mettre au jour en interrogeant l'œuvre d'un anthropologue singulier dont la pensée, comme celle de tout être humain, appartient à ce déconcertant champ des possibles qu'aucun individu ne crée séparément des autres, et que nous appelons culture'.

[164] For this reversal see A Brett, *Changes of State: Nature and the Limits of the City in Early Modern Natural Law* (Princeton NJ, Princeton University Press, 2011).

[165] Pottage, 'Introduction', 6 on the in-between spaces that produce legal form.

[166] We return to the Roman law legacy in Part I below. The point is not to demonstrate any (doubtful) continuity between the Roman law of the conflict of laws and that of contemporary private international law, but to point to a triple, less visible, linkage (of which the various parts will be further developed below). Firstly, the influence of Carl von Savigny on the modern model of the conflict of laws coincides with the aspiration of the Germanic historical school in the nineteenth century towards a Romanist legal pedigree. Secondly, classical Roman law first gave rise to a specifically legal epistemology (*ius*) of which the heritage marked modern Western/European metaphysics and thereafter modern law (including modern private international law). Thirdly, the exploration of what we mean by 'Roman law' itself uncovers successive and variegated strata with equally diverse functions in society, harbouring the same duality (the double scenography) described in the text above.

[167] Latour, *Body Politics*, and McGee, *Latour and the Passage of Law*, describing legality in general. Here, the metaphor of the ecosystem can be understood to describe legality as a mode of existence beyond any particular 'ecological' signification. But here, of course, the implication is that the latter is included within a second, deeper meaning.

It is not then that the various positive incarnations of the conflict of laws have been in any way immune to more dominant separatist ideologies within the law, nor that the discipline did not spur on the distortions of the political economy or encourage the exclusionary universalisation of 'civilised' values. On the contrary, as will be seen in Part III below, the conflict of laws was (and still is) instrumental both in reinforcing geopolitical boundaries and in spreading the neoliberal tendencies of contemporary legality in the name of individual autonomy. But in the shadow of the more portentous, symbolic divisions between sovereigns accomplished by its public international counterpart, it has also stood for a more invisible labour of connection, translation, and mending. It represents the intimate and the homely, as opposed to the grandiose; the in-between as opposed to closure and determinacy. The jurisprudential promise of the discipline lies in this very paradoxical duality; its own bipolarity reflecting the broader schism within international law. And while such schizophrenia is obviously true for legality in general (or specific institutions, embodiments or offshoots thereof, such as rights, courts, equality, tradition, rules, etc), the contention in this book is that the conflict of laws' peculiar relationship to alterity provides an appropriate lens through which to bring an ecological horizon back into legal focus.

VIII. LAW'S RESIDUES AND THE SHADOW STORY

It is arguably in law's (deep) 'nature' to oscillate between poles.[168] *Ius* and *lex*; law and *nomos*. But while the (ontological, temporal, philosophical, religious) bifurcation of our world is traceable to a specifically legal vision embedded in Christian theology and liberal economics, it is important to contextualise and nuance each of the paradigm ruptures that marked this singular trajectory. In themselves and whatever their subsequent significance, singly or conjointly, they often represented resistance to previous forms of obscurantism or oppression. As Philippe Descola observes, early modernity acknowledged the necessity of nature's 'splendid alterity'. Even in Buffon's great *Epoques de la Nature* (1780),[169] the destinies of earth and humanity were still interconnected. And while the giddy cycles of (European) natural law had no doubt served above all to define civilisation as the ultimate schism within human nature,[170] the shadowy survival of other non-modern cosmologies (largely marginalised as primitive or peripheral) along with their alternative forms of normativity and inclusive collective life that have never sought to sever nature and sovereignty,[171] open

[168] On this aspect of law's specific mode of existence (on which more follows below in Part II), see K McGee, 'On Devices and Logics of Legal Sense: Toward Socio-technical Legal Analysis', in McGee, *Latour and the Passage of Law* 61–92. A similar sense of oscillation is arguably also present in various works on specific fields of legality, such as international law: see for a prominent example, M Koskenniemi, *From Apology to Utopia* (Cambridge, Cambridge University Press, 2005).

[169] GL Le Clerc de Buffon, *Les Epoques de la Nature* (1780).

[170] Human nature, observes Descola, is the 'great oxymoron' of the West: *Par delà nature et culture* 313.

[171] In Descola's vocabulary and classification, these non-modern cosmologies are 'non-naturalist' (insofar as they do not naturalise the distinction between nature and culture). For forms of non-exclusive inclusiveness, see H Lindhal, *Authority and the Globalisation of Inclusion and Exclusion* (Cambridge, Cambridge University Press, 2018). Such inclusiveness involves learning to live inside, with the consciousness that there is no escape to the outside: Latour, *Où suis-je?*

the alternative pathway that weaves its way through this project.[172] Such a pathway can also be understood as the elusive and changing tracks through the 'swamp', the intimations so faint that the only way across is an extreme attention to the signs emitted by myriad other minuscule life forms which we have devoted centuries to making invisible.[173]

The idea then is that certain traces, residues or intimations still present in legality's own deeper ecology, can suggest ways of inhabiting the earth's fragile 'crisis zone' alongside its non-human beings and inanimate things. Tracing such intimations of different visions within the law requires an archaeological unearthing of what Peter Goodrich has called, strikingly, 'law's residues';[174] these are embodied in what he calls law's 'minor jurisprudences'.[175] There is, he writes, 'a history of the dark side of law, of its other scene, of that which it does not know and so cannot control. It is in this sense a history of the desires that survived law. A catalogue of fictions, images and possibilities discarded or repressed by law'. In the shadow, then (or the swamp?[176]), of law's conventional role as conveyor of the great severance between humankind and its others, lies its 'other scene', far removed from the legal ontologies, aesthetics and paradigms that structured the dichotomic architecture of modern thought. Here plays out the destiny of law at its last frontier. The irony may be that this is the very threshold at which the frontiers that conferred such apparent invulnerability to the purveyors of modernity, must disappear.

IX. BRICOLAGE, INTERDISCIPLINARITY AND METHOD

As will already be evident from various allusions in this introduction to a wide variety of fields of knowledge, the quest in this book for a new design – that is, for the alternative legal forms underlying the specific technologies of private international law – appeals to an interdisciplinary perspective. The conceit of such an approach, which rests inevitably on incursions into other sciences (with correlative losses in translation), may no doubt seem methodologically unacceptable to experts from the latter.[177]

[172] The idea of excavating alternatives lying beneath monolithic accounts of history is of course a recognisable move in legal critique: see for example, L Esclava, M Fakhri, V Nesiah (eds), *Bandung, Global History, and International Law: Critical Pasts and Pending Futures* (Cambridge, Cambridge University Press, 2017). On genealogies, see below 69.

[173] On the ethics 'emitted' by the beings that exist alongside us (and within us), see below 292 and Latour, *Où suis-je*. On peregrination through dark or shadow pathways, see S Tesson, *Les chemins noirs* (Paris, Gallimard, 2015); on 'deambulation' (with a legal twist), see S Vaxenum, 'Du droit de déambuler. Le paysage comme lieu de passages' (2021) 19 *Les Cahiers de l'Ecole de Blois* 10–19.

[174] Goodrich, *Law in the Courts of Love*.

[175] Significant from an ecological perspective, 'residues' are also part of the critical vocabulary of various disciplines, including the political economy (value), linguistics (meaning), contemporary Italian theories of biopolitics, sovereignty and law (life: for instance, in Agamben's terms, *homo sacer* is a remnant of Roman law, a lingering, marginal enigma at the very edges of perceptibility): *Homo Sacer: Sovereign Power and Bare Life, Meridian : Crossing Aesthetics* (Palo Alto CA, Stanford University Press, 1998).

[176] On the metaphor of the swamp, a discursive trope in the conflict of laws, see below 177.

[177] Indeed, even Bruno Latour's formidable Inquiry generated criticism from purists speaking from within each of the multiple modes of existence whose values he attempted to identify through decades of ethnographic work. On such critique, see Latour's own account in his ' Biography of an inquiry: On a book

Moreover, even supposing that scientific accuracy or plausibility is ever attainable from the disciplinary outside, there remains a further, methodological conundrum in respect of the choice of the various strands, schools, concepts, texts, or authors that within any field of knowledge are necessarily part of a holistic body of learning. In selecting and decontextualising, the risk is to misinterpret, deform, underestimate, or omit any one given element. The particular form of 'bricolage'[178] practised in this book abandons any claim to the 'proper' – that is, fulsome and fully accurate – apprehension of any learning from outside or indeed inside – but this point will be the object of further developments (below) – of the law. It rests for a large part on deliberately 'naïve' readings (perhaps indeed mere language games) of texts or concepts that appear, beyond the frontiers of the law, to echo a specifically legal idiom, or conversely, within the latter, to carry a specifically ecological signification.[179] The methodological choice, then, is to take the surface or semantic value of (Latourian) 'semiotic objects' very seriously. The new jurisprudential design to which this book aspires entails an excavation of meaning underlying the vocabulary and grammar of legality, while alternative legal forms may emerge in the invisible ink of language from law's own outside.

Thus, law's own remarkable propensity to resort to metaphors and fictions creates a constant supply of 'naturalist' imagery (the 'body' of law; the 'nature' of legal relationships; and indeed again the 'swamp' of legal knowledge ...). Conversely, resolutely literal understandings of various notions borrowed from other disciplines will be used to create a bridge between legality and concepts from distinct fields that contribute to an ecological jurisprudence. Among many examples are the reference by Jacques Derrida to the 'conflict of laws' (within the law of hospitality), Emmanuel Lévinas' paradox of self as alterity (*l'être en tant qu'autre*), Carl Schmitt's *nomos of the earth* (in which the ultimate state of earthly lawlessness is invested with a telluric meaning), Balkin/Valverde's jurisdictional 'chronotopes', Ratna Kapur's search for legal epistemologies 'beyond the fishbowl', and many more.[180] In this respect, horizons, conflicts, boundaries, linkages, relations or indeed swamps (a term that has become a near canonical description of the intricate and often messy legal assemblages involved

about modes of existence' (2013) 43(2) *Social Studies of Science* 287–301. On the losses in translation that practices of interdisciplinarity may often entail due to inaccurate representations of one discipline by another, A Riles, 'Anthropology, Human Rights, and Legal Knowledge: Culture in the Iron Cage' (2006) 108(1) *American Anthropologist* 52–65, providing an example relating to debates between critical international lawyers and anthropologists about cultural relativity and human rights (see below spec. 285).

[178] The reference is of course to the metaphor proposed by Claude Lévi-Strauss in the first chapter of his *La Pensée Sauvage*, in 1962. Its use here is probably the very illustration of the risks (of oversimplification, or deformation) identified in the text above. In anthropology and philosophy, bricolage is an extremely sophisticated concept: see A Mélice, 'Un concept lévi-straussien déconstruit: le « bricolage »' (2009) 5 (656) *Les Temps Modernes* 83–98.

[179] Playing language games instead of doing 'proper' science (or science properly) is indeed a critique addressed to 'French anthropology' from which much is borrowed in what follows. See M Fischer, 'The lightness of existence and the origami of "French" anthropology: Latour, Descola, Viveiros de Castro, Meillassoux, and their so-called ontological turn' (2014) 4(1) *HAU: Journal of Ethnographic Theory* 331–55.

[180] All these works are discussed and referenced below.

in the conflict of laws) will be taken as it were at their face value. The wider endeavour is one of translation (a cultural, interpretative process, but also the uncovering of an ontology of the in-between, as will be seen below) with the purpose of excavating the deeper, often alternative, meaning of concepts and categories that appear quite 'naturally' to belong to the law, and what is more in an invariable format or content. In other words, this unorthodox exercise in interdisciplinary thought is designed to make available a 'shadow' version or avatar of this particular discipline, with the design to 'ecologise' legal thinking more generally.

X. WHAT IS ECOLOGICAL ABOUT THIS ALTERNATIVE JURISPRUDENTIAL DESIGN?

The object of this book is not 'environmental law', either as an exercise in judicial case tracking, *légistique*,[181] or as the search for legal technologies such as human or natural rights that would further the ecological cause. As seen above, the claim here is that it is both unfeasible and implausible to approach cultural (law included!) and biological diversity as distinct phenomena. Making room for the latter inevitably involves a radical transformation of our understanding of the former. To ecologise, according to Latour's definition, is to move in a direction that is exactly opposite to that in which the 'Moderns' have become engulfed and which has led to the denial and destruction of alterity (whether in the shape of humanity, foreign cultures, other life forms or indeed ecospheres). Modern law must prepare for a change of jurisprudential shape; such a change commands its ability to accommodate the demands of alterity emanating from what we perceive to be our natural surroundings. The ecology of the conflict of laws serves in what follows as an avatar, a guide through legality's often 'dismal' swamp in search of traces of an alternative jurisprudence.

XI. PLAN AND PROJECT

How then do we go about this return to the terrestrial,[182] the 'juridical touchdown'[183] or legal 're-earthing' from modern law's disembodied or disembedded orbit? Does

[181] For the anglophone reader, '*la legistique*' is the (Napoleonic) art of rational legislation (combining law, sociology and linguistics). The official website of the French government contains a guide which promises 'l'ensemble des règles, principes et méthodes qui doivent être observés dans la préparation des textes normatifs: lois, ordonnances, decrets, arrêtés'. This is of course a reminder to keep in mind that French-style rationalism-formalism as core to *lex*, or 'Law I', is in many ways extreme as compared to some of the common law tradition of the past century. Nevertheless, and perhaps paradoxically, the common law tradition of *lex* has arguably gone further than its civilian counterpart in the 'capture of the international' through the use of traditional modern-legal concepts, as will be seen below in Part III.

[182] On the terrestrial as opposed to the territorial, see Lindhal, *Authority and the Globalisation of Inclusion and Exclusion*.

[183] See R Wai, 'Transnational Liftoff and Juridical Touchdown' (coining this term in a different context, to which we shall return below in Part III).

the ultimate frontier threaten the very existence of legal prescriptivity as we know it, in the same way that the ontological revolution that was the secularisation of the modern world, replaced religion as a form of transcendence by reason (framed once again as natural law)? Will law undergo a similar displacement and eclipse, in favour of equally awe-inspiring or terrifying forms of (algorithmic and digital) combined de-spatialisation and mechanisation?[184] Is there any chance of accommodating in legal form the radical alterity of the 'heathen earth'[185] and thereby ensuring the responsiveness we owe to those living and inanimate entities that depend upon us for their, and not just our, survival?[186] How can the status of our natural surroundings as radical exteriority become an injunction to recognise our environment as part of ourselves? Might law's own ontological model or epistemological schemes contribute in turn towards the enriching of political-ecological, eco-aesthetic or earth scientific thought?

By way of a very partial response, the use of private international law as a heuristic opens several avenues that will unfold successively below. They posit that law's encounter with alterity is the core axis of what might be called an ecological *nomos*. While alterity in this context is usually understood as foreign norms or alien cultural practices, it can also be related more specifically to the 'splendid otherness of nature', animality and other life forms.[187] The demonstration then draws on the constant interweaving of two different accounts of such encounters. The first corresponds to a largely asymmetrical vision of otherness as a mirror image of self. It is present within the conflict of laws as the dominant methodological model. The foreign – here, foreign law – will be allowed to cross the threshold of the host legal system to the extent that it 'fits' or complies with a broader institutional and epistemological scheme. The latter is monist in the sense that it accepts only one legitimate perspective of (social, cultural, biological) reality.

The second account embodies a minor jurisprudence or shadow avatar of this conventional perspective. The concept of an 'avatar' evokes certain animist indigenous cosmologies, for which there are invisible bridges between plural worlds: this world and the next. In this respect, particular attention will be paid below to the aptitude of the avatar to inhabit a specific space of the 'in-between'. The significance of the 'shadow' in this context refers to an aesthetic and an ontology of the subterranean, the denied or repressed, the haunting, eerie or uncanny. However, in an additional twist, borrowing from feminist and psychoanalytical theory, the shadow

[184] On de-spatialisation of law as the consequence of the digital revolution, see A Garapon, J Lassègue, *Le numérique contre le politique* (Paris, Presses Univ de France, 2021), or indeed as characteristic of the coming era, after the Anthropocene, the 'Novacene' (the expression is James Lovelock's, in *Novacene, The Coming Age of Hyperintelligence* (Boston MA, MIT Press, 2019).

[185] K McGee, *The Heathen Earth, Trumpism and Political Ecology* (Goleta CA, Punctum Books, 2017).

[186] Latour, *Enquête*, 441 et seq.

[187] See again Lévi-Strauss, *La Pensée Sauvage*, reminding us that the same frontier raised by the West between humanity and nature, 'constantly pushed back', also serves to divide humanity.

also evokes something that is both mimetic, indetachable, and at the same time form-giving or shape-providing.[188]

The contrast and paradoxical linkages between these indissociable legal modes will serve to probe the ideological (in the sense of epistemological, ontological, aesthetic, ethical or political) underpinnings of the lens through which law understands, and reacts to, extraneous cultures, alien values and foreign life forms.

PART I introduces the methods and epistemology of private international law. It resonates with Descola's observation that instead of trying to reduce, through simplistic explanatory schemes, the diversity of ways of inhabiting the world, the important point is to ask what makes all these compatible without reducing them to sameness or oneness.[189] The real need, then, is for a syntax of translation[190] that allows for the coexistence of multiple cosmologies. This is the self-assigned task of the conflict of laws, to the extent at least that the latter qualify as a legal form – a central point in the discipline's methodological controversies. Here we propose an exploration of the conceptual landscape of the discipline as shaped in this respect by its Roman heritage[191] in search of insights into the epistemological framework of our

[188] J Benjamin, *Shadow of the Other. Intersubjectivity and Gender in Psychoanalysis* (Abingdon, Routledge, 1998); and on cognition and the ways in which the social construction of a binary opposition between 'masculine' and 'feminine' has influenced the social construction of science, see E Fox Keller, *The Mirage of a Space Between Nature and Nurture*: at every moment of perception of the world around us, we isolate objects as discrete entities with clear boundaries while we relegate the rest to a background in which the objects exist.

[189] Descola, *Par delà nature et culture* 689. In international and comparative legal scholarship (and incorporated within legal artefacts, including the US dollar), within or without the conflict of laws, there is much emphasis on unity in diversity (*E pluribus unum* …; juridical 'harmony' without unification, as will be seen below, etc). However, these may nevertheless be (possibly diluted) forms of monism/universalism that aspire to commonality and correspondence, and are not necessarily associated with the pluriversality envisaged as an alternative jurisprudential design, outlined below in the rest of this book.

[190] On the idea of translation itself as a third language or *lingua franca*, see below 187 et seq. A key point here is that commonality or commensurability does not signify sameness or uniformity, even though that is indeed a correspondence that monological forces always seek to attain.

[191] The 'statutist tradition' covers the methods first devised in the late Middle Ages by Bartolus (1313–57) and the Commentators of the *Corpus Iuri*. See P Stein, *Roman Law in European History* (Cambridge, Cambridge University Press, 1999) 71 et seq. Initially, for Bartolus and the Commentators of the late Middle Ages, the *ius commune* provided the methods with which to interpret local statutes, and in such a way as to restrict the opportunity for derogation. Later attitudes varied considerably from place to place towards the *Corpus Iuris* and Roman law more generally, but the conviction remained that conflicts between local, secular laws took place in the shadow of an overarching normative scheme (whether *Corpus, Institutes*, Roman classical culture, or natural reason) that commanded a uniform method of delimitation of local statutes or customs. The same can be said of premodern conceptions of law (customs, status) underlying the emerging discipline of the conflict of laws in early continental European modernity. Because local customs were still understood as interpretative variations on Roman law as the sole depositary of a legal essence or authority, the focus of the intense juridical labour of the post-glossators was the spatial (personal or territorial) projection of forms that were recognised as unquestionably juridical. In continental Europe, their methodological heritage would endure despite the vicissitudes of the authority and perceptions of the *ius commune* and the highly variegated political scene, until the great revival of classical (pre-Justinian) Roman-Christian law as reason, culture and ethos in the nineteenth century. Neo-statutism is the version developed in the mid-twentieth century by American scholars, for the purposes of intranational federal conflicts of laws. These approaches are often (confusingly) named 'unilateralism', as opposed to the 'multilateralism' (or bilateralism) that was to characterise 'Savignian' methods of choice of law. On the particular method associated with the influential opus of Carl von Savigny, see below 72 et seq.

legal understandings of difference. The conflict of laws' particular methodologies for approaching alterity are understood in this context not as neutral modes of allocation of laws, but as the legal expression of various attitudes towards the foreign, emerging and declining according to historical contingencies and contemporary ideologies in legal thought.

Redefined as the channels through which law encounters alterity, these methods shape and are shaped by multiple ideas, debates, fictions, representations and polemics surrounding individual and collective exposure to difference. Such exposure often leads to (politically and psychologically) defensive reactions that involve a rejection of any form of plurality.[192] However, the conflict of laws shows that there exists an alternative. In line with the lessons of the era of the 'the post',[193] the comforts of legal monism in terms of certainty, linearity, centrality of decision, and the overarching position of the legal interpreter (or national judge) are left behind. In the conflict of law's minor jurisprudence, the (dangerous) legal method[194] of dealing with alterity is (politically) pluralist – and, as will be seen in the following parts, (aesthetically) de-centred, and (ethically) hospitable.

PART II connects the singular legal ontology and aesthetics of the conflict of laws. It recalls that our relationship to forms of life other than our own, whether cultural or natural, visible or invisible, are and always have been indissociable from a specifically legal understanding of the world order. As Bruno Latour explains, we need to be attentive to 'the passage of law' – emblematically visible in private

[192] On the relationship between political or collective ethno-legal nationalism and defences deployed within the individual psyche, see Mazurel, *L'inconscient ou l'oubli de l'histoire*; F Benslama, *La psychanalyse à l'épreuve de l'Islam, Flammarion, «Champs» Essais* (Paris, 2002) 84; on the place of collective identity in populist and xenophobic 'nativism', see M Lazar, 'Du populisme à gauche: les cas français et italien' (1997) 56 *Vingtième Siècle. Revue d'Histoire* 121–31. *Cf* on the idea of a collective subconscious composed of shared archetypes and instincts, C Jung, *L'Energétique psychique* (Geneva, Georg, 1973) 99. On the continuity between legal ethnocentrism and its contemporary avatar of 'global centrism', see M Xifaras, 'The Global Turn in Legal Theory' (2016) XXIX (1) *Canadian Journal of Law & Jurisprudence* 215–43.

[193] On the post-structuralist, post-modern 'era of the post', see Xifaras, 'The Global Turn in Legal Theory'. This era undoubtedly includes 'post-monist' jurisprudence: see N Roughan and A Halpin, *In Pursuit of Pluralist Jurisprudence* (Cambridge, Cambridge University Press, 2017). The conflict of laws is very present in this new post-monist literature: see PS Berman, *Global Legal Pluralism: A Jurisprudence of Law Beyond Borders* (New York, Cambridge. University Press, 2012); R Michaels, 'Globalizing Savigny? The State in Savigny's Private International Law and the Challenge of Europeanization and Globalization' in M Stolleis and W Streeck (eds), *Dezentralisierung. Aktuelle Fragen politischer und rechtlicher Steuerung Im Kontext der Globalisierung* (Baden-Baden, Nomos, 2007) 119; G Teubner, *Constitutional Fragments: Societal Constitutionalism and Globalization* (Oxford, Oxford University Press, 2012); and (dismissing the conflict of laws in this context) Neil Walker, *Intimations of Global Law* (Cambridge, Cambridge University Press, 2015). As will be seen below, there is a triad of theoretical challenges to monism – analytical, meta-jurisprudential, or pertaining to political or moral legitimacy (see J Fabra-Zamora (ed) *Jurisprudence in a Globalized World* (Cheltenham, Elgar 2020)) reopening the quest for a jurisprudential exploration of the 'intimations' of global legal pluralism. Some of these strands are analytical or jurisprudential, some historical, some embedded in societal (or other) constitutionalism and others still others venture into multidisciplinarity.

[194] On Jung's characterisation of psychoanalysis in these terms, see J Kerr, *A Most Dangerous Method* (London, Vintage Books, 1994), www.psychanalyseactuelle.com/ textes/a-dangerous-method. Jung conceived psychoanalysis as a cultural theory. See M Vannoy Adams, *Interdisciplinary Applications of Jungian Psychoanalysis* (Abingdon, Routledge, 2014).

international law's 'labour of connection' – in order to retrieve something of the world's connectedness.[195] The latter was largely shattered by the 'jurisdictional jurisprudence'[196] that presided over a vast emptying of place and a repression of histories through the agency of law. Seeing legality itself as an 'ecology of ligatures' contains the promise that it might reflect, or shape a greater responsiveness towards our natural surroundings.

In this respect, private international law's specific legal methods allow for the coexistence of a plurality of perspectives. They have rarely, if at all, been explored from the angle of legal aesthetics. A canonical example of the latter can be found in Pierre Schlag's 'Aesthetics of American law', in which the author explores the (various, evolving) styles of legal forms understood as tropes, metaphors, methods, concepts, structures and modes of reasoning.[197] However, PG Monateri's recent reflection on geopolitics and the styles of law beyond the state and after the global turn, have drawn attention to the types of resistance that legal forms in various traditions may oppose to the encroachment of an increasingly homogeneous normative space, leaving room nevertheless for processes of translation.[198] In a similar vein that takes us from the aesthetic to the metaphysical, the so-called ontological turn in (legal) anthropology invites us to imagine the means to bring together, on an epistemic plane, phenomena (entities, relations) that appear at first sight to be incommensurable.[199] Such a conversation about modes of assembling the (juridically) heterogeneous, or imagining a syntax of translation and reinterpretation,[200] is precisely one way of defining the conflict of laws. Moreover, with strong echoes in feminist and eco-aesthetics,[201] the

[195] Latour (*Enquête*), 357 et seq. On an analogous idea of connectedness in relation to law and cross-border social ligature, see too C Scott and R Wai, 'Transnational Governance of Corporate Conduct through the Migration of Human Rights Norms: The Potential Contribution of Transnational "Private" Litigation', in C Joerges et al, *Transnational Governance and Constitutionalism* (Oxford, Hart, 2004) 287–320.

[196] McVeigh, *Jurisprudence of Jurisdiction*.

[197] P Schlag, 'The Aesthetics of American Law' (2002) 115 *Harv L Rev* 1047, 1055; 'Normativity and the Politics of Form' (1991) 139 *U Pa L Rev* 801.

[198] P-G Monateri, *Geopolitica del diritto. Genesi, governo e dissoluzione dei corpi politici* (Rome/Bari, ed Laterza, 2013).

[199] P Descola, *Les formes du visible* (Paris, Le Seuil, 2021).

[200] With reference to the work of Michel Serres, *La Traduction. Hermès III* (Paris, Les Éditions de Minuit, 1974). See too on the processes of translation and alteration, crucial to all modes of existence, Latour, *Enquête*, 53, 207.

[201] 'Eco-aesthetics', a relatively new sub-field of philosophical aesthetics that has come to comprise the 'aesthetics of the everyday', is pursued today by several Chinese aestheticians (*Stanford Encyclopedia of Philosophy*, V° Environmental aesthetics, by A Carlson). Of particular interest in the context of this book (see Part III below) is Huiching Chen Ruyu, Hung: 'E. Levinas' Ethics of Responsibility-for-the-other and its Implications for Ecological Thinking', noting that 'Levinas' ethical thinking enlightens our ecological thinking. When facing nature, all things in the Universe are endowed with infinity and transcendence, while they also summon our infinite responsibility to protect nature' (https://pesa.org.au/images/papers/2012-papers-English/E18.pdf). This point is made too by C Pelluchon, *Pour Comprendre Levinas* (Paris, Seuil, 2020); *Les lumières à l'âge du vivant*, in which she shows the proximity between Levinas's thought and the phenomenological turn in contemporary ecological approaches. Allen Carlson's account cites one prominent version of Chinese aesthetics accessible in English, that embraces, as the 'four keystones of ecological aesthetic appreciation', not only the centrality of ecological knowledge and the rejection of the duality of humanity and the natural world, but also the overarching value of ecosystem biodiversity and health and

call of indigenous cosmologies to adopt the standpoint of the 'in-between'[202] evokes once again its shadow version.[203] In this respect, 'dwelling in the border' also refers to a non-modern decolonial[204] or pluriversal ontology[205] and evokes a more fluid, earth(l)y epistemology of boundary-crossing and re-emplacement.

PART III explores both the political-economic and ethical dimensions of the conflict of laws. It shows how, on the former terrain, it contributed to the rift within the *oikos* between the economy and the ecology, suggesting that there is something 'natural' to the economic determinism at the heart of global governance and its neoliberal world order. This economically determinist view rests on the idea that there exists a universal, apolitical, market rationality to which 'society' is subject, as if animated by mysterious forces that escape politics.[206] In making the idea of individual autonomy the foundation of the latter, it also enabled a radical distortion of the Enlightenment's ethic of virtues.[207]

However, on this ethical register, the conflict of laws demonstrates the possibility of expressing radical hospitality in legal form. Its shadow version contains a model for accommodating the 'face of the other' within the law.[208] Thinking about the face of the other within the law is a means of transforming the separation between self and other into an understanding of the other as part of ourselves. In this respect, it resonates once again with the contemporary phenomenological turn in eco-aesthetics.[209] In ethical terms, this might pave the way towards a moral economy of

the continued guidance of ecological ethics (ibid). These need to be related to strong strands of feminist eco-aesthetics, such as Donna Haraway (*Simians, Cyborgs, and Women: The Reinvention of Nature*, and below 173, 179 et seq., 289 et seq, and above 3).

[202] Mignolo, *Local Histories/Global Designs*; E Viveiros de Castro, *Métaphysiques cannibals* (Paris, PUF, 2009), and collected writings by this author in *The Relative Native: Essays on Indigenous Conceptual Worlds* (HAU, 2016).

[203] For further accounts of indigenous cosmologies and their 'shadowy' relationship to modern law, see notably (for Canada), J Borrows, *Drawing Out Law. A Spirit's Guide* (Toronto, University of Toronto Press, 2010); see too, by the same author, *Canada's Indigenous Constitution* (Toronto, University of Toronto Press, 2010).

[204] On decoloniality, see Mignolo, *Local Histories/Global Designs*. As Ralf Michaels explains ('Globalizing Savigny?'), decoloniality draws attention to the dark side of modernity, irrevocably paired with coloniality. *Cf* the production of the 'legal barbarian' as the Other of the modern subject, in Maldonado Bonilla, *Legal Barbarians*. We shall return below to the co-production of the modern state and its colonial other. 'Disalienation' means the reversal of the great bifurcation in our mental and emotional universe (with reference to the work of Frantz Fanon, Félix Guattari or Michel Foucault), as distinct from the dream of a return to a pre-modern past.

[205] Mignolo, *Local Histories/Global Designs*.

[206] Kjaer, *The Law of the Political Economy* 22.

[207] On this distortion (to which we shall of course return), Pelluchon, *Les Lumières à l'âge du vivant*.

[208] Part III below will explore the relevance of Emanuel Levinas' phenomenological account of the face-to-face relation that entails an inescapable and infinite responsibility for the other: *Totalité et infini* (1961) (*Totality and Infinity*, 1969), then *Autrement qu'être* (1974) (*Otherwise than Being*, 1981). For the purposes of our project, it is significant that Levinas finds 'alterity within the self'. The 'self as other, other as self' or '*Ich und du*', and more broadly, hospitality and relational ethics, have a distinctive and more recent French, continental and theological pedigree (Ricoeur, Buber, Derrida etc). At the source of this tradition, the specific features of the work of Levinas that are of particular importance in this book are its phenomenological dimension, the replacement of the philosophical conception of truth by that of horizon and the metaphor of the 'split horizon', hospitality as the ethical obligation of substitution of self and other.

[209] As seen above, 6–7, and Parts II and III below.

responsiveness towards our surroundings and those beings, including the unseen and inanimate, whose survival hangs upon the thread of each of our decisions. The world emits morality on a specific wave-length, writes Latour, through all the entities 'that call upon us in order to save us'.[210] A jurisprudential horizon comes progressively into focus, made of responsibility towards the earth[211] on which we depend for survival and all the foreign forms of life that depend in turn upon our own hospitality.

[210] Latour, *Enquête*, 454.

[211] A Pottage, Colloquium, LSE/Sciencespo, London 2021. One of the most debated contemporary legal-philosophical questions concerns the framing of new models of 'planetary responsibility'. All manner of public, private or international lawyers are engaged in attempts to adjust older patterns of individual liability, linear conceptions of causation, and more conservative notions of harm, so as to include state liability for climate change, ecological harm, the interests of future generations, or indeed the legal standing of animals or non-sentient entities in the court room. Comparative private international law reveals multiple instances in which, in recent years, such changes are visible in transnational litigation – and indeed the transnational has been at the fore in many cases of global environmental damage. It also seems to show up a deeper thread, that connects many of the structural changes within the law of jurisdiction, judgments or applicable law to the – often unnoticed – presence of ecological issues, as if an unseen driving force – the return of Gaia – was at work within the more conventional categories of legal reasoning.

Part I

Epistemology and Genealogy: Struggling for the Soul of Method

PART I INVESTIGATES the epistemological axes of the discipline[1] of the conflict of laws. Beyond the usual textbook accounts of the methods, categories and values that surface throughout its (long) history, this is an attempt to uncover the stakes underlying a multi-secular struggle between two broad methodological schemes. Each of these provides a set of lenses and tools by means of which the law constructs and organises its own interactions with exogenous forms of legality.[2] These juridical interactions give rise to what might be described as opposing meta-theories of linkages. As will be seen in detail below, the latter are potentially tight or loose, transformative or coordinatory, hierarchical or lateral, reflexive or static, defensive or open, compromissive or coalitionist. They involve a vast array of technical modes such as translation, transformation, substitution or hybridisation, and can also include highly sophisticated metaphorical forms of cross-dressing, ventriloquism, *bricolage* or *métissage*.[3] Moreover, the inner workings of these schemes

[1] On what is meant by a 'legal discipline' in epistemological terms, see F Audren, S Barbou des Places, *Qu'est-ce qu'une discipline juridique?* (Paris, LGDJ Lextenso, 2018). The conflict of laws (private international law: see above 23–24) is a sub-discipline within the legal field, with a changeable pedigree and location inside the latter, attaching it successively and diversely either to the civil (private) law (the Roman and neo-Roman *corpus iuris*, unsurprisingly dominant in the continental civil legal tradition) or to the law of empire, sovereignty or public international law (and its issues of prescriptive jurisdiction). For readers who are non-lawyers, or for lawyers unfamiliar with its modes and methods, further explanations will be supplied below.

[2] As from the nineteenth century, these normative systems were understood as being composed of *private* law, both in the continental tradition and in the (pre-legal-realist) common law world (as will be seen below). The public counterpart of the discipline deals with relations between states (primary subjects of the international legal order) but is not usually framed as addressing the interactions of different national legal systems (including the public law of different nations), of which the interaction stands in a form of legal limbo: see C McLachlan, *Foreign Relations Law* (Cambridge, Cambridge University Press, 2017). On the rise and fall of the public/private law distinction in general, see D Kennedy, 'Stages of the Decline of the Public/Private Distinction' (1982) 130 *U Pa L Rev* 1349; for its implications in private international law, see the further canonical scholarship assembled in H Muir Watt, *Private International Law and Public Law* (2 vols) (Cheltenham, Elgar, 2017).

[3] In the vocabulary of the law of the conflict of laws, these are devices that belong to the 'general theory' (such as characterisation, renvoi, incidental questions, etc) or to a process known as 'adaptation' (adjustment, substitution, equivalence, etc), on which more below. Cross-dressing means putting oneself judicially 'in the shoes' or in the clothes of the foreign court, while ventriloquism means speaking for the foreign law. The metaphorical life of the conflict of laws is particularly rich: Raape's 'bronze rock', Rabel's legal 'drawers', renvoi as eternal tennis match, Francescakis' 'recipe' for choice of law, and defining the discipline as a whole, the 'dismal swamp', to which we return below.

deploy extraordinary fictions[4] that modify the location of reality in time and space, creating mysterious alchemies that transform policies and affects into science.[5] Deep down beneath the technicalities are profound, conflicting belief systems as to whether we inhabit one normative world or a pluriverse, whether humanity is ontologically separate from or superior to its natural surroundings, and whether what we perceive (and often fear) as other is outside or indeed inside ourselves.[6]

More visibly, such oppositions engage evolving (and still largely unconscious) premises about ecology and culture, law and politics, persons and things, and more. These dichotomies command the structure of our knowledge of reality and all have powerful implications in respect of the ways in which alterity – including the splendour of nature's otherness[7] – finds its place within our *nomos* or legal consciousness.[8] The continual combat within the law as to how political communities should relate to the foreign, between deference and rejection, inclusion and exclusion, universalism and pluralism, echoes far wider frays between order and disorder, harmony and chaos, of which the terms hark back to the premodern, Roman origins of Western modernity and its specific, idiosyncratic, legal tradition.[9] That the latter was largely formative, or at least co-productive, of modern scientific and political thought (as seen above), and thereby steeped in implications for ecology, invites exploration of the deeper underpinnings of the various legal methods that compete for supremacy in framing our relationship to difference.

[4] These devices will be examined in detail below. Seeing law as fiction questions the modern distinction between legal method as rational and scientific (as in the use of inductive or deductive legal reasoning, the weighing of interests, etc) and mythologies or make-believe (which 'we' tend to attribute to pre-modern indigenous, religious or traditional cultures). Symmetrical anthropology teaches however that there is very little to choose between the two (see for instance below 199 et seq. on the signification of the two burlesque figures of the shaman and the jaguar, and their connections with the conflict of laws).

[5] On law's alchemy, see R Mangabeira Unger, *The Universal History of Legal Thought* (Deep Freedom Books (ebook), 2021) 14: 'The persistence of a similar view of the nature and work of legal doctrine in so many different legal traditions and across such a broad range of historical time and space only makes the riddle of its subject matter more significant and more striking ... The work is the representation and reconstruction of law, tested against particular case and circumstance, as an ordering of social life that the participants in a particular society can understand and embrace, in the light of the interests that they recognize and of the ideals that they profess. The alchemy to be performed by legal doctrine is therefore the revelation or the transmutation of what would otherwise be the brute fact of the way things are into an order that can be the subject and the outcome of a discourse. The discourse concerns the forms that human association can and should take in different domains of social life'.

[6] Cross-cutting this point are conflicting framings of law's spheres in terms of geographically delineated spatiality, versus geography-agnostic functional/teleological terms.

[7] Descola, *Par delà nature et culture*.

[8] And within the construction of what 'our' is at a given time and for a given purpose. See more below for the important concepts of *nomos* (as developed by Robert Cover) and legal consciousness (as advanced by Duncan Kennedy). However, at this stage, it may be important to signal that the apparently narrow exploration of legal methods undertaken in this Part is designed to go beyond the insights of critical legal studies (as deployed by the two influential authors just cited). Special thanks to Jorge Esquirol for drawing attention to the relevance in this respect to Joseph Gabel's account of the Marxian idea of 'false consciousness' as defined as a *non-dialectical* (reified) perception of social reality ('Effets pervers et fausse conscience' (1987) Juillet-Décembre *Cahiers Internationaux de Sociologie* 339–54).

[9] On the idiosyncratic endo-European experience of modernity, see P-G Monateri, *Geopolitica del diritto* (Einaudi, 2013). On the inner conflict between chaos and order that marked the very origins of Roman law, see below 69 et seq, 96 et seq, 179.

Overall, then, the current conceptual economy of the conflict of laws comprises two broad modes of reasoning ('methods') in respect of foreign law.[10] This duality can be correlated to two underlying models of legality: a modern, or monist, scheme, embodied during the nineteenth century, that seeks closure, order, decisiveness, objectivity and predictability from a purportedly neutral (or Archimedean) standpoint; and a further pluralist version, geared to diplomatic negotiation, reflexivity, the perpetual oscillation between poles and the refusal of separation between the observer and the observed, or between application and interpretation. The argument developed in this Part is that some elements of the second model, eclipsed by the first, may be envisaged as a residual jurisprudence[11] with a premodern pedigree.[12] As such, it resurfaces continually in the chinks of its conventional, more recent and widespread other.[13] This methodological binary is linked in turn to a specific foundational 'story of origin' or genealogy, itself the object of borrowings, variations, twists and entwinements between different legal traditions. In other words, the discipline lends itself particularly well to a comparative legal study of the production of knowledge, and provides food for further thought in respect of law's epistemology more generally.[14]

In the genealogy of Western thought, epistemology emerged as the study of principles that govern the production of scientific knowledge, as understood in the context of modernity. To the extent that its very terms are shaped by a certain vision or cosmology, modern epistemology (an understanding of facts as being distinct from values[15]) is currently under critical fire from many quarters: critique of epistemological neutrality has spread from the study of the social and to the 'earth sciences'. While law has tended to remain aloof from these movements,[16] multiple strands of critical

[10] 'Law' here can mean rules, institutions, jurisdictional parameters, legal authority, or particular judgments. As will be seen below, different epistemological stances understand law in different ways for the purposes of legal method.

[11] On this concept, see Goodrich, *Law in the Courts of Love*. It is conventionally dismissed as having the 'worst defect that could ever affect a legal theory', that is, its lack of positive legal status (meaning that no legal system has actually adopted it as legal method): see P Gothot, 'Le renouveau de la tendence unilatéraliste' (1971) *Rev crit DIP* 1.

[12] See below 112.

[13] This is in no way to imply that within the dominant modern tradition, there have not been (ample) attempts to pursue justice, fairness, or relationality, with moderation, nuance and proportion, and care and attention to context and individual needs. Examples can be found in the work of the great 'humanist' thinkers in the conflict of laws in the course of the twentieth century (or indeed in the previous one: see R Banu, *Nineteenth Century Perspectives on Private International Law* (Oxford, Oxford University Press, 2018); on the earlier modern Roman legal humanists, see P Stein, *Roman Law in European History* (Cambridge, Cambridge University Press, 1968)). H Batiffol, *Aspects philosophiques du droit international privé* (Paris, Dalloz, 2002) could be cited here, or the most prominent example from across the Atlantic, the legal-realist David F Cavers, whose (humanistic-antidogmatic) 'A Critique of the Choice of Law Problem' (1933) 47 *Harv L Rev* 173 triggered the American realist revolution (or 'crisis') in the conflict of laws (as seen below). See AT von Mehren, 'Choice of Law and the Problem of Justice' (1977) 41(2) *Law and Contemporary Problems* (Contemporary Perspectives in Conflict of Laws: Essays in Honor of David F Cavers) 27–43. However, the question addressed in this Part is whether the underlying epistemological premises of the conventional accounts of the conflict of laws live up to the requirements of an ecological jurisprudence today.

[14] On epistemology and method in respect of law, drawing largely on Roman legal history and comparison, see GH Samuel, *Epistemology and Method in Law* (Aldershot, Ashgate, 2003).

[15] This is the definition of modern epistemology in Latour, *Enquête* 21, 115.

[16] Hence the importance of the question raised by Geoffrey Samuel, 'Is Law Really a Social Science? A View from Comparative Law' (2008) 67(2) *The Cambridge Law Journal* 288–321. The author surmises that

ecological, historical, anthropological, feminist, queer and decolonial thinking invite us, elsewhere, to reflect on the schemes of intelligibility that have dominated our world, with devastating effects on our relationship with humanity and the planet.[17] Alternative cosmological schemes challenge the modes of veridiction of modern (social and hard) sciences, that is, the 'abstract-universals' and Archimedean standpoint through which we accede to, and make sense, of, reality. At their core, there is a powerful call to revisit our understandings not only of objectivity and perspective, but also of identity and difference, outside and inside, self and other. Despite the general indifference of legal scholarship towards these alternative (non-modern or postmodern) epistemological strands, many have significant implications for legal thought, notably insofar as they question the separation of the principles that govern knowledge of reality of facts (epistemology) and their interpretation (hermeneutics).

As far as private international law is concerned, the question of alterity (the foreign, the unfamiliar, the outside) along with all the individual and collective relations or attitudes that are expressed in respect of it in legal terms, is evidently central. Moreover, conventionally – and still today, at least in the European continental tradition – the discipline makes a particularly strong epistemological claim: it puts scientific neutrality at its methodological core; a sort of abstract-universal *par excellence*. Formalised in the nineteenth century concomitantly with its separation from the law of nations, its classical legal pedigree explains its quasi-existential investment in the smooth uniformity of the (territorialised, state-centred) legal order[18] and its affinities today with neoliberal governance discourse (to which we shall return later on in this book). Notwithstanding the power of this convention, however, alternative, non-modern epistemologies still resonate (faintly) within the discipline, echoing pluralistic or mosaic-like (or indeed, perhaps melting-pot or *métissage* …) patterns of legal thinking that developed in the course of its premodern history in the

it is not so, as long as law is dominated by an authority paradigm (like theology) and not an empirical one (involving the possibility to disprove a given finding empirically).

[17] These schemes are criticised as being, variously, modern, naturalist, universalist, abstract (or unsituated), colonial, gendered, capitalist, (neo)liberal. Much of this critique, which means that situated knowledge replaces objectivity, and standpoints are multi-sided, will resurface in various contexts in Parts II and III of this book. At this stage, see for example, for a prominent feminist ecological critique: Haraway, *Simians, Cyborgs and Women* (opposing situated knowledge to the concept of objectivity); for influential queer epistemology, see E Kosofsky Sedgwick, *Epistemology of the Closet* (Berkeley CA, University of California Press, 1990) and J Butler, *Gender Trouble: Feminism and the Subversion of Identity* (Abingdon, Routledge, 1990); on 'the postmodern condition' and the critique of modern meta-narratives or *métarécits*, JF Lyotard, *La Condition postmoderne : rapport sur le savoir* (Paris, Minuit, 1979); on the geophilosophical concept of rhizome, see G Deleuze and F Guattari, *Capitalisme et Schizophrénie II, Mille Plateaux* (Paris, Minuit, 1980); on pluriversality, W Mignolo, *Darker Sides of the Renaissance* (Durham NC, Duke University Press, 1995) (seeking to 'decolonise' the assumptions that continue to undergird the production of knowledge in the West and its claim to exclusivity); for further examples of pluriversal thinking and alternative spiritual epistemologies, Reiter, *Constructing the Pluriverse* (calling attention to understandings of time and space as non-linear or 'pluri-topical' and embodying 'border gnosis', while epistemologies are themselves 'mosaic-like'). See too the account by Descola, *Par delà nature et culture* 144 et seq of the epistemological split between the two autonomised spheres of nature and culture (science of nature and science of mind or culture) at the end of the long German nineteenth century.

[18] On the smoothness of modern metaphysical space and the resistance provided by the ontological diversity of two principal European legal traditions (common law/civil law) in the world order, see Monateri, *Geopolitica del diritto*. See too below p 165, 175, 227 et seq.

multipolarity of medieval Europe.[19] While these were repressed progressively by the rationalist project of modern legal thought,[20] they remained in the form of subterranean residue[21] under the surface of the latter, inscribed within what we might think of as an underground or hidden narrative. In this Part, then, the study of the conceptual economy of private international law will serve as a heuristic[22] for thinking about law's epistemological foundations more broadly, and the ways in which the latter have shaped our relation to otherness.

At this point, it is important to emphasise that the two opposing models of legality present within this discipline will be presented below as two ideal types. The first, which can loosely be characterised as monist, is usually known as 'multilateralism' (somewhat confusingly – but such semantic confusion may signal part of the deeper substantive problem). It is the (ostensibly) dominant paradigm, and easily illustrated with examples from positive law and doctrinal presentations. The second, embracing a pluralist pattern, usually carries the (equally mystifying) label of 'statutism', 'neo-statutism' or (worse) 'unilateralism'. It was long eclipsed by the former and even now tends only to appear in its chinks. Less easy therefore to discover in unadulterated form in legal praxis, the essential point about it as an alternative model is that it opens the doors of the forum to foreign law on the terms of the latter, according to its own vision and institutional make-up.

The first chapter below will return to the dominant 'story of origin'.[23] This story tells of the genesis of the conflict of laws as a triumph of legal monism in the mid-nineteenth century, in the form of a specific methodology (known under different and abstruse names, largely misnomers, such as 'multilateralism', 'bilateralism' or 'conflictualism').[24] At that point, it prevailed over its earlier, medieval counterpart, reputedly bringing enlightenment and order through rational legal method based on Roman law. This is a narrative of a world governed by private law, from which modern statehood and politics were evicted. Paradoxically, however, it survived the final advent of statehood, and, in a curious twist, came to tie the latter to the very idea of law: thereafter, there was no legality beyond or outside the will, consent or delegation of the sovereign state. In this respect, it is an artefact of modern law, inherent in the modes of legal ordering that we associate broadly with a whole series of notions: the Westphalian settlement and the Atlantic revolutions, secularism and

[19] On the Roman legal history of medieval Europe, in which the conflict of laws played a crucial part, see Schiavone, *Ius*; Stein, *Roman Law in European History*.

[20] The rationalist project became particularly pronounced in international law. This was already true of its predecessor, the law of nations (the *ius gentium* of Vitoria and Suarez), and remained constant with philosophical and legal thinkers as diverse as Wolff, Kant and Blackstone, in their rationalistic approach deriving nature from reason. However, from early modernity, there has been a powerful tendency to think that international society occupies a privileged place in the 'book of nature', governed by its own 'natural' laws.

[21] On 'residue', see above 28.

[22] A heuristic is an epistemological device that serves as a 'short cut' in the production or communication of knowledge. In its uses below, it will occasionally be synonymous with the concepts of metaphor, model, pattern, style or template

[23] This term borrows from the vocabulary of genealogical analysis, as will be seen below.

[24] On the relationship of these terms to monism or monologism, see below.

territoriality, Western rationality and the disqualification of peripheral normativities. Broadly speaking, thereafter, in this new universe of sovereign states, alterity in legal form was to become a mirror image of self. In the specific vocabulary of the conflict of laws, foreign legalities appear as reflections of the law of forum, and are assumed to subscribe to its own particular architecture, distinctions and categories. Receiving foreign law in such conditions comes at the price of potential denial of difference. The latter makes itself felt, however, through various forms of methodological upheaval, category trouble or methodological conundrums.

The second chapter will use these in order to pick up the traces or residues of alternative eclipsed, largely marginalised schemes of legal plurality. Lurking under the powerful rationalist narrative, these hark back to an alternative scene of multiple forms of normativity that the contemporary 'loss of centre'[25] is bringing once more to the surface in a form of de-centred perspective. As the structural opposite of the first, it accepts the existence of self-styled, alternative or non-state embodiments of legality, including the non-secular, the customary and the indigenous, that it acknowledges along with their self-understandings, that is, with their specific unfamiliar or idiosyncratic morphology and 'intellectual style'.[26] It understands law's specific mode of existence as distinct from – beyond and prior to – the state form, thereby claiming both a premodern pedigree and, key to its contemporary success, a predictive value in the transformation of jurisprudence in the global turn. Most importantly, the mediation it undertakes with alterity takes place *on the terms of the other*. Law is inclusive of what is self-defined as such, and not restricted to formal or institutionalised norms created or endorsed by a fellow nation state. This is what can be termed the 'shadow version' that haunts the conventional story of origin of the conflict of laws. Herein, as seen above, lies the key point we are attempting to make in this book. The value of exploring this discipline lies in its heuristic potential for the framing of an alternative jurisprudence harnessed to the ecological needs of our planet.

However, before engaging in this exploration, a brief preliminary section will present private international law's conceptual economy as a complex assemblage of linkages and loops,[27] axes and categories, all operating in the light of the binary foundational story briefly outlined above. It may be of little interest to specialists of the discipline who are perfectly aware of the technological sophistication or distinctive 'intellectual style' of the discipline.[28] However, for those who are unfamiliar with

[25] The loss of centre is generally considered to be the feature of globalisation. It may also be a 'loss of control': see S Sassen, *Losing Control? Sovereignty in the Age of Globalization* (New York, Columbia University Press, 2015).

[26] The latter expression is borrowed from K Knop, A Riles, 'Space, Time and Historical Injustice: A Feminist Conflict-of-Laws Approach to the "Comfort Women" Agreement' (2017) 102 *Cornell Law Rev* 853.

[27] Arguably, of course, the loop or reflexivity is a feature of the law more generally. François Cooren asks what it means to 'speak in the name of the law' and likens the law to the puppet that moves the ventriloquist, as much as the reverse. In Latourian terms the idea is that law has its own agency and that outside beings lend it their voices (see 'In the name of the law: Ventriloquism and Juridical Matters', in McGee (ed), *Latour and the Passage of Law* 235 et seq; the fascination for ventriloquism is shared by J Derrida, *Psyche: Inventions of the Other* (Palo Alto CA, Stanford University Press, 2007).

[28] On 'intellectual style' in this field, see Knop and Riles, 'Space, Time and Historical Injustice'. There is a further feature of legality – contrasted with other objects of historical research on the one hand, or with the social sciences on the other – that is particularly salient in the case of the conflict of laws.

its various comparative historiographies, it may be useful to highlight the particular methodological forms that have been present throughout its long history and have occupied an exclusive (and unusual) place within its conceptual layout. Furthermore, this will be the opportunity to emphasise the properly ecological stakes that underlie this somewhat juridical discussion.

I. AN INITIAL GLIMPSE: PRIVATE INTERNATIONAL LAW AND ITS INNER CONFLICTS

This book is not intended as a presentation of positive legality in the field (*lex* or 'Law I', meaning, as seen above, collections or codes of texts, case law, regulatory principles, etc) from any singular national perspective.[29] However, for readers unfamiliar with the conceptual economy of the conflict of laws, and who may well indeed be daunted by its 'quaking quagmire',[30] the purpose of this brief preliminary introduction is multifold: to draw attention, as in a nutshell,[31] to the specificity of the various juridical devices (choice of law rules, regimes of recognition, legal fictions, categories, limits and divides …) that compose what are known as the 'methods' peculiar to this discipline and that, typically, are then treated as incarnating a specific positivised form (tracking territorial jurisdiction and 'local' laws); to highlight the ways in which

From an epistemological perspective, we know that access to knowledge of a given discipline passes through the study of its specific methods. However, in law – and strikingly in the case of the conflict of laws – such a study is indistinguishable in turn from a historical account, that can easily be mistaken for the very essence of the methods themselves (GH Samuel, 'Taking Method Seriously' (2007) 2 *Journal of Comparative Law* 94, 210). There is a short explanation for this feature with respect to private international law. The latter is quintessentially methodological, meaning that it is entirely composed of modes of reasoning that are often described as 'procedural' to the extent that they do not operate on the register of substantive legality. In other words, to coin an aphorism borrowed from the field of law and digital coding, 'method is law'. As every student of the conflict of laws is taught, its rules will never provide a concrete outcome on the merits of a case, but will merely point to the jurisdiction whose courts, laws or judgement will be relevant to the latter. The longer answer pertains to the conflict of laws' Roman pedigree, and will be developed progressively in the course of this Part.

[29] Readers are reminded again here that this book is in no way an introduction to the positive legal dimensions of the discipline of the conflict of laws, on which there are many excellent handbooks or textbooks. For a collection of canonical or otherwise significant cases drawn from multiple jurisdictions, with accompanying explanations (that attempt to deviate from more conventional 'case note' mode in order to introduce critique and a measure of interdisciplinarity), see the case book *Global Private International Law* (published in English by Elgar in 2017 and in French by Pédone in 2020).

[30] For this figure, see above n 22. The current controversy over the 'restatement' of the state of the law in this field in the United States by the American Law Institute (the Third Restatement of the conflict of laws) is sparked in large part by a debate over how best to make the field intelligible to an outside or specialised judicial audience. As L Brilmayer and D Listwa state: 'The public perception of choice of law in the United States has never been a particularly positive one Dean William Prosser famously called the field "a dismal swamp, filled with quaking quagmires" – and, by adding this theoretical framework, the hope, as the Reporters' Memorandum to the draft *Restatement* explains, is to make the choice-of-law methods more "intelligible to nonspecialists" and more "align[ed] with the ordinary process of legal analysis." In other words, by offering a theory of choice of law that the drafters themselves view to be attractive … they hope to win over judges and lawyers who may be intimidated by or otherwise wary of choice-of-law rules and principles' (L Brilmayer and DB Listwa, 'Continuity and Change in the Draft Restatement (Third) of Conflict of Laws: One Step Forward and Two Steps Back?' (2018) 128 *The Yale Law Journal*, Forum).

[31] On the underestimated importance of 'nutshells' on representations of legality and legal history, see A Watson, 'The Importance of Nutshells' (1994), https://digitalcommons.law.uga.edu/fac_artchop/668.

these tools are caught up in a long historical controversy over the most appropriate modes of legal reasoning with which to frame the encounter with foreign law;[32] and above all to unveil the deeper stakes that connect these recurring, contested (and apparently superficial, minor or technical) issues of legal epistemology to contemporary, highly political debates involving our (Western, modern) relationship with other cultures and our (humanity's) natural surroundings.

A concrete case exemplifying the state of cross-border environmental litigation will serve here as a lens through which to view the bigger picture of the discipline as a whole (section II below). Indeed, as will be seen throughout the book, questions of scale – from what distance or through what lens phenomena are viewed – are essential to any jurisprudential approach to law and jurisdiction.[33] Using the terms of Barthes' photographic theory,[34] this singular case will serve as the point (*punctum*) that concentrates the gaze and gives colour to the rest (*studium*). Closest to earth, then, the focus will be on the distinctive methods, techniques, style and assumptions of the conflict of laws (section III). To better understand their heuristic value in the specific context of this book, they will then be replaced within a broader, bird's-eye view of the whole discipline (section IV), allowing for a brief return to the stakes of the methodological discussions it entails (section V). These preliminary approaches should prepare the reader for a more in-depth exploration of the struggle for method, undertaken in the further chapters of Part I of the book.

II. AN EXAMPLE: CROSS-BORDER ENVIRONMENTAL LITIGATION

Broadly speaking, private international law or the law of the conflicts of laws in judicial practice concerns how courts go about framing and deciding legal disputes when the facts play out in (relevant) geographically or jurisdictionally complex patterns. An example of the type of issue that courts are called upon to decide by means of the specific technologies of private international law might relate to the legal consequences of (alleged) cross-border environmental harm. When the latter occurs, say, in the course of mining operations in one country, whereas the (corporate) operator is located in another, questions may arise as to (i) which country's courts have jurisdiction over the claim;[35] (ii) what levels of safety and

[32] 'Law' in this context (*Lex* or 'Law I') can mean rules, institutions, jurisdictional parameters, legal authority, or particular judgments. As will be seen below, different epistemological stances understand law in different ways for the purposes of legal method.

[33] M Valverde, *Chronotopes of Law: Jurisdiction, Scale and Governance* (Abingdon, Routledge, 2015). For instance, scale changes the way we see phenomena (persons/things) as distinct (or unitary), or oppositional (or compatible) and indeed whether there is a separation in the first place between subject and object, an ontological issue that engages our perception of the ecology as outside (environment) or as part of us.

[34] R Barthes, *Camera Lucida: Reflections on photography* (trans R Howard) (New York, Hill and Wang, 1980) distinguishes the *studium* (historical, social or cultural meanings extracted via semiotic analysis) from the *punctum*, that points to a feature of the photograph that conveys a meaning outside any apparent symbolic system. The 'punctum effect' requires the viewer to repudiate prior knowledge in order to allow details to appear that are unintended or uncontrolled by the photographer.

[35] This apparently simple question raises further issues: how to identify the defendant within a corporate group or conglomerate; whether a given entity (collective, such as a class or association; or fictional, such as

standards of reparation are applicable;[36] and (iii) whether acknowledgement would be given to a judgment, obtained in either place, within the other legal system.[37] The response to all these questions in the terms of the conflict of laws is to trigger a set of idiosyncratic methods that (in a sequence that is neither chronological nor necessarily logical) respectively (i) regulate the exercise of jurisdiction by domestic courts; (ii) determine the legal system applicable to the substantive issues; and (iii) set the conditions of enforceability of decisions issued by foreign courts, or define (by recognition of legal effects) some sort of relevant legal status decided by a foreign judgment.[38]

The deployment of extractive industries by large (Western) corporate groups in developing, ex-colonised countries (in the global South) has given rise to a recent surge in cross-border environmental litigation in the courts of the states where such groups are headquartered, accompanied by expanded and increasingly sophisticated private international legal issues. For instance, in an English case, *Vedanta Resources PLC v Lungowe*[39] involving allegations of extensive, enduring and ongoing water pollution by the defendant group in the course of copper mining operations in Zambia, litigation took several years to wind its way through the mere periphery of such issues. At a very early stage in the proceedings,[40] the Supreme Court of the United Kingdom had to determine (inter alia) whether the claims against the local

a personified river) has legal standing; if emergency measures are available. Moreover, a further specification is that there can be intrastate, federalised jurisdictions that private international law treats as if they are countries or nation states. One tricky doctrinal point in this respect is the difference between internal conflicts dealt with like those between the laws of nation states and 'self-limiting' substantive rules that delineate their own geographical/topological scope (such as rules that apply only to rural areas, or only to the metropolis, for example: on these, a much-cited account is K Lipstein, 'Inherent Limitations in Statutes and the Conflict of Laws' (1977) 26 *ICLQ* 884.

[36] In turn this issue also includes the extent to which different kinds of damage are repairable, and the modes of such reparation.

[37] This refers to its aptitude to prevent or estop further proceedings, or justify enforcement.

[38] The latter are understood in (widely shared) doctrine and practice, as the jurisdictional institutions of nation states, along with the content of (domestic or municipal) positive law (*lex*) in force within any of the latter.

[39] *Vedanta Resources PLC and another (Appellants) v Lungowe and others (Respondents)* [2019] UKSC 20 (Appeal from [2017] EWCA Civ 1528). In this one example among many, contrary to earlier disputes in similar circumstances (see on 'creeping ecologisation' of the case law, below 58), the ecological damage was central. Here, citing the unanimous opinion of Lord Briggs §1), the claimants complained of toxic emissions from the Nchanga copper mine in the Chingola District of Zambia. These were a group of some 1,826 Zambian citizens living in four communities within the Chingola District. They were, by any standards, very poor members of rural farming communities served by watercourses which provide their only source of water for drinking (by themselves and their livestock) and irrigation of their crops. They claimed that both their health and their farming activities had been damaged by repeated discharges of toxic matter from the Nchanga copper mine into those watercourses, from 2005 to date. At a later point in the case, the Court picked up the words of the Court of Appeal, §90: 'the claimants were at the poorer end of the poverty scale in one of the poorest countries of the world ... they had no sufficient resources of their own (even as a large group) with which to fund the litigation themselves ... they would not obtain legal aid for this claim and nor could it be funded by a Conditional Fee Agreement ('CFA') because CFAs are unlawful in Zambia.'

[40] The Court emphasised from the start (§4) that 'this appeal is all (and only) about jurisdiction; that is, the jurisdiction of the courts of England and Wales to determine those claims against both defendants'. The jurisdictional difficulty was to secure English jurisdiction over the 'anchor' English defendant, so as to be able to bring a claim in England both against the latter and its foreign subsidiary (a defendant to a closely connected claim).

'anchor' defendant (Vedanta, the parent company domiciled in England) disclosed 'a real triable issue' (exclusive of abuse of process in the attempt by the foreign claimants to sue the foreign subsidiary in the English courts).

This question in turn depended upon whether the parent company (reasonably or arguably) owed a duty of care under English tort law[41] to the claimants, inhabitants of the contaminated area in Zambia.[42] In this respect, it was alleged (and finally judicially considered) to have exerted a 'very high level of control and direction' over the mining operations formally conducted by its local Zambian subsidiary. One of the important novelties here, in the light of previous case law,[43] was that the damage had been suffered abroad and moreover by third parties (neither employees nor contractors of the defendant), thereby raising the question of the personal and geographical reach of the (potential) duty of care as a necessary prerequisite for liability in tort.[44]

This case fully displays the exuberant complexity, or Escher-like quality, of private international law. Whereas questions relating to jurisdiction are generally to be decided before questions relating to applicable law, the reasonably arguable existence of a duty of care on the part of the parent company towards foreign third parties, on which jurisdiction of English courts depended, is an issue of substantive law that required identification, in the first place, of the applicable national rules. Because of the preliminary nature of this issue, the potentially relevant legal regime was present as it were by anticipation – a masterly fictional or *as if* move.[45] In this respect, Zambian law had (provisionally) been deemed to be applicable by the Court of Appeal.[46] By a lucky stroke, Zambia's colonised past meant that its legal system could be said to belong to the common law tradition, so that (very) recent (post-colonial) developments in English tort law could be ascribed to Zambia, including an enlarged duty of care. It was indeed finally accepted that 'it was arguable that the Zambian courts would identify the relevant principles of Zambian common law in accordance with those established in England' (even if the potential extension of the

[41] The vocabulary borrowed from English tort law 'puts the cart before the horse' in the sense that at this early stage in the chain of legal reasoning, we do not know yet whether the applicable law will be familiar with such a concept. This is a widespread error (see for a similar one, the French *Lautour* case (Cass civ, 1re, 25 May 1948, below 53), in which the court sought to determine the law governing liability 'for the custody of things', unconsciously using French civil law, art 1384-1 – now 1242-1 – as a parameter for a supposedly neutral or objective distribution of legal issues). It illustrates the point made below according to which operations of characterisation prior to the designation of the applicable law project a mirror image of self on foreign law.

[42] As against the parent company, Vedanta, the claimants relied upon Art 4 of the Recast Brussels Regulation (Regulation (EU) 1215/2012 on Jurisdiction and the Recognition and Enforcement of Judgments in Civil and Commercial Matters). As against the Zambian subsidiary (KCM), beyond the reach of the latter instrument, the claimants relied upon what may loosely be called the 'necessary or proper party' gateway of the English procedural code for permitting service of proceedings out of the jurisdiction (para 3.1 of CPR Practice Direction 6B).

[43] *Chandler v Cape plc* [2012] 1WLR 3111, Court of Appeal.

[44] On the ways in which territorial jurisdiction has largely shielded corporate groups from being called to account for extraterritorial damage, see below 242 et seq.

[45] On 'borrowing' foreign law, see above, n 41.

[46] Although this point was not discussed before the Supreme Court, Zambian law as the law of the country in which the harm occurred would have been applicable under the conflict of laws rules resulting from the EU 'Rome II' Regulation (in force at the time). This would have been supported by the general rule (Art 4-1) or, if identified as environmental damage, on the choice of the claimants, under Art 7.

duty of care had not yet been enacted: another masterly *as if* move[47]). Back thereafter to square one: English jurisdiction could be exercised, the claims heard against both parent and subsidiary, and indeed arguments over the applicable law rehearsed anew, no doubt laying the ground for settlement[48] (before a further turn of the wheel towards any of the further issues evoked above).[49]

It may be observed that in this particular dispute there was no invocation before the (pre-Brexit) English court of non-municipal law, whether in the form of international principles, human rights enshrined in the European Convention, or European Union treaties or secondary legislation (whether substantive or private international).[50] Nor did the polluted river, subterranean waterways or animal life claim legal standing in the English court, any more than non-human entities such as future generations (although the defendant was a composite juridical person).[51] Nor was the environmental damage invoked as a self-standing form of legally reparable harm; the same goes for the existence of an ecocide (in respect of the biodiversity contained in the rivers) or indeed an epistemicide (in respect of the cultural modes of life rendered impossible by the contaminated waterways).[52] While the claimants were numerous and the defendant group part and parcel of a wider extractive industry, the collective dimension of the dispute was scarcely perceptible; it had no influence on the framing of causation, for instance, which continued to rest on ideas of individual agency.[53] Furthermore, the background responsibility of the state of incorporation or indeed its producers and consumers, was not envisaged as the grounds for a distributive or equitable move beyond mere legal liability.

Of course, most such ideas may have seemed to be beyond the semiotic pale[54] for the English court. In this case, as we have seen, the legal fiction of identity between foreign and local law was available, but any of the categories at play could have been loosened up (assuming lawyers prescient and skilled enough to think to invoke them in the first place, as against the shrinking semiotics of legal argument). Importantly,

[47] This move has its roots in a venerable legal fiction known as the presumption of identity between the law of the forum, English law, and the rules of the applicable foreign law (unless the contrary is pleaded and proved to the satisfaction of the court. On this presumption, see R 'Fentiman, 'Foreign Law as Local Law: a Case of Mistaken Identity?', *Liber Amicorum Monika Pauknerová* (Wolters Kluwer, 2021).

[48] Settlement is a crucial part of the Escherian litigation landscape in cross-border disputes. Once past the crucial (jurisdictional or 'reasonable cause of action') threshold, the case is practically 'won'. This does not necessarily mean however that the process does not have a normative effect: for a recent example before the Supreme Court of Canada, *Nevsun Resources Ltd v Araya*, 2020 SCC 5 and then a practitioner's point of view: M Rogge, 'Nevsun puts Canada's Corporate Decision Makers in the Human Rights Zone', working paper no 70, 2020, Corporate responsibility Initiative, Harvard Kennedy School.

[49] For further moves (settlement) in the *Vedanta* case, see www.reuters.com/article/us-zambia-mining-vedanta-idUSKBN29O1EL.

[50] In countries bound by the European Convention on Human Rights, the extraterritorial scope of such rights (in the form of the right to a clean living environment under Art 8) might have been argued. Similar litigation in the United States brought under the Alien Tort Statute might (at least at one point) have given rise to various challenges, including the availability of federal jurisdiction in respect of a foreign corporation. See below 149, footnote 109.

[51] See below 275.

[52] See below 215.

[53] On the ethical dimensions of the structure of legal process, see below 285 et seq.

[54] See D Kennedy, 'A Semiotics of Legal Argument' (1991) 42 *Syracuse Law Review* 75.

all the moves suggested above are legally imaginable. In other countries, hemispheres or cultural traditions, any one of them might have been more audible and changed the modes of reasoning involved.

III. DOWN TO EARTH: *PUNCTUM*

Recall that the primary feature of modes of reasoning specific to private international law is that they operate at a methodological or meta-level when the factual circumstances of the case are deemed to extend across jurisdictional borders.[55] As we have just seen, an example of the type of issues that courts are called upon to decide by means of its specific juridical technologies might relate to the legal consequences of (alleged) cross-border environmental harm.[56] When the latter occurs in the course of mining operations in one country, whereas the (corporate) operator is located in another, questions arise as to which country's courts have jurisdiction over the claim; which legal system determines whether a given entity (collective, such as a group or association, or fictional, such as a personified river) has legal standing to bring it; if emergency measures may be enforced overseas; the potential implications of human rights and their extraterritorial reach; what levels of safety and standards (and modes) of reparation are potentially applicable; and how much credit would be given to a judgment, obtained in either place, in the eyes of the other legal system.[57] The response to all these questions in terms of the conflict of laws is to share them out, in a particular sequence, between different legal 'systems'. The latter are understood in widely shared doctrine and practice as the jurisdictional institutions of the nation states, along with the state of (domestic or municipal) positive law (*lex*) in force within any of the latter.

As this example shows, the law of the conflict of laws does not address directly the 'substance' of legal disputes (meaning concrete outcomes in terms of status and title, rights and obligations), but comprises a protocol or set of processes designed to navigate, as it were upstream, the preliminary questions of which (national) court has jurisdiction over a particular relationship (or duty, title, etc) and, once that is determined, where (in which national system) it must look for the relevant legal materials with which to make its ultimate decision in a particular case. As a specific legal technology, in the absence of any particular prescriptive content,[58] its function is presented as essentially allocatory: it provides, as it were, the signposts, parameters or boundaries that serve to allot, divide up or distribute the scope, reach or thrust of

[55] The question of the threshold of the international is in itself a complex and highly circular conundrum, on which see below 229.

[56] Again, in *Vedanta Resources PLC v Lungowe* [2019] UKSC 20, the dispute focused on the jurisdiction of the English courts in respect of the latter but not (as yet) on the ultimate, concrete destiny of the claim (although, as seen above, in order to determine the first issue, there had to be a perilous 'as-if' exercise in judicial anticipation of the seriousness of the latter).

[57] Meaning, its aptitude to prevent or estop further proceedings, or justify enforcement.

[58] At least if the latter is understood in relation to the habitual legal mode of (private) law in adjudication, insofar as it operates to enforce promises, establish titles, modify the status of persons and things or repair harm.

jurisdictional claims or sets of legal rules.[59] Gathering moss from diverse strands of juridical and political doctrines (or public and private forms of legality), over centuries of judicial and legislative controversies, hesitations, cross-fertilisation among various legal traditions and recurring encounters with unfamiliar foreign institutions, private international law grew, incrementally, a set of highly complex juridical tools.[60]

As will become rapidly apparent, the whole arsenal of legal devices specific to the conflict of laws is a result of the complex weaving together (*cum plessis*) of sedimented histories, metaphors, tropes, structures, categories or modes of reasoning, all evolving through confrontation, translation and transfer.[61] These somewhat baroque assemblages constitute what are usually named 'methods'.[62] At play in the encounter between local (law) and foreign (law), these methods are shaped by and reflect an invisible and multi-layered backdrop that determines in turn all manner of symbolic significations and concrete outcomes.[63] Like all legal methods, they function within a fictional universe. Here, the latter is as it were a metaverse – an equally singular world (constructively) situated 'beyond the state'.[64] People, things, entities, events and relationships cross geopolitical and metaphorical borders, legal systems are seen to interact and, as seen above, call for coordination 'as if' they might clash.

It can also be said, therefore, that this site of interaction is a virtual space in which law encounters its own other.[65] In this respect, all these diverse legal tools appear to fall into a distinctive, dualistic pattern, which weaves through the discipline of the conflict of laws across diverse cultural settings, in a curious relationship of opposition, exchange and succession. Thus, two main methodological schemes geared to the encounter with alterity in the legal world appear as paired structural opposites, each with its own internal consistency. Moreover, each of these models is linked in turn to an idiosyncratic representation of its own genealogy. Broadly speaking, as already noted above, these correspond to legal monism on the one hand and legal pluralism on the other. As the conventional story of their relationship unfolds, it reveals how this dualistic foundational narrative serves as an epistemological filter, giving an enduring shape to the distinctive architecture, categories, divisions and

[59] An important legal distinction (that often escapes continental lawyers) opposes adjudication of largely private law issues as enumerated above and judicial review, which verifies the legality (conversely in terms of public constitutional law) of the legal enactments *(lex)* of legislative or administrative authorities. The ambivalence of private international law is that it sits between the two. It is deployed through private law issues but its allocatory function determines, as if under a supranational constitutional regime, the ultimate source of legal materials relevant to any case.

[60] That these often emerged as much the result of category mistakes and methodological confusion than deliberate design, see below 81.

[61] The idea of 'translation', crucial in comparative legal studies, will also be deployed below, Part II.

[62] For a similar reflection on the eclectic content of 'Method' in comparative legal studies, see Monateri, *Geopolitica del diritto* 10 et seq.

[63] These can be considered in their epistemological dimension as specific modes of veridiction. Many have significant governance implications – for instance, on the expansion or regulation of corporate extractive industries – and engage equally foundational issues of political ecology.

[64] R Michaels, 'Globalization and Law: Law Beyond the State', in R Banakar and M Travers (eds), *Law and Society Theory* (Oxford, Hart, 2013).

[65] As seen above, the methodologies present in the conflict of laws might be seen as instantiations, in legal terms, of the syntax of identification and relationality by which Philipe Descola proposes to classify the diverse cosmologies and models of society that coexist in the world.

schemes of intelligibility of contemporary private international law.[66] According to the traditional narrative, legal monism triumphed in a moment of revelation during the nineteenth century – a paradoxical moment that produced a timeless form of modernity from a turn back to an imagined Roman past. Unsurprisingly, then, this account is betrayed by a series of aporia underlying the prevalence of the monist model and revealing its own other, shadow version in its chinks.

Such inner conflicts provide us with the thread that will weave through the first part of the book below. According to the predominant grand historical narrative that tends to prevail across legal cultures (albeit a variegated and internally conflicted one, as will be seen further below), the modern foundations of this discipline were laid in the second part of the nineteenth century, at the time of the emergence of public international law as its (equally modern) homologue. The paternity of this moment (along with the nomenclature 'private international law') is attributed to Joseph Story, later to become United States Supreme Court Justice, in his prior academic quest for a means of peaceful legal settlement between slave and non-slave states over the fate of fugitive slaves, in the fraught era preceding the American civil war.[67] However, the most influential conceptual enterprise took place more or less contemporaneously across the Atlantic in Carl von Savigny's extraordinary restatement of the *Institutes* of Justinian.[68] His underlying concern was that of national German unification on the basis of a common Roman Christian cultural heritage, in the face of the expanding sway of the French Civil Code and its underlying Napoleonic imperial ambitions. In both cases, the conflict of laws served a nation-wide political project on a register that was purportedly devoid of politics either because it was imagined as solely legal, or indeed specifically private. In England, following suit, Dicey's doctrine of vested rights played similarly on a dual plane, tightening through juridical form the private personal and commercial linkages and networks that constituted the fabric of empire. Such duality is unsurprising: is not the endless dialectic between law and politics the very signature of modern Western thought?[69]

Be that as it may, by the mid-twentieth century, the desire for a removal of law from the sphere of politics after two Western 'world' wars and the Holocaust led not only to a new fervour for human rights[70] but also to a renewal of interest in the governance implications of the legal technologies of the conflict of laws, in respect of social and economic interactions 'beyond the state'. That these included the replacement

[66] The importance of these, not solely as an academic matter but in the deep schemes that shape our international legal order (including its various embodiments of neoliberal legality) and our relationship to the alterity of the natural world, will unfold throughout the book.

[67] On Joseph Story and the birth of a concept, see JR Paul, 'Comity in International law', *op cit*.

[68] C von Savigny, *System des heutigen römischen Recht*, 8 vols (1840–49); French translation: *Traité de droit romain*, 8 vols (Paris, Firmin Didot Frères, 1855–59); English translation of Vol 8 by W Guthrie, *Private International Law. A Treatise on the Conflict of Laws* (London, T & T Clark, 1869).

[69] On the distinction between law and politics, *ius* and *lex*, and their specific rationalities, see Schiavone, *Ius* 14 and below, 183.

[70] Of course, the above in no way purports to be an exhaustive or even accurate world history. Human rights (in international law post-Nuremberg and in the European Convention of Human Rights in 1950) were 'produced' at a time when communism was also an alternative governance project in a significant part of the world (on the consequences of the eclipse of the latter on the function of the former, see S Moyn, *The Last Utopia. Human Rights in History* (Cambridge MA, Harvard University Press, 2012).

of colonialism by less visible forms of legal coloniality is rarely mentioned in the textbooks.[71] The latter focus, rather, on the rise of cross-border trade and investment, the promise of consolidating peace through trade, the rise of mass travel (of people) and expanding volumes of transport (of merchandise): all these phenomena coincided with the crystallisation in Western legal consciousness of a methodological consensus around the need for openness towards the (legal or jurisdictional) foreign.[72] Never again![73] The brave new liberal post-war era was made of internationalism and universalism, in which the conflict of laws occupied pride of place.[74] Hence, the institution of a worldwide regime for international arbitration (the New York Convention of 1958). This accompanied the free movement of capital,[75] the intensification of treaty-making by the Hague Conference for private international law,[76] and the growing success of 'party choice' as a guiding principle in a world of individuals endowed anew with political freedoms and novel economic rights.[77] The terrain was prepared for the 'global turn' thereafter, accelerating the circulation of people, things and capital, and requiring an adjusted legal regime. Corporate activities abroad intensified, markets spread, capital spun itself into financial assets. The earth became encircled by myriads of investment treaties, logistical value belts and virtual block chains. All these moves were undergirded by rules of jurisdiction and choice of law[78] that the courts were called upon to 'apply' but in actuality, in many cases, had to forge from scratch.

However, a longer and slightly different history can be told. Despite the various (re)incarnations of the discipline in the nineteenth and twentieth centuries, the modes

[71] On coloniality within the conflict of laws, see below 248.

[72] In comparative conflict of laws, a series of (for the most part, tort) cases in France, England and the United States marked a new post-war generation of thinking in the conflict of laws. In these three jurisdictions, using very different modes of reasoning, three leading cases reached the same outcome (see *Babcock v Jackson*, 191 NE 2d 279, 12 NY2d 473 (NY 1963); Cass Civ 25 mai 1948, *Lautour, Rev Crit* 1949 89, note Batiffol; *Boys v Chaplin* [1971] AC 356) and were each perceived in their own context as a leap forward from previous, more closed methods that tended to favour the systematic application of the court's own law (*lex fori* : *cf* today, EU Regulation Rome II (cited above), Art 4-2). These moves, issuing from much cross-fertilisation, prepared the terrain for the intense mosaic-like production of the Hague Conference mentioned in the text. In terms of jurisdictional parameters and the recognition and enforcement of judgments, a similar movement of liberalisation took place at roughly the same time. See for instance, for the United States, *The Bremen v Zapata Off-Shore Co*, 407 US 1 (1972) (introducing choice of forum: see below 264); for the United Kingdom, new moves in *forum non conveniens* in *Spiliada Maritime Corporation v Cansulex Ltd* [1987] AC 460 (HL); for France, Cass civ, 21 June 1948, *Patiño*, JCP 1948II4422, note Lerebours-Pigeonière opening access to jurisdiction to 'foreign' disputes not captured by arts 14 and 15 of the Code Civil, the *Lautour* case (cited above) in 1948 introducing liberal 'international' public policy, and the *Munzer* case, 7 janvier 1964, Bull Civ n°15, allowing for recognition of foreign judgments with differing content in terms of substance and choice of law.

[73] On the question of human rights, universalism (and cultural relativism) see below 282 et seq.

[74] An interesting example is the post war faith in 'principles of universal justice' (albeit embodied in a local vision and version) of which the conflict of laws (and its specific mechanism of public policy), which is evidenced in a case such as the famous French 1948 *Latour* case cited above (along with H Batiffol's approving commentary).

[75] On which see below 239.

[76] On this small international organisation and its century of production of conventions on uniform private international law, see www.hcch.net/en/publications-and-studies/publications2/general-information-brochure.

[77] See below 258.

[78] On the idea that markets are constituted, see below 222.

of reasoning used today still bear earlier traces of the legacy of the medieval European world dominated by Roman law (as we shall see in further detail below).[79] The content of this inheritance has evolved over time and space, under the influence of a series of factors: legal transplants, cross-germinations and imaginaries induced from past centuries of inter-polity[80] and imperial projects; the itineraries of individual explorers and commercial actors; and profound changes in both the economic and geopolitical context.[81] In other words, the changing incarnations of the discipline are indexed on equally unstable ideas about the international, statehood, frontiers, citizenship, legal orders and the societies they govern; the economic and political regimes in which such interactions take place; conceptions of procedural and substantive justice (and their mutual relationship); visions of the interests involved; the litigation strategies by the (often very unequal) parties involved; and much more.

The idiosyncratic dimension of these legal technologies explains, moreover, over time, the abundance of scholarly controversy over the place of the conflict of laws in relation to the categories, hierarchies or typologies that are usually seen as inherent to quintessentially modern legality. The conjunction of all these strands mentioned above has meant considerable (and therefore existential) uncertainty in respect of the 'nature' or location of the (sub)discipline within broader representations of legal systems. Since it intervenes, typically, in cases involving litigious relationships between non-state actors, it is often seen, as its name indicates, as part and parcel of private law (as usually expounded in 'continental' European 'general theories'[82]).

[79] For the sake of clarity, the argument here is about the epistemological legacy of Roman legality in the construction of modern legal categories and divides and does not claim any specific continuity between Roman (whether classical or medieval) and contemporary rules governing cross-border relationships. Nevertheless, below, it will be argued that the renewal of Roman conflicts of laws methods in the high Middle Ages triggered the tradition known as 'statutist', providing a template for the 'shadow' version of private international law presented in the text above as an ideal type. Under a further caveat, 'Roman law' was not itself a smooth continuum, but displayed considerable epistemological differences between its early content and modes of reasoning, the later classical period and the Digest, and indeed its rediscovery and reconstitution at the threshold of modernity. PG Monateri observes that the the history of the European legal tradition is one of a series of disruptions, so that 'the renewal of Roman law throughout the ages does not demonstrate a peculiar capacity in Roman law itself, but rather the peculiar capacity of later lawyers, especially in the civil law transition, to adopt newer rules and to attach to them the authority of the old Roman texts' as a strategy of legitimisation: 'Early Roman Law and the West', in H Pihlajamäki, M Dubber & M Godfrey (eds), *The Oxford Handbook of European Legal History* (Oxford, Oxford University Press, 2018) 179.

[80] The concept of 'inter-polity law' is Lauren Benton's: see L Benton, 'Possessing Empire. Iberian Claims and Interpolity Law', in S Belmessous (ed), *Native Claims. Indigenous Law against Empire, 1500–1920* (Oxford, 2012) 19–40; L Benton and N Perl-Rosenthal (ed), *A World at Sea Maritime Practices and Global History. The Early Modern Americas* (Philadelphia PA, University of Pennsylvania Press, 2021). Others have used 'inter-society' to similar ends in analogous contexts, as for example B Slattery, 'The Grounds of Human Rights', https://ssrn.com/abstract=3846427 or http://dx.doi.org/10.2139/ssrn.3846427.

[81] Indeed, public international law can be viewed from underneath, or on the receiving end, through a decidedly *mestizo* lens: see A Becker Lorca, *Mestizo International Law: A Global Intellectual History 1842–1933* (Cambridge, Cambridge University Press, 2016).

[82] On this tradition of general theories of private international law, see D Bureau and H Muir Watt, *Droit international privé*, 5th edn (Paris, PUF Coll Thémis, 2021), vol 1, §55 and ibid for a proposal (implemented at vol 2, §1119 et seq) to reverse the respective relationship (principle/exception) of the general and special parts of the discipline in the light of EU private international law developments. More broadly (beyond the sole continental tradition), the epistemology of modern legality presupposes that knowledge of the law issues from ordering, stratification and categorisation.

However, because it is devoted to the specification of the scope (spatial or personal) of other legal rules or statutes (as in medieval 'statutist' or contemporary American neo-statutist theories), or indeed to the determination of the limits of imperial or national sovereignty (*Cunctos populos …*[83]), or again to the conditions of judicial enforceability of rights (as in early modern Dutch and later common law doctrines), it has also been deemed indissociable from public international law (or its predecessor, the 'law of nature and nations', or again in a contemporary version, human rights law[84]). At the same time, because it is neither substantive, nor properly international, nor indeed geared to public law, it is also seen more modestly as mundanely procedural, ancillary and unambitiously, parochially statal.

Now, if the fictional allocation of law and assignment of judicial disputes followed territorial lines (a recurrent belief, as will be seen below[85]), the division of sovereign power by the principles of public international law of jurisdiction would suffice.[86] Similarly, if the geopolitical dimensions of legal conflicts could be bracketed entirely in favour of a purely 'private law' allocation of legal relationships, then (as famously argued by an Etienne Bartin[87]), it would be enough to 'project' the (supposedly rational and apolitical) institutions of the civil law onto all social relationships as if there was a universal (or natural) understanding of their 'legal nature' and thereby of their applicability or spatial scope.[88] In either of these hypotheses, the disciplinary

[83] *Cunctos populos, quos clementiae nostrae regit temperamentum:* Edict of Thessalonicus AD 380, issued jointly by the Emperors of the East and West (Theodosius I, Gratian and his junior co-ruler Valentinian II), subsequently incorporated into Book XVI of the Theodosian Code and later recodified in Justinian's *Institutes*. Importantly, the preclassical discipline of the conflict of laws emerged (notably in the work of Bartolus in the high Middle Ages) as a theory of derogations from a fictional unity of the Roman people and (equally fictional) positivity of Justinian's code (see N Hatzimihail *Preclassical Conflict of Laws* (Cambridge, Cambridge University Press, 2021); Stein, *Roman Law in European History*; Schiavone, *Ius*).

[84] On the natural law of nations, see below 72, 112, 125 and above, 11, 43; on human rights, see below spec. 285 et seq.

[85] On the focus on territory as part of the problem, see below 152 et seq.

[86] The problem of course is that these principles are elusive in themselves. See FA Mann's two canonical courses on international jurisdiction at an interval of 20 years : 'The doctrine of jurisdiction in international law' (1964) 111 *Recueil des cours* and then, 'The Doctrine of International Jurisdiction Revisited after Twenty Years' (1984) 186 *Recueil des cours*, in which he writes (p 20): 'In the United States of America, as will appear on more than one occasion, there exists a strong tendency to found international jurisdiction on the existence of interest and a process of balancing of interests. Indeed, a casebook edited by prominent authors (*International Law, Cases and Materials*, by Henkin, Pugh, Schachter and Smit (1980), p 421), suggests in terms that "under international law the jurisdiction of a State depends on the interest that State, in view of its nature and purposes, may reasonably have in exercising the particular jurisdiction asserted". There is, however, outside the United States no support for such a theory to be found in any of the traditional sources of international law, and it should be firmly rejected. Since in the present world sovereignty is undoubtedly territorial in character, in assessing the extent of jurisdiction the starting point must necessarily be its territoriality such as it was developed over the centuries and defined by the Huber Storyan maxims: as a rule jurisdiction extends (and is limited) to everybody and everything within the sovereign's territory and to his nationals wherever they may be.' Again, on territoriality, see below 147 et seq.

[87] E Bartin, *Etudes de droit international privé* (1899) 11: 'les règles de conflit sont des règles nationales, dans chaque pays, au même titre que les institutions de droit interne dont elles circonscrivent le domaine. Elles leur restent liées comme l'ombre au corps, parce qu'elles ne sont autre chose que la projection de ces institutions elles-mêmes sur le plan du droit international'.

[88] Even Bartin acknowledged a more political description, however, in *Etudes de droit international privé:* '[l]e conflit des lois devient ainsi, pour la législation sur laquelle on raisonne, *comme un procédé permanent de contrôle*, dans l'ordre du droit civil interne, *du principe des institutions de droit privé* : il oblige le civiliste à dissocier, pour chaque institution de droit privé, dans le conglomérat de raisons plus

division – present even in the common law tradition since the decline of the natural law of nations in the eighteenth century and its later replacement by the statalised, positivised public/private dichotomy – between the public and the private international legal order would be pointless.[89] The same could be said in respect of any further distinction between the thrust of (sovereign) law and the reach of (individual, human) rights and freedoms, which sit somewhere on the fence between the public and the private and do not carry any simple answer as to their scope, although they are often assumed to have an easily determined 'extraterritorial' (if not universal) thrust.

However, legal praxis has always shown that neither the geopolitical definition of territory (or its juridical expression, territoriality) nor the pervasive presence of any single legal tradition,[90] nor indeed the somewhat magical notion of fundamental (and universal) rights, can provide a satisfactory response to the type of issues that are traditionally covered by the conflict of laws. The latter is involved in a labour of constant arbitration between equally plausible sovereign jurisdictional claims and multiple adjustments among heterogeneous legal rules spread over an infinite number of fact patterns and suspended in complex configurations of time, space and values. It is this distinctive conceptual process resting on a sophisticated sequence of steps, moves, devices and contrivances that is perceived, diversely, either as a seductive intellectual game of logic or language rarely to be found in other areas of the law, or, in legal-realist mode, its denunciation as a quaking quagmire.[91] We shall return much later to the signification of the latter, heathen metaphor in an ecological-legal context.[92] For now, we need to rise above this earthy perspective to take a bird's-eye view of the discipline as a whole.

IV. BIRD'S-EYE VIEW: *STUDIUM*

In many contemporary accounts, the conflict of laws is said to be attuned to the attainment of 'conflicts justice',[93] meaning the purportedly special needs of adjudication of

ou moins cohérentes qu'on donne de cette institution, les raisons qui méritent d'être retenues, de celles qui ne méritent pas de l'être'. By pre-war 1939 (in *Principes de droit international privé*, tome II, p 9, § 223), his ideas seem to have veered towards a more sovereignty–based approach, in which 'le droit international privé n'est pour moi que la somme, dans un Etat donné, des effets de la souveraineté de cet Etat dans l'ordre des intérêts privés'. This can be taken to be a fair rendition of what was to become the standard doctrinal point of view.

[89] See below on the question (bracketed here) whether or not the separation of public and private (international) law has any sense 89 et seq.

[90] The same can be said of comparative legal knowledge, even though it is undoubtedly more helpful than belief in the universality of one tradition alone. However, while comparative law produces (or should produce) thick contextual knowledge about law in various locations by means of a particular focus on the singularity of each (see P Legrand, 'Foreign Law: Understanding Understanding', 6(2) *Journal of Comparative Law* 67), it does not typically address the issue of frontiers as the place of encounter with the other, as does the conflict of laws.

[91] See above 5, footnote 22.

[92] The reference is to K McGee, *Heathen Earth: Trumpism and Political Ecology* (Punctum Books, 2017). The mix of bio-ecological metaphors here is of course entirely intentional.

[93] The idea of 'conflicts justice' (as opposed to substantive justice in private law adjudication) is traceable to American legal-realist doctrines largely embodied in the *Second Restatement of the Conflict of Laws*

'private' legal disputes in factual situations that cross or sit astride national borders.[94] To this end, it serves the cross-border 'coordination of legal systems',[95] the 'international harmony' of (virtual or real) judicial decisions,[96] the avoidance of situations in which individuals are addressees of contradictory rules of conduct,[97] or sovereigns offended by the exorbitant exercise of legal power by their peers.[98] In this respect, its register is one of what might be described as high legal fiction, or the metaphysics of metaphor (as in the recurring idiom of 'localisation' or the constant allusion to the 'nature of legal relationships' or again the 'reach of rights'). If law more generally is, to borrow from Agamben's terms, the mother of all signatures (understand: fictionality),[99] private international law accentuates this singularity. Indeed, it never claims to be performative in the real world[100] when it purports to share out jurisdictional power

(see for an overview: S Symeonides, 'Material Justice and Conflicts Justice in Choice of Law', in P Borchers, J Zekoll (eds), *International Conflict Of Laws For The Third Millennium: Essays In Honor Of Friedrich K. Juenger* (Transnational Publishers, 2001) 125–40. Section 6 of the (soon to be extant) *Second Restatement* defines Choice of Law Principles as follows: '(1) A court, subject to constitutional restrictions, will follow a statutory directive of its own state on choice of law. (2) When there is no such directive, the factors relevant to the choice of the applicable rule of law include (a) the needs of the interstate and international systems, (b) the relevant policies of the forum, (c) the relevant policies of other interested states and the relative interests of those states in the determination of the particular issue, (d) the protection of justified expectations, (e) the basic policies underlying the particular field of law, (f) certainty, predictability and uniformity of result, and (g) ease in the determination and application of the law to be applied'.

The corresponding trope in the continental European tradition might be the opposition between the quest for the international 'harmony' of outcomes (or the alignment of the different courts of the world on one solution so as to avoid 'forum shopping') and the concern for internal 'harmony' or coherence inside a legal system (for a much-cited example, see J Maury, 'Règles générales des conflits de lois' (1936) III *Rec Cours Acad Droit Internat* 325–570; ascribing to Franz Kahn the first coinage of the term, 'harmony of laws' ('*Gesetzes Harmonie*'). Mediating between the two might be the legal-realist theories in the United States that insist on ways to seek out 'false conflicts' so as to make the disorder disappear (on 'governmental interests analysis', see below 79, 83).

[94] As seen above, the location of this threshold is in itself a moot issue. As will become apparent below, border-crossing and border-dwelling are more than simply a matter of private law and justice.

[95] See, for example, H Batiffol, 'Réflexions sur la coordination des systèmes nationaux' (1967) 120 *Rec Cours Acad Droit Internat*, and for his philosophical reflections on such coordination, *Aspects philosophiques du droit international privé* (Paris, Dalloz, 1956).

[96] Hence the attention paid to such devices as 'incidental questions': see W Wengler, 'Die Vorfrage im Kollisionsrecht' (1934) 8 *RabelsZ* 149 (emphasising in this context the importance of '*Gesetze Harmonie*').

[97] This is a leitmotif of the schools of thought attached to statutism (or 'unilateralism'), as explained by Gothot, 'Le Renouveau de la tendance unilatéraliste'.

[98] See for example the Supreme Court (majority opinion, p 5) in the *Kiobel* case (*Kiobel v Royal Dutch Petroleum Co*, 569 US 108 (2013), on which see below 149, 241) evoking 'the danger of unwarranted judicial interference in the conduct of foreign policy … magnified in the context of the ATS, because the question is not what Congress has done but instead what courts may do. This Court in *Sosa* repeatedly stressed the need for judicial caution in considering which claims could be brought under the ATS, in light of foreign policy concerns. As the Court explained, "the potential [foreign policy] implications … of recognizing … causes [under the ATS] should make courts particularly wary of impinging on the discretion of the Legislative and Executive Branches in managing foreign affairs." Id, at 727; see also id, at 727–728 ("Since many attempts by federal courts to craft remedies for the violation of new norms of international law would raise risks of adverse foreign policy consequences, they should be under-taken, if at all, with great caution").'

[99] G Agamben, *The Signature of All Things: On Method* (New York, Zone Books, 2008) 33 (and see below, on the aesthetics of signature).

[100] In the sense of 'doing things' with legal utterances (as in JL Austin, *How to Do Things with Words*, 2nd edn (Cambridge MA, Harvard University Press, 1975). For example, a 'renvoi' entails no material displacement of a file, any more than acting 'like a foreign court' implies any theatrical move (in terms of geography, disposition of the courtroom, costume, etc). These all take place in the imagined space beyond

among courts or defines the spatial reach of legal rules: on the contrary, it operates very deliberately in an 'as if' mode.[101] The latter requires the formidable fictional division of the whole legal world (at a macro level) for the purposes of the fair disposal of any one (micro) case.[102]

The important point here is that the legal 'boundary work' of private international law opens the chink through which plurality can and has been acknowledged within the law. In Ralf Michael's words, the conflict of laws, as the doctrine of the border, pushes law to 'the very margins of legal thinking'.[103] Simultaneously, however, because it was restricted to 'private legal relationships' at the time of its first modernisation in the nineteenth century (as will be seen below), the discipline tends to enact a somewhat mundane encounter with alterity (through contract, matrimonial property, various torts, marriage …). But this everyday navigation of otherness may be the very key to why the law of the conflicts of laws, with its specific frontier location at the junction of the foreign and the familiar, puts it in a privileged position to challenge law's own grand universalist claims that have otherwise little occasion to be questioned. Evidence of this can be found in the contemporary trends in comparative approaches to the conflict of laws, in the context of the current global turn: an overview of the most recent judicial moves around the world reveals an intriguing, perhaps improbable form of creeping 'ecologisation'. Thus, a large proportion of cases framed within traditionally sealed categories of public and private law (contracts, land, civil liability, etc) bear witness to increasing challenges to universalism and its assumption of the 'sameness' of the other. Disputes arise in respect of the (ab)uses of rights over land, the (over-)exploitation of natural resources, the (un)balancing of global markets in raw materials, the power (and failures) of global value chains, the (lack of) stewardship of waterways and forests, the (mis)treatment of animals, the (displaced) status of land-based customs, the (dis)respect inspired by unfamiliar cosmological beliefs, and more.[104]

This initial glimpse of the potentially subversive introduction of alterity within the operations of the law is enough to suggest that it may be worth testing out the heuristic value of this discipline, in the context of the quest pursued in this book for an ecological jurisprudence. This means using it as an explanatory device of which the promise lies in its ability to exemplify or magnify various dimensions of legality in general. Firstly, then, it occupies a strategic position at law's 'final frontier', that is,

the state and have no direct bearing on the litigants in terms of changes in status, rights and obligations, or enforcement (that may of course ensue once the substantive dispute has been decided). A decidedly performative exception specific to private international law is *exequatur*: once granted, *exequatur* (let the foreign judgment be enforced!) empowers immediately by enjoining local bailiffs or administrative authorities to enforce the foreign decision through seizure of assets, location and return of an illegally displaced child, etc.

[101] H Vahinger. *The Philosophy of 'As If'* (Fakenham, Cox & Wyman, 1968). This echoes Bentham's theory of fictitious entities (on which see Schofield, *Utility and Democracy: The Political Thought of Jeremy Bentham*). More on as-if, fictionality and the conflict of laws below 191.

[102] As will be seen below, this can be seen as an ontological feature of law in general.

[103] R Michaels, 'Law and recognition: Towards a relational Concept of Law', in N Roughan & A Halpern, In Pursuit of Pluralist Jurisprudence (Cambridge, Cambridge University Press, 2017) 95.

[104] As noted above, these aspects are novel for the conflict of laws and not present in the more traditional *Vedanta* case used as illustration at the beginning of this preliminary section.

where law encounters foreign forms of normativity that are not aligned with modern Western views of legality, or claims that are illegible in law's cultural language. It operates at the very confines or external limits of legal systems, performing a particular type of boundary labour in the sense that its whole purpose is to work at the threshold, on the dividing line between the familiar and the foreign, inside and outside. It is an excellent place from which to reflect upon the ontology of the border and the jurisprudential aspects of jurisdiction; to identify the resonances between visions of the world's legal order and perceptions of our relationship with other biological and biographical forms of life. It is the place where various legal world views clash, and where modern law, called upon to define its own outside, threatens to unravel – unless something is done to change its settings (whether methodological, epistemological, ontological, aesthetic, political or ethical).

In this respect, literally, this discipline is concerned, as we have seen, with movements across borders in law – that is, over the frontiers between different national legal systems or the boundaries between territories. This is why it is also the scene of 'boundary struggles'. With a little help from metaphor, the conflicts of laws can be seen as the site and endgame of collisions between social spheres – however much its (academic) conceptualisms and its (judicial) praxes have traditionally worked to drain the life-blood from the real-world dimensions of these struggles and encounters with others and their differences.

Secondly, however, the argument that will be further developed in the following chapters is that the conflict of laws as a discipline contains a shadow pattern, an alternative avatar. Its own historiography features an innate duality that harks back to its Roman legal pedigree with its accompanying dialectic between order and disorder. Here, what might be described as its residual jurisprudence makes available, in legal terms, an alternative world view. According to the latter, the conflict of laws has a singular ability to embody, in a juridical mode, the entanglement of all the life forms, familiar and foreign, cultural and natural, that are present on the planet.[105] Such linkages are complex, reflexive, multidirectional. They are mirrored, emblematically, in the specific modes of reasoning of the conflict of laws. As has been observed by 'symmetrical' legal-anthropological scholarship in this particular field, these modes present various unfamiliar features of experimental, lateral, as if, reflexive and in between legal thinking.[106] Moreover, contrary to the severance and exclusion associated with naturalism, the conflict of laws' own alternative or shadow mode of connective existence embodies a radical form of hospitality towards alterity. Once again, alterity stands in here for all the other (cultural) lifeworlds and (biological) forms of life that – often imperceptibly – co-inhabit our earth alongside of ourselves, and upon which we depend for our own survival and to whose call we must respond.

[105] In this respect, it exemplifies legality's mode of existence as a 'juridical ecology of linkages' (once again in recognisably Latourian terms), carrying out the endless labour of re-stitching or 'reprisal' (a word borrowed from old French (see again below pp 181, 215)) of these broken connections that is required of us, urgently, if we want to come back down to earth.

[106] See Knop and Riles, 'Space, Time and Historical Injustice'. On Latour, symmetrical anthropology and its 'ontological turn' see above 35 and below Part II.

In this respect, the conflict of laws contains the traces of a residual jurisprudence as seen above, which comes back to haunt us as the disaster of the Anthropocene unfolds.

Thirdly, the discipline can be seen as a repository of normative ideas about the foreign, and more metaphorically, about the other (the alien or the different). Foreign law can be taken here as a symbolic representation of alterity more generally: the legal methods through which private international law accommodates the foreign to varying degrees contain as many attitudes towards difference, declined in ethical or political terms. Such methods, as we have seen, compose a baroque assemblage of highly elaborate legal concepts, theories, doctrines, definitions and tools, which are often understood on an exclusively technical register, meaning that they are devoid of any political significance beyond the allocation of rights and reciprocal duties as between private parties. In this respect, the field might seem no different from the (other) social sciences in the assumption, or the dogma, of scientific neutrality – except that the latter have progressively become detached from such dogma and now rarely adhere either to an Archimedean view of society, or to a conception of their own forms of knowledge as 'scientific'. The law lags on this point may be linked to specific features of legal epistemology. But private international law has certainly developed its own 'exceptionalism' – standing in isolation from the rest and elaborating its own account of itself as a form of transcendent objectivity, removed from the local mess of politics.[107]

Lastly, the semantic register of the conflict of laws, visible in all the considerations above, is singularly suggestive. Its specific vocabulary of 'attachments' or 'reattachments' (*rattachements*) evokes the linkages it labours to establish between (legal and factual) phenomena and various jurisdictions, within the allocatory scheme described above. Attachment is again an important concept in anthropology, where 'forms of attachment' designate the various types of relationality or dependency that various entities entertain among themselves. Law's conventional 'jurisdictional attachments', writes Shaun McVeigh, can be understood as a technology or set of techniques, devices of judgement, categorisation and administration that have dominated the processes of capture or attachment of persons, things, events and effects to the body of law. Conversely, however, in an imagined new age of 'reattachments', legal thought, like all the other disciplines that produce and order modern knowledge, needs to abandon the idea of human exceptionalism (or exemptionalism), to accept that our critical zone on earth has no outside, to understand that 'environment' is not distinct from self and that things (inanimate, technological, artefactual, cultural) lead us just as much as we, in all our imagined autonomy, drive them. In other words, we need to come back down to earth, in legal as in other terms. Law in this perspective is not disembedded, but belongs to the world. It takes place, but does not stay in place. This brings us to the question of the stakes in method.

[107] Perhaps the clearest sign of its own archaic epistemology is the treatment of foreign law as fact – meaning either that it is 'merely' so, and therefore undeserving of further, properly legal, attention, or conversely, that it is set in stone or intangible and thus deserving of deference (see on the law/fact distinction, below 118).

V. THE STAKES IN METHOD

It might well be asked what the point is of discussing the genealogy and style of these idiosyncratic modes of legal reasoning (methods) when the ecological stakes outlined above are so far from (one might further say) trivially juridical.[108] As emphasised above, most representations of the history of the conflict of laws frame the latter as a (largely circular) debate between two broad methodological forms (monism vs pluralism). One particular (contemporary) avatar of this debate is the transatlantic opposition between a rule- or principle-based (largely syllogistic and frequently dogmatic) approach and a policy-driven analysis of all manner of interests involved in a particular case.[109] In order to better grasp its wider significance in terms of a horizon of ecological jurisprudence, it is useful to ask three important questions. Firstly, how does this juridical debate between monism and pluralism relate to broader (non-legal) controversies over theories of truth? Secondly, what exactly is ecological about the debates over the nature of legal method? And thirdly, how does all this relate to the question of alterity?

A. Monism vs Pluralism and Theories of Truth

Pragmatism[110] in law is associated with the advent, in the United States, of legal realism and certain forms of legal pluralism. A first significant element in response to

[108] The point made in this preliminary section is about reciprocal influences, travelling metaphors, and the interdisciplinary (sometimes mis-)translation of ideas. Law is not often part of the conversation (and of course, the conflict of laws even less so). However, in the discussion above on the stakes of method, the following anecdote or concatenation is worthy of reflection. William James, whose influence on Bruno Latour is clear (one point of intellectual encounter was the Gifford Lectures, Edinburgh, delivered by each), devoted his work on pragmatism to the memory of John Stuart Mill ('from whom I first learned the pragmatic openness of mind'). Mill himself was a complex figure, having spent a large part of his career in the East India Company, where he opposed direct rule (see on his personal history and doctrines of liberalism, Poole, *Reason of State*). The *Encyclopedia Britannica* notes that 'Pragmatism first received philosophical expression in the critical group discussions of the "Metaphysical Club" in the 1870s in Cambridge, Mass. In addition to Peirce and James, membership in the club included … Oliver Wendell Holmes, Jr.' As far as Mill is concerned, the same source also recounts that from May 1820 until July 1821, Mill was in France with the family of Sir Samuel Bentham, brother of Jeremy Bentham, the English utilitarian philosopher, economist, and theoretical jurist. Copious extracts from a diary kept at this time show how methodically he read and wrote, studied chemistry and botany, tackled advanced mathematical problems, and made notes on the scenery and the people and customs of the country. He also gained a thorough acquaintance with the French language. On his return in 1821 he added to his work the study of psychology and of Roman law, which he read with John Austin. On travelling metaphors in comparative legal studies, see R Michaels, 'The Functional method in comparative law', in M Reimann and R Zimmermann (eds), *The Oxford Handbook of Comparative Law* (Oxford, Oxford University Press, 2008) 340, observing the interdisciplinary borrowing of functionalism: p 344: 'Ernst Cassirer transposed the notion from mathematics and science to philosophy; sociologists from Comte and Spencer via Durkheim to Parsons and Luhmann borrowed biological concepts; lawyers like Jhering and Pound were inspired by sociological ideas of function'. But, he warns, 'such cross-fertilization, as comparatists know well from the legal transplants debate, is not immune to misunderstandings and alterations, known or unknown'.

[109] As already suggested above, this traditional framing of the transatlantic cultural opposition is a caricature. The current debate in the United States over the methodological grounding of the *Third Restatement* of the Conflict of Laws shows a nested opposition within this (realist and policy-based) tradition between an open-ended and a black-letter approach (see below 79).

[110] In this context, Bruno Latour's own work invites us to explore that of William James on (scientific and philosophical) pragmatism ('A New Name for Some Old Ways of Thinking' (1906/07), www.gutenberg.org/ebooks/5116). See too on the intellectual crossings between law and science, above, 4.

the question above lies in the link between pragmatism as a theory of truth and what is known as the North American legal-realist or functionalist 'revolution' (specifically in the conflict of laws).[111] Pragmatism represented a rejection of inductive logic in science in the early twentieth century. According to William James, observing an initial 'singular unanimity as to what the laws of nature and elements of fact means',

> the notion has gained ground that most, perhaps all, of our laws are only approximations. The laws themselves, moreover, have grown so numerous that there is no counting them; and so many rival formulations are proposed in all the branches of science that investigators have become accustomed to the notion that no theory is absolutely a transcript of reality, but that any one of them may from some point of view be useful. Their great use is to summarise old facts and to lead to new ones. They are only a man-made language, a conceptual shorthand, as someone calls them, in which we write our reports of nature; and languages, as is well known, tolerate much choice of expression and many dialects.[112]

Pragmatism, then, is the name for a new state of mind produced by this evolution. It is described by James in the same passage as 'the attitude of looking away from first things, principles, "categories", supposed necessities'; indeed 'the true is the name of whatever proves itself to be good in the way of belief, and good, too, for definite, assignable reasons'.[113]

A second important step is to point out the resonance of the same debate within the contemporaneous legal-methodological opposition between monism and pluralism ('multilateralism' and 'statutism') in the conflict of laws. A further citation from the work of William James supplies the connection:

> The great monistic *denkmittel*[114] for a hundred years past has been the notion of the one knower. The many exist only as objects for his thought – exist in his dream, as it were; and as he knows them, they have one purpose, form one system, tell one tale for him. This notion of an all-enveloping noetic unity in things is the sublimest achievement of intellectualist philosophy.[115]

He continues:

> The world's oneness has generally been affirmed abstractly only, and as if anyone who questioned it must be an idiot. The temper of monists has been so vehement, as almost at times to be convulsive; and this way of holding a doctrine does not easily go with reasonable discussion and the drawing of distinctions. The theory of the Absolute, in particular, has had to be an article of faith, affirmed dogmatically and exclusively. The One and All, first in the order of being and of knowing, logically necessary itself, and uniting all lesser things in the bonds of mutual necessity, how could it allow of any mitigation of its inner rigidity? The slightest suspicion of pluralism, the minutest wiggle of independence of any one of its parts from the control of the totality, would ruin it. Absolute unity brooks no degrees …[116]

[111] On this 'revolution', see S Symeonides, 'The American Revolution and the European Evolution in Choice of Law: Reciprocal Lessons' (2008) 82 *Tul L Rev* 1741.

[112] W James, Lecture II: 'What Pragmatism Means', in James, *A New Name for Some Old Ways of Thinking*.

[113] Ibid.

[114] *Denkmittel* refers to the means by which we handle facts by thinking them.

[115] James, Lecture IV: 'The one and the many', in James, *A New Name for Some Old Ways of Thinking*.

[116] James, Lecture VI: 'Pragmatism's Conception of Truth', in James, *A New Name for Some Old Ways of Thinking*.

As will be seen later, this monistic *denkmittel* is highly relevant to the methodological debate within the conflict of laws, at least at the (late) high tide of legal realism in the field, in the mid-century. Famously, Gerhard Kegel's Hague lecture on the 'Crisis of the Conflict of laws' drew attention to the dangers of allowing pragmatism to interfere with the smooth functioning of syllogistic reason.[117]

Pluralism on the other hand (continues William James) has no need of any such dogmatic rigour.

> Provided you grant some separation among things, some tremor of independence, some free play of parts on one another, some real novelty or chance, however minute, she is amply satisfied, and will allow you any amount, however great, of real union. How much of union there may be is a question that she thinks can only be decided empirically. The amount may be enormous, colossal; but absolute monism is shattered if, along with all the union, there has to be granted the slightest modicum, the most incipient nascency, or the most residual trace, of a separation that is not 'overcome'.[118]

Pragmatism, then

> pending the final empirical ascertainment of just what the balance of union and disunion among things may be, must obviously range herself upon the pluralistic side. Some day, she admits, even total union, with one knower, one origin, and a universe consolidated in every conceivable way, may turn out to be the most acceptable of all hypotheses. Meanwhile the opposite hypothesis, of a world imperfectly unified still, and perhaps always to remain so, must be sincerely entertained. This latter hypothesis is pluralism's doctrine. Since absolute monism forbids its being even considered seriously, branding it as irrational from the start, it is clear that pragmatism must turn its back on absolute monism, and follow pluralism's more empirical path.[119]

The ideological stakes of the monism-pluralism debate are clearly outlined. But what exactly is ecological about them?

B. The Ecological Nature of Method

The ecological stakes underlying the design of legal method lie in the possibility of disentrenching a Cartesian version of nature from the law. Once again, it is useful to turn to sources outside the law to help understand the problem. In this respect, if we turn from modes of veridiction in science to political economy, an important observation by Engels can be transposed to law's characteristic mode of categorising reality and separating the parts from the whole. Thus,

> The analysis of Nature into its individual parts, the grouping of the different natural processes and objects in definite classes, the study of the internal anatomy of organised

[117] G Kegel, 'The Crisis of Conflict of Laws', *Collected Courses of the Hague Academy of International Law*, vol 112 (1964).
[118] James, Lecture VI: 'Pragmatism's Conception of Truth', in James, *A New Name for Some Old Ways of Thinking*.
[119] Ibid.

bodies in their manifold forms – these were the fundamental conditions of the gigantic strides in our knowledge of Nature that have been made during the last 400 years. But this method of work has also left us as a legacy the habit of observing natural objects and processes in isolation, apart from their connection with the vast whole; of observing them in repose, not in motion; as constraints, not as essentially variables; in their death, not in their life.[120]

William James provides further fuel for this argument about the influence of our modes of legal thought and our encounter with nature. Once again, a citation is in order:

All our conceptions are what the Germans call *denkmittel*, means by which we handle facts by thinking them. Experience merely as such doesn't come ticketed and labelled, we have first to discover what it is. Kant speaks of it as being in its first intention a *gewuehl der erscheinungen*, a *rhapsodie der wahrnehmungen*, a mere motley which we have to unify by our wits. What we usually do is first to frame some system of concepts mentally classified, serialised, or connected in some intellectual way, and then to use this as a tally by which we 'keep tab' on the impressions that present themselves. When each is referred to some possible place in the conceptual system, it is thereby 'understood'.[121]

This notion of parallel 'manifolds', with their elements standing reciprocally in 'one-to-one relations', is proving so convenient nowadays in mathematics and logic as to supersede the older classificatory conceptions. There are many conceptual systems of this sort; and the sense manifold is also such a system. Find a one-to-one relation for your sense-impressions anywhere among the concepts, and in so far forth you rationalise the impressions. But obviously you can rationalise them by using various conceptual systems. The old common-sense way of rationalising them is by a set of concepts of which the most important are these: Thing; The same or different; Kinds; Minds; Bodies; One Time; One Space; Subjects and attributes; Causal influences; The fancied; The real. We are now so familiar with the order that these notions have woven for us out of the everlasting weather of our perceptions that we find it hard to realise how little of a fixed routine the perceptions follow when taken by themselves.[122]

James then provides in turn an aptly ecological example:

Were we lobsters, or bees, it might be that our organisation would have led to our using quite different modes from these of apprehending our experiences. It might be too (we cannot dogmatically deny this) that such categories, unimaginable by us today, would have proved on the whole as serviceable for handling our experiences mentally as those which we actually use.[123]

Beyond method, the question of other possible *epistemes* will be further developed below. However, the main point for the time being is the link between the

[120] F Engels, 'Socialism: Utopian and Scientific', in *Marx & Engels: Collected Works*, vol 24 (1874–83) (New York, International Publishers, 1989) 299.

[121] James, Lecture VI: 'Pragmatism's Conception of Truth', in James, *A New Name for Some Old Ways of Thinking*. It is interesting to emphasise here that this very debate – is reality or experience 'out there' before we ticket and label it? – is central to the conflict of laws, in the context of the intellectual process known as characterisation (see below 81, 184).

[122] James, Lecture VI: 'Pragmatism's Conception of Truth', in James, *A New Name for Some Old Ways of Thinking*, Chapter 5.

[123] Ibid.

modern-Cartesian refusal of plurality and a further dimension of modern thought, which lies in its Archimedean viewpoint. Referring to the work of Isabelle Stengers,[124] anthropologists D Danowski and E Viveiros de Castro observe:

> the Great Divide which has for the last centuries opposed those peoples who allegedly lived in an oneiric, phantasmatic relationship with the Earth, and a 'we' that took itself for an impersonal 'one', an abstract Third Person: the anonymous point of view from which 'one' could apprehend nature's real essence, and of which we Moderns were the zealous guardians.[125]

This observation is clearly relevant in turn to grasping the tensions that traverse the conflict of laws. Here, the historical and apparently technical opposition between monism and pluralism has vast, unsuspected implications for the ways we approach not only our foreign cultural others but also our natural world with its biological lifeforms.

C. Approaching Alterity in Legal Form

The philosophical contests presented above are helpful when reading the most usual textbook accounts of the discipline of the conflict of laws, where it appears as the sedimented result of a timeless dichotomic opposition between two approaches towards alterity in legal form. Indeed, this incursion into philosophical controversy helps make explicit the assumptions underlying the positions of either 'camp' within this specifically legal discipline (even though, as will be seen below, these are constantly moving positions). Basically, the choice is between monist and pluralist approaches that correspond broadly to those defined by William James, often (but not always) coextensive, moreover with the pair formed by syllogistic logic and pragmatism. While (thickly) clothed in legal technique, they are also the site of a political combat for ideas. The object of the strictly methodological discussion that interests us here is diversely described as about how to 'coordinate legal systems', or how to ensure the 'harmonious' fit of legal rules of heterogeneous origin. As seen above, in more concrete terms, the issue is what type of legal reasoning should be used by a court when confronted with a dispute that involves opposing claims of which one or more are framed in the light of foreign legal norms. If any such claim appears legitimate, how can it make sense (or be made to produce sense) within a heterogeneous order or framework?

The predominant contemporary approach ((mis-)named multilateralism[126]) adopts an Archimedean standpoint towards the coordination of different legal rules (artefacts, objects, contrivances, constructions) borrowed from various normative

[124] I Stengers, *In Catastrophic Times. Resisting the Coming Barbarism* (Open Humanities Press, in collaboration with Meson Press, 2015) (first published in French, *Au temps des catastrophes. Résister à la barbarie qui vient* (Paris, éd La Découverte, 2009).

[125] Danowski and Viveiros de Castro, *Ends of the World* 111.

[126] As already signalled above, these opposing intellectual camps are (somewhat inappropriately) named 'multilateralism' or 'conflict of laws proper' vs 'statutism' or 'unilateralism'.

sources. It uses an old anthropological device, the *as if* of legal fiction,[127] as if the court (or the observer) were removed from the equation. This is also a form of universalism, insofar as it assumes that others think and act (in legal terms) as oneself (as within 'a community of laws'[128]). Coordination can therefore take place – if not without distortion, then at least with minimal technical tweaking. A caricature of this position can be found once again in Etienne Bartin's (early twentieth-century) idea that private international law maps out the world's legal systems as if in the name and place of an absent supranational legislator.[129]

Later, post-universalist approaches[130] attest to more pragmatic influences. Here, it is accepted that a viewpoint can only be one's own (that of 'the country of the forum') even while its thrust is still deemed to be universal. This new position came to be known, somewhat confusingly, as 'particularism': confusingly because while the singularity or subjectivity of any viewpoint is acknowledged, the external standpoint is maintained and there is still an underlying project to make the rest of the world fit with it. At this point, there had to be practical concessions to pluralism or pragmatism so as to make things work on the ground. This more reflexive stance can be found, for instance, in the influential work of Henri Batiffol on the coordination of legal systems[131] or, on the other side of the Atlantic, in the more contemporary syncretic representation of the discipline by Symeon Symeonides.[132]

On the opposite front, there are those who attempt to abandon this overarching perspective, in the idea that alterity should be allowed in, not in the terms of monistic understanding of the world, but *on its own terms*. This stance is far more demanding because the right 'fit' of the foreign within the host legal order (or within ourselves) is more difficult to attain unless in the shadow of an overarching legal order (such as Roman law) or uniform legal culture (such as the Roman Christian legal tradition, or again the common law, or indeed a shared belief in territory as a defining principle[133]).

[127] On the legal device of *as-if*, see below 191.

[128] On Savigny's influential expression, see below 70.

[129] '*Dédoublement fonctionnel*' ('functional doubling-over'): a notion made popular at the time by constitutionalist George Scelle (*Précis du droit des gens*, 1933) and meaning very basically that one agent can serve the purposes of another. See E Bartin, 'Une conception nouvelle de l'empire de la loi locale par opposition à la loi personnelle et à la loi territoriale' (1935) 52 *RCADI* 583–642.

[130] The slow abandon of universalism was linked to the incremental awareness that private international law is only national or municipal, no longer attributable to the 'natural' law of nations (in Anthea Roberts's terms: *Is International Law Really International?* (Oxford, Oxford University Press, 2018), challenging the conception that international law is universal and that international lawyers exist in a single 'invisible college'). The idea that it is 'private' because it is linked to non-state actors is still tenacious in civil law tradition, as will be seen below.

[131] See notably Batiffol, *Aspects philosophiques* : that such systems are designed to 'dégager ce que le droit positif contient d'enseignements sur les réalités sociales que constituent les matières régies par le droit et le droit lui-même'. In this spirit, while deliberately distancing his own position from the nationalistic tendencies of the war years, he accepted that in exercising its coordinatory function, given the lesser state of development of the international legal order as compared with municipal systems, the latter had to shoulder a large part of this task. The tone is resolutely pragmatist.

[132] See S Symeonides, 'Codification and Flexibility in Private International Law', in KB Brown and DV Snyder (eds), *General Reports Of The XVIIIth Congress Of The International Academy Of Comparative Law*, (Springer, 2011). Here, under clear North American pragmatist influence, the current state of the art across the board appears as methodological syncretism or *bricolage*.

[133] As will be seen below, these various background assumptions of commonality correspond respectively to doctrines of continental multilateralism, to the North American legal-realist vision that provides the example given in the text, and to vested rights theories that travelled from early Dutch scholarship (notably that of Ulrich Huber) to the Anglo-American world.

An example will be taken from what has come to be known as 'interests analysis', as formulated at the start of the North American 'revolution' during the high tide of legal realism, by Brainerd Currie. Although he envisaged only intra-national (federal) cases, and assumed a background of American common law, the latter was not enough to ward off strong differences in legal policies and outcomes. His idea was that where a given dispute could give rise to potentially conflicting results in different jurisdictions, the court had to search for the policies and interests underlying all of these, not solely from its own perspective, but from that of all the others as well. This would encourage a spontaneous form of virtual negotiation, and the discovery in many instances that the apparent conflict was a 'false' one, because in all likelihood, not all such jurisdictions would actually have a concrete interest in furthering their policy in the light of their factual connections with the case. However, precisely because the Archimedean (or federal) viewpoint was out of bounds, the same court would have to refrain from deciding between them every time the conflict was a 'true' one, incapable of resolution through spontaneous compromise. In such cases, it would have no choice but to decide the case under the law of the forum (its own law). While the 'positive' legal landscape is mixed, a certain number of state legislatures or judiciaries have adopted this methodology in practice.[134]

Whatever the methodological rights and wrongs of this particular (and highly controversial) theory,[135] this second camp is resolutely pluralistic (and here, pragmatist), in that it accepts from the start that there are many truths, or many normative universes (pluriverse). The argument in favour of the respect for the various forms in which the latter are given legal expression places the choice of approach on largely ethical grounds. It sees the conflict of laws as carrying a double burden of translating or making sense of alterity within the host legal system and ensuring by the same token that every legal phenomenon is in its right place. This challenge may explain why there is a comparative dearth of contemporary doctrines of legal pluralism in continental private international law.[136] In practice, the closest courts come to reasoning in such a way is through the idea of recognition of legal relations created abroad, initiated (controversially) by the European Court of Human Rights in the name of the right to privacy.[137] In this context, the latter right is used to justify the protection of a personal or family relationship (adoption) shaped abroad on the terms of a foreign law, even when such terms do not align with the vision of the receiving (or host) state,

[134] See the panorama drawn up by Symeonides, 'Codification and Flexibility in Private International Law'. Another group of states follows the Second Restatement (closest connection method) and a further group still subscribes to the old English 'vested rights' doctrine.

[135] On the analogous terms of the current debate in the United States over the *Third Restatement* of the conflict of laws, see above 5, 45 and below, 79. It must be emphasised that Currie's governmental interest analysis is described here as one incarnation of pluralistic methodology. But it is not an ideal one; its DNA is largely marked by mid-twentieth-century intra-federal social and economic change in the United States, where the common law of the various states was in flux as the nationwide market expanded, mobility increased, industry begot accidents and products liability began to serve as insurance.

[136] Beyond the premodern medieval statutists, notable contemporary exceptions, as will be seen below, can be found in the work of Rolando Quadri, Pierre Gothot and Didier Boden, and in a slightly different mode, Karen Knop and Annelise Riles.

[137] Privacy or the 'respect for private life', including family relationships constituted abroad (Art 8 ECHR). In *Wagner and JMWL v Luxembourg* (2007) ECtHR App no 76240/01, Luxemburg was obliged to give legal effect to an adoption that had been awarded in Peru but that did not fit with Luxemburg's own choice-of-law rules (until then, a valid reason for refusing to recognise the existence of a foreign adoption).

whether in terms of the appropriate allocation of jurisdiction or the categorisation and shape of a 'legal relationship'.

But in a context wider than the (United States federal or specifically European) examples just cited, a pluralistic model might be described as one that takes on a specific type of boundary work in between many worlds, weaving together the various pieces of the broader normative puzzle. In this capacity, it can be seen as playing a properly constitutional role in seeking to allow all legal Others to keep their world views, imaginaries and fantasies, with as little distortion or loss in translation as possible. Its philosophical affinities are unhesitatingly pluralistic, resonating with theories of the in between and the pluriversal, as we shall see below. By now, then, the ecological implications of jurisprudential debates in legal method between monism and pluralism should be apparent, particularly insofar as they oppose the validity and legitimacy of an Archimedean viewpoint. Such stakes appear once again in the following comment by Eduardo Viveiros de Castro, according to which, as long as we are obsessed with the ideal model of rational, objective knowledge (the 'legislating' Understanding), capable of bringing all of the earth's peoples into agreement with each other, we will remain incapable of establishing with these other peoples relations worthy of that name.[138]

NATURE AT THE STAKE

The ecological stakes of an alternative jurisprudential design lie then in the *affects* or attachments[139] of our juridical universe and the ways in which they shape our approaches to 'nature' as an ideological concept. Law is profoundly entwined in our views of nature as (or not as) a social problem, in other words, with our understandings of the relationships between ecology and culture, the natural and social sciences, or simply persons and things. As will be shown below, unpacking legal methods by searching for their underlying mental schemes, accompanying genealogical narratives or constitutive myths is essential for understanding the ways in which law weighs in the struggle between 'first' and 'second' natures, the economy and the ecology and of which the outcome may change our planetary future.

The possibility of such relations conditions in turn our ability to respond to the appeal of all the other heterogeneous forms of life that surround us, provide our habitat on earth's crust and indeed compose our very being.[140] This is the cue to inquire in more detail, through the lens of private international law, whether and how far modern law has led us astray and is able to reverse its own trajectory.

[138] Once again, see Danowski and Viveiros de Castro, *Ends of the World* 111, and the important citation in the text above referring to the 'Great Divide' between those '"peoples" who allegedly lived in an oneiric, phantasmatic relationship with the Earth, and a "we" that took itself for an impersonal "one", an abstract Third Person: the anonymous point of view from which "one" could apprehend nature's real essence, and of which we Moderns were the zealous guardians'.

[139] On critical 'affect' theories, close to psychoanalysis and queer theory, see for example, E Sedgwick, *Touching Feeling: Affect, Pedagogy, Performativity* (Durham NC, Duke University Press, 2003). On the affects of law and the relevance of this concept for 'jurisdictional jurisprudence', see below 156 et seq; see too, 11, 40, 142, 229. For an ironic use of this term, B Latour, 'On some of the Affects of Capitalism', Lecture given at the Royal Academy, Copenhagen, 26 February 2014.

[140] See Part III below.

1

The Story of Origin

APPLIED TO THE emergence of this legal (as any other) modern discipline, a genealogical perspective is proposed here that differs from a strictly historical account.[141] The latter (and most conventional) approach focuses on the chronological appearance of various ideas and doctrines, notably those that are seen to embody a radical break with a previous paradigm.[142] In the case of the conflict of laws, the focus of most historical narratives usually starts with the multiple, successive strains of 'statutism' deployed from the (late) Middle Ages in the shadow of Roman law in order to reconcile diverging local customs in medieval Europe.[143] Thereafter, the emphasis shifts to the grand methodological resequencing that took place in the nineteenth century.[144] The protagonists are a triad of founding fathers,

[141] On this distinction (which we owe to Michel Foucault's *L'archéologie du savoir* (Paris, Gallimard, 1969), see A Rasulov, 'New approaches to international law: images of a genealogy', in JM Beneyto and D Kennedy (eds), *New Approaches to International Law: The European and the American Experiences* (TMC Asser-Springer, 2012) 151–91. A genealogy rejects any account of the birth of a discipline as the intellectual brainchild of a 'founding father', in favour of that of a myriad of smaller mutations across various areas of thought and practice. In this respect, it resembles the idea of a Kuhnian paradigm shift (as in *The Structure of Scientific Revolutions*, 3rd edn (Chicago, University of Chicago Press 1996). It can also be framed as archaeology, to the extent that it questions the historical accuracy of a received account, preparing the terrain for an analysis of its ideological function. On the power of archaeology to challenge myths and overthrow dogma through its unpredictability, its capacity to surprise and upset conventional wisdom, see the exchange between David Wengrow and Kwame Anthony Appiah in 'The Roots of Inequality: An Exchange', *NYRB* (13 January 2022). For a comparative approach to 'visions of law-in-history', see Monateri, *Comparative Legal Methods* 51.

[142] On the relevance of the Kuhnian paradigm for the understanding of legal epistemology, see Samuel, 'Taking Method Seriously'. The important point about scientific revolutions made by Kuhn himself, is that paradigms do not 'just' change radically, without multiple, often imperceptible prior moves and later lingering residues. Foucault outlines a similar approach to the embodiment of a new *epistemè*. In particular, the so-called 'Copernican' change ascribed to the opus of Carl von Savigny within the conflict of laws was obviously prepared by multiple smaller changes and indeed the 'revolution' was far less generalised than is usually thought: see for example, B Ancel, 'Destinées de l'articles 3 du Code civil' in *Le droit international privé: esprit et méthodes – Mélanges en l'honneur de Paul Lagarde* (Paris, Dalloz, 2005) 1–18.

[143] The origins of the modern discipline can be traced to the growing perception that local customary divergences from Roman law created a dilemma, at least if Roman law was to be considered as universally authoritative· The responses varied according to the status accorded to Roman law, as reason, science, custom, sovereign will, etc and the ways in which universalism combined, say, with humanism or scientificity. This was the very moment from which something recognisable as a 'Western legal tradition' took shape: see H Berman, *Law and Revolution. The formation of the Western Legal Tradition* (Cambridge MA, Harvard University Press, 1983) 5.

[144] In this context, see D Kennedy, 'Three Globalisations': the mid-nineteenth century saw the ravages of the industrial state in England, the rise of liberal economy according to Adam Smith, and the emergence of Marxist critique. In Germany, in reaction to British political economy there also emerged a mixture of Hegelian thought and Catholic social doctrine, accompanying an intense interest in Germany's national past.

drawn from various parts of the Western world (old and new).[145] However, a genealogical analysis differs from an historical study in that it uncovers the disparities, contradictions and dispersion hidden beneath a linear retrospective reconstruction.[146] Thus, the representation of the birth of the modern discipline is underwritten by the fantasy of a revolutionary dawn of enlightenment through method across various cultures and contexts, as will be seen in section I below.

Such an account focuses on the emergence of a particular type of legal reasoning designed to govern interactions within a 'community of laws' – that is, among like-minded German-Roman-Christian polities salvaged from the ashes of the Holy Roman empire. In such a context of shared legal categories and institutions, it was easy to believe in an apolitical world of private law overseen by a neutral coordinatory scheme. However, such a belief overlooks the momentous geopolitical context in which this scheme was progressively deployed. The methodological shift that supposedly opened a new modern era (albeit by returning to an imagined Roman past) accompanied the (late) entry on stage of the Hegelian state,[147] in the throes of German unification and nation-building, Napoleonic imperial expansion and decline, the transatlantic revolution, the invention of contemporary public international law and the expansion of the colonial project along with industrial capitalism. Moreover, the foundations and trajectories of the common law in the anglophone tradition were different enough to create tensions within this account. Section II below will attempt to winkle out the ideological vision underlying these purported moments of revelation, questioning their legacy.

Three decades on, the rise of Bismarck and the proclamation of the unified German State in 1871 led to war with France. *Cf* JP Chazal, 'Le propriétaire-souverain: archéologie d'une idole doctrinale' (2020) 4 *Rev trim dr civil*.

[145] Because the conflict of laws as we know it today emerged as an academic discipline in the nineteenth century (on this point, see N Hatzimihail *Preclassical Conflict of Laws* (Cambridge University Press, 2021), drawing attention to the danger of anachronism in the reading of its history), subsequent historiographical accounts tended (and still tend) to focus on the contribution of 'great men' rather than on the circulation of ideas. For a critique of the conventional ways of 'doing' the history of the discipline in this respect, see JL Halpérin, *Entre nationalisme juridique et communauté de droit* (Paris, PUF, 1999), recalling the work of Dutch jurist Eduard Meijers (some of whose work is accessible in French: 'La question du renvoi' (1938) 38 Bull Inst Int 191).

[146] According to Foucault's account (*L'archéologie du savoir*), behind the great historical events or beneath the 'grand narrative' (see Lyotard, *La Condition postmoderne*), it is far more likely that there are a multitude of smaller moves, that are not necessarily coherent as between themselves nor indeed the result of a univocal direction of history. Moreover, significant contextual events may be sidelined, so that significance is conferred in retrospect on a particular selection of past events, to the exclusion of others. See too the interesting reflection on modern time developed by A Appadurai, 'The Past as a Scarce Resource' (1981) 16(2) *Man* 201–19 (Royal Anthropological Institute of Great Britain and Ireland), pointing to a third kind of past (beyond the abstract or the purely pragmatic) whose essential purpose is to debate other pasts. It generally partakes of both ritual and everyday kinds of discourse and indeed makes it possible for people to pass from one to the other.

[147] On the late, twentieth-century emergence of the fully fledged modern sovereign, see H Brunkhorst, *Critical Theory of Legal Revolutions: Evolutionary Perspectives* (London, Bloomsbury, 2014); see too the review of the latter by P Kjaer, (2015) 42 *Journal of Law and Society* 312–18. *Cf* M Koskenniemi, observing that the history of international law is that of statehood, situated in the realm of the 'international', conceptualised as a terrain of war and peace, diplomatic conflict, and cooperation, in which little is visible of the many turns from professional historiography to social history and genealogy, to the complex jurisprudential understandings of the meaning of 'law' ('Expanding Histories of International Law' (2016) 56 *American Journal of Legal History* 104–12, 107).

I. GENEALOGY AND METHODOLOGY

According to a first (grand) narrative, the 'story of origin' of the conflict of laws tells of the advent of enlightenment through methodology.[148] There is a clear connection between this account of an enlightened dawn and a certain representation of the discipline as a rationalist governance project. The invention of a whole new way of approaching colliding norms took place more or less simultaneously across the (Western) legal world. As the story goes, during the second half of the nineteenth century, the three founding fathers[149] of the modern discipline, coming from different legal traditions and in various political contexts, all broke with the legal consciousness of the past, turning their backs on archaic doctrines associated with medieval scholarship. Modernity was to have dawned at that (somewhat late[150]) point, with the advent of a novel theoretical framework that contrasted with the previous confusion of the dark ages of unscientific pragmatism and disorder.[151] It was in this favourable context that the conceptual axes of the discipline took shape, in the principled form of 'multilateralist' rules, to which a 'general theory' or a set of 'fundamental problems' would soon be adjoined (section I.A).

That this paradigmatic moment had occurred in a historical context of intense political and ideological turmoil is invisible in the retrospective account, as already suggested above. However, this troubled background, together with increasingly visible geographical variations in cultures of political theory and jurisprudence in the early twentieth century, may explain why a further, supporting, historical claim exists, whereby the current configuration of the discipline is the result of a long and reiterative confrontation between opposing methodological poles. Thus, the rationalist revolution is but one (albeit always ultimately victorious) stage within a longer pendulum-like evolution, swinging endlessly in a constant dialectical exchange.[152]

[148] For a brilliant critical study of this narrative, P Gothot, 'Simples réflexions à propos de la saga du conflit des lois', in *Le droit international privé: esprit et méthodes, Mélanges en l'honneur de Paul Lagarde* (Paris, Dalloz, 2005).

[149] As will be seen below, these were Joseph Story in the United States, Carl von Savigny in continental Europe and Albert Venn Dicey in England. The great Italian scholar and statesman Pasquale Stanislao Mancini (1817–88) was highly influential at the time in the promotion of a universalist-personalist doctrine embedded in a 'principle of nationality' drawn from public international law, but was eclipsed by the others within the retrospective account of the foundation of the modern discipline; his doctrine was not in phase with the separation of the public and the private characteristic of the legal consciousness of the early twentieth century.

[150] See Brunkhorst, *Critical Theory of Legal Revolutions.*

[151] This widespread representation of past chaos may be due very largely to Savigny's rejection of previous strands of legal humanism as unscientific and the return to the textual (or indeed mathematical: see Schiavone, *Ius* 38) purity pursued by Justinian, who had forbidden interpretation of the *Digest.* On this point, see A-H Neidhart, 'The Transformation of European Private International Law. A Genealogy', PhD Dissertation, European University Institute, 2018. Whatever the political reasons for wishing to represent the move as a return to the past, the account of an enlightened renaissance was reinforced by later scholarship. It is noteworthy of course that at the same time, public international law was also replacing eighteenth-century humanism and the law of nations by the regulation of state sovereign equality (see M Koskenniemi, 'Expanding Histories of International Law').

[152] This exchange takes place in a-historical time (from the threshold of modernity to the contemporary era), and in a metaphorical space (between the common law and civilian traditions).

This second narrative of reiterative contest and reciprocal conquest is similarly reflected in a moving, binary architecture: dichotomies and divisions, encounters and reactions, principles and exceptions, all surface and dissolve, only to assemble anew in the opposite structural configuration (section I.B).

A. The Consensual Tale

Progressively, by the turn of the twentieth century, at the time of the great universalist project of comparative law and the concomitant emergence of public international law as distinct from the venerable *ius gentium*,[153] a 'convergence thesis' developed around the methodological reversal embodied in Carl von Savigny's opus,[154] which was retrospectively described as 'revolutionary'.[155] Remarkably, despite very different political contexts and intellectual frameworks, the genesis of the discipline unfolds along similar lines in civil and common law traditions. Emerging some time after the (scholarly[156]) events in question, the account of the purported paradigm change is affected however by a (first) paradox: at the foundational moment, and for obvious political reasons in each case, none of the founders claimed to be doing more than reordering existing practice.

Thus, as is widely known, Savigny's account signalled the revival of Roman law in the form of a Christian-Germanic heritage, mirroring the doctrine of historical jurisprudence; as such, it was a political project of German unification and an antidote to the Napoleonic appropriation of the civil law through the French Civil Code of 1804.[157] The methodological strategy consisted in reinterpreting existing local practices through the schemes of intelligibility derived from Roman law, itself

[153] A change in terminology had occurred (following Jeremy Bentham, 'Principles of International Law' in J Bowring (ed), *The Works of Jeremy Bentham* (Edinburgh, 1838–43), vol II), from the 'law of nations', as directly descended from the *ius gentium* (both evocative of natural law) to positive 'international law' (whence private and domestic institutions were banished).

[154] *System des heutigen römischen Recht*. In later parts of this book (see in particular, Part II below), this opus will be discussed in its further dimension as the re-actualised (*heutigen*) project of a complete formalisation of life, following a cosmological system of 'invisible proportions' and displaying the aptitude of legal knowledge to detach itself from its object (Schiavone, *Ius* 60). Well before writing his great opus, in 1814, Savigny had launched a form of manifesto for the new German historical-scientific school, with its own review ('Zeitschrift für geschichtliche Rechtswissenschaft'). See O Jouanjan, *L'esprit de l'école historique du droit* (Strasbourg, Presses University Strasbourg, 2004).

[155] The dubbing of this reversal as a 'Copernican revolution', seems to be attributable to P Neuhaus, 'Savigny und die Rechtsfindung aus der Natur der Sache' (1949/50) *IS RabelsZ* 364, 366. Schiavone, *Ius* 38 proposes a very different analysis of Savigny's contribution to the knowledge of Roman law more generally as a form of minor historicism that rapidly became a conservative apology within a wider romanist myth of a classical law.

[156] On the peculiar feature of private international law as 'droit savant', see B Oppetit, 'Le droit international privé, droit savant', Collected Courses of the Hague Academy of International Law (vol 234) (1992), III, 331.

[157] See FC von Savigny, *Vom Beruf unserer Zeit für Gesetzgebung und Rechtswissenschaft* (1814, revd 1828). Codification cut the 'umbilical cord' between the life of the nation and its law, that required an ongoing, inductive or empirical spread of the *volksgeist* from case to case. The 'nature and nurture' political legal imagery of the umbilical cord here is significant: see on the constant presence of imaginaries of nature in legal thought, above, 8.

supposedly, in turn, part of the *Volksgeist*.[158] From this perspective, then, the new learning was located within the wider context of a celebration of the Roman heritage, while emphasising the historical continuity between the latter and the intellectual and cultural community of the Germanic peoples.[159] In terms of content, Savigny's might be described as an emphatically holistic[160] approach, in the sense that it appealed to the overall, systematic structure of Roman law (as restated in the seven preceding volumes of his great *Treatise*). It consisted in the identification of the natural 'seat' of a legal relationship – a largely metaphysical concept that would in turn ensure a rational determination of the applicable law – that is, without the risk of overlap or hiatus that had (purportedly) plagued the earlier statutist approaches.[161] Nature and science converged, then, in ensuring a 'harmonious'[162] non-conflictual distribution of 'legal relationships' among legal systems.

A parallel account of a foundational moment, where the chaos of ancient doctrines was replaced by a principled approach, is shared in the common law world. Thus, across the Atlantic, Joseph Story's systematisation of the discipline in his *Commentaries* of 1834 was written in the context of imminent conflict among the states of the Union over the status of fugitive slaves.[163] Its influence was immediate and widespread.[164] Methodologically, the central feature of his doctrine was the

[158] As emphasised above, there is a striking osmosis between the conflict of laws and comparative legal methods. In Savigny's work the two fields combine to project a certain idea of Roman law. In respect of this vision, largely the projection of a myth, PG Monateri (*Comparative Legal Methods* (Cheltenham, Elgar, 2021) 57) reminds us that the sudden emergence of Germanic historicism in the nineteenth century, presupposing an organic link between law and the essence of a nation contributed to an 'insulated' or exclusivist conception of Roman law largely coincidental with local custom, organically regenerated by the combined genius of each. This was an alternative to natural law, embodied in a legal history. When mingled with comparativism (including linguistic theories), it produced in turn a model of the 'Western' tradition and efforts to reconstruct the original law (*Urrecht*) with strong ethnic (Indo-European) dimensions. On the parallelism in this respect between trends in comparative law and with comparative linguistics, see by the same author, 'Black Gaius. A Quest for the Multicultural Origins of the "Western Legal Tradition"' (1999) 50 *Hastings Law Journal* 1.

[159] On the paradox of the axiological value conferred on (national) culture by 'a people without unity', see Descola, *Par delà nature et culture* 142, observing in respect of the German anti-Enlightenment movement (from Herder to von Humboldt) 'à quel point un peuple dépourvu d'unité politique a pu être obsédé par les interrogations sur ce qui fondait son caractère propre'.

[160] For want of a better term, 'holistic' here is used to designate a systematic rationalisation of the whole (and not in the pragmatic or pluralistic sense that will be developed in the alternative account below).

[161] Savigny famously asserted that his proposed methodology for the solution of the conflict of laws (beginning with the location of the 'seat' of the legal relationship within Roman categories) consisted in reframing the central question posed by the statutists ('what is the scope of a given statute?'), but he also maintained that the new and the old methodologies remained otherwise strictly equivalent.

[162] 'Harmony' is a recurring term within continental doctrines of the conflicts of laws (usually referring to a desirable state of compatibility of judicial decisions from different jurisdictions, obtained for example through the use of renvoi or the 'foreign court theory', by one or each of them).

[163] Joel Paul (in 'Comity in international law') makes the point that slavery was crucial in the formation of modern thought in the conflict of laws. See too, in the English context, *Somerset v Stewart* (1772) 98 ER 499 in which Lord Mansfield extends the protection to a slave on English soil, preventing his forced return (as a stolen chattel) aboard ship to Jamaica. For another point of view on the body of the slave (and the question of portable personal status) as foundational to 'our' legal ordering, see the interesting observations by Janet Halley, https://youtu.be/95v6ftXIdwI at 39 minutes (discussing the work of Judith Surkis on personal status in French colonised Algeria. see below 249 et seq).

[164] On this resounding and immediate success of Story's account, see Paul, 'Comity in international law' 159.

concept of a foreign, territorially vested, right, to which courts could give effect without violating the jurisdictional and prescriptive monopoly of the local sovereign. The inspiration for this territorialist conception lay in the writings of European late medieval scholars, notably of the Protestant Dutch School, available in Latin.[165] Notably, Story took up Ulrich Huber's reference to the (much misunderstood) *comitas* of nations as the grounds for the application of foreign laws.[166] Under this doctrine, the enforcement of foreign rights was mandated by the deference due (on the grounds of 'courtesy' or goodwill among nations, not law) to the foreign sovereign within whose jurisdiction such rights had vested.

In 1896, Dicey's comprehensive *Digest* followed suit in England[167] with resounding (and perennial) success.[168] Embracing the territoriality of laws and its corollary, vested rights, in the wake of Story (and the Dutch Protestant school), the *Digest* nevertheless excluded the recourse to *comitas* as the foundation and justification of the conflict of laws. Dicey qualified the latter as 'a singular specimen of confusion of thought produced by the laxity of language'.[169] Courts, it is said, give effect to foreign laws and judgments for reasons of justice, not by courtesy to foreign sovereigns.[170] Suffice it to observe at this point the role of the late emergence of the conflict of laws in England[171] and the concomitance between enlightened dawn and consolidation of empire.[172] The parameters of jurisdiction and domicile would continue to ensure the prevalence of English law and *mores* in personal and family matters involving colonial territories and subjects.[173] While the new opportunities of international

[165] Notably, Ulrich Huber's *De Conflictu Legum Diversarum*, on which, see E Lorenzen, 'Huber's *De conflictu legum*' (1918–19) 13 Ill LR 375, 199. Huber's three maxims were: '1. The laws of each state have force within the limits of that government and bind all subjects to it, but not beyond. 2. All persons within the limits of a government, whether they live there permanently or temporarily, are deemed to be subjects thereof. 3. Sovereigns will so act by way of comity that rights acquired within the limits of a government retain their force everywhere so far as they do not cause prejudice to the powers or rights of such government or of their subjects'. On the relationship between Huber and his contemporaries, the Voets (father and son), see Lorenzen, 'Huber's *De conflictu legum*' and Hatzimihail, *Preclassical Conflict of Laws*, emphasising the importance of Protestantism (and resistance to the Spanish Church) in the emergence of what this author sees as the first modern doctrine of the conflict of laws.

[166] See above, maxim 3. Comity, diversely understood, offers an explanation as to if, why and the extent to which sovereign states are compelled to apply foreign laws (see Paul, 'Comity in international law'; H Yntema, 'The Comity Doctrine' (1966) 65 *Mich L Rev* 9). Story saw comity as 'the most appropriate phrase to express the true foundation and extent of the obligation of the laws of one nation within the territories of another', *Commentaries on the Conflict of Laws* § 38 (1883).

[167] On nineteenth-century English conceptions as imbued with continental legal consciousness, Neidhart, 'The Transformation of European Private International Law. A Genealogy' 198 et seq.

[168] A Venn Dicey & J Bassett Moore, *A Digest of the Law of England with Reference to the Conflict of Laws* (London, Sweet & Maxwell, 1896).

[169] Dicey, Morris & Collins, *The Conflict of Laws,* 15th edn (London, Sweet & Maxwell, 2012), 1-008.

[170] As seen in the latter observation, the key to the enduring misunderstanding over the concept of comity lies in the shifting terrain of the question of the appropriate theoretical foundation for the conflict of laws, oscillating between a focus on the relations between sovereigns (deference, courtesy, reciprocity) and a focus on the duties or office of the local courts when asked to acknowledge foreign legal norms.

[171] Flagged by *Dicey, Morris & Collins*, 1-018.

[172] Moreover, of course, the emergence in this nexus of public international law as we now know it, after the vanishing of the law of nations and the equally sudden arrival on the scene of fully fledged statehood (see below 165).

[173] See below 164.

commerce[174] led to an opening (at least, discursively) in respect of foreign law and judgments, nevertheless, the predominance of the *lex fori* and the lack of enthusiasm of English courts for exercising jurisdiction in cases governed by foreign law (by staying on grounds of *forum non conveniens*) has lived on (despite some punctuated breakthroughs[175]).

By the early twentieth century, then, and whatever the variations in theoretical grounding or technical approach, a consensus had emerged on each side of the Atlantic as to the appearance and superiority of the 'multilateralist' methodology, born of the converging genius of the founding fathers. A form of new international common sense prevailed, so that forerunning, dissident, or alternative accounts were forgotten – as indeed the significant divergences within the new wisdom due both to various historical and geopolitical contexts and to conflicting epistemological (or legal-philosophical) visions of the law were eclipsed. Despite these potential sources of division, English-speaking authors did not hesitate to cite Savigny's *Treatise* in translation (Savigny having in turn referred to Story's *Commentaries*[176]) reflecting a first Western globalisation of legal consciousness, here as in other fields.[177] The scene was set for the flourishing of a form of methodological universalism at the turn of the century,[178] as if, like its public international counterpart, the understanding of the discipline was (subject to minor concrete adjustments) shared throughout the ('civilised'[179]) world. According to this 'convergence thesis',[180] while the content of legal traditions varied, agreement could nevertheless be found on a common recipe

[174] New or old? On the path dependency of 'connectivity norms' (in trade and value chains) in the wake of colonial trade routes, see P Kjaer, 'Constitutionalizing Connectivity: The Constitutional Grid of World Society' (2018) 45 *Journal of Law and Society*, and the specific version developed by Kjaer from the perspective of choice of law, 'L'idée sociologique de connectivité et le droit international privé' (2019) *Rev crit DIP* 929.

[175] Such as *Lubbe v Cape Plc* [2000] UKHL 41, in which the stay was not granted, although in the end restriction of judicial aid to foreign victims of personal injuries limited the real thrust of the case. Later, this breakthrough was severely curtailed (see the *Vedanta* case, above).

[176] On this intellectual relationship, see G Kegel, 'Story and Savigny' (1989) 37(1) *Am Journ Comp Law* 39–36.

[177] D Kennedy, 'Three Globalizations of Law and Legal Thought: 1850–2000', in D Trubek and A Santos (eds), *The New Law and Economic Development. A Critical Appraisal* (Cambridge, Cambridge University Press, 2006); by the same author, 'Towards an Historical Understanding of Legal Consciousness: The Case of Classical Legal Thought' (1980) 3 *Res In Law and Soc* 3–24.

[178] Of which a positivist variety emerged, through the foundation of the Hague Conference of Private International Law in 1893.

[179] References to 'civilisation' were frequent and can be found within the works of the founding fathers themselves. Such references bear an obvious relationship to colonial capitalist expansion. See N Tzouvala, *Capitalism As Civilisation: A History of International Law* (Cambridge, Cambridge University Press, 2020).

[180] Private international law provides an excellent example of the widespread and persistent epistemological bias in favour of similarity or convergence within comparative legal scholarship. For the most powerful critique of this bias, present in dominant comparative methods such as 'functionalism', see P Legrand, 'The Same and the Different', in P Legrand & R Munday (ed), *Comparative Legal Studies: Traditions and Transitions* (Cambridge, Cambridge University Press, 2003) 240–311. *Cf* for a similar position in comparative anthropology, Descola, *Les formes du visible* 26 On functionalism and its classical methodological alternatives (notably, structuralism) in comparative law, see Monateri, *Comparative Legal Methods* 3 et seq, 8 et seq. The (strong minoritarian) contemporary objections to functionalism in this field are largely valid too for the 'interests analysis' in the conflict of laws (cherry-picking 'purposes', risk of anachronism, assumption of coherent legislative will, etc) as will be seen below.

for coordination between laws, for the teleologically posited benefit of an increasingly mobile citizenship and thereafter for international trade and investment more generally.

In this respect, the triumph of 'multilateralism' would progressively be flagged, in retrospect, as synonymous with that of (epistemologically) modern and (politically and economically) liberal values.[181] The brave new vision of the conflict of laws had induced an epistemological shift, away from a focus on the (near literal) thrust of sovereign power embodied in national statutes towards the systematic, or conceptual, architecture of a legal system.[182] Crafted at the time of the ultimate collapse of the Eastern Roman empire, this reversal of perspective, from imperial power to a metaphysics of legality, also paved the way for a representation of the discipline as essentially apolitical. In turn, such a reversal enabled a framing of the function of the conflict of laws as allocatory and orchestrated from an Archimedean point, external to the laws to which it applied.[183] The new perspective that prevailed inside the discipline, born from but now ironically conceived as distinct from the public international ordering of interstate relationships, was that of a coordinated legal realm beyond the reach of state politics. Under the aegis of the 'private', it sheltered itself at the same time both from parochial struggles encased in (growing) domestic public or regulatory law and from (equally expansive) colonial appetites that found support in its public international counterpart.[184]

Such a representation was certainly in phase with the legal consciousness that prevailed at the time of this reconstruction.[185] The era that saw the dawn of a golden age of (Roman or common law) private legal values and modes of reasoning within a new, scientific, apolitical learning, was that of classical legal thought in national (Western) domestic settings.[186] Meanwhile, an important shift occurred in the prevailing vision of the international legal world.[187] By the turn of the twentieth century,

[181] On these political-economic aspects, see below Part III 277.

[182] As explained by Ralf Michaels in respect of Savigny's methodology, this reversal had a double component. On the one hand, Savigny was able to assert an argumentative primacy of the legal relation over the applicable law. It was not the lawmaker who decides what situations he wants to cover, but the situation which determines the appropriate lawmaker. This emphasised the private, apolitical character of the choice-of-law process as opposed to statutism, which had a political, public overtone (Michaels, 'Globalization and Law: Law Beyond the State' 289).

[183] The dualism statutism/multilateralism persisted in a further difference between definitions framed in public or private law terms, as distribution of prescriptive jurisdiction or of relationships between various national legal orders. On the reasons for the persistence of such dichotomies, see below, section II.

[184] On the colonial division of Africa consummated in 1870, see M Koskenniemi, *The Gentle Civilizer of Nations: The Rise and Fall of International Law 1870–1960* (Cambridge, Cambridge University Press, 2001). The turn to positivism at this point seems to have lifted any natural law break on colonial appetites (international law was a 'thin' commitment: see S Ratner, *The Thin Justice of International Law. A Moral Reckoning of the Law of Nations (*Oxford, Oxford University Press, 2015). There exists however a further, eminently humanistic and feminist account of the (much earlier) foundational moments: MT Guerra Medici, 'The Mother of International Law: Christine de Pisan' (1999) 19 *Parliaments, Estates and Representation* 15–22.

[185] See again Kennedy, 'Three Globalizations' and Neidhardt, 'The Transformation of European Private international law. A Genealogy'.

[186] And of its nascent global reach. See Schiavone, *Ius* 57, observing the correlation between the various morphologies of power and the models of legal thought.

[187] At this point, modern, positive, 'international law' banished private and domestic institutions from its scope. Modern private international law emerged, as it were, from public international law's move to positivism.

the public and private spheres had become radically disjoined.[188] A shared perception of the conflict of laws emerged, then, as a mode of legal governance of private relationships that transcended politics. After this point, rising above local struggles and aloof from the conflicted geopolitical sphere, the private international legal order was subject to a distinct, depoliticised, legal regime.[189] Pursuing a resolute quest for 'international harmony', in the light of the universalist aspirations of the time, it proved remarkably weatherproof in respect of the later geopolitical events that were to shake the Western world. Indeed, the return of sovereignty concerns (and the rise of national identity[190]) between the two world wars in the first half of the twentieth century served, paradoxically, to strengthen and extend geographically the sway of a methodological model that had been expressly designed, in Savigny's highly political project for the unification of Germany, to ensure the articulation of difference in a culturally and politically homogeneous legal setting. And, again curiously, far from weakening this project, the (largely colonial) discovery of radical legal difference[191] gave rise to the (remarkably intense) doctrinal production of 'general theories' of the conflict of laws in a quest to reintroduce harmony against all the odds of evident disunity in a rapidly expanding world.[192]

B. Frictions and Contradictions

The conventional representation of a common disciplinary genesis, epistemology and methodology is problematic in many ways. Unsurprisingly, on closer scrutiny, accounts of the further evolution and contemporary status of private international law differ quite radically among legal traditions. Diverse geopolitical strategies or philosophical influences obviously contribute to such disparity; each culture spins a specific dominant yarn of its own defining moments, adheres to an idiosyncratic perception of its essential schemes, and produces its own categories, conceptual grammar and vocabulary. Underlying or flowing from such differences are varying ideas of law as authority or reason, or again as individualised norms or a holistic form of ordering, and these differing constructions impact in turn upon the central focus of legal reasoning and the attendant tools (rules, judging, rights, logic, equity, proportionality, etc). Such accounts come moreover with contrasted ideas as to the function of the conflict of

[188] Thereafter, public law was local law (see Neidhardt, 'The Transformation of European Private international law. A Genealogy'.).

[189] As seen above, the representation of the legal order beyond the state as 'depoliticised' does not mean, of course, that the whole Savignian project did not pursue a clearly political agenda in the context of the move towards the unification of Germany.

[190] National identity as a principle of public and private international law was championed by the remaining, fourth 'father' of the discipline, the Italian jurist Mancini (see above 71, footnote 49).

[191] This was also to lead to the demise of the 1900 comparative legal project as the 'Word Fair of legal thought' (see Mireille Fournier, 'Comparative Law gets entitled', Thesis, University of Victoria 2018, p 15, chapter 2).

[192] See more below on the various devices that emerged progressively to deal with the difficulties raised by non-universalisable legal concepts. The poetic irony of this unintended detachment of Savigny's thought from its context is that it replicates the very same distanciation as between legality and reality that affected the law of classical Rome (which Savigny purported to revitalise): see Schiavone, *Ius* 35 et seq.

laws, regardless of the legal tradition involved (common law/civil law; United States/Europe). Some narratives tend to dwell on the just apportionment between laws or on the pursuit of justice in private cross-border relationships, while concurrent versions are harnessed to the protection of sovereignty, the effective enforcement of regulatory policies or the facilitation of regulatory competition. Correlatively, asperities appear underneath the consensual tale of a common origin. In particular, three significant difficulties reveal the artificial fracture of the story of a shared Enlightenment.

The first problem is that the representation of a shared new start glosses over a reciprocal cultural misreading. Although Savigny's *Treatise* was reminiscent at first glance of Story's systematic exposition of the field of the conflict of laws, the resemblance was largely superficial. In Story's *Commentaries*, as indeed in Dicey's *Digest*, the Dutch statutist legacy of territorially vested rights[193] had indeed morphed into apparently multilateralist rules.[194] However, when compared with their continental counterpart, the search for the metaphorical location of the legal relationship,[195] by means of an analysis – both axiological and teleological – of legal categories, shows up as missing.[196] This is because the intellectual focus of the discipline was far from shared across civilian and common law traditions. On Savigny's side, as recalled above, the new method was rooted in a comprehensive, holistic inquiry into the conceptual and functional structure of (Roman) civil law, whereas the common lawyers were more concerned with providing descriptive accuracy and a comprehensive account of existing judicial practice.[197] In other words, there was an epistemological gap between the two accounts, mirroring differences in common law and civilian understandings of legality in general.[198]

That despite apparent similarities, the English-speaking tradition had followed a distinct trajectory became very clear a century later, at the time of the methodological controversy between 'Savignian' multilateralism and policy-based interests analysis[199]

[193] Huber, *De conflictu legum*.

[194] For example: 'Generally speaking, the validity of a contract is to be decided by the law of the place, where it is made.' Commentaries § 242. Movables were subject to the law of the owner's domicile (indeed, '*mobilia sequuntur personam*' 'has so general a sanction among all civilised nations, that it may be treated as a part of the *jus gentium*.' §380); and so on.

[195] On the fact that 'place' in Savigny's conceptual scheme was metaphysical, not geographical, location, vs Michaels ('Globalization and Law: Law Beyond the State').

[196] B Audit, 'Le caractère fonctionnel de la règle de conflit (Sur la crise des conflits de lois)' (1984) 186 *Recueil des cours* 219 et seq).

[197] VE Lorenzen, 'Story's Commentaries on the Conflict of Laws – One Hundred Years After' (1934–35) 48 *Harv L Rev* 15, noting that at the time of the Commentaries, upwards of 500 decisions by Anglo-American courts relating to this subject existed, which called for a 'comprehensive exposition'.

[198] On these aspects of comparative legal epistemology, see G Samuel, 'Epistemology and Comparative Law: Contributions from the Sciences and Social Sciences', in Mark Van Hoecke (ed), *Epistemology and Methodology of Comparative Law* (Oxford, Hart, 2004) 35–77. The common lawyers attempted to organise (restate) a selection of solutions into a list (a commentary à la Blackstone, or a Digest of rules). Even as the European account accentuated historical continuities within a community of Roman legal consciousness, contemporaneous Anglo-American scholars had tended in turn to emphasise the role of local (indigenous?) ingenuity in the rise of a new legal discipline.

[199] Succinctly: the current draft Third Restatement of the conflict of laws Restatement (Third) of Conflict of Laws cmt c (Am Law Inst, Council Draft No 2, Sept 12, 2017) embodies this methodology (See ibid § 501 cmt b describing Brainerd Currie's governmental interest analysis theory as embodied in the 'two-step' model). Section 502 (a) reads: 'A court will decide a choice-of-law issue by determining whether there exists a material difference among relevant laws and, if so, deciding which of the conflicting laws will be given

in the United States[200] that came to a head in the 1970s. We shall return to this controversy below, but the point here is that the American functionalist 'revolution' addressed the territorialist legacy of the Dutch school of vested rights, but left the core of Germanic/French continental doctrine untouched. What had migrated from eighteenth-century Holland to the nineteenth-century Protestant Anglo-American world of Story and Dicey was both a vision of law as the expression of sovereign power and the conviction that the (purportedly) descriptive principle of territoriality sufficed to ensure the ensuing allocation of legal relations among the several laws of nation states. Paradoxically – or perhaps not so curiously, in the light of the obvious inadequacy of territory as a normative principle[201] – in the course of the supposedly 'Copernican' revolution that took place yet a century later in the United States, the novel framing of 'interests' that called for a 'functionalist' or policy-based consideration in each case were strongly reminiscent of those that structured Savigny's legal categories and, in his own metaphysical (and decidedly un-legal-realist) vision, mandated the distribution of 'legal relationships' according to their nature (imagined as inherent).[202]

A second problem is what was rapidly omitted or forgotten from Savigny's *opus*, that is, the careful circumscribing of the new methodology to shared *Volksgeist* or normative community of the culturally close polities comprised within the remit of what was to become the (relatively) unified German state – the heritage of the Holy Roman Empire common to the Germanic peoples.[203] In this respect, the project underlying the *Treatise of Roman Law* was clearly to put an end to the confusion deriving from imperial disintegration and the correlative decline of the idea of a higher natural order that might govern interactions between the subjects of different local laws. But Savigny's intellectual authority survived the transplantation of his doctrine into the world beyond the Germanic 'legal community', for which the doctrine had not been designed.[204] This provides the key to a further epistemological

priority'. This priority stems in turn, according to interests analysis, from an assessment of the respective strength of the policies of the various implicated states This methodology itself is in turn controversial, along the lines of a further, recurrent, nested, conflict between open-ended principles and predictable hard rules (see Brilmayer and Listwa, 'Continuity and Change in the Draft Restatement (Third) of Conflict of Laws': 'The new Draft Restatement aspires to achieve both the predictability of rules and the sensitivity to state substantive policy of an ad hoc method. But these goals are fundamentally irreconcilable. The drafters seek to accurately determine "interests" or "scope" and embody them in a general rule; to keep exceptions to the general rule to an absolute minimum; and to do this at a time that it cannot even be known what states will be involved in a particular case and what their laws are'. The draft, they write, 'surrenders enthusiastically to the mid-twentieth century, "modern", choice of law revolution'.

[200] Not in England, where legal-realism left a very modest imprint in the form, notably, of JHC Morris's discovery of the 'proper law of the tort' during his academic stay in the United States: 'The Proper Law of a Tort' (1951) 64 *Harvard Law Review* 881–95. The point here is that the American policy-based 'revolution' revealed, retrospectively, the former differences in approach between the common law world and the continental civilian tradition.

[201] As just suggested. This inadequacy will be addressed more fully below, Part II.

[202] For instance, the need for permanence of personal relationships leads to retain domicile as a connecting factor. See Audit, 'Le caractère fonctionnel de la règle de conflit'; *cf* the reference to the 'rich vein of legal writing led by Currie', in *Dicey, Morris & Collins*, vol II, 35.005, fn17.

[203] Remarkably, the 'concert' of European nations at the Vienna Congress of 1815 comprised over 40 Germanic entities.

[204] As Ralf Michaels points out ('Globalizing Savigny'), it was the use of natural law, or at least the naturality of Roman categories, that paradoxically led to 'universalising Savigny', even when it was clear that the commonality that conditioned the possibility of this alternative methodology was limited to the Christian-Roman legal tradition.

conundrum. The conflict of laws might seem to be inherently pluralistic in that it provides for interaction between different sets of legal rules and between courts in different jurisdictions, complete with their respective cultural and procedural set-ups. Further, any horizontalist doctrines of respect for or giving effect to foreign laws and courts self-presents as respect for legal difference, albeit as constituted solely by statal boundaries. However, broadly speaking, in the Roman conceptual scheme, conflicts were vertical, between the overarching (general or transcendent) and the local (singular and deviant) and not lateral, as among the plural laws of different polities or localities. Transplanted out of context, the scheme retained something of its original shape however, viewing difference through a monist lens.

The resulting transplanted strand of legal thought – claiming Savignian pedigree – has been eloquently dubbed 'savignism',[205] in order to denote its distance from the actual content of the great Romanist's doctrine and to emphasise the paradox of its cultural influence beyond the confines of the fallen Roman empire and its first Germanic invocation. It began to be used in the new context of the international[206] and its allocatory function became infused with considerations of state sovereignty. Moreover, with increasing cultural diversity of the substantive content of the laws involved, various aporia surfaced: the ideal of harmony[207] collapsed with different understandings of the 'nature' of the legal relationships that were required to be allocated (or the scope of legal categories in which various disputes were meant to be fitted). These divergences were frequent, even among supposedly similar civilian systems; instances of endo-European conflicting classifications fed expanding judicial practice in the conflict of laws in the first part of the twentieth century.[208] Such conflicts were however particularly marked when the colonial context brought modern secular law into contact with the local, indigenous, often religious laws of the colonised.[209]

The ensuing difficulties in the deployment of the 'Savignian' method warranted a series of devices designed to restore the initial 'harmony' (*Gesetzesharmonie*[210]). Such devices, often ad hoc judicial inventions – the notable example being 'renvoi'

[205] On this term, see Gothot, 'Simples réflexions à propos de la saga du conflit des lois' 343. It designates, in particular, the French strain of multilateralism incarnated in Bartin's scholarship at the turn of the twentieth century.

[206] The new sphere of the 'international' was so termed by Bentham as a constructed reality (as opposed to visible or tangible reality) that required naming in order to exist (on invisible forms of reality, see below Part II). On the later appearance of the fully-fledged sovereign state as constitutive of the emergence of the inter-statal as late as the early twentieth century, see Brunkhorst, *Critical Theory of Legal Revolutions*.

[207] On the recurrence of the idea of 'harmony' to be restored, see above 73. The underlying imaginary is that of a rational legal order beyond the state, in which accidental asperities, gaps or contradictions can be corrected by wielding the appropriate tools.

[208] Perhaps the most famous example (of a thoroughly French contribution to the conflict of laws!) is the Franco-Bavarian *Forgo* (inheritance) saga, that gave rise to the device of renvoi as seen immediately below in the text (see the *Forgo* case: Cass Civ 24 June 1878 et Req 22 February 1882, sous Cass, req, 22 févr 1882, Recueil Sirey 1882 1 393, note Labbé and the report of judge Demangeat; B Ancel and Y Lequette (eds), *Grands arrêts de la jurisprudence de droit international privé* (Paris, Dalloz, n° 8). Innumerable famous cases with methodological implications (for instance as to the validity (or incestuous nature) of a marriage between uncle and niece; or the morality (and legal effect) of going abroad or changing nationality in order to divorce; or disagreement as to the (contractual, non-contractual or personal) nature of pre-nuptial engagement (or *fiançailles*)) all arose in an endo-European context.

[209] On comparative aspects of colonial jurisprudence see below Part II.

[210] See above 73.

that allowed the French state to claim the inheritance of a Bavarian citizen, which was deemed vacant by the grace of a divergence in choice of law rules[211] – became the bread-and-butter of private international legal scholarship. Redubbed 'general theory', a set of remedial contrivances – characterisation, 'renvoi', *Vorfrage* (or incidental questions), adaptation and substitution, *conflits mobiles*, the exception of public policy – occupied several decades of academic controversy and judicial invention.[212] Each one developed its own variants and internal oppositions, appealing in turn to sovereignty or private law concerns, or to international, as opposed to material or substantive, justice. Most strikingly, all these devices represented a

[211] Among the voluminous literature on renvoi, see recently, E Agostini, 'Le mécanisme du renvoi' (2013) *Revue critique de droit international privé* 545, describing the 'revelation' of the problem by the author of the note, Labbé, and the ensuing 'religious war' that took place between the 'zealots' (Gabba, Rundstein, Isaac, Vareilles-Sommières, Polydore …), the 'recent converts' (Westlake, Anzilotti, Niboyet, Lerebours-Pigeonnière, …), and the 'incorrigible pagans' (Kahn, Bartin, Buzzati, Laurent, Ligeoix, Despagnet …).

[212] Renvoi arises out of the divergence between the connecting factor of the law of forum used to designate a foreign law (in cases of personal status, say the law of the foreign domicile of a national of the country of the forum) and the factor retained by that foreign law itself (which might on the contrary consider that the same issue should be governed by that citizen's foreign nationality). The contrasting virtues of nationality and domicile as connecting factors (the first in the context of the rise of the 'principle of nationality' in continental Europe and the end of the nineteenth century; the second 'domicile of origin' subsisting as the core jurisdictional attachment for the officialdom of the British Empire), were at the heart of a battle for the soul of personal status, creating moreover an apparently endless mirror-effect in cases that were split between countries that aligned with one or the other (see *Dame Birchall c Birchall* (1939) 9 *Recueil Gazette du Palais*, 1.962; (1939) 34 *Revue critique de Droit international privé* 472, note JP Niboyet. The following passage of Professor Niboyet's annotation (at p 476) is translated by Martin Domke ((1943) 5 *The University of Toronto Law Journal* 95–112, 100): 'The result of the renvoi theory is finally to admit of subjecting foreigners domiciled in France to our law provided their national law does not link up the status personae with nationality regardless of domicile. The *lex patriae* cannot, of course, be evaded with respect to other foreigners (Germans, Italians, Poles, etc), as their law declares itself competent. That is for us an immense disadvantage … It would be much better to abolish art 3 par 3 of the Civil Code, the enactment of which was an inconceivable mistake, and to return to the traditional *lex domicilii* followed by French law before the Civil Code. In this way, all foreigners, when established in France, will have the opportunity of complying with our law'). Another problem ('characterisation') is that apparently similar legal categories proved to have diverging scopes or purviews (what's in a 'marriage'?) or to signify dissimilar values (does succession law limit the testator's freedom in order to protect the family lineage?), generating considerable losses in translation. One striking example, particularly relevant to the theme of this book, is linked to the inadequation of the civilian categories of property and things to account for indigeneous conceptions of a collective or tribal relationship to sacred objects: see the *Hopi mask* case, below, 279. Moreover, seemingly easy decisions as to the applicable law did not prevent sub-conflicts ('incidental questions', such as determining the law applicable to the issue of who is a 'spouse' or 'son', when this status is required by the foreign law applicable to the succession; choices internal to multi-cultural religious legal systems, such as when 'Lebanese law' or 'law of the United States' is applicable to the personal status of a citizen of these countries). These appeared in unexpected, nested, ways (for a complicated example, see the Australian (tort) case, *Neilson v Overseas Projects Corporation of Victoria Ltd* [2005] HCA 5, on which see A Mills, 'Renvoi and the Proof of Foreign Law in Australia' (2006) 65 *The Cambridge Law Journal* 37–40. Chinese law was applicable to an accident in China, and under Art 146 of the Chinese General Principles, the choice of law rule in tort in China also selects the *lex loci delicti*. However, unlike the Australian rule, Art 146 provides for an exception: 'If both parties are nationals of the same country or domiciled in the same country, the law of their own country or of their place of domicile may also be applied.' There was significant judicial debate here as to what kind of sub-issue (renvoi or 'incidental application') was raised 'within' Chinese law). A figure such as *conflit mobile* (with further reflexive variations as in a hall of mirrors, such as *conflits de systèmes*), is an interesting example of a 'chronotope' (on which, see below 212), a spatial-temporal assemblage in which the applicable law changes when the thing (or right) to which it applies is displaced (is prescriptive acquisition of moveable property established on expiration of the delay required by the country of origin, if the moveable is displaced to a country where such a delay is longer?).

creeping and largely unacknowledged return of statutist forms of legal reasoning, initially repressed or banished from the multilateralist model.[213]

Indeed, a third problem with the conventional account lies in the very hybridity of each tradition. As we have just seen, despite quite virulent methodological debates over issues such as characterisation (*lege fori* or *lege causae*?) 'renvoi' (single, double, 'foreign court theory', or not at all?), or preliminary questions (recourse to the conflict rules of the forum, or those of the law applicable to the main question?), concessions to the alternative, competing visions were made regularly, nevertheless, in either camp. Such *métissage* is generally denied,[214] yet on each side there is a further shared story of ceaseless confrontational exchange between the two traditions. At an undetermined point in the narrative, the common moment of past enlightenment fades away in favour of a dialectical progression, through movement and countermovement towards an indeterminate, future synthesis. The history of the discipline, it is (re)told, is one of perpetual oscillation or exchange between two methodologies, each moreover standing in for a particular vision of the world, or indeed governance project. Today, they are seen to be merging or converging, to an as yet unspecified extent.[215]

Certainly, since the end of the nineteenth century, there have been at least three major occurrences of a reciprocal shift, as if the earlier vicissitudes and oscillations in the career of the venerable *ius commune* were prolonged on the international scene under a new shape. Firstly, as seen above, Protestant Dutch statutist theories of vested rights crossed the Atlantic in the nineteenth century to infuse early accounts of the conflict of laws in the common law tradition, before crystallising there into a set of universalist rules based on territory. Thereafter, they gave rise to a neo-statutist, policy-driven backlash, propelled by the 'revolutionary' discovery of the virtues of 'interest analysis'.[216] Paradoxically, as already observed, this shift served only to

[213] Nowhere was this more clear than on the francophone scene, very prominent in the early part of the twentieth century in the areas of both comparative law (recall the Paris Congress of 1900, evoked above) and private international law, no doubt because of the strongly civil law flavour of the conflict of laws in continental Europe, where the Napoleonic code still retained its prestige. (On the significant Belgian tradition, see D Foussard, 'Le droit international privé de Foelix ou l'art périlleux de la transition (1840–1847)' (2020) *Rev crit droit international privé* 449). Antoine Pillet had advocated (post-Savigny) the return to a principled form of statutism (*Principes de droit international privé* (Paris, Pédone, 1903). Some decades later, Jean-Paulin Niboyet staged a spectacular 'conversion' to 'unilateralism' (statutism), based on his reflection on renvoi (which he believed to be mandated by deference to the foreign sovereign's own definition of the scope of its laws: see his note under the *Birchall* case: Req, 10 mai 1939 *(Birchall*), S.42.1.73). He was seen at that point as a traitor within his own camp. On the resurgence of statutism within the various devices comprised within the 'general theory' of the conflict of laws, see D Boden, 'L'ordre public: limite et condition de la tolérance: recherches sur le pluralisme juridique', PhD dissertation, Paris I, 2002.

[214] See for instance the indignant defence of the Savignian tradition against American influence by G Kegel, 'The Crisis of Conflict of Laws', *Collected Courses of the Hague Academy of International Law*, vol 112 (1964). For a provocative analogy between the desire for the purity of law and legal origin and the belief in the purity of language, with arrestingly sinister overtones, Monateri, 'Black Gaius'.

[215] Evidence of this lies in the remarkable spread of (similar) codes: see Symeon Symeonides, *Codifying Choice of Law Around the World: An International Comparative Analysis* (Oxford, Oxford University Press, 2014).

[216] On 'interests analysis' (a form of functionalism or policy analysis), see above 67, 78. This purportedly revolutionary discovery was a rediscovery of a statutist form of reasoning. See A Bucher, *L'ordre public et le but social des lois en droit international privé* (1993) II *RCADI* 9, and 'Vers l'adoption de la méthode des intérêts ? Réflexions à la lumière des codifications récentes' (1996) 12 *Trav Comité fr dr inte privé, Année* 209–37.

separate the American tradition from its territorialist beginnings and bring it closer in substance to the previously disqualified Roman-continental model. The concept of 'policy' analysis was undoubtedly repugnant to a European consciousness steeped in (Roman) private law. Nevertheless, in no time, as global legal consciousness entered the 'era of the social',[217] the multilateralist model sought, conversely, to accommodate a greater spectrum of collective and category-specific interests, with the beginnings of a labour-protective, consumer-focused and child-prioritised orientation in private international law.

Today the picture is blurred. The methodological models have lost their previous distinctive outlines; indeed the very idea of 'conflict' in the encounter of different legal institutions is controversial.[218] Such encounters are notoriously more complex than they might seem at first sight. Even under (still frequent) dogmatic or highly technical visions of legal order that leave out the possible divergence of underlying world views or cosmologies (to which we shall return below[219]), they are not necessarily understood as confrontational. Sometimes indeed, they are 'false'.[220] In other instances, they imply that a law deliberately 'offers' its competence but will defer to a refusal.[221] More frequently, they signify that several laws are concurrently available for possible use, on any issue of private law: in a world of potentially equivalent or universalisable (Roman law-based) reason, what counts is the *ratio legis* (as distinct from the scope of substantive rules claimed through possibly divergent choice of law rules).[222] Occasionally is there a concession to the more violent reality of interjurisdictional competition and economic lawfare, involving exclusive and incompatible claims of multiple regulatory states.[223] Nevertheless, while the focus is on the encounter of

[217] Kennedy, 'Three Globalizations'.

[218] Broadly put, private international law understands 'conflict' in terms of three ideal types: thus, simultaneous assertions of jurisdiction in respect of a single situation or the issues to which it gives rise are theorised as giving rise to either confrontation, cooperation or competition between the contending laws or legal systems.

[219] See Part II below.

[220] As in Currie's 'governmental interest analysis', in which a key concept is that of true/false conflicts. The latter involves an attack on traditional methods that create conflicts through an excess of abstraction or dogmatism (this was the case of the *lex loci delicti* in the leading legal-realist case *Babcock v Jackson* 191 NE 2d 279, NY 1963) and a correlative lack of focus on the unexpected policy conflicts that may lie under the surface (see D Cavers et al., 'Comments On Babcock v Jackson, A Recent Development In Conflict Of Laws' (1963) 63 *Columbia L Rev* 1212.

[221] As in renvoi.

[222] For instance, in the area of international contracts, the assumption is that national legal systems are composed of default rules (except when they contain derogatory, internationally mandatory rules or *lois de police*). This is a way of saying that their content is in principle equivalent or that differences are immaterial in the absence of issues of public policy. Contract law is thus a 'homogenous legal product' (see A Ogus, 'Competition Between National Legal Systems: A Contribution of Economic Analysis To Comparative Law' (2008) 48 *International and Comparative Law Quarterly* 409). Such a view of a shared legal rationality, dominant in civilian private law traditions, is strongly opposed by policy-based analysis.

[223] As in 'lois de police' or 'overriding mandatory norms' (for foreign mandatory rules, see for instance Art 9 EU n° 593/2008 of the European Parliament and of the Council of 17 June 2008 on the law applicable to contractual obligations ('Rome I Regulation'). And yet again, some such claims may merely be 'given effect' incidentally as bare data (see for example, Art 17 of Regulation (EC) No 864/2007 of the European Parliament and of the Council of 11 July 2007 on the law applicable to non-contractual obligations ('Rome II Regulation').

norms that self-define, meet, clash or combine, usually only marginal attention is given to phenomena that emerge independently of state borders, in further reflexive patterns of unstable and recursive interaction. In other words, the dominant understanding of conflict leaves in the shadow an alternative reality, which has had to struggle to maintain its own relevance in the face of more potent narratives.

II. MYTH AND LEGACY

Whatever its historical accuracy, the story of the origin of modern private international law served to consolidate a double legacy.[224] Indeed, the analysis proposed above suggests that what is important for understanding the way in which the field has evolved is neither to identify some inherent dynamic of legal change, nor indeed to subscribe to any specific chronological account, but rather to reflect upon the ideological function of the underlying myth in this particular context. On the domestic front, the conventional account provided the foundations for a mantra of neutrality.[225] This mantra reflected the spirit of classical private law that prevailed in the formative moments of the modern discipline, justifying the Archimedean standpoint from which it proceeded to allocate legal relationships (civil law) or cross-border legal disputes (common law).[226] It outlived its substantive law counterpart (the classical legal dogma of neutrality of private law), however, becoming increasingly irrelevant as a mode of dealing with new cultural forms of alterity as expressed in legal terms (section II.A). On the international plane, the same account accompanied a deliberate strategy of self-insulation from the inroads of geopolitics, international relations or indeed the potentially disruptive claims of foreign states or associated public entities. It came thereby to apportion and distribute jurisdiction in ways that proved equally and increasingly inconsequential within the wider discursive world of (public) legal governance, even as they served the interests of a seamless imaginary of private global ordering (sction II.B).

[224] As D Danowski and E Viveiros de Castro observe, the semiotic regime of myth implies perfect indifference to the empirical truth or falsity of its contents (*The Ends of the World*, 12). *Cf* A Appadurai, 'The Past as a Scarce Resource' (1981) 16 *Man* 201–19 arguing (as against the more conventional anthropological claim that all human societies have two modes of cognition: one universal and the other, pragmatic) that 'there is a third aspect of the past, which is culture-specific, and which consists of a set of norms whose sole purpose is to regulate the inherent debatability of the past in the present. Such a normative organisation of discourse concerning the past, I propose, is the ghost in Bloch's otherwise elegant machine. This normative framework permits an orderly symbolic negotiation between 'ritual pasts and the contingencies of the present' (ibid, 219). Among these control devices are myths and other stories we tell about ourselves.

[225] Law's neutrality has a venerable pedigree. Schiavone, *Ius* 399 traces the genealogy of (private) law's neutrality in the Western tradition to Cicero's discourse on imperial legitimation (*Pro Caecina*). From this point, writes Schiavone, law was suspended between myth and reality, science and ideology, dissociated from both fact and power (whether social, economic etc).

[226] The civilian tradition tends to focus on abstractions (legal relationships) while common lawyers usually talk about disputes or issues. The first tends to adopt a deliberately universalist meta-vision while the style of the latter is more grounded in understanding national particularisms, while attempting to cope with the more down-to-earth cross-border dimension of legality. These cultural differences may explain why the mantra of neutrality described in the text above made the classical law on the conflict of laws vulnerable to the onslaughts of legal realism in the United States, even while in continental Europe it prepared the terrain, rather, for its reinforced coordinatory function (at least within the European Union).

A. The Domestic Front: Irrelevance

Whatever (once again) its historical accuracy, the retrospective narrative of a triumphant birth or revival of a new scientific, apolitical learning, served to accomplish a shift in the prevailing vision of the international legal order. Crafted (somewhat paradoxically) in the light of the universalist aspirations of the turn of the nineteenth century, and consolidated during times of later chaos by a resolute quest for harmony through law, the new world vision was that of a private ordering beyond the reach of state politics. From this point, despite the (again somewhat paradoxical) survival of sovereignty concerns in the (remarkably intense) doctrinal production of 'general theories' of the conflict of laws in the early decades of the twentieth century,[227] the private international legal order was seen both as transcending local struggles and disconnected from the geopolitical sphere, thereby becoming subject to a distinct, and – most importantly – depoliticised legal regime.[228] The radical inaccuracy of this representation of the public/private legal divide, along with its political economy, is not the question here.[229] Certainly, what we think of as the international legal order split (in a nebulous golden age) between bodies politic and private persons, has always been a very mixed assemblage of both.[230] The point at this stage is the myth that served (and continues resolutely) to support a representation of the private international sphere as neutral, non-instrumental or apolitical.[231]

Perceived as a central element of the turn to Enlightenment in the nineteenth century, after the purportedly dark ages of sovereign struggle for power, the idea of the neutrality of a meta-method had in fact surfaced continuously, from medieval times, when it was linked to the transcendent rationality of Roman law. In its pre-classical form, Roman law provided the over-arching principles that allowed for

[227] Under this appellation or otherwise. 'General theories' of the conflict of laws, as seen above, cover the series of corrective contrivances devised by courts or doctrinal scholarship to redirect the operation of 'Savignian' conflict of laws rules that no longer 'work' outside their initial context. Sometimes, the question of 'methods' (multilateralism versus statutism) is also part of these presentations.

[228] As one example among many, in 1929, Max Gutzwiller wrote in substance in his general Course at the Hague Academy that whereas the great civil codes are deeply impregnated with the social and economic conditions of their time … private international law is absolutely foreign to such material conditions. Issues of conflict of civil laws are of a purely legal, indeed technical, nature (see 'Le développement historique du droit international privé' 29 *RCADI* 222 et seq: 'N'oublions pas toutefois une particularité du Droit international privé qui n'est pas sans importance. Alors que les grands codes civils sont fortement empreints des conditions sociales et économiques de leur époque … le Droit international privé est absolument étranger à ces considérations matérielles. Abstraction faite de ses fondements, qui le rattachent au Droit international public et à la souveraineté personnelle et territoriale de l'État (notions, elles aussi, essentiellement abstraites), les questions des conflits des lois civiles renferment un problème purement juridique, voire technique, abandonné dans une mesure bien large aux décisions d'un petit comité d'experts').

[229] On the political economy dimension of this development, see below Part III.

[230] Kjaer, *The Law of Political Economy;* Brunkhorst, *Critical Theory of Legal Revolutions.* These mixed assemblages are also the starting point of various theories in the 'transnational' field (an alternative appellation that suggests not conflicting national laws but rather forms of substantive legality that extend beyond state borders): for example, see GP Callies, P Zumbansen, *Rough Consensus and Running Code: A Theory of Transnational Private Law* (Oxford, Hart, 2010).

[231] As observed by Roland Barthes, ideology parades as *doxa.* R Barthes, *Mythologies* (Paris, Seuil, 1957).

what would be described today as the 'glocalisation'[232] of a set of tools sufficiently abstracted from substantive content as to be able to be shared across legal cultures, while leaving ample room for their local appropriation and adjustment to specific or particularistic content of various national domestic legal orders. Remarkably, as will be seen below, similar features of neutrality and apoliticity were attributed to the market itself in eighteenth-century liberal democracies, before coming to qualify the whole area of domestic private law that governed it, notably through property rights, party freedom and individual liability. These features are replicated in the underlying, liberal vision of international society as a cosmopolitan community of private individuals from which states were largely absent.

In the particular case of contemporary private international law, two specific factors have combined to renew, reinforce and sustain such an ideal. On the one hand, on the public international scene, the law of supposedly united nations has been at least partially discredited and the object of both third-world critique and first-world scepticism: intimately embroiled in the colonial land grab by Western European states, on the one hand, it had failed equally dismally thereafter to prevent the ensuing endogamic conflicts that were the two world wars. Private law's specific rationality appeared as a way to sidestep these political 'appetites' and imbroglios.[233] On the other hand, on the municipal plane, the story of origin of the conflict of laws was constructed in the context of the (first and potent) globalisation of classical legal thought.[234] At its core were private law and legal positivism. Deductive forms of legal reasoning prevailed, deployed within a supposedly coherent and autonomous legal order and expressing an ideal of legal science. Civil codes flourished (first the French, then, *contra* Savigny, the German[235]) as constitutional orders of private law,

[232] 'Glocalisation', a term that became popular in a legal-sociological resistance to the idea of globalisation (see P Legrand, 'On the Singularity of Law' (2006) 47 *Harvard International Law Journal* 517–30) can be understood as the local cultural reappropriation of purportedly uniform or universal legal rules and institutions.

[233] As a contemporary legal historian puts it : 'Même s'il prend en charge l'intérêt général, il évite de se mêler par trop aux agitations de la cité, et il reste à l'écart des ruptures liées aux codifications ou aux révolutions, qu'elles soient d'ordre politique ou intellectuel' (Foussard, 'Le droit international privé de Foelix'); *cf* B Ancel and Y Lequette, *Grand arrêts*, n° 1, justifying the superiority of the emerging 'multilateralist' methodology by its particular fit with apolitical, private law (under a venerable case, *Busqueta*, before the Royal Court of Paris 13 June 1814, the first in the conflict of laws to be decided under the Civil Code: see B Ancel and Y Lequette, *Grands arrêts de la jurisprudence de droit international privé* (Paris, Dalloz, 2005). Paradoxically, the new faith in private law led to a renewed if not unprecedented surge of private corporate power (as we shall see below, Part III).

[234] Duncan Kennedy's influential analysis of the different ages of globalisation ('Three Globalizations') sees the mid-nineteenth century as the opening of such an era within Western legal consciousness. He notes that economic life had been commodified (land, labour and capital) while the ensuing market economy was fully juridified in the sense that it was governed by a judicially enforced regime of private law based upon autonomy of the will. On the existence of a critical strand at the time, see MC Belleau, 'Les juristes inquiets: classicisme juridique et critique du droit au début du XXème en France' (1999) 40 *Les Cahiers du droit* 507–44. Flourishing before the First World War, this anxiety about the social consequences of individualism largely bypassed the field of the conflict of laws.

[235] The heated Savigny-Thibault debate over the virtues of codification (in mid-nineteenth-century Germany), a canon of comparative legal studies, resurfaced in Europe in the equally violent controversies over a possible uniform substantive European civil code: see P Legrand, 'antivonbar' 1 *Journal of Comparative Law* 1, 13; R Zimmermann, 'L'héritage de Savigny. Histoire du droit, droit comparé, et émergence d'une science juridique européenne' (2013) XXVII *Revue internationale de droit économique* 95–127; M Bussani, 'Current Trends in European Comparative Law: The Common Core Approach' (1998) 21 *Hastings Int'l & Comp L Rev* 785.

with private property and contract at their core. Formal equality and individual freedom constituted the political ideal.[236]

Thereafter, perhaps largely due to its distance – its meta-position[237] – in respect of substantive concerns (or also perhaps because a certain political economy bled into the discipline as a whole – a consideration to which we shall return in Part III below), the conflict of laws remained by and large the same, through the age of the social and beyond, unscathed by post-colonial, feminist and racial critique, or more recently, decoloniality and alternative ecological epistemologies. Whatever the reasons for such a contrast with the breadth and depth of political contestation in its public international counterpart (as we shall see), the perceived need to protect a purportedly non-parochial, non-political legal rationality from geopolitical turmoil secreted an enduring ideal of legal neutrality that indubitably acquired dogmatic status. In other words, the discipline managed, by and large, to sustain a foundational myth.

In order to fulfil its powerful ideological function the myth requires the making of an idol: an illusion or simulacrum that emphasises the authority of tradition at the expense of new idea.[238] Like all idols, as a French author has recently noted in respect of property law, it has magical powers in the perception of believers, a performative effect both on the symbolic structure of society and, by way of consequence, upon legal substance. Thus the social imaginary takes over and becomes constitutive of

[236] Kennedy, 'Three Globalizations'.

[237] As noted at several points already, it is conventionally taught that private international law's rules operate at one remove from the substantive content, or domestic policy considerations, of the national laws that it allocates, including those of the forum state. This is appropriate (as the account goes) because it is concerned only with legal relationships between non-state actors; indeed, since its methods are allocatory and not substantive, it is 'blindfolded' or impartial in respect of the distinction between the foreign and the domestic and equally innocent from geopolitics. This purported non-instrumentality of the discipline as largely methodological was inseparable from ideas of 'private' law as apolitical, either because it is deliberately sheltered by the liberal state from the policy arena, or by virtue of its spontaneous generation from markets, custom or reason. Indeed, while 'private law' has many potential meanings (according to whether it refers to a particular sphere of the law of social relations, or to the origin, or creator, of the norm), both continental and common law traditions have seen a form of apoliticity as the hallmark of the private, as opposed to its public counterpart – albeit perhaps in different degrees (civil law taking formal rationality to a higher degree due to the centrality of doctrinal scholarship).

[238] See for the following account, JP Chazal, 'Le propriétaire souverain: archéologie d'une idole doctrinale' (2020) 1 *Revue trimestrielle de droit civil* on the mythical dimension of French property law: 'a hagiographic portrait was drawn of the sovereign-property-owner, bestowing upon him the legitimacy of tradition, and the appearance of scientificity'. In this context, February 1848 marked a revolutionary moment ; jurists rallied at that point in defence of the existing social order and theorised absolute property rights as (natural) unlimited prerogatives. Borrowed for the purpose from eighteenth-century economic doctrine, the concept of the sovereign property owner was attributed retrospectively to the Civil Code. The point made by Chazal's study is that the conditions of possibility for the emergence of a legal discourse of this kind were not fulfilled in France before the mid-nineteenth century; the terrain was prepared at that point by economic doctrines of free trade and production that reduced the role of the state in the direction of the economy. Thereafter the function of law was to guarantee individual freedom through the protection of private property. This (late) conversion of legal scholarship into a natural law doctrine marks the appearance of property as unfettered individual freedom at the heart of the political economy. From that point, man-made restrictions were perceived as hindrances to the natural law of the economy (see below, Part III). The (more or less) contemporaneous construction, within the domestic laws of emerging liberal democracies, of the doctrine of property along with its mythical dimension is striking: see the seductive power of the 'false tree of liberty' at the time of the enclosures in England (S Marks, *A False Tree of Liberty. Human Rights in Radical Thought* (Oxford, Oxford University Press, 2019).

reality: the world we see is one of common sense, free of contradiction.[239] Reality is 'hidden in plain sight' and a new type of discourse becomes possible. At that point, the myth becomes hegemonic, chasing out alternative or competing visions. The social or legal repertoire is limited to those that are cognitively conceivable, normatively legitimate, instrumentally feasible within dominant discourse. It narrows the field of the legally sayable.[240] Moreover, inaccuracies or incoherence are of no import: they are topically part of the very process of mythification.[241]

In the making of modern private international law, all these ingredients are present. As seen above, savignism was the process of transformation of a set of ideas historically formulated by Carl von Savigny in a highly specific context, into a dominant doctrine that had little to do with its initial meaning or ambition. Such doctrine became hegemonic – meaning that once it emerged and prevailed among competing discourses, it became self-perpetuating, limiting the alternatives that did not fit its logic. The legal repertoire is limited to arguments that are cognitively conceivable, normatively legitimate and instrumentally feasible within the primary discourse. The 'idol' then that came to be endowed with magical properties was the personified ('Savignian') methodology that happened to carry the liberal ideal. The prevailing common sense became such, moreover, that it was (and still to some extent is) difficult to voice either an alternative methodology, or even a revised historiography. This does much to explain why the mid-twentieth-century transatlantic methodological controversy over the place of policy analysis in the conflict of laws[242] was placed on such high moral ground. Observing from across the Atlantic the turbulence of the social 1960s that swept through American legal thought in this field, in the aftermath of legal realism, Gerhard Kegel famously identified a 'crisis of the conflict of laws' in the battle for the neutrality of method.[243]

[239] In Paul Ricoeur's words, 'l'imagination sociale est constitutive de la réalité sociale', in *L'idéologie et l'utopie* (Paris, Seuil, 2005) 19.

[240] On a legal-sociological variation, borrowing from structuralist linguistics, see D Kennedy, 'A Semiotics of Critique' 22 *Cardozo Law Review* 1147.

[241] On this process, see P Veyne. *Les Grecs ont-ils cru à leurs mythes ? Essai sur l'imagination constituante* (Paris, Christian Jacob, 1985).

[242] Already alluded to above, see below 98.

[243] Kegel, 'The Crisis of Conflict of Laws'. In this context, the prized non-instrumentality of European-style choice of law rules covers a series of quite different ideas, including resistance to political influence in the form of state policies, or the condemnation of the preferential treatment of nationals. Of course, the categories used in the text above (civil vs common law; United States vs Europe, etc) are in themselves excessively broad and would require to be nuanced in a deeper historical study. In each tradition there have always been 'hold-outs' that have attracted contemporary dismissive attention in the mainstream: see for instance, in Max Gutzwiller's General Course cited above, the reference to the 'unfortunate' minoritarian alternative accounts to that of Savigny, notably that of Pillet. However, the study of the latter is designed to show up some of the strengths of the former (p 359: 'On a beaucoup critiqué cette doctrine savignienne. Ces critiques se résument toutes en des considérations que M. Pillet a formulées en ces termes: Vouloir rechercher dans la nature des choses la solution des conflits de lois, est une idée juste, mais point assez précise pour servir de principe à une doctrine. Et en effet, dans l'enquête qu'il poursuit en vue de déterminer le siège de divers rapports de droit, Savigny lui-même emprunte aux domaines les plus divers ses motifs de décision, argumentant tantôt de l'intention des parties, tantôt de la situation de l'objet, tantôt de telle ou telle autre circonstance à laquelle il attache arbitrairement une influence prépondérante'). For an interesting attempt to revisit the doctrines of the (European) nineteenth century and rehabilitate a minoritarian voice, that of Jitta, see R Banu, *Nineteenth Century Perspectives on Private International Law* (Oxford, Oxford University Press, 2018).

What is more surprising is that the myth has endured far beyond later shifts both in modes of legal thought (successive turns to the social or to the neoliberal), and in geopolitical configurations of the world (through decolonisation, the Washington consensus, the emergence of the European Union, or indeed the 'awakening' of China[244]). In defining its relationship to its own outside, private international law in the continental tradition still purports to draw a natural[245] line that largely excludes the public, political sphere.[246] In the United States, the principles that define the international reach of federal rules are deemed to present analogous virtues of technicity, in contrast to the policy-infused content of interstate conflict rules.[247] Yet, the location of the discipline at law's symbolic (domestic-political and international-geopolitical) frontier might have made it particularly receptive to contemporary changes in legal thought and practice wrought by globalisation (at least to the extent that the latter means accelerated and amplified encounters with cultural difference). Paradoxically, it is the reverse that seems to have occurred: it has become self-insulated from the transformative trends in legal thought that occurred elsewhere during the twentieth century.[248]

In this respect Martti Koskenniemi makes a striking observation about the received narratives of the history of international law, drawing attention to this self-effacement of the private side:

> [W]hile international legal histories have meticulously traced the legal trajectories of the foreign policy of states, they have paid much less attention – virtually no attention – to the private law relations that undergird and support state action that become visible only once analysis penetrates beyond the official statements or formal acts of governments and diplomatic chancelleries.[249]

In other words, the peculiar legacy of the mantra of neutrality is the riddle of the contemporary lack of relevance of private international law both for understanding modernity's own past and for the future structuring of law's relationship to the surrounding world.

[244] On the geopolitics of private international law in the context of the mega global value chains of the new Chinese silk routes (One Belt One Road initiative) see H Muir Watt,'Le droit international privé au service de la géopolitique : Les enjeux de la nouvelle Convention de la Haye du 2 juillet 2019 sur la reconnaissance et l'exécution des jugements étrangers en matière civile ou commerciale' (2020) *Rev crit droit international privé* 427. This book was written many months before the momentous geopolitical events linked to the Russian invasion of Ukraine in 2023.

[245] Meaning that, it naturalises (makes natural-seeming and invisible) the dividing line between public/private, and internal/external. And as it does so, it de-politicises, meaning that (as a highly political move) it keeps the domesticated private sphere pure, free from the claims of 'political appetites' (as seen above).

[246] Today, references to the neutrality of conflict of law rules can still be found in contemporary judicial decisions· (as seen above). European doctrine has remained at least formally hermetic to the attraction of American-style policy analysis and still excludes claims by states or public entities grounded in their public law (as evidenced in all the European Union private international law instruments) with constant attendant frontier skirmishes (and a large volume of case law on the part of the European Court of Justice).

[247] On territoriality as the parameter of the international scope of federal law (including jurisdiction), see below 145 et seq.

[248] With calamitous consequences in terms of law's political economy and its effects on the planetary ecology, as will be seen below (Part III).

[249] 'Expanding Histories of International Law' (2016) 56 *American Journal of Legal History* 108. This author's heroic account of this 'expanded' and integrated history of the public and the private dimensions of international law and power is to be found in M Koskenniemi, *To the Uttermost Parts of the Earth: Legal Imagination and International Power 1300–1870* (Cambridge, Cambridge University Press, 2021).

B. The International Front: Self-Isolation

According to most historical accounts, the new duality of the public and private legal order that displaced the previous *ius naturae et gentium*[250] during the long nineteenth century is due to the emergence, from the earlier, archaic, strains of humanism and cosmopolitanism, of a modern international law, formally devoted to the mutual relationships between (European) nation states (and the division among them of the 'great (colonial) pie' of purportedly unpopulated and unappropriated lands and resources available for the taking by the outside world).[251] Thereafter, there was (supposedly) a clear delineation between public and private spheres, divided by their subjects, their rationalities, their 'sources' and indeed their values and objectives. In this era of classical legal thought, public international law dealt in the business of statehood and geopolitics, while the focus of its private counterpart was on the facilitation of markets and transnational commerce between subjects, natural or corporate, of domestic law. A key point, as Martti Koskenniemi shows, is that this commitment to the disciplinary separation within the international is as strong on the public side as it is on the private – with analogous blind spots as to the ways in which power was deployed within the political economy.[252]

Certainly, the imaginary of the private side of international law became sidetracked from the second half of the nineteenth century, into an epistemological closet from which it has had great difficulty emerging. On the receiving end of legal transplants from its powerful public counterpart, it rested on the assumption of the alignment of legal authority and territorial sovereignty, the separation of law and politics, and the ontological difference between states and private (corporate) persons.[253] Meanwhile, occupied with 'reason of state'[254] and the colonial project,

[250] The (Western) natural law tradition goes back to the Spanish scholastics (sixteenth century), reappearing later in the Protestant works of Northern Europe (in the Dutch school of Hugo Grotius in the seventeenth century: see P Haggenmacher, *Grotius et la doctrine de la guerre juste* (Paris, Presses Universitaires de France, 1983)). The role of founding father of international law is often ascribed to Samuel Pufendorf's *De jure naturae et gentium* (1688 ed Frank Böhling) (English trans. CH Oldfather and WA Oldfather, in *De jure naturae et gentium libri octo*, vol 2 (Oxford, Clarendon Press, 1934). As M Koskenniemi notes ('Expanding histories of international law'), these voices of rationalist universalism were treated retrospectively with great respect, if not reverence, as a voice of justice and reason in a violent world, as opposed to Machiavellian statecraft and the egoism of sovereign statehood, and carried into the account of the birth of contemporary international law. However, as he further shows, this genealogical connection is far more troubled than it is usually represented to be.

[251] On the contemporaneity (and causal entanglement) of the emergence of modern public international law and the colonial project, A Anghie, *Sovereignty, Imperialism and International Law* (Cambridge, Cambridge University Press, 2003).

[252] M Koskenniemi, 'Expanding Histories of International law' (2016) 56 *American Journal of Legal History* 107 et seq. This is a point to which we shall return below.

[253] As the argument went (and often still goes, as seen above) in the European tradition, the conflict of laws' pre-modern Roman legal roots set it apart from (and above) the geopolitical disruptions that accompanied the rise of the Leviathan (or the birth of modern sovereignty) and a later (public) order of sovereign territorial states. The Anglo-American tradition told a similar story of separation, for exactly the reverse reason: the conflict of laws was derived directly from the principle of territorial sovereignty. There was no perceived need for a further specific body of law for the relationships between emerging sovereign states, whose commerce was not perceived as distinct from that of all the roaming maritime traders, ambassadors, pirates or slaves engaged (willingly or not, officially or not) in the business of crossing local frontiers or sailing on the high seas. The few principles that composed the law of nations were dedicated to securing the status of these mobile constituencies and were indeed deemed to be part of the common law.

[254] On the relationship of 'reason of state' and public international law, see Poole, *Reason of State*.

public international law readily left its lesser side to deal with the more trivial, and supposedly timeless, needs of transnational trade and commerce between private actors. The latter embodied, as we have seen, a romantic revival of Roman law as applicable to a wider (Germanic) community, prolonging the thrall of imaginaries of natural reason and substantive private law beyond or across the newly congealing formal frontiers of states. Therefore, reciprocally, the political appetites and strategies of national public policy-makers were seen as incompatible with the ontology of private law. The business of sovereignty was beyond the pale or essence of private legal principle or reason.[255]

However, beyond this story of separation, a closer look shows that for some time, the two faces of international law were not necessarily perceived as disjoined.[256] Beyond the disciplinary divide, the public side drew heavily on principles of private law, while, conversely, in allocating the private laws governing relationships between citizens of various states, private international law (at least in the civilian tradition, with its legacy of pan-political Roman imperial imaginary) described itself as a supranational legislator by default. Moreover, the genealogical links between the old (presumptively universal) law of nature governing both individuals and bodies politic and the new public international order is doubtful. If, as Martti Koskenniemi surmises, the avatar of the law of nations was more accurately economics (alongside the science of the reason of state projected onto external relations), this signals, rather, its proximity to the private side of the new ordering.[257]

Moreover, whatever its genealogy, this binary division of international law was neither watertight nor stable. As the colonial project advanced, along with industrial capitalism on the home front, immunities, privileges, taboos[258] and non-justiciability or act of state doctrines applicable to public entities crossed the divide into municipal courts in the course of private international adjudication; attempts to cordon off the public from the private, or political from the legal, did not prevent the evident osmosis or travelling of legal concepts between the two. On either side of the divide, law became 'politics by other means'.[259] In this respect, one of the most powerful critiques of the disciplinary divide focuses on the structure of argument deployed on one side and the other. As Joel Paul shows, the structural similarities are striking.[260] Each pursues or moderates common sets of values: principles of contract (or expectations of individuals); public policy (or state interests) and comity (or interests of

[255] Seen from the private side, the implication of the account of separation is the moral superiority of private law, resistant to the politics and appetites unleashed in the public sphere.

[256] On which the canon is Hersch Lauterpacht's doctoral dissertation, *Private Law Sources and Analogies of International Law With Special Reference To International Arbitration* (1927), see M Koskenniemi, 'Lauterpacht: the Victorian Tradition in International Law' (1997) 8 *Eur J Int'l L* 215.

[257] Despite the apparent structural analogy between the old and the new. See M Koskenniemi, 'International Law and raison d'état: Rethinking the Prehistory of International Law', in B Kingsbury and B Straumann (eds), *The Roman Foundations of the Law of Nations* (Oxford, Oxford University Press, 2010).

[258] Famously, the 'public law taboo': see for example, WS Dodge, 'Breaking the Public Law Taboo' (2002) 43 *Harv Int'l LJ* 161.

[259] According to Carl von Clausewitz's famous aphorism about war (*Vom Kriege* (Berlin, 1832)), law impermissibly becomes 'politics by other means' ('der Politik mit anderen Mitteln'). It is important to be aware again at this point of the risk of 'category errors'. As will be seen further below, 'Law I' has an evident political dimension, but 'Law II' has its own, specific 'mode of existence'.

[260] J Paul, 'Comity in international law', 32 *Harv Int'l LJ* 1.

the wider community of states). None of these mandates any particular substantive outcome. The difference is that public international law works 'downwards' from comity to contract,[261] while its private counterpart works 'upwards' from individual expectations to broader concerns of the international community. The structure depends directly on a choice as to how the problem is framed, as it were from the top or the bottom.[262] In the process, there emerges a thoroughly ordo-liberal idealisation in terms of where the public/private (policy/law) divide should be drawn.[263]

Despite this evident imbrication, private international law retreated massively into technique. The relationship between the two bodies of specialists and areas of knowledge developed into one of autonomy or mutual indifference so that the private side missed out on the rise of critical third-world thought in public international law. Only recently has the latter begun to surface through the critique of law's political economy, in studies of the imbrication of the production and trade of commodities in the global South (sugar, coffee, rubber) and the expansion of colonial capitalism.[264] At the same time, however, given the affiliation of the conflict of laws to the *ius gentium*, it was also self-insulated from wider trends in legal consciousness in domestic law. In view of this double discontinuity, it is easier to understand why private international law still represents, within the law, an historical anomaly[265] and how it also largely escaped from wider trends in legal consciousness linked to the 'rise of the social' in the early part of the twentieth century. Only decades later did policy analysis sweep into the conflict of laws[266] (later still crossing the Atlantic) before a powerful

[261] It might be important to point out that, as this analysis shows, the 'private' in private international law is often largely considered to be coextensive with contract, accentuating the market orientation of the discipline; the latter is indeed often associated with a new off-shoot in the form of commercial arbitration. Tort law is somewhere on the brink: traditionally 'private law' in the civilian tradition, it tends nevertheless to be more openly affected by (non-neutral) policy considerations (protective of third parties).

[262] Paul compares two issues, one supposedly public (legality of a foreign expropriation) and another purportedly private (enforcement of an arbitration clause), to show that in the end, comity defines the limits of contract, contract defines the limits of public policy, and public policy defines the limits of comity.

[263] For instance, commercial relations anywhere in the world come to be exempted from national statutes on state (public) immunity, whereas (private) torts are exempted only if they occur on a state's territory (see C Scott, R Wai, 'Transnational Governance of Corporate Conduct Through the Migration of Human Rights Norms: The Potential Contribution of Transnational 'Private Litigation' in C Joerges, I-J Sand & G Teubner (eds), *Transnational Governance and Constitutionalism* (Oxford, Hart, 2004) 287.

[264] See, representing the 'twail moment' (third world approaches to international law, under the intellectual aegis of David Kennedy) in public international law, Anghie, *Imperialism, Sovereignty, and the Making of International Law*. The blindspot in private international law extends to subaltern, critical race, gender and more broadly critical studies in the political economy (on which see below).

[265] On this exceptionalism, see Neidhardt, *The Transformation of European Private International Law*.

[266] In the domestic sphere in the United States, legal realism displaced or destabilised many of the classical ideals and schemes, followed between the post-war period and the millennium by the arrival of policy analysis, neo-formalism, adjudication and human rights. In the domestic setting, the public/private divide came under fire from the legal realists in the early twentieth century and thereafter entered, mainly in the United States, into various stages of decline. However, their critique was slow to reach the international sphere – no doubt because critical energies were devoted essentially to the strengthening of social state intervention in the domestic market. The realist contribution is visible in the conflict of laws in the works of David Cavers ('A Critique of the Choice of Law Problem' (1933) 47 *Harvard Law Review* 173) or Brainerd Currie (*Selected Essays on the Conflict of Laws*, Duke University Press, 1963) and in judicial reasoning from the famous *Babcock v Jackson* decision in 1963 (12 NY 2d 473). Today, as seen above, the methodology on the intrastate or federal front is mixed, while formalism has returned to the international arena (see below 93).

countermove pushed legal formalism back to the front of the scene, through the channel of 'external relations'.[267]

In Europe, the increasingly 'engaged' or instrumental character of contemporary private international law within the internal market has seeded doubts as to the accuracy of the foundational myth of political innocence.[268] Nevertheless, the field has remained (largely) impervious to the subsequent critical strands (of various post-colonial, feminist or critical race theories) that surfaced in the public sphere. In its conventional form, it has retreated too far into a closed, inward-looking sphere to be able to exit its confinement without a radical overhaul. Attempts to move into a wider political debate come under attack however by the usual set of objections that are deployed when the politics of legality are challenged. Judicial misuse of 'proper' methods of reasoning, or lack of scientificity of legal method, betray the conviction that there is indeed a right answer, dictated by the accurate, scientific use of legal method. As such, private international law has become an exemplary terrain for the 'hermeneutic of suspicion' described, when transposed into the field of legal argument, by Duncan Kennedy as 'the charge of abuse of legal method with ideological intent'.[269] According to Kennedy's analysis, the transformation in contemporary legal thought, of a law-centric paradigm to one centred on judging, or, in another vocabulary to a general empowerment of judges, the spread of judicial balancing and the emergence of the 'total constitution' has led to an ever more insistent societal demand that legal rules be applied in a strictly 'neutral', 'objective' and 'apolitical' manner. Indeed, 'it is still a key legitimation claim that conflict occurs within a framework that is stable, neutral between persons, and democratically legitimate'. This tension gives rise in turn to the hermeneutic of suspicion, born of a sense both of the inevitability and unacceptability of ideology in legal judgement, projected onto the actor whose ideology is opposed to one's own.

In other words, as a result of the conflict of laws' self-insulation, retreat into technique and attendant near lack of introspective scholarship, the field as it stands is largely impotent or irrelevant in law's confrontation with the further social, economic and ecological challenges involved in the global turn. Curiously, as suggested above, this stands true too for the United States, where legal realism led progressively to the contemporary decline of interest in the whole discipline rather than its opening up into a terrain of contestation for more global issues. Furthermore, equally paradoxically given its own self-definition as operating at the very confines of state, the broader

[267] Emblematic of this regressive move is the current success of the 'presumption of territoriality' that has restored law to its purportedly natural domain or scope, as will be seen in detail below (Part II).

[268] A brief overview of the private international law of the EU suffices to shows the prominence of consumer, labour and insurance-holder protection addressed to residents and users of the market and the pursuit of these substantive objectives through various devices such as jurisdictional options for the weaker party, or alternative choice of law rules *in favorem*, or more. Even in private law, therefore, formal equality as a value has given way for a greater focus on the protection of categories of individuals (children, consumers, workers), or on the eradication of discrimination based on gender, race or sexual orientation (whether in the workplace, the market, or the family). The jury is out on whether this protects citizens or the market. On aspects of political economy, see below, 227 et seq.

[269] D Kennedy, 'The Hermeneutic of Suspicion in Contemporary American Legal Thought' (2014) 25 *Law Critique* 91–139.

political stakes involved in many private disputes are made invisible.[270] A whole range of considerations have been screened out, associated diversely with contemporary reflections on democracy, feminism and race theory, anthropology and cultural studies, science and technology and the earth sciences, that by contrast have been carried (to a degree) by critical strands of public international law. This is not to say that the public side of international law has always been less morally impeachable, but rather that the disjoining of the two dimensions served to consolidate the regressive trends embedded in each, despite their respective adherence to higher principles.[271]

THE RETURN OF THE REPRESSED

At the end of this initial exploration of the conventional account of the conflict of laws, it is important to point out the existence of certain significant, albeit minoritarian, counter-moves.[272] These include the revitalisation of early humanist ideals[273] in the name of social progress. While these had been largely swept aside until very recently, forms of 'relationality' embraced by contemporary private law seem to be seeping back into the private international legal field.[274] Above all, contemporary quests for a 'pluralist jurisprudence'[275] have induced a renewal of interest in the earlier, premodern 'statutist' methodological model of the conflict of laws (briefly encountered above), that was expelled from the nineteenth-century genesis of its current, monist version and subsequently relegated to the margins of the conventional history of the discipline. In the following chapter, we shall attempt to show how suppressed

[270] For instance, when the private claim involves modern forms of exploitation, expropriation and extraction, the latter are often invisible under the layers of dispute over jurisdiction: see below, 232 et seq.

[271] In terms of the political economy, to which we shall return below, this self-isolation of private international law from its public counterpart has always triggered a series of disastrous effects. Public international law largely facilitated the colonial project in the name of ideals of individual equality and collective civilisation, while the retreat of its private side in the name of neutrality left no brakes on the ensuing corporate appropriation of natural resources in countries of the South. The distinction served both the (public) colonial project and (private) empire. Today, increased indeterminacy of law and fact, the renewal of ideas about time and space, the polymorphism of conflicts, geopolitical changes, the normative role of science and expertise, new social practices, patterns of religious belief, all require an open debate as to the shape of law among other forms of normativity and the morphology of statehood in respect of concurrent communities. The self-isolation of private international law sterilises the terms in which it – and legality more generally – could be deployed to confront these challenges.

[272] The more radically critical moves involving aesthetics, ethics or the political economy will unfold below in the following Parts of this book.

[273] On Savigny's struggle against the previous legal humanism of the eighteenth century in the name of science and the return to the purity of Justinian's text (or mathematics?) see Schiavone, *Ius* 38 and above 71), see Neidhart, 'The Transformation of European Private International Law. A Genealogy' (and above 71, footnote 151) and on the contemporaneous transformation of public international law as replacing eighteenth-century humanism (and the law of nations) in the name of state sovereign equality see Koskenniemi, 'International Law and raison d'état' and above 74).

[274] H Dagan, *Reconstructing American legal realism & rethinking private law theory* (Oxford, Oxford University Press, 2013); A Somek, *The Legal Relation. Legal Theory After Positivism* (Cambridge, Cambridge University Press, 2017); R Banu, *Nineteenth Century Perspectives on Private International Law* (Oxford, Oxford University Press, 2018). The caveat here is that there are various ways of understanding relationality (see too in the context of the ontological turn in anthropology, below Part II).

[275] Roughan and Halpin, *In Pursuit of Pluralist Jurisprudence*.

plurality has come back, as it were, to haunt us.[276] This shadow version of the conflict of laws has always existed in subterranean ways, often troubling the smooth surface of the dominant scheme.[277] The argument (as deployed throughout this book on further registers) is that it provides a potent alternative understanding of alterity in legal form that might serve, more broadly, as a model for law's role in the struggle for the future of the biosphere.

[276] On the return of the repressed, see H Marcuse, *Éros et Civilisation* (Paris, Seuil, 1971 [1955]) 23 (and below 97).

[277] On hauntology in global governance (on which, Derrida, *Specters of Marx*), see below 158 et seq (and again, Monateri, *Dominus Mundi* and Santner, *The Royal Remains*).

2

The Shadow Account

MODERNITY INVOLVED A radical ontological mutation, in the guise of a rationalist project of statecraft, ordering the political world through law.[278] As seen above, this new legal form was monist, in the sense that an essential part of this project was the 'definitional exclusivity' of modern law.[279] The latter was progressively to become synonymous with rules produced by the sovereign state ('Law I'), disqualifying other normative orders.[280] By this token, it excluded heterogeneous forms of prescriptive authority (whether religious, moral, cultural, etc), alternative levels of power (whether of feudal lords or metaphysical *dominium*, natural or divine), and indeed (from the perspective of each sovereign the commands of its foreign counterparts.[281] Today, four centuries later, this monist perspective is troubled by 'intimations'[282] of decline.

[278] On law's formative role in modern (Western and European) metaphysics and political theory, and indeed in the emergence of the very idea of *Occident*, see Schiavone, *Ius*, particularly ch 1, pp 13 et seq and 25. An account of linear temporality as emerging in the work of the jurists, in a quest for the permanence of the body politic, can be found in E Kantorowicz, *Les deux corps du roi* (Paris, Gallimard, 1989), ch VII 'Le roi ne meurt jamais', p 867 et seq.

[279] N Roughan and A Halpin, *In pursuit of pluralist jurisprudence* (Cambridge, Cambridge University Press, 2017) 5.

[280] Modern law turned its back on the medieval plurality, or multipolarity, of terrestrial authorities and its unitary, transcendent cosmological order. The historical moment described here coincides with the collapse of the Catholic spatiality and the territorial partition of religious belief after the bloody endo-Christian and endo-European Thirty Years War (1618–48). Thereafter, the 'nomos of the earth' as propounded by Carl Schmitt (to whose doctrine on this point we return below: this reference does not signal the importation of the 'whole package' of Schmittian ideas) was a concrete, secular, political world order (C Schmitt, *The Nomos of the Earth in the International Law of the Ius Publicum Europaeum* (New York, Telos Press Publishing, 2006)): see P-G Monateri, *Dominus Mundi. The Political Sublime and the World Order* (Oxford, Hart, 2018) 77 et seq). The new *nomos* that accompanied the emergence of the territorial Leviathan was state-centred and secular (see below, Part II). It fractured the universal empire of the *Dominus mundi*, with profound consequences for the understanding of legality and its specific (territorial) spatiality and (linear) temporality. Today, as if in echo, specialists of international relations see the rebirth of unstable multipolarity as a new paradigm of world order (for instance, https://knowledge.insead.edu/leadership-organisations/what-it-means-lead-multipolar-world: 'After decades of living under the illusion of a unipolar world, the multipolar reality is hitting us in the face. How did we fail to anticipate, address or mitigate so many challenges?').

[281] This project must be understood in the medieval context of the terrifying wars of religion, clashing terrestrial and ecclestiastical authorities, extreme poverty, and a political scene of generalised suspicion that undermined social fabric. An excellent rendition of all these can be found in Umberto Eco's classic, *Il Nome della Rosa*.

[282] N Walker, *Intimations of Global Law* (Cambridge, Cambridge University Press, 2015). On the notion of 'intimations' in the collective (sub)conscious of the intimate (to which we shall return, below), see Mazurel, *L'inconscient ou l'oubli de l'Histoire* 187 et seq.

The distinct resurfacing of archaic, alternative, pluralistic epistemologies[283] might be seen as a sudden reflowering of multipolarity induced or facilitated by the internal contradictions of (late) modern law: a return of the repressed.[284] The moment has come, then, to craft novel, inclusive legal forms, unmoored or detached from the modern state's prescriptive monopoly.[285] An invitation, in other words, to unearth (or re-earth?) the 'minor jurisprudence'.[286] contained in the shadow version of the conflict of laws.

Indeed, globalisation is necessarily pluralistic, writes Hans Lindahl.[287] The most salient feature of the 'global turn' in law[288] is an unleashing – or more accurately, a new visibility – of non-state normativities, ontologies, cosmologies and rationalities. Unaligned with political geographies, informal orders of various types – private, customary, religious, indigenous – intermingle, clash and combine irrespective of state boundaries or the dogmatic distinctions on which the Westphalian paradigm rests.[289] Modern legal technique no longer deludes us into believing that the cosmos is anything but chaos; our contemporary legal consciousness is one of disharmony, relativity and multiplicity.[290] At its furthest confines, moreover, there is an increasingly uneasy awareness that various alternative non-modern modes of relating to nature and the universe, previously disqualified as primitive, are at least as authentic, legitimate, and productive as our own.[291] And yet it is anything but easy to undo Western modernity's tight association between law and the triad of state, rationalism and secularism. Law, emphasises Poul Kjaer, is essential for the constitution of state, but the reverse appears equally true; in a characteristically circular mode or radically

[283] For work in private international law that bears witness to these trends, see S Brachotte, 'The Conflict of Laws and Non-Secular Worldviews: A Proposal for Inclusion', Doctoral Dissertation, Sciences Po, Law School, defended May 2022.

[284] According to Walter Mignolo (*Local Histories/global Designs: Coloniality, Subaltern Knowledges, and Border Thinking*, 260), these other models are resurfacing in a 'multipolar' pluralistic world, as a result of internal contradictions within the dominant Western forms of knowledge production. On the significance of 'shadow' in this context, see above 59.

[285] For the grounding of this moment, see the invitation to imagine political assemblages in which the interests of all sentient and non-sentient forms of life are represented, by B Latour, 'Composing the New Body Politic from Bits and Pieces', in B Latour, S Schaffer, P Gagliardi (eds), *A Book of the Body Politic. Connecting Biology, Politics and Social Theory* (Cini Fondazione, 2017) 19.

[286] In Peter Goodrich's terms: *Law in the Courts of Love.*

[287] H Lindahl, *Authority and the Globalisation of Inclusion and Exclusion* (Cambridge, Cambridge University Press, 2018) 36 et seq.

[288] Xifaras, 'The Global Turn in Legal Theory'.

[289] See Roughan and A Halpin, *In pursuit of pluralist jurisprudence.*

[290] On the continuing presence of chaos at the roots of the cosmos as allowing modern politics, see C Castoriadis, *L'institution imaginaire de la société* (Paris, Seuil Sciences humaines, Essais, 1999); on the theme of struggle and its implication for politics and law within the modern *episteme*, see Foucault, *Les Mots et les Choses*; in international relations and law, D Kennedy, *A World of Struggle – How Power, Law, and Expertise Shape Global Political Economy* (Princeton NJ, Princeton University Press, 2016); on generalised suspicion, see D Kennedy, 'A Political Economy of Contemporary Legality', in P Kjaer (ed), *Law's Political Economy* (Cambridge, Cambridge University Press, 2020) 89.

[291] An increasingly important ecological argument is that more careful agricultural methods can actually enrich the earth and increase its productivity in order to feed the world's population without further destruction. D Kanter et al, 'Gaps and opportunities in nitrogen pollution policies around the world' 3 (11) *Nature Sustainability* 956–63.

'reflexive loop', the modern state was itself a construction, or a co-production, of the very legal order it produced.[292] How, then, to be post-monist?

In private international law, pluralism, as we have already seen above, has always been present as an alternative project. Within the law of the conflict of laws, it takes on the form of a method first known as 'statutism' – whether in its initial medieval guise (as applicable to early city *statuti*[293]), or as a legal-realist style of policy analysis (in the context of legislation or statutes against a common background in the United States), or indeed (in continental rights-based doctrines) as a mode of recognition of foreign legal status or title.[294] Rather than assuming a predetermined allocation of legal issues or distribution of laws, it commands a more fluid acceptance of other normativities *on their own terms*, partly based on an insistence that the forum has the right to assert itself on its own terms as well. True, in most of these cases, its distinctiveness is hardly visible against the background of a unitary, overarching (Roman, or common law, or rights-based) legal culture. Outside such commonality, statutism has always been kept at bay – as we shall see below, as a perceived political threat to what was understood as a project of apolitical meta-national legal ordering.[295] In many instances, it was discursively excluded and yet used, as it were under cover, as sticking-plaster when the various assumptions of monism fell apart and generated logical conundrums.[296] Such interweaving of a dominant and alternative methodology certainly partakes of the notorious 'exceptionalism' of the conflict of laws as a discipline.[297] Moreover – and somewhat confusingly, given the influence of the largely monist story of origin explored above – according to a widespread representation, the subsequent evolution of the conflict of laws oscillates between the two prongs of this same methodological dichotomy, framed as an ideological opposition.[298]

Two orders of critical analysis of this standard account may be helpful to the pluralist project – the focus of this chapter – of untying legality from its exclusive state

[292] Kjaer, *Law's Political Economy*. On the reflexive loop, the reference is to autopoiesis and Luhmann's social systems theory, of which the application to law is to be found in the work of G Teubner, *Law as an Autopoietic System* (Oxford/Cambridge, Blackwell Publishers, 1993). For critiques of the continuity of statism in legal philosophy, see D Patterson, *Legality's Borders: An Essay in General Jurisprudence* (Oxford, Oxford University Press, 2010); K Culver & M Giudice, *The Unsteady State: General Jurisprudence for Dynamic Social Phenomena* (Cambridge, Cambridge University Press, 2017).

[293] The first treatise of *statuti* is attributed to Alberto Gandino, *Quaestiones statutorum* (circa 1284). See M Sbriccoli, *L'interpretazione dello statuto. Contributo alla storia della funzione di giuristi nell'età comunale* (Milan, 1969).

[294] See above, 50.

[295] Against the background of a common substantive legal culture, conflicting laws were seen as derogations from a shared standard. In the absence of the latter, an allocatory framework is seen as essential to hold plurality together. See above, 76.

[296] As seen above, much if not all of what is known (in continental Europe) as the 'general theory of the conflict of laws' is composed of a set of devices (renvoi, preliminary questions, distinctions between the creation and recognition of legal rights, and more) used by courts or imagined by scholars in order to redress the troublesome effects of the *refoulement* of monism's methodological other.

[297] On exceptionalism of the conflict of laws see Paul, 'The Isolation of Private International law'; in respect of family law, Neidhart, 'The Transformation of European Private International Law. A Genealogy'. On the well-known image of the discipline as a 'dismal swamp' full of abstruse theories, see below, Part II.

[298] Such oscillation does not mean that the same accounts do not give primary importance to one of the (Savignian) poles over the other, nor that the movement itself is not seen as sporadic rather than regular.

form. Once again, the idea here is that the study of the conflict of laws might serve as a heuristic[299] for shedding light both on the challenges encountered by modern law in a radically transformed context and the subsequent possibility of pluralising (post-monist) legality. Thus, firstly, in epistemological terms, the conceptual economy of private international law shows up under a deconstructive lens as being structurally 'nested',[300] or shaped by the constant assembling, disassembling and reassembling of conceptual opposites, embedded, in turn, within wider, interchangeable, intellectual pairs (section I). Secondly and in turn, a genealogical critique reveals the knots or incoherences that muddle the apparently smooth reconstitution of the conventional story of origin and questions the values that this story serves to support (section II).

I. DIALECTICAL TENSIONS

Section I represents a search for possible keys to the peculiarly circular narrative of change that is characteristic of most historical and comparative accounts of private international law. It tells of a binary opposition and a dialectical evolution.[301] The pendulum of history swings from 'statutism' to 'conflictualism' to 'neo-statutism' and back, setting in motion a further dynamic between opposing conceptual binaries such as the territoriality or personality of laws; the individual or society; public law or private law; universalism or particularism. Every so often, in various contexts of geopolitical, domestic or intellectual transformation, a shift occurs, within an endless unsteady sequence of ebbs and flows of these two opposing models. Earlier and indeed subsequent fractures appear in this alternative story as discrete episodes within a timeless dialectical exchange. Beyond its own oscillating content, this account evokes a broader impression of *déjà vu*, as if in echo to the struggle between two models of world governance that have coexisted in constant tension in the Western tradition – global imperial rule versus a fragile equilibrium between fragmented, territorial polities.

Thus, from a standard contemporary continental European perspective, the nineteenth-century Anglo-American model of the conflict of laws has come to be identified with an archaic past made of concerns – territoriality, particularism, statutes, public law, sovereignty, vested rights – that savignism[302] supposedly left behind. The latter rejected as overly political the understanding of the thrust of statutes as expressions of sovereign will, linked as they were to the expression of Protestant, independentist and essentially localist claims or ideals in the era of the Atlantic revolution. From the same continental standpoint, an analogous opposition re-emerged, a century later, when the neo-statutist theories of the so-called American functionalist

[299] As defined above, a heuristic is an aid (in the form of a mental shortcut) to learning, discovery or problem-solving. A metaphor is just such a device.

[300] See, for the idea of 'nested sovereignty', Simpson, *Mohawk Interruptus. Political Life Across the Borders of Settler States* (Durham NC, Duke University Press, 2014). Here, the topic is nesting of dichotomic forms of legality.

[301] An example of this narrative can be found in Oppetit, 'Le droit international privé, droit savant'.

[302] See above, 75.

or policy-based revolution, embodied in governmental interests analysis, were seen to threaten the stability of the purportedly apolitical, technical, 'multilateralist' and European allocatory model.[303] However, from the reverse viewpoint of the common law tradition, particularly in the wake of legal realism in the United States, the continental Roman law paradigm steeped in universalist ideals and naturalist thought was seen as representing a bygone, romantic vision of the law. Moreover, its appeal to the purported 'essence' of legal relationships and their metaphorical correlation to geographical space was denounced in emblematically pragmatist terms as both metaphysical and nonsensical.[304]

However, this opposition between two poles was and still is certainly more chaotic than meets the eye, pervaded by 'irritants'[305] that are not captured by the idea of a simple dialectic. For this binary methodological account coexists with an intense hybridisation of each of the opposite prongs, as seen above. Instead of a regular rise and fall of each of the latter, there were continuous, unstable internal mutations that steadily muddle the picture. In other words, recurring sets of conceptual pairs move within, as much as between, each legal tradition, so that any attempt to tell the story of one leads into elements that turn, reverse and borrow from the other. This complex struggle is therefore both diachronic, because it tracks the internal changes within each model (statutism evolves into neo-statutism), and synchronic, as it opposes at any given time two distinct but contemporaneous approaches (statutism versus conflictualism). The 'swing of the methodological pendulum' narrative has to concede therefore that, beyond a dialectic of exchange, each scheme is in a state of constant recomposition.

At each step, other dynamics are at work and new combinations occur. These may involve equally dualistic theories of the relationship between law and state, the distinction between the public and the private, the respective importance of the individual or society, the opposing attraction of territoriality or personality of law as a guiding principle; all these divides are underwritten furthermore by differences in legal traditions or belief systems, and historical and geographical contexts. Whatever the specific features attributed at a given time to either pole, each provides the frame for an endless assemblage, disassemblage and reassemblage of recurrent ideational binaries. The latter are composed of nature and reason, policy thinking and science, organic and atomistic visions of society, cosmopolitan ideals and protectionist concerns, and all combine in various ways with the two available methodologies, justifying alternately their respective fortune and decline. Section I.A below will study these pairs in terms of the paradigm dichotomies specific to Western legal thought. Section I.B will envisage them under a deconstructive analysis as examples of 'nesting'.

[303] See above, 76.

[304] On pragmatism, see above: 62. These opposing perspectives embody a wider mismatch that is at the heart of much debate within comparative legal studies over the extent of contemporary convergence or divergence as between common law and civilian traditions. We return to these below in a discussion of the presumption of commonality or similarity in comparative legal epistemology: see 262.

[305] As in G Teubner, 'Legal Irritants: Good Faith in British Law or How Unifying Law Ends Up in New Differences' (1998) 61 *Modern Law Review* 11–32.

A. Paradigm Dichotomies

The epistemological structure of Western legal thought is shaped by the remarkable ubiquity and protean nature of the Roman legal legacy.[306] Periodically reborn or rediscovered over the centuries in an extraordinary variety of forms and contexts, influential in the fields of philosophy, ethics and logic, alternately identified with religion or science, reason or naked power, natural law or local cultural genius, travelling beyond the geographical remit of the vestiges of the Roman empire, Roman legal thought continues to shape our own intellectual paradigms and schemes of intelligibility.[307] Such a legacy is, as we know, peculiarly significant in respect of the conflict of laws. Deliberately central in Savigny's great opus, this also applies to the common law tradition, where Roman frameworks were imported into the conflict of laws through the teachings of the Dutch statutists.[308] This suggests that the binary structure through which the history of private international law is told is emblematic of a much broader model of legal thought. In turn, this is important for the rethinking of modern jurisprudence in a global, ecological perspective.

Indeed, the Roman division of persons and things, *res/persona*, still structures our (modern, Western) consciousness in ways that are, in Alain Pottage's terms once again, 'profoundly juridical'.[309] Moreover, this divide is considered in philosophy and anthropology as foundational in the further bifurcation of mind and body, nature and culture. Thus, Italian philosopher Roberto Esposito claims that the codification by Roman law of persons, things and actions (categories and distinctions that had hitherto been widely accepted in Roman societies) became the presupposition of all types of thought, including philosophy, politics and economics.[310] Indubitably, then, this initial dichotomy runs deep in our legal consciousness. Of interest here, in particular, are the complex patterns of imbricated binaries that stemmed from this initial categorisation. While humans came to be irreconcilably separated from things, the person came to be divided in turn, between body and soul; unless it was, vice versa, that body and soul led to the severance of humanity from its surroundings, subject from object, facts from values, etc. In other words there have been continual re-articulations of the primary divide, with a hiatus, displacement or loss in translation at each move. Hence Roberto Esposito's thesis that the body is neither a person nor a thing, but

[306] See below 179.

[307] GH Samuel, *Rethinking Legal Reasoning* (Cheltenham, Elgar, 2018). Importantly, this is valid not only in the continental European context but for Western modern thought more generally. In respect of the Roman legacy in the *legal* field, the specific areas of the conflict of laws shows up an interesting feature, to the extent that the common law tradition has embraced civilian influence (as seen above 75).

[308] See above, 73–74.

[309] See above 15. A Pottage, 'Introduction: The fabrication of persons and things', in A Pottage & M Mundy (eds), *Law, Anthropology, and the Constitution of the Social: Making Persons and Things* (Cambridge, Cambridge University Press, 2004) 4. Similarly, building on Latour's account of Law II as a mode of existence, Kyle McGee points out that the dichotomies of person/thing and body/soul are ingrained in legal reasoning and explains 'why chains of reasoning take the shape they do': K McGee, 'On Devices and Logics of Legal Sense: Toward Socio-technical Legal Analysis', in K McGee (ed), *Latour and the Passage of Law* (Edinburgh, Edinburgh University Press, 2015) 61.

[310] R Esposito, *Person and Things: From the Body's Point of View* (Cambridge, Polity Press, 2015).

a non-binary, 'impersonal' category, capable of dissolving this dichotomy.[311] Donna Haraway's cyborg bears a similar signification.[312]

The endless bifurcation of persons and things evokes a further strand of specifically epistemological exploration. Thus, in respect of modern Western legal thought in general, Geoffrey Samuel observes that the whole career of modern legality is dominated by the continuity, under different guises, of 'paradigm dichotomies'.[313] Suggesting that (Western) law's epistemological development 'remains trapped in the seventeenth and eighteenth centuries', he looks for the cause of the arrested categories of our categories of legal knowledge in the prevalence of the authority paradigm. This is the paradigm that, as opposed to inquiry, prevails in theology, or belief systems that appeal to a higher being (God or Nature).[314] In Western legal thought, the history of law is so much entangled with that of (largely Christian, Catholic) theology that the survival of an analogous proximity in modes of knowledge production is hardly surprising. Such a paradigm explains, and in turn results from, the extraordinary career of Roman law throughout the modern history of legal (and metaphysical) thought. Gaius' *Institutes* were not only a set of ordered rules but above all a way of viewing, and making accessible, social reality – a 'gateway' to knowledge.[315]

In what we would now identify as political theory, throughout the long career of the Roman empire, the *Dominus Mundi* embodied the divine order of the world.[316] At the time of the renewal of Roman law during the European Middle Ages, the belief continued in the authority of Roman law as text (that one might qualify variously as timeless, sacred, received …) supported by either divine will or naked political power. Remarkably, such belief survived still further through the revolutionary ontological upheaval that took place in sixteenth-century Europe. In a radical intellectual shift, the humanists destroyed the medieval faith in the embodied authority of Roman law as text. The result, however, was still not to abandon the authority paradigm (that is, to take the text as embodying a non-empirical or non-demonstrable truth), but to propel the modern reconstruction of a wholly rational system of private law, of which the primacy derived from that point from its internal (natural) coherence and the possibility of using it as a basis for deductive or syllogistic reasoning.[317]

[311] Ibid.

[312] Haraway, *Simians, Cyborgs and Women.*

[313] Samuel, *Rethinking Legal Reasoning* 279 et seq.

[314] The characteristic of the authority paradigm is that it leaves no room for falsification (following Karl Popper, such falsifiability is the parameter for scientific theory). Legal knowledge, like religion, cannot be proved empirically to be true or false. Schiavone, *Ius* similarly observes that law resembles religion because it seeks to harmonise the world of belief with that of truth. There is an additional take in the *Enquiry* of Bruno Latour, who suggests that POL (politics) also belongs to this group (LAW, REL) because there is no reliance on (or governance by) exterior facts. These three modes relate to 'quasi-subjects' (as opposed to technology, fiction and reference, which are all 'quasi-objects').

[315] On the lack of initial systematicity of Roman law BC, the late appearance of a 'recognisably modern' compilation of Roman rules as from the eleventh century, and the transmutation of the initially humble *Institutes* of Gaius (AD 161) as a 'gateway to knowledge' in law through printing efforts as from fifteenth century, see A Watson, 'The Importance of Nutshells' (1994) 42 *Am Jour Comp Law* 1, 3, 9 et seq.

[316] The reference is to Monateri's *Dominus Mundi.*

[317] See Stein, *Roman Law in European History.*

Savigny's systemic treatise of Roman law, of which the last volume was devoted to the conflict of laws, subscribes to this particular paradigm orientation. This does not exclude, however, a series of internal inconsistencies, already evoked in the preceding chapter. We know that the great Romanist scholar was also the founder of the historical school, emphasising (against the claims of codification, against the influence of Napoleonic institutions, against the competing arguments of Mancini's universalist-personalist doctrine drawn from public international law) the genius of local folk legal culture. Yet he claimed all the while a Roman law pedigree for Germanic law and a striking coincidence between the latter and natural reason. Thus, his work also reflects an organic vision of legality with a belief in the normative force of national consciousness. Unsurprisingly, then, several of his own premisses were actually shared by his adversaries, notably in the context of the famous controversy over the codification of German law.[318]

A closer look shows that within the authority paradigm (again, signalling that the word embodies a truth that is not empirically demonstrable), many possible schemes of intelligibility may combine in various, possibly contradictory, ways. Indeed, beyond the paradigms (or within each one), as Geoffrey Samuel explains, on a 'lower' epistemological register, schemes of intelligibility also appear as binaries (holism/atomism, universalism/particularism, naturalism/positivism), that are also constantly reassembling, but not necessarily steadily or in sync. In turn, the history of legal methods is, 'at a very broad level … a history of what might be called dialectical tensions or movements between competing poles or approaches'. These different epistemological registers all play out dialectically, in various combinations, with still further pairs of methods.[319] The latter intervene at a still lower level, and in similarly binary form, with particular relevance for private international law. For example, the dualism between universalism and particularism is further reassembled through the dichotomies between empiricism and rationality, casuistic and axiomatic reasoning, argumentation and reasoning, or the axiomatic and the axiological, functionalism and actionalism, literalism and teleology etc.

These multiple dialectical tensions explain not only the internal inconsistencies within Savigny's doctrine, but also why posterity retained from it, selectively and paradoxically, both the naturality of the seat of legal relationships and the scientificity of the proposed approach. Moreover, every one of these various epistemological schemes affected successive representations of the conflict of laws and the hiatus of loss in translation that occurred at every turn. In the writings of Bartolus, local law was subordinated to Roman law;[320] Huber promoted a doctrine of territorial

[318] On the codification debate opposing Savigny and Thibault, see above 86 and on this particular point, M Reimann, 'The Historical School Against Codification: Savigny, Carter and the Defeat of the New York Civil Code' (1989) 37 *Am Jour Comp Law* 95, 97–98.

[319] Samuel, *Rethinking Legal Reasoning*, 273 et seq.

[320] Bartolus' (short)(post-) gloss on the *Cunctos Populos* was part of a wider study (*Si Bononiensis*) on the extraterritorial application of the urban statutes of (northern Italian) city states, exemplified by the dilemma of the judging of the citizen of Bologna in Modena. Bartolus' role in the founding of the conflict of laws as what we would now recognise as a discipline is controversial and perhaps overrated (given that he was occupied above all by the extent of admissible derogations to Roman law), particularly in respect to that of his pupil Baldus (on whom see JD Wilson, 'Baldus de Ubaldis' (1902) 12 *Yale Law Journal* 8–20).

independence that was nevertheless still regulated by the *ius gentium;* Savigny's account of (national) diversity took place against the backdrop of a (universal, or at least European/Roman) legal or normative community. None of these abandoned the authority paradigm that subscribed to the truth of the (Roman legal) Word, and, in the context of apparently opposing theorisations, many subscribed to a preference for a given intellectual model (holistic, naturalistic, scientific, or axiomatic …) that had at least partly inspired their predecessor, or indeed their adversary.

B. Nesting

At this point, a second, further lens for the reading of this long history of private international law can usefully be borrowed from deconstruction theory and its heritage of structural (Saussurian) linguistics. Two ideas are key in deconstructive reading. These are 'différance' and 'trace', as proposed by Jacques Derrida, to describe the mutual dependence and differentiation of concepts within a text.[321] Another way of putting a similar idea in a deconstructive mode is, as Jean-Luc Nancy writes, that every norm produces its own opposite contrary.[322] If, as we have just seen, the outcomes resulting

Bartolus and Baldus are identified with the Italian school of the 'post-glossators', which succeeded to that of the initial commentators of the (rediscovered) *Corpus Civilis* (from the end of the thirteenth century). The (widespread) influence of the *Mos Italicus* was challenged in the sixteenth century by the legal humanism of the French Renaissance (the *Mos Gallicus*) led by Cujas, with the (paradoxical) aspiration to abandon the sedimentation of centuries of commentaries and return to a properly recontextualised version of the Roman texts. Free however to relativise and adapt the ancient script, several paid particular attention to the conflict of laws. This was particularly the case of Charles Dumoulin (1500–66), whose famous legal consultation on the law applicable to matrimonial property is seen as the beginnings of the idea of free party choice of law in contract ('party autonomy', on which below 258). For more on Bartolus, see below 152, 168.

[321] J Derrida, 'La Différance' (conference before la Société française de philosophie, 27 January 1968, published in *Le Bulletin de la société française de philosophie* (juillet-septembre 1968) and in *Théorie d'ensemble* (coll Tel Quel) (Paris, Seuil, 1968); *Marges de la Philosophie* (Paris, Minuit, 1972). On the importance of these ideas for law *(generaliter)*, see C Younes, 'Le droit et la différence', PhD thesis, University Paris 1, 2004. An example of 'differance' is an attempt to invert hierarchies of concepts, so as to show that, within the opposition between a dominant and a subordinate term, the dominant term bears some form of conceptual dependence to the subordinated one. On the other hand, 'trace' is 'the retention of absent concepts in our understanding of other concepts'. As Jack Balkin observes ('Nested Oppositions' (1990) 99 *Yale LJ* 1669), claims of similarity and difference can be reinterpreted as conceptual oppositions, so that they can also be reinterpreted as forms of nested opposition. Post-Derrida, important work in public international law mapped out either the structural (Kennedy) or the rhetorical (Koskenniemi) inevitability of polarised thought: see D Kennedy, *International Legal Structures* (Baden-Baden, Nomos, 1987); M Koskenniemi, *From Apology to Utopia. The Structure of International Legal Argument* (Cambridge, Cambridge University Press, 2005); 'What is Critical Research in International Law? Celebrating Structuralism' (2016) 29 *Leiden Journal of International Law* 727–35. On the underrated role of structuralism in methods used in comparative and historical legal studies, see G Samuel, 'Comparative Law and Jurisprudence' (1998) 47(4) *International and Comparative Law Quarterly* 817–36. In private international law, arguably, the same point had been made, drawing, differently, on moral philosophy to set out the idea of opposing polar principles: see O Schachter, 'International Law In Theory And Practice General Course in Public International Law' (Vol 178), *Collected Courses of the Hague Academy of International Law* (first published online 1982).

[322] Normalisation, according to Jean-Luc Nancy, 'dessine les contours de la marge et de l'anormalité, monde sublunaire et dégradé. Car si les normes, explicites ou tacites, forment et conforment les êtres, les choses et les mots, *c'est toujours accompagnée de son contraire que la norme constitue ses objets.*

from the combination of multiple epistemological levels may seem paradoxical or contradictory, it is because the apparently opposite conceptual pairs, both initial and subsequent, are 'nested'.[323] As Jack Balkin explains, this means that each of the terms of a conceptual opposition either contains the other, or shares something with the other. Roberto Esposito provides a similar account of 'polarised' thought, 'that is able to proceed only in a logic of counterposition and assimilation, but which in reality is perpetuated in the effort (or the illusion) of remedying and resolving in a literal sense every problematic node revealed by a reality that nevertheless transcends it and leads it back to the limit from which it moves: the human condition'.[324]

Thus, 'nesting' also explains the propensity for legal argument to unfold in successive stages in which each borrows or reincarnates elements of the other. Not only does each term of the dichotomy tend to produce the meaning assigned to the other, but in the process of their interpretation, sub-doctrines arise that borrow directly from the opposing intellectual cluster.[325] In other words, in a strange reversal, such sub-doctrines rely on the same arguments initially used to justify the opposite concept. The argument used to legitimise an initial choice between two values or principles reappears whenever we consider sub-rules that flesh out their meaning. The debate between these principles is replicated within each subsequent debate over the content of the initial principle. The conflict of laws provides some very good examples of this dialectic.

A clear instance is the heated contest between partisans and opponents of renvoi in the early part of the twentieth century, evoked above. All the protagonists belonged to the majoritarian, multilateralist (as opposed to the statutist) methodological camp (by definition, since renvoi was conceived, as a corrective device or a complement, as an appendix to multilateralist or 'Savignian' choice of law rules). Both sides appealed to the exigencies of sovereignty, and particularly the respect due to foreign sovereigns in their legislative capacity, in support of their position. The coup de théâtre took place when the most prominent and staunch supporter of multilateralism, the French scholar JP Niboyet, 'turned statutist' as an outcome of participation in the (virulent)

La plupart du temps en effet, les normes s'ordonnent à la logique des oppositions binaires qui déclinent leurs valeurs antagonistes, à commencer par celles du normal et de l'anormal. Nous sommes ainsi constitués par des normes qui, infiltrant tout, commandent notre être au monde, c'est-à-dire comment vivre, travailler, penser ou aimer pour participer à la normalisation générale, être normé, normatif et normal' (C Fallen, *L'anomalie créatrice* (Paris, Kime, 2012) Preface. We return to this point about normalisation (rather than dichotomies) below, 132.

[323] See critical legal scholar Jack Balkin, 'Nested Oppositions'. In his account of 'nested oppositions', Balkin defines the deconstructive move that this analysis implies in respect of the logic of similarity and difference in the following terms: 'All conceptual oppositions can be reinterpreted as some form of nested opposition. This follows from the contextual and relational nature of conceptual oppositions. Because opposition depends upon context and relation, recontextualization of a conceptual opposition may reveal similarities where before we saw only differences, or historical or conceptual dependence where before we saw only differentiation …'.

[324] See the closing pages of *Communitas: Origine e destino della comunità?* ['Communitas: The Origin and Destiny of the Community?'] (Torino, Einaudi, 1998); see too R Bonito Oliva and T Campbell, 'From the Immune Community to the Communitarian Immunity: On the Recent Reflections of Roberto Esposito' (2006) 36 *Diacritics*, T Campbell, '"Bios", Immunity, Life: The Thought of Roberto Esposito' (2006) 36 *Diacritics*, 70–82.

[325] Balkin, 'Nested Oppositions'.

'renvoi' debates at the time: he shifted positions as it were on the strength of his own argument, redeploying sovereignty in support of the very opposite methodology to the one that he had initially promoted.[326] Once again, nesting explains the constant interweaving, reversals and reappearances of the authority paradigm, combined with various schemes of intelligibility, as well as the various 'odd' polarisations.[327]

Applied more broadly to representations of the history of the conflict of laws, nesting shows each of the conceptual binaries encountered above – holism vs individualism, territoriality vs functionalism, statutism vs multilateralism, etc – to be tightly imbricated. Highlighting patterns of shifting succession and recomposition of doctrines, such an approach implies that conceptual opposites share, to a variable degree according to context, a common ground. For instance, to return to the example of the many historical lives of Roman law in European legal thought, the apparent antinomy between nature and reason, or custom and code, universalism and particularism, humanism and scientism, can be seen more as a constantly shifting exchange between ideational clusters.[328] This means that modernity's rationalist

[326] Sovereignty was initially and predominantly deployed to justify why the forum state, having defined the thrust of its own laws, should in no way defer to the diverging views of another sovereign (as expressed in different connecting factor: the forum decides that the (foreign) law of the domicile of an individual governs her personal status, whereas that law disagrees on this match and 'sends back' the same issue to the law of that same individual's nationality (as in the *Birchall* case, cited below). However, as redeployed, the sovereignty of the foreign state can be understood as commanding deference to its own, differing definition, choice or policy. How indeed (argued Niboyet) can the forum impose upon foreign law a scope that the latter does not want to occupy? The only solution to this conundrum is that each defines its own spatial delimitation. Niboyet came to this conclusion in annotating *Birchall v Birchall*, Req, 10 mai 1939, S, 1942.1.73, note Niboyet.

[327] Among these, as seen above, the paradoxical support of the historical school for the scientificity of Roman law; later traces of statutism within multilateralist doctrines; or the presence of balancing in the most dogmatic of concepts. The semiotics of contemporary legal argument provides an interesting twist. Thus, commenting on the (odd) polarisation of contemporary legal thought today as reflecting a hermeneutic of suspicion, Duncan Kennedy (in *International Legal Structures*) observes 'a situation in which the surface of supposedly non-ideological argument suggests the very thing that it firmly denies'.

[328] In turn, this can be related to the two contradictory accounts of the modern genesis and subsequent evolution of the discipline that coexist within the conflict of laws, as seen above (77), each federating at a given time a series of purposes or principles (justice or sovereignty), schemes (scope or seat) objects (laws or legal relationships) categories (territories, persons) etc. The first is the tale of a rationalist revolution in the second half of the nineteenth century, when statutism was replaced by multilateralism. The second is the account of an ongoing evolutionary dialectic and a cultural opposition between these two opposing models. Both accounts are frequently repeated, even though most students or scholars of the discipline would readily accept the historical inaccuracy or approximation of either or both. This is precisely a characteristic feature of myth (legal or otherwise). Thus, the first tale rests upon various imaginaries about the nature of law and legal change that hark back to the era of classical legal thought and ground a peculiarly widespread and resilient belief in the political neutrality, or non-instrumentality, of the discipline as a whole. The second, structuring the foundations of the conflict of laws in binary terms, suggests moreover that knowledge of the field lies a series of determinate concepts and their antonyms (systematicity, sovereignty, territoriality, individualism, functionalism, rights, etc). A clarification might be useful at this point as to the ambit of the epistemological account above. It is (merely) designed to explain how and why legal thinking has operated within a binary 'box' and is not intended as a response to a far bigger question as to whether this corresponds to a particular account of what it means to be human (or a 'language being') in which all life is mediated through combined thought and language that is inherently and necessary dualistic. In the text above, binaries are but one step from monism (or an effect thereof), although of course it might be argued that there can be a pluralism of pairs.

project of governance through law rests on a constantly moving ground. The question for private international law is now, in the light of an emerging awareness of plurality, whether our contemporary monist, model, with all its current epistemological settings, can be reversed in favour of the opposite, shadow model of interlegality.

If so, might such a move serve to challenge the deeper paradigmatic and deeply juridical separations between person and thing, mind and body, self and other, subject and environment, nature and culture, that have served to bolster our indifference towards 'nature's splendid alterity'?[329] As we have seen, a genealogical analysis aims to highlight the disparities, inconsistencies and dispersions underlying the historical or chronological reconstitution of the events that purportedly led, in linear mode, to the appearance of a given concept or scheme. Applied to the story of modern private international law, as it is supposed to have emerged in the guise of an enlightened methodology in the nineteenth century, such an approach makes visible a series of contradictions, uncertainties or incoherences. In this respect, this first section has shown the shifting ground on which apparently stable legal categories are constructed. In order to sustain an illusion of consistency, law has to engage, then, in an intensive form of epistemological 'boundary work' as we shall now see.

II. COMPETING IMAGINARIES

Such 'boundary work'[330] covers the fashioning of the lens or categories through which law apprehends the world outside itself, the social reality to which it applies and that it contributes to shape. As Gunter Frankenberg writes, 'legal formalism, supported by sociological positivism, produces and informs distinctions that function as borderlines and cornerstones. These distinctions limit the law externally and structure it internally'.[331] In the conflict of laws, such labour takes the form of a series of epistemological distinctions by which law defines its own frontiers, in relation to statehood, fact, domestic society, the foreign, the international public arena, or indeed private agreements. In all these respects, the prevalence of legal monism has required a considerable amount of technical maintenance at its confines. This has entailed the exclusion of alternative sources of legality within the state,[332]

[329] Descola, *Les formes du visible*. For the 'profoundly juridical' nature of these distinctions, see A Pottage, 'Introduction'.

[330] On this term in the context of epistemology, see M Lynch, 'Circumscribing Expertise: Membership categories in courtroom testimony' in S Jasanoff (ed), *States of knowledge* (Abingdon, Routledge, 2006) 164. 'Understood in the coproductionist idiom, boundary work does not simply trace or retrace a line that is already inscribed at the boundary [between law and science] … it is more like a line in the sand that contentiously, provocatively and sometimes successfully divides sciences from its other.'

[331] 'Critical Comparisons: Re-thinking Comparative Law' [1985] 26 *Harvard International Law Journal* 411, 423 on the subject of 'cognitive control' within comparative legal studies.

[332] This consequence of modernity for law will be explored further below. As will be seen, albeit in an uneasy relationship with the vestiges of a transcendent world order among nations, law-making was to become, formally, a monopoly of the sovereign state. The multiple overlapping and concurrent legalities of trans public and private collectives (professional guilds, churches and other corporate bodies such as the great trading companies) disappeared from the very definition of law and were relegated to the infra-state or private spheres.

shoring up the autonomy of the legal world in respect of the social reality outside it, keeping legality distinct from politics, and relegating the foreign to the realm of fact beyond it.[333]

However these boundaries are all increasingly uncertain in a world in which the state's monopoly over the production of legality is challenged, the foreign discredited as a meaningful category, and indeed the realm of fact uneasily distinguishable from the empire of law or values.[334] This is not to say that any of the divides devised by modernity were ever anything else than legal fictions or normative constructions.[335] Nor that they were without political reason, or epistemological consistency, when they emerged. But they continue to be supported by a dominant common sense despite the changes in the initial context and indeed, over time, have become dogmatic or detached from the surrounding reality. However, in law as in other areas of modern thought, in the face of competing imaginaries, such categories and distinctions are likely to be exposed as artificial, particularly to the extent that they contradict the collective values carried by the belief-system in which they were embedded initially. This is the case today in the philosophical arena, in respect of modernity's ethic of virtues.[336]

As far as the law is concerned, the legal technologies put into place along with modern statehood have gradually outlived their purposes in important ways and are singularly challenged as the ideologies, power structures, and political economy of the real-world change. It is clear that legal monism was never able to prevent a certain epistemological oscillation in respect of the limits of law, when confronted with the multiplicity of prescriptive claims from beneath or beyond the state. The pre-Westphalian religious disorder that law had sought to tame through the harnessing of natural or secular reason (and successfully kept at bay for a time) never completely disappeared. Religious contention was resolved by the division of territorial sovereignty among European states. The later rise of the liberal state maintained religious freedom in pockets of value pluralism, meaning that beliefs were relegated formally[337]

[333] Modern legal philosophy supplied elaborate exclusions and distinctions in this respect: theories of 'legal sources'; normativism and the divide between law and fact; positivism and the rationalist exclusion of cosmological visions based in nature, and more. On the coproduction by law of the nature/culture divide, see below Part II.

[334] These various uncertainties are linked respectively to 'private' codes and standards (multiple non-state authorities exercising quasi-prescriptive power beyond the reach of the rule of law, particularly in transnational settings, from forestry stewardship bodies to market associations such as ISDA (International Swaps and Derivatives Association)); the multiple components of chains of production and their applicable legal regimes; and the multiplication of modes of legal reasoning that incorporate policy-orientated, balancing or proportionality tests and attention to concrete, individual cases.

[335] See GH Samuel, 'Is Law a Fiction?', in M Del Mar, and W Twining (eds), *Legal Fictions in Theory and Practice* (Springer, 2015) 31–54; on *as-if* philosophy, Vahinger, *The Philosophy of 'As If'*; for its use in the conflict of laws, see A Riles, 'Cultural Conflicts', in K Knop, R Michaels and A Riles, 'Transdisciplinary Conflict of Laws' (2008) 71 *Law and Contemporary Problems* 273.

[336] C. Pelluchon, *L'éthique des vertus: une condition pour opérer la transition environnementale* (Paris, PUF, 2017). We shall return to the ethical dimension of plurality below, Part III.

[337] Of course, less visibly, the new secular international order (that did not prevent sovereign states from having official religions), was haunted by the religious (see Monateri, *Dominus Mundi*). Hence multiple troubles with distinctions between religion and sect, or secularism and ideology (see E Balibar, *Des Universels, Essais et conférences* (Galilée, 2016)).

to the sub-legal, private sphere and the practice of religion protected by freedoms attached to the person.[338] The foundational legal fiction was that law was a unitary phenomenon.[339] However, there may be a threshold beyond which a legal fiction becomes overly artificial, elaborate or systematic, or requires too wide a leap between the objective pursued and law's aspiration to reflect reality, to remain socially credible and legally sustainable. Yan Thomas' discussion of the elaborate self-imposed limits of fictions in the medieval reinterpretation of Roman law strongly suggests that such a breaking point may exist today at an imminent juncture.[340]

All this is true of private international law. Its specific technologies were gradually co-opted into modernity's new theorisations of territorial political sovereignty and the Leviathans that were to ensure the supremacy of the new secularised order.[341] From the nineteenth century, it was knitted into tight separations between state and non-state, foreign and domestic, the legal order and its own outside, the latter. Moreover, the whole ingenious construction came, little by little, to be natural-seeming; it was difficult thereafter to conceive of a legal world without states, territorial jurisdiction, or a theory of legal sources exclusive of empirical social reality. The ruses of naturalism are at work inside the very world of legal fiction itself.[342] Here, then, the tensions roused by the global turn are particularly acute, since they all imply, in one way or the other, a probing of forms of legality taking shape 'beyond the state'[343] – the gradual re-emergence of modern law's outside. In this regard, they also point to an aporetic triad of distinctions[344] of which the careful conservation and maintenance have constituted the specific 'boundary work' falling to the conflict of laws: state/non-state; law/fact; and foreign/domestic.

[338] And, to an extent, to communities distinct from their members (in how the private international law of human rights in Europe handles the combined 'legal' and 'sub-legal' status of religious freedom, see L Harms, *Faith in Courts* (Oxford, Hart, 2022, forthcoming).

[339] Fictions, as Yan Thomas observes, are not default settings for the truth but what we know to be false: 'Les artifices de la vérité en droit commun médiéval' (2005) 3–4 *L'Homme, Revue française d'anthropologie* 113–30.

[340] Yan Thomas ('Les artifices de la vérité en droit commun médiéval') sees legal technique (fiction) as the most enduring and historically adaptable form of intelligence produced by the human world. However, he shows that the limits of fictions for the medieval jurists lay in ontological boundaries: 'Le corps et l'âme, le physique et le spirituel, le visible et l'invisible, l'éternité de l'invisible au-delà de la mort du corps: voilà une division fondamentale de l'anthropologie chrétienne que les juristes du Moyen Âge projetèrent sur l'univers du droit romain pour en classer les opérations fictives et leur donner un sens; pour les contenir dans les limites mêmes de leur univers religieux'.

[341] This strangeness is emphasised by Monateri, *Dominus Mundi* (for example, in his study of the genealogy of political modernity p 101 et seq).

[342] Once again, the ruse of naturalism (Descola, *Les formes du visible*).

[343] This expression is used by R Michaels, 'Globalisation and Law: Law Beyond the State' in R Banakar, M Travers (eds), *Law and Social Theory* (Oxford, Hart, 2013) 287. One may note more traditional uses of this same expression to refer to the 'supranational' conception of international or European law (as in, for instance, J Weiler, (ed), *European Constitutionalism Beyond the State* (Cambridge, Cambridge University Press, 2009) or indeed to polarised conceptions of public international law as being 'beyond the state' but still state-centred (see C Pavel, *Law Beyond the State* (Oxford, Oxford University Press, 2021). In each case, these usages are distinctly more monist than pluralist.

[344] One of modern law's aporias lies in the circularity of legal concepts when they shape the very terms of the difficulty to be solved. One might say that such aporias are, at the same time, highly material productive dynamics!.

The question here is whether the methodological technologies of private international law are themselves too entangled in such divides as to be of any use in thinking about forms of legality secreted by collectives or assemblages other than the state body politic. In examining each of these three pairs in turn, the suggestion here is, once again, to plumb the premodern pedigree of the discipline in the governance of non-state plurality and its scheme of collateral coordination of the multiple claims to authority coexisting, within and across, different territories. None of the following riddles encountered by monism is problematic under the pluralist lens provided by the shadow version of the conflict of laws, suggesting various avenues that will be further explored in the two following Parts of this book. The first conundrum is that the very idea of non-state legality appears, through a monist lens, as a contradiction in terms (section II.A). A similar puzzle appears when law and fact are defined reflexively in respect of one another (section II.B) or when modern law encounters its own foreign other, on its own outside (section II.C).

A. State/Non-State

When the modern European world order emerged in the seventeenth century to put an end to the bloody wars of religion, law and theology became 'functionally differentiated', with far-reaching consequences for the organisation of society.[345] It was a foundational political moment; but it was also an ontological revolution[346] and, moreover, entailed a profound epistemological change. Its gradual consolidation, along with the accomplishment of legal monism, was the work of grand narratives

[345] This was the beginning of modernity: the world was on course for ever increasing fragmentation of disciplines, modes of existence, or (in the words of Teubner, *Law as an Autopoietic System*) 'social communicational spheres'. As Teubner explains, increasing functional differentiation within law itself was to lead to the specialisation of the conflict of laws as functionally distinct from its public international counterpart. The emergence of the two 'branches' of international law, each in its modern form, was contemporaneous, as seen above in chapter 1.

[346] The ontological change was the dissolution of the sublime or transcendent body of the *Dominus mundi* and its replacement by a divided world of territorial Leviathans. Of course, the metamorphosis of the sovereign body, from royal to political, took time to unfold, spanning several centuries of modernity's history. Indeed, neither the idealised Hegelian state – as *telos* and essence of evolution – nor the Weberian bureaucratic, capitalist state, appeared fully fledged in the seventeenth century; its later political form was predetermined neither by the Treaty of Westphalia itself nor by the conceptualisation of sovereignty in the works of Thomas Hobbes, King James I or Jean Bodin. The modern state actually materialised very late in its post-Westphalian trajectory; its development took a leap during the nineteenth century with its Hegelian elevation into a metaphysical superstructure, no less than 'the march of God through the world'. At this point, however, lest we succumb to a form of historical ethnocentrism, an alternative story of origin reminds us that the cosmopolitan state actually preceded its monist incarnation, while plurality (including empire and multi-level governance) was the rule: the national state, writes Hauke Brunkhorst, is a 'borderline case' of statehood (*Critical Theory of Legal Revolutions*). According to this account, the (Hegelian) notion of statehood is a kind of 'transitional semantics' which merely gained ground in the ford between traditional and modern society; it is a notion which is fundamentally provincial as it contains a strong eurocentric bias. The first insight which follows from this reconstruction is that, mainly in the form of empires, cosmopolitan statehood precedes national statehood. A second is that the modern state emerged around the 1930s (for the United States) because only then did an overarching and unitary form of public law-based power emerge which was capable of breaking institutionalised forms of private law-based power.

and legal fictions that were needed to shore up state law and ward off competing visions.[347] By the end of the nineteenth century, there could be but one, state-centred, conception of law. All others were banished, gradually, to the realm either of informality (common usage, gentlemen's agreements, standards, or indeed, sartorial[348] or social codes[349]), or the sphere of the private (religious practice, moral or political convictions, ecological habits[350]). Thereafter, if plurality still existed formally in the new secular legal realm, it was through the diversity of local laws, each contained within the territory of the various (European) nation states and most being treated as coterminous with national law, whereby sub-state divisions were still deemed internal to the sovereign state (attracting foreign acknowledgement only by dint of recognition of the outer layer of legality as attached to the nation state). Through a 'smart' technology of spatial distribution and containment, the Westphalian compromise enforced upon its sovereign creatures mutual toleration of (theological and legal) difference.[351] The concept of law, then, as opposed to its (increasingly) diversified substantive local content,[352] entertained a constitutive link to both state (in terms of origin) and spatiality (in terms of scope).

Thus, in its modern guise, legality acquired, in somewhat paradoxical terms, an inside and an outside.[353] On the one hand, in the internal or domestic sphere of each territorial sovereign, the national body politic was constituted as the font of legitimate authority and normativity, excluding any alternative forms that it had not created or endorsed.[354] Thereafter, legality was a continuum (from time immemorial and despite changes in the bodies of government, or the evolution of the state form) located within a vacuum (in respect of social reality, from which it remained conceptually removed). On the other hand, the new secular world was instituted as multiple; the (European) states were conceived as the sole actors in the Westphalian political order, in which they were several and equal. Their sovereign independence

[347] Older cosmological or theological ideas left traces: the haunting remanence of the 'royal remains' (Santner, *The Royal Remains*); nature (divine or human) either a model or the very font of the law (see above, 8).

[348] 'Sartorial' will refer largely in the text below to religious dress codes (hijab, turbans, monastic veils, or insignia such as crosses) but of course, to be entirely accurate, such accoutrements as wigs and robes are very much part of official, formal statal ceremonial garb.

[349] On the contemporary political-economic struggle to exclude such soft legal modes from the sphere of binding legality, see below Part III.

[350] Of course the uneasy status of custom, or the question of state religion, or the impregnation of (private) law with morality, are all signs of law's oscillations, mentioned above.

[351] On the status of territorial sovereignty as law or politics, see above 90.

[352] The full extent of such differences, as the formation of modern private international law shows, were not necessarily immediately visible (see above, chapter 1). Comparative law emerged as a recognised academic (and entirely eurocentric) discipline as late as 1900, still prisoner to the assumption that legal orders shared a similar architecture and meaning. Of course, that does not mean that legal comparison was unknown before 1900, particularly as a practice or argument (including in the colonial project): see for example, L Chen, *Chinese Law in Imperial Eyes: Sovereignty, Justice & Transcultural Politics* (New York, Columbia University Press, 2016) ch 2: 'Translation of the Qing Code and Colonial Origins of Comparative Chinese Law'.

[353] On the topic of the inside and the outside in relation to legality, see more generally, H Lindahl, *Authority and the Globalisation of Inclusion and Exclusion* (Cambridge, Cambridge University Press, 2018). See too on space, transcendance and exception as the three foundational elements of the world order: Monateri, *Dominus Mundi* 4. On spatiality and exclusion, see below Part III of this book.

[354] Such exclusivity translates into a 'theory of legal sources'' (or Latour's 'Law II': see above 21).

had however to compose first with the existing *ius gentium*[355] and then positive public international law, of which the authority came to rest anew upon an uncertain mix of consent, consensus and transcendent principle. In the middle, at the aporetical nexus between the definitional exclusivism of monism and substantive diversity of local content, the conflict of laws served as go-between, or operator of interlegality,[356] among the various domestic normative orders.

Beyond its uneasy location in between the two faces of sovereignty,[357] it was affected by a further paradox. The conceptual foundation of the conflict of laws in the European tradition, as we have seen, was embedded in the myth of the permanence of classical Roman (private) legal thought, reconstructed in the (Germanic) nineteenth century. This reconstruction largely espoused the modern project; it defined legality in terms of a metaphysical rationality, transcending context, above history and time. In this respect, as the Roman legal historian Aldo Schiavone observes, it focused a distantiated 'surgical' lens on the universe of people and things that it encompassed and classified according to invisible schemes of proportion and relationality.[358] And yet, the law of the Roman empire at its height was the scene of disorderly plurality and multi-layered governance, harbouring all the while a whole world of differences and contradictions. The very genius of Roman law, writes the historian, was precisely to elaborate ways of keeping such tensions in balance. Significantly, one such technique of governance was an early intimation of the conflict of laws.[359]

Given this pedigree, it is hardly surprising, then, that the deepest hiatus between monist principle and plural reality shows up most starkly in the latter field. The inconsistency affecting the conventional account of legality appears in particular in respect of two distinct figures of non-state law-making that have also been central to the contemporary revival of jurisprudential interest in legal pluralism. In her exploration of 'nomos without narrative'[360] – that is, of forms of legality unmoored from statehood – Talia Fisher emphasises that the claims to normative authority by different non-state collectives are analytically very different, according to whether they correspond to an economic 'privatisation' model, or to a 'communitarian' religious or cosmological belief-system. These opposing models of community derive from

[355] On the uneasy conceptual elaboration of the relationship between internal and external sovereignty in the seventeenth century and the (Roman) genealogy of sovereign equality as legal principle determining the extent of sovereign authority, see B Straumann, 'The *Corpus iuris* as a Source of Law Between Sovereigns in Alberico Gentili's Thought' in B Kingsbury and B Straumann (eds), *The Roman Foundations of the Law of Nations*, 101 et seq.

[356] The concept of interlegality is associated with the work of Boaventura de Sousa Santos. See for example, 'Law: A Map of Misreading. Toward a Postmodern Conception of Law (1987) 14 *Journal of Law and Society* 279–302 and below Part II.

[357] On the two-facing constitution, J Bomhoff, D Dyzenhaus, T Poole (eds), *The Double-Facing Constitution* (Cambridge, CUP, 2020).

[358] Schiavone, *Ius* 60.

[359] Thus, as recounted by Monateri (*Dominus Mundi*, 16 et seq), we probably owe to the classical Roman era the first formulation of a conflict of laws; the solution rested upon an ontological dilemma. *Dominus mundi sum; lex autem maris*, was the cryptic inscription by the hand of the Emperor ('Divine Augustus') (to the effect that applicable law was that of Rhodes), in the margins of Gaius' *Institutes*. Whether the law of Rome or Rhodes applied to the status of maritime bounty depended upon the nature – its amenability to terrestrial rule – of the wild unruly sea (on law's spatiality, see Part III of this book).

[360] T Fisher, 'Nomos without Narrative' (2008) 9 *Theoretical Inquiries in Law* 472. The reference is to Robert Cover's Foreword: *Nomos* and Narrative (to which we shall return below, Part II).

distinct ontological premises regarding law, community, social life, and the human subject.[361] The point here is that within the conflict of laws more specifically, this ontological duality corresponds to distinct conceptual tools. The study of the latter serves to reinforce Fisher's sociological analysis of legality and the challenges raised by these two non-modern forms of normativity for the definitional exclusivity of state law. These challenges are of two different kinds, however.

Firstly, the economic privatisation model is the location of a struggle between two opposing camps, deploying both ethical and economic arguments.[362] On the one hand, there are those for whom (modern) law, as a public good, is at risk of confiscation (by individual interests, lobbies or capital). On the other, partisans of the neoliberal (or the libertarian[363]) 'law market paradigm' support self-regulation, contractual autonomy and 'soft' non-binding legal forms of incentivisation and nudging (corporate social responsibility; *lex mercatoria;* environmental, social and governance 'ESG' standards). This controversy, largely specific to the market sphere (trade, industries including finance, investment, value chains), extends to private international law, in the form of longstanding debates over the permissible thrust of contractual 'party autonomy' (determinative of both the applicable law and the forum of dispute resolution) in international transactions.[364] The latter principle can be understood either as a technical device for determining the applicable law through contractual choice, subject however to the constraints of the public interest (liberally defined, or as an assertion of the ability for non-state rules such as private codes and standards (the transnational equivalent of business custom, often given normative force in domestic law in the context of commercial disputes) to govern cross-border business activities and flows of capital, untrammelled by social regulation.

The various regimes and devices developed over time within the discipline have translated these conflicting tendencies. While some of these have worked to ensure the primacy of public policy, or mandatory or overriding state norms, in certain circumstances, others have undoubtedly supported the emergence, in the name of free contractual choice, of closed dispute resolution processes that bind the immediate parties and indeed wider circles of participants, to the quasi-exclusion of any state law, regulation or oversight.[365] The point here is not to affirm the intrinsic virtues of state or public regulation: the latter is obviously vulnerable to capture and not necessarily democratic. Nor is it, at this stage, to delve into the political economy of private norms.[366] The focus of this argument is the tension created within a formally monist system: disqualifying from the category of legality all manner of non-state norms (corporate codes, industrial standards, ranking systems), has not prevented, and

[361] She suggests that alternative models 'have been solely occupied with taking a particular stance against the centralization model of state law, and have failed to engage in any debate amongst themselves as representatives of alternative legal decentralization schemes'.

[362] On this pattern, see below Part III.

[363] On the differences between neoliberalism and libertarianism, see below Part III, 239.

[364] On party autonomy, see below Part III, 258.

[365] The 'quasi' here refers to the fact that such exclusion actually involves the conscription or appropriation of state and interstate law (ICSID being a prominent example, in respect of the enforcement of arbitral awards: see below 236). One might more accurately say 'exclusion when needed; invocation when useful'.

[366] See Part III below.

indeed has arguably enabled, the emergence of a parallel informal or privatised world of authority and normativity beyond the state.[367] Relegating these various deployments of private power to the informal sub-legal sphere has, paradoxically, largely empowered unbridled 'governance through contract' rather than the reverse.[368] This 'return of the repressed'[369] is equally visible in respect to the second model of non-state law-making.

Indeed, a second challenge to monist legal theory lies in the increase in 'communitarian' claims to self-regulation. The presence of foreign religious, sartorial (as defined above), or aesthetic practices, beliefs, mindsets and tastes has become more apparent and, in many cases, has given rise to calls for specifically legal recognition. Such claims reflect the greater (or more visible) cultural heterogeneity affecting the populations encompassed within the territories of Western secular nation states as a result of successive, massive, historical (often post-colonial, but now war, economic and climate-change related) waves of immigration. In an inevitable, contemporary, backlash, 'assimilated' immigrant communities are claiming back the laws and courts of personal status in family matters and challenging by the same token the mutual constitution of legality and statehood. For the most part, however, the most common response on the part of secular, liberal, host societies has been to consign such claims to the informal sphere.[370] Just as, in the economic field, normative plurality has been left to contract, privacy is becoming an increasingly comprehensive category, catching issues related to intimate conviction, sexual orientation and the expression of religious belief.[371]

[367] At stake is the elusive parameter by which to measure the legitimacy of plural claims by non-state actors to law-making status. Often implicit in judicial reasoning, the predominance of the monist perspective in the conflict of laws finds a rare, formal expression in the official doctrine of the EU regulation on the law applicable to contractual obligations, alias Rome I (Regulation (EC) No 593/2008 of the European Parliament and of the Council of 17 June 2008 on the law applicable to contractual obligations). While the regime of international contracts is very specific, the understanding of law as state law (excluding the informal or non-state) is widely accepted (if more rarely judicially stated) as a general principle of the conflict of laws. The linchpin of this regulation is 'party autonomy', or the freedom of the parties to choose the applicable law or competent forum among all the national legal systems of the world (as we shall see below, in Part III). But why then, as the argument for greater freedom goes, should party choice (and other conflict of law rules) not extend to these expressions of non-state law, in conformity with social practice? Disappointing the partisans of a more inclusive conception of law (or a wider availability of applicable rules), this Regulation accepts as valid only those agreements that designate the 'law of a country', that is, that of another nation state. By way of compromise, its recital 13 emphasises that 'This Regulation does not preclude parties from incorporating by reference into their contract a non-State body of law or an international convention'. That such incorporation (by reference) is valid when validated by the applicable law went without saying, however. The premise is that (liberal) domestic laws all allow a large extent of party freedom, so that, unless there are peremptory policies that claim to apply to contracts outside the domestic sphere, there will be little real interference from the applicable law.

[368] See below 233.

[369] The 'repressed' here refers to that which has been made invisible or forgotten, as seen above 51. It is not necessarily synonymous with 'oppressed', although of course this might be the case too.

[370] For the most part: all depends of course on which polities are included in this category. For instance, if Israel is included, then religious personal law is state-endorsed: see I Shahar, *Legal Pluralism in the Holy City* (Abingdon, Routledge, 2015).

[371] On the human rights issues raised by the wearing of the burka in public (in France) discussed below, see *SAS v France* (App no 43835/11, 2014, ECtHR). Earlier case law of this Court (particularly separate opinions of Dutch Judge Martens) on transsexual identity had defined the latter as both a social and a personhood issue. The *SAS* case involved a full-face-covering veil, but semantically, the burka is often

This includes what could be termed sartorial codes;[372] as an example, the freedom to wear a *burka* in public, framed by the wearer as a religious injunction or the externalised expression of personal conviction.[373] Private international law once again bears witness to the variability of the confines of personhood (including 'gender trouble'[374]) at the core of these boundary struggles.[375] These confines of personhood are, once again, at one and the same time, those of the private sphere as opposed to the public (once again from the perspective of secular, liberal states[376]).[377] In this regard,

understood outside its Afghan use to extend to the hijab and nikab, often inaccurately assimilated as '*voile*' in French). The argument invoked the right to respect for privacy (Art 8 ECHR) as well as freedom of religious belief (Art 9) and non-discrimination (Art 14). While an extended right to privacy can of course mean protection against intrusive or arbitrary state power, its effect as seen here is also to relegate its objects to a sphere of infra-legality.

[372] See G Frankenberg, *Comparative Law as Critique* (Cheltenham, Elgar, 2019) ch 5: 'Muslim Veiling: Critique of a Comparative Discourse'.

[373] As an emblematic illustration, legal debates in France about the admissibility of the burka in public space resuscitate the troubled relationship between republican secularism (or *laïcité*) and the freedom of religion; in their contemporary shape, they also engage feminist doctrines, religious discrimination issues, conceptions of public order, security and police powers under the state of exception, and constitutional and human rights debates about personal freedom and choice.

[374] Butler, *Gender Trouble: Feminism and the Subversion of Identity*. For an example of a (French) private international legal case on the civil status in France of an Argentinian transgender person (and the accompanying commentary on 'limping sex'), see Paris, 1ère Ch C, 14 juin 1994, (1995) *Rev Crit DIP* 308, note Y Lequette. This case evokes, irresistibly, the first (French) conflict of laws case under the Code Civil, relating to the civil status in France of a defrocked Spanish monk, *Busqueta* (Royal Court of Paris 13 juin 1814, cited above). Both cases locate doctrinal controversy on high moral ground.

[375] The specifically private international legal issue raised by the burka (or head/face covering) is that of the scope of personal law – paradoxically the heir of 'personal status' – that has come home to roost. Access to citizenship (indeed, access to territory) in France for instance is conditional on renouncing a certain number of practices that are deemed incompatible with the *mores* of the Republic (for instance, polygamy). At the same time, public policy within the meaning of private international law concedes more (is more tolerant) where foreigners are concerned; a practice such as polygamy can sometimes produce effects despite its formal prohibition (in terms of succession, notably). However, as with the more traditional case of religious ceremonies, sartorial codes are categorised as part of the private sphere conceded (more or less) by the liberal state; they cannot be claimed as part of a concurrent normative framework governing personal expression in its own right. That the latter is the core of the definition of pluralism is a point to which we shall return. The point here is that, outside the realm of formal legality – in the realm of fact – religious communities are indeed living by different rules (whether sartorial codes, family rules), often enforced by specific tribunals. Post-colonial societies show that the traditional monist perspective has, at the very least, outlived the purpose for which it was designed, as a secular order imposed on warring European religious powers in early modernity. The objective of social peace through law (where theology had failed, or was precisely part of the problem) may require, today, the acceptance of more plurality within territorial populations, as the example of religious communities demonstrates. Or it may be, as shown by the clash of state law and indigenous cosmologies, that the state form is no longer a factor or guarantee of societal harmony. Furthermore, accentuating the pressure from earlier movements of population in the aftermath of decolonisation, new waves of economic and climate migrations from the global South compound the difficulties generated by monist definitions of legality in host countries. For instance, think of both notional and actual migration of Iranian citizens to Europe or Canada as helping produce the current dynamics of women's protest, which can be seen as both endogenous and exogenously stimulated.

[376] In the light of very contemporary developments, Iran has emerged as the mirror image of a forced sartorial choice. Of course, debate is then open on whether (beyond the type of penalty involved) the fact of being forced to wear a head/face covering is different/worse than the reverse (see Frankenberg, *Comparative Law as Critique*, whose point in the book is to raise this interrogation).

[377] The 'private sphere', 'right to privacy', and 'personhood' overlap in a complex dialectic. When large swathes of former colonised populations migrated to the metropolis in the immediate aftermath of decolonisation, the cohesion of metropolitan society was considered at threat from the strangeness of religious (or other) institutions – more so than when it surfaced in the far-away periphery as an object

the Roman legal category of 'personal status'[378] was transformed in the colonial nineteenth century into a sphere of (purported) tolerance for local, religious law in family matters, by exception to the rule of the sovereign metropolis. In this context, drawing on the then emerging disciplines of legal anthropology and comparative law, it was used in reality as a technology of imperial management, entailing the subordination of local, indigenous or autochthonous legality.[379] In post-colonial states, personal status in private international law has again come to signify a space conceded to the informal (or not properly legal) belief systems of indigenous or religious communities and their distinctly non-modern rationalities, normativities or cosmologies.[380]

The question prompted by these two ontological models of non-state legality is whether, once unharnessed from the sphere of state, all attempts to identify the features of law are doomed to fail. The principal objection to legal pluralism is that it cannot answer the question of just how open its approach can be in bestowing the status of law on the claims of competing contenders. In their 'pursuit of pluralist jurisprudence', Nicole Roughan and Andrew Halpin point to the risk of diluting the requisite credentials of legitimacy, to the point that the status of law, too readily conferred on 'anything from bus queues to tea ceremonies', loses all meaning and practical usefulness.[381] How can a legal theory claim to be such in the absence of any parameter by which to draw the limits of legality? In private international law, this

of anthropological curiosity. The exception of public order (conjoined with citizenship and immigration rules) began progressively to whittle away the margin of social tolerance; moreover, more radically, the shape of the traditional category of personhood, modelled on Western distinctions between law and custom, secularism and religion, and more, excluded practices such as sartorial codes or religious ceremonies, leaving them to be regulated directly by local public law. Examples are Muslim head/face coverings (as seen above) and religious ceremonies, for instance in marriages. See for a Greek Orthodox ceremony, qualified as a (mere) requirement of formal validity governed as such by local law, the French case *Caraslanis* (Cass civ I, 1er février 1955, 55-02.067 (1955) *Rev crit DIP* 723, note Batiffol).

[378] The origins of this category can be found in the work of the medieval statutists, the post-glossators of the fourteenth century, who had set about both to justify both the prevalence of (revived) Roman law over vernacular custom and to facilitate the mobility of merchants and traders issuing from various jurisdictions or city-states. In Savigny's widely accepted account, the concept of the 'personality' of certain statutes as an indication of their scope, thrust or object (their application to persons, wherever located) came to designate a category of legal issues that were to be governed by an individual's personal law (law of domicile or later, nationality).

[379] As we shall see further below 250, during colonial rule, 'personal status' came to be the linchpin of the (secular or civil) legal regime, a carefully crafted exception to the laws of the metropolis (see Surkis, *Sex law and Sovereignty in French Algeria*, 14). To take the example of Algeria, family institutions (such as polygamy) were allowed to survive, whereas real property was subjected to French civil law. In the tradition of the British Empire, colonies and Commonwealth, further legal tools appeared to subordinate local or indigenous normativities. In North America, rather than the category of personal status, constitutional concessions were made (or treaties signed) in order to accommodate a sphere of relative autonomy to original or aboriginal peoples, in terms of title to land and territorial sovereignty. In Canadian jurisprudence, however, the Crown 'wearing two hats' has managed to take away through the interpretation of treaty rules as much as what it initially conceded (see M Valverde, 'The Crown in a Multicultural Age: The Changing Epistemology of (Post)colonial Sovereignty' (2012) 21(1) *Social Legal Studies*).

[380] The Canadian judicial jurisprudence of 'reasonable accommodation' of plural standpoints is an attempt to translate the social scientific idea of recognition into legal terms. Its practice however may still leave much to be desired insofar as it remains monist in its exclusion of alternative cosmologies from the definition of legality. See Brachotte, 'The Conflict of Laws and Non-Secular Worldviews'.

[381] Roughan and Halpin, *In Pursuit of Pluralist Jurisprudence*, 5. See too Culver and Giudice, *The Unsteady State*, which sought to define a 'law-ness' that is non-state in essence.

objection exactly mirrors the complaint of impotence that has always plagued statutist methodologies. How can a method of conflict resolution claim to be such in the absence of any external criterion by which to choose between the laws in conflict?[382]

From either of these perspectives, the resilience of monism would seem to lie in its ability to provide a simpler or safer answer to the legitimacy dilemma evoked above (albeit unsatisfactory at the margins). The requirement that law be moored in statehood provides a workable parameter for sifting out normative claims that are minoritarian or insufficiently representative of the local community, ideologically inacceptable, or insufficiently 'law-like'. On balance, as the argument goes, this requirement filters out these risks, even if, admittedly, a number of state laws are undemocratic or arbitrary (even within the earlier-posited paradigm of secularism, liberalism, etc). In the conflict of laws, similarly, the parameter of statehood filters out claims to legality that are unendorsed by other like-minded (or like-constituted) statal legal orders. This may exclude, in the same way, claims of infra-state communities, or indeed alien forms of law practised in cultures beyond the pale of the modern 'concert of nations' and disqualified as 'merely' religious or cosmological. The difficulty is that in either case, these supposedly residual, non-modern forms of law-making are becoming increasingly visible, even within the hitherto culturally homogenous societies of the former metropolis.

At this point, the shadow, statutist version of the conflict of laws may serve to provide a more inclusive definition of legality. As we know, the initial Roman statutist tradition provided a lateral (non-hierarchical) scheme of coordination of the multiple claims to authority coexisting, within and across, different local jurisdictions (customs, municipalities, city-states, princedoms, etc). The focus in cases of conflicting laws was on the scope to be assigned to various legal rules rather than on definitional parameters of legality.[383] In this respect, far from being incomplete, however, this non-modern methodology took as its starting point the self-definition of each contending system.[384] But then, it might be objected, do we not circle back to the classical problem of 'anything goes': is law whatever claims to be so?[385] In response, as we shall see in Part II of this book, an ecological vision of the body politic introduces the interconnectedness of all the components of our social and natural worlds into the very constitution of legality. Monist law's 'definitional exclusivity'

[382] For such an argument, see for instance Ancel and Lequette, *Grands arrêts de la jurisprudence de droit international privé*, 7–10 (under n°4, the *Busqueta* case).

[383] Initially, as we have seen, coordination was ensured by the overarching framework of Roman law, of which plural local laws or customs represented contextualised, sometimes derogatory, embodiments. Once again, therefore, it is useful to recall that statutism methodologies were seen initially as a response to the clash between the universalism of Roman law and its local incarnations. Only in the nineteenth century with the rise of nation states did foreign law become a 'problem' (see Paul, 'Comity').

[384] See above 33, 66, 98 and below 127, 282, 313.

[385] On the recurring objection to pluralism according to which 'anything goes', it is interesting to read William James once again on possible objections to pluralism: 'May not the claims of tender-mindedness go too far? … Must all be saved? Is no price to be paid in the work of salvation? Is the last word sweet? Is all "yes, yes" in the universe? Doesn't the fact of "no" stand at the very core of life? Doesn't the very "seriousness" that we attribute to life mean that ineluctable noes and losses form a part of it, that there are genuine sacrifices somewhere, and that something permanently drastic and bitter always remains at the bottom of its cup? I cannot speak officially as a pragmatist here; all I can say is that my own pragmatism offers no objection to my taking sides with this more moralistic view, and giving up the claim of total reconciliation.

can be replaced, as Ralf Michaels has suggested, by an initial condition required of any form of normativity aspiring to the status of legality, that it demonstrates an openness in respect of other laws (that is, we might add, alien legal forms).[386] K Culver and M Giudice propose similarly that a 'key element of the legal order' (beyond the 'unsteady state') might be inter-institutional mutual reference.[387] Instead of demanding of law that it present a series of predetermined features, all presupposing the background attachment to statehood, the existence of law *qua* law would be evidenced by an attention to scope, coordination or interlegality. The content and operation of such a mode of lateral interaction will require further excavation below. For the time being, the point is the potential of the non-modern shadow version of the conflict of laws in untying from statehood the terms of the double question of legality and scope and reversing the sequence in which such questions are framed.[388]

B. Law and Fact

A similar potential exists too in respect of modern law's incessant boundary work in respect of law and fact.[389] Of course, the distinction between law and fact is a

The possibility of this is involved in the pragmatistic willingness to treat pluralism as a serious hypothesis. In the end it is our faith and not our logic that decides such questions, and I deny the right of any pretended logic to veto my own faith. I find myself willing to take the universe to be really dangerous and adventurous, without therefore backing out and crying "no play." I am willing to think that the prodigal-son attitude, open to us as it is in many vicissitudes, is not the right and final attitude towards the whole of life. I am willing that there should be real losses and real losers, and no total preservation of all that is. I can believe in the ideal as an ultimate, not as an origin, and as an extract, not the whole. When the cup is poured off, the dregs are left behind forever, but the possibility of what is poured off is sweet enough to accept' (ibid, ch VII). This point will come up again in Part II below on ethics and pluralism, and engages within the conflict of laws the question of the ethical moment of public policy.

[386] R Michaels, 'Law and Recognition: Towards a Relational Concept of Law,' in N Roughan, A Halpin (eds), *In Pursuit of Pluralist Jurisprudence* (Cambridge, Cambridge University Press, 2019) ch 5, pp 90–115; see below 205.

[387] Culver and Giudice, *The Unsteady State*, 91. This is a key book about 'inter-institutionalism' (albeit without mention of the conflict of laws as such).

[388] For a philosophical insight into the ways in which questions and responses are framed see H Lindahl, 'Place-Holding the Future: Legal Ordering and Intergenerational Justice for More-Than-Human Collectives' (2021) 10 *Journal of Legal Philosophy* 313–30: 'What is it for a legal order to *respond* to a demand for justice? To *represent* anew. Responsiveness is not a fortuitous feature of representation; representation is responsive representation. A collective's responsive representations never only 'follow' questions, in the twofold sense of coming "after" and "obeying". Instead, responsive representations are *retroactive* in that the question to which they respond only becomes manifest in the responses themselves. The dynamic of question and answer unfolds a double asymmetry marked by the precedence of the question and the retroactivity of the response.' This passage illustrates in powerful philosophical terms the critical potential of 'resequencing' as embodied juridically in private international law: see above 69. We return to it in the context of the ethic of responsiveness, below Part III.

[389] On the problematic nature of the law/fact distinction from an anthropological point of view, see Viveiros de Castro, *The Relative Native. Essays on Indigenous Conceptual Worlds* (Chicago, Hau books, 2015) 15, observing that the problem is epistemological, that is, political. 'It speaks to the properly transcendental question of how to decide on the legitimacy of discourses that enter into a relationship of knowledge. In particular, it speaks to the manner in which relations of order are established between these discourses – these relations are in no way innate, after all, and nor are their enunciative poles. No one is born an anthropologist and, as curious as it may seem, even less a native. As indeed Marilyn Strathern has observed, "The problem begins when we begin to produce descriptions of the world".'

difference not of natural fact, but of (factually imagined modern) law.[390] The law/fact binary is as much part of (Western) law's self-definition as of its constructed vision of its own outside.[391] The latter, the factual, is usually conceived of as the social, or (perhaps, at a pinch) the natural, world. In the context of the conflict of laws, law's factual outside is composed of foreign law and (oscillating) public international law, introducing an extra twist to the traditional law/fact binary. Foreign law (and often heterodox supranational sources) is neither entirely fact nor completely legal. The difficulty stems from the monist definition of legality, under which law is coextensive with the geographical limits of the nation state. Foreign law is therefore, as it were, beyond the pale. In other words, in the same way that legal monism (as secular, Western, rationalist legal form) disqualifies from the sphere of legality all forms of normativity *unlike itself*, its expression within the conflict of laws similarly excludes from the realm of legality (as national, jurisdictionally anchored legal form) all claims *outside of itself*.[392]

This explains why, in modern private international law, foreign law, having no authority within the forum state's home territory is considered, traditionally, as devoid of legal status before the courts of that country. Of course, the disqualification has to be nuanced because foreign law can nevertheless be applied or given effect *as if* it has such authority.[393] But the point here is that, just as non-state forms of normativity are relegated to the realm of the (private, informal) non-legal (without nevertheless being divested of all effect, as we have seen), foreign laws are equally disqualified, this time as 'mere' (though 'hard' or intangible) facts. Legal monism rests on a vision of the outer limits of law: it excludes any claim of foreign law (its exogenous other) to operate directly within the same territory (this would be a violation of local sovereignty). This exclusion can be correlated to the monist theory of legal sources: the latter also excludes foreign law from the pyramid of norms (in absence of any delegation or habilitation traceable to the fundamental norm of the local system).

The potential contribution of the conflict of laws to a post-monist rethinking of the law/fact distinction, in the elaboration of an ecological jurisprudence, will require substantial further explanation throughout the rest of this book. For now, we can offer some initial thoughts. In this respect, it is important to see that the careful separation of the worlds of legal prescriptivity and the social or factual universe it is designed to regulate, is intimately linked to the decontextualised – defactualised – form of legal

[390] A Pottage, 'Introduction', 1, 8. *Cf* GH Samuel observing that Law being the ultimate arbitrator of law and fact is what makes fictions so revelatory of the artificiality of the institution, its ontology ('Is Law a Fiction?', 229 et seq).

[391] Constructed or 'augmented': K McGee, 'For a juridical ecology of ligatures', in B Latour, S Schaffer, P Gagliardi (eds), *A Book of the Body Politic, Connecting Biology, Politics and Social Theory* (Giorgio Cine, 2017) 175, 177. Law's outside, composed of social reality, or a universe of things, persons and events, is also its very own, constructed object.

[392] A point of doctrinal clarification may be in order here for uninitiated readers: this exclusion of heterodox claims (emanating from foreign laws) denies the latter any direct legal binding force but (paradoxically) these are treated as valid within their own (largely territorially defined) sphere. Their status as hard facts gives them moreover an (apparent) intangibility that is greater than that of domestic law (that the court can change or make evolve).

[393] On the *as if*, see below 191.

knowledge that developed within the Western tradition.[394] Aldo Schiavone makes a forceful point – of singular relevance for private international law – about the epistemology underlying the renewal of Roman law in the nineteenth century. Savigny, he observes, (re)discovered the aptitude of legal knowledge to detach itself from its own object, in an abstract and distantiated form: a 'surgical lens' directed at the world in search of 'invisible relationships and proportions between persons and things'.[395] In other words (those of Kyle McGee), in fulfilling its course through modernity, law constructed its own mode of knowing: a realm of augmented reality through which to view social facts, correlatively ordered and pasteurised through their 'semantic doppelgangers'.[396]

This epistemological dimension of classical European legal thought as it emerged in the course of the nineteenth century (with remarkable staying power in the conflict of laws, as we have seen) is of course of very particular interest for private international law, in view of the osmosis that occurred at that time, notably through the work of Savigny, between the rediscovery of Roman law and the modern genesis of the conflict of laws.[397] The search for invisible relations and proportions between the entities that populated the virtual legal world (persons and things) is a very exact definition, or metonym, for the Savignian vision of the conflict of laws. The latter appears, emblematically and more broadly, in Roman-influenced legality more generally, as a realm of a certain set of intellectual operations: splitting, categorising, reducing or suppressing.[398]

The maintenance of this segmentation between the two worlds of fact and law has proved singularly problematic in the legal universe itself, requiring an inordinate amount of (legal and other) boundary work. Moreover, this separatism can be viewed, as it were, from either side of the law/fact divide. Thus, from a monist perspective, as Gunter Frankenberg writes, 'law is located 'out there' in a 'social vacuum' in the sense that social phenomena are interpreted within the framework of 'objective' classificatory patterns, earmarked by strictly scientific methods and data.[399] Analytical legal theory has therefore had to fend off the rising tide of social scientific interest in the relationship between law and society and more generally, the empirical or phenomenological world. *Quis judicabit?* Who, pope or emperor, gets to decide what is law and what is not?[400] The conflict of laws is once again at the forefront of this very

[394] Both Alain Pottage and Kyle McGee (in their respective works just cited) hypothesise that this foundational dichotomy within Western legal reason harks back to its Roman law pedigree in the divide between persons and things, that came in turn to be embedded in the Cartesian dichotomy between mind and body. The bifurcation of nature and culture may well have a similar origin. One might also approach this dualism conceptually through the pair thought/language. In treating such relations and proportions as 'real' in the same way as in the physical world through interpersonal interactions, a distinctly legal-fictive move is made.

[395] Schiavone, *Ius*, 60.

[396] McGee, 'For a juridical ecology of ligatures'.

[397] See above 72.

[398] Pottage, 'Introduction'.

[399] Frankenberg, 'Critical Comparisons', 324. On the proximity of modes of veridiction of natural law and various novel, contemporary modes of governance, see above 9.

[400] On the investiture struggles that are arguably (according to Kjaer, *Law's Political Economy*) at the origin of modern law as we know it, see above 26.

singular 'investiture conflict' – a struggle over the boundaries of law itself understood here in opposition to its foreign, factual other.

As Geoffrey Samuel writes (in a reflection appropriately devoted to 'resonances' between law and fact and fact and law), the great epistemological difficulty for modern Western thought is that of locating a frontier between fact and knowledge.[401] This has echoes in Bruno Latour's critical definition (seen above) of modernity in science as a belief in the distinction between facts and values. Indeed, opposing fact and law is fraught with similar epistemological difficulties to those raised within the natural sciences as to the separation between scientific knowledge and perception. Lawyers move constantly from law to fact and fact to law; from the universe of normativity to that of description. Such an ability to move between registers (or universes) was, as Samuel observes, the very genius of Roman law.[402] Moreover, an important insight of sciences and technology studies is not only that scientific expertise about the natural world is characteristically fuzzy, but that law itself coproduces the very definition of science and scientific fact that it is then reused on both sides of the divide.[403] Once again, we run into the problem of epistemological circularity and the ensuing indeterminacy of a distinction that is commonly posed as natural.[404] The assumption (again the 'ruse of naturalism'[405]) underlying these separations, that seem to dispense with all justification, is that of the certainty of the factual world: the latter calls quite simply to be observed, recorded or evidenced. Legal comparativism (of the Savigny-influenced sort) is caught up in the very same conceit.[406]

Once again, private international law illustrates, emblematically, this entanglement between law and fact. Beyond its highly technical dimensions,[407] the point here

[401] GH Samuel, 'Imitation of Life: Resonances Between Law and Fact and Fact and Law', in S Taekema, B van Klink & W de Been (eds), *Facts and Norms in Law* (Cheltenham, Edward Elgar, 2016).

[402] Samuel, ibid; also, 'Taking Methods seriously' (Part II), JCL 2.2.

[403] Jasanoff, *States of Nature.*

[404] The difficulty is equally present in the social sciences, where the divide between the observer and the observed is classically subject to caution. See on circularity in legal reasoning within the conflict of laws, above 30, 44, 50, 76.

[405] Descola, *Les formes du visible.*

[406] Comparative legal studies are a case in point. See again Frankenberg, 'Critical Comparisons', 325. 'The objective posture allows the comparatist to present and represent her own assumptions and what she observes in a scientific logic, with the balances and measures that project neutrality and conceal the weigher's complicity with both selection of the units on the scale and the objects to be measured. This ethos of value freedom suppresses how language, interests and experiences, which even the comparatists concede are culture-based, contribute to the comparison'.

[407] Its most venerable quandary concerns the procedural status of foreign law: R Fentiman, *Foreign Law in English Courts: Pleading, Proof and Choice of Law* (Oxford, Oxford University Press, 1998). Holding foreign law to be (as a matter of procedural) fact has practical consequences within the courtroom (relating to issues of pleading and proof, or the respective roles of judge and litigants). The assimilation is susceptible to degrees as far as judicial notice is concerned. On this last point, different legal systems impose more or less extensive duties on the courts in terms of gathering evidence on foreign rules and ascertaining meaning. The factors involved are whether the system is adversarial, and whether information is readily available (also to be factored in are language-skills and the unreliability of translation). Most higher courts do not usually risk engaging in hazardous determinations, given the linguistic and interpretative risks presented by foreign legal concepts; even among like-minded jurisdictions, the rate of error is high. The proceduralisation of foreign law is an *as-if* move, as seen above. But the law/fact distinction raises myriad further, more or less familiar, legal conundrums in respect of foreign law. Some pertain to the place of the social norm within the make-up of a legal rule; the issue arises for instance in connection with the law of unrecognised states, or in respect of the local 'rules of conduct' that can be invoked defensively by

is the light it might shed on the wider dilemmas relating to the production of legal knowledge evoked above. Taken (as it is traditionally in the context of the conflict of laws) as a largely procedural principle in respect of the law of other nations (a subtly *as-if* move that reduces law to fact), the essential justification of the disqualification of foreign law *qua* law is that of the deference due to the foreign sovereign: the state of the forum cannot (legitimately) participate in the interpretation or evolution of foreign law and must therefore do no more than passively observe, record and receive evidence of it as external reality. A widespread simile is that of photography, likened to the ascertainment of the content of foreign law at a given time: documentary evidence or expert witnesses are called upon to provide objective knowledge of the state of foreign law as it is 'out there' at that particular point. Paradoxically, then, the 'photography' or quest for objectivity, epistemologically impossible – unless under the most extreme expressions of legal formalism[408] – when the applicable rule is 'real' law (that is, domestic law), becomes possible (and indeed mandatory) when that rule is fact (that is, foreign law).

But of course the image of photography, if designed to illustrate objectivity, largely misses the mark; the assumption of objectivity runs into immediate trouble. The guesswork involved reintroduces in respect of foreign law an unsustainable conceptual distinction between the legal norm (whatever its form, legislative, judicial etc) and its meaning, or between application and interpretation, or even between cores of legal certainty and penumbral discretion.[409] Unsurprisingly, then, when called upon to be photographers, or objective observers, of foreign law, courts find themselves involved in a great deal of awkward guesswork,[410] while experts battle over the content and meaning of unfamiliar rules, in the light of foreign precepts of interpretation, constitutional values, analogous cases or dicta. Errors are frequent (including through linguistic mistakes or losses in translation) and raise the issue of the desirable degree of involvement of supreme courts in hermeneutical or other controversies over the content and meaning of foreign law.[411]

Belying monism's self-distanciation from social reality, such muddling signals that the distinction between law and fact, in this context as in others, cannot be sustained without a significant degree of artificiality or as-if fictionality (as if the court of the

the defendant in a tort claim (for instance, under EU 'Rome II' Regulation, Art 17). See on the use of 'data' in this context and within the conflict of laws more generally, S Symeonides, 'Rome II and Tort Conflicts: A Missed Opportunity' (2008) 56 *American Journal of Comparative Law* 173–222.

[408] The critical canon on this point is Duncan Kennedy's *A Critique of Adjudication: Fin de Siècle* (Cambridge MA, Harvard University Press, 1997) 105–07.

[409] Again, D Kennedy, 'A Left Phenomenological Alternative to the Hart/Kelsen Theory of Legal Interpretation' in *Legal Reasoning, Collected Essays* (Aurora CO, The Davies Book Publisher, 2008).

[410] For a good illustration of one of these conundrums, see K Lipstein, 'Proof of Foreign Law: Scrutiny of its Constitutionality and Validity' (1965) 42 *BYIL* 265.

[411] There is also the problem of whether a foreign court's interpretation of the forum court's own law, observably or potentially divergent from its own, can or must be accepted as proper legal grounds for the purposes of enforcement of a foreign judgment (see for example, the divergent interpretations of French law as between French and English courts in *Dallah Real Estate and Tourism Holding Co v Ministry of Religious Affairs, Government of Pakistan*, in the context of the enforcement/nullity of an arbitral award: on which, J Kleinheisterkamp, 'Lord Mustill and the Courts of Tennis – Dallah v Pakistan in England, France and Utopia' (2012) 75 *The Modern Law Review* 639).

forum state were the foreign court[412]) that may become deleterious or counterproductive at a certain point. However, once more, a closer comparison between the two concurrent methodologies of the conflict of laws in respect of the epistemological status of foreign law, or the definition of law's outer limits in relation to fact, shows that such contortions may actually be remarkably suggestive. While monism (and its Savignian or multilateralist expression) presupposes the existence of predefined limits between fact and law, the alternative statutist epistemology sees no difference between law and fact, between the pre-existing operation of law and its abstract content or potential, or between context or interpretation.[413]

An example can be provided from within the common law tradition, where an idiosyncratic ramification related to the status of foreign law appears in the guise of the doctrine of vested rights, borrowed from the Dutch statutist school.[414] This is a characteristic form of legal-fictional as-if reasoning,[415] passing as factual certainty. Under this theory, the court of the forum can only ever register, acknowledge or recognise legal events occurring within foreign territory in the shape in which they are framed, concretely or hypothetically, in foreign law. When there is a concrete and individual instantiation of the latter, notably as in a foreign judgment, it must therefore be registered as such. But a right thus embodied may also be a mere potentiality, requiring an anticipation of what the foreign court would surely do, were it to exert its jurisdiction.[416] This signals a specific non-modern or non-linear temporality, because it deliberately embroils the distinction between past application and future 'vesting' of a legal rule. By the same occasion, it also crosses the dividing line between self and other by commanding the former (the court of the forum state) to incarnate the latter (or put itself into the shoes of another court, operating in a foreign territory).

By way of conclusion on this point, it is useful to return to a further twist inside that very Roman tradition that gives its pedigree to monist-multilateralism. As seen above, according to Geoffrey Samuel, it is this same pedigree that confers upon law as a discipline an epistemological advantage in respect of other fields of knowledge (or 'science'[417]). 'The *Institutes* of Gaius', he writes, 'is more than just a systematic and coherent model of legal rules. It is a way of viewing social reality and social fact,

[412] On 'foreign court theory', see P Picone, *La méthode de la référence à l'ordre juridique compétent en droit international privé* (Rec. Cours Acad. Droit international de la Haye, vol 197).

[413] As seen above, nowhere is this more clear than under the vested rights doctrine, which systematically transformed foreign normative potentiality into a pre-existing, individualised fact invoked before the court of the forum state.

[414] See above 74.

[415] Vahinger. *The Philosophy of 'As If'*; for its use in the conflict of laws, see Riles, 'Cultural Conflicts', 273.

[416] This as-if device has another, further variation in the form of the 'foreign court theory', that invites the court to undertake a vast fictional adventure in guessing and following exactly what a given foreign court would do if seized of a factually identical case (for an interesting example involving Chinese law before Australian courts, see *Neilson v Overseas Projects Corporation of Victoria Ltd* [2005] HCA 54). Continental 'renvoi' tends to be understood as directing the court towards the abstract content of foreign law including its private international law rules, whereas within the common law tradition (or the foreign court theory), the fact of foreign law is the anticipation of the foreign decision (including its own use of renvoi ... wheels within wheels).

[417] GH Samuel, 'Is Law Really a Social Science? A View from Comparative Law' (2008) 67 *The Cambridge Law Journal* 288–321.

providing the means by which one can move with ease from fact to law and law to fact.'[418] Law is, in other words, a *passeur*, able to travel between different worlds or registers.[419] Law oscillates constantly between two registers of thought, fact and law, the general and the particular, the abstract and individual.[420] This signals an epistemological and an ontological problem with the law/fact divide. Importantly for the direction in which this book unfolds below, it also suggests that rather than being part of the problem, the muddling of this distinction may be an important aspect of the rethinking of an alternative, post-monist methodology. But before we get there, we need to gather some last, additional moss from the study of a third divide, between foreign and domestic, that (reflexively) sustains the two others.

C. Foreign/Domestic

A further field of inquiry, in response to the (pluralist) question of whether legality exists beyond its monist, state form, is the distinction, specific to the cross-border or to the field of the conflict of laws, between the foreign and the domestic. One instance of the latter is of course the modern legal and political gulf between national and foreigner. It grew out of early distinctions surrounding citizenship in the late Middle Ages, although it seems very doubtful that belonging to a community was thought of at that point as exclusionary.[421] The jurisdictional division of the various customs of Northern Italy and France along personal law lines was designed more to ensure a form of elective proximity between multiple, largely stable (and small-scale) populations and their modes of social regulation, than as the exclusive political marker that nationality would have become by the end of the nineteenth century.[422] Moreover, at the time of the early modern tracing of the territorial borders of statehood, these seem to have been places of passing or of itineraries of constant crossing and recrossing, rather than the reverse.[423] These boundaries gradually took on greater significance as state territory became inscribed within modernity's definition of law: they determined law's internal empire within the sovereign state and its other, on its foreign outside.

[418] Samuel, *Rethinking Legal Reasoning*, 143 et seq. See too Watson, 'The importance of Nutshells', prec.

[419] As will be seen in Part II of this book, this quality can be seen as part of legality's specific mode of existence. We shall return then to law as nomos, or a vision of law as social reality. The point here is only the epistemological one.

[420] This oscillation is of course particularly true, and indeed emblematic of legality, in (domestic) policy-focused analyses, economic regulatory law, or in constitutional or human rights approaches that involve balancing or proportionality tests. It also explains why conservative doctrines (notably in the French dogmatic tradition) discount such instances as being not 'properly' legal. See B Oppetit, 'Droit et économie', *Archives de philosophie du droit* (Sirey, 1992) 19–28.

[421] On this point see the study by P Gilli, 'Comment cesser d'être étranger? Citoyens et non-citoyens dans la pensée juridique italienne de la fin du Moyen Âge', in *Actes des congrès de la Société des historiens médiévistes de l'enseignement supérieur public*, 30ᵉ congrès, Göttingen, 1999. *L'étranger au Moyen Âge*, 59.

[422] Hence the 'principle' of nationality in Mancini's (subsequently marginalised and, post-world wars and post-fascism in Italy, much discredited) doctrine of private international law, a unitary conception of international law, straddling the public/private divide: see above 92.

[423] A Brett, *Changes of state. Nature and the Limits of the City in Early Modern Natural Law* (Princeton NJ, Princeton University Press, 2011).

In private international law, the spatial dividing line follows an apparently unproblematic definition of a threshold for the conflict of laws. The latter can only arise as such in international[424] collisions of norms, ones that do not fall within the space assigned to the sovereign's prescriptive monopoly. Simple at first glance, this parameter has proved highly elusive in practice, when confronted with the messier world beyond the monist imaginary of state – particularly when viewed as a territorial unit. The global turn has made law's work even more arduous, in the presence of both increasingly heterogeneous communities and greater interconnection across borders. First of all, at the margins, the divide between inside and outside raises a series of traditional difficulties. Thus 'national law' excludes, notably, conflicts involving unrecognised states;[425] it requires interpretation in cases of intra-federal conflicts (when the law of a federal state is designated by the choice of law rules of a third country);[426] and it also leaves out a-territorial transnational norms, that require specific theories of applicability.[427]

There are deeper complications that are less easily solved, however, because they trouble the very foundations of the monist model as reflected within private international law. Indeed, the latter's own 'theory of the frontier' assumes that collisions occur at the point at which state laws reach out, or individuals or things move, across territorial borders.[428] The formative nineteenth century, it is said, was the age of territory.[429] But far earlier still, in the conceptions of the early modern Dutch school,

[424] As Bentham would have it, 'between nations' (see above 80) as opposed to the *ius gentium*, applicable indiscriminately to public and private actors alike, across national divides.

[425] It has been noted, for instance, that in cases involving the inhabitants or property in territories of unrecognised states (that is, unrecognised by the forum state), courts have shown considerable flexibility, from time to time, in bypassing the formal requirements for citizenship in favour of more factual concepts of belonging. Whether in respect of Palestinian claimants, or migrants without citizenship, social effectivity has prevailed (in some cases) over formal recognition: K Knop, 'Citizenship, Public and Private', 71 *Law and Contemporary Problems* 309–42; M Karayanni, 'Choice of Law under Occupation: How Israeli Law Came to Serve Palestinian Plaintiffs' (2009) 5 *J Priv Int'l L* 1. See too D Gruenbaum, 'From Statehood to Effectiveness: The Law of Unrecognised States in Private International Law' (2022) 86 *Rabels Zeitschrift für ausländisches und internationales Privatrecht* 577–616 (40) arguing that applying the law of unrecognised states reveals the potential for the conflict of laws to grapple with non-state rules and with interactions of normative orders of all different sorts, regardless of their state pedigree.

[426] The conceptual conundrum is analogous here to more traditional issues regarding the admissibility of renvoi, or the treatment of conflicts of successive norms within the foreign order. The theoretical circularity is similar. According to the function assigned to the choice of law rule, the conflict will take place 'inside' the foreign order, or prior to reaching it. As far as territorial units of sovereign states are concerned, a distinct and context-sensitive practice has developed in the uniform private international law of the Hague Conference, as to the extent to which it will bypass the local choice of law rule and thereby modify the local ordering. The question here is where the frontier is drawn and further, the articulation with the (public) international law of treaties (see O Lissitzyn, 'Territorial Entities Other than Independent States in the Law of Treaties' 125 *Rec Cours*, préc).

[427] These include interrogations over the legal value of the *lex mercatoria* (as seen above), or the status of 'autonomous' substantive rules such as those of the 1980 Vienna Convention on the Sale of Goods when the buyer and seller are not both domiciled in contracting states, and more. These conundrums are often considered as belonging to the uncertain discipline of transnational trade (or commercial) law.

[428] The reference to J-P Niboyet's 'phenomenon of the frontier' is part of the canon of the conflict of law's 'general theory', as defined above 81. Metaphorically, or in terms of social geography, the political limits of the nation state are crossed similarly when citizens engage in dealings or personal relationships with foreigners, even in the forum state's territory (although, doctrinally, only in some areas of 'private' law).

[429] Charles S Maier hence proposed to acknowledge territoriality as the defining principle of the century between roughly 1860 and 1970, which he consequently classified as the 'Age of Territoriality'; CS Maier, 'Consigning the Twentieth Century to History: Alternative Narratives for the Modern Era', (2000) 105

prolonged over the centuries within the common law tradition (as we have seen above), vested rights were already events that 'took place' (as it were, literally), by the operation of a metaphor or fiction,[430] within the local jurisdictional sphere of the foreign legal system.[431] By contrast, civilian legal thought maintained a distinction, that bore the legacy of canon law, between personal and real statutes; the former had no need to take the form of a metaphorical or virtual entity such as a vested right because they were portable or extraterritorial, attached to the person even when crossing jurisdictional boundaries.[432]

This may help explain why, beyond the conventional clear-cut account of law's frontier, the line between the national and the foreign, the domestic and the external, or indeed the territorial and the extraterritorial has always been drawn according to very diverse patterns, reflecting multiple imaginaries, interests and policies. That its allocatory grid integrates a whole series of other parameters while purporting to defer to a cartography of territorial sovereignty is supported by Jacco Bomhoff's seminal exploration of the three distinct grammars of the 'reach of rights'.[433] As shown by this author, the question of the spatial scope of law receives different answers according to the characterisation of the problem for which it is framed (whether of the extension of human rights, constitutional theories of state action or conflict of laws). These of course were but new iterations of the multi-secular definitional debate between real and personal statutes.[434] That spatiality is not synonymous with territoriality does not come as a surprise, moreover. Multiple parameters have always defined law's space, even in the name of territorial sovereignty. In the end, there is no fixed point at which the national stops and the foreign starts.[435] While modern private international

American Historical Review 807–31. See too above 55, footnote 86 the citation from FA Mann's influential Hague lecture on 'The Doctrine of International Jurisdiction Revisited', p 20, in which he asserts, contrary to what he sees as contemporary erroneous ideas in the United States: 'As in the present world sovereignty is undoubtedly territorial in character, in assessing the extent of jurisdiction the starting point must necessarily be its territoriality such as it was developed over the centuries and defined by the Huber-Storyan maxims : as a rule jurisdiction extends (and is limited) to everybody and everything within the sovereign's territory and to his nationals wherever they may be'.

[430] On the feature of fiction as a fact we know *not* to be true, see Thomas, 'Les artifices de la vérité en droit commun médiéval'.

[431] Sometimes, as seen above, as in the theory of vested rights, foreign laws deployed their legal effects by way of the recognition of the 'fact' of their anticipated existence by the courts of the forum state; such facts were anticipated, and enforced as virtual reality (before the foreign sovereign itself had translated them into individualised public acts). In another version, rights were deemed 'transitory' and able to travel by themselves to a new location where they could glide into the local legal order.

[432] On portable personal status, see the early French decision on the defrocked Spanish monk *Busqueta* (Paris, 13 juin 1814, cited above); on portable citizenship and portable sovereignty, see more below 152.

[433] J Bomhoff, 'The Reach of Rights: "The Foreign" and "The Private" in Conflict-of-Laws, State-Action, and Fundamental-Rights Cases with Foreign Elements' (2008) 71 *Law and Contemporary Problems* 39–72.

[434] See above 99.

[435] The determination of the dividing line between what is inside and what is outside the domestic sphere creates a still greater dilemma when it is the cue for the entrance of the principle of 'party autonomy' (encountered above 113). Under this principle, international contracts are governed by the law chosen by the parties, while domestic contracts, contained within the domestic legal sphere, remain subject to local domestic law (and its specific rules on 'party autonomy'). On either side of the bright line, the difference of legal regimes is considerable. Transnationally connected or 'pluri-located' parties may contract out of otherwise applicable national regulatory frameworks (though not, as seen above, of state law as such) in favour of more liberal or more appropriate) regimes provided by foreign nation states. Contracts in the field of finance, investment, securities or insurance for instance, can and do benefit from the provisions of

law has always, formally, taken the geopolitical map of the world as a given, it has always been apparent that the dividing line between the domestic and the foreign is fundamentally indeterminate, and that ways of differentiating persons can follow a large variety of lines (or links), whether territorial, personal, situational or virtual.[436]

The point here, then, is to emphasise, under the conventional methodological approach, the definitional circularity of the place (the frontier) or the moment in time (the crossing) at which a situation could be said to be foreign for the needs of the conflict of laws. The only possible criterion is contained within the choice of law rule that designates a foreign law, since only then will it appear that there is indeed a conflict of laws to be solved; however, the application of such a rule is triggered in turn only when the law of the forum is involved in a conflict with a foreign law.[437] A lesson from the more pluralist vision provided by statutism is once again in order here. To circumvent this difficulty, it offers a legal fiction. The latter interposes

English law or New York law, usually in conjunction with contractual forum selection (including arbitration clauses), however strictly regulated at home. The only limit to this extraordinary empowerment of participants in the international market, it is usual to point out, is in the form of exceptional protective devices: public policy (within the meaning of private international law) or what are known as 'internationally' overriding or derogatory 'mandatory rules' or *lois de police* (as for instance in the EU Rome I Regulation on the law applicable to contractual obligations, Art 9). Unsurprisingly, however, the parameters of this bright line between domestic and international contracts have always proved elusive. Courts, legislators and international treaties have attempted all manner of geographical and economic 'tests'. But in the end, as underlined in the text above, there is no fixed point at which the national stops and the foreign starts.

[436] This does not exclude location, nor the importance of place, however, as private international law shows. Phenomenology makes this point when it postulates that all human experience must be embodied, or 'take place' (as we shall see below 139). As Hans Lindahl points out, even eBay is located *somewhere* ('Place-Holding the Future',) – even though it must be added that such necessary emplacement is also inevitably constructed (by dint of corporate choices, whereabouts of servers, bits, etcetera) and can be multiple (or ubiquitous?). A similar observation extends to law's temporality, that is far from reflecting modernity's linear or chronological model.

[437] This logical difficulty is sometimes signalled, in certain (civilian, or non-adversarial) legal systems, in connection with the procedural regime of the choice of law rule, where it appears as the problem of 'internationality'. When a situation extends beyond the domestic sphere, the court is (sometimes) under a duty to either to draw the attention of the litigating parties to the possible consequences of the foreign element (or 'element of extraneity') in terms of displacement of the law of the forum, or, more directively, to indicate the applicability of a foreign law under which they must then present their claims. This presupposes identifying a situation that is potentially subject to foreign law by reason of the presence of foreign elements; it may turn out however, in the end, that the possibly relevant choice of law rule does not designate such foreign law as applicable and the situation falls back into the domestic sphere. If such is the case, however, then the duty of the court to take notice of the internationality of the dispute also falls of its own accord and we are back to square one. A good example is the drafting history of the Rome Convention, now the 'Rome I' Regulation, between Member States of the European Union (the then European Community) Art 3§3. The carefully negotiated text could do no better than specify that 'Where all other elements relevant to the situation at the time of the choice are located in a country other than the country whose law has been chosen, the choice of the parties shall not prejudice the application of provisions of the law of that other country which cannot be derogated from by agreement'. Whereas the whole point of the text was to set in stone the principle of party choice as the mainstay of the common, internal, market, the definition of the conflict of laws was designed to outlaw fraud. But it then becomes apparent that not only is the internationality of contract impossible to define but that its counterpart, fraud, is equally elusive. It has happened that, in the end, some courts have given up trying to define the limits of the domestic sphere and referred back to the will of the parties to define the internationality (or lack of it) of their contract (for an example, Cass civ I, 4th October 2005, 02-12.959, n° de pourvoi 02-12.959: 'dans la commune volonté des parties, la situation n'avait pas de caractère international').

a suspended, 'instant of reason', during which the court can proceed *as if* such a conflict existed, explore the potentially applicable laws and validate the result once all the potential claims have been examined and their respective weight assessed. This *as if* moment suspends the ordinary chain of legal reasoning.[438] It involves a form of imaginary diplomacy, in which a first unsatisfactory outcome can be revisited until a more palatable version of each claim can be found. In other words, it displays the 'sublime art of compromise'.[439]

In this respect, the problem with the distinction between inside and outside is perfectly identified by Hans Lindahl as linked to the 'Cartesian residue' that continues to command our modern idea of spatiality[440] and the binary oppositions between inside and outside, or self and foreign.[441] As this philosopher points out, contemporary sociologies of globalisation are themselves prisoner of the idea that the world is an abstract space.[442] This point can be taken further here, to emphasise that there is no a priori reason, given contemporary transformations of political spatialities, to distinguish methodologically between conflicts of norms occurring on the 'inside' and the 'outside' of each national polity, or, between situations which are domestic and those which are international.[443] Another way of acknowledging the same point is to say that cultural (or, looking ahead, ecological-environmental) conflicts occur in similar ways whether or not the protagonists are separated by national frontiers. The disorder and fragmentation of our normative universe points to modern law's difficulty in dealing with the loss of centre or an Archimedean point.[444]

[438] This particular form of *as-if* is at the very core of American 'interests analysis', notably because the combined 'interests analysis' and jurisdictional argument can lead to finding no actual conflict (the 'false conflict' hypothesis (above, 83).

[439] Latour, *Enquête*.

[440] And indeed temporality. As we shall see below 212, private international law illustrates the extraordinary plurality of legal 'chronotopes', in which differences of scale, chronology and perspective combine in equally multiple ways.

[441] The ontological conundrum raised by the status of the sea in Roman law, as seen above (is the sea of an essence such that it remains outside the empire of [Roman] law [and the authority of the Roman emperor]?) has a contemporary incarnation in the elusive legal regime of cyberspace. Is the virtual world different in essence from the real (or terrestrial) or is it only dispersed in multiple locations? As Hans Lindahl observes, an affirmative reply presupposes that cyberspace and the immaterial or dematerialised events and operations that compose it are ontologically different from our tangible reality. But of course, as he says ('Place-Holding the Future' 153) there is only one world! New technologies are only one more instance of the multiplication of practical and conceptual means of communication and action.

[442] Lindahl, 'Place-Holding the Future' (see the passages on 'Globalisation as localisation', p 15 et seq).

[443] See H Muir Watt, 'Conflicts of laws unbounded: the case for a legal-pluralist revival' (2016) 7 *Transnational Legal Theory* 313–53.

[444] The familiar 'legal fragmentation' in international law can also be formulated in terms of language games, postmodernity, social communication systems, hyper-specialisation, etc (for instance, JF Lyotard, *La Condition postmoderne. Rapport sur le savoir* (Paris, Minuit, 1979) announcing the end of the grand narratives (*'grands récits')* typical of modernity (the history of humanity as enlightened progress, for example)). See X de la Vega, 'Jean-François Lyotard (1924–1998) – La fin des grands récits', *Sciences Humaines*, Hors-série N° 6 – Octobre–novembre 2007: 'À l'âge postmoderne, chaque domaine de compétence est séparé des autres, et possède un critère qui lui est propre. Il n'y a aucune raison que le « vrai » du discours scientifique soit compatible avec le « juste » visé par la politique ou le « beau » de la pratique artistique. Chacun doit donc se résoudre à vivre dans des sociétés fragmentées où coexistent plusieurs codes sociaux et moraux mutuellement incompatibles.' On this point, see again two classic works in Anglo-Canadian-American political philosophy, C Taylor, 'On the Diversity of Goods' in *Philosophical Papers, Philosophy and the Human Sciences* vol 2; M. Walzer, *Spheres of Justice: A Defense of Pluralism and Equality* (Basic Books, 1983).

The post-monist alternative vision of law locates it in a non-territorial 'terrestrial'[445] place, disconnected from state. Its project is not to restore unity, but to make sense of disorder or hybridity writ large.

But (it might be objected) does law not require, emblematically, a judgment in the sense of a final closure through veridiction (jurisdiction) that leaves no room for hesitation? In the eyes of law's modern forms, it is certainly paradoxical to promote a jurisprudence made of rhizome-like[446] modes of legal reasoning, that move in between the self and the other.[447] This is tantamount to preaching a suspension of judgement or *epochē*, a posture of non-involvement.[448] However, on the one hand, there is a different way to understand the latter. In phenomenological terms, Husserl saw scepticism as a practice of Cartesian doubt, methodic and tentative, that should lead to a bracketing or transcendental suspension of all common-sense beliefs relating to the natural-empirical world, without ceasing to believe in them, nevertheless.[449] This is certainly an essential part of a critical legal consciousness, particularly when informed by an awareness of the temporal and spatial relativity of all legal institutions.[450] On the other hand, as we shall now see in Part II below, methodic doubt can be correlated with an alternative view of law's mode of existence. The latter can be understood as ceaseless oscillation, weaving in and out and back and forth between different arguments, rather than being braced on impossible distinctions such as those that separate fact and law, the national and the foreign or state and non-state forms of legality.

ECLOSION

The heuristic value of the above account for possible transformation of legal-theoretical visions of law and in the light of current ecological imperatives, lies in the unknitting of all these peculiar dualisms. Proceeding from the more general conviction that the fabric of legal thought affects our perceptions of our surrounding world, the exploration above takes seriously the specific techniques deployed by the methodologies of the conflict of laws. In this respect, like all modern legal forms, the conflict of laws has been traversed historically by changing ideas of nature and

Similarly, Ludwig Wittgenstein's '*Investigations philosophiques (Philosophische Untersuchungen)* (published posthumously 1953) tells of the plurality of language games each subject to its own rules that are incommensurable in respect of the others.

[445] On terrestriality as a form of anti- or non-modernity, see B Latour, *Où suis-je? Leçons du confinement à l'usage des terrestres* (Paris, La Découverte, 2021).

[446] On the metaphor of the rhizome as opposed to linearity (and hierarchy), see G Deleuze, and F Guattari, *A Thousand Plateaus,* trans B Massumi (London and New York, Continuum, 2004). Vol 2 of *Capitalism and Schizophrenia* 2 vols 1972–1980. Trans of *Mille Plateaux* (Paris, Les Editions de Minuit). See too below 174.

[447] On the important concept of in-between as a legal ontology, see below 181.

[448] In other words, a posture of non-involvement allowing the attainment of peace of mind in everyday life, promoted by the classical Greek Sceptics.

[449] Enc Britannica, V° 'Epochè'. On the ecological turn to phenomenology, see below 271.

[450] See, promoting this stance, Frankenberg, *Comparative law as critique*; see too, H Muir Watt, 'Discours sur les méthodes'.

society; of time and space; of knowledge and power and their mutual relationship. Operating beyond the confines of state, it has, to a large extent provided an echo chamber to modern epistemological thought. However, its own peculiar trajectory also suggests that under this conventional surface, there exists an alternative jurisprudential vision of legality that gives place to plurality, entanglements and hybridity. It is no surprise, then, that recent interdisciplinary feminist scholarship has identified in this trajectory a specific 'intellectual style' for dealing with complexity.[451]

[451] Knop and Riles, 'Space, Time and Historical Injustice' (on which see more below 213).

Part II

Aesthetics and Ontology: Constructing the *Nomos* of the In-Between

Nomos, in the words of Robert Cover, is the normative universe we inhabit.[1] It is the legal expression of our *episteme*,[2] or lifeworld.[3] In this respect, our *nomos* must be understood as both form-giving and provider of meaning.[4,5] This Second Part of the book is largely then about the relationship between legal form and substance.[6] It suggests that the conflict of laws, in all its methodological

[1] 'Nomos and Narrative', is an axis of the law and humanities canon (R Cover, 'Foreword: *Nomos* and Narrative' (1983) 87 (4) *Harv LR* 4, 5: 'No set of legal institutions or prescriptions exists apart from the narratives that locate it and give it meaning. For every constitution there is an epic, for each decalogue a scripture. Once understood in the context of the narratives that give it meaning, law becomes not merely a system of rules to be observed, but a world in which we live … The varied and complex materials of that *nomos* establish paradigms for dedication, acquiescence, contradiction, and resistance … To inhabit a *nomos* is to know how to *live* in it … In this normative world, law and narrative are inseparably related … This *nomos* is as much "our world" as is the physical universe of mass, energy, and momentum.' He adds in a footnote (10): 'I mean here to suggest a rough correspondence to the Kuhnian understanding of "science" not as a body of propositions about the world nor as a method, but as paradigms integrating method, belief, and propositions – a doing.' On the contrasting Schmittian conception of *nomos*, see below.)

[2] Foucault, *Les Mots et les Choses*; analogous concepts are schema (Pelluchon, *Ethique de la Considération*), collective imaginaries (Mazurel, *L'inconscient ou l'oubli de l'histoire*), belief-system (J D'Aspremont, *After Meaning. The Sovereignty of Forms in International Law* (Cheltenham, Elgar Studies in Legal Theory, 2021), paradigms (Samuel, *Rethinking Legal Reasoning*), (legal) consciousness (D Kennedy, 'Three Globalizations of Law and Legal Thought: 1850–2000' in D Trubek and A Santos (eds), *The New Law and Economic Development* (Cambridge MA, Harvard University Press, 2010). On hegemony, as a means of understanding how these mental frameworks exert power over our lives, see below 256 (23, 167).

[3] The concept of 'Lifeworld' is associated with Husserl's phenomenology (the phenomenological environment from which we draw our subjectivity, see below, Part III), and with the vision underlying indigenous epistemologies (see A Mills, 'The Lifeworlds of Law: On Revitalizing Indigenous Legal Orders Today' (2016) 61(4) *McGill LJ* 847, 862: 'The roots of a society are its lifeworld: the story it tells of creation, which reveals what there is in the world and how we can know. Creation stories disclose what a person is, what a community is, and what freedom looks like').

[4] On the idea that 'mankind' is suspended in semiotic webs of signification (or 'culture') that it has woven for itself see C Geertz, *The Interpretation of Cultures* (Paris, Macat, 2017) 256).

[5] See from a legal-anthropological perspective, Pottage, 'Introduction'. From a social-legal perspective, Poul Kjaer writes that 'a central contribution of law to the rest of society is form giving, in which a social exchange becomes an economic exchange when given legal form and status through instruments such as contracts and property rights, and a social exchange becomes a political act when unfolded as formal legally-framed decision-making or when relying on legally-constructed citizen rights, such as the right to vote, and other constitutional principles' ('The law of political economy: an introduction', in *The Law of Political Eonomy*, 12).

[6] For the canon on legal form and substance, see O Wendell Holmes, *The Common Law* (1900; published by the Gutenberg Project in e-book form): 'The life of the law has not been logic: it has been

and epistemological duality (described in Part I above), can serve heuristically to underscore two (broad) opposing patterns or models of law,[7] this time through their aesthetic and ontological dimensions.[8] On the one hand, the dominant shape and content of Western legality[9] has evolved in cadence with statehood, secularism and capitalism (with its intrinsic colonial dimension and successive trans-formations).[10] The main achievement of the moderns, as Bruno Latour wryly observes, has been to universalise these (legal) forms. The latter have facilitated the collective cecity and amnesia that allow the 'anthropocentric machine'[11] to hurtle on regardless, devastating life in its path and devouring the very resources it needs to survive.[12]

On the other hand, however, this scheme is at once challenged by an emerging alternative and is haunted by its very own shadow opposite,[13] which resurfaces

experience … The substance of the law at any given time pretty nearly corresponds, so far as it goes, with what is then understood to be convenient; but its form and machinery, and the degree to which it is able to work out desired results, depend very much upon its past.' For the equally canonical demonstration of the solidarity between form and substance in private law, see D Kennedy, 'Form and Substance in Private Law Adjudication' (1976) 89 *Harvard Law Review* 1685.

[7] As will become apparent, this opposition or duality opposes (very broadly) dominant Western modern models of legal thought versus the non-modern (or, 'naturalism' as in Descola, *Par delà Nature et Culture*, versus all the others). However, this pairing does not imply that 'the rest' (the non-modern or non-naturalist) are one or monolithic. As Descola shows, the world contains multiple non-naturalistic schemes (or modes of conceiving relationality and identity) that should clearly not be 'lumped together'. The same goes for categories such as 'indigenous' approaches to the world (and to law). Nevertheless, in some contexts, the assemblage of all the latter on one (the other) side of the divide between currently dominant modern versus minoritarian non-modern is necessary for the purposes of critique (particularly of law as shaped by neoliberalism). Beyond the context of this critique, the project in this book is resolutely pluralistic and recognises the world's 'pluriversality' (as seen below).

[8] The 'ontological turn' in French anthropology (covering Latour, Descola and Viveiros de Castro, to whose work we return frequently below) has been criticised as merely another name for Wittgensteinian or Lyotardian language games (see Fischer, 'The lightness of existence and the origami of "French" anthropology'). Analogous critiques were addressed in their time to former incarnations of (philosophical) French theory. What follows draws resolutely from this 'turn' (and includes its play with words).

[9] In this context, our contemporary condition is described in various terms in as many disciplinary vocabularies: late-modern, anthropocentric, capitalocentric, neoliberal, or naturalist. As suggested above, 'our' here refers to a perspective either of individual liberal and supposedly free subjects; of the Western tradition as superior, more rational or more 'civilised' than all others; or again of humanity as naturally endowed with specific intelligence and virtues in respect of other species. The common factor linking these various labels is a world view that separates human society from nature, empties places of all other belief systems and neglects other forms of life (see for example, Mick Smith's 'extinction studies', in which he confronts the sense of the world and senseless extinction in ecological terms: *An Ethics of Place: Radical Ecology, Postmodernity, and Social Theory* (SUNI, 2001)). Legality has participated in the shaping of this perception as we shall see progressively below. However, as will become clear, what follows is *not* an indictment of modernity as such, nor of enlightenment per se, nor indeed of technology. Nor does it signify that our *nomos* cannot change, as we shall see.

[10] H Brabazon (ed), *Neoliberal Legality: Understanding the Role of Law in the Neoliberal Project* (New York, Routledge, 2016).

[11] G Agamben, *Open: Man and Animal* (Palo Alto CA, Stanford University Press, 2002), taking up Descartes' concept of the 'animal machine'.

[12] On the political-economic dimension of the Anthropocene, see below Part III, which also questions the fruitfulness of exploring both (non-modern) indigenous cosmologies and (Western) post-Holocaust phenomenology as a means of accessing the world after extinction, or once 'breakdown' taken place.

[13] The idea that a norm secretes its own opposite, a central part of the deconstructive critique of law (as seen above) can also be related to the structure of our *nomos*. Normalisation, writes Jean-Luc Nancy, 'dessine les contours de la marge et de l'anormalité, monde sublunaire et dégradé. Car si les normes,

faintly and unexpectedly from time to time. It coexists then with an alternative 'minor jurisprudence',[14] an 'abyssal' model[15] made of (ontological) hybridity or interstitiality and (aesthetic) entwinement and oscillation. The argument that unfolds below is that the resilient presence of 'nature' within the form and substance of modern law entails an (often twisted or aporetical) dialectic between a rationalist project of legal ordering (monism) pursued from an overarching external standpoint, and a shrouded (or less rationalist) penumbra of entanglement[16] between multiple normative worlds. This perspective shows up shadows, but also reflections and invisible forces – as in Lynn Margulis' 'symbiotic planet' as a matter of evolutionary biology,[17] or in Eulalia de Valdenebro's 'metanthropical principle' as expressed in art forms.[18]

Aesthetics, writes Georgio Agamben, is 'signature' and law is emblematically such.[19] It gives a visible shape to our reality; a lens through which we read the

explicites ou tacites, forment et conforment les êtres, les choses et les mots, c'est toujours accompagnée de son contraire que la norme constitue ses objets. La plupart du temps en effet, les normes s'ordonnent à la logique des oppositions binaires qui déclinent leurs valeurs antagonistes, à commencer par celles du normal et de l'anormal. Nous sommes ainsi constitués par des normes qui, infiltrant tout, commandent notre être au monde, c'est-à-dire comment vivre, travailler, penser ou aimer pour participer à la normalisation générale, être normé, normatif et normal' (Préface, C Fallen *L'anomalie créatrice* (Paris, Kime, 2012)). On law's binaries, see above 103.

[14] P Goodrich, *Law in the Courts of Love: Literature and Other Minor Jurisprudences* (Abingdon, Routledge, 1996).

[15] The term is borrowed from B de Sousa Santos, *Demodiversity: Toward Post-Abyssal Democracies* (Abingdon, Routledge, 2020). Its connotation is positive here.

[16] Entanglement is a metaphor to be found very frequently in ecological thought of all kinds, and is often used (as it will be hereafter) in opposition to linear or grid-like division between humanity and nature induced by modern 'jurisdictional thinking'. Some of the important points made below follow the path drawn by socio-technical legal studies (or science and technology studies as applied to law). The latter emphasises, importantly, that in humanity's entanglement with nature, technology cannot be left out of the picture, since it is inextricably linked with both: see S Jasanoff, *States of Knowledge: The Co-Production of Science and Social Order* (London, Routledge, 2004); B Latour, 'Love your monsters: Why We Must Care for Our Technologies As We Do Our Children' in M Shellenberger (ed), *Love Your Monsters: Postenvironmentalism and the Anthropocene* (Breakthrough Institute, 2011); Haraway, *Simians, Cyborgs, and Women*, presenting the cyborg as a material/semiotic figure that implodes the dichotomies of nature/technology, human/non-human, male/female; E Fox Keller, *The Mirage of a Space Between Nature and Nurture* (Durham NC, Duke University Press, 2010), observing that the vulgarisation of Darwinism sees the 'struggle for existence' as nothing but the competition for some environmental resource in short supply, ignoring the large body of evidence about the actual complexity of the relationship between organisms and their resources. Indeed, organisms do not simply use resources present in the environment but, through their life activities, produce such resources and actually 'manufacture' their environments. In Part III below, we return to the ravages caused by the vulgate of Darwinism as political or economic theory.

[17]] For a convenient access to this highly complex ecological thought, much celebrated by Bruno Latour, see L Margulis, *Symbiotic Planet: A New Look at Evolution* (Basic Books, 1998).

[18] On the description of private international law as a dismal swamp, see above 45. On the aesthetic of the swamp, the work of Brazilian literary critic Silviano Santiago (*The Space in-between: Essays on Latin American Culture* (Durham NC, Duke University Press, 2001) is particularly interesting on the idea (developed in the 1970s) of the swamp as an 'in-between space' (*o entre-lugar*, in Portuguese). On the swamp as a place from which to build an alternative vegetal cosmovision or '*principe métanthropique*', see the work (botanical painting, videos, texts) of artist and ecosophical theorist Eulalia de Valdenebro, 'Le principe métanthropique: Faire lieu à partir d'une épistémè végétale possible', PhD thesis, Univ Paris 8, 2022. As this work shows, the swamp contains all manner of shadows, reflections, blurring of lines, echoes and (as in the imprint of wind or fog) invisible forces.

[19] If aesthetics is 'signature', then law is the mother of all signatures (Agamben, *The Signature of All Things* 33 et seq, referring to the core *episteme* of the treatise of Paracelsus, *De Natura Rerum*, according to which all things bear a sign or signature that manifests and reveals their invisible qualities, in correspondence with the cosmos). The language of the law is the archetype of *signature* – meaning that before

world.[20] As Pierre Schlag writes, 'legal aesthetics covers all the representations, tropes, and imageries that we associate with legality and that actually shape the way we think about the world'.[21] Law, he observes, is

> an aesthetic enterprise. Before the ethical dreams and political ambitions of law can even be articulated, let alone realised, the aesthetics of law have already shaped the medium within which those projects will have to do their work. In this conception, the aesthetic pertains to the forms, images, tropes, perceptions, and sensibilities that help shape the creation, apprehension, and even identity of human endeavours, including, most topically, law.

Law indubitably co-produced the aesthetic of modernity in its mapping out of space in visual terms.[22] It drew frontiers – between territories and empires, centres and peripheries, sovereigns and proprietors, simultaneously extending empires and enclosing land. This legal enterprise of division and classification, hierarchisation and structuration, carved up both society and planet in an obsessive 'rage for order'.[23] Such a particular, obsessional form of legal ordering – in the name of science, nature or reason – reinforced the severance of humanity from its surroundings. A separatist approach to 'nature' in such terms rests upon assumptions that are analogous to modern legal views of alterity in cultural, political or human form.[24] In stark contrast

being signification, it belongs to the sphere of *forms* that manifest and reveal invisible qualities and meanings. Signature, he writes, is what allows us to trace the genealogy of modern law's secular concepts back to something else, such as theology, for example. This follows on M Foucault, *Les mots et les choses, Une archéologie des sciences humaines* (Paris, Gallimard, 1966) 40 et seq, describing 'the secret order of things', where deep analogies appeared as signs at their surface. This cosmology prevailed in European thought (on its 'obsessional' form see Descola, *Par delà Nature et Culture* 358) until the Renaissance reversed the relationship between the visible and the invisible (Foucault, ibid, 41; on the dramatic 'decomposition' of this cosmology in Europe on the coming of modernity, Descola, ibid, 329, 428). It is also that of non-Western 'analogist' belief systems (ibid, 359). Its role in medieval thought prior to modernity may explain why such signatures are so apparent within the law. As can be seen in the text above, metaphors – particularly with a 'natural' dimension, such as bodies, organisms, human nature, Gaia – play a particularly salient role in law, while, conversely, scientific (life and earth sciences) thought borrows from legal imagery. Defining images as 'agents of the social', making visible the cosmological schemes of continuity and discontinuity between humans and non-humans, see P Descola, *Les formes du visible* (Paris, éd du Seuil, 2021). This insight is particularly relevant in law and singularly so in the conflict of laws, where perspective – the great discovery of modernity that originated in art (E Panofsky) – is central, as we shall see later. See moreover in respect of law, the use of art (the photographic portraits of Omar Victor Diop) by Daniel Maldonado Bonilla (*Legal Barbarians. Identity, Modern Comparative Law and the Global South* (Cambridge, Cambridge University Press, 2021)) to illustrate the othering of non-Western subjects or 'legal barbarians'.

[20] Again, on the foundational role of the Roman invention of legal epistemology in this respect, see above 16, 22.

[21] P Schlag, 'The Aesthetics of American Law' (2001–2002) 115 *Harvard Law Review* 1047 draws on the Greek etymology of our term aesthetics (*aisthetikos*), meaning perception or sensation. Among law's tropes, nature (along with the 'organic' structure of legal systems, the 'body politic', the body corporate and more), as we have seen, occupies a substantial discursive place and has allowed multiple displacements of focus and perspective. Law's imagery, fictions and metaphors can be seen as the aesthetic 'signature' of deeper, underlying ontological, epistemological or ethical projects or beliefs: Agamben, *The signature of all things*.

[22] On the denial of the irrational and the reign of the visual, see Descola, *Les formes du visible*. On the idiom of co-production, as between law and science/technology, see Jasanoff, *States of Knowledge*.

[23] Benton and Ford, *Rage for Order*.

[24] It is sometimes rightly pointed out that environmentalist politics, following an eminently modern universalist ideal, tends to leave out the colonial aspect. But this objection is not relevant in respect of the many strands of political ecology that take this connection to be essential, as will be seen progressively below.

to this dominant legal aesthetic, a shadow model helps address the question of what the legal signature of entangled, symbiotic lifeworlds might look like.[25] Following Philippe Descola's invitation to explore the (often invisible) 'forms of the visible',[26] an alternative vision, to be found in various non-modern (ecological) epistemologies and (indigenous) cosmologies, might help us 'disincarcerate' the subject/object divide[27] and increase our awareness of the interdependence of all forms of biological and cultural life on a planetary scale. This aesthetic of fragile entanglement can be correlated in turn to a 'moral economy of intimacy',[28] in which (market) exchange is an endless reciprocal flow of gift and counter-gift.[29]

Indeed, (aesthetic) representations of nature have also played an essential role within the further (ontological) register of law's mode of existence. Modern legality has often been depicted by means of metaphors that partake in the 'ruse of naturalism', insofar as they make a given world-vision carried by law seem to go without saying or '*allant de soi*'. But of course, any such imagery presupposes in turn a certain conception of nature itself,[30] variously understood over time as composed of the cosmos and its signs, or the body and its organs, or the biosphere, and depicted equally diversely as harmony or wilderness, celestial order, or the uncanny sublime.[31] As the metaphor of the 'body politic' shows, throughout the history of modernity,

[25] In aesthetic terms, there is a contrast to be expected between the forms or styles induced by coloniality (as defined by W Mignolo, see below) and those of entanglement. On the aesthetic dimensions of deep ecology ethics and ecofeminist thought see below, Part III.

[26] Descola, *Les formes du visible*. This work invites an important observation in respect of what is portrayed in this book as the 'shadow' version of the conflict of laws – or, as will be further seen below, with regard to its relation to the metaphor of the 'dismal swamp'. The idea of the shadow also includes reflections, echoes and invisible realities underlying visible forms. On pp 31–33 of Descola's book (under the title 'Le signe incarné', p 31), there is an illuminating account of different modes of visible 'representation' of invisible realities whose original forms are unknowable to us. A rock may be the visible incarnation or a receptacle of a divinity, an iconic 'representation' of a spirit in the same way that a diplomat can be said to 'represent' their country: not a mimetic figuration but the visible image of a nation in the eyes or the gaze of the host country. On hospitality towards alterity in whatever visible shape it chooses to take, see below 292 et seq.

[27] Latour, *Enquête* 10. Borrowing from another perspective would partake of a 'symmetrical anthropology' of the moderns. Such a gaze turned on self would mean, in legal terms, observing one's own legal world (see below 282, 300).

[28] Marcel Mauss's famous discovery of the relations of entanglement induced by exchange as gift provides a social model that is an alternative to neoliberal atomisation, and a grounding of the economy that contrasts with that of market or profit; see below. In his canonical *The Gift: Forms and Functions of Exchange in Archaic Societies* (London, Cohen & West, 1966; reprinted in Paperback, 2011, with an introduction by EE Evans-Pritchard); in French: 'Essai sur le don. Forme et raison de l'échange dans les sociétés archaïques' (1923–24) *Année Sociologique*, republished in *Sociologie et anthropologie*, 4th edn (Paris, PUF, 1968)), he compares gift-giving and exchange in 'archaic' societies, in which gift creates a moral bond and the return of the gift involves honour and respect. On the moral economy of gift, see further, Descola, *Les formes du visible* 541 describing a cosmic economy of sharing, a constant flow of gifts and counter gifts, a sort of moral economy of the intimate, ending in a form of ontological entanglement.

[29] Descola, *Par delà Nature et Culture* 349.

[30] Trees (with branches and roots), webs (the common law), living organisms (the Napoleonic Civil Code; the European Convention of Human Rights …), the 'life of the law' (Holmes), the wilderness beyond civilisation or the pale of the law … not to mention 'natural law'). Nature is also depicted in legal-theoretical literature as a metaphorical void of lawlessness occupied by the sovereign exception (as sublime – awesome, unruly, violent, irrational): see too above 11.

[31] See C Tang, *The Geographic Imagination of Modernity* (Palo Alto CA, Stanford University Press, 2008); Globinar, Sciences po, September 2021; Monateri, *Dominus Mundi*.

complex, reflexive borrowings between *nomos* and *physis*, biology and biography, have either founded the political community on various forms of transcendence, theological or secular, or, reciprocally, modelled scientific understandings of the natural world on the life of the law.[32]

In this respect, the Western metaphysical tradition has given rise to a belief in the 'natural' severance of society (or culture, or Man) from the surrounding world, over which it exercises an innate mastery. In other words (those of Philippe Descola), the separatist understanding of our relationship to our surroundings (biological and geological, sentient and non-sentient, visible and invisible, human and animal) has largely supported the assertion of 'humanity's ontological privilege' over all other forms of life.[33] It rests on the (self-)ascribed essence of 'human nature', understood as exclusively endowed with rationality (or intelligent access to reality). Legal modernity reflects and reinforces this understanding through the axial categories through which it channels our access to the real world, splitting mind from body, persons from things, agency from environment.[34] Indeed, law was present at the very origin of this severance of nature from society. Gradually detaching its abstract forms from the materiality of life,[35] it shaped modern metaphysics,[36] co-producing the conditions for humanity's subjugation of its surrounding world. Modern law's 'first' nature is to be found, then, in the terms of the bifurcation between the natural and cultural or social worlds that reflected the original Roman legal[37] (and Byzantine theological) distinctions between mind and body, persons and things.[38]

[32] Transformations in science fed legal imaginaries in turn, while simultaneously being shaped by law. So much so that in turn, a distinctly legal metaphor such as the body politic travelled back to the natural sciences, with significant epistemological consequences, losing much in translation (as shown in Latour's 'body politics', see Latour et al, *The Body Politic)*. Monateri shows, in *Dominus Mundi*, how the sublime body of the king hovered between nature and imaginary. Moreover, as Derrida contended, the beast (representations of nature) and the sovereign (conceptions of the political) are connected, because neither animals nor kings are subject to the law – the sovereign stands above it, while the beast is excluded from below (*L'animal que donc je suis* (Paris, éd Galilée, 2006). This suggests an intriguing triangulation between law, sovereign power and nature (on which, below 156 et seq; 166 et seq).

[33] According to Descola's already much-cited expression, *Par delà Nature et Culture* 306.

[34] See above 101.

[35] Schiavone, *Ius* 277.

[36] On this point, see above, 17. On a critical view of (modern, Western) metaphysics that links the aesthetics (form) to the substance (meaning), see J Derrida, 'La mythologie blanche' (1972) *Poétique* 5: 'white mythology' is 'metaphysics which has effaced in itself that fabulous scene which brought it into being, and which yet remains, active and stirring, inscribed in white ink, an invisible drawing covered over in the palimpsest'.

[37] In this respect, the twin fathering of (asymmetrical) anthropology and (modern) comparative law in Henry Summer Maine's *Ancient Law* (1863) began from the premise that Roman law still governed the institutions of civil(ised) society (*Ancient Law: In Connection with the Early History of Society and its Relation to Modern Ideas* (London, 1863)). On the contribution of Summer Maine to the foundation of (modern) comparative law and anthropology, see the critical account by V Corcodel, *Modern law and otherness: the dynamics of inclusion and exclusion in comparative legal thought* (Cheltenham, Elgar, 2019).

[38] As this book goes to press, France's national museum, Le Louvre, is showing an art historical exhibition on 'Les Choses. Une histoire de la Nature Morte', curated by (and for the first time, acknowledged as 'authored' by) L Bertrand-Dorleac (www.louvre.fr/en-ce-moment/expositions/les-choses#presentation). It explores the relationship between life and things, and the multiple, ineffable links between thing-ness and personhood, the visible and the invisible, the archaic and the postmodern, through artistic representation of things from the very ancient or archaic to the very contemporary. This use of the aesthetics of (un)still life as a way of challenging some of the embedded distinctions put in place by modernity fits perfectly within this Part of the book, as will be seen below.

The distinction between *res/persona* still structures our thought (as seen above) in ways that are properly juridical.[39] In the terms of Kyle McGee, significantly, it explains indeed 'why chains of legal reasoning take the shape they do'.[40] The initial divide between persons and things was mirrored in turn by further epistemological separations between subject and object, self and environment. Law – along with science and technology, sovereignty and politics, metaphysics and economics – partook thereby in the vast co-production of modernity. Such categorisations have become unsustainable in the context of an ecosystem of ever-increasing intricacy between humans and non-humans, science and mythology, society and nature, life and technology.

Moreover, equally importantly, humanity's ontological privilege over its non-human surroundings is refracted in turn through an analogous prerogative asserted by Western modernity in relation to the rest of the (culturally 'primitive') world and its inhabitants (possibly devoid of soul or fully human nature).[41] This visual ordering of nature endorses coloniality as a negation of alterity,[42] insofar as there is an evident mirror effect or echo between the legal shape of humanity's relationship to the so-called *natural* world (whether composed of animals, minerals or things, visible or invisible) and the form it gives to interactions, hierarchies and divisions within the *social* world. Law's contribution to the ontological distance between the social and the natural[43] also enabled the unrestricted appropriation of the earth's resources and the correlative neglect of alterity in terms of biological and cultural forms of life. As Pierre Schlag again observes in his study on (American) legal aesthetics, the conceptual architecture of law not only carries differential distributive consequences for the real economy, but in conceptualising, formalising, and naming the stakes in the first instance, it has already enacted an allocation. This is true, very literally, for private international law. Indeed, the conventional account of the latter does much to reinforce these aesthetic and ontological dimensions of legality.[44] However, as will now

[39] As seen above, Pottage, 'Introduction' 4.

[40] K McGee (ed), *Latour and the Passage of Law* (Edinburgh, Edinburgh University Press, 2015) 78, 102. This text must be understood with reference to Wesley Newcomb Hohfeld's canonical 'Fundamental Legal Conceptions as Applied in Judicial Reasoning' (1917) 26 *Yale Law Journal* 710. According to McGee, Hohfield proposes an 'immanent modalization of each transformation composing a chain of legal reasoning'. McGee goes on to evoke the role of such modalisation within the hidden 'universe of the infra-juridical' or the invisible 'locus of beings of law'.

[41] On the Spanish scholastics and the controversy of Valladolid, see M Koskenniemi, 'Empire and International Law: The Real Spanish Contribution' (2011) 61 *University of Toronto Law Journal* 1.

[42] On coloniality as a negation of alterity (on various registers) see the work of literary critic S Santiago, in A Gazzola (ed), *The Space in-between: Essays on Latin American Culture, Latin America in translation* (Durham NC, Duke University Press, 2001); on coloniality as ontology from a legal perspective, as a distinct, broader concept than colonialism in the sense of a particular form of imperial regime, see W Mignolo, 'Foreword. On Pluriversality and Multipolarity', in B Reiter (ed), *Constructing the Pluriverse. The Geopolitics of Knowledge* (Durham NC, Duke University Press, 2018) ix et seq.

[43] The question is the process by which, in Latour's words, the moderns deprived themselves 'for ever' of the connections between the order of Nature and the order of Society (*Enquête*, 22).

[44] A recurrent trope of doctrinal discourse within the discipline is its association with the smooth, secure harmonious ordering of the transnational economy (or of non-state relationships more generally). This has an echo in contemporary governance discourse, that as Poul Kjaer observes (*The Law of Political Economy*), represents capitalism's all-inclusive global stateless (or in which states are in the background) economic space, coded by law, in the form of 'flows' and 'networks', somehow streaming into place naturally, smoothly and correlatively de-politicised. And yet all the while, we realise, the 'grand project of de-structuring the common' (*The Law of Political Economy* 22) is *en marche*, setting the stage in its most

be seen, there is an alternative way of reframing the status of its specific technologies as an emblematically non-modern frontier discipline.

Chapter three below is an attempt, then, to use the conflict of laws as a means to address the state of our late-modern *nomos* insofar as it relates in these terms (ontological and aesthetic) to our understanding of our ecology, or our natural surroundings. It will probe our separatist or 'jurisdictional' jurisprudence[45] and the ways it has led to an emptying of the world of its diverse life forms (whether biological or cultural). In this respect, the discipline of private international law is (self-) represented as a rationalist project, conducted from an overarching perspective and designed to harness the normative disorder generated by cultural diversity. Indeed, our metaphysical and legal tradition produces, and is dominated by, a particular type of 'jurisdictional thinking' that reflects an eminently spatial and grid-like representation of the world. It embodies in turn a specific mode of legal rationality that pursues order from a monist or Archimedean stance. This aesthetic of dividing lines or jurisdictional frontiers rests upon the correlative ontological assumption of the severance of society and nature. The challenge here again is to denaturalise the separation induced between humanity and the planet it co-inhabits by our dominant belief-system, *theologicum et juridicum*.[46]

Chapter four will then explore how to reintroduce greater plurality within law's separatist aesthetic and binary ontological scheme. The existence of a shadow avatar of the discipline of the conflict of laws[47] will serve to show that there is nothing inevitable, nor above all universal, in this particular understanding of law's 'second nature'.[48] In terms of legal aesthetics, an alternative *nomos* derived heuristically from

recent expressions for 'surveillance capitalism' (S Zuboff, *The age of surveillance capitalism: the fight for a human future at the new frontier of power* (Profile Books, 2019)), to the tune of general indifference, resignation or apathy (when it is not enthusiasm!). From a political economy perspective, Honor Brabazon writes ('Introduction. Understanding Neoliberal Legality' 7 et seq) that the significance of the neoliberal turn in law 'extends beyond the content of the laws in question to the form of law itself'. Moreover, she observes that, while 'neoliberalism is not reducible to merely juridical phenomena … the specificities of the legal form enable law to play a unique and crucial role in this process that extends beyond law's previous mediation of social relations'.

[45] McVeigh (ed), *Jurisdictional Jurisprudence*.

[46] Joao d'Azevedo, *Tribunal Theologicum, et Juridicum contra subdolos Confessarios in Sacramento: Penitentiary ad venereum solicitantes ereptun* (typ Mich Rodrigz, 1726).

[47] On the shadow version of the conflict of laws see above 96 et seq. On the figure of the avatar and its particular relevance in this Part, see below 197 et seq.

[48] On the first and second natures, see above and (in connection with the economy) Latour, *Enquête* 381. To recall the findings in Part I above: various fragile cracks in the surface of private international legality, shadowy shapes, a blurring of lines and signs of deeper disorder, that signal or prefigure law's 'second nature'. Significantly in this respect, it is the question of the environment that has displaced jurisdictional lines in the past decade, as a semiotics of repressed entanglement, resurfacing spontaneously and incrementally. At the margins of modern legality, private international law shows up the dubious sustainability of the various distinctions and severances that were purportedly deduced from the legal 'nature of all things': between law and fact, inside and outside, natural and cultural institutions, territory and extraterritoriality. Such distinctions involve denials that have in turn produced contorted figures (such as renvoi or conflicts of characterisation) that are both the trace of a former legal ideal of transcendence and universalism, and the inklings of deeper entanglements with the world around us. It might be said that law's political ecology suggests that underneath the current emptying of the world, multiple dependencies surface every time its boundary work lets up the pressure.

its minor jurisprudence,[49] in the penumbra of the former, resonates strongly with ideas of plurality, interstitiality and in-betweenness currently developed in the field of indigenous ecological epistemologies.[50] Here, the suggested path involves a reversal of standpoint, the embracing of a 'perspectivist' aesthetic.[51] In stark contrast to 'jurisdictional thinking' that empties, divides, disenchants and flattens the world, separating humanity and the planet (us and them; the body politic and its surroundings), the alternative, shadow scheme that has always haunted the history of the conflict of laws resonates with an ecological 'jurisprudence of the border',[52] drawing our attention to the paradoxical centrality of the 'in-between'. It understands frontiers not as exclusionary dividing lines but as a passing-places, in which existence can 'take place' in a hybrid and inter-mediating mode. In this respect, instead of dividing and sundering apart, legality might also give expression to a 'non-naturalist' ontology: a mode of being in the (legal) world as interdependent and enmeshed, linking up all the infinitely various forms of life that co-inhabit the earth's fragile crust, each with its own world view or mode of access to reality. Such enmeshment between self and alterity can be expressed in phenomenological terms (as will seen later on in this book, in Part III). For now, borrowing from non-modern cosmological schemes of intelligibility, this alternative legal mode 'dwells' in the interstices of entanglement[53] or indeed on the borderline of law itself.

[49] As Michel Foucault reminds us (*Les Mots et les Choses*), supposedly 'primitive' forms of analogism were current in Western thought until the end of the sixteenth century and see Descola, *Par delà Nature et Culture* 358).

[50] Quite obviously, there is a risk of essentialisation in suggesting that all such epistemologies form a single homogeneous block. Descola's quadripartite scheme of various traditions of relationality in respect of alterity is evidence enough of their diversity (see above 132). Nevertheless, indigenous communities throughout the world do form a sort of transnational epistemic alliance of the non-modern, with a common refusal to distance themselves from nature (and animal life) as understood in the West (Descola, *Par delà Nature et Culture*, on the various non naturalist cosmologies that beyond differences share a non-exclusionary relationship to the natural or non-human world; on the strategic alliance, see the aboriginal scholar Naomi Metallic's Comment on 'Deference and legal Frameworks Not Designed By, For or With Us', https://www.administrativelawmatters.com/blog/2018/02/27/deference-and-legal-frameworks-not-designed-by-for-or-with-us-naiomi-metallic/; R Sieder, '"To Speak The Law": Contested Jurisdictions, Legal Legibility and Sovereignty In Guatemala' (2020) 43(2) *PoLAR – Political and Legal Anthropology Review*). We must also remember, however, that 'prejudices, in the neutral sense used by Gadamer, can only be managed, not eliminated' (Ruskola, *Legal Orientalism* 51).

[51] Schlag, 'The Aesthetics of American Law': 'perspectivism' is one of the three models of legal aesthetics (along with 'grid' and 'energy') that he proposes.

[52] Mignolo, 'On Pluriversality and Multipolarity', evoking a border ontology, epistemology and gnosis: 'a pluriverse is not a world of independent units, but a world entangled, then a way of thinking and understanding that dwells in the interstices of entanglement, at its borders, is needed. To think pluritopically is to think from within the borders'. *Cf* too R Simenel, *L'origine est aux frontières* (CNRS, Éditions de la Maison des Sciences de l'homme, 2013) (whose project is to articulate 'deux vecteurs de la représentation de l'espace-temps, habituellement distingués par les champs disciplinaires mais ici réunis par la « pensée indigène»: l'« origine » et la « frontière ». L'origine, objet de l'histoire, et la frontière, objet de la géographie, se trouvent ici combinées dans une ethnographie dont la démarche est d'associer l'ordre du temps à celui de l'espace pour mieux comprendre la manière dont un lien social se bâtit en référence à l'altérité'.

[53] Mignolo, ibid. On the productive idea of 'dwelling', see below 172.

3

Jurisdictional Jurisprudence

THE RUSE OF naturalism, incarnated in a narrative of historical progress, is to make us believe that the social world obeys some sort of innate or immanent order. It owes much in terms of both form and substance to the prevalence of a 'jurisprudence of jurisdiction'.[54] On the one hand, on an aesthetic register, it subscribes to an abstract, grid-like vision of the earth, divided into independent sovereign spaces that often have little relevance to the reality on the ground.[55] Such emptying or flattening of space and time is the hallmark of our modern disenchantment.[56] In this respect it is the precondition of various forms of alienation – disembodiment, dematerialisation or disembeddedness – that are (and have long been) the target of critique in terms of the political economy or political ecology. A world emptied of diverse life forms and cultural difference – shaped according to a linear scheme of ontological architecture, to use the terms of Alain Pottage[57] – is far easier to dominate, expropriate, commodify and appropriate. On the other hand, as Costas Douzinas observes, the metaphysical significance of jurisdiction lies in its institution of a 'life before the law':[58] it implies an idea of place, or location, subject to rule ('attachments'[59]) and persons and events 'articulated as juridical through processes

[54] McVeigh (ed), *Jurisdictional Jurisprudence*. This expression will be used repeatedly below. See too, bearing a similar meaning, A Kaushal, 'The Politics of Jurisdiction' (2015) 78 *The Modern Law Review* 759–92, showing how traditional understandings of this concept (government, authority, territory), on the one hand, overlook the implication of the political community that is tethered to jurisdiction and on the other, make invisible the presence of jurisdiction in theories of sovereign exception. This double point will also be made below in this chapter that follows.

[55] Typically, modern colonial creation of states 'took place', that is, outlined territory without consideration or knowledge of the terrestrial reality on the ground. This is of course emblematically true of the division of the 'great pie of Africa' between the colonial powers in the nineteenth century, but the same can be observed, through the eminently aesthetic lens of the Louvre, on the creation of modern Greece in the mid-nineteenth century by the great European powers: see J-L Martinez, 'Paris-Athènes. Naissance de la Grèce moderne (1675–1919)', Le Louvre, Paris, exhibition, October 2021.

[56] The canonical reference to *Entzauberung* is to Max Weber's account of bureaucratic, secularised modernity and its devaluation of religion; further on the collective subconscious roots of disenchanted thought, see the historical-psychoanalytical analysis by A Mazurel, *L'inconscient ou l'oubli de l'histoire* (Paris, La Découverte, 2021), on the social metamorphoses of our libido, with reference to H Marcuse (*Eros et Civilisation* (Paris, ed de Minuit, 1963)) and N Elias (*La Dynamique de l'Occident* (Paris, Pocket Agora, 2003)).

[57] Pottage, 'Introduction'.

[58] 'The metaphysics of jurisidiction', in McVeigh (ed), *Jurisprudence of Jurisdiction*, Chapter 2.

[59] Jurisdictional 'attachments', flagging (as it were) a semiotics of jurisdiction, are echoed in the French term of art '*rattachement*' (or re-attachment) which translates as 'connecting factor' in the conflict of laws.

of codification or marking'. In this respect, jurisdiction contains a project of world governance, linked to modernity's abstract ontologies of spatiality and temporality.[60] From such a perspective, once again, the world 'before the law' is *terra nullius*, a void, devoid of affects, available for appropriation, enclosure or taking.

At first sight, these assertions might appear irrelevant as far as the private side of international law is concerned. As we have seen in Part I of this book, the rise of public international law in the 'long' Western, nineteenth century, with its claim to order the world, eclipsed both the *Corpus juris civilis* and the law of nations, pushing the private dimension of legality to the sidelines. Nevertheless, the incessant jurisdictional boundary work[61] of the latter has been a cardinal, if less visible, force in the building of a crucial, structural 'nexus' between sovereignty, statehood and territory, on which our late-modern worldview still rests.[62] These are the indissociable axes of the rationalist modern project with its universal claim, the building blocks of our political and geopolitical universe. The latter have tended to eclipse alternative schemes, both in our own past (intercity medieval customary plurality, personal laws, 'interpolity' legality[63]) and in other contemporary traditions (indigenous or transcendent rationalities).[64]

In order to understand the constitutive role of this nexus and the ways in which it has led (albeit under a distorted late-modern avatar) to the neglect (through the economisation?[65]) of life itself, we need to see it as co-produced by multiple forms of knowledge (geographical, political, natural-scientific and of course eminently legal), all refracted through law. None of its elements (at least as later interpreted) had any necessary links with the content (retrospectively) ascribed to the Peace of Westphalia, the legendary legal foundation of the modern secular world order.[66] Inextricably linked to modern conceptions of time and space, to the discovery of perspective and the mapping of the known world, they were shaped by the needs of early capitalism and empire, and the contemporaneous reconstruction of social order in the wake of endo-European religious wars.[67] As Jürgen Osterhammel observes, the state form

[60] On which, see below 146. Once more, there is a tight complementary between the vision of the world as presupposed and produced by the conflict of laws and comparative law. The observation of P-G Monateri in respect of 'the impressive power of comparative law in the production of a spatial picture of the world' (*Comparative Legal Methods*, 22) is entirely valid for the conflict of laws.

[61] Law's 'boundary work' follows the boundary struggles between social spheres (on the latter, see N Fraser and R Jaeggi, *Capitalism, A Conversation in Critical Theory* (Cambridge, Polity Press, 2018), and below, Part III 219 et seq).

[62] This nexus is observed by S Dorsett and S McVeigh, 'Introduction' in McVeigh (ed), *Jurisdictional Jurisprudence* 3 et seq. It tells of a progressive rationalisation of spatiality through the simultaneous action of law, cartography and other modes of measurement of space (p 12).

[63] L Benton and A Clulow, 'Empires and Protection: Making Interpolity Law in the Early Modern World' (2017) 12 *Journal of Global History* 74.

[64] Both past and other are made invisible by modernity's accelerating and amnesiac projection into the future, and universalisation, that blinds us to coexisting forms of alterity. On this invisibility, see Mills, 'The Lifeworlds of Law'.

[65] On 'economisation' (aspects of our political economy), see below Part III.

[66] On Westphalia, see above 2.

[67] On the science of cartography, the emergence of territory, modernity and the political development of liberal humanist governance, see Tang, *The Geographic Imagination of Modernity*; R Ford, 'Law's Territory (A History of Jurisdiction)' (1998–99) 97 *Michigan Law Review* 889.

appears 'without explanation' towards the very end of the eighteenth century in accounts of international law, replacing the law of nations.[68] In this context, a set of (largely indeterminate) principles that came to be known as the 'rule of law'[69] were understood as providing the foundation of either (or both) municipal, constitutional democracies and the international legal order.

Further patterns emerge, notably the co-appearance on the one hand of public (state) and private (corporate) legal forms (endowed with agency and personhood), on the other, of (state) sovereignty over bordered territory and sprawling imperial and colonial enterprises.[70] Various 'jurisdictional devices' had facilitated all these moves, including, progressively, a certain fetishisation of 'law's territory'.[71] Progressively, ideas of sovereignty and territory became embroiled within the imaginary of nationhood,[72] linking the space of territory to a historical past.[73] At that point, other newly discovered non-Western cosmologies, as well as more archaic cultures in the West's own past, were (and continue to be) seen as more primitive stages on the narrow road to progress and civilisation,[74] a universal imperative necessarily embodied in the sovereign territorial nation-state and legitimised by the secular rule of law in liberal democracies. This composite assemblage (between sovereignty, secularity, the nation-state, the rule of law, democratic liberalism and territoriality) operated the 'naturalisation' of its foundations and served to justify its imposition on other, supposedly primitive, archaic or less enlightened cultures. It became the driving

[68] J Osterhammel, *The Transformation of the World. A Global History of the Nineteenth Century* (Princeton NJ, Princeton University Press, 2014).

[69] On which there is a consensus not on its definition but on its conceptual elusiveness (see further below Part III). Its content is the composite result of the 'ratchet effect' (H Brunkhorst, *Critical Theory of Legal Revolutions: Evolutionary Perspectives* (London, Bloomsbury, 2014)) of the various (legal) Atlantic revolutions (see for instance the repertoire established by the Council of Europe's Commission of Venice). But the rule of law is clearly a two-pronged fork, particularly when seen in the colonial and neocolonial context (U Mattei, L Nader, *Plunder: When the Rule of Law is Illegal* (Wiley-Blackwell, 2008).

[70] T Poole, *Reason of State* (Cambridge, Cambridge University Press, 2015); Benton and Ford, *Rage for Order*.

[71] Dorsett and McVeigh, 'Introduction'. Fetishising territory may be the reverse side of orientalising non-territorialised legal traditions (on which, see Ruskola, *Legal Orientalism*).

[72] On political power as always resting on an original fantasy, see A Mbembe, *De la Postcolonie. Essai sur l'imagination politique dans l'Afrique contemporaine* (Karthala, 2000) (with a chapter devoted in particular to the aesthetics of vulgarity, p 139 et seq).

[73] On the imaginary of modern statehood and its temporal dimension, see B Anderson, *Imagined Communities: Reflections on the Origin and Spread of Nationalism*, revised edn (Verso, 2006). For a particularly striking example, see J Baskin, 'The Unbearable: Toward an Antifascist Aesthetic' reviewing Karl O Knausgaard's six-volume autobiography, *My Struggle*, (Archipelago, 2018), and a film, Terrence Malick's *A Hidden Life*. Picking up on Knausgaard's statement that 'Nazi Germany was the absolute state. It was the state its people could die for', Jon Baskin, describes this as an 'attempt to reconstruct the thoughts and emotions of those who were attracted to National Socialism, under the principle that it is impossible to understand the emergence of Nazism – 'the last major utopian movement in the west' – without understanding what moved the people of Germany, and later of other European countries, to embrace it. And what moved them, in Knausgaard's view, was not the Nazis' promise to redistribute income, or Hitler's analysis of world affairs, or even, initially, their hatred of the Jews. What moved them was, rather, the joyful feeling of togetherness and community, of being able to transcend not only the fragmented democracy of the Weimar period but politics altogether (www.nybooks.com/daily/2020/08/14/the-unbearable-toward-an-antifascist-aesthetic/).

[74] Bonilla, *Legal Barbarians*.

political project at the heart of public international law proper (as distinct from the earlier law of nations[75]) and its 'civilising mission'.[76] Non-modern forms of legality were disqualified as such (and relegated into the sub-legal, private sphere of practice, custom or belief[77]).

Operating at the boundaries of territorial statehood and the fuzzier confines of empire, private international law bears witness to the construction of this enduring paradigm, to which it has also largely contributed.[78] Its own brand of 'jurisdictional jurisprudence' has refined distinctions between persons and things, foreign and domestic, public and private, territory and its outside, labouring towards an ordering of the world; emptying, disembodying, disembedding and disconnecting spaces; and negating the multiple interdependencies and entwined trajectories that cross through our social, biological, political and economic collective lives. *Terra nullius!* In other words, as suggested above, the various jurisdictional divides to be found at the core of the private international legal order have also underwritten the severance of humanity from its natural surroundings and reinforced its 'ontological privilege' over other forms of life. Alternative life worlds became invisible as not worthy of consideration. Nature was reduced to resource, and space emptied of all its invisible entities.[79]

Today, this jurisprudence has increasing trouble in subduing power within geographical confines.[80] 'Nested' forms of non-state sovereignty are found to be niched moreover within territorial states, along with violent tensions over legitimacy and jurisdiction.[81] Such 'law trouble'[82] extends to the various separations on which the cohesion of the nation-state depends, burying the materiality of bodies and things beneath abstract legal concepts; separating society from what it perceives as its external environment; denying reality to the invisible; and more broadly, distinguishing near and far, time and space. Nevertheless, the axes of 'jurisdictional thinking' have remarkable staying power. The private side of international law is still acutely involved in an enterprise of ordering and allocation based on the assumption (or project) of a compartmentalised, territorial, political-legal order. In what follows, we shall attempt to follow this deployment of the jurisdictional nexus described above as it empties of life and sense of place the very spaces and institutions it seeks to map and define. This nexus is, in other words, part of the (ecological) problem.

[75] On this point, *supra* 9.

[76] M. Koskenniemi, *The Gentle Civilizer of Nations. The Rise and Fall of International Law 1870–1960* (Cambridge, Cambridge University Press 2001.

[77] See above 110 et seq.

[78] As was already apparent in Part I, the geopolitics of the conflict of laws – or the impact of shifts in political power on legal methodologies – are entirely similar to those of comparative legal studies. The obvious example is the instability of the Germanic element in the groupings of legal families, echoing the ambivalence of the *Volksgeist* in the work of Carl von Savigny on the conflict of laws, and mirroring swings in geopolitical equilibria (see Monateri, *Comparative Legal Methods*, 37).

[79] On the visual turn in modernity, see above 134. Examples of legal emptying of space will follow below.

[80] On the onslaughts of legal pluralism, see Part I 109.

[81] See A Simpson, *Mohawk Interruptus. Political Life Across the Borders of Settler States* (Durham NC, Duke University Press, 2014). Audra Simpson has also applied these ideas to the conflict of laws in 'Subjects of Sovereignty: Indigeneity, The Revenue Rule, and Juridics of Failed Consent' (2008) 71 *Law and Contemporary Problems* 191–216 (see below 148, 163, 197).

[82] The reference is to Judith Butler's term of 'gender trouble', which also points to the difficulty in maintaining boundaries and binaries. On the queer ontologies of non-sovereign states, see below 151, 165 et seq., 248.

A first aspect of this nexus, in terms of legal aesthetics, is that territory, or its private international law avatar, 'territoriality', signifies that law's spatial scope is coterminous with geopolitical space. In this respect, private international law fits legality within a grid of bounded territories, even while it does much to undermine the relevance of territoriality as a useful category (section I). A second, this time ontological, thread leads us to sovereignty. While shying away ostensibly from the operation of (state) power, private law is involved nevertheless invisibly but potently in a project of world governance, displacing or revealing the locus of the sovereign within its own version of the international legal order (section II).

I. *TOPOS* AND *TELOS*

Territory as a constitutive component of political and legal sovereignty, indissociable in the latter respect from statehood, is a recent concept, emerging slowly in the imaginings of modernity.[83] According to a historiographical convention, two contemporaneous, inextricable events mark, symbolically, the emergence of political and legal modernity.[84] On the one hand, a new world order of states, each sovereign contained within defined geopolitical frontiers, was inaugurated by the peace treaty of Westphalia of 1648 that put an end to the bloody endo-European religious wars.[85] On the other, the contemporaneous accession of James I to the throne of England, incarnation of Hobbes' *Leviathan*, marked the transition from the arcane, theological and esoteric Elizabethan reign of the 'faery queen', to that of the modern sovereign body politic, both terrestrial and territorial, rational and representative of the people.[86]

However far this narrative of progress was from the reality of the time,[87] there was certainly a 'rush for (global) order' from the very threshold of modernity.[88] Insofar as it was projected onto the geopolitical layout of the world, it was a secular, and moreover specifically legal project. Displacing the unruly multipolarity of terrestrial

[83] See Tang, *The Geographic Imagination of Modernity*, underlining the recent emergence of legal-political territory.

[84] On the multiple topologies of time, linked to perceptions of space, and the emergence of quantitative (as opposed to cosmic) time, along with modernity's technologies (such as the watch, maritime commercial transport, postal services …) see Pomian, *L'ordre du temps* 253 et seq.

[85] Theological choice belonged thereafter to the domestic politics of each sovereign in its allotted space. This technique of spatial allocation among warring belief systems is at the very origin of the contemporary conflict of laws as an international discipline: see on Joseph Story's reflection on the legal solution to the problem of fugitive slaves as between violently divided states prior to the American Civil War, above 73.

[86] On this transition, see Monateri, *Dominus Mundi*, 75 et seq.

[87] Even in this (solely) endo-European context of what is usually described as 'world' peace, the settlement did not succeed in putting an end to religious war, nor did it mark the sudden substitution of a secular ontology. Moreover, territory had emerged progressively, prior to Westphalia, as a political-jurisdictional unit. The arcane mysteries of royalty (and the influence of the doctrine of the king's two bodies) were still to endure. Statehood as we know it only emerged in the early twentieth century, at the very moment of its decline in the global turn (see above 70).

[88] L Benton, *A Search for Sovereignty. Law and Geography in European Empires 1400–1900* (Cambridge, Cambridge University Press, 2010).

authorities and the overarching theological cosmology of the prior world, modernity involved a radical ontological mutation, in the form of a rationalist scheme of ordering of political life through the rule of (secularised) law. The new *nomos* that accompanied the emergence of the Leviathan was state-centred and anthropomorphic.[89] It fractured the universal, divinely ordained empire of the *Dominus mundi* into separate sovereign units with profound consequences for the understanding of legality and its specific (territorial) spatiality and (linear) temporality.[90] It was linked to scientific (meaning rational) ways of perceiving time, space, nature, causality and agency that involved a deep (and certainly very progressive) metaphysical change: the invisible beings that peopled the premodern, theological world were phased out in favour of legal (neither natural nor divine, but no less invisible) forms: sovereign statehood, corporate bodies[91] and, ultimately, autonomous subjects and their imagined national communities.

Concomitantly with the building of maritime trade routes, intense technological discoveries, cartography[92] and a new political economy, legality (internal and external, domestic and international) took part in an equally dense conceptual change in the architecture of the normative world.[93] Law, as Lauren Benton notes, was always an important part of modern, imperial constructions of space – 'even when conflicts prompted talk of the limits of law'.[94] This last point is of evident significance for what follows below in terms of private international law. But while the ingenious political compromise of Westphalia certainly helped bring an end to the bloody religious wars, 'terrifying scenes of empire' were soon to replace them.[95] The point

[89] On the interpretation of the frontispiece of Hobbes' *Leviathan*, in which the strange composite body (politic) of the sea-monster has the face (and crown) of King James I, see Monateri, *Dominus Mundi* 120. For some strikingly analogous composite figurations produced by other artistic, political and aesthetic traditions, see Descola, *Les formes du visible*, esp ch, 8 'Exercices de Composition', p 297 et seq, and picture 81 (demons driving a soul in the shape of an elephant, full of animal parts: Mughal, sixteenth century, p 325).

[90] Monateri, ibid.

[91] On the chartered companies of the Indies and their quasi-sovereignty, already a powerful presence in the world of Hobbes, see Poole, *Reason of State*. Both Marx and Mills had been struck by the disastrous saga of the debt of the Carnatic: see *Nabob of The Carnatic v The East India Company* [1789] EngR 1625, (1789–1817) 1 Ves Jun Supp 223, (1789) 34 ER 761 (B), in which the East India Company was treated as an as-if sovereign (and the Nabob who had incurred large debts to it, secured on his public revenues and on part of his territory, had no recourse before municipal courts). See Poole, ibid; and on the context of the judicial saga, J Phillips, 'A Successor to the Moguls: The Nawab of the Carnatic and the East India Company, 1763–1785' (1985) 7 *The International History Review* 364–89.

[92] See Tang, *The Geographic Imagination of Modernity*, on the coproduction of legal-political territory by the invention of cartography in the seventeenth century, that substituted for the idea of the universe as a finite and well-ordered whole, the idea of an infinite universe unified only by the composition of the basic laws of Euclidean geometry.

[93] The change led to the mapping of territories, the construction of modern European states and empires and, by the eighteenth century, the 'discovery of man' (Foucult, *The Order of Things*) or the formation of the individual subject endowed with rights (on the effects of this discovery in terms of law and rights, see below Part III).

[94] Benton, *A Search for Sovereignty* 1. Benton observes that contemporary legal scholars saw fragmented geographies as an integral part of imperial sovereignty, contrary to the received idea that such territories awaited incorporation into the sovereign state.

[95] As Latour writes (*Enquête*, p 27), terrifying scenes of empire and the butchering of the planet took place thereafter in the name of reason, in a tragic indifference to the beings, bodies, practices and things that compose the ecosystem on which we depend.

here is to probe the ways in which ideas stemming from the jurisdictional nexus of statehood, sovereignty and territory contributed to the severance between society and the natural world; more specifically still, how geographical place was articulated in private international legal terms in such a context. Unsurprisingly, its methodologies are fraught with contradictions. This is true whether the territorial spatialisation of the world is designed as a natural-seeming description of law's place (section I.A), or invoked notwithstanding its evident inaccuracy to solve conflicting sovereign claims (section I.B).

A. Territoriality as Natural Description

'Jurisdictional thinking', then, takes territoriality as the basic, modern, epistemological category through which to think about both the thrust of sovereign power and modern law's spatial empire.[96] In this context, territory is homogeneous and bounded space, coextensive with the reach of sovereign rule in whose name jurisdiction is exercised. Within this same scheme, moreover, the territorial sway of jurisdictional power is mirrored by the equally clear-cut scope of state law. The narratives of late-modern jurists about the origins and structure of (public) international legality undoubtedly partake of this vision; it is also relayed within its private counterpart by legislators and courts.[97] Thus, according to Charles S Maier, the (also long) twentieth century produced a 'territorial imperative' in the form of an 'overarching spatial imagination'.[98] In this context, as suggested above, 'territoriality' refers to an inherent quality of the law, suggesting that its scope – that is, the things, events, or persons to which it applies – is naturally coextensive with the geopolitical space (territory) occupied by the sovereign state. From its status as descriptive common sense, territoriality derived its remarkable influence as an organising principle of order between sovereigns.

But territoriality is not a descriptive concept. It takes part in an 'assignment of (jurisdictional) attachments'.[99] Unsurprisingly, then, as the yardstick of the legitimate exercise of state power, a reference to the physical ('territorial') frontiers of sovereignty is clearly inadequate to account for a series of phenomena related to the issue of law's largely metaphorical spatial scope. This is true not only for the enduring 'personal' thrust of various legal statutes in the ordinary context of the conflict of laws, but also for the reach of human rights in a cross-border setting,[100] or indeed for contemporary delegated or functional modes of deployment of prescription and

[96] Benton, *A Search for Sovereignty*.

[97] According to art 3§3 of the French Code Civil, changed since 1804, French law applies throughout national territory to all occupants therein, at least to the extent that is penal or police.

[98] C Maier, *Once within Borders: Territories of Power, Wealth, and Belonging since 1500* (Cambridge MA, Belknap Press of Harvard University Press, 2016). But see Benton, *A Search for Sovereignty* 7, fn 13, who queries the prevalence of this paradigm.

[99] McVeigh (ed), *Jurisdictional Jurisprudence*. On its status as value judgment, see below.

[100] See Bomhoff, 'The Reach of Rights: "The Foreign" and "The Private" in Conflict-of-Laws, State-Action, and Fundamental-Rights Cases with Foreign Elements' (2008) 71 *Law and Contemporary Problems* 39–72.

enforcement composed of non-territorial practices.[101] Furthermore, as indigenous ways of dwelling in the land (explored below) remind us, populations, traditions and governance arrangements that existed well before the arrival of modern colonial settler states, continue today to straddle the borders of the latter or bear witness to 'nested' forms of sovereignty.[102] Indeed, territorial states, while formally sovereign, have 'lost control', both of their policies and of their borders.[103] The vocabulary dies hard, however, as does the accompanying imaginary. Territoriality is usually paired with 'extraterritoriality', considered as an outrageous anomaly,[104] an exception to the received principle that law (or political power, hard or soft[105]) does not extend beyond the physical borders of the polity. In terms of the law, we live, we are also told, in an 'age of extraterritoriality', suggesting that territory remains the natural parameter, however far we have strayed away from it.[106]

Territory and territoriality take on a specifically legal meaning in the context of clashes between far-reaching policies, regulations and measures (and countermeasures) involving geopolitical stakes or deleterious consequences for individuals or corporations.[107] Once judicialised and framed in the terms of private international law, courts determine the respective scope of legislative enactments, weigh their degree of intrusiveness vis à vis individual entitlements in the light of the public interest,

[101] See for example, MA Slaughter, *A New World Order* (Princeton NJ, Princeton University Press, 2009). The new vocabulary of food sovereignty, supply chain sovereignty, or digital sovereignty illustrates this change. The other basic units of modern statehood that presuppose the significance of borders (that is, a stable population and effective government) are equally affected by the global turn, in a despatialised world (of digitalised finance, massive displacement of populations, etc).

[102] See Simpson, *Mohawk interruptus*, to which we return further below.

[103] S Sassen, *Losing Control – Sovereignty in an Age of Globalization* (Columbia University Press, 1996); on the loss of border control in the name of other imperatives such as humanitarian intervention, see J Bartelson, *Sovereignty as Symbolic Form. Critical Issues in Global Politics* (Abingdon, Routledge, 2014), observing that sovereignty has been turned into something granted, contingent upon its responsible exercise in accordance with the norms and values of an imagined international community. Humanitarian intervention is a striking example of a departure from the purely Westphalian model of international law and territorial sovereignty, reversing its perspective (or symbolic form) while still operating within its framework.

[104] Making this point about the term's 'connotations with illegitimacy and outrageousness', see C Ryngaert, *Jurisdiction in International Law* (Oxford, Oxford University Press, 2008) 7.

[105] The semantics (and connotations) have become common to international law and international relations to describe the reach of power (hard and soft) of major state actors, denoting thereby intrusion or undue influence or other forms of domination (see for example C Woll, *Economic Lawfare: The Geopolitics of Corporate Justice* (Cambridge MA, Harvard University Press, 2021).The imagery of sovereignty extending across borders is used in this respect to describe either the creation (or neo-colonial maintenance) of the economic dependency of weaker states (in respect, say, of China's empire over the states that are crossed by the new Silk Routes), or the exorbitant reach of regulation designed to serve the political and economic interests of the hegemon (as in the case of American antitrust or other market regulation in the early part of the twentieth century, or more recent practices of 'extraterritorial' economic sanctions), or indeed, the deployment of executive power over occupied territories in the context of military operations or occupation.

[106] Observing that 'extraterritoriality' assumes the naturality, legitimacy and authority of territorial jurisdiction, whereas the assertion of legal authority beyond/despite territory has always played a role in the consolidation of sovereignty (see D Margolies, U Ozsu, M Pal, N Tzouvala (eds), *The extraterritoriality of law: history, theory, politics* (Abingdon, Routledge, 2019).

[107] Or indeed any entities that are in a position to claim rights. For an example of sovereign entities claiming individual rights in this respect, see the *RJR Nabisco* case discussed below.

assess their compatibility with local public policy and, in the course of such enquiries, engage in difficult interpretations of foreign legal content.[108] However, despite the recurrence of references to territoriality (and by implication, to its brazen twin, extraterritoriality) – whether in defining the legitimate scope of national legislation, or in disqualifying foreign measures, or indeed to trace the line between the national and the foreign – such concepts prove to be embarrassingly unclear. Examples abound, despite judicial attempts at clarification.[109]

Such indetermination makes sense if we turn to the genealogy of territory as a legal concept. Modern understandings of law's scope have always integrated a whole series of parameters in which territoriality and its extraterritorial other respond to variable and equally uneven patterns, reflecting multiple interests and policies. As Lauren Benton shows in her 'Search for Sovereignty' in early modernity,[110] the geography of law was far more complex than is suggested by the simple equation implicit in the 'jurisdictional nexus' between sovereignty, state and territory. On the contrary, as seen above, perceptions of territory as homogenous legal space were largely formed, and projected retrospectively, at the end of the nineteenth century, when modern international law emerged full-fledged, along with the figure of the nation state.[111] Constructed by law in the context of particular needs, projects, ideals or ideologies (particularly those of the mutations of empire and industrial capitalism), this is one more sign of the 'naturalisation' of the territorial state. A further fallacy is that the modern territorial state once existed in a fairly clear-cut form but that its frontiers became blurred at a more recent stage (the global turn) with the privatisation of the

[108] For a particularly controversial (counter?) example of the judicial confining of foreign law to foreign territory as grounds to refuse the 'extraterritorial' application of Iraqi law applicable to the claims for compensation brought by Iraqi citizens against the British government for harm caused by the occupying allied forces in Iraq, see *Ministry of Defence v Iraqi Citizens* [2016] UKSC 25 per Lord Sumption, proposing an embroiled conflict of laws reasoning on the law applicable to prescription and limitation of their action in tort (that might reasonably have been suspended on the terms of Iraqi law in the light of the inability of these collateral victims to bring a case either to the Iraqi courts by reason of an allied order applicable on occupied territory, or to the English court for obvious actual reasons).

[109] The recent saga involving the legitimacy of the exercise of judicial jurisdiction by the federal courts of the United States over 'extraterritorial conduct' of corporations on the basis of the 1789 Alien Tort Statute provides ample illustration of this uncertainty. The territoriality (territorially limited scope) of (public regulatory, and here, jurisdictional) statutes must prevail presumptively, unless Congress decides otherwise (see notably *Kiobel v Royal Dutch Petroleum Co*, 569 US 108 (2013). Yet, in this context, the respective meanings of territoriality and extraterritoriality are (and always have been) indeterminate. The same can be said of the dividing line between the domestic (what 'touches and concerns' home territory and the foreign (that which is located on the outside: see again the *Kiobel* case). Outside the Alien Tort Statute, an example of the elusiveness of the concept of territoriality can be taken from a recent case, *RJR Nabisco, Inc v European Community*, 579 US ___ (2016), in which the US Supreme Court engaged in deliberately pedagogical clarification of the method to be followed in the determination of the territorial or extraterritorial nature of a particular statute. The issue arose here in connection with the thrust of the RICO anti-corruption legislation (Racketeer Influenced and Corrupt Organizations Act: 18 USC §1962 (a-d), which contains provisions for an individual, or 'private attorney general', action for punitive or exemplary damages (§1964-c). The benefit of the latter was invoked by claimants (states of the European Community) in respect of harm (allegedly) suffered outside the United States. The Court ruled that only in the event of the exceptional and express will of Congress may the scope of legislation be extended beyond the limits of the territory of the United States. It then engaged in a two-step test involving the identification of the 'focus' of a statute (on this circularity, see below 155).

[110] Benton, *A Search for Sovereignty.*

[111] Brunkhorst, *Critical Theory of Legal Revolutions.*

political economy. As Poul Kjaer observes, this chronological account ignores the permanence of the interwoven assemblages that have always straddled these conventional epistemological divides.[112]

Thus, the texts of early modern jurists portray a far more fluid picture of the scope of law between nations and the spatial confines of empires.[113] Once again, Lauren Benton's account of the construction of (imperial) space since (very) early modernity highlights the co-productive role of law and geography in its definition, and the broader interrelation of cartography, colonial legal discourse and international law. In the initial years of overseas expansion from the West, she writes, 'law formed an important epistemological framework for the production and dissemination of geographic knowledge, while geographic descriptions encoded ideas about law and sovereignty'.[114] The modern conception of the spatial layout of the world was a fascinating mixture of cosmographic,[115] geographical and legal epistemologies and imaginations; the experience of explorers, travellers, sojourners and mariners with their thick descriptions of faraway locations; and scientific discourse linked to cartography and perspective.[116]

Moreover, more significantly still, far from producing homogeneity, such epistemologies 'awarded a place of privilege to anomalies in the accumulation of knowledge and the developments of understandings about the global order'.[117] From the early centuries of modernity, as Benton explains, European imperial pursuits, sharing a repertoire of Roman and canon law, produced 'uneven' legal geographies. Space was neither smooth nor flat, but full of corridors, enclaves, passageways, sea lanes and imagined rich, interior realms. Geographical tropes were used to describe the uneven deployment of sovereignty over distant and rugged parts of the earth's surface, also suggesting that the characteristics of geographical categories such as hills or islands, or distant latitudes such as the South, posed problems of legal order; these were the natural locations of barbary, remoteness and wilderness, with all that these labels implied, as a contrast to imperial centres of civilisation. Furthermore, these tropes came to evoke a variable intensity of imperial sovereignty, in the forms of more or less loyal subjecthood or political solidarity on the part of the inhabitants of these regions.[118]

[112] *The Law of Political Economy*, pointing to the further paradox that more statehood in the twentieth century has meant ever more transnationalism.

[113] As Benton notes (*A Search for Sovereignty* xiv), the fluid politics and confines of empires were traceable to the texts of leading jurists of international law such as Gentili, Grotius, Bentham, Maine and more. Remarkably, these texts are all canons of the private (international, economic and comparative) side of the law.

[114] Ibid p 9.

[115] Ibid, on the (sixteenth-century) yearning for a 'true and perfect geography' of the world that aligned all newly discovered lands on a cosmography of astronomical markers.

[116] Ibid, on the European sponsoring of mapping exercises, while mariners often filtered such geographical information through legal reports or in connection with legal cases.

[117] Ibid p 298.

[118] Ibid pp xii, 7 and 296: geographical tropes figured prominently as a shorthand way to describe the spatial variations of imperial law, associating geophysical properties and qualities of law and sovereignty. For instance, islands and hill regions could be correlated to wilder or more primitive cultures, imperial enclaves whose characteristics posed problems of legal order.

This would tend to undermine the historical accounts of territorial world ordering crafted retrospectively in the nineteenth century, that continue to prevail today. However, there are significant continuities between the early modern anomaly-centred forms of knowledge and very contemporary perceptions of geopolitical spaces that emphasise the presence of 'irregular' places such as islands (sometimes governed as states of exception[119]), enclaves such as indigenous reserves (sad vestiges of the purportedly unoccupied lands of the new world), or 'veiled' protectorates (that can otherwise be cast as occupied territories).[120] To which can be added further 'deviant' structures such as nomadic peoples, diasporas, and massive encampments of economic migrants and asylum-seekers. In other words, sovereignty, to the extent that it is understood as power embodied in law and assigned to place, with internal and external dimensions, has always come in different shapes and sizes.[121]

Moreover, common perceptions – originating in colonial representations of the conquered world and reinforced under the intellectual influence of Carl Schmitt[122] – of an extra-European space of lawlessness, are historically dubious, since various avatars of a largely maritime 'law of nations' certainly predated the West's imperial control of the oceans.[123] Thereafter, extraterritoriality was understood and practised in early modernity as an (entirely legitimate) extension of municipal law into the seas, with multiple and unequal ties to various sovereigns. In this respect, as Benton surmises, European law was probably neither exceptional nor isolated. Its sway coexisted with spatially diffuse legal cultures and highly irregular or heterogeneous territorial (including and perhaps even largely maritime) claims.[124] Furthermore, she points out, Jean Bodin's contribution to the conceptualisation of sovereignty in the sixteenth century is notable for its utter lack of attention to, or even mention of territory. For Bodin, the principal mark of sovereignty was the aptitude to give law to all, without anyone else's approval. This lack of heed to territory would have been consistent with early modern constructions of sovereignty as 'spatially elastic': territory was no more than a contingent element of imperial rule, incidental to sovereign jurisdiction of which the properties resided elsewhere.[125] Because subjects could be

[119] The traces of these imaginaries are present today in the exceptionalism of the legal-political status of islands (ibid p 299); for instance on the private international legal dimensions of the migrants' camp on Manus Island, Australia, see S Corneloup, J Verhellen, on 'Privatisation of international migration flows' in H Muir Watt et al, *Global Private international law* (Cheltenham, Elgar, 2019) 548 et seq.

[120] For an unedifying, early twentieth century account of British 'protective' rule in Egypt, its 'veiled protectorate', see HJ Carman, 'England and the Egyptian Problem' (1921) 36 *Political Science Quarterly* 51, that reveals the beginnings of the later neo-colonial global investment regime, equally purported to bring development aid to striving, non-modern economies (more on which, see below Part III).

[121] Thus, Gentili himself defined pirates as 'non legitimate sovereigns', while the chartered East and West Indian trading companies, as seen above, were granted a form of quasi-sovereign personality.

[122] To whose depiction of space and sovereignty we shall return below 157 et seq.

[123] On the presence of the sea in the imaginaries of early Roman and later early modern ideas of power, see Monateri, *Dominus Mundi* 16 et seq On the Asian (pre)history of Chinese imperial maritime control, see Tang, *The Geographic Imagination of Modernity*.

[124] Lauren Benton points to a shift in the division of the Atlantic as late as the mid-eighteenth century, following the jurisdictional location of laws of amity as opposed to zones of war ('Legal Spaces of Empire. Piracy and the Origins of Ocean Regionalism' (2005) 47 *Comparative Studies in Society and History* 700–24.

[125] Benton and Ford, *Rage for Order* 288.

located anywhere, writes Lauren Benton, and the tie between sovereign and subject was defined as a legal relationship, legal authority was not bound to territory.

What better description of the allegiance underlying the conceptions of personal status in the works of Bartolus de Sassoferrato and the post-glossators, in their labour of interpretation of the *Corpus juris* in the fourteenth century?[126] This premodern 'extraterritorial' authority of personal status underwrote ideas of subjecthood and citizenship, fluid categories that allowed the assertion of sovereignty over non-homogeneous, irregular, expanses of land and sea.[127] Mobile citizenship and portable sovereignty went together. In this light, the descriptive value of territoriality, particularly posited as a permanent historical feature of legality, is highly dubious.

B. Territoriality as Value Judgement

The conflict of laws often presents territoriality as a principled answer to the question of the spatial scope of clashing (overlapping) legal regimes. As seen above, well before the formation of sovereign states, early medieval reconstructions of Roman law contrasted the territorial scope of certain statutes and the personal application of many others. The latter 'followed' the members of a community beyond the geographical limits of the jurisdiction to which they belonged or owed allegiance. At the time of the early modern tracing of the territorial borders of statehood, such borders seem to have been places of passing or of itineraries of constant crossing and recrossing – notably in the interests of trade – rather than the reverse.[128] Indeed, although inklings of citizenship were enmeshed in these early ideas about the scope of statutes and customs, along with the gradual dissolution of feudalism, it is doubtful that the fact of belonging to a given community was understood at that point as exclusionary of other affiliations, or geographical mobility. The jurisdictional division of the various

[126] See Stein, *Roman Law in European History;* N Hatzimihail, *Preclassical Conflict of Laws* (Cambridge, Cambridge University Press, 2021). The foundational work on personal status is widely considered to be that of Bartolus of Sassoferrato (1314–57), commenting on the *Glossa Ordinaria* of Accursius, of the first words of the first provision of the *Corpus iuris, 'Lex cunctos populos'*. In that provision, the Roman emperor 'wills that all peoples whom the due temperance of Our clemency rules live in accordance to that religion which the Divine Apostle Peter gave to the Romans' (meaning that if a Bolognese is sued at Mantua he ought not be judged according to the statutes of Mantua to which he is not subject). According to what Hatzimihail qualifies as a later caricature, Bartolus is credited with a binary distinction: personal statutes followed the person, whereas real statutes applied only locally. 'We have inherited this caricature from ancestors who themselves inherited it from pre-classical scholars fighting their own battles, often against Bartolists. It seems that by the sixteenth century the mentioned rule had been regarded as the criterion par excellence for distinguishing between real and personal statutes, leading to disagreement by Dumoulin or d'Argentré (who appears to have viciously attacked Bartolus, calling the rule futile, childish, and a sophistry)' (Hatzimihail, p 34). Interestingly, as Stein points out, Bartolus' Commentaries contain a fifth section, usually omitted as not pertaining to the conflict of law, on whether statutes and customs of the laity bind the clergy (nos 28–31). This category englobes personhood and family relationships as understood in the Western tradition; it excludes many issues or areas of the law that are tightly linked to these institutions in other cultures, whether succession to property, religious ceremonies, specific forms of dress, etc).

[127] Benton, *A Search for Sovereignty* 297.

[128] A Brett, *Changes of State: Nature and the Limits of the City in Early Modern Natural Law* (Princeton NJ, Princeton University Press, 2011).

customs of Northern Italy and France was designed more to ensure a form of elective proximity between multiple, largely stable (and small-scale) populations and their modes of social regulation, than as an exclusive political marker.[129]

It was only in the eighteenth century, in the context of religious strife and imperial expansion, that the influential doctrine of vested rights developed by the Dutch statutist school opposed the newly minted principle of territorial sovereignty to any deployment of foreign law on home ground (meaning that foreign law could not aspire to authority before the courts of the forum state). This was an act of Protestant resistance towards the personal thrust of canon law, or its exorbitant claim to extend its government over the constituency of the (Spanish) Catholic Church to the very limits of the vast Spanish empire.[130] It was also a means of easing the tensions between the various Dutch provinces, caught up in the turmoil of internal religious factionalism.[131] As we have already seen above, the concept of vested rights, according to Ulrich Huber, concentrated a triad of legal principles that were designed in this troubled political-theological and economic context to legitimise the operation of foreign law within the territory of the 'host' sovereign. Thus, firstly, all states have sovereign power within their territory, but not beyond. Secondly, the state has sovereign power over any person within its territory. And thirdly, when the court gives effect to rights created by foreign law in the territory of the foreign sovereign in the exercise of the latter's own sovereign authority, it so acts out of (mere) *comitas* (as distinct from binding law), as to ensure (in the interests of a sort of international *vivre-ensemble*) that the laws of each nation having been applied within its own boundaries retain their effect everywhere so far as they do not prejudice the power or rights of another state or its subjects.[132] In sum, foreign law could not be 'applied' as such, but could be acknowledged as having a factual existence once, or as if, vested in the form of a concrete right recognised by the foreign territorial sovereign within the latter's own jurisdiction.

[129] See too above 103.

[130] JR Paul, 'Comity in International Law' (1991) 32 *Harvard International Law Journal* 14 et seq on Huber's role in the appearance of comity in (private) international law.

[131] Paul ('Comity') writes: 'Understanding the historical context sheds light on the doctrine's original purposes. The Dutch of the seventeenth century had a strong sense of being God's chosen, having reclaimed their land from a jealous sea and defeated Spain to create the first truly middle-class society in Europe. They also had the sense that their existence was threatened by internal factionalism between Catholics and Calvinists, and further between Armenians and Orthodox Predestinarians. In addition, tensions existed among the various provinces and between noble and merchant interests vying for greater influence over a weak central government. In this context, a theory of conflicts seemed necessary to complement the unification of the Dutch provinces by easing the strains among them. A theory of conflicts had to address the question of when it was appropriate to apply the law of one province over another, or of a foreign sovereign over the law of the republic, and justify and explain instances of yielding to the law of another. Moreover, the theory had to be consonant with the expansion of trade with other European powers, as well as within the emerging Dutch colonial empire'.

[132] U Huber, *De Conflictu Legum* (Leipzig, 1707). For an English translation of this work, see E Lorenzen, 'Huber's De Conflictu Legum' (1919) 13 *Illinois L Rev* 375, 401–18. As further explained by Paul ('Comity'), the Dutch jurists built upon the statutists' legal programme. The initial contribution by Paul and John Voet, father and son, was a novel construction asserting that all laws were territorial except personal statutes, which operated within the territory of another sovereign by the will of the forum sovereign. However, the credit for this set of principles went largely to Huber, who integrated the (most controversial, or most misunderstood) 'comity' dimension.

These ideas appealed a (broad) century later, across the Atlantic, to Joseph Story in analogous historical conditions – that is, in a similar situation of secession of a Protestant (Puritan) colony from the (decadent) British Empire and likewise moreover in the context of a threat to the unity of the young American federation through the internal factionalism that would lead to civil war. Coining the new vocabulary of 'private international law', Story systematised the whole of the field around the idea of territorial application of the law, all the while embracing Huber's 'comity' as a mediating principle between free and slave states.[133] Thereafter, in a curious reflexive loop, the concept of vested rights – divested however of the comity doctrine – travelled back over the Atlantic to the metropolis, where it was instituted by AV Dicey as the foundation of the (English) conflict of laws.[134] Territorial sovereignty signified that there could be no judicial application of foreign law, except in the guise of an extraordinary fiction: anticipated, virtual rights (as if the foreign sovereign had made a ruling) were in effect deemed 'transitory', that is, endowed with cross-border mobility and enforceable before home courts. Meanwhile, multiple adjustments and refinements were required in order to determine which component of a chain of events, actions, things or persons operated to attach or connect the whole to a particular territory. Fictions and presumptions were called in to ensure that the domicile of colonial administrators or agents remained within the jurisdictional limits of the home country (or homeland).[135] Fierce competition for commercial influence between European maritime powers led to the investing of ships as spaces of sovereignty, since the sea itself could not be divided.[136]

It was also at this (late) time that global rivalries of the great powers focused more squarely on the consolidation of land rule (and the construction of ordered imperial bureaucracies to ensure its administration).[137] The rise of the concept of territorial sovereignty, projected retrospectively back to the beginnings of modernity, was linked to the reinforcement of colonial control over bounded, homogeneous, geographical space.[138] However, this is precisely the time when territoriality as a (new) quality of law began to show its most serious cracks. Its indeterminacy became visible with early judicial attempts to define the scope of burgeoning public regulatory law (in areas such as competition and securities), when illegal conduct took place outside the country and generated effects within.[139] This quandary of plurilocated torts

[133] Paul, 'Comity', 20.

[134] On the founding fathers in the common law tradition, see above 71 et seq.

[135] Law was making a particularly strong contribution to the colonial imaginary of the 'homeland' (as opposed to native soil), through the (now-waning) notion of 'domicile of origin', for instance, a jurisdictional 'attachment' acquired by birthright and difficult to displace.

[136] On the early Atlantic divisions, see above 151. The concept of law passed down by the Dutch statutists, redolent of Hobbes' *Leviathan*, was certainly coextensive with territorial power – a secular idea of which a residue remains today in respect of the international law of enforcement jurisdiction.

[137] Benton and Ford, *Rage for Order* 8.

[138] See below 164.

[139] There was (and still is) a remarkable parallelism, cross-fertilisation or analogy between the assumptions, trends, grammar and vocabulary of the conflict of laws and the burgeoning twentieth-century area of the law of 'external relations' (on which see C McLachlan, *Foreign Relations Law* (Cambridge, Cambridge University Press, 2017)) governing the external thrust of public regulatory law, or the constitutional rights of foreign citizens (on this parallelism, see Bomhoff, 'The Reach of Rights'). This analogy reinforces the idea of that the conflict of laws played a constitutive and constitutional role in the construction of empire as a set of 'rules about rules' or law of laws as will be seen below.

continues to haunt the contemporary 'presumption against extraterritoriality'. Even presented as a highly rational two-step methodology,[140] the latter is clearly unhelpful. That centuries of doctrinal controversies have been unsuccessful in discovering objective parameters by which to determine the focus of legal statutes, is both the drama and the very justification for the existence of the conflict of laws as a discipline. Such an apparently simple legal 'test' remains indeterminate or 'beyond meaning'.[141]

The whole point of Savigny's methodological revolution (encountered above) was indeed to bypass these quandaries, although the replacement of a search for the reach of statutes by the identification of connecting factors only served to reintroduce further highly subjective refinements that arguably evolved (or degenerated) from method to mere 'recipe'.[142] These of course are but fresh iterations of the multi-secular definitional debate between real and personal statutes. They are moreover enmeshed in further distinctions such as foreign/domestic or local/international, to the extent that territory is used to define foreign elements located 'outside the state'.[143] This conclusion is supported by Jacco Bomhoff's exploration of the three distinct grammars of the 'reach of rights'. As shown by this author, the question of the spatial scope of law receives different answers according to the problem for which it is framed (whether of the extension of human rights, constitutional theories of state action or conflict of laws).[144]

[140] On the example of the purportedly pedagogical *RJR Nabisco* case, see above 149. The first step is to ask whether Congress intended the statute to apply extraterritorially 'that is, whether the statute gives a clear, affirmative indication that it applies extraterritorially' (in this case, the answer was affirmative for the regulatory parts of the RICO Act, but not for the provisions instituting the individual action). If not, then the second step is then to ensure that territorial provisions are not made to apply, as it were, out of bounds: 'we do this by looking to the statute's "focus." If the conduct relevant to the statute's focus occurred in the United States, then the case involves a permissible domestic application even if other conduct occurred abroad; but if the conduct relevant to the focus occurred in a foreign country, then the case involves an impermissible extraterritorial application regardless of any other conduct that occurred in U.S. territory'. As pointed out by Justice Ginzburg in her dissent, it is somewhat confusing that 'focus' is directed here to conduct, whereas the end point in dispute is the harm or damage.

[141] In Jean d'Aspremont's terms (*After Meaning)*. Generations of controversies as to the scope of various categories of rules have never succeeded in formulating a satisfactory objective test, that is, a clear-cut parameter that distributes them according to their respective (personal, or territorial) nature or object without recourse to the most intricate, controversial and subjective analyses.

[142] This description (by P Francescakis, *La Théorie du renvoi* (Paris, Dalloz, 1958)) was considered highly innovative or indeed subversive in its time (on European resistance to legal realism in the midst of the 'crisis' of the conflict of laws, see above 88).

[143] As already seen above, private international law's very own 'theory of the frontier' assumes that collisions occur at the point at which state laws reach out, or individuals or things move, across territorial borders. The point here is to emphasise, under multilateralist methodology, the definitional circularity of the place (the frontier) or the moment in time (the crossing) at which a situation could be said to be foreign for the needs of the conflict of laws. The only possible criterion is contained within the choice of law rule that designates a foreign law, since only then will it appear that there is indeed a conflict of laws to be solved. However, the application of such a rule is triggered in turn only when the law of the forum is involved in a conflict with a foreign law. To circumvent this difficulty, a frequent fiction consists in interposing a suspended, 'instant of reason', during which the court can proceed as if such a conflict existed, explore the potentially applicable choice of law rule and validate the application of the latter to the extent that it designates a foreign law. In this respect, the problem with the distinction between inside and outside is perfectly identified by H Lindahl (*Authority and the Globalisation of Inclusion and Exclusion* (Cambridge, Cambridge University Press, 2018)) as linked to the 'Cartesian residue' that continues to command our modern idea of spatiality and the binary oppositions between inside and outside, or self and foreign.

[144] Bomhoff, 'The Reach of Rights'.

Such contemporary quandaries affecting the legal idea of territoriality are the traces of the tensions prior to the ultimate emergence of modern statehood, as seen above. Territoriality, then, is a stubborn part of modernity's imaginary of law, but at the same time, its maintenance requires the intensive boundary work traditionally assigned to the conflict of laws. As Lauren Benton's (already much-cited) historical study of imperial legality shows, this discipline fulfilled an essentially constitutional function and took on a highly political significance in the construction of empire and the external relations of the imperial centres of power. This is an aspect to which we shall return below, in the exploration of sovereignty. Here, the point is that both fundamental norms and allocative 'rules about rule' were included within the capacious and elusive concept of the rule of law – of which, perhaps not so coincidentally, AV Dicey was also the most prominent promoter.[145] Although modern statehood and public international law took over this role at the end of the nineteenth century, the conflict of laws continues to bear the traces or residues of these earlier conceptions: undercurrents that on occasion threaten to resurface in unexpected ways and locations.

Indeed, while assertions of prescriptive and adjudicative jurisdiction still purport to defer to a legal cartography of territorial sovereignty, there is very little to tie territoriality to geography or place within private international law's allocatory grid. Territoriality and its opposite are perfectly unhelpful in terms of defining the reach of legal provisions as to the acts, events, persons or things to which they should apply. Frequently (increasingly) invoked as if they were analytical-legal concepts grounded moreover in a mere description of spatiality,[146] they are quite obviously full of (jurisdictional) affects.[147] Furthermore, as we shall now see, the vicissitudes of territoriality are echoed by similar conundrums affecting understandings of sovereignty. The private side has ostensibly retired from this particular arena, leaving it to the sway of the public. At the same time, however, it has retained or retrieved its historical significance as a 'rule of rules' within the neoliberal legal ordering. In other words, the ontology of private international legality is both ostensibly devoid of sovereignty and yet provides its very locus.

II. SOVEREIGNTY

Among the central debates concerning sovereignty in contemporary legal and political theory is the determination of law's 'outside', or its relationship to politics.

[145] The 'founding fathers' of the conflict of laws, as seen above, were all political theorists and constitutional lawyers: see on this point C Wasserstein Fassberg 'The Public in Private International Law', in Y Emerich, L Saint-Pierre Harvey (eds) *Le public en droit privé* (Yvon Blais, 2019).

[146] In jurisdictional terms, extraterritoriality might be likened to 'extra-terrestriality', as defined by B Latour in 'On some of the affects of capitalism' (Lecture before the Royal Danish Academy of Sciences in Copenhagen, 2014) when he notes that at the end of the twentieth century, when its last enemy, communism, had itself disappeared, the economy (capitalism) had reached its 'extraterrestrial' status: unbound at last, unregulated, infinite.

[147] On affects theory, see M Gregg & G Seigworth, *The Affect Theory Reader* (Durham NC, Duke University Press, 2010). On affects (or attachments) as political and cultural artefacts, see S Ahmed, *The Cultural Politics of Emotions* (Edinburgh, Edinburgh University Press, 2004); on their presence within the law, see A Katsiginis, 'The Affective Structures of Human Rights', PhD Sciences Po Law, forthcoming; on their ability to attach to anything, E Sedgwick, *Touching Feeling: Affect, Pedagogy, Performativity* (Durham NC, Duke University Press, 2003) 62. *Cf* Latour, 'On some of the affects of capitalism'.

While the latter issue can be understood in several ways, it will be framed here in terms of the relationship of the rule of law to the exception. Recurring references to Nature appear in this context, of which the most controversial is Carl Schmitt's *Nomos der Erde*.[148] This work contains a prediction (based on the biblical Book of Revelation) of the collapse of the current world order in the ultimate struggle of humanity for the resources of the earth and the disappearance of the sea. Resonating in dramatic and sinister ways with the current ecological crisis,[149] this imagery also highlights the potent aesthetic dimensions of sovereignty, to which recent historical scholarship of the 'Italian School' of political theory has done much to draw attention.[150] Sovereign

[148] *Der Nomos der Erde im Volkerrecht des Jus Publicum Europaeum (*Berlin, Duncker & Humblot, 1950; 2nd edn, 1974); English translation, *The Nomos of the Earth in the International Law of the Jus Publicum Europaeum* (Telos Press 2006). Schmitt predicts the end of the legal-political order that has regulated the world for the past three centuries (the modern era). Schmitt is mainly known (or notorious) among (public) international lawyers for these views on the political foundations of the world order that opposed him frontally in the troubled first third of the twentieth century to the specifically legal theory of Hans Kelsen. The broader contest involved the ideological consequences of each of these conceptions, the first of which was adopted by Nazism, the second framed as resistance. On the private side, while Kelsen's theory of the *Grundnorm* is usually adopted as going without saying in continental doctrine, there is very little discussion of its political dimension and no mention at all of Carl Schmitt. As PG Monateri points out (referring in turn to M Koskenniemi, *The Gentle Civilizer of Nations: The Rise and Fall of International law 1870–1960* (Cambridge, Cambridge University Press, 2004) 436), in his earlier work, *Der Begriff des Politischen*, Schmitt modified his discussion about the limits of the 'political' (between the first (1927) and the second (1932) editions. In the first edition, the 'political' had existed alongside such other realms as economy, morality, law, culture, etc in an apparently equal position as one of the aspects of a community's life, distinct from its other aspects. In the second (and third) editions, the political stood out, however, from such delimitations so as to encompass all of them. Now politics had no intrinsic limit: every aspect of life could manifest the friend–enemy opposition and thus transform itself into political struggle. Politics has no substance, it describes the 'intensity of association or dissociation of human beings' (Monateri, *Dominus Mundi*, p 6).

[149] On the ecological implication of Schmitt's *nomos*, see B Latour, in 'How to remain human in the wrong space? A comment on a dialogue by Carl Schmitt' (2021) 47 *Critical Inquiry* 699–718; see too A Pottage, 'Why Nature Has No Rights', forthcoming in A Alvarez Nakagawa & C Douzinas, *Non-Human Rights. Critical Perspectives* (Cheltenham, Elgar, 2023) observing that 'the challenge now is to rematerialize law as a truly Earthly discourse, a "discourse" forged in an encounter with the Earth itself, and mediated by the materials and competences of the Earth itself. A beginning is offered by Latour's reflections on Schmitt's nomos, which translate Schmitt's sense of the normative order of the Earth [*das Sinnreich der Erde*], or the capacity of the Earth to yield law, into a broader refiguration of nature. The argument will be familiar: whereas the law of the "moderns" assumes that the Earth is the normatively inert ground for the foundation of human society, Schmitt understood that it interpellated humans with a call that was answered and actualised as law through the operations of mensuration, demarcation, and cultivation. Through the figure of space, we understand that our terrain is produced by a process of production is political in the sense that terrain is always at stake: "whenever someone qualifies real space to be empty and neutral, we are called upon to understand that for some reason some power has emptied and neutralised the territory of someone else". In the era of Anthropocene, these contests are quite radically about life and death; they are contests in which we have to address an enemy, someone who does not share our ground of existence. The Earth itself is at stake. And the contest is all the more existential because it is not subsumed into historical process. Schmitt's friend/enemy distinction articulates a principle of negation that is non-Hegelian in the sense that it is absolutely flat rather than cumulative: "An historical truth is true only once".'

[150] These Italian authors include Georgio Agamben, Toni Negri, Roberto Esposito. P-G Monateri's study of *Dominus Mundi*, already much cited above, will serve here as a reference on the aesthetic aspects of sovereignty. For Monateri, however, these authors, while clearly ideologically not aligned with Schmitt are nevertheless 'epigones' of the latter in that they subscribe to the Schmittian theory of political theology the critique of which is the central point of *Dominus Mundi*). For an additional twist, see F Luduena Romandini, *A comunidade dos espectros. 'La comunidad de los espectros. I. Antropotecnia*' (Buenos Aires, Miño y Dávila, 2010) and particularly the second part, in his discussion of sovereignty and normativity, '2. Espectrologia I: Iconologia de un fantasma; 3. Espectrologia II: necropolítica da Modernidade'.

power is described as ineffable, incapable of representation,[151] in the same way as nature itself is pictured as sublime.[152] These ideas will be borrowed here, to the extent that they shed light in turn on the underlying tropes, imageries and fictions[153] at work in private international law in its invisible operation as the 'rule of rules'.

At stake in Schmitt's *Nomos* is the success or failure of 'an attempt to bypass law' through politics or sovereignty.[154] The genealogy of this debate emphasises that the struggle for the legality of the world order is visible within a (further) structural nexus: spatiality, transcendence, and exception.[155] Once again, this has immediate echoes in the various conceptions of world ordering through law. Similarly, then, to the tensions affecting the role and determination of territory, this (second) structural connection can be related to further conceptual turmoil visible beneath the traditional surface of private international law. Thus, firstly, by elevating the latter from the register of legal technique to that of governance, it unveils the 'second nature' of private international law as the legacy of wider struggles for the rule of law within the world order. The discipline appears historically as a specific incarnation – ancestor or avatar – of a spatialised 'rule of law', a 'rule of rules' endowed with a transcendent, constitutional function (section II.A). Secondly, by framing the classical conundrum of 'public policy' as implicating the relationship between law and its outside, it brings to the surface, in terms both aesthetic and ontological, the troubled question of the status of the sovereign exception and its relationship to the norm (section II.B).

A. The Law of Laws

Central to the conflict of laws, the relationship of the rule of law to place, spatiality and location is an important part not only of the history of (territorial) statehood, as seen above, but also, within the world order, of contemporary debates on global governance.[156] As P-G Monateri explains in his remarkable political-legal exploration of the looming imperial Roman figure of the *Dominus Mundi*, by the (modern)

[151] C Lefort, *Essais sur le politique, 19e-20e siècles* (Paris, Esprit/Seuil, 1986) 29: modernity was not content to render power to the people (through the constitutional and representative republic) but carried 'l'idée d'une société désormais vouée à accueillir l'irreprésentable'. For an analogous account of the void underlying the sovereignty of the people, illustrated in aesthetic terms by the famous painting by David of Marat's death in which half the frame is a black void, signifying the irrepresentable sovereign void, see E Santer, *The Royal Remains – the people's two bodies and the endgames of sovereignty* (Chicago IL, Chicago University Press, 2011).

[152] Or similarly beyond belief or representation. On these allusions to the sublime and the ineffable in the work of authors as different as Burke and Agamben, see Monateri, *Dominus Mundi* 135 et seq.

[153] For Pierre Schlag's definition of legal aesthetics, see above 35.

[154] Monateri, *Dominus Mundi* 8 et seq.

[155] Ibid. This echoes McVeigh's jurisdictional triad of territoriality, statehood and sovereignty, as seen above 142.

[156] The end of the (imaginary) Westphalian world order, now dissolved into a state of indeterminacy between fact and law, is a diagnostic shared by many more contemporary observers of international relations or (in the newer idiom) of global governance. It also evokes the hypothesis of extinction (see above 16, 132, and below 215). Monateri observes *(Dominus Mundi* 135) that we are now able to see 'the parable of the *Dominus Mundi* in its entirety, because we are experiencing the dissolution of its dissolution, in other words, the end of the Westphalian world order'. We know that Schmitt's prediction of the end of the liberal world order is linked to the disappearance of the political, while Schmittian 'epigones' see the root, or the rot, within the liberal order itself.

concepts of space and location 'we mean both the creation of an inside/outside dimension as well as a placement within the locus of authority and power'.[157] This further provides the key to the reflection that follows below, in respect of the conflict of laws: 'such an inquiry into the locus of difference and power and its consequences may be needed to provide a different vision of the "political", as well as a new arrangement of law and its categories'.[158] This diagnostic aptly prepares the terrain for an exploration of the relationship of private international law to the political realm, beyond its (ostensible) distanciation from concerns of sovereignty in the course of the nineteenth century.[159]

The starting point of this trend of thought is the hiatus induced by the 'global turn' between the imaginary of the Westphalian political-legal order based on (territorial) sovereignty (as seen above) and other forms of (largely economic[160]) purportedly depoliticised global rule. Indeed, the political sovereign is a diminished figure[161] and our world is becoming placeless.[162] In Agamben's words, moreover, the global order is located on the unstable threshold of un-decidability between *anomie* and *nomos*, between life and law, between *auctoritas* and *potestas*.[163] These tensions at work within the rule of law itself entail important consequences in terms of traditional conceptions of spatiality. Not least because the 'loss of control' of nation states has obvious geopolitical effects; boundaries count less as the locus of sovereignty moves towards a 'new, mutable experience' of power channelled through paradoxically spatialised exceptions and exclusions.[164] In the international sphere, the political diversity that was instituted with the Westphalian territorial order is, arguably, fading away in favour of exclusive forms of universalism,[165] while modes of neoliberal (purportedly) depoliticised governance come with a loss of 'scruple'[166] – that is,

[157] In stark contrast to the premodern universe of the *Dominus Mundi*, where the whole physical globe (with the question of the ontological exceptionalism of the sea) was under a unitary and uniform legitimate political authority. This world was without an inside or an outside because its sovereignty was all-encompassing (Monateri, *Dominus Mundi* 4).

[158] Ibid, 168.

[159] See above, 88.

[160] See below on the economisation of the world, 220.

[161] On the diminished figure of the sovereign, see A Orford, 'A Jurisprudence of the Limit', in *International Law and its Others* (Cambridge, Cambridge University Press, 2006) 1–32: 'the rapid growth and proliferation of nativist policies illustrates powerfully that the sovereign, though still "able to kill, starve, exploit, imprison and subordinate" those within and beyond its territory, is a "smaller, more absurd and ridiculous figure" than often imagined by lawyers and theorists'.

[162] Lindahl, *Authority and the Globalisation of Inclusion and Exclusion.*

[163] Agamben, *The signature of all things*, presenting the state of exception as the axis of the juridico-political machine. It institutes a threshold of un-decidability between *anomie* and *nomos*, between life and law, between *auctoritas* and *potestas*.

[164] There are of course many further examples of the production of other forms of placelessness ('despatialization') induced, for instance by the massive recourse to purportedly depoliticised algorithmic governance and its epistemological implications (see A Garapon and J Lassègue, *Justice digitale. Révolution graphique et rupture anthropologique* (Paris, PUF, 2018)).

[165] As Philippe Descola reminds us, all schemes are universal to the extent that they represent a worldview that is necessarily 'true' from their own perspective, but they are not necessarily exclusive in that they do not necessarily imply that all others are required to share it. The reverse trends characterise both modern Western political thought (theories of universal human rights or of neoliberal global economic order) and Islamic conceptions of a universal caliphate, neither of which accept the legitimacy of political diversity.

[166] On the loss of 'scruple' in favour of economic 'calculation' (and the common etymology of these terms) see Latour, *Enquête*, 442 et seq and below 220, 224. According to Latour, the contemporary risk is not just the loss of democracy, but the loss of politics itself.

an ability to moderate sovereign desire (both public and private) for capture and appropriation. The resulting disruption in the formal legal categories of law is reflected in violence, warfare and ecological devastation and all that these stand for in terms of neglect or rejection of alterity.[167]

Now, it was precisely the emptying of the world order of political form that was lamented by Carl Schmitt. His own response, a claim for the revival of a political *Nomos der Erde*, was notoriously influential on Nazi doctrine.[168] The urgent question, then, is whether in sharing the diagnosis of a neoliberal, placeless or depoliticised world, we need to endorse this violent vision of law's earthly rule. This difficult interrogation is precisely central to Monateri's political-legal study of the figure of the *Dominus mundi*. In response, his own exploration of the Roman-Byzantine roots of political sovereignty is resolutely anti-Schmittian and takes the shape of a fascinating counter-theory to the foundational idea of 'political theology'.[169] Importantly, Monateri also reintroduces a missing, specifically legal dimension to other equally exciting contemporary attempts to understand the ontological implications of the migration of sovereignty to the body politic.[170] Nevertheless, as he also emphasises, it is important not to forget the latter, so as to contextualise Schmitt's claims within the various interconnected dimensions of his thought.[171] Here, we shall attempt to follow this brilliant effort of contextualisation in order to better understand the relationship of space and location to sovereign rule, and the consequences that this understanding may have in turn for the function of the conflict of laws as a 'rule of rules'.

Firstly, the Schmittian doctrine described as 'political theology' rests on the idea that the secularisation of the modern or Westphalian world order involved not a disappearance of theology (as is, or was, perceived conventionally) but its migration to a political register. According to Schmitt, it bled into the general theory of the state and continues to govern us subliminally, even in our secular world, purportedly emptied of religion or transcendence.[172] This is the point at which various further and deliberately non-Schmittian strands of thought take up the theme of the 'royal

[167] Once again, viewed in terms of a relationship to alterity, colonial conquest, racial capitalism and ecological devastation, are indissociable.

[168] Notably through its condemnation of liberal democracy. Poole, *Reason of State*, explains Schmitt's *political romanticism* as a political critique of the passivity induced the romanticisation of experience. Such romanticism represents a secularisation, subjectification and privatisation in which God is replaced by the modern emancipated private individual. As it were, the whole world decays into an occasion for the subjectivity of the subject. Romanticism is conceived by Schmitt as an 'endless talk' fit for a bourgeoisie incapable of real political action, where for him this constitutes a neutralisation and a denial of the true essence of the true political, as long as it rests on the capacity to decide (as we shall see below).

[169] His counter-theory is that of a 'demonological inversion' rather than a transfer of the religious to the political (*Dominus mundi* 101). He deviates very deliberately from the direction taken by Georgio Agamben (described as an 'epigone' of Schmitt, since, even if ideologically opposed, he retains the same political theology framework).

[170] See in particular, Santner, *The Royal Remains* and also his *The Weight of All Flesh* (Oxford, Oxford University Press, 2015).

[171] Monateri, *Dominus Mundi* 7 et seq.

[172] Ibid, noting that this thesis is the prolongation of Kantoriwicz's doctrine of the king's two bodies, in which the body politic becomes the continuation of the sublime body of the king. In other words, sovereignty and politics have replaced God but have not eliminated theology: we still live in (what we might call) a subconscious theological setting.

remains' within secular sovereignty.[173] Notably, Eric Santner connects the migration of sovereignty from the royal (sublime) body (of the king) to the body politic (of the people) as the source of a soma, a frenzied somatic state of agitation (*lex animata*) that propels our (neoliberal) political economy.[174]

Secondly, still following Monateri, Schmitt's conceptualisation of the world order is linked, crucially, to his specific 'concept of the political'. The latter involves a choice between friend and foe, the aptitude of each territorial Leviathan to declare warfare. In this respect, it appears to derive directly from Bodin's theorisation of sovereignty,[175] and is precisely a reflection of the Westphalian world of independent political units that are each empowered to decide, with no other transcendence or higher limit, between war and peace against each other.[176] This was the new settlement, a political compromise[177] which replaced the previous religious order, instituting parallel, equal, territorial entities invested with 'double-facing' sovereignty.[178] From then on, as emphasised by Martti Koskenniemi, the primacy of the political meant that it had no intrinsic limit: every aspect of life was potentially affected by the friend–enemy opposition and thus prone to give rise to struggle, calling in turn for resolution.[179] At this point, sovereignty came to be understood as the power to suspend the rule of law, that is, as a political decision, to trigger the exception. This account of the exception, as Monateri notes, is taken up by Giorgio Agamben, for whom the state of exception was thereafter the veritable axis of the 'juridico-political machine'.[180] For Schmitt, the '*Kompetenz über Kompetenz*' was the sublime mark of supreme authority over war and peace, life and death. As Thomas Poole writes, at the core of the 'mystery of lawlessness' is the question of who gets to decide when normality exists?[181] *Quis judicabit?*[182] Or, to go back to the conflict of laws, the first known Roman precedent

[173] Santner, *The Royal Remains;* P Kjaer emphasises in turn the importance of the investiture conflicts (opposing Pope and Emperor) for the formation of modern European political order, in which religion was expelled from the public sphere.

[174] On Santner's analysis of the political-economic dimension of our 'busybodiness', see below 256. Interestingly in this respect, the legal and theological genealogy of the metaphor of the body politic is also the focus of Bruno Latour's investigation of the political ecology, or 'body politics' and its implications for (equally irrational) scientific representations of our earth. Latour, *Enquête*, and for the politics of bodies, see below 294.

[175] 'For he is absolutely sovereign who recognizes nothing, after God, that is greater than himself. I say, however, that power of the sovereign. Thus declaring war or making peace is one of the most important points of majesty, since it often entails the ruin or the preservation of a state' (Jean Bodin, *Les Six Livres de la République*; see Monateri, *Dominus Mundi* 108 et seq).

[176] In his own pursuit of an anti-Schmittian account of modern political, P-G Monateri proposes an iconoclastic interpretation of the 'Concept of the Political' as 'an intricate gloss to the ideas that Bodin developed as a trial judge in witchcraft cases. And it is a climax of irony that this concept can, at least in part, be traced back to a kind of pro-Semitism that caused its author to be condemned as heterodox in the very moment he was establishing the modern political orthodoxy of the West' (ibid).

[177] Or stalemate, from which the apparatus of modern legal-political concepts was produced. The latter include the very concept of the political (ibid).

[178] On the double-facing constitution, see J Bomhoff, D Dysenhaus, T Poole (eds), *The Double-Facing Constitution* (Cambridge, Cambridge University Press, 2020).

[179] M Koskenniemi 'Carl Schmitt and International Law', in J Meierhenrich and O Simons (eds), *The Oxford Handbook of Carl Schmitt* (Oxford, Oxford University Press, 2017).

[180] G Agamben, *State of Exception* (Chicago IL, Chicago University Press, 2005).

[181] Poole, *Reason of State*, 217.

[182] A Orford, 'Who Decides? Who Interprets?: Jurisdiction, Recognition and the Institutionalisation of Protection', in *International Authority and the Responsibility to Protect* (Cambridge, Cambridge

in the field might as well be the one that established, by imperial authority, the jurisdiction of the emperor over jurisdictions: *Dominus Mundi Sum.*[183]

Thirdly, in Schmitt's doctrine, the *Nomos* encoding the political power to institute the state of exception is grounded upon a concrete spatial (territorial) order, derived in turn from an original act of land-taking. In that regard, as Monateri observes, the great religious endo-Christian conflict in Europe, the Thirty Years War (1618–48), ended as a purely political compromise, a vast state of exception on a continental level that shaped the modern idea of territorial sovereignty.[184] This first taking, an analogy of the exercise of *dominium* as a form of private property, is the *imperium* constitutive of the modern state.[185] Its rise is also linked in Schmitt's thought to his (fallacious[186]) representation of an extra-European world of lawlessness and warfare. Here, the important point is that, for Schmitt, the modern Westphalian order could not be reduced, as Kelsenian normativism would have it, to a *pure theory of law* or a merely formal frame of rules devoid of substantive (political) content.[187] Still according to Schmitt, this concrete territorial order collapsed between 1890 and 1918 in the face of a sea-based, economically driven, Anglo-American universalism, reducing the (recently instituted, liberal) international law to an empty abstraction of rules.[188] The collapse is induced by the incapacity of democratic liberalism to incarnate the political, as seen above.

The primary objection to this terrifying vision of the world can be raised from the perspective or with the help of private international law. It tells us that while the rule of law comprises an eminently spatial dimension, the latter is in no way tied or reducible to territory. If we turn back to Lauren Benton's exploration of the spaces of colonial empire (in which territory as we know it, in the form of homogeneous

University Press, 2011) ch 4. Orford states that 'when Hobbes argued that the lawfulness of authority was grounded upon the capacity to protect, he was playing a part in a much broader struggle between church and state, or spiritual and temporal authority. Central to that struggle was the question of whether the Pope had jurisdiction to declare that a ruler was unlawful and should be deposed or resisted.'

[183] On the original conflict of laws case that instituted the jurisdictional authority of precedent (by recognising the authority to the claim to world authority by the 'Divine Augustus', see above 112.

[184] See above, 110.

[185] On these twin concepts in Roman law, see Schiavone, *Ius*, 33. See again, on the analogy, M Koskenniemi, 'Sovereignty, Property and Empire: Early Modern English Contexts' (2017) 18(2) *Theoretical Inquiries in Law* 355, observing that private property and contract law created empire as much as they allowed Locke to create sovereignty, and were at the centre of the colonial legal endeavour. The rationalist project of world ordering through law and the colonial project were contemporaneous. This point has now been taken up by Koskenniemi more recently in his opus *To the Uttermost Parts of the Earth* (Cambridge, Cambridge University Press, 2021).

[186] Lauren Benton challenges the Schmittian argument according to which the construction of European legal sovereignty required, on the outside, the lawless other, the exception, a bracketed zone of war. Such an account of the extra-European world as a zone of lawlessness pays insufficient heed, she shows, to the variegated patterns of sovereignty and politics of empire that took place within the latter, not outside it (*A Search for Sovereignty: Law and Geography in European Empires, 1400–1900* (Cambridge, Cambridge University Press, 2010).

[187] Kelsen's *Pure theory of law* depicted the legal order as a mere nexus of valid norms, the *Grundnorm* – the fundamental norm from which all other norms derive their validity – being a pure logical postulate. On the contrary, Schmitt maintained the conception of the constitution as a concrete order based on a material apprehension and division of spaces and resources.

[188] This political vision of the *nomos* corresponds to the Nazi conception of law. Contrary to a frequent misreading, Nazism did not favour an emptying of legal content in favour of value-neutral formalism (O Jouanjan, *Justifier l'injustifiable. L'ordre du discours juridique nazi* (Paris, PUF, 2017)).

space, was a late arrival), she makes the important point that the rule of law evolved as a 'rule about rules', and that in such a context, it is the shape of jurisdiction (not land, territory or geographical place) that is crucial.[189] This observation is of course loaded with significance for the conflict of laws, and all the more so that, prior to the formation of the modern state, spatiality was produced by the personality of law and 'mobile sovereignty'.[190] In other words, the delimitation of legal spaces 'took place' not through the territorial world order underwritten by public international law, but through the specific jurisdictional politics of private international law in which the latter's 'second (constitutional) nature' transpires. Today, increasing consciousness of this function may well explain the growing or renewed interest in the conflict of laws as 'foreign relations law',[191] or indeed the recent quest for a 'constitution' of this discipline.[192] The latter might find room for non-sovereign states or stateless sovereigns, queer ontologies half visible in the semi-peripheries.[193] This brand of scholarship is driven by the idea that the constant allocatory labour of private international law must have significant governance implications in its own right. Such implications are located interstitially, either in the 'diagonal' space in which nation-states interact with foreign citizens and are called to account for the violation of their rights,[194] or on the invisible lines that trace the perimeters of communities beyond the state.[195]

In other words, the locus of sovereignty is not, or not exclusively, in a Schmittian (public) land-based order, but also and very emphatically in the private legal politics of jurisdiction. As we have seen, *dominium* and *imperium* are structurally analogical and ontologically intertwined.[196] The pair operate together in ways that have always allowed 'quasi-sovereign' beings to coexist, under specific legal regimes, on the private side of the fence that maintains their formal separation with nation states.[197] This schizophrenic duality of law and sovereignty resurfaces within the contemporary political economy, where the modern Leviathan, the 'true political', seems to have escaped from the (public legal) body of the state so as to reincarnate in the (private legal) corporate bodies of global economic conglomerates.[198] In dramatic

[189] Benton, *A Search for Sovereignty*.

[190] On this point, see further below 164.

[191] McLachlan, *Foreign Relations Law*.

[192] J Bomhoff, 'The constitution of the conflict of laws' in H Muir Watt & D Fernandez Arroyo, *Private international law and global governance* (Oxford, Oxford University Press, 2014) 262.

[193] See again, Simpson, *Mohawk interruptus* and more below 197.

[194] McLachlan, *Foreign Relations Law*. For an example of the type of case involved, see *Ministry of Defence v Iraqi Citizens*, UKSC, discussed above 149.

[195] Bomhoff, 'The constitution of the conflict of laws'.

[196] Modern sovereignty emerged from a complex constitutive network of private economic (trade, investment and property) relations (see M Koskenniemi, 'Empire and International Law: The Real Spanish Contribution') while the latter all suppose an enabling backdrop of state institutions and public enforcement (see Kjaer, *The Law of Political Economy*).

[197] The latter being the supposedly exclusive bearers of political sovereignty. On the example of the role of the chartered trading companies for the Indies in the establishment of empire, see above 146; the example evokes contemporary role of multinationals in global governance (see below Part III).

[198] This is the theme developed by F Capra and U Mattei, *The Ecology of Law. Toward a Legal System in Tune with Nature and Community* (San Francisco CA, Berrett Kohler Publishers, 2015). P-G Monateri adds (*Dominus Mundi*, 165) that it is not that the political has ended; rather, it has traded its place. The new Leviathan lives on in the private corporation.

terms echoing his own account of the conditions of the emergence of modern sovereignty, P-G Monateri likens the 'political' to a demon wandering in search of bodies to inhabit.[199] He observes that corporate bodies – deploying a mixture of hybrid powers – have assumed a major political role in comparison with states and in effect, have taken over the control of the planet. The world that was governed by the unitary *Dominus* and then by multiple Leviathans is now dominated by amorphous, non-Westphalian legal creatures, animated nevertheless by the intangible essence of the political.[200]

If we turn back to the genealogy of this ontological entanglement of law and sovereignty, Lauren Benton's observation of the entwinement of geographical discourses and legal practices embodying early modern European imperial claims discloses two further theses that are crucial in this context, insofar as they both point in the direction of the private legal dimensions of sovereignty. The first is that the emergence of modern statehood and empire were indissociable, as were the twin concepts of public *imperium* and private *dominium*. The specific argument Benton is making here is the long irrelevance of territory within this history.[201] Thus, if law travelled from the imperial centres of power to the confines of empire,[202] it was through the 'portability of subjecthood', forms of self-delegated legal authority through personal belonging and the private 'management of extraterritoriality' by all sorts of colonial actors. In other words, it was the personality of laws, not their territoriality, that created these imperial geographies.[203] As Benton further observes, this was not without difficulty for the self-understanding of the sovereignty of the Crown and the rule of law it purported to ensure.[204]

Secondly, this account confirms, as seen above, that modern statehood, and a concept of state sovereignty linked to the exercise of control over bounded space,[205]

[199] Ibid, 168 et seq.

[200] Ibid.

[201] This argument is of course also to be related back to the vicissitudes of territoriality in the legal construction of jurisdiction.

[202] Confines of empire, borders of states: on the notion of confines, see Tang, *The Geographic Imagination of Modernity*.

[203] Much of the construction of imperial space depended on the intensively legal work of individual agents, often self-proclaimed carriers of parcels of sovereignty to the known limits of the world. These were imperial functionaries, but also traders, mariners, disbanded naval captains and even pirates, claiming both imperial allegiance and delegated authority on the oceans. Once again, within the conflict of laws, this explains (for instance) the extraordinary fictional device of the 'domicile of origin', that ensured that functionaries and agents of the Crown remained subject to the law of the imperial centre in all respects deemed socially and economically important (marriage, succession), even if their lives ran their course in the periphery (for a similar result with a comparative colonial dimension, see *Ponnoucannammalle*: French colonial administrators were not considered as married to indigenous 'natives' under the law of the metropolis).

[204] Benton sees these multiple non-formal exercises of legal authority as a further factor of the (uneven) extension of empire. The unregulated actions of self-proclaimed individual bearers of sovereignty created difficulties for the self-understanding of the Crown. See, couched in the terms of private international law, a series of recent cases in the context of British military action in Iraq, resuscitating ideas of Crown privilege and justiciability (*Rahmatullah v Ministry of Defence and another* [2017] UKSC 1 and [2017] UKSC 3; Case ID. UKSC 2015/0002) and recalling various strands of early case law in an imperial context, notably in relation to the ascription to the Crown of various acts of ship's captains and other privateers at the uttermost confines of the oceans or empire.

[205] Benton, *A Search for Sovereignty*, 8.

was a product of the end of the nineteenth century, contrary to the genealogical narrative (or story of origin) developed retrospectively at that point. Statehood did not appear fully formed at Westphalia nor did it spring from early modern political thought (that is, from the conceptualisation of sovereignty in the works of Jean Bodin, Thomas Hobbes, and James I). The metamorphosis of the sovereign body, from royal to politic, took time to unfold, spanning the several centuries of modernity's history.[206] If Jean Bodin did not mention territory in his theorisation of sovereignty, Hobbes' own world was one of private entity quasi-sovereign bodies that laboured in the construction of empire.[207] The post-Westphalian political space was populated, in Brunkhorst's terms, by conglomerate quasi-feudal empires with strong privatistic and multi-level features, not nation states.[208] These were queer ontological forms indeed. Such queer legal shapes at the confines of sovereignty appear moreover in the case of Egypt as veiled protectorate, in the blurry status of the Nabob of the Carnatic, or, on the private side of imperial forms, in the (experimental) law of corporate veiling in British India.[209]

As we have already seen at several points above, in its idealised incarnation – as *telos* and essence of evolution – the modern state materialised very late, and quite suddenly, according to Osterhammel, in its post-Westphalian trajectory, in the replacement of natural law at the end of the eighteenth century.[210] Its development took a leap during the nineteenth century with its Hegelian elevation into a metaphysical superstructure, no less 'the march of God through the world'. The implication is that cosmopolitan private sovereigns and vast empires with fuzzy confines actually preceded their monist, territorial incarnation, while plurality (and multi-level governance) was the rule: the national state, writes Hauke Brunkhorst, is actually a 'borderline case' of statehood.[211] Prior to this move, but still faintly perceptible beneath the smooth homogeneous surface of the spatialised rule of law, the 'rule of rules' ran invisible roots into private forms of interlegality. Suggestive of a potent, unruly, ineffable disruption, this is ontology of the exception. Once again, it has a particular resonance within the private underside of international law.

[206] Nor did older cosmological or theological ideas disappear without trace. On the contrary, historical accounts of the contemporary political economy point to the haunting remanence of the 'royal remains' (Santner, *The Royal Remains*), while contemporary political ecology reminds us of the extent to which nature (divine or human) was called upon to provide, recurrently, either a model or the very font of the law (see above 8 et seq.).

[207] See again, Poole, *Reason of State*.

[208] On the European continent, these quasi feudal arrangements remained in place right up to the implosion of the multinational Austro-Hungarian, German, Ottoman and Russian empires in the wake of World War I.

[209] On Egypt as veiled protectorate, see 151, 165); on corporate veils in British India, see R Birla, *Stages of Capital: Law, Culture, and Market Governance in Late Colonial India* (Durham NC, Duke University Press, 2009); on the in-between status of the Nabob of the Carnatic in 1791, see above 146; on colonial legal orientalism in this same vein, see Ruskola, *Legal Orientalism*, J Surkis, *Sex, Law, and Sovereignty in French Algeria, 1830–1930, Corpus Juris: The Humanities in Politics and Law* (Ithaca NY, Cornell University Press, 2019) (and more below 250).

[210] Osterhammel, *The Transformation of the World*.

[211] Brunkhorst, *Critical Theory of Legal Revolutions*.

B. The Status of the Exception

P-G Monateri provides the following insight to Schmitt's political-theological definition of the exception.[212] According to Schmitt, 'the state of exception is to Jurisprudence what miracles are to theology'.[213] Thus, if the 'sovereign' is he who decides on the state of exception, the latter occupies in political theory the same place as does the miracle in theology. At this point, the concept of the 'political' as a decision between friend and foe also assumes a theological and ontological trait. The bulk of Schmitt's theories, as Monateri further argues, consists in the creation of a specific paradigm which captures the ineffable, intangible, sublime side of law and politics within a theological framework.[214] Indeed, even today, contemporary accounts of the exception, or of the essence of sovereignty, reproduce the imagery of irruptive, uncontrollable violence, a vortex of darkness and void often likened to the sublime dimension of nature.[215] Such representations contrast with the Enlightenment account of the clarity, predictability and rationality of the rule of law. In stark contrast, the aesthetics of the exception flag its strange, uncanny ontology.

In this account, echoing Agamben's, the exception represents the locus of manifestation of this surplus of immanence as an exercise of 'bare power'; the expression of potency, secret or occult, unknown or undefined, unpredictable or unspeakable. In a state of emergency, the legal and moral ontology of the world collapses into this indeterminate state, 'displaying the inner transcendence of the political as that which can never be completely ontologised, that is, something not made of fixed stuff'.[216] Moreover, importantly in terms of the law, the exception does not exist per se, but springs from the way it is located in discourse and within a given political order.[217] As for transcendence, as Monateri further surmises, it means 'that which goes beyond words, that which defies our lexicon, but to which we refer to as a kind of ultimate justification for legal or political action'. Therefore, it need not be religious; it can be purely mundane, a kind of surplus of immanence, as he explains. It corresponds to what we feel when we say that 'there is more than that' in a legal text or in a political fact, that opens an uncanny horizon of indeterminacy 'beyond meaning'.[218]

[212] Monateri, *Dominus Mundi*, 7; see too Poole, *Reason of State*, on the connections between the Schmittian exception and 'reason of state'.

[213] For further analysis on *homo sacer* as miracle, see T Christiaens, 'Agamben's Theories of the State of Exception: From Political to Economic Theology' (2021) 110 *Cultural Critique* 49–74.

[214] P-G Monateri's own particular historical and resolutely anti-Schmittian thesis is that, far from there being a (subliminal) continuity between premodern theology and modern politics, modernity produced an inversion, a 'demonological rupture'. Both Bodin and James I of England wrote (scientifically) on demonology at the very time they theorised sovereignty, while the legal texts drafted under the Stuarts bore witness to the struggle between the King and the Pope to exercise power over the witches that had persistently troubled the Elizabethen world (Monateri, *Dominus Mundi* 101 et seq).

[215] P-G Monateri shows how the aesthetics of the exception in political theoretical accounts captures this dark side through references to the sublime – that awe-inspiring, wild, mystery – in nature. The aesthetics of the sublime take us back to the imperial '*Stupor Mundi*'», the terrifying and unbelievable appearance of the Emperor of the world as against the forces of Chaos. This mixture of mystifying and terrific aspects was well represented by the red purple of the Emperor's mantle, signifying that he had the power to shed blood (Monateri, *Dominus Mundi* 50 et seq).

[216] Ibid, 11.

[217] Ibid.

[218] On this point see above 190.

It is something like the hidden, never fully verbalised background notions such as legitimacy or hegemony.[219]

The jurisprudential question, then, is whether this 'ineffable immanence' is outside or inside the rule of law. Is it contained within, or by, the law, or is it indeed, in the radical and paradoxical Schmittian reversal, the lawless grounding of the legal order itself? Prolonging this debate within contemporary political theory, the answer that Agamben provides is that the exception is *simultaneously* within and without the law. At the very heart of the law, then, lies a lawless space,[220] a dark location where 'bare life' – the bodily life of the *homo sacer*, divested of legal form but maintained in mere existence nevertheless by the law[221] – is subjugated to the direct discipline of sovereignty in the form of biopolitics ('bio-power' or 'body politics').[222] By way of parenthesis at this point, it is remarkable that the (premodern) institution of *Habeas corpus*[223] – the judicial injunction to produce the body as the primary guarantee against arbitrary police power and as such at the historical and ethical font of the liberal political order – is still law's best response to the capture, arrest and confinement of prisoners and internees of military or national security camps, reduced to bare bodily life before the law.[224]

While this (neo-Schmittian) vision is controversial on many counts (particularly in that it reduces the liberal order to the camp[225]), it provides an important key to the understanding of the quandary of the status of the exception (within or without the rule of law?) as linked to the schizophrenic nature of sovereignty itself.[226] At its very

[219] Ibid 10.

[220] In Agamben's theory, Western law (prevailing in modern liberal democracies) is centred upon the void space of the state of exception, inversing the democratic order. Thus, the figure of the camp is a central, not an exceptional, place (as for instance relegated to a far-away island). For a critique of Agamben's shared (with Schmitt) fascination with the extraordinary, see G Frankenberg, *Political Technology and the Erosion of the Rule of Law. Normalizing the State of Exception* (Cheltenham, Elgar, 2015). On the void space, see E Santner's analysis of its artistic expression and symbolism in David's dramatic painting of the death of Marais (Santner, *The Royal Remains)*.

[221] The *homo sacer* is a figure of ancient Roman law (or more properly, theology), who is banned from society (banished) and accursed, as he may be killed by anybody. Yet he is not entirely outside the law because he cannot be sacrificed in a religious ritual. In this respect, reduced to 'bare life', *homo sacer* is a shady hauntological figure (see above 29). Hence the analogy with the figures of migrants, the homeless, the mad, or internees in prisons or camps.

[222] Guantanamo Bay or Manus Island would be contemporary examples of lawless spaces of dominion that are still *within* the legal framework, but are now legitimised places of *extra*-legal disciplinary bio-power. The extra-territorial legal status of island camps (Guantanamo Bay) is an additional factor of exceptionalism. This indeterminacy is why the camp, for Agamben, is the *nomos* of the Modern (*Homo Sacer*, ch 7), the very essence of the liberal legal order.

[223] *Habeas corpus ad subjiciendum et recipiendum* emerged to ensure the due process of law through the injunction to 'produce the body' of the accused (that is, to hear the defence) in order to ensure against arbitrary arrest and detention (addressed to the police or other officers of the law, 'we, the Court, command that you have the body of the detainee brought before us'). It was codified as the essence of English liberal modernity as the *Habeas Corpus* Act in 1679, but can be traced back to more ancient (Roman) roots.

[224] *Boumediene v Bush* (nos. 06-1195 and 06-1196, USSC) held that statutory *habeas* jurisdiction extended to Guantanamo.

[225] On the ethical virtues of the Enlightenment, see below.

[226] As P-G Monateri observes: 'The *Dominus Mundi* is the perfect paradigm of what could be defined as the inner ambiguity of human institutions, due to the encounter of classical political theory with the Christian revelation. The *Dominus Mundi* displays in its multifarious characterisations the unfathomable threshold of what is godly and what is demonic in the world order.' (*Dominus Mundi*, 3).

core, explains Monateri, two opposing models are entwined in an inextricable and terrible embrace. These models are the continental imperial *Dominus mundi*, a unitary world order with no outside, on the one hand, and on the other, the English Leviathan, the territorially contained unit acknowledging no legitimate superior authority.[227] The former was ousted by the second, at the price of bloody wars and ages of terror, but has returned today as a *refoulé* to haunt its previous empire.[228] Hence the unsettling indeterminacy of the current world order, of which it has been aptly observed that, as symbolic form, it has undergone a total reversal, with no satisfactory outcome.[229]

Here is the cue to return to the role of the jurists in the formation of the ideas that lie at the origin of these paradigms. Of particular interest, first of all, to private international law and the claim that it can provide some clues to the jurisprudential debate over the place of the exception, is the work of Bartolus de Saxoferrato, widely considered (as seen above)[230] as giving form to the premodern discipline of the conflict of laws in the fourteenth century. Hovering at the ontological transition from the ancient theological ages to the secular modern era, his contribution to a theory of sovereignty in Western legal thought is (perhaps unexpectedly) foundational insofar as it was in substance a claim to order the world through the *corpus juris*.[231] Thus, as far as the relationship of *imperium* to *dominium* is concerned (today, we would say, that of the public to the private), Bartolus defines a particular legal ontology under which the world as a whole can be at the same time 'one thing' and 'many things', under different (universal and local, public and private, eminent and individual) ownerships.[232]

[227] Ibid. The first model 'allows no fracture, resulting in a strong and compact spatial construct where there is no possible distinction between an inside and an outside, and the world is conceived of as a unique spatial entity whose government is concentrated in a single *locus* of authority'. The second, on the contrary, coinciding with the rise of the modern emancipation of politics from religion, arose from the collapse of Holy Roman Empire. Its place, along with its ontological spatiality, was taken by the political powers of the world (the European kings as Leviathans) and divided up among them, under the formal legal instruments of international law. Modern sovereignty meant the acknowledgement of the impossibility of world dominance by any *legitimate* superior authority. This 'normative inversion' founded the legal theory upon which the sovereign territorial state of early modern times later developed.

[228] Ibid: 'Our theory is, then, that the current context of globalisation represents the reappearance of the ghost of the *Dominus Mundi*, which lay dormant as a repressed political figure, a *refoulé*. The reappearance of its sublime and, at the same time, rotten nature. From this standpoint, the clash that we are currently experiencing between populism and globalism could ultimately be seen as two sides of the same ghostly coin, since the *Dominus* was both a national sovereign and a global Lord. But what is more important is that the sublime-kitsch-rotten nature of the political has been left to wander about and must be "recaptured" in its proper significance, superseding the neoliberal dream of a totally depoliticized world.'

[229] See Bartelson, *Sovereignty as Symbolic Form*.

[230] See above 152 and below 203.

[231] Again the *body* of law. As Monateri again points out (*Dominus Mundi*, 15), in the consciousness of the time, this metaphor of the *corpus*, of the body of the law, represented a real ontological experience. The empire, as a single *real* body (constituted by the universally practised Holy Communion), was ruled not by discretion but by the body of rational prescriptions forming the Justinian compilation (the *corpus juris*) as a peculiar revelation of the law. This character of *revelation* of the *corpus juris* and the belief in the unity of the *corpus christianum*, the mystic unitary body of Christendom, represented the ontological unity of a world which continued to be substantially the same as that of the Romans. The *corpus juris* was a physical object, thought to be the written revelation of Reason as applied to the legal and political domain, just as the Empire was a physical body united by Holy Communion. This conception was, of course, political theology at its height.

[232] Bartolus took part in the underlying theological debate on the relationship between *imperium* and *dominium*. The world in its entirety can be considered a single *res*, one thing, and as such it belongs to the emperor, but the various things composing the world, the *singulae res*, may also belong to others. This was

Once again, the law served both to establish a divine right of the emperor, but also to limit his power. On the other hand and similarly, Bartolus discusses the status of free-cities – those whose local laws would derogate from the transcendent Roman *Corpus juris* and enter into lateral conflict – within the larger spatiality of the empire. Here again, the emperor was the true *Dominus Mundi*, but his dominion consisted in a general overarching jurisdiction and did not prevent the self-government of the free cities (with their own customs or self-regulating normative practices), nor did it interfere with the privileges of earthly king (and their royal decrees).

If we go back to the political and legal theorisations of sovereignty, we see that this early modern ontology entailed, paradoxically, a secular, technical approach to political problems that purported to neutralise political clashes through a formal legal framework. As observed again by P-G Monateri, this early modern Romanist approach represented a formalisation of the political and the theological through legal language. Transcendence becomes embodied within the framework of the law and political decision disappears, in favour of logical findings that flow from accepted, pre-existing premises and distinctions.[233] Thus, one of its inherent characteristics is a denial of any need for an ultimate exercise of political power – of pure sovereignty. 'If the world is legally defined, and social relations are legally framed, there is no longer any real room for a pure political decision: a solution of any problem will be found in the reasoning and the subtle distinctions of the jurists.'[234]

This obviously contrasts with the coming of the violent (Hobbesian-Schmittian) Leviathan, and the accompanying supremacy of the political over the law. From a practical viewpoint, it was 'a way to transform *essentially contested concepts* – concepts susceptible to rival and competing meanings, such as the concepts of sovereignty, war, and peace – into a system of defined legal relationships'.[235] Remarkably, an idea has re-emerged in contemporary private international law from an entirely different, feminist anthropological perspective. In their analysis of the 'comfort women saga' in terms of the conflict of laws – used here as a mode of thinking or 'intellectual style', rather than in the form of accumulated positive rulings in comparative case-law – the authors emphasise the virtues of the technical side of private international law as a mode of transforming (not reducing) political conflicts into legal disputes.[236]

the civilian theory of *universalities*: the world is a *universitas*, a thing made of other things, like a flock or a library. On the cardinal place of *imperium* and *dominium* in classical Roman law, see Schiavone, *Ius*, 33: they were the foundations of the (formalising) legal order, so powerful as to 'irradiate' the categories of sovereignty and freedom.

[233] Ibid, 44 et seq.

[234] Ibid.

[235] Ibid. On the presence of these Roman legal ideas in the work of Carl von Savigny, see Schiavone, *Ius* 33.

[236] K Knop, A Riles, 'Space, Time and Historical Injustice: A Feminist Conflict-of-Laws Approach to the "Comfort Women" Agreement' (2017) 102 *Cornell Law Rev* 853. The concept of 'intellectual style' is attributed by Riles in turn to anthropologist Diane E Fosythe (see A Riles, 'A New Agenda for the Cultural Study of Law: Taking on the Technicalities' (2005) 53 *Buff L Rev* 973, 1003; D Forsythe, *Studying Those Who Study Us: An Anthropologist in the World of Artificial Intelligence* (Palo Alto CA, Stanford University Press, 2001) 44. On the notion of 'legal style', more familiar in comparative legal studies, see P.-G. Monateri, *Comparative Legal Methods* (Cheltenham, Edward Elgar, 2021) 38 defining it as 'the way the mind arranges legal institutions with an effect on the rules as well'. Style thus understood 'moulds substance', a point central to the demonstration of Pierre Schlag ('The Aesthetics of American Law') to which we shall return below.

In a similar vein, secondly, the work of the early Roman jurists within the conflict of laws sheds light on the status of the sovereign exception through a central – apparently 'merely methodological'[237] – dilemma. The latter has never ceased to trouble legality's commitment to neutrality in this context, in terms of both politics and morality. Its focus is the exception, labelled *ordre public* or, translated somewhat approximately, public policy, by which a given legal order protects its own (moral, political or cultural) values by refusing a request to apply a foreign law or to enforce a foreign judgment.[238] The point is that it is both an existential element within the coordinatory function of private international law – so much so that it has not disappeared today from the close-knit 'judicial area' within the European Union (any more than it was absent from the Savignian world of the community of laws)[239] – and at the same time its content remains notoriously elusive. Named as 'values', national or international, interests, morality, policies or 'justice', it is the uncanny 'something else' within a rational project that seeks in vain to confine it to 'manifestly exceptional' cases. It is a form of overflowing from (purportedly) predictable legal frameworks, of which examples abound in comparative legal practice.[240] Manifestly, 'the law governs us more than we can govern it', remaining always partially ineffable.[241]

In other words, the exception can be seen as an irruption of the irrational, political among the more policed forms of interlegality. The real focus of contemporary methodological debate in private international law is precisely the dialectic of the norm and the exception, the definition of the political and the place of the exception in respect of legality. Again, *Quis judicabit*?[242] Who has the last word as to what is inside and what is outside the law? As we know, two opposing models are interlocked in the history of the discipline. On the one hand, under the statutist scheme, there was no need for any derogatory device, because the political element was already within, and dominated, the law. This is particularly evident in a policy-based analysis, in the American neo-statutist style, but clearly present in previous iterations of Protestant territorialism.[243] In the continental model, on the other hand, the ordinary application of the law under universalist parameters calls for the exceptional intervention of politics or morals, 'value judgements' that escape any legal definition.[244]

[237] That the 'merely technical', typical of private law, always covers deeper substance, see Kennedy, 'Form and substance'.

[238] On the social construction of the inacceptable and the exclusionary values of 'imagined communities' involving the legal regime of life and death, sex and belief, see below 282.

[239] It is its rooting in sovereignty that still makes this exception Schmittian, as opposed to an ordinary (unexceptional) exception (carved out of a rule).

[240] Texts that attempt to define and restrict the exception of *ordre public* (for instance, in EU regulations on the conflict of laws and cross-border recognition of judgments) and case law that gives it substance worldwide are multifarious and impossible to synthesise here. As seen above, behind these judicial interventions, the triggering of the exception is usually associated with deeper questions of sex and bioethics, life and death, honour and punishment.

[241] Monateri, *Comparative Legal Methods*, 166.

[242] See above 120 and below 183, 229, 236.

[243] See above 99.

[244] There is a fascinating comparative legal dimension here. If we go back to the early nineteenth century debates over the contribution of the rights paradigm ('rights of man' or 'human rights') to conceptions of legality, we find early incarnations of controversies that continue to run through private international law today. Simply, the debate is now '*à front reversé*' because the opposition to (human or fundamental) rights comes largely from France or francophone legal doctrine. For Burke, then, 'French philosophy' was

This suggests the intrinsic duality (or schizophrenia) of each model, and, beyond this particular instance, the deep enmeshing of the law and the exception. It is also the sign of our world's current 'state of indetermination between fact and law'.[245] In this respect it can be taken as a cue to look towards all the other existing ontologies that confer a sense of meaning to these very entanglements by 'dwelling in the between' and constantly crossing from one register to another.

TRANSITION(S)

As we have seen, the quality of our[246] relationship to alterity, whether in the realm of the ecology or in respect of alien cultures or other parts of humanity, is victim to our rage or obsession for order. The latter undergirds the whole paradigm of jurisdictional thinking. It reveals a series of fallacies, or, using the specific lens of private international law, widening cracks in our 'jurisdictional jurisprudence'. The primary chasm is linked to the prevalence of a flattened, monist perspective (the grid or territorial map) that was co-constitutive of, as much as it was enabled by, the emergence of statehood and empire in early modernity. However, the flattening out of the world by this 'rule of rules', committed thereafter to a constant labour of boundary-drawing, did not prevent the return of the *refoulé* in the guise of an all-engulfing (ineffable, political) exception.

The quest for an alternative jurisprudential vision here is obviously not a desire to swing back to the primacy of sovereignty over law – a return to the political sublime.[247] It is a project to change the foundational terms of the deadlock – the dreadful embrace – between law and sovereignty. In this respect, law as a symbolic form is undoubtedly in a position to provide, on an aesthetic register, a vision other than that of a divided world and, in ontological terms, an idea of sovereignty other than exception. Indeed, as the shadow avatar of the conflict of laws shows, legality can also take on a different shape, acknowledging the coexistence of diverse world views and their mutual dependency. The project here is to mine this potential so as to outline a reaction to the lack of nexus between worlds that lies at the core of jurisdictional jurisprudence. In this respect, different morphologies of legality with diverse underlying visions of alterity and ways to relate to it can be found both in other existing cosmological schemes and indeed within the history of the Western legal tradition itself. These open the way in turn for an ontological turn in legality, a transformed legal aesthetic of which alterity might be the epicentre.

to be condemned not so much for having created the conditions for the Revolution, as for having perverted the notion of the law, making the exception the paradigm and the basis on which the whole legal order is rebuilt and redesigned. This is why it was the first *total and philosophical revolution*. It stretched the concept of the political beyond its limits to the point of imagining a redesign of the whole of society.

[245] See above 158, 159 on Agamben and the threshold of un-decidability between *anomie* and *nomos*, between life and law, between *auctoritas* and *potestas*.

[246] Once again, on the meaning of 'our' in this context, see above 1, 269.

[247] Nor the suggestion that there is any salvation in a Schmittian war over the earth's limited resources.

4

A Jurisprudence of the Border

An 'ontology of the border'[248] is a mode of existence that weaves in-between[249] different lifeworlds and cultural forms, crossing frontiers, changing shape, creating hybridity and revealing our enmeshed interdependence with alterity. It acknowledges the coexistence on our planet of multifarious universes[250] that are not separate or exclusive, but overlapping and interacting.[251] In aesthetic terms, this ontology resonates with a radical change from modernity's Archimedean, linear perspective, in favour of a reflexive, multi-sided or 'pluritopical' standpoint.[252] 'Dwelling'[253] at the threshold of multiple worlds (in 'pluriversal' mode[254]), it involves an ability to decentre and adopt the lateral standpoint of the other – that is, of each of these interlocking cultural and natural ecosystems. Taking

[248] Mignolo, 'On Pluriversality and Multipolarity'.

[249] On the in-between as a critical concept borrowed from decolonial literary critique, see above 139.

[250] See K Eitel, M Meurer, *Exploring Multifarious Worlds and the Political Within the Ontological Turn(s)* (Berliner Blätter, 2021) 84.

[251] In *Pluriversal Politics: The Real and the Possible* (Durham NC, Duke University Press, 2020), *Arturo* Escobar defines this concept as 'a world where many worlds fit' (p 9).

[252] Mignolo, 'On Pluriversality and Multipolarity'. The contemporary turn to eco-aesthetics as part of political ecology is to be contrasted with the modern (eighteenth century) aesthetics of nature the classic formulation of which can be found in Immanuel Kant's *Critique of Judgement*, taking nature as an exemplary object of aesthetic experience. The intimate connection with law appears here insofar as all judgement (including legal judgement) is aesthetic.

[253] The idea of 'dwelling', central in Mignolo's pluriverse, is also a focus of (Western) anthropology under its ontological turn: see T Ingold, 'The Temporality of Landscape' (1993) 25 *World Archaeology*. Ingold's 'dwelling perspective' has spread to other disciplines such as landscape architecture, as an attempt 'to reconcile the separation between man and landscape by imagining the landscape as a continually unfolding story. The landscape bears witness to the passing of time; it contains a living memory of all who have lived in it. To perceive the landscape is to carry out an act of remembrance – one is immersed in this unfolding, gathering details and impressions that can be related again': J Abelman, Response to Tim Ingold, www.groundcondition.com/essays/the-dwelling-perspective/.

[254] For the use of pluriversality in private international law, see the Max Planck Institute research project, 'Decolonial Comparative Law' led by Ralf Michaels and Lena Salaymeh. *Cf* further on private international law and 'plurilateralty', A Benoistel, 'Le concept de renvoi mobile: une théorie de la reconnaissance entre le droit international privé et les libertés de circulation européennes', PhD thesis, Université Paris 1 – Panthéon Sorbonne (2018). William James, whose critique of monism is discussed above 61 et seq., can also be credited with the invention of the notion of the 'pluriverse': see K Ferguson, *William James: Politics in the Pluriverse* (Parlux, 2005), noting that 'James contended that engagement with the foreign, the difficult, and the uncomfortable makes us who we are. Rather than mitigating differences or attempting to resolve conflicts, he embraced them, wholeheartedly advocating the opportunity to be transformed' (Preface, xxiii).

its cue from various strands of feminist-ecological[255] and eco-phenomenological thinking[256] in the West, and from indigenous cosmologies and art forms in the global South,[257] its clear political message is that the only adequate response to our late-modern obsession for division, closure, classifications and hierarchies is to 'dwell in the border', inhabit the 'in-between'.[258] Importantly, here, the latter signifies a radical reversal of coloniality as an attitude in respect towards alterity.[259]

Borrowed from literary critique,[260] the 'in-between' as a significant conceptual category has emerged in multiple fields of knowledge as diverse as linguistics, political theory, history, anthropology, sociology, psychology, art, gender studies and philosophy. Artforms and landscape design are not linear, stable and unidimensional, but multi-sided, moving and ephemeral.[261] Environment itself is not separate but

[255] See, commenting on 'the mirage of a space between nature and nurture', E Fox Keller, *The Mirage of a Space Between Nature and Nurture*; see too, paraphrasing Bruno Latour's famous dictum 'we have never been modern', D Haraway and N Gane, 'When We Have Never Been Human, What Is to Be Done? An Interview with Donna Haraway' (2006) 23 *Theory, Culture, Society* 13, asserting that 'we have never been human': 'The dichotomies between mind and body, animal and human, organism and machine, public and private, nature and culture, men and women, primitive and civilized are all in question … they have been "techno-digested"'; by the same author, the famous Cyborg Manifesto and its progeny: *Manifestly Haraway*: *The Cyborg Manifesto and the Companion Species Manifesto* (Minneapolis MN, University of Minnesota Press, 2016).

[256] See C Pelluchon, *Les Lumières à l'Age du Vivant* (Paris, Le Seuil, 2021) and below on relevance for law of Levinassian phenomenology in approaching alterity, see 271 et seq.

[257] See for an instance of interdisciplinary explorations at the frontiers of art forms, museology, history and law, the work of Patricia Zalamea (for example, 'En diálogo con un mundo antiguo: las pinturas de las casas coloniales de Tunja en el marco de un Renacimiento global' (2019) 36 *Revista Historia y Sociedad* 161–94) or of Eulalia de Valdenebro, *Le principe métanthropique*. Such work is emblematic of the contemporary retrieval of 'Humanity(s)' as an intellectual stance. Along these lines, see too C Gordon-Walker, 'Beyond Inclusion: Canadian And Indigenous Sovereignty In Mainstream Museums' (2018) 199 *The British Columbian Quarterly* 129–49. On the idea of 'indigenous ontologies' as a block of common resistance to (late or colonial) modernity (notably in respect of relationships to land, natural resources, non-humans, see above 196).

[258] In addition to the works of Mignolo, De Sousa Santos, Viveiros de Castro and Ingold already cited, see M Wildcat and J De Leon, 'Creative Sovereignty: The In-Between Space: Indigenous Sovereignties in Creative and Comparative Perspective' (2021) 19 *Borderlands Journal* 1–28 arguing that indigenous sovereignties exist in the in-between space between what is and what is possible.

[259] As Silviano Santiago writes, 'Colonization through the spread of Faith and the Empire is the negation of the values of the Other … To be more precise, it is a triple negation of the Other: first, from a social standpoint, because the Indian loses his freedom as he becomes the subject of a European crown. Second, the Indian is forced to abandon his religious system (and everything implied by it in economic, social, and political terms) and is transformed – by the power of catechism – into a mere copy of the European. Third, he loses his linguistic identity, gradually expressing himself through a language that does not belong to him … Therefore, colonization through the expansion of Faith and of the Empire is above all the lack of respect (and not mere intellectual curiosity) in relation to the Other, it is intolerance with the values of the Other. It is the main effect of the narcissistic European gesture that aimed at seeing its own image repeated throughout the universe. In full glory, the so-called universal history begins with European expansionism. The New World is only the occasion for another mirror, and the native is the clay to mould a double, similar figure – and add more violence and destruction', in A Gazzola (ed), *The Space in-between: Essays on Latin American Culture*, 13 (in the context of an essay entitled 'Why and For What Purpose Does the European Travel?' ibid, 9).

[260] Silviano Santiago, ibid.

[261] On an eco-feminist account of multi-sidedness, see V. Methta, 'Anekantavada: The Jaina Epistemology', *Constructing the Pluriverse, op cit*, p. 259.

tightly enmeshed with the inner life of organisms (the holobiont).[262] Time and space are enmeshed,[263] where 'origin (history) is frontier (geography)'.[264] Persons are intimately enchained to things,[265] life to technology.[266] Moreover, disciplines (in all senses of the term) are not independent silos, but interlinked in subterranean rhizome-like fashion.[267] For instance, as Evelyn Fox writes, the binary compartmentalisation of gender has influenced the social construction of science.[268] Indeed, the travelling of metaphors between science and politics, law and biology is but a further 'body-political' example of this interpenetration of centres (or factories[269]) of knowledge production. What we term the political ecology includes, as we have seen, inputs from hard climate science, anthropology, science and technology studies and feminist theory.[270] This is why, in what has come to be called the 'ontological turn',[271] recent calls for a 'flat ontology' resonate in analogous ways in fields as supposedly diverse and separate as contemporary philosophy,[272] physics,[273] queer theory[274] or

[262] Writing on natural symbiosis (or 'multi-species aggregation'), Mike Lynch asks 'what might it mean to consider ourselves, as actors, to be continuous, indeterminately growing interactive trajectories, adapting to changing conditions? … We are more like mycorrhizal fungi than we imagine. This makes an enormous difference for our theories of 'human' action in the world. How can humans act as an autonomous force if our 'we' includes other species that make us who we are? … Reimagining ourselves as interactive trajectories might get us thinking about how we act together with other species to make the world. Living in indeterminacy is a form of freedom we share with other species. If we want to know how multispecies aggregates act, this is a better place to start than reason' ('Sem(b)iosis and the Political Economy of Nature', in Latour et al *The Body Politic*, 89).

[263] On pluritopicality see Mignolo, 'On Pluriversality and Multipolarity'; on 'chronotopes' and their relevance for the law of jurisdiction, see M Valverde, *Chronotopes of Law: Jurisdiction, Scale and Governance* (Abingdon, Routledge, 2015).

[264] 'The frontier is origin', writes ethnographer R Simenel, *L'origine est la frontière*, explaining that his ethnographic approach is to 'associer l'ordre du temps à celui de l'espace pour mieux comprendre la manière dont un lien social se bâtit en référence à l'altérité'.

[265] R Esposito, *Persons and Things: From the Body's Point of View (Theory Redux)* (Cambridge, Polity, 2015).

[266] Latour, *Enquête*, 211 et seq.

[267] On the metaphor of the rhizome to depict postmodern modes of thought, see G Deleuze and F Guattari, *Mille plateaux* (Paris, Minuit, 1980).

[268] Above 2, 16 et seq.

[269] The image is Latour's (*La fabrique du droit. Une ethnographie du Conseil d'État* (Paris, La Découverte, 2004).

[270] As K Eitel and M Meurer (*Exploring Multifarious Worlds and the Political Within the Ontological Turn(s)* (Berliner Blätter, 2021) 84) emphasise, this includes anthropology and science and technology studies (from Latour to Jasanoff, *States of Knowledge*).

[271] See Eitel and Meurer, 'Introduction' in *Exploring Multifarious Worlds*, 19, investigating 'eerie moments' which 'exist in common but non-contemporaneous environments appearing in between … jumble time and ontological orders, granting us insights into automatic modes of action that normally go unseen.

[272] See for example, LR Bryant, *The Democracy of Objects* (Open Humanities Press, 2011) proposing an 'object-oriented ontology' (OOO), that draws on the thought of Gilles Deleuze, Niklas Luhman, Jacques Lacan, Bruno Latour and more.

[273] See for example, A Wendt, *Quantum Mind and Social Science, Unifying Physical and Social Ontology* (Cambridge, Cambridge University Press, 2015): working on the hypothesis that seemingly non-material phenomena such as life, consciousness, and social structures are all ultimately made of the material stuff ostensibly described by physics.

[274] Ruskola, *Legal Orientalism*, introducing an aesthetic *nuancier* imported from the arts and humanities, revealing queer and more exotic forms of sovereignty *en demie-teinte*, of which decadent and lawless China was no doubt the epitome; K Connell, 'Objects in Human Drag: The Queerness of Object-Oriented Ontologies' (MA thesis 2016, Contemporary Art, Design and New Media Art Histories, OCAD University, Canada, http://openresearch.ocadu.ca/id/eprint/777/1/Connell_Katherine_2016_MA_CADN_THESIS.pdf).

architecture.[275] These are all part of our *episteme* or *nomos* that provides us with schemes of intelligibility of our world.

In this respect, the primary lesson to be learned from 'dwelling in the border' is that our normative universe is not one (in the sense of unique or exclusive) but multiple (in that a plurality of modes of access to reality coexist in time and space). Moreover, these alternative strands of in-between thinking all seek to make visible beneath the (modern) binaries and categories that construct our vision of the world or affect our sense of belonging, the fuzziness of confines (metaphorical or geographical) and the multitude of traces, residues, practices and concurrent imaginaries that contribute to form our subjectivities. Importantly, then, these are all attempts, in diverse disciplinary idioms, to unearth and trace the constitution of power asymmetries niched within our *nomos*.[276] Dwelling on the border is a reaction or resistance to colonial forms of universalism,[277] or, in respect of law, to the 'jurisprudence of jurisdiction' that flattens lifeforms and empties the world of its alterity.[278]

Such ideas, then, have potentially radical implications for legal form and substance, in the 'jurisdictional' mode described above.[279] They are beginning to outline an alternative legal shape and ontology, a 'jurisprudence of the border'.[280] Most of the contemporary moves in respect of the law originate in struggles to save and give voice to non-modern life worlds in the Global South[281] or in indigenous minorities in Western colonial states such as Canada or Australia.[282] They seek to track the sinuous operation of power and the embedding of hierarchies under the smooth, neutral-seeming surface of our linear, monist and universalising jurisdictional grid. Above all then, their exploration is also an injunction[283] to look beyond modern law's metaphysical,

[275] See for example, P Campbell, 'The Sea as a Hyperobject: Moving beyond Maritime Cultural Landscapes' (2020) 8 *Journal of Eastern Mediterranean Archaeology and Heritage Studies* 207–25, arguing that the flat ontologies of speculative realism and object-oriented ontology (OOO) can be used to understand the sea as a new type of entity – a hyperobject. In this approach, the sea is not a landscape or facilitator of human activity but an entity of vast geographical and temporal scale that possesses agency.

[276] *Cf* on the work of E Fox Keller (*The Mirage of a Space Between Nature and Nurture)* the review by R Lewontin, 'It's Even Less in Your Genes'(NYRB, 26 May 2011): 'In trying to analyse the natural world, scientists are seldom aware of the degree to which their ideas are influenced both by their way of perceiving the everyday world and by the constraints that our cognitive development puts on our formulations. At every moment of perception of the world around us, we isolate objects as discrete entities with clear boundaries while we relegate the rest to a background in which the objects exist'.

[277] As seen above 36, 137, 'colonial' here must be understood in opposition to 'decoloniality' (and as distinct from colonialism as a particular regime of appropriation). Decoloniality is an ontology of asymmetrical power relations (that can of course be found at the very centre of the colonial metropolis) and thus embodies a particular relationship to alterity. On different modes of universalism, exclusive or relative, see below 214.

[278] On naturalism's blanding of difference, see Descola, *Par delà Nature et Culture* 671–72 et seq. From a political economy perspective, on the voiding effect of neoliberal legality see below 219 et seq.

[279] See for instance, C Younes, 'Le droit et la différence', Thèse de doctorat en Droit privé (dir. Étienne Le Roy) (University Paris 1, 2004), presenting a project of allowing an 'other law' to emerge, a figure of the in-between (*entre-deux*) in a process of 'mutual alteration'.

[280] Mignolo, 'On Pluriversality and Multipolarity'.

[281] As seen above, the leading contemporary examples are the work of de Sousa Santos, Mignolo, and Viveiros da Castro, relayed too by the critical Western anthropologists (Latour, Descola, Ingold) who are ready, in the tracks of Lévi-Strauss, to turn their gaze reflexively onto our own modernity.

[282] See for example the work of Aaron Mills, Rachel Sieder, Naomi Metallic cited above.

[283] Or 'enjunction' (see R Janda and R Lehun, 'The Conflict of Human and Nonhuman Laws' in Irus Braverman (ed) *Animals, Biopolitics, Law: Lively Legalities* (Abingdon, Routledge, 2017)).

geopolitical or epistemological schemes so as to make way, over the legal threshold, for an ontology of interstitiality, and an aesthetics of entanglement.[284] In sum, to renew contact with the 'beings of metamorphosis' whose invisibility and mystery are part of their very 'terms of reference'.[285]

In legal terms, the concepts of frontier, interlegality,[286] threshold, hybridity, interstitiality, border-crossing, connections, plurality and of course alterity all evoke the idiom of the conflict of laws. The hypothesis developed in this chapter is that the alternative, shadow avatar of the latter may serve as an 'intellectual style'[287] in which to give shape and flesh, or form and substance, to alternative modes of 'dwelling within the law' more generally. Indeed, by virtue of the very boundary work that put it at the centre of jurisdictional jurisprudence (as seen above), the conventional account of private international law also carries the traces or residues of an alternative jurisprudence,[288] that of the border, as Walter Mignolo suggests. The various spatial, temporal, social, economic, political and psychological disjunctions observed above, ascribed variously to 'naturalism', modernity, or neoliberalism, can be seen as forms of discipline or repression of plurality and disorder.[289] However, like the 'royal remains',[290] vestiges of past or denied legal forms tend to return in unexpected or eerie ways, as we have seen.[291] Traces of these ontological (hauntological) forms[292] continue to resurface from time to time, outside or

[284] The increasing 'juridification' of such alternative epistemologies may indeed already be changing our perception of the ecology and our social relation to alterity. On the juridification (meaning the translation into the vocabulary of Western law) of these claims, the process and its risks, see Sieder, '"To Speak The Law": Contested Jurisdictions, Legal Legibility and Sovereignty In Guatemala'.

[285] Latour, *Enquête*, 187. According to Descola, *Par delà Nature et Culture* 427 et seq, the being of metamorphosis has no ascribable essence: it is at once and at the same time human, animal and spirit, friend and enemy, adjutant and opposant, prey and predator; it incarnates a mystery that fascinates humans and generates controversy among them. It lives in the threshold zone located at the frontier of the known, inhabited social world, and 'the remainders of the world' where there proliferates everything that exceeds human understanding. See too, in the Palo Alto tradition, the idea of 'man-trace' or *Ichnos-Anthropos* that perceives and interprets signs through a non-dualist 'body-trace' (in which body and spirit are one).

[286] B de Sousa Santos, *Toward A New Legal Common Sense: Law, Globalization, and Emancipation*, 2nd edn (London, Butterworths, 2002) 437, describes interlegality as the phenomenological counterpart of legal pluralism; see too R Wai, 'The Interlegality of Transnational Private Law', *Law And Contemporary Problems* 107; Valverde, *Chronotopes of Law*, 50). De Sousa Santos also uses the concept of 'transconflictuality' (which might also be the phenomenological equivalent of intersectionality).

[287] Knop and Riles, 'Space, Time and Historical Injustice'.

[288] On residual jurisprudence, see Goodrich, *Law in the Courts of Love*. The themes of residues and traces will resurface in the rest of this chapter and indeed (along with the idea of dwelling at the threshold) in Part III below.

[289] See above 141 et seq. In respect of 'naturalism', the critique of the jurisdictional ontology and grid-like aesthetics of modern legality will unfold in this Part. The underlying assumption of community or identity as closure will be challenged in favour of a picture of our interwoven relationship with the world we co-inhabit with other beings and things. With regard to neoliberalism, Part III below will attempt furthermore to reconfine the economy within the limits of the *oikos*, in view of a reversal of the ongoing devastation of our planet's resources.

[290] On the idea of 'the royal remains', see Santner, *The Royal Remains* and above 160.

[291] We might say therefore that the inner conflicts within law's collective subconscious (including the conflicted existence of the conflict of laws) actually drive and produce its contradictory and multidirectional trajectories.

[292] Jacques Derrida defines (hau)ntology as a 'logic of haunting' that is 'larger and more powerful than an ontology or a thinking of Being', and that 'harbor[s] within itself, but like circumscribed places or particular effects, eschatology and teleology themselves' (Derrida, *Specters of Marx: The state of the debt, the*

despite the grid of jurisdictional jurisprudence. Norms begin to wander[293] away from their fixed locations[294] and their contours melt into various forms of indeterminacy and hybridity.[295] Modern law's project of global order cannot contain (in the sense of both content and containment) the underlying entanglement of life forms, mental categories, temporality and spatiality. Here, the point is that these alternative modes of dwelling can be productively unearthed (or perhaps more appropriately, re-earthed), so as to allow legality to resonate with deep-ecological descriptions of the world as biodiversity and entwinement.[296]

Evocative of the latter, the 'dismal swamp', then, comes into its own.[297] Navigating in-between spaces, thresholds of uncertainty,[298] the shadow avatar of the conflict of laws proposes two distinctive features of an alternative scheme of legality. These might be described in terms of law's ontology as its diplomatic, 'go-between' function, and, in terms of legal aesthetics, its interstitial and multi-sided location at the very crossing of borders, that opens on different vistas or ways of seeing. On the one hand, instead of dividing up and severing, it reconnects and repairs. On the other, it contains an invitation to stand and look back at ourselves, not from law's traditional unitary or monist standpoint, but from the lateral and necessarily plural, perspective of the other. These are the two – equally interwoven – ideas developed below.

work of mourning, and the new international (New York, Routledge, 1994) 10). It is a study of spectrality and spectres – that is, entities and processes that exceed any definite categorisation; accordingly, it inevitably questions the established notions of being, thereby transforming the status of the objects and subjects of knowledge, and contesting the possibility of objectivity: see E Lorek-Jezińska, K Więckowska, 'Applied Hauntologies: Spectral Crossings and Interdisciplinary Deconstructions' (2017) 8 *AVANT. The Journal of the Philosophical-Interdisciplinary Vanguard* 15–23.

[293] A Boureau, *L'errance des normes. Elements d'éthique scholastique (1220–1320) La Raison Scholastique* (Paris, ed Les Belles Lettres, 2016) on the distancing of religious taboos and the delegation of the production of ethical norms to the (emerging) subject. Interestingly for the theme of planetary responsibility and the shape of legal norms, this early 'wandering' of norms is shown to have woven around a juridical-moral ethic of responsibility.

[294] Is there a return to 'wayfinding' today? See R Macfarlane's review of three books on navigation, both human and animal (NYRB, 1 July 2021). The piece expands into a meditation on the value of wayfinding, which he describes as 'an ethic', rather than simply the ability to get from point A to point B. Wayfinding requires 'collaboration and cooperation between humans and their environments', an active engagement with the landscape that we are on the path to losing (with our overreliance on GPS). On the right to roam or (Latourain) 'deambulation', see S Vanuxem, 'Du droit de déambuler. Repenser la liberté d'aller et venir à l'âge de l'anthropocène' Conference, Sciences po, Faculty Seminar, Spring 2022. For a reflection on law and place, displacement and place-holding, see Lindahl, *Authority and the Globalization of Inclusion and Exclusion*; and 'Place-Holding the Future: Legal Ordering and Intergenerational Justice for More-Than-Human Collectives'.

[295] Interestingly, the idea of 'hybrid legal systems' is used in comparative legal studies to refer to mixed legal traditions (Roman-Dutch, for instance) that serve as an irritant to enterprises of classification into legal families: see R Zimmermann, K Reid, D Visser (eds), *Mixed Legal Systems in Comparative Perspective: Property and Obligations in Scotland and South Africa* (Oxford, Oxford University Press, 2005).

[296] As mentioned above, the point here about unearthing, or indeed the unearthly, resonates with the Levinassian notion of a 'split horizon' in presence of alterity, as will be seen below (Part III).

[297] On the description of private international law as a dismal swamp, see above 45. On the aesthetic of the swamp, the work of Brazilian literary critic Silviano Santiago (*The Space in-between: Essays on Latin American Culture* (Duke University Press, 2001) is particularly interesting, having developed (in the 1970s) the idea of the swamp as the 'in-between space' (*o entre-lugar*, in Portuguese). On the aesthetic of the swamp and the portrayal of private international law as such, see above 177.

[298] On the ethical signification of the threshold, see below.

As a symbolic form, first of all, and in stark contrast to its 'jurisdictional' embodiment as rational order, law appears in this shadow account as a 'juridical ecology of ligatures'.[299] The residues of archaic forms, along with increasing awareness of the (threatened) plurality of legal worlds, are an invitation to seek alternative ontological accounts of legality in view of the evident failures, or distortions, of the previous, opposing model. The avenue to explore is Bruno Latour's unique transdisciplinary effort to depict legality in ecological terms.[300] Rather than attempting to provide a static definition of law,[301] the move here is to flesh out the imagery of law's 'passage', that emphasises its ontology or mode of existence as re-connection or reattachment ('*rattachement*'[302]) of which the conflict of laws provides an emblematic form (section I). This same depiction of law as a pluralist ecosystem of linkages can be correlated, in turn, to a specific – and again peculiarly ecological – aesthetic. The cracks in the surface of jurisdictional jurisprudence, as described above, are the cue to use the conflict of law's own shadow scheme in order to explore the means and implications of a legal perspective that would abandon a grid-like view of the world in favour of a 'perspectivist' or multi-sided approach[303] (section II).

I. A 'JURIDICAL ECOLOGY OF LIGATURES'

Exploring the invention of law in the West, the legal historian Aldo Schiavone suggests that the specific mode of existence of Roman law lay in its ability to institute a complete formalisation of social life.[304] We can return again here to this author's account, mentioned above, of the ontology of prescriptivity as evidenced within the great (re)invention of Roman legal science in the sixth century AD in Justinian's momentous *Digest*. In the new Roman learning, on the one hand, abstract legal concepts were not merely mental categories, but metaphysical figures of being ('jurimorphs' or semiotic objects in circulation, in Latourian terms[305]), real actants endowed with a life of their own and an incontestable objectivity, of which legal knowledge was the mere reflection. The underlying cosmopolitical dimension[306] of this project was to enclose

[299] K McGee, 'Introduction', in *Latour and the Passage of Law* 1–16.

[300] See the very helpful intermediation, for lawyers, of the collective edited by McGee, *Latour and the Passage of Law.*

[301] The difficulty of the quest for such a pluralist jurisprudence is evidenced and analysed by N Roughan and A Halpin, *In Pursuit of Pluralist Jurisprudence* (Cambridge, Cambridge University Press, 2017).

[302] This is the French technical term for 'connecting factor' in the conflict of laws.

[303] Schlag, 'The Aesthetics of American Law'.

[304] Schiavone, *Ius*, 279.

[305] Latour, 'The Strange Entanglement of Jurimorphs', in McGee, *Latour and the Passage of Law* 331.

[306] Here, the compound term is taken at its face value to signify a juncture of cosmology as (universalised) world view and an (imperial) political project. However, cosmopolitics (as distinct from Kantian and indeed Beckian cosmopolitism: see U Beck, *Qu'est-ce que le cosmopolitisme?* (Paris, ed Aubier, Alto, 2006)) has come to take on a further meaning as coined by Isabelle Stengers (in the midst of the contemporary 'science wars' in which Bruno Latour himself was engaged. The message it contains (about the production of scientific truth) is very important for the theme in this book as developed below in this chapter. It is emphatically not the defence of a homogenised world state. Philippe Descola proposes a further, original definition, which has its place more particularly in what follows: cosmopolitics situates multiple worlds

all of (bare) life within a transcendent scheme of classifications, proportions, and linkages: again, a metaphysical clockwork operating according to its own temporality. The early emergence of legality as a mode of existence responded to the risk of social disintegration in times of intense political struggle following the founding of Rome.[307]

In terms borrowed from Bruno Latour, a whole 'juridical ecology of linkages and trajectories' was put in place through Justinian's imperial project of world governance through law.[308] Law's passage takes (its) place, as Kyle McGee in turn explains, within the 'unwritten order of the universe of things', an ongoing universe of interactions and symbiosis.[309] This depiction of law is anything but traditional.[310] The same goes

on an epistemic plane that seeks to link within a loose assemblage all manner of beings and relations that appear to be ontologically incommensurable (*Les forms du visible* (Paris, Seuil, 2021)). In this context, a cosmology corresponds to the forms such assemblages take on for those who inhabit them.

[307] In later centuries, and in profoundly changed circumstances, the imperial claim to rule the world was still grounded on a specific 'political theology', in which law and revelation, legal form and liturgy were long indistinct (as seen above). The divide between law, politics and religion would take shape with the final fall of the *Dominus Mundi* (in the East) and the institution of a new (Westphalian) secular order (that put an end to endo-European religious struggle in the West). However, it was again the work of medieval (largely English and French) jurists in a quest for the legitimation and continuity of royal power, that had prepared the advent of political modernity and the rise of the Leviathan. The later transformations of modernity, framed by an autonomous legal rationality, must again be understood on an ontological register. Human reason and human nature replaced transcendent order and divine right as a mode of governance of the world. The path was opened for the emergence of the 'jurisprudence of jurisdiction' observed in the previous chapter.

[308] Schiavone, *Ius* 19: in Justinian's 'majestic and global' vision, the clairvoyance and wisdom of the sovereign emperor were the channel through which Providence would accomplish its grand design of perfection and salvation through law.

[309] McGee, *Latour and the Passage of Law.*

[310] Bruno Latour's momentous *Enquiry into Modes of Existence* is (deliberately) unclassifiable in disciplinary terms (one self-description by the author of his own opus, that is particularly apt here as will be seen below, is as a 'sociology of translation'). The concept of 'modes of existence' is inspired from Etienne Souriau's definition of speech acts, each with its own conditions of felicity and infelicity (*Les différents modes d'existence* (Paris, Presses Universitaires de France, 1943; republished 2009, with an introduction by Isabelle Stengers and Bruno Latour)) along with their specific itineraries of veridiction. This is a way of acknowledging the existence of 'plural worlds' (to which we return below). Latour's own intellectual ambition is to compile no less than a vast (symmetrical, or reflexive) 'anthropology of the Moderns'. Its crucial axis is a (pragmatist) reflection on the production (or manufacture) of truth, or, better, of a plurality of truths. Insofar as it affects the law, it can be seen as a (strange) mix of legal ethnography and legal semiotics (McGee, *Latour and the Passage of Law*, 2), in which translation is a 'key part' (through Michel Serres, on whose work on 'translation' it is useful to read SD Brown, 'Science, Translation and the Logic of the Parasite' (2002) 19 *Theory, Culture & Society*). On semiotics, Latour acknowledges the key role of P Fabbri (see for instance on the semiotic turn, his *La svolta semiotica* (Rome, G Laterza, 2001)), who drew attention to non-human actants, to the circulation of (scientific) truths along 'chains of inscriptions' (the latter reference is to J Derrida, *De la grammatologie* (Paris, Minuit, 1967)) and to the existence of worlds of objects with their own magic, protocols and even morality. This also connects Latour's work to the 'cyborg' of feminist scholar D Haraway (*Simians, Cyborgs, and Women: The Reinvention of Nature)* as a material/semiotic figure that implodes the dichotomies of nature/technology, human/nonhuman, male/female). Singularly, at least in view of law's minor status within other social scientific projects, the specific ontology of legality is given considerable attention by Latour (*Enquête*, ch 13, 'Le passage du droit et les quasi-sujets', p 357 et seq. To fully understand this chapter, it needs to be emphasised here (once again: see above 21) that legality thus understood relates to *jus* and not *lex*, as explained by Schiavone, *Ius*. Indeed, one reiterative mistake (a 'category error' induced by the perverse pseudo mode 'Double Click') in legal theory is to mistake law's own internal 'theory of sources' for an ontology of law; another is to mistake legal interpretation (translation) for 'pure information', as if it was objectively 'out there'. In Latour's

for Latour's equally striking idea that ontology is the science of 'being-as-other'.[311] Nevertheless, both notions have obvious resonance within contemporary accounts of the conflict of laws. The link is provided of course by Carl von Savigny's opus of 'actualisation' of Roman law in the mid-nineteenth century (with particular attention in the eighth and ultimate volume to the question of conflicting, derogatory norms), constructed on this understanding of *ius*, foundational to the *Corpus civilis*.[312] As Schiavone writes of the *System des heutigen römischen Rechts*, published as Berlin was preparing to conduct the political unification of the German nation, it was an extraordinary 'short circuit' in the field of law between the ancient and modern worlds, between the subject of empire and the modern individual, that subtracted the ontology of Roman law from its historical context and projected it forward as the very path of civilisation.

In echo to this holistic ordering of the world through a 'whole ecosystem of relations and interactions',[313] the emblematic core of the conflict of law's own connective work at the boundaries of the foreign can also undoubtedly be described as a labour of ligature, located within a complex ecology of interactive trajectories beyond the borders of the state. Strikingly evocative in this respect is the imagery of private international legality as a biosystem, providing a space for the operation of vital exchanges and interdependencies.[314] In particular, the biological notion of entanglement[315] – multispecies symbiosis or holobiont – serves as a metaphor for an ecological body politic, a collective made up of the interactive trajectories of all interdependent beings (including the non-sentient and the invisible). 'We have never been individuals' is the 'symbiotic view of life'.[316] Instead of taxonomies, we would have assemblages of relations.[317] However, depicting law (or *ius*) as an 'ecology of

presentation, beyond the moderns' subject/object binary, law's beings are classified (like, for instance those of politics) as 'quasi-subjects', offers of subjectivities (as it were) that come to fill the empty planes of enunciation made ready by 'quasi-objects' (such as the beings of fiction or technology): see *Enquête*, 371. On the links between this philosophical-anthropoligical project, including his symmetrical ethnography of the Conseil d'Etat in *La Fabrique du Droit* (Paris, La Découverte, 2002), and his current concerns with the plight of the planet, see D Saunders, 'From the Conseil d'Etat to Gaia: Bruno Latour in Surfaces and Depths', in McGee, *Latour and the Passage of Law* 17 et seq).

311 *Enquête*, final chapter, and in particular p 479.

312 As Aldo Schiavone reminds us (*Ius* 31), Savigny himself was writing at a time at which a 'secret resemblance' was established between the 'natural' maxims and principles of Roman reason, proportion and measure, both objective and rigorous, and Leibniz (re)discovery of infinitesimal calculus (of which Kant had just investigated the gnoseological implications).

313 These expressions are taken from Kyle McGee's 'Introduction' to *Latour and the Passage of Law*.

314 There are evident echoes here of Justinian's great project to institute a complete formalisation of social life, and again in Savigny's own ambition for the revival of Roman law (along with its conflict of laws component), even if Savigny harked back to a pre-Justinian, uncodified state of the classical purity/maturity of Roman law. We return to this point below.

315 On entanglement theory, see D Haraway, *Staying with the Trouble: Making Kin in the Chthulucene* (Durham NC, Duke University Press, 2016).

316 S Gilbert, J Sapp, A Tauber, 'A Symbiotic View of Life: We Have Never Been Individuals' (2012) 87 *The Quarterly Review of Biology* 325. This of course is in deliberate echo to Bruno Latour's *Nous n'avons jamais été modernes: Essai d'anthropologie symétrique We have never been modern* (English translation: Cambridge MA, Harvard University Press, 1993).

317 Taking the cue from indigenous cosmologies, Jean-Baptiste Morizot writes that ontology, understood as the essence of all interdependent human and non-human, visible and invisible beings, would then be second to the way we relate to them. See *Esthétique de la rencontre*, co-authored with E Zhong Mengual

ligatures' is not necessarily easy for a legal mindset shaped by jurisdictional jurisprudence and its ontology of taxonomic categories (as seen above). This is the cue to turn to the shadow, pluralistic, version of the conflict of laws, where it has obvious resonance (both semantic and conceptual). It enjoins us to take this novel observation of law's 'passage' very seriously. This is what the two paragraphs that follow will attempt to do.

The starting point is to see law as continually 'passing through' in a constant labour of mending or reparation of broken links.[318] In this regard, it performs on a diplomatic register as go-between,[319] maintaining plurality while weaving interstitial connections. A linguistic analogy will be helpful here to further flesh out what this means (section I.A). Further, however, in its own dynamic course, its endless action of 'boundary-crossing' is repetitive, unstable and decidedly non-linear. The genius of the operative mode of *ius* lies in its ability constantly to change register or 'gear' (weaving in and out from the general to the particular, from principle to fact, from rule to exception).[320] Private international law amplifies this inherent ontological agility by virtue of its constant navigation of legal frontiers (section I.B).

A. Law as Go-between

Law's labour, in Latour's vision of its 'passage', is an endless weaving in between utterances and their authors, deeds and their doers, actions and those responsible for them. It involves a 'litany of semiotic objects' all caught up in a trajectory that is unmistakably legal.[321] This vision proscribes all references to 'system' or 'order'.[322] It is one 'regime of truth'[323] among many, that serves to stabilise collectives of humans and non-humans by producing 'durable correlations'. Such correlations are not pre-established; they must be created anew each time through the action of legal connection. Thus, the originality of law, observes Latour, lies in its constant 'countermovement of reprisal that reattaches what the continual movement of dispatches

(Paris, Seuil, 2018); *Wild Diplomacy. Cohabiting with the Others Among Us* (New York, State University of New York Press, 2019). See more on this point below.

[318] See McGee, *Latour and the passage of law*.

[319] Roughan and Halpin (*In Pursuit of Pluralist Jurisprudence*) observe that pluralist legality operates on a go-between register (at risk of undermining the quality of decisiveness that is central to monist arguments).

[320] This point about the genius of Roman law is made by G Samuel (above 119); the metaphor of change of gear or 'débrayage', is omnipresent in Latour's *Enquête*.

[321] McGee, *Latour and the passage of law*, 'Introduction', 3.

[322] See in particular, a recent prolongation of the Enquiry that relates to the conditions of possibility of a renewed body politic, beyond the holistic concept of 'society' in the social sciences. Inspiration is drawn here from numerous areas of study, including the natural sciences, where exploration covers the working of collectives such as anthills or again, the holobiont. The urgency of the task is compounded by the Anthropocene, and awareness of looming ecological devastation. See B Latour, S Schaffer, P Gagliardi (eds), *A Book of the Body Politic. Connecting Biology, Politics and Social Theory* (ed Cini Fondazione, 2017).

[323] Each mode of existence (law, politics, science etc) has its own 'mode of veridiction', that is of access to reality (or truth). On the mode of veridiction of natural law and its residues of rebirth among newer forms of governance (such as 'nudging' or algorithmic governance), see above 10.

never stops detaching'. The central intuition is that, in the course of this perpetual reiterative, shuddering and hesitant performance, law 'passes'.[324] 'Something called law' iteratively and repeatedly follows a fragile itinerary through semiotic objects: allegations, proofs, rhetoric, texts and the indispensable '*libido judicandi*' that 'structure and dictate how imputations should be established'.[325] In this respect, law contains a series of devices or processes that catch all sorts of 'matters of concern' within a recognisably legal trajectory, producing legal effects. These include operations such as fictionalisation, rescaling, reorienting, bending[326] and are all part of 'law's strange gait', constantly shifting gear or shuttling between semiotic registers from 'value-object' to obligation.[327] This, then, is what it is like to 'walk the walk of the law', a strange, slow,[328] wavering gait that bridges a specific 'discontinuity' shifting constantly from facts to principle and back, each of the latter being itself inherently unstable.[329]

[324] The imagery of the 'passage of law' evokes, on the one hand, running water, in a state of constant redefinition, in contrast to the mirage of the pre-constituted, hard and fast lines of modern law. In respect of the interstitial operation of legality, William Twining has drawn attention to the ways in which globalisation has affected its modes of diffusion in time and space. Using Sousa Santos's concept of interlegality (on which we shall return below) to refer to relations between legal (and normative) orders, he suggests that their interaction 'is often more like that between waves or clouds or rivulets than between hard, stable entities like rocks or billiard balls' ('Diffusion and Globalization Discourse' (2006) 47 *Harvard International Law Journal* 507–16, 513). The hermeneutical turn in legal theory has long drawn attention to the evolutionary, contextual character – the elusiveness – of meaning and its potential for perpetual, aquatic, recomposition (see, on public international law in this respect, J d'Aspremont, *Beyond Meaning*). It echoes moves in social and political theory to associate late modern sovereignty with the notion of liquidity (Z Baumann, *Liquid Modernity and Beyond* (Cambridge, Polity, 2000)). However, 'passage' in this context also suggests porosity of membranes. In the context of the transition to legal pluralism, this means that the relationship between the domestic and the foreign, or law and fact, is one of permanent osmosis, and not, as legal monism would have it, of strict separation. The word-game (law's 'passing') also refers to the idea that there is a discursive style, or 'pre-position', that is unmistakably law-like: 'ça passe' (or not) as a successful legal argument. To 'go down well', it has to be well fabricated: see F Cooren, 'In the Name of the Law: Ventriloquism and Juridical Matters', in McGee, *Latour and the passage of law* 235, 250.

[325] Latour, 'The Strange Entanglement of Jurimorphs', in McGee, *Latour and the passage of law* 331, 332. McGee, ibid, Introduction, p 3. This vision of law's 'performance' results from his ethnography of the French Conseil d'Etat (*La fabrique du droit* (Paris, La Découverte, 2002)). Admitted inside the very core of a central, if idiosyncratic, jurisdictional institution, Latour set out to observe the multiple actants (from paper-clips to legal 'grounds'), and 'fragile trajectories' of legal arguments involved the intimate clockwork of (administrative) legality.

[326] Bending the rule to breaking point, but not quite. Law never goes as far as 'bridging the unbridgeable': K McGee, 'On Devices and Logics of Legal Sense: Towards Socio-Technical Legal Analysis', in McGee, *Latour and the Passage of law*, 61, 78. And of course, these operations affect the law as much as the law commands them.

[327] Ibid.

[328] This suggests an analogy (see Saunders, 'From the Conseil d'Etat to Gaia' 36) between Latour's description of law's suspended, procedural slowness in its strange 'hall of mirrors' (S Gurtwirth, 'Providing the Missing Link: Law after Latour's Passage', in McGee, *Latour and the Passage of law*, 122), and Heidegger's thought on temporality (on which, see further, MA Gillespie, 'Temporality and History in the Thought of Martin Heidegger' (1989) 43 *Revue Internationale de Philosophie* 33–51, 'Heidegger (1889–1989)).

[329] McGee, *Latour and the Passage of law* 5. Law's aptitude or vocation to bridge such discontinuity is why law can never be considered as a mere channel of 'objective' information or knowable 'facts' in epistemological terms. As seen above, in Latour's own words, the difference between law and science is precisely that law does not transport knowledge. Asking it to do so is like trying to 'fax a pizza' (ibid, p 48).

Thus, its specific mode of existence confers on law several distinctive features that accompany, support or explain its action as go-between. Firstly, law's 'passage' is indissociable from that of its 'superficiality'. Latour emphasises a 'peculiar lack' – that of 'any reflexivity other than (law's) own; it is its own metalanguage'.[330] It is indeed the only mode of existence that perpetually archives its own moves, retaining traces of its own passage everywhere, with no particular domain of its own.[331] At first sight, the connotation of law's 'superficiality' or lack is distinctly negative. However, the point being made here is that, by contrast with other modes of being such as politics (including *lex*),[332] the virtue of legality (*jus*) lies in its ability, in the course of its ubiquitous and perpetual labour of linkages, to connect anything and anybody. Without law, nothing could bind space and time in any form of continuum.[333] It operates as a go-between all forms of animate and inanimate actants, events or discourses, 'plunging into everything'.[334] But in 'linking together the mostly wildly disparate actors', it reveals that its distinct power lies in its 'astute devoidness of any other content than its connectedness'.[335] At this point, we can recall the ontology of Roman law and its extraordinary project of the total formalisation of life, as described (above, section I) by Aldo Schiavone. Furthermore, in terms of Latour's own thought, it is precisely law's ubiquity, weaving in and out on the 'lifeworld of surfaces',[336] that will allow the 'reassembling' of everything (including of course, non-human actors) that our encounter with Gaia requires.[337]

This superficiality comes as a form of immense relief. It 'disencumbers' law from the formidable injunctions of the *Rechtstaat*, or *l'Etat de droit*,[338] that a repeated category error keeps transferring from the political sphere of Law I (*lex*) to the juridical register of Law II (*jus*).[339] It is a grave mistake (the ruse of Double Click[340]) to

[330] Latour, 'The Strange Entanglement of Jurimorphs', 334.

[331] G Harman, 'Politics and Law as Latourian Modes of Existence', in McGee, *Latour and the Passage of law* 38, 48–50. It might be said (with a risk of misunderstanding) that law has no content, in the sense that it is fully identical with its own conditions of enunciation (McGee, *Latour and the Passage of law* 63).

[332] Coded as POL (politics), in which we find *lex*, or Law I as seen above.

[333] G Harman, 'Politics and Law as Latourian Modes of Existence', 50.

[334] Ibid.

[335] *Enquête*, 33.

[336] Saunders, 'From the Conseil d'Etat to Gaia' 34.

[337] Ibid, 36. This is the link between Gaia and Latour's 'Actor Network Theory' (on the latter as 'reassembling the social' see, published under this title, B Latour, *Reassembling the Social: An Introduction to Actor-Network Theory* (Oxford, Oxford University Press, 2005). The gathering of everything (all beings) is the civilisation to come. Importantly, then, legal action includes (renders answerable for their deeds, utterances or actions) all actors. All associations we register as legal make society, the latter being entangled with law (McGee, *Latour and the Passage of law* 5). This raises the question of residues, or the 'plasma' (beings without trace) that is left out, as will be seen below, Part III.

[338] Gurtwirth, 'Providing the Missing Link: Law after Latour's Passage'.

[339] See above 20 et seq. See too above 170 et seq. on the status of the exception and the conflict (*quis judicabit?*) between the rule of law and the realm of politics (or religion). Here, law's rule drives concepts such as power and legitimacy into a state of redundancy or suspension (McGee, *Latour and the Passage of law* 3).

[340] Double Click, as seen above 8, is the ruse or 'pseudo-mode' whose agency must be resisted. It leads us to the disastrous category errors of those who think they are Moderns. It also refers to a contentious device that Google installed on smartphones, that – of interest from the perspective of private international law – has recently given rise to a spectacular transnational class action in the United Kingdom *(Lloyd v Google* LLC [2021] UKSC 50).

assign the objects of other modes of existence (politics or POL; organisation or ORG; or technics TEC) to law. It is for these other ontologies to shelter these values, but not for law, 'which justifies nothing but its own assignation'.[341] At the same time, however, this very project of remaining at the surface of all things requires of legality an immense (superhuman?) effort. Firstly, staying afloat as it were in the new 'depth game'[342] means resisting the comfort of the Moderns' hegemonic abstractions,[343] a fully ontological task of encapsulating all that the latter have repressed.[344] Secondly, for each minuscule case it is called upon to consider, it has to mobilise (virtually) the totality of the interdependent elements of the entire 'body of law'. By virtue of law's own mode of veridiction, its superficiality is correlated to the multitude of intricate correlations it needs to maintain: between the infinitely numerous and microscopic legal 'sources' and the few elevated general principles; between humble facts and the constitutional rule of law.[345]

Kyle McGee describes this 'juridical ecology of ligatures' as a 'factory of stabilising bonds'.[346] The specific legal mode of existence of *jus* (as opposed to the political mode of *lex*) is one of an unending 'labour of connection'. Following the 'hesitant composition of fragile trajectories' it seeks to link together disparate actors or actants, things or events, 'in order to suture, with lace-like thread, the planes of enunciation emitted in other controversies, other practices, other scenes'. This points very clearly to law's existence as relationality, not taxonomy. Interestingly, a recent anthropological study of the idea of 'status' in indigenous cosmologies points to the idea that 'status' is above all 'relation', not category.[347] The primacy of relationality (over taxonomies) in indigenous epistemologies resonates all the more forcefully within the conflict of laws that this relational notion of 'status' is described as an encoding of alterity on an ontological register, through constant and inextricable interweaving (or *allers retours*).

[341] *Enquête*, generally, and see McGee, *Latour and the Passage of law* 4. This argument ties up with Samuel Moyn's point about human rights as 'the last utopia' (see below 288 et seq): rights are being wrongly burdened with the labour of POL or FIC.

[342] Saunders, 'From the Conseil d'Etat to Gaia' 34.

[343] It works as an antidote to the 'incarceration' of thought (or the enchantment of reason?) into modernity's abstractions (see McGee, *Latour and the Passage of law* 3). As Kyle McGee writes on this point (ibid, 61), we need to focus attention away from the latter towards law's 'wonky artefacts'.

[344] Ibid, 35.

[345] In an idiom more familiar to analytic legal theory, one might speak of law's systematicity. A judicial application of the law cannot ignore the need for coherence, or the fact that any decision may have ripple effects throughout the system. This is particularly well-illustrated in the conflict of laws, where theories of characterisation (or fitting foreign institutions into the categories of the forum) come with elaborate corrective devices of adjustment or adaptation (of which the canonical account is G Cansacchi, 'Le choix et l'adaptation de la règle étrangère dans le conflit de lois' (1953) 83 *RCADI*) in order to limit the collateral or ripple effects of disturbance caused by the introduction of alien legal practices (a well-known example of the legal irritation produced by the encounter of two very different models – civilian and common law – lies in succession law, and a (canonical) judicial illustration of the care needed in this respect to find the right category to house a foreign institution, can be found in a famous judgment of the (French colonial) Court of Appeals of Algiers of 24 December 1889, in which the widow *Bartholo* claimed a poor spouse's quarter, unknown to French law. This affair inspired Etienne Bartin's own equally famous 'discovery' of the 'problem of characterisation', concomitantly with that of Kahn in Germany (see above 80).

[346] McGee, *Latour and the Passage of law*. The expressions in inverted commas below in the text are borrowed from here.

[347] Morizot, *Esthétique de la rencontre*. See above 180.

Moreover, the idea of an ecology of ligatures and a labour of 'reprisal' (a term with a decidedly ambivalent meaning, since the return loop it implies could be either vengeance or mending …[348]) signals that law has a reparative, tailoring quality. This signifies that, whatever its changing political content, legality operates as it were as the stabilising factor – or weaving thread – that keeps the social fabric together. In this respect, of course, it embodies a radical reversal of the separative effects of modern law, as seen above. Juridical ligatures bridge gaps and bring together whatever is at risk of being sundered. One might see the very constitution of private international law as directing it towards the rebonding of people and places, communities and responsibility, duties and liability, conduct and remedies, when the connections are lost or made fuzzy by geographical dispersion and the multiplicity of potentially applicable rules.[349] Wherever there are boundaries that divide or distinguish (categories, places, cultures …), law can 'come to pass' through, beyond or in-between. In this vision, law is precisely an 'in-between actor that produces form'.[350]

Finally, in addition to law's 'superficial' formalisation of life and its constant labour of rebonding, it is driven by a specific dynamic. In reconnecting human interventions and their consequences, law reconstitutes a 'sequential relay of legal beings' (such as powers, capacities, rights, duties and obligations). Such sequencing impells or prompts action. This is because it 'catalyses and sustains different forms of agency'. This action of catalysation may involve a reordering or resequencing of events (by revisiting causation, for instance) or reinsert a missing link, working backwards in its specific legal 'directionality', from consequence to cause, from enunciation to actor, etc. In resequencing or reassembling events, beings and things, it works through a series of legal processes described by Latour as imputation, habilitation or recognition.[351] This 'conceptual topography' reconfigures jurisprudence. Registering any being, as we have seen, law exerts a series of contractions, condensations and extensions, so as to produce a 'juridical linearisation' within its complex folds.[352]

Private international law is an amplification of all these apparently strange virtues attributed to legality in general. In this respect, it stands apart among conventional legal disciplines, refusing to be absorbed in any particular substantive field: its

[348] On hospitality/hostility as a similarly conflicted term, see below 273.

[349] On the constitution of the conflict of laws as creating community, see Bomhoff, 'The constitution of the conflict of laws'.

[350] On law as an actor-producing form, see Pottage, 'Introduction, The Fabrication of Persons and Things' 6. Similar (critical) imaginaries of law as reprisal can be found in contemporary strands of law and humanities that appeal to the idea of the reparative in-between. For example, in a project that brings together law and theatre, entitled 'Staging repair', such repair-work emerges 'in dissent to the state', and can be found 'in spaces that are not characterised as formal legal institutions, emerging from actors who do not occupy roles within these institutions.' VD Sheikh, 'Staging repair' (2021) 25 *Law Text Culture* 144–77, https://ro.uow.edu.au/ltc/vol25/iss1/6.

[351] Such legal ligatures are created according to three technical modes: imputation, reparation, recognition. These schemes correspond, on the public side, to the habilitation/delegation processes at the heart of constitutional or administrative law; on the private side, they evoke both the constitutive action of law in generating links such as title to property, contracts, or family bonds, and liability and remedies in tort law.

[352] McGee, *Latour and the Passage of law* 10. N van Dijk, 'The Life and Deaths of a Dispute: An Inquiry into Matters of Law', in McGee, *Latour and the Passage of law* 160 et seq, on the de-grounding and re-grounding of jurisprudence.

superficiality means that it is 'meta-dogmatic', a 'tertiary norm' (as we have seen above) designed exclusively to ensure, collaterally, the coordination of other normative systems. Moreover, the quintessential *modus operandi* of law-as-ligature is encoded more specifically within its shadow version. The latter shows up, as we know, in the cracks and disjunctures at the core of our 'jurisdictional jurisprudence'. By contrast with the latter, it embodies legality in its reparative quality, mending broken connections as it passes through a contested, pluralistic environment. It very literally 'reattaches' (*rattachement*[353]) diverse semiotic beings (often those that were sundered apart by its jurisdictional counterpart, as seen above) in its hesitant, reflexive trajectory, weaving in and out of borders and constantly reinventing[354] and changing gear between fact and law. If Latour's depiction of law's labour in this respect relates to domestic law (whether in the form of administrative law within the *Conseil d'Etat* or as substantive legality in general), what better description could be found of the conflict of laws 'beyond the state'? The singularity of these processes as they operate within the latter lies in the fact that they address spatial dislocation as a particularly visible form of disconnection. Furthermore, the reparative mandate of law's processes as they work 'beyond the state' is directed towards a specific type of (cross-border) discontinuity:[355] it requires a resetting of spatial ordering, or re-emplacement, against the unstable backdrop of multiple substantive normative claims.[356]

At this juncture, a linguistic analogy to law's passage, or go-between agency, may be helpful. After all, 'jurimorphs' involve, quintessentially, translation: contentious matters of concern are 'transmogrified' into discursive legal devices.[357] The idea of translation as extended beyond text (in the mode of Michel Serres) is of particular importance in understanding the non-modern ontology of plural worldliness (or pluriversality).[358] Moreover, along the lines (familiar to comparative legal studies) of law and ventriloquism (*lex loquitur*),[359] it could be said that all operations of

[353] See above 186.

[354] This reinvention stands in opposition to the more 'uncanny' replications ascribed to dominant jurisdictional jurisprudence (see for example, on the Crown's weird repetitive incarnations, M Valverde and A Weaver, '"The Crown wears many hats": Canadian Aboriginal Law and the Black-boxing of Empire', in McGee, *Latour and the Passage of law* 93 et seq.

[355] Indeed, the somewhat hackneyed notion that private international law pursues a peculiar value system labelled 'conflicts justice' (as opposed to its substantive variety) might be revitalised here in order to emphasise this mission.

[356] The idea of using private international law as an intellectual style capable of 're-sequencing' the order of the terms in which legal issues are framed finds strong further support here. This idea has been advocated by recent scholarship, in the various works of R Michaels, K Knop, and A Riles cited above.

[357] On 'jurimorphs' as translation (of value-objects into legal beings), see McGee, *Latour and the Passage of law* 8. For a science-and-technology approach to the courts as sites of translation and mistranslation of scientific findings, see Jasanoff, *States of Knowledge*.

[358] M Serres, *La Traduction. Hermès III* (Paris, Minuit, 1974), following the operation of translation in various fields (inside canonical knowledge and its history, through encyclopaedias and philosophies, on sites of art and text) and the transformation of the message into differential versions at the limits of betrayal. In other words, as in Latour, the paradigm of translation is extended beyond text. Perhaps indeed translation is a metonym for all modes of communication. See above on the influence of Michel Serres' thought on translation on Latour's account of the (non-modern) ontology of plural worlds.

[359] This metaphor is used to flag the (classical legal) illusion that courts are the 'bouche de la loi' (the mouth of the law). For the use by Latour of the metaphor of the autonomy of the marionette, see *Enquête*, 158; and in a Latourian mode, F Cooeren, 'In the Name of the Law: Ventriloquism and Juridical Matters',

interpretation or making sense of the law involve lending it voice (to the point that it is difficult to ascertain whether the puppet manipulates the ventriloquist or the reverse). In more traditional terms, it might be said that this linguistic analogy is of significance, first of all, because of the structural links between language and law.[360] Indeed, all of the points made above are relevant to the former as a mode of communication and the carrier of a world view. Language has a similar paradoxical depth of superficiality, both devoid and full of (its own) signification. It is both reiterative and reparative, constantly beginning again, giving voice, shuttling back and forth between different meanings, tones, registers and weaving links among diverse actors.[361] Of particular, immediate interest here is its border-crossing dimension, as it 'passes' over from one culture to another.

A recent historical study of the Mediterranean lingua franca[362] illustrates these features in a particularly striking way. This study explores the relationship of this singular language to ideas of identity and community through several centuries of interaction between Islam and Christianity. For the shadow version of the conflict of laws, it deserves particular attention because of the specific non-modern context to which it refers, its spectacular go-between quality, and the centrality of alterity in its own particular ontology or mode of existence. Adopting a (rare) historical perspective, this approach is deliberately distanced from the more usual analysis of *métissage* from a linguistic perspective; moreover it does not focus on the language imposed by later French colonial domination on the inhabitants of Algeria and large swathes of the Arab world.[363] In other words, the study is not about the Derridaean expropriation or dispossession of self through the language of the other. Neither of these issues is denied, but the message of the book is rather that of the conceptual and ethical possibility of a third, neutral linguistic space, located in between existing traditions, connecting them without detracting from any of them. Moreover, the lingua franca was not an indeterminate wishwash or sabir or pidgin (to use terms with a distinctly colonial, derogatory overtone), but a distinct medium with its own identity and regime. This then was a language of intercultural communication between diverse world views, spoken from the very threshold of modernity until as late as the mid-nineteenth century, and notably, during the Crusades.

in McGee, *Latour and the Passage of Law*, 235. Using the metaphor, see J Derrida, *Psyche: The Invention of the Other* (Palo Alto CA, Stanford University Press, 2007).

[360] On this vast question, see for example, S Glanert (ed), *Comparative Law – Engaging Translation* (Abingdon, Routledge, 2014).

[361] Moreover, in anticipation of a point to which we shall return below, it is shamanic in that it can remain the same while taking on different forms.

[362] J Dakhlia, *Lingua franca. Histoire d'une langue métisse en Méditerranée* (Actes Sud, 2008). This particular account of the lingua franca is not necessarily the only valid reading (see, for an alternative account, A von Busekist, 'Idealism or pragmatism? Ad hoc multilingualism and Open English', in PA Kraus and F Grin (eds) *The Politics of Multilingualism: Europeanisation, globalisation and linguistic governance* (Studies in World Language Problems, 2018) 305–32). However, what counts in this context is the idea (whether or not historically accurate) of a third, hybrid, go-between language, composed of inputs from all sides (and constantly changing with each mutation of the other historical languages) – a form of coalescence without compromission. Interestingly, studies of the Mediterranean as a space of legal pluralism are rare. see however, in contemporary context, V Zeno-Zencovich. 'The Mediterranean And Legal Pluralism' (2021) 1 *Comparative Law Rev* 1.

[363] On law and French colonialism, see below 250.

The lingua franca was shared by all manner of Franks and Turks – seamen, diplomats, adventurers, or sultans. It was not the language of a people, a race, or a culture; indifferent to territorial or imagined spatial limits, it was an additional device that allowed constant intercourse and exchange between people of diverse tongues, milieux and genders, even in times of extreme 'civilisational' conflict. It was not translation, nor the creolisation of a purer, original model, but a communicational, third, space of meeting and mixing of diverse tongues. It was, in other words, a go-between, an interstitial area of communication, detached from territory, disconnected (*détissage* or unwoven, rather than *métissage*) from national identity and divested of values (such as purity and closure) other than communication itself. The fascinating (and sparsely documented) history of the lingua franca, then, tells the story of a weaving of (linguistic but ineffable) links between human societies that are not exclusive of a wider background of conflictuality. Most importantly, it highlights hybridity as the very means of understanding and demarking not only the other but self.[364] Here, as Jocelyne Dakhlia writes, we have a modality of the in-between and the relationship to otherness that takes place through negotiation: by the same token, whatever is not negotiable becomes more, not less, visible. There can be a language, then, that is common but that is not spoken in one voice. Moreover, a shared language does not prevent the simultaneous existence of frontiers and communities with their own identities. Very close to the concept of law-as-ligature that this reading of the lingua franca is designed to illustrate is a vision of translation according to the Senegalese philosopher Bachir Soulemane Diagne: the real lingua franca is translation itself.[365]

This inter-language as a neutral or third space is precisely also an apt metaphorical representation of the boundary work that falls to private international law. In this context, the categories through which law 'passes' allow, too, for weaving together, not division, mending and not splitting apart. Borders, in other words, become places of passing and exchange rather than separation. Accepting that communities or identities are porous and multiple is a way of reinterpreting the boundaries that define them as a site of constant border-crossing and borrowing rather than a wall.[366] Moreover, the lingua franca is not a substitute for various local or domestic substantive normative orders, but exists as a third medium, weaving in-between jurisdictions. It is a threshold discipline, working to ensure the mutual accommodation of different cultural forms of life. It assumes not one universe, but

[364] For analogous ideas, also outside the law, in the philosophical work of William James ('the foreign, the difficult, and the uncomfortable makes us who we are') and in art forms and ecosophy (as in E de Valdenebro's 'Le principe métanthropique'), see above 173.

[365] See in particular, *De langue à langue: L'hospitalité de la traduction* (Paris, Albin Michel, 2022). In his quest for linguistic diversity (hospitality) as key to good intelligence between diverse belief systems (and moreover, to 'decolonisation of philosophy through the medium and metaphor of language'), Diagne refers frequently to Goethe, for whom he who 'knows' only one language can in fact have no such knowledge. On the ethics of hospitality and its links with law and language, see below Part III.

[366] In this respect, the conceptual shadow of the Leviathan has largely hidden both the slow (and haphazard) creation of the frontiers that congealed into the territory of the modern state and more importantly here, their porosity. Annabel Brett presents a historical study of the progressive definition of such borders as places of passing and exchange rather than separation (*Changes of State: Nature and the Limits of the City in Early Modern Natural Law* (Princeton NJ, Princeton University Press, 2011).

a pluriverse that accepts alterity upon its own terms.[367] Again, as observed recently by Souleymane Bachir Diagne, one might say that the real signification of this or any lingua franca lies in the passage from one language to another, in other words in the very act of translation itself.[368] This insight is further accompanied by the view of translation itself as an act of mutual hospitality – a fundamental theme to which we return below in Part III.

For the time being, this view of translation as lingua franca can be seen as an apt image of law's labour of informal diplomacy, as exemplified in the conflict of laws. As go-between, it chugs back and forth beneath the radar of the geopolitical order. In stark contrast to the grid-like model encountered above, the jurisdictional lines of belonging are not fixed or closed, but are constantly redrawn. For example, informal 'private' definitions of citizenship that deviate from formal status (nationality),[369] overlapping circles of (plural) identity,[370] or the inclusion of the inhabitants of war zones, unrecognised states or occupied territories within collectives endowed with legal standing before the courts[371] are all illustrations of the possibilities or aspirations opened up by dwelling in the in-between – even if the available concrete, historical examples also show up (by definition!) the historical fragility or ephemerality of any one instantiation of this reiterative, adaptative, dynamic. The point here is that law's ability to change perspective, its endless labour of redefinition according to a dialectic that weaves together individual circumstance and context on the one hand and a broader, collective ethical horizon[372] on the other, is characteristic of legality's 'oscillating' mode of existence.

B. Law's Oscillation

A further feature in Latour's depiction of legality is of singular significance for the conflict of laws. Its trajectory in this respect – once again, its endless action of restitching, looping or 'reprisal' – is decidedly unstable and non-linear. In its labour of communication, it evolves, vacillates, and adjusts, in a form of constant, non-linear oscillation.[373] Such oscillation distances legality from the stability, linearity, and binary divisions of the traditional model of legal monism. Evocative once again of the conflict of laws, it relates to law's constant, unstable, negotiation of boundaries (of whatever kind). The pedigree of law's specific juridical ecology can be traced back, as we know, to the existence of foundational binaries in modern thought, such as those that separate persons and things, intentionality from corporeality, body from

[367] It is also an instance of what Bruno Latour calls the 'sublime art of compromise': *Enquête*, 459.
[368] *De langue à langue. L'hospitalité de la traduction* (Paris, Albin Michel, 2022).
[369] Knop, 'Citizenship, Public and Private'.
[370] Berman, *Global Legal Pluralism*.
[371] See on the (variable) parameters of jurisdiction, the example developed by M Karayanni, *Conflicts in a Conflict. A Conflict of Laws Case Study on Israel and the Palestinian Territories* (Oxford, Oxford University Press, 2014).
[372] On the location and signification of this ethical horizon, see below 270.
[373] In Latour's depiction, this is the (second) sign of law's passage.

mind, nature from culture, and theology (and indeed law) from politics.[374] However, the point here is that far from remaining static in their content, these ontological and epistemological divides are permanently navigated and renegotiated by law itself. Law's aptitude to shuttle back and forth over (provisional) limits is embedded as it were in its DNA. As Aldo Schiavone explains, the metaphysical existence of Roman legal concepts required of Reason a constant effort of adaptation; therein lay the true nature of law.[375] Boundary struggles, then, are endemic to legality's bicephalic, vacillating mode of existence; perpetual oscillation, collision, contestation, and contingency are built into the very economy of the legal-normative.

There is indeed 'something about the law', Kyle McGee surmises, 'that seems to demand this kind of movement, this kind of vacillation'.[376] McGee is peering here into legality's 'black-boxes', 'unscrewing the Leviathan', in an attempt to remedy the 'metaphysical failure' of legal doctrine to analyse the secret (and wonky) artefactual mechanics from which flow law's 'quasi-spiritual powers' (associated with such values as neutrality, legal security, objectivity, etc). Such oscillation, he writes, is

> a requirement or a constraint that is grounded in the bifurcation of person and body. We can see in legal doctrine, and even in contemporary legal practice, a repeated shuttling and shifting back and forth between two registers that are thought to exhaust the real: we would say materiality and discourse today, but we could also say naturalism and constructionism or ontology and epistemology or being and thought.[377]

Thus, legal events are inscribed within a 'generative trajectory', an intense circulation of legal-semiotic objects, perpetually composing, adjusting and refracting. As illustrated by any form of legal argument, whether based on text or precedent, law's concepts serve as dense 'transfer points'[378] for multiple meanings, policies, strategies or ideologies.

Moreover, just as in perceptions of the world in which the frontier between the animate and inanimate, animal and human, natural and cultural reveals blurry edges and queer confines, law is always similarly 'beyond meaning' or driven by something

[374] Descola, *Les formes du visible* 136 explaining that we Naturalists (or we Moderns) subscribed definitively to the primary anthropological divide between society and nature when man was 'invented' in the nineteenth century and recalling that Foucault's archaeological exploration of the archive of the social sciences led to the conclusion that 'man' was invented when society made it possible as a totalising whole (see above 13). This did not however prevent the regular revival of ideas of natural law. But we also need to recall that while law is an emblematically modern form – a form, in the words of Aldo Schiavone (*Ius*), that 'invaded modernity'-, the epistemological roots of these bifurcations take us much further back, to the metaphysics of Roman legality and its structural dualism. On this dualism as a feature or keystone of the semantic architecture of Western law, see Pottage, 'Introduction, The Fabrication of Persons and Things'.

[375] Roughan and Halpin, *In Pursuit of Pluralist Jurisprudence* 392.

[376] This and the following citations are taken from Kyle McGee's chapter, 'On Devices and Logics of Legal Sense: Toward Socio-technical Legal Analysis', in McGee, *Latour and the Passage of Law*, 61 et seq.

[377] As seen above, doctrinal skirmishes (in McGee's terms, law's organic and discursive oscillation between dissonant epistemic positions) are singularly visible in private international law, whose constitution is famously or notoriously '*savante*' or learned (as opposed to judicial), as seen above 72. However, more interesting is its constant oscillation between the familiar and the unfamiliar, self and other, outside and inside, rule and exception, home and foreign.

[378] Foucault used this expression to characterise the place of sexuality in Western thought. Even the most syllogistic or deductivist approaches to judicial reasoning by courts presuppose that opposing claims are made in the name of diverse nominally plausible interpretations.

that is not confinable to words.[379] In contrast to modern law's obsession with closure and line-drawing, it provides the model for law as a constant crossing of boundaries, a specific interstitial place that allows for alliances between outside and inside. It gives shape to a vision of legality that is emblematically inscribed within the in-between. It 'makes the difference' in this respect, embodying an ontological plurality that resets the nomos of spatial ordering. Moreover, it 'takes place' outside predefined spatiality. In this alternative conceptual economy, law appears as a form of existence that refuses to be confined within one locality, or restricted by any frontier; nor is it enclosed in chronological time. It takes place, but does not stay in place, resisting an inside/outside ontology. Preferring the interstitial to the linear, negotiation to closure, mutual supportiveness to autonomy, law thus understood is not disembedded or abstracted from its wider social, cultural or natural universe, but 'belongs to the world'.[380] In ecological terms, as seen above, this scheme of fragile connections reflects our interdependent terrestrial or planetary existence as a holobiont.

The mode of existence of the conflict of laws echoes this strange oscillating feature of law, emphasising the heuristic value of its shadow avatar in this context.[381] Weaving in and out of national legal regimes, its mission in responding to the challenges of normative diversity is to disregard pre-established frontiers or the hard lines of conceptual categories in order to mend broken connections between people and places, actions and events. Insofar as its methodologies are designed to operate in an unstable environment, they are reflexive, experimental, multi-step or process-like, lateral and fictional ('as if'). Indeed, some of the latter characteristics have been identified, very plausibly, as inherent to private international law's own 'intellectual style'. The discipline has ontology of its own, at least partially dissociated from that of a given body or tradition of substantive law. It is notably full of corrective devices (such as *forum non conveniens* for jurisdiction, or escape clauses in choice of law) that operate similar negotiations across the metaphorical borders of diverse domestic legal regimes, in the quest for adjustment and proportion in the allocation or distribution of social relationships or events.

In all instances, moreover, the final outcome in any individual case is determined by a series of intellectual arbitrages which, although undoubtedly at work in any domestic judicial decision, are once again quintessentially present within the specific methods of private international law. The latter was once famously styled, in culinary terms, as a 'recipe', unfolding in a step-by-step process that required, at every

[379] On ineffability (see above 158) and its particular relevance to the ontology of the common law, see P-G Monateri, *Geopolitica del diritto. Genesi, governo e dissoluzione dei corpi politici* (Einaudi, 2013).

[380] Mignolo, 'On Pluriversality and Multipolarity'.

[381] We can now return to the question of pluralism and its embrace of this oscillating 'second nature' of legality. Contrast the monist 'mirage of pre-constituted legal order', the fiction of certainty or unicity that masks such vacillation as problematic. The very uncertainties, controversies, reinterpretations, compromises and hesitations rejected by this determinist vision of the law are, in a pluralist perspective, an inseparable part of its constitution. These two opposing approaches are reflected within private international law itself. On the one hand, the aspiration of multilateralist or Savignian methodology is to smooth over the roughness generated by legal difference. On the other hand, under a pluralist reading, private international law has navigation and negotiation at its heart. Such a reading accounts more plausibly for its specific ontology.

turn, a deliberate judicial choice between several equally plausible possibilities.[382] It is through this intricate, oscillating process that private international law weaves its way between all things, mending broken links 'for connectedness' own sake'. All manner of distinct normative claims, understood on their own terms or in their own strangeness, can be connected to the facts, events or actors that call for a juridical shape. Such progressivity – or lack of predefined determination – in individual outcomes is also reflected, more broadly, in the idea that law's own constitution fully embraces what might be termed doctrinal and political controversies. As Robert Wai observes,

> with plural orders one should expect an interrelationship of normative contestation as much as an interrelationship of harmonisation or unification. Transnational private law as transnational governance highlights that some degree of contestation and conflict is the legitimate function of law as a place for disputation. The legitimacy of private law indeed comes importantly from that role: law, including private law, is not only about the efficient facilitation of transactions. It also is related to how individual actors in our global society can disagree about the right thing to be done in a particular transaction …[383]

Once again, to go back in more concrete terms to the field of 'environmental law' and cross-border litigation over climate change today, it is very difficult to state the law, here and now, on a whole series of crucial issues. This applies to whether 'ESG' standards have legal teeth in respect of corporate commitments to 'responsible capitalism' (are these norms forms of law?); whether a parent or holding company can be held to account for the actions for its subsidiaries abroad; whether financial actors or investors are under a duty of care analogous to that of producers or industries; how causation is to be understood in such cases; who has legal standing to bring such cases to court; whether the judicial branch is legitimate to intervene in scientific and social controversies; and much more. To the hard scientist's mystified query about the uncertainty of legal interpretation (what exactly does law say or mean?) in the face of contradictory theories, the pluralist's response is that 'law is all that' at the same time![384] It remains however to choose among law's own offer of *modes d'emploi* the one that best allows its rocky passage into the global ecology.

Here we move from the ontological register of unstable ligature to an aesthetic of the in-between, inviting exploration of law's own morphological plurality. The link between law's oscillating mode and hybrid 'forms of the (legally) visible' is provided by Philippe Descola's definition of the chimera, in the context of analogous cosmologies.[385] Thus, the chimera is composed of heterogeneous, disparate and sometimes contradictory attributes borrowed from diverse types of beings (humans, animals, plants, artefacts) but 'presenting a certain anatomical coherence', a 'unity of composition' assembled so as plausibly to represent a living form. The composition requires a certain 'cognitive constraint' if it is to be considered real. But it is a means of overcoming the 'panic of diversity', of combining the consciousness that each

[382] Francescakis, *La théorie du renvoi*, § 50.
[383] Wai, 'The Interlegality of Transnational Private Law', 109. On the concept of interlegality, see above 112.
[384] See McGee, *Latour and the Passage of law.*
[385] Descola, *Les formes du visible* 303 et seq, 598.

being or thing is irreducibly singular and specific with the hope that all these particularisms may hold together. However, the medium is not a self (a *moi*) reflecting itself in others, but an affinity between disparate connected parts. The visible image of the chimera (often in the form of uncanny composite masks) is designed precisely to draw attention to the assemblage of linkages itself. This is a remarkably apt representation of the often baroque normative hybrid produced by the operation of the conflict of laws, at least in its shadow mode as a jurisprudence of the in-between, an ecology of fragile connections. We now turn to this visible dimension, with a little further help from the shaman, the jaguar and other non-modern modes of access to the real.

II. LAW'S MORPHOLOGICAL PLURALITY

In a 'pluritopical' aesthetic vein,[386] indigenous ecological epistemologies invite us to adopt the cognitive standpoint of the other – to follow 'the gaze of jaguar',[387] think like a mountain,[388] enjoy life like a fish,[389] or imagine ourselves as mushroom spores[390] – instead of viewing the world – and dividing it up, flattening and emptying it – from a unitary, external, stable and overarching viewpoint.[391] At first sight, however, such ideas (and certain strands of Western eco-phenomenological aesthetics[392])

[386] That is, from multiple, moving perspectives all at once. On pluritopicality, see Mignolo, 'On Pluriversality and Multipolarity', 'Foreword', p xi: 'To think pluritopically is … to dwell in the border'. Border-dwelling must be understood as both an ontology and an aesthetic.

[387] E Viveiros de Castro, *Le regard du jaguar. Introduction au perspectivisme amérindien*, trans Pierre Delgado (Paris, Éditions la Tempête, 2021): 'En lieu et place d'une théorie évolutionniste (lato sensu) qui prétend que "les humains sont des animaux qui ont gagné quelque chose", les amérindiens disent: "les animaux sont des humains qui ont perdu quelque chose".'

[388] A Leopold, *Think Like a Mountain* (London, Penguin Classics, republished 2021). Or indeed, like a forest: Eduardo Kohn, *How forests think. Toward an anthropology beyond the human* (Berkeley CA, University of California Press, 2013). Or again, like a river: C de Toledo, 'Le fleuve qui voulait écrire. (Les auditions du parlement de Loire. Audition de Bruno Latour)' (Paris: Les liens qui libèrent, 2021).

[389] On Chinese eco-aesthetics, see A Carlson, 'Environmental Aesthetics', *Stanford Encyclopedia of Philosophy*, V° (Palo Alto CA, Stanford University Press, 2007).

[390] A Tsing, *The Mushroom at the End of the World. On the Possibility of Life in Capitalist Ruins* (Princeton NJ, Princeton University Press, 2015).

[391] This point is made forcefully by Descola in his exploration of the aesthetics of indigenous cosmologies, *Les Formes du Visible*.

[392] One point that will be made repeatedly below (including in Part III), in anticipation of the objection that the position unfolding in this section 'exoticises' indigenous cosmologies (within the meaning of 'legal orientalism', see Ruskola, *Legal Orientalism*) is that – with some serious excavation – a not dissimilar epistemological stance can be found within the Western tradition itself. On this point it is interesting to recall (with Carlson, 'Environmental Aesthetics') that a Western 'forerunner of contemporary ecological non-cognitive aesthetics' (known as the 'engagement approach'), was John Dewey, whose work is seen as close to Merleau-Ponty's phenomenology but also in certain regards to Marxist and feminist aesthetics. The 'engagement approach' rejects 'disinterested appreciation, with its isolating, distancing, and objectifying gaze, is out of place in the aesthetic experience of nature, for it wrongly abstracts both natural objects and appreciators from the environments in which they properly belong and in which appropriate appreciation is achieved. Thus, the aesthetics of engagement stresses the contextual dimensions of nature and our multi-sensory experiences of it. Viewing the environment as a seamless unity of places, organisms, and perceptions, it challenges the importance of traditional dichotomies, such as that between subject and object. It beckons appreciators to immerse themselves in the natural environment and to reduce to as small a degree as possible the distance between themselves and the natural world. In short, appropriate aesthetic experience is held to involve the total immersion of the appreciator in the object of appreciation.'

would seem to be particularly difficult to translate into a credible legal form.[393] Modernity has so accustomed us to the existence of a monist (or grid-like[394]) aesthetic in law – meaning a unitary viewpoint embodies in a rule of decision that operates 'closure' of legal conflicts – that plurality in law would seem to be a contradiction in terms.[395] The idea of a weaving, unstable, shamanic, legal form (to which we shall return below) is likely to meet with derision or condescension[396] and requires some further explanation with reference to the way in which law envisages perspective. The shadow avatar of the conflict of laws will serve to make visible these faint and alien shapes of law.[397]

To say that law has a morphology is a reference, once again, to the form-giving dimension of our *nomos*[398] and central in turn to thinking about alterity in legal form. Although the evocation of law and bodies certainly has a broader biopolitical and phenomenological significance (to which we shall return below),[399] the reference to legal morphologies and their plurality here highlights the variety of size and shapes of the body of law itself (the *corpus iuris*[400]), underwritten by all sorts of

[393] Insofar as they echo indigenous ecological cosmologies: see from the perspective of literary critic F Coelho, 'Improvisations of a Tropical Cartesianism' (2011) 7 *Brazilian Improvisations/Improvisações Brasileiras:* 'For some thinkers improvisation and its corollaries are proof that these countries and their people would live forever on the margins or in negative dialectics within the heritage of Enlightenment reason, (but) for others it is precisely there – in the possibility of reinventing reason from hybridisms, strategic appropriations, and re-readings – that the creative and autonomous potentials in the post-colonial world lie.'

[394] Schlag, 'The Aesthetics of American Law'.

[395] This is the point made by Roughan and Halpin, *In Pursuit of Pluralist Jurisprudence.* The same can be said of further, connected concepts of modernity such as 'the order of time' (on the multiple topologies of time, see Pomian, *L'ordre du temps*). Conversely, see too the observation by de Viveiros de Castro as to the necessary circularity of (metaphysical) monism that presupposes distinctions that are impossible to draw (see *The Relative Native*, 113): 'Humanity and world are literally on the same side; the distinction between the two terms is arbitrary and impalpable: if one starts from humanity (thought, culture, language, the "inside") one necessarily arrives at the world (being, matter, nature, the "Great Outdoors") without crossing any border and conversely. "Pluralism = monism", the magical formula sought by Deleuze and Guattari can also be written, when read by a Tardean sorcerer or an Amerindian shaman, as "Pan-psychism = Materialism"'.

[396] Or of course downright rejection, just as do deviations from dogmatic and syllogistic legal forms in modes of energy or dissociation (Schlag, 'The Aesthetics of American Law', again).

[397] In this regard, the function of the 'shadow' is all at once to haunt, to make visible, to reflect and to represent an underlying reality. See the passages in Descola, *Les formes du visible*, 31 et seq on the different realities underlying visible forms and the modes of 'representation' at work and on the definitions of avatars and totems in indigenous traditions. The avatar is a figure much used in political ecology, including as an art form (see for example, C Erb, 'A Spiritual Blockbuster: Avatar, Environmentalism, and the New Religions' (2014) 66 *Journal of Film and Video* 3–17). For the law, see J Borrows (Kegedonce), *Drawing Out Law: A Spirit's Guide* (University of Toronto Press, 2010) and below, 199 et s.

[398] See above 131 et seq. on the ideological or world-making dimension of our *nomos*.

[399] A further dimension of the legal status of (moving or displaced) bodies as bare life (*homo sacer*) in the context of colonialism, biopolitics and migration, will be seen below 221 and 302 et seq. On (feminist) environmental ethics and the phenomenological turn therein, or the increased significance of gendered bodies, materiality or corporeality in our perceptions of the world, see below 293. Moreover, see too, Schiavone, *Ius* 57 on the relationship between morphologies of power and models of legal thought.

[400] This metaphor is suggested by M Drakopoulou, writing on the underlying morphological (and gendered) imaginaries of the legal subject in Roman law ('Of the Founding of Law's Jurisdiction and the Politics of Sexual Difference: the case of Roman law', in McVeigh (ed), *Jurisdictional Jurisprudence* 33–60). On the relation of morphology and history, and the function of metaphor (here, the body) in the use of Freudian analysis of a past that remains inaccessible to conventional tools of historical analysis, Carlo Ginzburg, *Mythes, Emblèmes, Traces. Morphologie et histoire* (Paris, Verdier, 2010 (1986)).

different imaginaries.[401] In aesthetic terms, the world contains a great diversity of such bodies of law, all linked in turn to diverse perceptions of our natural surroundings (as cosmological signature, transcendence, symbiosis ... but also as inert resource to be appropriated and discarded), of the relationship of biological life to the invisible universe (peopled with metaphysical entities, divinities, ancestors or indeed legal persons such as states or corporations), of time and space (as separate and linear, or pluritopical) of interactions between humans and other species (according to different poles of identification and relation to alterity[402]), and of the signification of forms, rituals, procedures and symbols. These various legal imaginaries all translate into the images, categories and tropes that Pierre Schlag evokes in his study, cited above, on the aesthetics of law. This reminds us that the constitution of our modern legal ontology is largely visual and little shared in this respect by other cosmological traditions that give greater place to the invisible.[403]

There are many reasons for which it is crucial to take seriously this plurality of belief systems, forms, and the corresponding ideas of legality.[404] Indeed, the current renewal of interest in plurality in legal form,[405] particularly in eco-feminist, eco-aesthetic and indigenous epistemologies already evoked above[406] signals that it is impossible to overlook the morphological diversity of what is understood as 'law' (or what we can relate to as being 'law-like') in various cosmologies, if we want to work out the means of communicating with and among them. Much of this is due to growing awareness of the existence outside the Western universe[407] of lifeworlds that

[401] See Introduction above 16. On the emergence of the body on the (German) philosophical scene in the second half of the nineteenth century, first with Arthur Schopenhauer, then with Friedrich Nietzsche, see L Barbisan, 'Eccentric Bodies. From Phenomenology to Marxism – Walter Benjamin's Reflections on Embodiment' 2017 I *Anthropology & Materialism, Special issue, Discontinuous Infinities*, https://doi.org/10.4000/am.803. The duality of the body, this 'material thing of a certain nature which ... makes up a fundamental component of the real givenness of the soul and the Ego' is explored by Husserl (*Ideas Pertaining to a Pure Phenomenology and to a Phenomenological Philosophy: Studies in the Phenomenology of Constitution*, written between 1912 and 1928, trans Fred Kersten (Dordrecht/Boston: Kluwer, 1989) 165). Later, Benjamin 'exploits the rift that the philosophical splitting of the body opens in the individual in order to overcome the boundaries on which the concept of identity is grounded' (ibid, §9).

[402] See on this point, again, Descola, *Les formes du visible*.

[403] On mosaics and orality in indigenous forms of normativity, see Mills, 'The Lifeworlds of Law'. Modern law is not only visual but largely linked to the written form, which is why it is threatened by the digital turn, see Garapon and Lassègue, *Justice digitale. Révolution graphique et rupture anthropologique*.

[404] Some of these are linked to the ethic of hospitality in such a context and we shall return to this below, Part III.

[405] We have seen above (281 et seq) that a triad of theoretical challenges to monism – analytical, meta-jurisprudential, or pertaining to political or moral legitimacy (on this triad, see J Fabra Zamora (ed), *Jurisprudence in a Globalized World* (Cheltenham, Elgar, 2020)) have reopened the quest for a jurisprudential exploration of the 'intimations' of global legal pluralism. Indeed, as recalled above, jurisdictional thinking rests on the tight nexus between law and state, so that plurality in law's morphological forms would seem to be a contradiction in terms. Moreover, modernity has so accustomed us to the existence of a monist viewpoint – in law, this means a unitary rule of decision that operates 'closure' of legal conflicts, or an Archimedean standpoint from which to restore order between conflicting claims to govern – that there again, the coexistence of multiple perspectives seems equally to run counter to reason. On these points, see above 61 et seq.

[406] See further below, 289 et seq.

[407] The moderns' 'universe' is understood as one (unique). In-between thinking or pluritopicality signify that each cosmology is aware that it is one among many, within what can be termed a pluriverse.

possess alternative modes of access to reality, so that none of the conceptual categories and binaries through which we define or delimit law (legality and politics, religion and secularism, form and substance …) have any relevance or foothold whatsoever. As ethnographer Rachel Sieder observes, this is precisely what is specific about legal conflicts involving indigenous epistemologies.[408] The latter engage the relationship to alterity at deep underlying levels and cannot be apprehended by technologies that work only at the surface.

While it is important to acknowledge the rich plurality of specific schemes or patterns of identification and relation to alterity among non-modern legal epistemologies,[409] they are nevertheless largely united in their rejection of modernity's separation of nature and culture, humans and animals, biology and ideology, history and geography, so that the most promising avenue today to protect the planetary ecology is to take the cue from these alternative belief systems[410] in order to build a 'cosmopolitics' of law.[411] Once again, the argument that runs through this book is that 'our' modern relation to alterity (in human or cultural form) is indissociable from our understanding of the extraneity of our natural surroundings (and the things and species within them) and that both underlie our law as *nomos*. Moreover, as the prospect of Anthropocenic disaster begins (slowly) to destabilise modern notions of time and corresponding eschatologies, drawing attention to the plight of future (human) generations and other biological species and our (possible) duty towards 'them' (perceived as the other), we come to realise that this 'fear of breakdown', from the perspective of indigenous or colonised peoples, is an event that has already come to pass.[412] And what is more, this event has occurred within ourselves: this is the drama that plays out beyond history, in our 'life before the law',[413] beyond the modern state.

As we have seen, modern Western rationality with its exclusive universalising tendencies has been blind and amnesiac in respect of non-modern normative forms, treating them (but they are also 'us'[414]) with incredulity (through the lens

[408] Sieder, 'To Speak The Law'. On the question (also envisaged by this ethnographer) on nature as legal subject endowed with rights, see below, Part III 285 et seq.

[409] As seen in Descola's quadri-partite classification above. The point here is not to essentialise 'indigeneity' but to see common forms of resistance to the empire of modernity. On the risk of exoticisation of the indigenous 'noble savage', see below 197, 248.

[410] See above 29, 107 et seq.

[411] I Stengers, *Cosmopolitics I* (Paris, La Découverte, 1993). This work was written at the heart of the 'science wars' (already mentioned above 178), that challenged (modern) science's assumed superiority over (non-modern) mystical, occult, primitive, archaic or esoteric world views. The 'science wars' are affecting the law today – although there have been very few attempts to apply a symmetrical legal anthropology to Western legality. This is not to diminish the value of critical legal studies of all kinds, but to note that lawyers (working within the confines of modern law) have rarely worked to open the 'black box' of law (or 'unscrew the Leviathan' in cosmopolitical terms (with notable exceptions in the work of Jasanoff, Valverde and Pottage cited in this book).

[412] D Winnicott, 'Fear of Breakdown' (1974) 1 *International Review of Psycho-Analysis* 103: the fear of breakdown (*effondrement*) is the projection of an event that has already come to pass. *Cf* Viveiros da Castro (*Le regard du jaguar*) observing that the Amazonian Indian community 'a été ravagée par des missionnaires catholiques, et comme le citoyen d'un pays au bord d'un effondrement écologique et d'un ethnocide mené en partie *"au nom de Dieu"*'.

[413] C Douzinas, 'Postmodern Jurisprudence: The Law of Text in the Texts of Law', in ' McVeigh (ed) *Jurisprudence of Jurisdiction*.

[414] On the ontological question 'who are we?', see below 269.

of rationality), paternalism (exoticisation or orientalism[415]) or derision (dismissing them as arcane). In a monist legal framework (including its expression within the conflict of laws), the *nomos* of other non-modern human societies is relegated to the infra-state (or the private sphere) and labelled as cultural or informal (and in liberal systems, the object of tolerance,[416] like all other religious or ideological belief systems).[417] Underlying these labels, there is a strong temporal dimension (linked to philosophies of history and ideas of progress). Often in counterposition to the idea of 'development',[418] non-modern epistemologies are seen to be trapped in a primitive past made of archaic irrationality, and do not 'count' as law. This, it has been pointed out, amounts to 'a denial of the co-temporality of the other', an epistemological scandal that chases the other out of the temporality of the observer.[419] Furthermore, if it is true that the realm 'we' understand as religion is the real driver of change (rather than economic forces alone) and that all (modern?) revolutions have been legal,[420] it is clearly a mistake both to subscribe to an overly narrow understanding of 'religious' practice as opposed to legal form and conversely, to underestimate the extent of the unconscious and arcane dimensions of culture, including in its modern legal expression.[421]

Below is an attempt to renew the terms of the reflection on legal plurality in this vein, with reference to an alternative legal aesthetic. This penetration of another universe requires the aid, as seen above, of an avatar. Thus the shadow version of the conflict of laws helps us move from a grid-like linear vision towards a multi-sided or pluritopical understanding of our relation to alterity (whether as other lifeworlds, our surroundings, or other species) that is accessible only by agreeing to dwell in the in-between.[422] Taking its cue from indigenous epistemologies, it will appeal to two

[415] See below 248 et seq.

[416] On which see below 277 et seq.

[417] On the effects of this process on the (nested) sovereignty of indigenous peoples, see A Simpson, *Mohawk Interruptus. Political Life Across the Borders of Settler States* (Durham NC, Duke University Press, 2014); also, specifically from a conflict of laws perspective, 'Subjects of Sovereignty: Indigeneity, The Revenue Rule, and Juridics of Failed Consent' (2008) 71 *Law and Contemporary Problems* 191–216, showing how indigeneity and sovereignty have been conflated with savagery, lawlessness, and smuggling in recent history. The national problem of indigenous smuggling is reconstructed here as it was portrayed in the public eye, largely via the media, and then through conflict-of-laws cases concerning the interpretation and application of the revenue rule.

[418] See below 247.

[419] J Fabian, *Le temps et les autres. Comment l'anthropologie construit son objet* (Toulouse, Anacharsis, 2006). The denial of co-temporality is an epistemological scandal that evicts others from the temporality of the observer (p 257).

[420] As Brunkhorst reminds us: see above 143.

[421] H Mazurel, *L'inconscient ou l'oubli de l'histoire – Profondeurs, métamorphoses et révolutions de la vie affective* (Paris, La Découverte, 2021) 257, writing on culture and the subconscious, underlines the psychoanalytic resonance of critical anthropology and the triad of collective denials it brings to light in terms of actors, engagement with reality and our relation to history.

[422] Mignolo ('On Pluriversality and Multipolarity') emphasises the dimension of 'dwelling' pluritopically, or 'inhabiting' the border, as the reverse of Hegel's philosophy of history (as grounded in territory). The idea of 'dwelling' in our environment is also central to Tim Ingold's work (see *The Perception of the Environment. Essays in Livelihood, Dwelling and Skill* (Abingdon, Routledge, 2000), in which the 'dwelling perspective', is about perception, a view of the relational self in which awareness and activity in and of the world are rooted in an organism's active engagement with the world). On the importance of habitation or *demeure* in the phenomenological turn in ethics, see below 293.

non-anthropomorphic figures, the jaguar and the shaman,[423] to further this reversal. Firstly, to follow the 'gaze of the jaguar'[424] means to enter a reflexive web of mutual sensitivity: the contrary of imposing our own standpoint on others. Thus, in a radical form of decentring, the gaze of the jaguar turns back on oneself, the observer;[425] it brings us to scrutinise our own community or lifeworld (section II.A). Secondly, the shaman,[426] symbolic mediator in animist traditions between humans and the spirits of nature or the other-world, is witness to the plurality and permeability of other, different forms of life (both spiritual and material). In its mediating role, it can

[423] The jaguar and the shaman are twin figures of indigenous mythologies. Each represents a specific, decentred mode of encounter with the strange. While both inhabit the 'space of the in-between', the jaguar (whose gaze represents a reversal of perspective, an 'anti-narcisse') and the shaman (who takes on the shape of the other, including an animal, jaguar-like form) should not be conflated (on their distinctiveness, see E Viveiros de Castro, *Métaphysiques Cannibales* (Paris, PUF, 2009); on their signification, see P Clastres, 'Échange et pouvoir: philosophie de la chefferie indienne' (1962) *L'Homme*; *La Société contre l'État. Recherches d'anthropologie politique* (Paris, Éditions de Minuit, 1974); *Mythologie des Indiens Chulupi* (Louvain, Peeters, 1992); for further analysis of the derisive laughter with which the two figures, presented as burlesque, are greeted by the Chalupi Indians, see A-C Taylor, 'Pierre Clastres et la dérision du pouvoir chez les Indiens: un commentaire' (2013) *Terrain, Anthropologie et Sciences humaines* 114–21). These two burlesque figures are invested with a cathartic and highly constitutional function, inducing laughter in order to exercise power. In the context of this book, to follow the gaze of the jaguar is to see ourselves as seen by the other, while the shaman leads us into the underworld (or otherworld, the hinterland) by taking on the attributes of the other. Moreover, in enacting a specific relationship to alterity, the jaguar may devour the other (by eating the relation), while the shaman becomes the other by changing identities. On the further hybrid figure of the chimera in analogist ontologies, see Descola, *Les formes du visible*, 303 and see above 192.

[424] Perspectivism is a concept associated with Eduardo Vivieros de Castro's immersive exploration of the modes of thought of Amazonian Indian communities (see 'Perspectivisme et multinaturalisme en Amérique indigène' (2014) 3–4 *Journal des anthropologues* §§ 14, 21: 'Le perspectivisme amérindien connaît donc dans le mythe une place, géométrique pour ainsi dire, où la différence entre les points de vue est à la fois annulée et exacerbée. Dans ce discours absolu, chaque espèce d'être apparaît aux autres êtres comme à elle-même – comme humaine –, alors qu'en même temps elle agit dans sa nature distinctive et définitive d'animal, de plante, ou d'esprit … Pour les Amérindiens, l'homme n'est pas le seul à être une personne au sens fort. Tous les habitants du cosmos sont des humains, sous le vêtement des espèces, des corps, des formes distinctes. Si l'on prend au sérieux cette proposition et qu'on essaie de réfléchir dans cette perspective, c'est un autre monde qui s'ouvre à nous, multiple, ondoyant, vertigineux … Le perspectivisme n'est pas un relativisme, mais un multinaturalisme. Le relativisme culturel est un multiculturalisme qui suppose une diversité de représentations subjectives et partielles, ayant une incidence sur une nature externe, une et totale, indifférente à la représentation. Les Amérindiens proposent le contraire: une unité représentative, une phénoménologie purement pronominale, appliquée indifféremment sur une diversité réelle. Une seule « culture », de multiples « natures »; épistémologie constante, ontologie variable: le perspectivisme est un multinaturalisme car une perspective n'est pas une représentation.' The philosopher makes the point that this is also an essential resource for confronting the ecological crisis, which is all at once metaphysical, political and economic.

[425] *Renvoi* in the conflict of laws (or 'foreign court theory', its other, common law version) is emblematically, or perhaps anecdotally, the legal device that does exactly this reflexive move. See again, E Viveiros de Castro, 'Exchanging Perspectives: The Transformation of Objects into Subjects in Amerindian ontologies' (2004) 1 *Common Knowledge* 463–84.

[426] On the varieties of shamanism, see Descola, *Les formes du visible*, 428: In a strict sense (see D Pollock, 'Shamanism', *Oxford Bibliographies*), shamanism is specific form of religious practice found in Siberia, where the Tungus religious practitioner, or *šamán*, provided the model. Anthropology tends to use this concept to describe a set of religious phenomena of historical depth and wide ethnographic extent, across very diverse indigenous traditions (sub-Saharan Africa, East Asia, Latin America) that fulfil a variety of social roles (healing as well as harming) by intervention with spirits or through knowledge gained by communication with spirits.

take on multiple shapes, both human and animal, emphasising thereby the value and centrality of hybridity in an ontology of the in-between (section II.B).

A. The Gaze of the Jaguar

'For the Amerindians, when a jaguar sees itself in the mirror, it sees a human being.'[427] The ecological implications behind this striking representation by Eduardo Viveiros de Castro of the object of the jaguar's gaze are far-reaching.[428] They eradicate humanity's distance from other species. For the Western metaphysical and legal tradition, of which we have already seen that its relation to human (cultural) alterity is inseparable from its approach to the (non-human) natural world, the reversal is just as significant. The deflected mirror-effect of the jaguar's gaze suggests a world of confusing reflexivity, that upsets our modes of access to reality.[429] The mirror of the other sends back our own image, decentring being, as if the jaguar, the avatar, the incarnation of radical alterity, was part of our split self. It serves to remind us, within the Western eminently 'centred' tradition, that the divide between us and them, subject and object, runs through ourselves, and that however rational, civilised or in control we think we are, we are produced and driven by our shadow lives and histories. In terms that ring true to deconstructive, post-structuralist ears, the gaze of the jaguar teaches that it is the perspective that creates the subject, and not the other way round. This is singularly relevant in respect of the law, whose modern guise as order and closure certainly offers tenacious resistance to this reflexive, decentred aesthetic.

In order to understand the insights that can be gained in respect of the law from attempting to follow the 'gaze of the jaguar', it is certainly useful to recall, briefly,

[427] E Viveiros de Castro, *Le regard du jaguar. Introduction au perspectivisme amérindien* (La Tempête, 2021).

[428] At this point, it is useful to refer to Viveiros de Castro's own explanation of anthropological perspectivism (*The Relative Native*, 16–20), that sums up beautifully the point we are trying to make here in respect of legal perspectivism (if indeed it is dissociable from the anthropological): 'When it comes to the question of whether the object of anthropology ought to be the native's point of view, the response must be both "yes" and "no." "Yes" (certainly!), because my problem (is) to discover what a "point of view" is for the native. In other words, what concept of a point of view do Amazonian cultures enunciate – what is the native point of view on the point of view? The answer is "no," on the other hand, because the native concept of a point of view does not coincide with the concept of "the native's of point of view." After all, my point of view cannot be the native's own, but only that of my relation with it. This involves an essentially fictional dimension, since it implies making two entirely heterogeneous points of view resonate with each other … As stated above, the experiment I am proposing posits an equivalence *de jure* between the anthropologist's and the native's discourses, taking them as mutually constitutive of each other, since they emerge as such when they enter into a knowledge relation with one another … They reflect … a certain relation of intelligibility between two cultures, a relation that produces the two cultures in question by back projection, so to speak, as the "motivation" of the anthropological concepts. As such, anthropological concepts perform a double dislocation: they are vectors that always point in the other direction, transcontextual interfaces that function to represent, in the diplomatic sense of the term, the other in one's own terms (that is, in the other's own terms) – both ways. In short, anthropological concepts are relative because they are relational, and they are relational because their role is to relate.'

[429] On the mirror of self as a (modern) ruse of naturalism, see below 297 and above, 101, 133, 173. This is exactly the point of Haraway's 'cyborg' critique (*Simians, Cyborgs, and Women. The Reinvention of Nature*, 178) when she challenges the naturalising stories that still haunt the bodies of everyone marked as other, whose task is to mirror the self.

various elements already encountered above concerning the impact of methodological choices and their corresponding epistemological assumptions on the aesthetics of modern legality. Thus, from a conventional, monist perspective, the latter is an (exclusive or totalising) ontological order (for instance, a code, a nation-state constitution, or an imagined world legal system), all-encompassing, external and prior to social reality.[430] A denial, as it were, of 'life before the law'.[431] In private international law, this vision is instantiated by multilateralist methodology: choice of law is an exercise in fitting diverse national rules back into an overall frame administered by means of a set of complete, coherent and exclusive categories. In such a framework, conflicting norms are anomalous: they look somewhat like a disassembled jigsaw puzzle, of which the pieces must be returned to their proper place within a pre-existing (and of course, internally consistent) order. Difference – in the form of alternative rationalities, or other world-visions – is, as it were, flattened out, or 'squared', through a requirement of conformity with the forum's legal categories.

Conversely, statutism thinks of law in terms of prospective, negotiable assertions advanced outside any fixed, overarching frame. It involves a 'distribution of agencies',[432] a constant change and exchange of perspectives, in a methodological incarnation of legal pluralism. The world beyond the state is cluttered with disorderly heterogeneous claims, rather than self-regulated as order undergirded by coherent principles.[433] Conflicts of laws are generated by the unruly encounter of concurrent, virtual aspirations and normative vocations, all necessarily formulated from an 'internal' perspective – that is, from the standpoint of the would-be legal order, and not dictated by reference to an Archimedean point. They 'blur jurisdiction' and involve 'the sharing of juridical space'. As we have seen above, 'law passes', and indeed a pluralist account of private international law provides an emblematic illustration of legality's specific mode of existence in this respect. Far from being anomalous, the constant overlapping and negotiation of the claimed spatial thrust of different normative projects is an integral part of legality's mode of existence. A sort of legal 'cosmopolitics', to borrow from Isabelle Stenger's account of the body politic.[434]

Law's morphological plurality is underscored, therefore, when its multiple bodies meet and interact. Such encounters may highlight the multiplicity of broad

[430] As seen above in Part I, in the conflict of laws, this vision is well illustrated by the idea of a 'legal relation' central to Savigny's doctrine, deployed within a real or imagined community of laws. The legal relation was as it were, pre-configured before it became the object of normative conflict, in such a way that whatever the starting point (the applicable law or the social relationship), the result was the same.

[431] See C Castoriadis, *L'institution imaginaire de la société* (Paris, ed Seuil, 1999).

[432] See McGee, *Latour and the Passage of law.*

[433] On the conceptualisation of transnational legal authority outside or beyond the state as claim, in the language of legal sociology, see R Cotterrell and M del Mar (eds), *Authority in Transnational Legal Theory Theorising Across Disciplines* (Cheltenham, Elgar, 2016). Examples of a pluralistic approach in positive private international law today are, on the one hand, the recognition of foreign judgments (and its contemporary avatar, the recognition of legal situations on human rights grounds); on the other, 'governmental interests analysis' and '*lois de police*'. All these examples start from and centre around the claim itself, that may require renegotiation or redefinition when it conflicts with another. See below 281 et seq.

[434] I Stenger, *Cosmopolitiques I* (Paris, ed La Découverte, 2003); and by the same author, ' The Cultivation of Ways of Overlapping: a Matter of Reclaiming', in Latour et al, *A Book of the Body Politics*.

institutions or concepts, or singular rules or policies, as well as deeper normative and belief systems.[435] The historical rivalry between monist and pluralist methodologies in private international law shows that there is a significant normative choice to be made: either a claim based on foreign law is heard in its own language, on its own terms, along with its conceptual vocabulary and representation of spatiality, with the ensuing risk of irreducible mutual misunderstandings; or it is made to fit, at the risk of deforming all of its conceptual architecture and ideology, within the structure of the legal categories of the forum.[436] The former 'perspectivist' vision, inherent in legal pluralism, is embodied in statutist doctrines within the conflict of law: the idea of 'claim' is taken very seriously in this context. Thus, above all, such claims are accepted in their existing shape or garb: in other words, statutism, like pluralism, refuses to smooth over differences.[437] For example, the Muslim *kafalah* needs to be taken as it is understood in its own context, and not made to fit in the (unfamiliar) categories of the forum, as should indigenous peoples' non-proprietary ideas of land use and occupation, or alien *persona* endowed with agency by a foreign law.[438] Judicial practice in such cases reveal underlying and historically variable assumptions as to what counts as law (as opposed to religious institutions, primitive practices, or alien legal fictionality).

The point here, however, is that under a monist approach, where law is synonymous with formal legality produced by the state, the question of what counts as 'law' is pushed into the background (there is little point in asking the law of a state whether it thinks of itself as law) and the focus is displaced towards a second issue, that of the spatial thrust and coordination of different systems of state legality. The *kefalah* as a religious institution will command attention only if it is embodied in the foreign

[435] See, for a theorisation of such encounters between secular and non-secular legal cosmologies or epistemologies, see S Brachotte, 'The Conflict of Laws and Non-Secular Worldviews: A Proposal for Inclusion', Doctoral Thesis, Sciences Po, Law School, May 2022. For examples of the latter, this author uses indigenous relationship to land; religious arbitration; and ideological activism on moral or sexual issues, with extra-territorial effects.

[436] See above: this is the 'problem of characterisation' in the conflict of laws. If made to fit in an inappropriate category, difficulties or irritants may emerge downstream (*renvoi* or indeed conflicts of characterisation, *stricto sensu*, where the governing law thus designated in the light of an initial analysis of the 'nature' of a legal institution then responds in completely different terms). As seen above there are endless examples in which monism's devices are deployed – notably, characterisation *lege fori* – show how foreign law is ironed out when its shape or content appear alien or deviant. Indeed, the various conundrums produced by multilateralist methodology – typically, *renvoi* generated by conflicting characterisation within the foreign legal system – are a direct result of this initial elimination of whatever does not, by and large, fit or conform.

[437] Ensuing cases of irreducible conflicts between claims that will not concede or negotiate are admittedly more problematic, but in such cases a pluralist view consists in giving effect to the strongest (in terms of legitimacy or effectiveness). Statutism (as will be seen below) does not deny that this may entail a comparative, value-laden assessment of the strength and value of linkages in the context of particular cases. It says however that conversely to its monist counterpart, the initial opening to the other must be framed in the other's terms. This is a complete reversal of bias, but not a miraculous solution to all conflicts.

[438] These are all well-known examples of 'unfamiliar' categories that raise issues of characterisation in the conflict of laws. The example of unknown legal *personae* was usually illustrated by the problem of the appearance of the trust at the threshold of civilian legal systems, but has lost much of its punch by reason of a certain convergence around fiduciary institutions. However, the question of the legal standing of rivers and natural entities is more topical: see below 286.

state law governing (from the point of view of the court of a secular legal system) the personal status of the child; the same can be said of the indigenous usage of sacred land, that will be recognised as title only if formalised as such under the *lex rei sitae*.[439] The reach of (foreign) state law, as we know, has been the exclusive preoccupation of private international law since the early twentieth century. The irony of this, as we have also already seen, is that contemporary methods used in this context originated in circumstances where statehood was not the only parameter with which to identify legality. If there was no perceptible rupture in this respect in the nineteenth century, with the close entwinement of law and statehood, it was because the 'concert' of European nation states was still homogeneous: the displacement, into a wider international setting, of the methodologies initially designed to ensure the coordination of the laws of Germanic Roman Christian city states and princedoms[440] seemed 'natural' (or only to involve a very slight move). In reality, the change was considerable, because the state form that had eliminated all the other actors from the international order (or all other subjects from international law) by the early twentieth century in no way guaranteed that thenceforth, under law's formal and apparently homogenous framework, there was either a common substantive content (hence the rise of the conflict of laws as a discipline, along with its comparative counterpart[441]), or a shared conceptual architecture (thereafter appeared the problem of characterisation), or indeed an analogous vision of what counts as legality (now assimilated to state-based private law).

Indeed, as Robert Cover's definition of *nomos* reminds us, there is considerably more to law than rules. And this invisible part is as variable as is unitary the formal frame in which it is contained. Legal pluralism, then, can be seen as an attempt to see beyond the unitary legal form of statehood. It also changes the terms in which the interaction between different conceptions of legality takes place within the conflict of laws. As seen above, monism assumes a comfortable fit between (state) legal systems; since it does not need to dwell on definition, it can orchestrate their encounters from an Archimedean standpoint. On the contrary, under radical pluralism, no such comfort is available.[442] Of course, it is difficult to leave behind the comfort of modern law's linearity and its obsession with closure, 'legal security' and decisiveness. As Pierre Schlag observes, the power of self-definition (in respect of what counts as law) always runs the risk of degenerating into 'dissociation'.[443] The conflict of laws illustrates this riddle perfectly: this is the very reason for which its shadow avatar has been relegated to the margins. The latter represented the dominant form as long

[439] Even then categories of title to property can be instrumentalised: see on the infamous *Song Mao* case (involving Tate & Lyle and Cambodian 'blood sugar') H Muir Watt et al, *Global Private international law*, with commentaries by A Mills, H Harata and O Le Meur, 118 et seq.

[440] See above 108.

[441] On their joint effect in terms of the voiding or hierarchisation of space, see below 277 et seq.

[442] William Twining describes the instability of such interaction, that 'is often more like that between waves or clouds or rivulets than between hard, stable entities like rocks or billiard balls' ('Diffusion and Globalization Discourse', 513).

[443] Schlag, 'The Aesthetics of American Law'. The idea of dissociation has obvious psychoanalytical resonance (see above 194 and below 203).

as Roman law (or reason)[444] offered an overarching background from which local laws diverged,[445] but was rejected as archaic when statehood became the exclusive, universal source of legality towards the turn of the nineteenth century and public international law no longer the frame of reference for the conflict of private laws.

Ever since, attempts to reinstate a neo-statutist, pluralist methodology beyond a 'community of laws'[446] have largely failed by reason of their apparent impotence in the face of 'true conflicts',[447] or their inability to achieve closure or decisiveness: the semantics of the conflict of laws and legal pluralism are different, but the dilemma is identical.[448] Their common conundrum is that they espouse 'perspectivism' (or self-definition),[449] but in the absence of any overarching or monist stance from which to harness multiple viewpoints, their very plurality is likely to fall into chaos or dislocation.[450] The seemingly inextricable difficulty in both cases is that 'anything goes'.[451] If we allow each legal entity to deploy its own singularity, chaos (in the form of overlapping claims, in the language of the conflict of laws, or legal insecurity, in debates over pluralism) ensues. How then, in the absence of a stable frame or centre, does it prevent the potentially positive dynamic produced by constant exchange between multiple viewpoints from breaking down into a state of disarticulated shambles or dislocation? How can law reconnect, replace, reorder or reinsert disrupted sequences of things and beings, persons and events when it cannot rely on the guidance of an overarching scheme of things? How can it enact fluid and contestable interlegality,[452] rather than dislocation?[453] In this respect, most justifications of

[444] This is equally valid for the overarching or common background composed of the common law in American neo-statutism, or the belief in the strict territoriality of law as in vested rights.

[445] See Stein, *Roman Law in European History* 71 et seq. Initially, for Bartolus de Sassoferrato and the Commentators of the late Middle Ages, the *ius commune* provided the methods with which to interpret local statutes, and in such a way as to restrict the opportunity for derogation. Later attitudes varied considerably from place to place towards the *Corpus Iuris* and Roman law more generally, but the conviction remained that conflicts between local, secular laws took place in the shadow of an overarching normative scheme (whether *Corpus, Institutes*, Roman classical culture, or natural reason) that commanded a uniform method of delimitation of local statutes or customs. Because local customs were still understood as interpretative variations on Roman law as the sole depositary of a legal essence or authority, the focus of the intense juridical labour of the post-glossators was the spatial (personal or territorial) projection of forms that were recognised as unquestionably juridical.

[446] In Carl von Savigny's *opus*, this normative community was that of the Germanic city-states and princedoms. But the same concept could refer to the common law tradition as a whole, or indeed to a common regional legal area such as that of the European Union.

[447] This is the classical critique of 'governmental interests analysis' in the conflict of laws: see below.

[448] As Roughan and Halpin (*In Pursuit of Pluralist Jurisprudence*) formulate the conundrum: how to achieve pluralism without sacrificing closure?

[449] On perspectivism in the work of E Viveiros de Castro, see above 199.

[450] Or 'dissociation', in Schlag's words. These terms all have psychic implications, pointing to a risk of social self-destruction.

[451] See on this theme, M Hesselink, 'Anything Goes in Private Law Theory? On the Epistemic and Ontological Commitments of Private Law Multi-pluralism' (January 14, 2022). EUI Department of Law Research Paper forthcoming, https://ssrn.com/abstract=4009148 or http://dx.doi.org/10.2139/ssrn.4009148.

[452] On the concept of interlegality, see B De Sousa Santos, 'Toward a New Legal Common Sense', 437; on the analogy between interlegality and private international law, see Wai, 'The Interlegality of Transnational Private Law'.

[453] See above: a coordinating method, we are told repeatedly, cannot work if it is decentred. As we know, it is this very conundrum – the demise of statutist methodology when confronted with insoluble 'true conflicts' – that explains the enduring success of monist ideas within the conflict of laws.

legal pluralism fail to overcome the objection of the risk of chaos or dissociation. The same objection is equally familiar in the conflict of laws, in respect of statutist methodology, the internationalist avatar of legal pluralism: a method of conflict resolution that is impotent to solve conflicts is by definition unqualified for the job.[454]

The underlying assumption of the usual approaches to legal pluralism, still bearing the traces of the monist model, is that legality has to be defined (however loosely) before envisaging its coordination with others. As several strands of scholarship have pointed out, this particular sequence or order of questions may well need rethinking, or 'resequencing'.[455] In other words, the key to this familiar methodological riddle may lie in the way in which the problem itself is framed. Moreover, the problem itself – the disorder – may be part of the solution. Taking our cues from indigenous-ecological lateral thinking[456] or frontier-dwelling, we could say that decentring and mutual sensitivity, or readiness to interact mutually to the point of substitution or identification with the point of view of the other, is constitutive of the very existence of an ecological system (whether law or holobiont). Multi-sidedness and hybridity appear then as a promise to be pursued, rather than as an obstacle to be overcome, encouraging a reversal in our methodological assumptions. The importance of individual (psychic) ability to decentre self and collective (cultural) capacity to step outside community imaginaries is already an important part of critical 'post-Freudian' thinking in the West, bringing (historical) context back into understanding of the collective psyche and its denials.[457]

This then is the insight to be drawn from indigenous epistemologies: the gaze of the radical, animal other directed towards oneself is a form of 'constitutive alterity'.[458] As Eduardo Viveiro de Castro explains, seeing ourselves through the gaze of the jaguar goes as far as the complete identification of the other's point of view as directed towards ourselves. This does not mean a renouncement of critique, nor an invitation to blind submission or unconditional deference to the others (*autrui*[459]). It is an invitation however, as Descola explains, to come out of oneself to view self as a singularity from the standpoint of alterity.[460] It is a project to become-other, to carry in oneself the gaze of the other. On a collective register, it is similarly a foundational or constitutive requirement of community, not to lose one's own identity

[454] For a synthesis of the debate over Brainerd Currie's 'governmental interest analysis '(above 100), see K Roosevelt III, 'The Myth of Choice of Law: Rethinking Conflicts' (1999) *Faculty Scholarship at Penn Law* 1340.

[455] R Michaels, 'The Functional method in comparative law' in M Reimann & R Zimmermann (eds), *The Oxford Handbook of Comparative Law*, 2nd edn (Oxford, Oxford University Press, 2019) 340.

[456] There are strong links between laterality (on an aesthetic register), relationality (as ethics) and the in-between (ontology) in contemporary pluralistic theories of all kinds: see (as a significant sample) Pelluchon, *Les Lumières à l'âge du vivant*, 72; S Bachir Dgiane, 'Décoloniser l'universel', in NY Kisukidisee (ed) *La vie des idées*, 2 mai 2019; Morizot, *Esthétique de la rencontre*; B Latour, *Où suis-je* (Paris, La Découverte, 2021), on lateral mobility as an emancipated mode of existence in conditions of confinement.

[457] Mazurel, *L'inconscient ou l'oubli de l'histoire*.

[458] Descola, *Les formes du visible* 438–39: the Other is the guarantor of the constitutive virtues of the community and flags the gaze of the other that I carry within myself.

[459] See below on the (Levinassian) difference between the other and other(s), *autre* and *autrui*.

[460] Descola, *Les formes du visible*, 438.

or the singularity of one's own collective values, but to interiorise the existence of alterity beyond our own confines.[461] As we shall see below, in order to move into this new register of 'inter-alterity', that is, of communication and identity between radical others in legal terms, law – through the conflict of laws – has to operate a radical change of gear.[462]

The important point at this stage is that an approach that sees mutual sensitivity as constitutive of legal community effectively fields the double objection conventionally addressed to legal pluralism and the underlying assumption of the inevitability of statehood.[463] The very constitution or definition of legality would depend upon such an opening towards alterity and a willingness to enter into contact with foreign legal forms on their own terms. In such a vein, the recourse to a pluralist scheme borrowed from the conflict of laws is proposed by Gunter Teubner, in order to ground a 'global societal constitutionalism'.[464] In this account, in the absence of any other possible universal substantive principle, the conflict of laws would supply a meta-dogmatic norm to which all systems would adhere, to the extent that they make a claim to some sort of prescriptiveness. This norm would be without substantive content in the sense that it could only be a form of reciprocal deference, an ecological necessity[465] deriving from the reality of their interdependence. Identified as a form of pluralist jurisprudence, it points tentatively towards a pattern of open interaction among systems in which the matter of authority is not settled by one system accepting or deferring to another's, nor by each system claiming authority for itself. Instead, each system's claim can be understood as referring to some kind of interdependence, which entails the existence of the other's authority without amounting to deference to that other system.[466]

Under this reading of legality, every normative order (or claim) is authenticated on its own terms, but such authentication is conditional on its containing some sort of integrated mechanism that makes interaction possible. As Nicole Roughan and Andrew Halpin explain, there has to be a step between the 'initial pluralist recognition' of multiple claims to normativity or authority and 'the subsequent interaction between recognised members of that plurality'.[467] This would be a third order or

[461] Ibid, 439.

[462] See below Part III.

[463] On the lack of such inevitability in the legal history of the West, see 80.

[464] Teubner, *Constitutional Fragments*, 152. His insight is as follows: 'In a world society with neither apex nor centre, there is just one way remaining to handle inter- constitutional conflicts – a strictly heterarchical conflict resolution'. Teubner's system of networked reciprocity reconstitutes an ideal, constitutionalised system of conflict of law rules in which a significant place is given to non-state communities, their value systems and the sense of belonging. Moreover, this overarching framework is designed to impose a break, or a certain discipline, on the autonomous, self-expanding rationalities of privatised legal regimes, or 'codes of capital'. However, it remains somewhat unclear how a constitutional metanorm in the form of a (monist or multilateralist) set of universal conflict of laws rules can be reconciled with the essentially perspectivist stance that pluralism requires. Any given system or node may create its own coordination devices, and these will of course reflect axiological priorities and preferences that will prevail before its own courts or decision-makers. But this does not avert the risk of collapse or disjunction largely associated with pluralism. The text above attempts to respond to this difficulty.

[465] 'Ecological' here refers to a symbiotic relationship between the norm and its environment.

[466] Michaels, 'Law and Recognition – Towards a Relational Concept of Law'.

[467] Roughan and Halpin, *In Pursuit of Pluralist Jurisprudence*.

principle designed to foster interaction between the various units. It implies that all systems that make a claim to prescriptiveness must possess a sort of a constitutive, non-hierarchical coordination device based on a form of minimal mutual recognition: a 'tertiary rule of recognition' (named thus by Ralf Michaels),[468] a 'strictly heterarchical' conflict resolution (Gunter Teubner's 'dogmatic metanorm'),[469] or indeed, as we shall see below, their own shamanic go-between: a *persona* whose very existence is designed to ensure the mutual communication between heterogeneous worlds.

However, before we return to the art of the shaman (in the next paragraph, below) the relationship between such an inbuilt mutual recognition device and the very definition of legality needs to be highlighted. Here, a paradigmatic change in respect of classical analytical-legal approaches may be underway, since the usual directionality or 'sequencing'[470] of this relationship is reversed. The very qualification of a normative system as legal would then be conditional on its acknowledgement of its own interdependence in respect of other such systems, the latter being identifiable in turn by virtue of their own reciprocal acknowledgement of their readiness to connect, as it were to speak the lingua franca of interlegality.[471] Thus, reflecting on the constitution of a new ecological body politic, the philosopher Isabelle Stengers advises to start from the 'mutual sensitivity' of collectives or individuals (rather than from an atomistic approach that begins with the first and ends with the second). Her approach is deliberately reflective of the symbiotic, co-productive constitution of the ecosystem: not one of its components can exist without the others.[472] If what we perceive as our 'environment' outside is actually part of our inner existence (or that of our microcosm), then we need to reverse the order of our rational chains of reasoning, that always start from the centre of any object of study to consider its relationship with its own surroundings or periphery. The suggestion here is to flip the order of questions so as to start from the ecological or macrocosmic 'outside' of any being or form of life, on the reverse assumption that this outside is integral to their very core.[473]

The implications of this new ecological paradigm for law become clear if we compare Stenger's approach to an equally recent jurisprudential exploration of legal pluralism more directly related to the conflict of laws.[474] Here, Ralf Michaels proposes a resequencing of the issues of legality (its definition) and modes of interaction (between legal systems) as they are conventionally ordered or presented. Instead

[468] Michaels, 'Law and Recognition – Towards a Relational Concept of Law', 107.

[469] Teubner, *Constitutional Fragments*. Seeing multiple colliding rationalities as coexisting within a network justifies an obligation upon each to ensure the mutual accommodation of the others; the performance of that obligation is constitutive of their very existence as network nodes.

[470] Ibid, 94.

[471] See above.

[472] See above.

[473] I Stengers, *The Cultivation of Ways of Overlapping: a Matter of Reclaiming*, in Latour et al, *Body Politics*, 159. This also seems to correspond to Gunter Teubner's 'ecological' understanding of law in society, in which the conflict of laws acts as go-between between legality and its environment. It also ties in perfectly with the idea that sovereignty may not be sovereignty if it does not accommodate interdependency; such interdependency is once again part of what it means to be sovereign.

[474] Michaels is writing as a pluralist here, not, he says, as a private international lawyer.

of attempting first to define a normative system and then asking about its relationship to its own others, in other words, other legal orders (in the more traditional terms of the conflict of laws, its spatial scope), the latter question will come first.[475] Thus, not only can a system not make any (legitimate) normative claim unless it integrates a mutual recognition device, but the latter is as it were constitutive of the system itself, commanding its very existence *qua* system. A pluralist conception must work interlegality into the very fabric of law, of which it is constitutive (rather than being an 'afterthought',[476] as is clearly the case in a monist vision that starts from the essence of law before addressing the question of interlegality).[477]

This is the cue to loop back to private international law. An alternative scheme of the discipline provides a model of lateral coordination and accommodation according to which singular systems or units interact in a mutually supportive mode. A significant example of such lateral interlegality could be taken from the field of the recognition and enforcement of foreign judgments. In many ways, the latter are at the crux of coordination between systems, as demonstrated by numerous cases of interminable struggle at the ultimate, enforcement stage of legal disputes.[478] On a monist register, jurisdiction is usually determined unilaterally by each legal system and exercised independently of the effects it might have elsewhere.[479] However, by contrast, in the mode of lateral, mutual coordination, any judgement made in the home jurisdiction should imply an anticipation of its effects elsewhere and the commitment to mutually accommodate the reactions of other legal systems.[480] Far from undermining the value of decisiveness, a pluralist approach suggests that a mutually supportive

[475] Nicole Roughan and Andrew Halpin elaborate on this point: 'in circumstances in which more than one system of norms is implicated in a legal dispute … as a matter of legitimate authority, there may be no justification for one system/set for ignoring or excluding the other under the rubric of jurisdiction'

[476] See Michaels, 'Law and Recognition – Towards a Relational Concept of Law'.

[477] For an analogous 'dialogical' or 'relational' idea of sovereignty, see C Scott, 'Dialogical Sovereignty: Preliminary Metaphorical Musings', https://digitalcommons.osgoode.yorku.ca/all_papers/191; and in respect of indigenous law and sovereignty (on which above 173), see by the same author, 'Indigenous Self-Determination and Decolonization of the International Imagination' (1996) 18 *Human Rights Quarterly* 814–20 and leading from there, Iris Young, *Two concepts of self-determination*, 10.1017/CBO9780511489235.009; *cf* the plea for a dialogical mode of solidarity as opposed to a form of sovereignty as 'solitude': M Delmas-Marty, www.lemonde.fr/idees/article/2020/03/17/mireille-delmas-marty-profitons-de-la-pandemie-pour-faire-la-paix-avec-la-terre_6033344_3232.html. On the idea of relationality in private law and why it is (arguably) not enough, see below, Part III.

[478] An example of a struggle of this kind can be found in the notorious *Chevron* saga, in which the litigants threatened to fight 'until the oceans run dry' (see H Muir Watt et al, *Global Private international law*, 55 et seq with commentaries by D Fernandez Arroyo and L Caballo Pineiro).

[479] See Michaels, 'Law and Recognition – Towards a Relational Concept of Law'. It can be argued that the requirement of a 'close connection' in one form or another as a condition for the exercise of jurisdiction ensures the acceptability of any resulting judgment.

[480] In this respect, one clear example is what could be called a method of anticipation put into place by the Hague Convention on intercountry adoption of 29 May 1993 (to be found in various forms in further judicial practice on which see D Bureau & H Muir Watt, *Droit international privé*, n°203). The simple idea is that the adoption will not be granted if it is shown that it would not be recognised in the country with which the child has or might have close connections and a desire to return. In an older vocabulary, this is an attempt to avoid 'limping' relationships (recognised in one country but not in the other). It has also been theorised by Paolo Picone as 'Ordinamento competente' ('La méthode de la référence à l'ordre juridique compétent en droit international privé' (1986) 197 *Rec Cours Acad La Haye de droit international/Collected Courses of the Hague Academy of International Law* 239 et seq.

model of interlegality enhances the legitimacy and the predictability of any normative claim.[481] Both would depend upon the degree to which other concurrent projects are accommodated on their own terms. Isabelle Stenger's account of the symbiotic body politic has already provided significant evidence of the ecological resonance of this mutually sensitive jurisprudential paradigm. Such resonance is stronger still if we move to the question of hybridity. So, as it were, from the gaze of the jaguar, we must loop back to the figure of the shaman.

B. The Art of the Shaman

A shaman (of which the jaguar can be an embodiment[482]) is an emblematic '*passeur*' between multiple worlds.[483] Dwelling in the border,[484] the shaman operates a form of inter-world diplomacy[485] between the physical or biological world and the universe of spirits. Shamanic otherness, in-between two worlds, evokes the shadowy otherworldliness of unseen (off-scene) and uncanny (the Freudian *unheimlich*) encounters with alterity. It involves moreover a form of ontological transmutation. Rather than mere disguise, this is a means of becoming other.[486] Two particularly important aspects of the ontology of the 'in-between' are present here. Firstly, in order to fulfil important social functions,[487] the shaman can take on different shapes or avatars, undergoing a sort of double or two-way 'translation'.[488] Sometimes, the spirit of the shaman goes out of itself into the other-world where it can inhabit a form that can communicate with the inhabitants of another life. Sometimes, it invokes into its (our) world a being from another, controlling its spirit or borrowing its shape. It is both hybrid, protean and multiform, inside and outside, past and present, here and there, charged with plural identities.

Secondly, the shaman is witness to the interpenetration of different registers of being. As Walter Mignolo writes of what he calls 'pluriversality', the shaman evidences cosmological entanglement, a plurality of worlds that are not separate, nor organised in a hierarchical mode, but which overlap, overflow and interact.[489] Against jurisdictional thinking as defined above, it weaves reflexively in and out, mixing past and present, reversing far and near. Moreover, it produces hybrids as forms of communication or mutual sensitivity (as seen above). These must be sharply distinguished from

[481] Roughan and Halpin, *In Pursuit of Pluralist Jurisprudence*.
[482] See Viveiros de Castro, *Le regard du jaguar. Introduction au perspectivisme amérindien*.
[483] Descola, *Les formes du visible*.
[484] See above on the importance of this in-between location.
[485] On the importance of diplomacy in the imaginaries of the world in the shadow of extinction, see Latour ('the supreme art of compromise'), *Enquête*, 478; R Janda, *Panarchy* (forthcoming; cited and presented, Globinar, Paris, Sciences Po, May 2022).
[486] Hence the sacred character of certain masks that ensure this transmutation from world to another (on the Hopi mask case, involving modes of relations with alterity that are incommensurable with Western legal categories, see below 279).
[487] These are known to be variable: the shaman may heal or harm social relations.
[488] Mignolo, 'On Pluriversality and Multipolarity', 83.
[489] Ibid: these are not separate worlds but worlds that overlap and interact.

'cultural relativism'.[490] Hybridity in this context is not a non-choice or a failure of communication, but on the contrary, a highly sophisticated form of 'cosmopolitics', or in more familiar terms, an exercise in the 'sublime art' of compromise.[491]

In legal terms, these two aesthetic dimensions of the in-between as embodied in the shaman resonate within the shadow version of the conflict of laws. The first concerns the highly sensitive question of identity or belonging that is, or has become, a central concern of private international law in respect of the 'imagined community' of the nation state.[492] As we know, the central labour of this discipline can be seen as the reconnecting of persons and communities in different ways, when geographical dispersion threatens to disrupt or sever moral, cultural, material or emotional ties.[493] The two possible schemes available for this purpose offer contrasting visions of the world (our world), along with diverging methodological approaches for the determination of the most significant relationship in terms of belonging and emplacement.[494] The conventional assumption, present in monism, is that identity and community are totalising concepts: community membership is exclusive, while identity is stable and one-directional. The implications for private international law have been deployed on a similar register since the heyday of the nation state:[495] by and large,[496] an individual's

[490] To which we shall return below: we know that this is the frequent charge against legal pluralism. The point being made in this section is that hybridity or the supreme art of compromise is communication between two worlds. This means that the adoption of the other's viewpoint may change one's gaze. Understanding (as seen above) that cannibalism is a way of integrating alterity (see Descola, *Les formes du visible*, 544: 'le moyen paradoxal d'incoporer l'altérié la plus profonde tout en restant fidèle à soi-même'), that the incestuous relations of the survivors of the Bounty were precisely necessary to their survival, or indeed that other forms of punishment (alternatives to imprisonment, seen as barbaric) are already very important. However, it is difficult to stop there and to accept what appears in the vocabulary of the Enlightenment, human rights and pyschoanalysis, to be murder, child molestation, inhuman treatment etc. The exception of public order in private international law shows these conflicts to be intractable, notably when they involve shame (punishment) and morals (religion, sexuality). There may be a need at some point to put up a screen or a limit when foreign practices or belief systems intrude upon the host community, as we shall see below, but such a defence must avoid negating the seriousness of the other's access to reality.

[491] These are respectively the expressions of I Stengers and B Latour, cited above.

[492] This is illustrated by heated contemporary political-doctrinal debates on the legitimacy and effects of dual nationality, or, in the European setting, the contested idea and case law on European Union citizenship, for instance (see the Report of the EU Parliament: www.europarl.europa.eu/RegData/etudes/BRIE/2018/625116/EPRS_BRI(2018)625116_EN.pdf).

[493] All these components are present to different degrees in the composition of domicile and nationality, the two standard legal expressions of attachment or belonging. They tend to be spelled out in cases of conflict and uncertainty. Thus, in identifying the law applicable to personal status, the rules of the conflict of laws aim to ensure that family and interpersonal relationships are governed by the law that best represents the lifestyle and sense of belonging of those involved.

[494] Law's boundaries in this context are those of the post-Westphalian division of the world's entire surface into states. As the current trajectories of migrant populations show (at the Mexican border, at lines drawn across the African continent, and again at the confines of the European Union), such exclusion comes with a series of destructive consequences in terms of dispossession of 'the right to have rights', and more generally the unequal distribution of economic and social value, power and privilege. The expropriations (or expulsions) described by Saskia Sassen as the new global 'golden rule' apply to whole swathes of the world's population.

[495] A recent and brief moment, as Hauke Brunkhorst points out (see above, 165).

[496] Of course, as always there have been trends to the contrary and counter-moves, that show up alternative modes. Dual citizenship calls for further choices (such as the choice of the most effective or the preference for the law of the forum), and clashes may occur between nationality and domicile in the deployment of the connecting factor (*renvoi*), while interesting forrays take place from time to time in the modulation of

personal relationships must always be governed by the same law, defined moreover by means of a connecting factor (domicile or nationality) that remains the same for all purposes.

Unsurprisingly, given the nexus between legality and statehood seen above, there is a close analogy between the assumptions relating to community and those underlying the definition of modern legality: the latter excludes by definition, as Hans Lindahl points out, since it is a narrative written in the first person plural, in the name of a bounded community.[497] In both cases, barring exceptional instances, statehood offers a mutually exclusive alternative: you are either in or out, in the same way that an act is either legal or illegal. In short, on any register – moral, epistemological, geopolitical or legal – there is no in-between place to be. By contrast, under a pluralist approach, an individual may be a member of several communities simultaneously.[498] This is the sense in which a pluralist perspective can make available an in-between space, in which multiple identities overlap.[499] If communities are imagined[500] and their boundaries unstable, a sense of belonging or place is not necessarily exclusive. This is also a view that is resurfacing in contemporary private international law,[501] that makes frequent allowance for ever more complex individual and collective attachments, including in their temporal variations.[502] In a similar vein, the everyday lives of a collectivity may be governed by rules that are effectively followed even when not formally recognised as that of a state.[503]

The second point is hybridity. At the core of another controversy over methodological legitimacy, *métissage*[504] or 'creolisation' of law[505] is the object of a debate over

one or the other (for instance, in the case of adoption of a foreign child: see D Gutmann, *Le sentiment d'identité, étude de droit des personnes et de la famille* (LGDJ, 2000)). Strategic use (domicile of origin in the colonial era) or more social, or sociological trends (current popularity of habitual residence in EU law) also come into play.

[497] Lindahl, *Authority and the Globalisation of Inclusion and Exclusion*, in which Lindahl himself develops the postmodern ideal of in-between place.

[498] P Schiff Berman, *Global Legal Pluralism: A Jurisprudence of Law Beyond Borders* (Cambridge, Cambridge University Press, 2012).

[499] In this respect, it borrows psychoanalytical insights relating to the invisible realm of the subconscious, to the equally subliminal operation of the social norm.

[500] See Anderson, *Imagined Communities.*

[501] A view advocated by Schiff Berman, *Global Legal Pluralism.*

[502] In this respect, Gutmann identifies a progressive 'recognitive' function in the conflict of laws, allowing it to follow the progressive integration of a foreign individual into a host community: Gutmann, *Le sentiment d'identité.*

[503] On the ways in which private international law can sidestep public international law's requirement of state recognition, see Knop, 'Citizenship, Public and Private'.

[504] In public international law, the notion of mestizo has been elevated to a genre: A. Becker Lorca, *Mestizo International Law: A Global Intellectual History 1842–1933* (Cambridge, Cambridge University Press, 2016); see too on international law from the margins, F Antunes Madeira da Silva, 'The Conquest of the Devil's Paradise: International law, Frontier-making and Capitalist power', PhD dissertation, Sciences Po Law School, November 2022. Such a move is missing on the private side.

[505] The concept of 'creolisation' emerged at the end of the nineteenth century to signify processes of linguistic appropriation and adjustment in the encounter between the language of the coloniser ('*langue lexificatrice*') and the local language ('*substrat*'), from which a hybrid merged ('*le créole*'), borrowing structural elements from each (see D Véronique, 'Créole, créoles français et théories de la créolisation' (2000) 85 *L'information grammaticale* 33–38). The idea of lingua franca evoked above is distinct, as it is a third language, not a 'corrupted' form, and does not involve the asymmetry that underlies creolisation. F Laplantine and A Nouss, *Etudes des métissages, des hybrides et des circulations* (Paris, Flammarion, 2007) 257.

the respective virtues of legal pluralism and a liberal (monist) vision of the law.[506] This is a variation on a familiar charge made in the name of decisiveness and purity against legal pluralism's supposedly muddy conflict-solving methods.[507] Unable to choose between equal claims to govern, and prohibited from falling back on a predefined parameter of choice – the very allocation it sought initially to avoid – it collapses into an intermingling or hotchpotch of all the conflicting norms. From this perspective, the failing of pluralism's collateral mode of mutual accommodation lies in its inability to commit to the exclusive application of a unitary substantive rule.[508] Implicitly, this refers, once again, to law's purported need for a priori decisiveness and furthermore to the illegitimacy of any form of syncretism.

However, hybridity does not have to be viewed as a defect, any more than purity a virtue. To take up the linguistic analogy once again, PG Monateri's comparative legal study of the shadowy figure of 'Black Gaius' – a legal avatar of 'Black Athena' – points to the dangers of pursuing unadulterated pedigree as a value in either language or law.[509] Both indeed are made of countless residues and traces from all parts. This points once again to hybridity as belonging to the cosmopolitical value of the in-between. It is inscribed in the idea of pluriversality, in the sense that different coexisting worlds interact, combining and blending in various ways.[510] In any of its avatars, the conflict of laws illustrates this by means of its most ancient and foundational idea: the *lex franca* created from multiple and mutually reinforcing legal components. If we move from aesthetics to political philosophy, we could say that this composite, mosaic pattern benefits from an enhanced acceptability, to the extent that it reflects the very plurality and interdependence of all the contributing bodies of law.[511] In other words, the hybridity of the final normative outcome reinforces its legitimacy, as compared with a decision obtained by reference to one

[506] See the political-philosophical objections to Paul Berman's theory of global legal pluralism by A Galán, D Patterson, 'The Limits of Normative Legal Pluralism: Review of Paul Schiff Berman, Global Legal Pluralism: A Jurisprudence of Law Beyond Borders' (2013) *International Journal of Constitutional Law*. This debate extends to the question of the adequacy of liberalism to accommodate alterity (see below).

[507] As seen above, this charge is now more than familiar: these methods fail precisely in cases of real antinomy (from the Greek ἀντί, antí, 'against, in opposition to', and νόμος, nómos, 'law') referring to a real or apparent mutual incompatibility of two laws: Encyclopædia Britannica Online), or 'true' normative conflicts between the host legal order and the incoming norm. The worst defect for a legal method, we learn, is not being able to choose between two alternatives; a choice of law rule that cannot solve 'true conflicts' cannot serve as a method.

[508] D Patterson, *Legality's Borders: An Essay in General Jurisprudence* (Oxford, Oxford University Press, 2010).

[509] P-G Monateri, 'Black Gaius: A Quest for the Multicultural Origins of the "Western Legal Tradition"' (2000) 51 *Hastings LJ* 479.

[510] On pluriversality, see the scholarship cited above 42, 137, 139.

[511] A 'close-call' (5–4) Canadian Supreme Court decision provides a striking illustration of the 'mutual translation' metaphor that suggests juxapositional/combinational *métissage* – a judicial entering in-between space in a new norm-forging decisional mode: Supreme Court of Canada, 2020 *Araya v Nevsun*, www.canlii.org/en/ca/scc/doc/2020/2020scc5/2020scc5.html?resultIndex=2, in which Abella J's majority judgment cites C Scott (ed), *Torture as Tort: Comparative Perspectives on the Development of Transnational Human Rights Litigation* (Oxford, Hart Publishing, 2001). A final section of the article by the same author, 'Translating Torture as Transnational Tort' 45–64, contains the mutual translation metaphor. See below, 245.

legal system exclusively applied and imposed on all the other affected communities. Since the disputes involving conflicts of laws arise out of situations that are spatially dismembered between different jurisdictions, none of which has an exclusive claim to govern the whole, but each of which contributes a part, the final composition carries an enriched, and not a diluted, form of social legitimacy.[512]

Interestingly, what is true of law's aesthetic of spatiality is also valid in respect of its inscription in time. In 'taking place', concomitantly with the emergence of the modern linear perspective in space,[513] modern law secreted its own (eminently juridical invention) continuous chronological temporality.[514] By contrast, indigenous epistemologies support the idea of the non-linearity or 'pluritopicality' of time and its variability according to place.[515] An alternative temporal mode of the in-between is sometimes visible, however, behind modern legality's chronological time, mixing the past, present and future. Law has the power to conjure up history into the courtroom, to fictionally suspend or cut off the passing of time, or to give voice to future generations.[516] The shadow avatar of private international law, in particular, illustrates this entwinement of time and space, history and geography. Indeed, Mariana Valverde uses 'jurisdiction' as a conceptual category through which she proposes to explore the multiple 'scaling' of time and its own complex relationship to spatiality.[517] Her notion of 'chronotope' sees each legal order as occupying its own specific temporal-spatial nexus.[518] In the conflict of laws, the device of *ordre public* is an

[512] That in most (or all?) cases, it does not correspond to the law of any given system, or indeed, does not correspond to a foreign court's idea of what its own law is, is of no import: an inaccurate interpretation of foreign law is not an error of law. Moreover, it will be recalled that even in highly monist settings, in the context of the enforcement of foreign judgments (or arbitral awards), an error of interpretation of the forum court's own law is not, per se, a reason to refuse recognition. A good example can be found in the controversial *Dallah v Pakistan* case involving the alleged misinterpretation of French law by English courts, which illustrates, very forcibly, that there are other interests and objectives at stake in private international law than the integrity of a given substantive legal rule (*Dallah Real Estate & Tourism Holding Co v Ministry of Religious Affairs, Government of Pakistan* [2010] UKSC 46, 3 November 2010; Cour d'appel de Paris, 17 February 2011, *Gouvernement du Pakistan – Ministère des Affaires religieuses c Société Dallah Real Estate and Tourism Holding Company*, n° R/G 09/28533; *cf* the analysis by S Bollée, in *Global Private International Law* (Cheltenham, Elgar, 2018) and *Le Droit international privé et le tournant global* (Paris, Pédone, 2020) n°4.2).

[513] Bartelson, *Sovereignty as Symbolic Form*.

[514] The invention of the latter was linked to the specific need for a fictional continuity of the medieval king's sublime body: as explained by Kantorowicz, medieval lawyers created a specific legal temporality when struggling with the political consequences of the physical death of the king's metaphysical corporeality. The king is dead; long live the king!

[515] See, on the ability of the *griot* to manipulate, resequence and reassemble different forms of symbolic organisation in the world, passing through different temporalities, I Ouattara, 'The Griots of West Africa, Oral Tradition and Shared Knowledge', in B Reiter (ed) *Constructing the Pluriverse*, 151.

[516] Our collective subconscious has no sense of time; our forgotten history prepares a return of the repressed: see Mazurel, *L'inconscient ou l'oubli de l'histoire*. On 'future generations', an imagined collective that is in the process of acquiring legal standing, see Part III below 233.

[517] M Valverde, *Chronotopes of Law: Jurisdiction, Scale and Governance* (Abingdon, Routledge, 2015). Valverde borrows in turn from figures of time and space in literature and linguistics, as in M Bakhtin, 'Discourse in the Novel' in M Holquist, ed, *The Dialogic Imagination* (University of Texas Press, 1981).

[518] One striking example Valverde provides – that of the courtroom, where the use of procedural rituals or forms marks ends and beginnings in time and space – recalls the archaic pedigree of law, still so visible in contemporary judicial procedures and protocols.

emblematic embodiment of the latter. One of the most ancient debates it has generated concerns the imbrication of distance and past, and their combined impact on the legal force of the moral or political concerns covered by the elusive notion of 'public policy'. In cases where rights were vested abroad long ago, there is less reason to disturb individual and social expectations by refusing to enforce them. Conversely, greater 'proximity' between the context in which the legal entity (relation, status, situation, right) took shape (notionally, or by means of a legal judgment), creates a corresponding need for the host legal system to assert certain core legal values.[519]

This temporal-spatial in-between in (private international) legal terms echoes moreover the feminist critique of linearity and its place within the (largely masculine) aesthetic of modern law.[520] To illustrate how such linearity is an artificial projection of the modern state, authors Karen Knop and Annelise Riles use the example of the saga of Asian 'comfort women' enslaved by the Japanese army as prostitutes during the Second World War. The saga is composed of diplomatic skirmishes, judicial disputes and individual quests for moral or psychological reparation. It has given rise to ubiquitous disputes, rulings, and processes. Rather than conforming to an orderly chronological and spatial pattern, linearity is disrupted here, the past constantly intruding into the present and changing the shape of the conflict, while the object of the latter pops up endlessly, here and there. Interestingly, it was a pure symbol – a bronze statue, implanted extraterritorially, so to speak (outside a Japanese embassy in Korea and elsewhere) – whose haunting presence sparked the initial dispute, with political and legal repercussions worldwide.[521] Such an example chimes well with the exploration by social theorist Saskia Sassen of the spatialities and temporalities of the global, in which she reminds us that the era of the global is that of atemporal time and of space in flux.[522]

This is also the cue to turn back once again to the in-between properties of hybridity. The in-between *modus operandi* of the conflict of laws resonates in this respect with the 'mosaic-like' quality of indigenous legality.[523] If we turn back to the ontology of the conflict of laws, we find multiple examples of the 'adaptations' to which a given rule or institution lends itself when applied by an alien forum. Indeed, the whole enterprise of the conflict of laws produces hybridity, by definition, insofar as, at the very least, it implies the mixing of foreign substance and domestic procedure. The result is a complex composition of normative bits and pieces collected from here and there and assembled to form a coherent and acceptable picture.[524] There are

[519] On proximity as an axial principle in the conflict of laws, see P Lagarde, 'Le Principe de proximité dans le droit international privé contemporain' (1986) 196 *Rec Cours Académie de droit international de La Haye*.

[520] On sovereign time, see Valverde, *Chronotopes of Law*; Sieder, 'To Speak The Law'.

[521] 'Space, Time, and Historical Injustice: A Feminist Conflict-of-Laws Approach to the Comfort Women Agreement' (2017) 102 *Cornell L Rev* 853.

[522] S Sassen, *Losing Control. Sovereignty in An Age of Globalization* (Columbia University Press, 1996).

[523] CF Black, *A Mosaic of Indigenous Legal Thought. Legendary Tales and Other Writings* (Abingdon, Routledge, 2018); J Borrows (Kegedonce), *Drawing Out Law: A Spirit's Guide* (University of Toronto Press, 2010).

[524] As already suggested above, the etymological origin of the term 'complex' (*com plessis*) suggests a weaving together of disparate or heterogeneous elements.

countless instances of such hybridisation; the combination of legal rules borrowed from different legal systems delivers a result that does not correspond to any existing form in any one of them.[525] At the very least, the procedural rules of the forum will coexist with extraneous substantive law, in such a way that statutes of limitation can shorten or lengthen, rules of evidence can weigh upon outcomes, remedies can be provided where none were available.[526] This is the most familiar – and venerable – manifestation of the in-between in private international law, that accepts hybridity as a legitimate legal form.

Furthermore, however, as already seen above, the in-between *modus operandi* of the shadow version of conflict of laws resonates with Walter Mignolo's description of the properties of 'pluriversality' insofar as it acknowledges the plurality of legal worlds, each to be understood from their own perspective – including when their gaze is focused reflexively on one's own.[527] But it also provides the means to respond to the charge of cultural relativism traditionally levelled against pluralist projects of legality. As Walter Mignolo stresses, cosmological entanglement is (emphatically) not cultural relativism.[528] Each world 'universalises', but importantly, none devours the others. This is very exactly the claim made by Philippe Descola, under the provocative label of 'relative universalism'. Here, 'relative' is not to be understood as a clever play upon words (as in cultural relativism), but as pertaining to a relation.[529] What it takes, he writes, are subjects who do not prejudge the lived experience of others according to their own consciousness and who accept the equal value of other diverse modes of access to reality. Similarly for Mignolo in turn, a pluriverse of meaning builds upon the recognition of multiple worlds, none of which claims superiority for itself. All traditions are universal, in that they take their foundational values to be exactly that. But this does not mean that each has correlatively to deny the existence of the others and the value of their own modes of access to reality.

[525] On 'adaptation' as a technique of the conflict of laws, see above 184. A notable example is the famous *Patino* saga and conundrum, in which (through the effect of a *renvoi* from Bolivian (personal) law of the husband to Spanish law of the place of the celebration of their marriage) a couple could neither divorce nor be legally separated, although each of both potentially applicable laws allowed one or the other. The 'adaptation' consisted (on the grounds of *ordre public*) in allowing the couple to benefit from the minimal mode of legal separation under French law (Cass Civ, 15 May 1963, Bull n° 258).

[526] More striking examples can be found in the area of family law, including for example the succession of polygamist husbands in Western courts, where various assets are divided between several spouses and their children.

[527] This idea has been translated into the conflict of laws by means of the concept of 'plurilateralism' by A Benoistel, 'Le concept de renvoi mobile: une théorie de la reconnaissance entre le droit international privé et les libertés de circulation européenne', PhD dissertation, University Paris I, 2018.

[528] Mignolo, 'On Pluriversality and Multipolarity'.

[529] Descola, *Les formes du visible* 522: It is a form of universalism that does not assume any fixed essence to categories of nature and cultures, substances and spirits, first and second properties but (writing on a structuralist mode) relations of continuity and discontinuity, identity and difference, resemblance and dissimilarity that humans establish everywhere with tools that come from their own phylogenetics: body, intentionality, aptitude to distinguish, aptitude to link to others through attachments or antagonisms, domination or dependance, exchange or appropriation, subjectivation of objectivisation. It does not need a transcendental spirit or mind to confer immanence or meaning.

BEFORE THE LAW: AFTER EXTINCTION?

The challenge for Western modernity, therefore, is to untie itself from the conviction that the world is a unified totality[530] centred on self in order for it to make sense, and instead to allow meaning to emerge from the entangled diversity and hybridity of the world. One possible avenue towards an alternative *nomos* lies on the path traced by Latour's 'symmetrical anthropology'. It is an invitation, or injunction, to look back at our would-be modern selves through the lens of alternative ontologies, long reduced to the status of the primitive or the archaic. They remain (faintly) perceptible, despite the colonial imposition of modern, naturalist rationalities and their austere aesthetics of division and closure, of which the axis was humanity's privileged status in respect of nature. The project, then, would be to discover through their intermediation, the being-as-other, *l'être en tant qu'autre*.

In other words, these non-modern modes of relation to alterity have (still barely) survived the threat of extinction, of which the prospect is now haunting the Western ('developed' or 'civilised') world as it enters the Anthropocene. Latour's momentous *Enquiry* into modes of existence suggests not only that law – beneath, beyond, or despite the delusions, cunning and ruses of Double Click and its pseudo-rational epistemologies – may possibly 'embody the truth' of a world of trace-making[531] but, more to the point here, that the shadow avatar of the conflict of laws goes a long way, in turn, in giving legal shape to an alternative relationship to alterity. It opens the perspective of a pluralistic, lateral, interstitial, fronter-dwelling 'pluriverse'[532] in which the law itself is an avatar, weaving in-between multiple meanings and viewpoints, in a constant labour of ligature, communication, reprisal and repair.

But what of the risk of romanticisation (anew) of the 'noble savage'? Viveiros de Castro defines this risk in the following terms.[533] With the Enlightenment, nature was robbed of its mysterious properties, and became 'disenchanted,' in the Weberian sense, abiding by a set of mechanical but unknown laws, which could be discovered and mastered through careful study and observation under controlled conditions. Thus began the 'conquest' of nature, the quest to harness its forces so that they may serve the ends of mankind. Romanticism responded to this alienation from nature with a sense of tragic loss, and sought to regain what they saw as the fractured unity of man and nature, exalting the primitive. But however noble the savage, no significant change occurred to the conditions in which indigenous populations (or natural resources) were treated. Appropriation and expropriation accompanied extensive epistemicide[534] in the name of civilisation or (later) development. Today, indigenous

[530] *Cf* Mignolo, 'On Pluriversality and Multipolarity' (whether under doctrines of Christianity, liberal ism, Marxism …).

[531] L de Sutter, 'Plasma! Notes on Latour's metaphysics of Law', in McGee, *Latour and the Passage of Law*, 205.

[532] On pluriversality as developed within the 'jurisprudence of the border' by Walter Mignolo, see above 193; *cf* on 'plural worlds' (as opposed to cultural relativism) Latour, *Enquête*, 479.

[533] *The Ends of the World.*

[534] On epistemicide (as the genocide of world views), see B De Sousa Santos, *Epistemologies of the South. Justice against Epistemicide* (New York, Routledge, 2014), exploring the concept of 'cognitive injustice', that is, the failure to recognise the different ways of knowing by which people across the globe run their lives and provide meaning to their existence.

peoples and their various cosmologies are at risk of becoming the contemporary counterparts of the exoticised native (and indeed are perfectly aware of this).[535]

Interestingly, at the same time, the use of anthropology has come full circle and, if 'symmetrical', suggests the course of an antidote. From being an instrument of exoticisation of colonised autochtonous populations, notably supporting ideas about other cultures and surrounding nature that translated easily into legal categories and distinctions, it has become, with the 'anthropological turn', the most subversive of disciplines, opening the way to a rethinking of the world in what was formerly dismissed as 'primitive' terms. The Enlightment's idea of humanity, writes Viveiros de Castro,

> must give way to those who Latour has called Terrans: all beings taken as parts of the world and as so many points of view the overlap of which constitutes the world – and which are as such (if it is at all possible to think them 'as such') discordant monadological expressions of a World without antonym or antagonist, as it is not an Object waiting for a Subject to bestow it with synthetic unity from a transcendent perspective.
>
> Indeed, the cogitation peculiar to anthropology: one that allows anthropology to take on the virtual presence of an Other who is also its condition[536] – the condition for passage from one possible world to another – and that is only as a consequence able to determine the derivative and vicarious positions of subject and object'.[537]

As we have seen, the shadow of extinction modifies the terms of the ontological question, who are 'we'? (and who is the other?) and its juridical expression. Thus, as the same author suggests, the end(s) of the world(s) will be 'necessarily thought from another pole, a "we" that includes the (syntactic or pragmatic) subject of the discourse on the end'. Crucially, however, he observes, discourses rooted in the perspective of the modern West never seem to doubt who the 'we' is, what is understood as 'human' or as 'person' by other collectives consensually regarded (by 'us') as humans (and at any rate never goes beyond the limits of the species as an extensive taxonomic category).[538] This is the cue, then, to attempt to take this path – once again, in the terms of law. As Part III will confirm, our current *nomos*, explored above on an

[535] Pachamama, the 'Mother of World-Time' is sometimes (erroneously) represented as akin to Gaia (see Latour, *Face à Gaia*, 369). Pachamama is a deity that originally had no attributes that we would consider 'characteristically maternal' (as is in fact the case with all terrestrial deities of Andean and Mesoamerican cultures, as D Danowski and E Viveiros de Castro point out, in *The Ends of the World*). But after the Conquest of the so-called new world, Pachamama was progressively domesticated through its association with the Virgin Mary; its image as 'Good Mother Earth' is a New Age addition to the myth, which did not fail to stir some perplexity and/or metacultural adhesion (a 'strategic Pachamamismo'?) among the indigenous of South America's plateaux. On devices of exoticisation or orientalisation of the Other, see Ruskola, *Legal Orientalism*; on legal barbarians, D Bonilllo, *Legal Barbarians*.

[536] See below 272 et seq on the Other as the condition of possibility of all perception.

[537] E Viveiros de Castro, *The Relative Native. Essays on Indigenous Conceptual Worlds*, 112: 'what the native forces the anthropologist to do is, precisely, to put into question what a subject can be.'

[538] Ibid, 25. As Viveiros de Castro further points out, there are various strands of ecological feminist thought (cited above, such as Stenger's Gaia, Haraway's 'staying with the trouble', Povinelli's 'geontology' (inspired by Australian aboriginal worlds), that might be described as innovative transformations (double structural twists, as Levi-Strauss would put it) of the mythical scheme of a 'world without humans'. Notably, the world itself can be seen as a multiverse traversed by multiple non-human ontologies, implicated in a 'becoming'(Haraway) that demands that we learn how to follow it.

ontological and aesthetic register, is in turn the reflection of deep schemes within our political economy. These too have worked to sever our ethical consciousness of all these other worlds, thereby diminishing our awareness of and receptivity towards alterity. The consequence has been the reduction of nature to the status of external, material resource, the voiding of space, the racialisation of capital, and the multiplication not of the uncivilised luxuriance of natural life forms but of 'sacrifice zones' of lifeless wilderness.[539] The approach proposed here leads back to earth.[540] It takes seriously the 'ends' of our multiple worlds in the shadow of extinction, helps establish a minimum of commensurability between indigenous cosmologies struggling for survival and various strands of thought within the Western tradition. Paradoxically, as we shall now see, in order to achieve, in ethical terms, a 'split horizon' in presence of alterity,[541] we need first to remedy the split that has sundered apart the modern *oikos*.

[539] Gonzalez, C and Mutua, A, 'Mapping Racial Capitalism: Implications for Law' (2022, forthcoming) *Journal of Law and Political Economy*.

[540] Latour, *Ou atterrir*.

[541] On the Levanissian split horizon, see below.

Part III

Economy and Ethics: Repairing the Split in the *Oikos*

THE POLITICAL ECONOMY[1] of late modernity rests on a radical severance within the *oikos*,[2] whereby the 'economisation' of the ecology signifies a radical lack of accountability of humanity towards the natural world. This abyss is a further instantiation of the split within humanity itself along social, cultural and geopolitical lines, as seen above, with a correlative neglect or negation of alterity.[3] The central question of political ecology today converges, then, with the eminently socio-economic concerns of earlier reflection on modernity's 'great transformation':[4] how, when and why did the economy become our 'secular religion',[5]

[1] The term 'political economy' carries several meanings. As Poul Kjaer explains (*The Law of Political Economy*), it emerged as a concept in the early seventeenth century, and as an independent area of scholarly enquiry (a discipline) in the eighteenth century (as developed by the French physiocrats). A further angle draws from Foucault and contemporary explorations of neoliberalism as a totalising rationality that produces particular types of subjects and social relations (Althusser, Gramsci and Polanyi, see below). This attention to the subjectivities produced by a particular political economy usefully counters the impression that society can simply be changed from one ideology to the next.

[2] The *oikos* emerged in ancient Greece as an ethical sphere for the wise management of the household: see for the history, including its later Byzantine mutations, D Leshem, *The origins of neoliberalism: modelling the economy from Jesus to Foucault* (New York, Columbia University Press, 2016). *Oikonomia* was the law of prudent management of resources ('squeezed between ethics and politics', in the words of Martti Koskenniemi ('International Law and raison d'état: Rethinking the Prehistory of International Law' in B Kingsbury and B Straumann (eds), *The Roman Foundation of the Law of Nations: Alberico Gentili and the Justice of Empire* (Oxford, Oxford University Press, 2010) 334). Importantly, the *oikos* was *opposed* to the market (conducive to wantonness); its relationship to the *polis* however is more controversial (the art of the household and the art of politics were not necessarily distinct).

[3] See notably above 172, 173 on decoloniality as a negation of alterity in ontological terms.

[4] K Polanyi, *The Great Transformation: The Political and Economic Origins of Our Time* (New York, Farrar & Rinehart, 1944); tellingly, it was published a little later in England in 1945 as *The Origins of Our Time* (reissued by Beacon Press, 1957). The most cited passage *(Great Transformation*, p 57) is the following: 'The control of the economic system by the market is of overwhelming consequence to the whole organisation of society: it means no less than the running of society as an adjunct to the market. Instead of economy being embedded in social relations, social relations are embedded in the economic system'. The proximity of this observation is striking with that of Michel Foucault in his *Naissance de la Biopolitique* (Paris, Seuil-Gallimard, 2004). On the contemporary political-economic relevance of Polanyi's thought in the translational legal order, see C Joergs and J Fal (eds), *Karl Polanyi, Globalisation and the Potential of Law in Transnational Markets* (Oxford, Hart, 2011).

[5] Polanyi describes how, in spite of the threat to social order, the philosophy that came to be called 'laissez faire' was '[b]orn as a mere penchant for non-bureaucratic methods … [and] evolved into a veritable faith in man's secular salvation through a self regulating market … as if God fixed the market price' (obs P Monateri, Globinar, Sciencespo, Autumn 2021, noting the structural similarity between the belief in autonomous markets and *Dominus mundi*).

the 'great dispatcher'[6] of all things? The broad hypothesis underlying this Part of the book is that one key (among many) lies in the legal dimension of the political economy[7] (whether under colonial capitalism or its later avatars and replications[8]). That is, legality has always been instrumental in the various dislocations evoked above – in the disembedding of markets from society, in the dissociation of risk and responsibility, in the severance of calculus from scruple,[9] in the screening off of Mississippi behind Manchester[10] – with disastrous consequences for both humanity itself and the planet.[11] The argument here, more specifically, is that such 'bifurcations'[12] that harnessed legality to the neoliberal economy, are exemplified and amplified by analogous dynamics unfolding within the apparently innocuous arena of private international law.

However, legality's inherent duality, its innate ability to harbour a residual version of itself (as already seen above) suggests that it also has the potential to 'ecologise rather than modernise'.[13] A sustainable or responsible mode of inhabiting the planet[14]

[6] Or '*metarépartiteur*': Latour, *Enquête* 442. This elevation is all the more mystifying as until the time of Karl Marx and John Stuart Mill, philosophers generally held economics to be an integral element of moral philosophy. Today, while values – moral, aesthetic, and cognitive – still dominate philosophical discourse, contemporary philosophers rarely hold economics to be integral to moral philosophy.

[7] Law is usually neglected in this debate. Yet, the idea of a natural order governing economic exchange dates back to the physiocrats (physiocracy is the government of nature) in the second half of the eighteenth century (Quesnay, Turgot) who believed that any political decision (such as laissez-faire, as seen above) must conform to the natural law of the economy. A century later (Walras, 1871), the appeal to (natural) law had given way to the idea of (pure) science. Law reappeared however, yet a further century on, in the context of the so called 'law and economics' movement, that entailed for the most part an absorption of the former by the latter under the influence of the Chicago School (to the detriment of earlier, more subtle neo-institutional analyses). But a countermove, already present in critical legal studies (see the entry by Duncan Kennedy on 'law-and-economics from the perspective of critical legal studies', *The New Palgrave Dictionary of Economics and the Law* (ed Peter Newman) (Basingstoke, Macmillan, 1998) 46), is visible today under the pressure of the ecological crisis, in respect of neoliberal regulation: see Brabazon (ed), *Neoliberal Legality*; B Golder and D McLoughlin, *The Politics of Legality in a Neoliberal Age* (Abingdon, Routledge, 2018). As already seen above, one important argument of this critical scholarship is that within the contemporary political economy, law (meaning Law I or *lex*) is marked by a specific aesthetic (consistent with, but distinct from previous forms of liberal-capitalism).

[8] On the replication of colonial history through artificial intelligence, see the MIT study on digital apartheid in South Africa: K Hao and H Swart, 'South Africa's private surveillance machine is fueling a digital apartheid', *MIT Technology Review*, 19 April 2022.

[9] Latour, *Enquête*, 459.

[10] N Fraser and R Jaeggi, *Capitalism, A Conversation in Critical Theory* (Cambridge, Polity Press, 2018) 39 et seq.

[11] Ibid, describing the idea of sustainable capitalism as an environmental goal as a 'tragedy-cum-farce' – a political economic critique that also unfolds on an ethical register, as in Latour, as 'a distorted accounting … that sees external nature – water, air, living species – outside th[e] system of exchange … as a "free gift"'. On the original juridical dualism of head and body, persons and things, see above 137.

[12] Latour, *Enquête*.

[13] Ibid, 23: this would mean reintroducing the plurality that Law, Religion and Science each stamped out in various ways, within an enriched ecosystem.

[14] One key to thinking about responsibility in (or for) our 'catastrophic times' is to turn to the figure of Gaia, in Isabelle Stenger's representation (*In Catastrophic Times: Resisting the Coming Barbarism* (Open Humanities Press/Meson Press, 2015)) of a form of transcendence that responds, implacably, to the equally brutal irresponsibility of our economic system (what one [*on*] used to call development: see below 247). Gaia becomes the name of an implacable equation in ethical-juridical terms: the effect that *should* affect those who caused it, but is in fact least likely to do so. To name Gaia then, is an operation which seeks to elicit from 'us' [Moderns], a 'we' in the place of a 'one' [*on*].

points in the direction not of profit and discharge (or *quitus*, an accounting formula that suggests a severance or discharge of all links),[15] not of extraction and indifference to consequence, but towards an economy of gift and solidarity.[16] In this respect, non-modern practices of production and consumption, intimately linked to ways of relating to alterity (whether in alternative forms of social interaction but also attitudes towards other forms of life), signal what is needed to bring about this admittedly monumental change. The relations of entanglement induced by exchange as gift[17] belong to a model of society that is entirely different from the neoliberal atomisation of (exclusively) human interaction,[18] and a grounding of the economy that contrasts with that of market or profit. Within the law, the de-centred perspective offered by private international law mirrors this alternative template, serving once more as a heuristic (or horizon[19]) for introducing a transformative scheme. It enjoins us to replace the frenetic and competitive pursuit of gain for an ethos of hospitality towards the foreign or the alien, whether cultural or natural, human or animal. Resisting the severance between the economy and the ecology, such a scheme resonates with a legal duty of care towards all the forms of life that surround us.[20] In the ethical vocabulary of responsibility, this is what the law of the Anthropocene might look like.

The two chapters below will attempt to give 'flesh' to this double life of the law. As they unfold, the body – lost in the cracks of modernity's legal-ontological division between person and things – will appear, not as sublime[21] but in its phenomenological mode,[22] not as sovereign subject but as bare life[23] – as a guide towards the care required in respect of our planet and the variety of inhabitants that depend on its fragile crust, and its expression in legal form. While the etchings of an 'eco-phenomenological' scheme in the field of law borrow heavily from non-modern cosmologies, this very term also implies that its constitutive elements are already present – albeit as residue – within the Western philosophical tradition.[24] The conflict of laws will serve here as a bridge, suggesting that our relationship to otherness in

[15] Or 'Être quitte'.

[16] Marcel Mauss' momentous anthropological work of the economy of the gift (*The Gift: Forms and Functions of Exchange in Archaic Societies* (London, Cohen & West, 1966); 'Essai sur le don. Forme et raison de l'échange dans les sociétés archaïques' (1925) *Année sociologique*), recognised by Lévi-Strauss as inspirational for his own *La Pensée sauvage*, revealed modes of exchange that were not price-based but an ontology and moral economy of the intimate: see Descola, *Les formes du Visible* 541. For a similar, contemporary argument for solidarity from the perspective of the Global South, see de Sousa Santos, *Epistemologies of the South*.

[17] See above: gifts generating endless series of entangled new gifts (or debts generating counter-debts.

[18] On interaction in the non-human and invisible world, see above.

[19] On the metaphor of the horizon and its obvious ecological implications, see below.

[20] What a legal duty of care might look like and why it is not the same as conferring rights on nature, see below 270 et s.

[21] E Kantorowicz, *The King's Two Bodies,* (Princeton NJ, Princeton University Press, 1957), arguing that, of the king's dual body, physical and sublime, the latter is at the origin of the body politic.

[22] On the phenomenological turn in ecological thought, see below. On Husserl and the phenomenological body, and on eco-feminist thought, see above 131, 195 and below 273.

[23] The reference is to the bare life of G Agamben's *Homo Sacer: Sovereign Power and Bare Life* (Stanford CT, Stanford University Press, 1998). On a feminist register, see Judith Butler, *Bodies that Matter: On the Discursive Limits of Sex* (London, Routledge, 1993).

[24] See Pelluchon, *Les lumières à l'âge du vivant*.

legal form could find expression in what might be termed a law of interalterity.[25] However, this ecological horizon[26] is so very faint in our late modern (legal) tradition that it is imperative to return first to the causes, or forces, that prevent us from approaching it. In other words, the starting place has to be the profound chasm that lies at the core of law's current political economy. This abyss can be correlated to the void or *terra nullius* induced by our jurisdictional thinking, the blindspot in our epistemology, or the collective denial of history in our collective subconscious.[27]

We can start with what has been described as a monumental epistemological mistake of modernity. According to Bruno Latour, this mistake is accountable for the extraordinary primacy acquired by economics over other modes of existence (whether law, ethics, or politics).[28] Since Locke, he writes, it is as if the Market were the beginning and the end.[29] Modernity's great 'category error' has been to believe that economics is a science, an objective form of knowledge, capable not only of formulating laws based on the same ontology of causation as those of Nature, but also of serving as ultimate arbitrator of all the other modes of veridiction.[30] Indeed, he observes, as soon as Darwin had repainted the portrait of Nature as non-providential and 'ruthlessly just', economics appropriated this heritage.[31] Fuelled by the most prestigious of the 'hard' sciences,[32] the economy imagined itself thereafter (in Nancy

[25] See for a previous formulation of this concept, Muir Watt, *Discours sur les méthodes*.

[26] The horizon is central in the thought of Emmanuel Levinas, as we shall see below. This horizon, again according to Levinas, is 'split' insofar as it is constituted by alterity. In *Pour Comprendre Levinas* (Paris, Seuil, 2020), Corinne Pelluchon observes (p 37) that in contemporary philosophy, the notion of horizon has replaced the traditional concept of truth.

[27] On this void at the heart of democracy as the 'empty space of power', see C Lefort, *Essais sur le politique (XlXe-XXe siecles)* (Paris, Seuil, 1986) 331; on the legal concept of the *terra nullius*, see below; on abyssal thinking see de Sousa Santos, *Epistemologies of the South;* on the (subconscious) collective denial of history, see Mazurel, *L'inconscient ou l'oubli de l'histoire.*

[28] To recall the findings of Latour's attentive *Enquête*, our world is filled with multiple modes of existence each with its own beings and forms and modes of veridiction. These may be legal, political, ethical, technological, scientific, artistic, or more, and they may command their own deployment in a variety of ways. Accounting (calculation, economics) has its own place and identity alongside the others. But under the deleterious empire of the pseudo-mode, Double Click, it (calculation) has colonised the latter. Another way of putting the same idea is that there is no such thing as an autonomously 'economic matter'.

[29] Locke and various further 'robinsonades'; ibid, 447. The latter term (in German, *Robinsonade)* was invented by Karl Marx to designate both a theoretical error characterised by its circular logic (categories that call to be explained are assumed to exist) and an ideological justification of the capitalist mode of production (presented as an historical and thereby unsurpassable fact).

[30] *Enquête*, 462. *Cf* (in translation) p 468: 'this, then, was capitalism, that simply changed the name of the Creator and presided over the great secular ideological wars between the State and the Market'.

[31] *Cf* for a similar critique, Pelluchon, *Les Lumières à l'âge du vivant*, 84, observing that there is no reason for Darwin's theory on evolution to have become an economic theory of the survival of the fittest. But as she points out, this is in no way to diminish Darwinism's breakthrough as the definitive modern break with teleology. See too for a critique of Darwinism as having established the various concepts through which Europe self-defined itself from the eighteenth century (art, culture, history, etc) as universal standards of evolution, Descola, *Les formes du Visible.*

[32] How rational the moderns felt (Latour observes, p 473 et seq), in encountering other cultures with different gods, whose gifts entangled rather than severed the various ties and dependencies between economic agents, engaged in an endless, escalating and all-encompassing Darwinian struggle! This struggle has no natural ceiling: once it becomes international, it has an inherent tendency to escalate to the level of states, with disastrous consequences for the system itself, for humanity and for the planet.

Fraser's terms) as a self-propelled machine,[33] endowed (according to the account of Roberto Esposito) with a form of self-immunity.[34] It became embroiled thereafter in an endless, escalating and all-encompassing competitive struggle, both destructive and self-destructive,[35] increasingly and paradoxically careless of its own conditions of possibility – that is, of the existence of alterity (whether in human form, as alternative modes of inhabiting the earth, or as natural resource).

That law has played a role in the self-immunisation of the market economy is confirmed by a more specific genealogy of the 'natural' law of the market in the international field. Exploring the enigma of the 'prehistory' of international law, Martti Koskenniemi observes that when, by the late nineteenth century, natural law had finally 'fulfilled its program', turning progressively away from theology and elevating Nature to a position of moral and political authority, it had 'become economics'.[36] Law, then, has often been tightly entwined with these paradoxical (or oxymoronic) ideas of nature,[37] whether as metaphor or model for the invisible clockwork of the economy, or, conversely, as vulnerable to its inexorable injunctions (both are present in the Hayekian 'natural law of the market'). This is eminently true for the international economic order, which, as Fraser and Jaeggi further remark, is often also represented as a (Hobbesian) state of nature.[38] Such a representation means that it is, politically, a lawless jungle (of Leviathans) and in economic terms, subject to mysterious, autonomous market forces beyond our control.[39] In other words, what has come to be known as the 'governance turn' in the international sphere has done much to cut the economy adrift (or 'disembed' it[40]) from political processes. Among the latter

[33] See Fraser and Jaeggi, *Capitalism. A Critical Conversation* 51.

[34] R Esposito emphasises the etymological links (*munus*: the gift given and received) between *communitas* and *immunitas*. In a world emptied of divinity, the munus became instrumentalised. The community becomes immune and expels the other, or the foreign or the strange. R Esposito, *Immunitas: The Protection and Negation of Life* (Wiley, 2011); see T Campbell, 'Bios,' Immunity, Life: The Thought of Roberto Esposito' (2006) 36 *Diacritics* 2–22. In turn Eric Santner frames the market as the flight of the *soma* to our 'busy-bodies'.

[35] At what point did the economy 'take off' or become unmoored in this way? In *Carbon Democracy: Political Power in the Age of Oil* (London, Verso, 2013), Timothy Mitchell dates this autonomisation to the time the limits of 'first nature' became apparent, that is 'around 1945, when "the Economy" was invented once and for all – an infinite and boundless domain totally indifferent to terrestrial existence and the very notion of limits, and entirely self-centered and self-governed. Whereas before the war there still existed, in what was still called "political economy", the idea of scarcity and allocation of rare goods, the Economy began to be entirely unmoored from any limitation.'

[36] M Koskenniemi, 'International Law and Raison d'Etat: Rethinking the Prehistory of International Law', in B Kingsbury and B Straumann (eds), *The Roman Foundations of the Law of Nations* (Oxford, Oxford University Press, 2010). Koskenniemi's argument is that there was no continuity between modern international law as it emerged from liberal legal activism in the great colonial adventure of the late nineteenth century, and the earlier strands of naturalist jurisprudence (*ius naturae et gentium*), developed successively by Gentili (the mythical founder of the law of nations), then the second Spanish scholastics, then the Protestant humanists, the French Enlightenment and finally the German natural law tradition.

[37] The 'modern law of nature' is a great oxymoron (Descola, *Les formes du Visible* 132 et seq).

[38] Fraser and Jaeggi, *Capitalism. A Critical Conversation* 90 et seq (on 'Capitalism's historical natures').

[39] Describing the contemporary 'governance turn' in the law of the global political economy (under the impetus of the World Bank, and other international organisations, such as the IMF and the OECD, and, of course, the EU), Poul Kjaer points to 'an ontological assumption as to the prior existence of some sort of given holistic unity which tends towards equilibrium upon the basis of mysterious forces' (*The Law of Political Economy*, 22 et seq).

[40] Polanyi, *The Great Transformation*.

is the possible protection of the biosphere from the purportedly natural law of the market.

The *oikos*, then, can no longer house the economy and the ecology (or 'nature') together, under their common etymology.[41] The first crowded out the second, so that it faded into the background – to take up its place among the 'background conditions' of capitalism.[42] The latter thrives on the free availability of the Earth's resources as much as it depends on an endless supply of labour or brainpower. But the great paradox of capitalism, its destructive dialectics, lies in the way that it devours its own conditions of survival,[43] with the compulsion to search for ever new sites of extraction.[44] In the 'capitalocene',[45] the finger of Gaia points not at humanity itself, nor indeed at modernity or enlightenment thought *per se*, but towards the economic model that encourages humanity to ride free on nature's abundance with no care or concern for the consequences. Behind the scene – that is, inside the economic calculus, beyond the political model of economic freedom, under the surface of legal entitlements – the natural world serves both as tap (for precious minerals, energy, petrol, nutrition, and of course labour) and sink (for refuse and waste of all kinds[46]).

In this respect, the point that will be developed below is that while law has played a key role in the sundering of the *oikos*, subscribing to the great 'economisation'[47] that has eaten its way into our values and world views,[48] its agency in the international

[41] Similarly, scruple could no longer remain with calculation. On the etymological links between the two (*scrupus*, pointed stone), see the Dictionary of the French Academy: *scrupule-calcul-et-gravelle*, www.academie-francaise.fr/scrupule-calcul-et-gravelle.

[42] See Fraser and Jaeggi, *Capitalism. A Critical Conversation* on this important distinction between foreground and background conditions of capitalism.

[43] In 1944, Karl Polanyi published his great work, *The Great Transformation*, pointing out the ways in which the growth of capitalist markets paradoxically impaired or destroyed the very social and environmental conditions needed for further expansion or indeed survival. The discovery of ever-new resources to extract (including the immaterial and extraterrestrial) has slowed down the reckoning he anticipated, but has not prevented the incremental accumulation of signs of our 'catastrophic times' (Stengers, *In Catastrophic Times: Resisting the Coming Barbarism* (Open Humanities Press, 2015)).

[44] The new resource to be extracted after the depletion of all the rest is of course personal data (see Zuboff, *Surveillance Capitalism*). In the same vein, methods of research themselves can be extractive: see G Graddy-Lovelace, *The Power of Seeds & the Politics of Agricultural Biodiversity* (Cambridge MA, MIT Press, 2019).

[45] A term that is preferable to Anthropocene, if one considers that it is not humanity's sole presence on the planet that is the source of the contemporary depletion of natural resources but the ways in which the latter have been extracted, immoderately and without any concern for their replenishment.

[46] The sink evokes 'waste colonialism', meaning the exportation-externalisation of waste from North to South, the abode of racialised, disposable, populations (see Gonzalez, C and Mutua, A, 'Mapping Racial Capitalism: Implications for Law' (2022) 2 *Journal of Law and Political Economy* 127).

[47] See Fraser and Jaeggi, *Capitalism. A Critical Conversation*, 51, warning against using the idea of 'economisation' to suggest that economics invaded other more innocent forms of social life, as if it were a self-propelling machine (or virus?), or a sort of self-fulfilling metaphor.

[48] The very foundation of critical social theory (Adorno) is that life is relegated by capitalism to the status of epiphenomenon, alienating alterity in its multiple forms. A '*triste savoir*' (as opposed to a '*gai savoir*'). Hence the 'Conversation' *(Capitalism, A Conversation in Critical Theory)* proposed by Fraser and Jaeggi as to what preconditions would be necessary to institute a more dignified social and political order. Similarly, observes the eco-phenomenologist Pelluchon (*Les Lumières*, 30), the institution of utility and self-preservation as the parameters of truth is the work of the Schema, the hegemony of organisational principles of society and all the representations of social, political and economics that constitute its matrix.

sphere is even greater than in the domestic arena. In other words, private international law – the law of the political economy as derived from nature, as we have just seen – has been particularly powerful in enthroning neoliberal rationalities. As will be demonstrated in the first chapter, this means that the central guarantor of both public interests and individual freedom is a form of law 'beyond the state', meaning that is unanchored to social phenomena. As such, it bolsters the underlying conception of the global economy as the central driver of societal evolution, fuelled by the logics of profit generation, welfare maximisation, and creative destruction.[49]

This diagnosis of the problem of law's political economy highlights the Herculean difficulty of dissolving a hegemonic scheme that has gone far in capturing our entire world – right up to the very idea of the future, as we shall see. It also shows very clearly that the only way ahead for law's alternative political ecology lies in the inscription within the law of an ethical responsibility towards the other forms of life and beings that surround us. It is through the appeal of these others, as Latour explains, that ethics are encoded within our very world.[50] In chapter six we shall see that the key, for the law, is to ensure that we hear such an appeal and respond with due hospitality. The cue at this point for the conflict of laws lies in its ability to give legal form to this demanding injunction in respect of alterity.

[49] Kjaer, *The Law of Political Economy.* The critique of the current state of the global political economy extends to notions of development in global governance discourse, or corporate social responsibility in the context of 'compliance'.

[50] Latour, *Enquête*, 454.

5

Private International Neoliberal Legality

I. TOEING THE LINE

NEOLIBERALISM HAS DONE much to entrench an economically determinist vision of society, subtracting global economic governance from political processes.[51] This blackboxing of power stifles any consideration of a range of other available policy options and institutional arrangements. Law enters the picture at this point, in the form of 'neoliberal legality'.[52] Markets are legal, political (and, therefore, regulatory) products, not spontaneously arising, pre-regulatory, pre-legal and pre-political phenomena which would thereafter be subjected (selectively) to regulation. In Fraser's and Jaeggi's depiction, capitalism's 'foreground' conditions, its economic constitution, are all the stuff of private law: property rights, corporations and contracts are all legal institutions, sources of power shaped in a certain way.[53] Importantly, the widespread understanding that this surface is

[51] P Ireland, 'Property, Private Government and the Myth of Deregulation' in S Worthington (ed), *Commercial Law and Commercial Practice* (Oxford, Hart, 2005) 85. As Paddy Ireland further remarks, 'power is the great absentee of neoliberal thought. Stifling alternatives, it rests on the idea that there exists a universal, apolitical, market rationality. In turn, a key move in critical thought is to reintroduce power into the equation. Markets are not neutral spaces for social interaction, but sites in which often very unevenly distributed power is exercised'. Similarly, for Kjaer (*The Law of Political Economy* 18), under neoliberalism, '"society" is factually equalled to the market and animated by mysterious forces that escape politics'. Thus, society is understood as being predominantly structured by economic interests, while the invisible hand of the economy is the true driving-force of societal evolution. Any notion of equilibrium, or balance, however, pre-supposes a whole which can be 'in balance'. This is also expressed by the common day stylisation of the market as a *persona* with autonomous agency, as expressed in statements such as 'the market expands', 'the market rebounds' or 'the market expects'. This rejoins Nancy Fraser's concept of the 'self-propelling' market.

[52] Brabazon, *Neoliberal Legality*.

[53] Thus, a further significant critical legal move is to identify the role of law within the economy as not just to correct exceptional failures of otherwise natural processes of exchange between (pre-legal) economic actors, but to provide all the (equally invisible) background rules that allow markets to operate, and all the while giving legal form to economic power. The law (not politics) gives form to this economic constitution by allowing markets to self-regulate (barring the unfortunate case of 'market failures ', when the laws of the economy go awry and public regulatory policies are required). There is nothing natural about exclusivity (of land rights), opacity (of corporate personality) or autonomy (of agreements). As Paddy Ireland notes ('Property, Private Government and the Myth of Deregulation'), lawyers are well placed to know the significant part played by legal and political constructs, since they are, or should be, aware that 'there is really no such thing as a free market'; that 'a market cannot be defined except with

self-propelling or 'natural' focuses political attention on the discursive foreground concept of individual freedom[54] and thereby obscures the presence of an equally indispensable series of (extra-legal, one might also say extra-territorial) 'background conditions': behind Manchester is Mississippi.[55] Moreover these conditions are in turn nested:[56] beyond the – already racialised[57] – low-paid labour, there is further, unpaid, gendered, social reproduction. Under it all, there is expropriation, both of humanity and nature.[58] Again such expropriation is extra-legal rather than illegal: it takes place out of the sight of the law (that of the forum, or colonial, territorial state) and not irregularly within its sway. As such, it is obscene (off scene).

The juridical screens that cut off part of reality are part and parcel of the broader work of neoliberal legality. In this respect, the way in which such economic processes are sustained is by the drawing of invisible – or abyssal (to borrow from Boaventura de Sousa Santos[59]) – lines within its operative settings. As Fraser and Jaeggi explain, different modes of capital accumulation (industrial, extractive, financial, digital mining etc) can be seen as as many ways of demarcating economics and politics, and subsequently, exploitation and expropriation, centre and periphery, domestic and international, reproduction and production.[60] Law, with its various distinctions (territorial vs extra-territorial; family vs labour market; public vs private, etc) appears as the ultimate arbitrator of these divides, that is, of the (ever-expanding) threshold between the economy and various other spheres potentially subject to political deliberation, moral rights, privacy or the requirements of the common good. Although there is nothing inevitable about these distinctions themselves, nor anything natural about where the separative boundaries are drawn, they are always very difficult to dislodge and indeed are hotly defended by vested interests whenever challenged.

reference to the specific rights/obligations structure that underpins it, and that since these rights and obligations are determined through a political process … all markets have a fundamentally political origin'. Katharina Pistor makes a similar point about the role of law and lawyers in the coding of capital (*The Code of Capital. How the Law Creates Wealth and Inequality* (Princeton NJ, Princeton University Press, 2019). In the global turn to governance the talk is more of investment, development, financial products, capital flows or social corporate responsibility and more, but this is all equally the stuff of (private and international) law. On critical moves in legal scholarship, see J Esquirol, 'Making the Critical Moves: A Top Ten in Progressive Legal Scholarship' (2021) 92 *University of Colorado Law Review* 4.

[54] Such freedom allows the individual to consent to be subjected to exploitative conditions in the labour market, the latter being a legal institution. Importantly, in Marxian theory, the foreground of legal exploitation (Manchester) is to be contrasted with an extra-legal background of expropriation or extraction (Mississippi), as seen in the text above.

[55] Fraser and Jaeggi, *Capitalism. A Critical Conversation* 28 et seq.

[56] On nesting, another deconstructive, critical critique from outside legal scholarship but particularly useful in the understanding of text, see above 105.

[57] On the origins of the concept of racial capitalism and its broad definition as the mutual dependence of capitalism and racism, see A Kundnani, www.kundnani.org/what-is-racial-capitalism/.

[58] A significant critique of the commodity capitalism (sugar, cotton, rubber) dating back to early colonial conquest links the fate of local populations and Nature (see for example JW Moore, 'Madeira, Sugar, and the Conquest of Nature in the "First" Sixteenth Century Part I: From "Island of Timber" to Sugar Revolution, 1420–1506' (2009) 32 *Review (Fernand Braudel Center)* 345–90); for the role of commodities in the construction of international law in the peripheries or margins of European empires see F Antunes Madeira da Silva, 'The Conquest of the Devil's Paradise: International Law, Frontier-Making and Capitalist Power', PhD dissertation, Sciences Po Paris, 2022.

[59] de Sousa Santos, *Epistemologies of the South.*

[60] Fraser and Jaeggi, *Capitalism. A Critical Conversation* 54.

Where the line is drawn (and who has authority to draw it – *quis judicabit?*) reflects the dynamics of a particular scheme, *epistemè* or vision of the world[61] that shapes, in turn, our understandings of society, self, intimacy, work, art, relationships, personhood, belonging, family, morality and more.[62]

These observations, valid on the domestic scene, are particularly relevant 'beyond the state' and are well illustrated in respect of the role of private international law in the constitution and distribution of economic power.[63] Indeed, the current neoliberal 'turn to governance' entails increasing depoliticisation of the economic exchanges that cross the threshold of the international.[64] In this way, multiple anomalies, whether portrayed as natural or institutional but always mysteriously 'beyond our control' – such as corporate unaccountability, asymmetrical value chains, distorted financial markets, child labour – are also the structural consequences of legal rules. The latter draw their own limits, not always aligned with geopolitical borders,[65] that allow nevertheless for variegated forms of 'boundary-crossing' for capital and 'extraterritorial' exploitation and extraction. Far from ensuring the world's prosperity, these legal designs of global governance lead to the depletion of natural resources (notably in the global South), generalised climatic disaster, populations living under the poverty line, warfare, gendered injustice, and perpetually indebted nations. Massive displacement of populations ('migration') ensues, with far greater difficulty – boundary-crossing in the real world – than the metaphorical cross-border flows of foreign investment and financial return.

Private international law is a well-focused lens through which to view this muddling of jurisdictional lines between politics and economics: a metonym, it might be said, 'for all the rest'.[66] A logic of calculation, competition, and profit-seeking – 'economisation' – has crowded out, in whole or in part, other (political, ethical, scientific) concepts such as responsibility, accountability, solidarity, or humanity – all concepts that we associate with modernity and enlightenment. The 'culprit' here is not the latter, or indeed modernity *per se*, but the ways in which such concepts have been co-opted by economic calculation and redeployed in the furtherance of unscrupulous profit-seeking.[67] The role of legality has been to make such creeping

[61] See above 97 et s.

[62] On the making of common sense, see B Latour ('On some of the Affects of Capitalism', Lecture given at the Royal Academy, Copenhagen, 26 February 2014) on 'agnotology', the science of the making and unmaking of public ignorance (in response to the question why it is that we've come to accept commodity production and exchange as a naturally given 'fact of life', and what might be done about it).

[63] From this perspective, again as Paddy Ireland writes ('Property, Private Government and the Myth of Deregulation'), the growing power of financial interests which underlies the neoliberal revolution is in significant part a product of enhancements to the bundles of rights possessed by financial property owners, not least their right to move freely around the world (financial liberalisation) and to claim protection from state interventions that diminish their value, even if democratically mandated (the new constitutionalism). This is the result of a combination of public international economic regimes and private international law.

[64] This once again is the illusion of self-propulsion.

[65] As seen in Part II above 141 et s.

[66] As Susan Marks observes in respect of enclosure: *A False Tree of Liberty, Human Rights in Radical Thought* (Oxford, Oxford University Press, 2019).

[67] Examples range from the selling of indulgences (meaning entry into heaven) that set off the Protestant reformation no less, to prostitution, both literal and metaphoric, meaning the sale of something that

economisation seem 'natural'[68] – that is, ascribable to non-political causes (once again, 'beyond our control'[69]). However, when power is reintroduced into this largely depoliticised account, the encroachment of alien rationalities into spheres where logics other than competition and calculation might otherwise prevail can be seen as a form of 'capture'.[70] In the field of climate science, the metaphor of capture has been applied to expert knowledge and indeed to regulation lobbied on the basis of the latter.[71] It has also been used in several further settings that have an immediate resonance in private international law, including in respect of the future[72] and the international.[73] The examples explored below are designed to shed light on the ways in which capture is enabled by law's own technologies of power.

A. Debt and the Capture of Human Collateral

Debt[74] supported by human collateral as mortgage provides a first emblematic illustration of the severance between capitalism's (legal) foreground and its (hidden)

in principle is not supposed to be bought and sold. See Sarah Churchwell's article in the *New York Review of Books* on debt, slavery and the Lehman saga (to which we return below), www.nybooks.com/daily/2019/06/11/the-lehman-trilogy-and-wall-streets-debt-to-slavery/.

[68] When extended to the 'natural' collateral constituted by non-renewable resources, such a system 'operating at a distance' is made further invisible or 'naturalised' by the very idea of an international 'carbon market' in which the 'right to pollute' has an exchange value (see J Ellis, 'Calculative Practices in International Environmental Governance: In (Partial) Defence of Indicators' (2020) 9 *Transnational Environmental Law* 297–321).

[69] S Sassen, *Losing Control? Sovereignty in the Age of Globalization* (Columbia University Press, 2015).

[70] On the idea of 'capture' (of bodies) in Marxian theory, see DM Levin, 'The Body Politic: Political Economy and the Human Body' (1985) 8(3) *Human Studies* 235–78, www.jstor.org/stable/2000894; and on the work of Walter Benjamin, see E Geulen, 'Pour une généalogie du genre dans l'œuvre de Walter Benjamin' (2004) *Tumultes* 161–88, https://doi.org/10.3917/tumu.023.0161.

[71] On the idea of 'regulatory capture' and its application to private international law, see H Muir Watt, 'Aspects économiques du droit international privé' (2004) 307 *Rec Cours Acad Droit international de la Haye*; C Devaux, *La fabrique du droit du commerce international; réguler les risques de capture* (Bruylant, 2019).

[72] By T Mitchell, 'The Body Politic that Captured the Future,' in B Latour, S Schaffer, and P Gagliardi, (eds), *A Book of the Body Politic*, 49–59.

[73] By S Pajuha, 'Conserving the World's Resources?' in J Crawford and M Koskeniemmi (eds), *Cambridge Companion to International Law* (Cambridge, Cambridge University Press, 2012).

[74] Debt is not only a fundamental Roman legal category (and as such, in the guise of obligation, remains essential to the civil law) but it may, as GH Samuel suggests, provide the key to the structure of the common law as it emerged at the very threshold of modernity ('Classification of contracts: A view from a common lawyer', in FJA Santos, C Baldus and Helge Dedek (eds), *Vertragstypen in Europa: Historische Entwicklung und europäische Perspektiven* (Berlin/Boston, Otto Schmidt/De Gruyter European Law Publishers, 2011) 117–52.). Its role in the emergence of the capitalist economy is crucial, to the extent that it explains the invention of both credit and money. Debt instruments drove the whole economy. As Sara Churchwell observes in her historical study (cited above), 'from such seemingly routine transactions an entire political economy can arise'. Commodities markets, title to property, loans, financial credit systems, securities are all legal institutions of private law that spring from the basic structure of debt. When, very rapidly, the growth of vast empires required massive exportation, adding in maritime transport with its increasingly complex legal devices (bills of lading), private international law upheld the infrastructure so as to allow trade to move more efficiently. On the close connection between army, debt, state, money and markets, this age-old or rather empire-old combination that lies at the heart of the dual power of state and market up to the present day, see D Graeber, *Debt: The First 5,000 Years* (Melville House, 2011).

background conditions.[75] The relationship between capitalism and slavery[76] begins with the accumulation of racial capital deriving from the global slave trade, which formed an integral and indispensable part of European expansion and settlement of the New World.[77] One instance of the role of law in this picture[78] is exemplified by the development of debt instruments in the transformation of industrial economies during the first part of the nineteenth century.[79] Such instruments were secured by the use of slaves as collateral, reducing 'human' capital to a form of financial asset.[80] As Sarah Churchwell explains in a historical study of Wall Street's debt to slavery,[81] the value of chattel slaves was incorporated into private law constructs such as mortgages, securities, and bonds. Thereafter, these instruments were sold to investors nationally and internationally. In a striking example of the schizophrenic rift between the foreground and background conditions of capitalism, this meant (as Churchwell rightly points out) that with the growth of international markets, the financialisation of slave-assets allowed even those countries that had formally or ostensibly outlawed the slave trade (the United States in 1808, Great Britain in 1833, France after Napoleonic vicissitudes in 1848), to continue to profit indirectly from slavery. Despite the moral or religious anti-slavery stance that became widespread during the eighteenth century (with a culmination in the French revolution), their populations (as Churchwell observes) had access to the immense profits generated from the world's first system of multinational production for a mass market – production of sugar, tobacco, coffee, chocolate, rum, dye-stuffs, rice, spices, hemp and cotton.

As Churchwell further writes, such an account discredits the widespread myth of a golden age of a 'real' or moral capitalist economy, that is, before contemporary financialisation made (late) capitalism irresponsible.[82] The Lehman bank, as she

[75] As defined above. In the Mississippi behind Manchester, there is gendered and racialised free labour.

[76] See E Williams's *Capitalism and Slavery* (University of North Carolina Press, 1944; republished with a new Introduction by CA Palmer, 1994).

[77] S Churchwell, 'The "Lehman Trilogy" and Wall Street's Debt to Slavery', *New York Review of Books*, 11 June 2019; on the infernal transatlantic triangle of the slave-value chains between Haiti (Saint Domingue) and France, see F Beauvois, 'L'indemnité de Saint-Domingue: "Dette d'indépendance" ou "rançon de l'esclavage"?' (2009) 10 *French Colonial History* 109–24.

[78] Of course this particular account in no way excludes further instances of the role of (canon or Roman civil) law in early modern forms of empire (on the use of canon law by the Spanish scholastics in the construction of a new world of economic private law, and indeed the political divisions among these scholars, see M Koskenniemi ' Empire and International Law: The Real Spanish Contribution' (2011) 61 *University of Toronto Law Journal* 1–36. Private international law provided the unseen backdrop to this construction.

[79] Following Sarah Churchwell's account ('The "Lehman Trilogy" and Wall Street's Debt to Slavery'), the cotton economy of the nineteenth century (accounting by most measures for more than half of the total goods exported from the US between 1820 and 1860), helped form many of America's current economic and social institutions: the carceral system, property laws, insurance industry, modern finance systems – all have roots in the Southern slave economy. The profits created by the cotton business helped fund vast empires of trade and industry, including shipping and railroads.

[80] In the course of the Lehman saga, as Sarah Churchwell explains ('The "Lehman Trilogy" and Wall Street's Debt to Slavery'), it emerged that JP Morgan had in the past accepted some 13,000 slaves as collateral, and taken possession of 1,250 more as capital.

[81] 'The "Lehman Trilogy" and Wall Street's Debt to Slavery'.

[82] There was no golden age, she writes, in which the Lehman bank traded innocent 'goods' that became degraded thereafter by late capitalism into mere financial tools of decadent speculation. The tragic (tragedy-cum-farce) story is the same if, remaining in the area of commodity production, we look to Poul Kjaer's account of 'connectivity norms' (*The Law of Political Economy*), that serves to highlight the ways

points out, had always traded in 'derivative' capital. This (as it were, collateral) story also alerts us to the darker sides of the supposed return to responsible capitalism that accompany the contemporary turn to 'green' investment – qualified by Nancy Fraser and Rahel Jaeggi as 'tragedy-cum-farce'.[83] Indeed, Churchwell's specific point here is that legal formalisation – the condensation of value into legal instruments – reinforced the 'naturalisation' of human capital, or the 'cognitive dissonance' that meant 'conceding the existence of slavery, while refusing to believe that it has anything to do with the story you are telling; … pushing slavery to the edges of your consciousness and being saved by the logic of exception'.[84] This analysis remains relevant today,[85] under the 'modern' form that human capital takes. As Churchwell again observes:

> The complex, sophisticated commercial systems that had developed along with colonial slave economies did not die when the slave trade was abolished; they merely operated from a greater distance.

This point signals the continued importance here of private international legal technologies[86] in the screening-off of labour conditions at the sites of production.[87] Profits derived from peripheral sites of extraction or agriculture are now channelled back to economic centres through global value chains.[88] The 'cognitive dissonance' of the ultimate consumers – and the impunity of those who benefit ultimately (whether the plantation owners, or the lead firms, or the financiers-investors) – is reinforced by the legally structured distance from the reality of the source of such initial profit.[89] As shown by repeated (hitherto vain) attempts in various fora at recapturing international

in which our contemporary value chains fit into the grooves of past colonial (and slave) trade routes. Sarah Churchwell further writes in this respect that the production of rubber, cotton, cocoa, tobacco or sugar not only traced the itineraries of the slave ships but provided a formidable impetus to 'the continuing importation of African labor to replenish a population that never came close to sustaining itself by natural increase. The demand for labour was especially acute in the tropical and semitropical zones that produced the staples and thus the wealth most desired by Europeans'.

[83] Above 220.

[84] Again, Churchwell, 'The "Lehman Trilogy" and Wall Street's Debt to Slavery'.

[85] Ibid. As in the case of the more recent subprime scandal, financial instruments rested upon collateral that were not 'assets' but homes, not objects but eminently human spaces and possessions.

[86] When extended to the 'natural' collateral constituted by non-renewable resources, such a system 'operating at a distance' is made further invisible or 'naturalised' by the very idea of an international 'carbon market' in which the 'right to pollute' has an exchange value (see Ellis, 'Calculative Practices in International Environmental Governance', 297–321).

[87] There is a considerable volume of case law (largely in the United States, due to the ephemeral revival of the Alien Tort Statute of 1789; see above 149) issuing from (largely aborted) attempts to give legal teeth to the managerial idea of corporate social responsibility in global value chains. Multinational firms remain legally unaccountable for human rights violations at the end of the chain (see for an example of quasi-success, *Nestlé USA, Inc v Doe*, 593 US ____ (2021); however, on the situation in the textile industry after the Rana Plaza disaster, or in the extractive industry, private international jurisdictional obstacles are still practically insurmountable, as current judicial sagas show. For an overview of Canadian case law on this topic, see G Saumier, 'L'ouverture récente des tribunaux canadiens aux poursuites dirigées contre les sociétés mères pour les préjudices causés par leurs filiales à l'étranger' (2018) *Rev crit droit international privé* 775–92).

[88] On the (colonial) path dependency of which, see Kjaer, *The Law of Political Economy*.

[89] It is still true that, as Sarah Churchwell writes of the financialisation of the slave trade, 'Every link in the financial chain profited. It was not the hand of the market that was invisible, but the slave labour in the production that was made so' ('The "Lehman Trilogy" and Wall Street's Debt to Slavery').

jurisdiction over 'modern slavery',[90] at stake is the legal status of borderless economic corporate power. The cunning of neoliberalism is to make governance through contract[91] seem perfectly compatible with a representation of the world of law as still divided by frontiers.[92] The impotence or neutralisation of public, territory-based jurisdiction in respect of borderless private power (yet another case of 'jurisdictional misfit', familiar in private international law[93]) signifies that when corporations have economic control or leverage over the market for a given commodity, such control is dislocated from any correlative duty of care, or vigilance, over the entire economic chain that generates value at every stage.[94]

An analogous 'naturalisation' of (unnatural) capital (human, social, racial) through its legal formalisation into a financial instrument can also be found on the public or sovereign side of debt, analogously 'captured'. The idea of 'odious debt' points to the unfairness of making contemporary populations – the future generations of the past, or '*futur antérieur*'[95] – bear the weight of undue debt incurred by previous (colonial, or corrupt) governments. The concept of odious debt was touted (in vain) during decolonisation in the name of the new international economic order. In this respect, the case of Haiti (among many other possible examples) is particularly illustrative of the ensuing vicious, egregious circle of transgenerational (legal) obligation. The shocking story of the requirement that the slave republic should compensate France for its own accession to independence (that is, for the loss of slave property incurred by the slave-owners) shows up the fragility of the distinction between the public and private legal channels through which a population may be burdened, enduringly, with the structural effects of debt and its capture of human collateral.[96]

[90] Lehman Brothers' massive subprime debt shows how financial crises can serve to confer considerable stakes on (private international) legal conflicts (see on the collapse of the Lehman bank from this perspective, H Muir Watt, *Global Private International Law*, 271 et seq). An unscrupulous (see above) rationality of calculation invaded everything that 'home' signifies: belonging, dignity, protection and effects. The singular egregiousness of the whole scheme showed up moreover in the largely racialised expropriation to which this regime of indebtedness and ensuing poverty led, within the territory of the United States.

[91] See AC Cutler, T Dietz, *The Politics of Private Transnational Governance by Contract* (Abingdon, Routledge, 2017).

[92] On this division, see above Part II. The point here is that the frontier appears to work one way only.

[93] See notably the use of the idea of 'misfit' by R Nagareda, 'Aggregate Litigation across the Atlantic and the Future of American Exceptionalism' (2009) 62 *Vanderbilt Law Review* 1.

[94] There is a significant contemporary move to institute a cross-border corporate duty of care or '*devoir de vigilance*' over the most egregious effects of global value chain structured production (for instance, in the European Union, the European Commission adopted a proposal on 23 February 2022 along the lines of the French *Loi sur le devoir de vigilance*, No 2017-399 of 27 March 2017), but for the moment, the concrete deployment of such an idea (which could actually be implemented through ordinary tort law, as in the English judicial initiative in *Vedanta Resources PLC and another v Lungowe and others* UKSC 2017/0185, 10 April 2019) is plagued by obstacles at the jurisdictional stage, or problems of corporate collective action.

[95] S Ludington et al, 'Applied Legal History: Demystifying the Doctrine of Odious Debts' (2010) 11 *Theoretical Inquiries* 247, 253. On the idea of '*futur antérieur*' or 'subjunctive subjectivity', see T Negri, 'Postface to the Complete Text of the Journal Futur Antérieur', Multitudes, www.multitudes.net/postface-to-the-complete-text-of/.

[96] See www.ayititoday.com/haiti-france-analyse-juridique-de-la-dette-de-lindependance/Haiti slave republic. The French state compensated the expropriated (French) private slave owners with the income produced by the debt incurred by the slave republic for the emancipation of its own citizens. This wealth chain (or debt chain) was supported at every step by various legal tools (international treaty, sovereign debt, private claims).

However, the very same story continues today, albeit under other – equally legal, and specifically private international legal – guises.

Thus, the syphoning of public resources from struggling economies through the ceaseless efforts of private 'vulture' funds[97] has become the contemporary embodiment of older forms of capture.[98] Beyond the highly mediatised (and only partially successful) struggle to 'ban the vultures' in various settings,[99] the legal framework within which sovereign debt is financialised and then enforced against an impoverished debtor state is less visible. This debt takes on the legal form of bonds bought up by speculative funds from impoverished sovereign debtors on secondary markets at 'bargain basement' prices.[100] A series of devices borrowed from private international law are then shaped through tireless litigation by the buyers, in such a way as to clear any legal obstacles to the enforcement of loans or bonds at their nominal value. The underlying strategic pattern is clear, although not always easy to trace because of the elusive identity and legal status of these funds.[101] Vulture-propelled forum-shopping

[97] These funds have been described as 'egregious predatory funds targeting the world's poorest nations' (J Goren, 'State-to-State Debts: Sovereign Immunity and the "Vulture" Hunt' (2010) 41 *George Washington International Law Review* 681, 689). Typically, 'vulture funds' – a particular variety of hedge fund usually incorporated in tax havens for the purpose of one particular purchase – purchase 'sovereign distressed debts' of a highly impoverished country for a reduced price; these are bonds corresponding to loans on which the borrowing sovereign has defaulted, which can be bought at far less than their face value on the secondary market. The vulture funds then invest in extensive litigation in national courts – generating precedent (in common law jurisdictions, particularly) on the way, in support of restrictions of sovereign immunity – for the full value of the claims (that is, the full nominal amount with the unpaid interest). On this strategy see J Blackman and R Mukhi, 'The Evolution of Modern Sovereign Debt Litigation: Vultures, Alter Egos, and Other Legal Fauna' (2010) 73 (Fall) *Law and Contemporary Problems* 47, 49.

[98] Resources that should find their way into public projects such as hospitals or housing are spirited away, to the detriment of current populations and future generations. There is abundant literature on the operation of such funds. See inter alia, Human Rights Council, 14th Session, Report of the Independent Expert Cephas Lumina on the effects of foreign debt and other related international financial obligations of states on the full enjoyment of all human rights, particularly economic, social and cultural rights, 29 April 2010 (A/HRC/14/21); the United Nations Human Rights Council initiative: www.ohchr.org/en/hr-bodies/hrc/advisory-committee/vulture-funds. For an overview of the crucial, specifically private international aspects, including an analysis of the vultures' litigation strategies, see H Muir Watt, 'Dette souveraine et main visible du marché: de nouveaux enjeux du droit international privé des contrats' (2015) *Rev crit droit international privé* 331–53. As J Lippert recounts in 'Vulture Funds: The Reason Why Congolese Debt May Force a Revision of the Foreign Sovereign Immunities Act' (2008) 21 *New York International Law Review* 1, at the outset, multinational corporate actors induce and recycle sovereign loans, backed by local (oil and gas) production. The proceeds of local production are then lent back through corporate screen lenders to the developing country at artificially high interest rates, ultimately generating more loans and worsening debt.

[99] Ibid for the ban the vulture legislation adopted after protest in the United Kingdom instituting an exception designed to protect humanitarian aid delivered to 'highly impoverished poor countries'. A similar initiative in the United States did not pass Congress, while in France, the courts have not always picked up the vulture dimension of apparently innocuous private international litigation. The ECHR has dismissed (at the admissibility stage) claims by a vulture fund based on its human right to property; however, conversely see *Dennis Grainger and others v UK* (App No 34940/10) rejecting the claim concerning the dealings of Northern Rock as manifestly ill-founded and inadmissible.

[100] See Muir Watt, 'Dette souveraine', for further references.

[101] They tend to appear and disappear, their trajectories through the legal systems of the world being difficult to trace because they are usually domiciled in offshore tax havens such as the Cayman Islands, under anodyne names such as NML Capital, Elliot, FG Hemisphere, Af-Cap, etc. Courts of the common law tradition have traditionally made hospitable fora, but courts belonging to the civil tradition are also joining the game. Brussels and Frankfurt have proved equally open to vulture claims. Thus, the vulture Elliott acquired debt issuing from a 1983 loan on which Peru had defaulted, and then refused to participate in an exchange or rescheduling agreement involving other creditors. It obtained a more than substantial

has led to the gradual whittling away of sovereign immunity in several accommodating legal systems and the incremental crafting of useful (and persuasive) precedents in various areas of private law that clear the way to enforcement.[102] Meanwhile, royalties or revenues are fictionally located outside the sovereign territory in order allow for seizure in payment of the debt;[103] *in pari passu* clauses in loan contracts are interpreted so as to reverse their apparent institution of an equal status between creditors, allowing hold-out funds to paralyse sovereign payments as they pass through international clearing houses; or again, a modification of the choice of law in the loan contract is imposed upon the state debtor in order to avoid the effects of a moratorium or other protective measures it might be tempted to take to protect its population from the syphoning off of international aid or other possible public resources that might otherwise serve to build infrastructures, hospitals, schools, etc.[104] The final touch has been the absorption of disputes relating to sovereign debt within the purview of investment arbitration, making its path thereafter even more untraceable.[105] As we

award against Peru in the United States from the Court of Appeals of the Second Circuit (*Elliott Associates, LP v Banco de la Nacion and The Republic of Peru*, 194 F 3d (2d Cir 1999)), which refused to entertain the champerty defence raised by the sovereign. It then applied successfully to the Court of Appeals of Brussels (the location of Euroclear) in order to block payments by Peru to the other (participating) creditors on the basis of the *pari passu* clause (*Elliott Associates LP*, General Docket No 2000/QR/92 (Court of Appeals of Brussels, 8th Chamber, 26 September 2000). It obtained an ex parte order on the ground that the *pari passu* clause – which was made to work rather like a most favoured creditor clause – gave the vulture funds, as holders of the rescheduled debt, the right to participate pro rata in Peru's payments to other foreign creditors. Since then, vulture investors have repeatedly used this strategy. It is not clear, however, that a *pari passu* clause really purports to do anything more than ensure that the creditor's loan will not be subordinated to the claims of other creditors in the event of the borrower's bankruptcy; it does not mean that the solvent borrower must make pro rata payments to all its creditors.

[102] Vulture tactics have generated a wealth of precedents eroding sovereign immunity throughout the Western world in connection with sovereign debt restructuring. A recent trend seems to be more restrictive, however, and may accelerate vulture flight towards investment arbitration described below. See the various immunity cases litigated by NML Capital against Argentina (in the UK: *NML Capital Ltd v Republic of Argentina* (2011) UKSC 31; in the US: *NML Capital v Banco Central* (2d Cir 2011), in which the Second Circuit held that the assets of the Argentine Central Bank on deposit with the Federal Reserve Bank of New York were immune from attachment under 28 USC § 1611(b)), but then in *NML Capital Ltd v Republic of Argentina* (2d Cir 2012), 10-4450-cv (L), it was judged that the bank account of a scientific research institution and instrumentality of Argentina, the Agencia Nacional de Promoción Científica y Tecnólogica, was not immune from attachment under the FSIA. The very fact that the funds are for market use, whatever the purpose, is enough to set aside sovereign immunity. In France, see however, Cour de Cassation 1re Ch Civ, 28 September 2011 n° 09-72057, maintaining immunity from enforcement against embassy assets.

[103] Various private international legal techniques are used for whittling away the jurisdictional immunity of the debtor state. Some serve to lift the sovereign veil of state-owned subsidiaries outside the sovereign debtor's jurisdiction, for example. In the United States, this strategy requires bypassing potential obstacles under the Foreign Sovereign Immunities Act linked to the destination (that is, the intended uses) of the royalties. An illustration can be found in the notorious *Af-Cap* cases, in which a vulture fund purchased a loan to the Congo at a 'bargain basement' price and then obtained garnishment of the royalties and taxes owed to the Congo by a group of Texan oil companies. See *Af-Cap*, 462 F 3d at 421; *cf FG Hemisphere*, 455 F 3d at 580.

[104] See the case of *Donegal v Zambia* [2007] EWHC 197 (Comm), recalling Zambia to its duty to respect its bargain (a constraint resulting from the law, even if the court acknowledged that law's injunction conflicted with its own sense of justice). Anthropomorphised, the 'highly impoverished' sovereign debtors are treated discursively as 'bad pupils', unable to manage their own budget or service their public debt. Undoubtedly, the action of corrupt governments is often involved. But the overall result of such arguments is to mortgage the future of whole populations.

[105] *Abaclat and others (formerly Giovanna A Beccara and others) v Argentine Republic* (ICSID Case No ARB/07/5).

shall now see, this last move is a variation on the line drawn between what is legal (and arbitrable) and what is political in the sphere of the international: again, and most literally indeed, *Quis judicabit*?

B. Foreign Investment and the 'Capture of the Space of the International'

The post-colonial international economic order put in place a series of financial institutions geared to the 'development' of the previously colonised world[106] and, in its name, a dense, expanding framework of (multilateral, regional and bilateral) trade and investment treaties. Resting on the (real or supposed) consent of the recently formed sovereign states,[107] massive private investment from the 'first world' would purportedly bring the economic prosperity and political stability required for the full deployment of the rule of law.[108] However, even as the sovereignty of the new territorial Leviathans over their own (vast) mineral resources, territorial waters, land and agriculture was solemnly recognised by the others (the 'international community'), this 'invitation' to host private (corporate) foreign investment was accompanied by a highly restrictive legal order, supposedly based again on (equally sovereign) consent.[109] The budding international investment regime prevented certain sorts of state intervention in respect of private property (for instance, nationalisation) but also prohibited 'creeping expropriations' or 'regulatory takings' – among which public health, environmental and social legislation were the primary targets. In such a context, human rights appeared not as limits to the transnational private appropriation of natural resources in the collective interests of humanity, but as insurance for private investment and guarantee of capital liquidity.[110] Once again, 'development' through investment has proved disastrous for whole populations and the planetary ecology alike.

The inhibitive content of the spreading web of investment treaties was accompanied by a further, less visible, double move on the private side of international law, which served to complete the neutralisation of the political margin of host states in

[106] S Pahuja, *Decolonising International Law. Development, Economic Growth and the Politics of Universality* (Cambridge, Cambridge University Press, 2013). On development discourse as the replication of wilderness (not ecological entanglement but barren, irradiated 'sacrifice zones', see Gonzales and Mutua, *op cit*.

[107] The governments of some of these newly independent states embraced this legal-economic order with apparent enthusiasm. For the complex situation (supported by narratives and myths) in Algeria after the Evian Agreement, see A Hassani, *La neutralité de l'arbitrage international – Essai de déconstruction d'un mythe*, PhD dissertation, Sciences Po Law school 2021, publication forthcoming.

[108] While the latter was to make their legal systems attractive (safe!) for private investment, as will be seen below. See K Miles, *The Origins of International Investment Law: Empire, Environment and the Safeguarding of Capital* (Cambridge, Cambridge University Press, 2013); A Leiter-Bockley, 'Making the World Safe for Investment: the Protection of Foreign Property 1922–1959', PhD dissertation, Melbourne Law School/Vienna Law School, 2019; N Perrone, 'Neoliberalism and economic sovereignty: property, contracts and foreign investment relations', in Brabazon, *Neoliberal Legality* 43–60.

[109] Consent was of course induced by fear of capital flight. For the private international legal dimensions of this locked-in syndrome, see H Muir Watt, *Aspects économiques.*

[110] M Sornarajah, *The International Law on Foreign Investment* (Cambridge, Cambridge University Press, 2010). Pahuja, *Decolonising International Law.*

respect of their natural resources. In particular, the background private international legal infrastructure has had profound and widespread distributional effects.[111] Its operation has consisted in the depoliticisation and privatisation of economic disputes arising in relation to the investments covered by the new regime, particularly in respect of host states' use of their regulatory powers (once again, in areas such as sanitary, social and environmental regulation). Depoliticisation in this context refers to the legal-fictional process by which these disputes were juridically elevated, by means of an ingenious intellectual device, to the realm of the international, meaning that they were located outside or above the scope of local or domestic legislation.[112] In a further displacement in the direction of privatisation, such disputes – the economic issues arising out of the investments enabled by the treaty regime – were deemed moreover to fall within the scope of private (largely contract) law. In other words, they were governed either by English or New York common law,[113] or ascribed to a set of rarefied, general principles (*lex mercatoria*[114]) governing the investment agreement (such as *pacta sunt servanda*): in either case, these regimes served above all to uphold the terms of (often egregiously unfair) bargains. The latter were – and still are – widely enforced by international arbitrators whose own mandate, it is frequently repeated, is to ensure the strict compliance with the terms and conditions of the parties' (purportedly) mutual understanding.[115]

[111] See I Feichtner, 'Law of Natural Resource Extraction and Money as Key to Understanding Global Political Economy and Potential for Its Transformation', in Kjaer, *The Law of Political Economy*, 152–80, exploring law's role (including norms of jurisdiction, ownership and use rights, and the justifications that accompany these norms of allocation), in the distribution and exploitation of natural resources, and the link between natural resource extraction and the financialisation of the global economy.

[112] The construction of the theory of state contracts rests on that of the legal fiction of the *Grundlegung*, developed to justify their internationalisation, that is, their 'natural' elevation to the status of contracts governed by international law, despite the presence of a private party, and not subject to international law. See P Weil, 'Droit international et contrats d'Etat', *Mélanges Reuter* (Pedone, 1981). However, the consequences of such internationalisation are surprising: once the *Grundlegung* is identified, it is then supposed to make a (secondary) reference to the set of legal rules governing the contract. Denouncing the *Grundlegung* as myth, see P Mayer, 'Le mythe de l'ordre juridique de base ou *Grundlegung*' in *Etudes offertes à Berthold Goldman* (Litec, 1983) 217; 'La neutralisation du pouvoir normatif de l'Etat en matière de contrats d'Etat' (1986) 113 *Journal du Droit International* 5–78.

[113] In a very broad comparative generalisation, the principles that go to compose the common law of contract ensure the upholding of (often unequal) bargains, more than, say, the French civilian model, which allows greater room for judicial intervention on grounds of fairness.

[114] On the concept of *lex mercatoria*, see B Goldman, 'Frontières du droit et lex mercatoria' (1964) *Archives de Philosophie du Droit* 177; for a dismissal of such arguments as sociology, not law, see P Lagarde, 'Approche critique de la *lex mercatoria*' in *Le droit des relations économiques internationales, Etudes offertes à B Goldman* (Litec, 1982) 125; on the comparative dimension to the debate about the legal nature of law-without-enforcement, see N Jansen and R Michaels, 'Private Law Beyond the State? Europeanization, Globalization, Privatization' (2008) 54 *American Journal of Comparative Law* 843; on the political economy of the *lex mercatoria*, see H Collins, 'Flipping Wreck: *Lex Mercatoria* on the Shoals of *Ius Cogens*', in S Grundmann, F Moeslein, K Riesenhuber (eds), *Contract Governance – Dimensions in Law and Interdisciplinary Research* (Oxford, Oxford University Press, 2015). The *lex mercatoria* is instantiated, in a paradoxical (codified, non-spontaneous) way by the Hague Principles on Choice of Law in International Commercial Contracts (2015), which 'sets forth general principles concerning choice of law in international commercial contracts. They affirm the principle of party autonomy with limited exceptions.'

[115] Under the terms of most bilateral investment treaties, 'state contracts' contain arbitral agreements, of which the legal 'autonomy' has been progressively cemented by the courts and international legislation alike. A large part of the success of this regime rests on that of investment arbitration as a flourishing

This move to depoliticise and privatise the international economic order certainly preceded the post-colonial treaty regime; it was already visible in the early twentieth century, in the era leading up to decolonisation, when international arbitration began to expand as an industry. In view of the predictable loss of resources, colonial capital required a supposedly neutral forum for investment disputes, again under the aegis of private law.[116] Prior to this – before the invention of the 'inter-national' in the nineteenth century – there was no 'realm of the international'.[117] Above all, there were no particular stakes in such a distinction under the older 'law of nations'. This is because the latter was part of the 'law of nature', differing from private law only by reason of its subjects. Empire, moreover, was an economy already firmly built on the institutions of private law (property, contract, credit, loans[118]) while, conversely, foreign relations law was geared to the protection of private property and trade routes overseas. Later, by the late nineteenth century, the schism within the law of nations that had taken shape between its public and private components was grafted onto a further separation between the political and the economic: the former belonged to the local while the latter became synonymous with the private and the international.

The delineation of all these categories has been and still is debated, endlessly. In private international law, as seen above, such controversies are existential and engage the very nomenclature of the discipline.[119] But in the context of foreign investment, the political and economic stakes of these particular 'boundary struggles' are starkly clear: corporate economic activities overseas (conducted in the past in the name of empire, and now in the name of development) have to be insulated from the sphere of local public and political decision-making. One of the main legal grounds or justifications for the elevation and insulation of foreign investment from the vicissitudes of democratic politics[120] derives from the 'theory of state contracts' mentioned above. Briefly summarised: only sovereign states can enter into treaties subject to public international law, so that the latter is neutralised when one of the parties to an investment agreement is a private corporation (albeit operating under the aegis of a bilateral treaty). But because this corporation is foreign, the local is equally disqualified and the agreement rises up into a rarefied legal atmosphere of largely private transnational law. This means a ratcheting-down of the sovereign

industry that generates in turn a body of largely self-referential norms somewhat analogous to case law. Regulation of the industry itself was and still remains decidedly light-handed; an insistence on 'transparency' allowing the structures themselves to flourish, insulating them from further critique. Furthermore, interference with the substantive content of the case law itself is kept to a bare minimum in the name of contractual freedom.

[116] A Hassani, *La neutralité de l'arbitrage international.*

[117] M Koskenniemi, 'International Law and raison d'état', 327 noting that in the 'prehistory' of international law, the natural law tradition embodied in the law of nations had no conception of such a realm as distinct from the principles of wise government as projected into foreign or distant territories. The 'international', as coined by Jeremy Bentham, is an example of a 'fictitious' concept. It is of course a fictitious political in-between space, but also a legal fiction.

[118] See above, 227 et s.

[119] See above, 189.

[120] U Baxi, *International Natural Resources Law, Investment and Sustainability* (Abingdon, Routledge, 2017).

state, deprived of its prerogatives through its own supposedly enlightened consent.[121] In short, once the threshold of the international is crossed, the separation between the local-political and the private-international ensures, through the legal tools associated with the latter, that the world is 'safe for investment'. By the same token, host states lose (or, under a contractual approach, renounce) sovereign control over their natural resources in favour of foreign extractive industries. Driven by financialisation, these industries have conducted expropriation on a vast scale.[122]

In this respect, Paddy Ireland draws attention to the parallel between neoliberal forms of domestic government policies (aiming to ensure the integrity of financial property) that routinely trump other economic and social objectives,[123] and their international avatars. This dense 'interlocking network of rules and rule-making structures'[124] provides investors with quasi-constitutional protection. In other words, this 'new constitutionalism'[125] locks countries into a neoliberal 'rule of (investment) law' which not only protects foreign investors from legislative and administrative actions that damage their investment interests, but confers on international organisations powers which, when exercised by states themselves, are usually referred to as 'sovereign powers'. Certainly, contemporary calls for greener investment or more responsible capitalism may seem to be changing the picture; after all, the market itself points to the unsustainability of certain predatory practices. However, if neoliberal legality involves the transformation of all law into private law,[126] then the 'capture of the international' in this context is the emblematic illustration of its *modus operandi* and not so easily dislodged. In all likelihood, as will be seen below, the most recent boundary struggles over the ecological impact of investment will simply provide more liquidity for an ever more concentrated ownership of capital.

[121] New boundary struggles break out, of course, from time to time. The fate of the failed transatlantic trade agreement is a case in point. Concessions follow, such as the contemporary multiplication of exceptions for environmental regulation, but their efficacy is limited either by the fear of capital flight or by the reluctance of the courts of the home country to sanction their violation. New scenarios appear, moreover, as the idea of corporate social responsibility, largely reappropriated as a laundering exercise by Western corporate interests, is now touted by Chinese entities investing in rare minerals in Africa. States, or the European Union, attempt to 'take back control' from private arbitration, but the area is too contested and the interests too vested, to trigger any visible change. Furthermore, at least until their demise in 2021, the World Bank's 'Doing Business' rankings signalled the readiness of host economies to provide 'good climates for investment' by aligning their legislation so as best to protect foreign private property.

[122] Feichtner, 'Law of Natural Resource Extraction and Money'. Current private international law litigation on environmental issues in English, Dutch and French courts (against ex-Royal Dutch Shell, Vedanta, Total, Perenco, and more) reveals how vast ecosystems such as the Niger delta have become human and natural 'sacrifice zones' (see below 241, 246).

[123] The OECD's Principles of Corporate Governance, for instance, seek to embed the Anglo-American shareholder-oriented model of the corporation around the world and to protect the interests of (*rentier*) shareholders. Although compliance with these standards is formally voluntary, in reality it is more or less compulsory if capital flight and investment strikes are to be avoided (see Ireland, 'Property, Private Government and the Myth of Deregulation').

[124] This shows once again that it is a fallacy to believe that deregulation means less regulation. Neoliberalism is compatible both with strong legal infrastructures such as those described, and liberal rights to ensure capital liquidity.

[125] The idea of a 'new transnational constitutionalism' provides a gloss of public legitimacy to a regime harnessed to the protection of private property.

[126] M Foessel, 'Néolibéralisme versus libéralisme?' (2008) Nov, *Revue Esprit, L'Etat entre néolibéralisme et régulation*.

C. Capital Structure and the Capture of Accountability

The (apparent) paradox of neoliberalism is that its diffusion of a rationality of calculation into ever-further social spheres distorts its own central pillar, that of accounting or 'accountability'.[127] Typically, the use of the economic concept of 'externalities' describes costs affecting other constituencies (labour, local communities, the 'environment') or interests (such as social equality, human dignity, democracy, or biodiversity) that are not reflected in the price of products and services. The real drawback of such a concept is that it suggests that such effects are measurable and can be compensated (as mere costs), and moreover are 'out there' (external) rather than enmeshed within ourselves, our lives and our activities. At the same time, it has a certain utility insofar as it shows that even on its own terms – that is, if we were really able to calculate 'social costs' and integrate them into price – the 'great book of accounts'[128] is radically skewed.[129] With respect to the idea of sustainable neoliberal capitalism, Nancy Fraser and Rahel Jaeggi analyse the playing out of this 'tragedy-cum-farce' as a form of 'distorted accounting … that sees external nature – water, air, living species – outside [the] system of exchange … as a "free gift"'.[130]

In (comparative, domestic) corporate law, then, capital is largely structured and governed in a mode that prioritises shareholder value and excludes objectives other than profit. While models vary in both these respects, and there have been, as we have seen, recent gestures towards 'responsible capitalism', it is unclear that capital's answerability, or vocation to be called to account, has significantly improved. This is the case moreover despite much lip-service to human, or social and economic, rights.[131] In this regard, neoliberal legality is perfectly compatible, indeed mandates, the values that constitute a robust rule of law. It seeks predictability for investment; a credible judiciary to enforce private agreements and ensure reparation of (non-efficient[132]) breach; protection from corruption; efficient corporate structures; etc.[133]

[127] Latour, *Enquête*, 463. The economy is not of itself a 'matter', ibid 465) or a social sphere, as seen above.

[128] Ibid.

[129] There is obviously nothing new here. Capitalism required that the connection between the regulated market (or legal exchange) and expropriation remain invisible in the great Book of Accounts.

[130] Fraser and Jaeggi, *Capitalism. A Critical Conversation* 35 et seq (on nature, moreover, as 'tap' and 'sink').

[131] One potentially interesting example is the creation in France of a new capitalistic 'style' in the '*entreprise à mission*' (a firm endowed with a social and environmental mission). See the official website gouv.fr: L'article 176 de la loi du 22 mai 2019 relative à la croissance et la transformation des entreprises (loi Pacte), introduit la qualité de société à mission. Il s'agit pour une entreprise d'affirmer publiquement sa raison d'être, ainsi qu'un ou plusieurs objectifs sociaux et environnementaux qu'elle se donne pour mission de poursuivre dans le cadre de son activité. The question is whether these self-proclaimed social and environmental objectives will have any legal teeth, or merely replicate new instances of 'purpose washing'.

[132] The notion of efficient breach, at the heart of conventional law-and-economics contract doctrine, postulates that the violation of an agreement through recourse to a more favourable deal offered by the market is efficient (does not give rise to reparation) if the breaching party stands to gain enough to be able to compensate for the loss.

[133] On all these conditions for 'understanding the role of law in the neoliberal project', see the Introduction of Brabazon, *Neoliberal Legality*, 1 et seq.

An excellent testing ground for the ethical standards of law's rule in these respects is to be found once again in private international law. Far from reining-in disembedded capital, it provides it with cross-border stability through freedom of contract and investment treaties, while supplying it with the means to stave off inroads from local courts or legislators, 'hard' international regulation,[134] or enforcement of supranational or regional human rights. Whatever the discursive concessions towards more social or greener corporate governance, accountability lacks teeth whenever (that is, in most cases) it concerns activities conducted abroad.

There is of course nothing new (or indeed modern) in the immunity from accountability of multinational corporate power, resting upon capital value equal to that of the economies of many sovereign states, when it operates outside its metaphorical 'home'.[135] The rise of the chartered trading companies in early modernity went with egregious forms of expropriation that took place beyond the reach (or out of sight) of the law.[136] These 'quasi-sovereigns', whether traders or pirates,[137] benefited from correlative prerogatives before the courts. Remarkably, their public or private status (and their location within the reach of the rule of law) was at the core of debates spanning the eighteenth and nineteenth centuries on the relationship between capitalism and democracy.[138] However, by the time massive corporate abuse, expropriation and extraction had attracted public concern, attention to the political dimension of the private right to seek economic profit had turned, with or despite Marx's *Capital*, towards the domestic sphere, leaving the new international realm to its own devices.[139] Here the complex concatenation of the public and the private; the

[134] On the need for protection from hard legislation (as opposed to soft law or self-regulation), U Mattei, 'Hard Code Now!' (2002) 2(1) *Global Jurist Frontiers* Art 1.

[135] On the idea of corporations having a 'home' (in which they can reasonably be sued, excluding thereby any basis for (US) jurisdiction over a 'sister' (Argentinian) subsidiary in a corporate group (of which the parent is in Germany), for gross human rights violations in the country of the latter, see *Daimler AG v Bauman* 571 US 117 (2014).

[136] On the East India Company in particular, see T Poole, *Reason of State, Law, Prerogative and Empire* (Cambridge, Cambridge University Press, 2015) 141.

[137] Defined by Gentili in 1580 as 'non-legitimate sovereigns', pirates have long haunted the jurisprudence of private international law in various ways. The question of 'who are today's pirates?' determined (partially) the line taken by the US Supreme Court in its Alien Tort Statute case law (see Justice Breyer's dissent in the *Kiobel* case, cited above, p 4: 'The majority cannot wish this piracy example away by emphasising that piracy takes place on the high seas … That is because the robbery and murder that make up piracy do not normally take place in the water; they take place on a ship. And a ship is like land, in that it falls within the jurisdiction of the nation whose flag it flies.'). The Statute itself was designed with piracy in mind, this being (in 1789) one of the few cases in which the common law identified a violation of the law of nations.

[138] On the various positions of Burke, Bentham and JS Mill, see Poole, *Reason of State, Law, Prerogative and Empire*, 165 et seq (on 'reason of state and the legislating empire').

[139] To take just one example, contemporary mining tragedies under regimes of private foreign ownership in the extractive industry (see below 246 the various cases brought against Shell in Nigeria, that are having difficulty in passing the jurisdictional stage; at the Cape, see in the UK, House of Lords *Lubbe*) recall the horrors of the early diamond boom in colonised German South West Africa in the early 1900s (see J Hammer, *The Horrors of the Diamond Boom*, www.nybooks.com/articles/2021/11/18/horrors-of-the-diamond-boom/).

local and the international; jurisdiction over title to land and private investment and finance; continues to ensure the ultimate (and brutal) sovereignty of capital.[140]

The first, and well-documented, explanation for this state of affairs is the way in which jurisdictional rules have remained largely traced – and indeed increasingly reinforced, as seen above – along territorial lines, while capital, in the form of investment in foreign corporate industrial activity abroad, has precisely erased such lines in the name of entrepreneurial freedom, or the importance of trade and investment for world peace. The hiatus between the political boundaries of states and unbounded private economic expansion, is striking. It is not difficult, therefore, to see the political economy of the design of states' international jurisdiction over corporate entities. The courts of the 'home state' (the country that houses the seat or 'home' of the economic entity or confers 'citizenship' upon it) have opposed systematic refusals – with a spatter of exceptions – to judicial intervention to ensure compensation for damage caused abroad in the 'host' state (the country on the receiving end of corporate investment and activities: a point to which we shall return below). A similar hiatus occurs in respect of the corporate form itself, where the choice of corporate citizenship or 'home' draws lines around the different notional locations of capital, so that the 'parent' company remains largely unanswerable for conduct that is legally imputable to an undercapitalised subsidiary in the host state. Here again, the corporate veil is lifted, sparingly, from time to time, but not enough to redraw the firewall and thereby impact upon the structure of corporate capital. The latter remains immune from accountability as long as power and politics – whether public or private – are kept out of the equation that commands the appropriate allocation of jurisdiction over 'extra-territorial' damage.

A similar analysis can be conducted, in the light of changing forms of capitalism, in respect of the legal regime of global value chains.[141] Here, different corporate participants – subcontractors of the lead firm – are distributed along a succession of different jurisdictions whose frontiers provide as many firewalls against the reflux of judgments from downstream that might call the lead firm to account for harm suffered in the course of this process.[142] Global commodities such as cocoa or rubber

[140] T Ferrando, 'About capitalism and private international law', in H Muir Watt et al (eds), *Global Private International Law*, 237–44, showing moreover, that corporate entitlement to influence local policy remains untouched and its domestic legitimacy unchallenged, at least in the eyes of the international legal order.

[141] On the private legal aspects of global value chains, see KH Eller and J Salminen, 'Reimagining Contract in a World of Global Value Chains' (2020) *European Review of Contract Law*, https://doi.org/10.1515/ercl-2020-0001. And on the specific form of 'hermeneutical' injustice carried by the (clearly inappropriate) private law model of contract, see LKL Tjon Soei Len, 'Hermeneutical Injustice, Contract Law, and Global Value Chains' (2020) *European Review of Contract Law*, https://doi.org/10.1515/ercl-2020-0008.

[142] An interesting element here is the role played by the legal regime governing the recognition and enforcement of foreign judgments. Traditionally – as amply illustrated by the notorious transatlantic drama in the *Lloyd's of London* case or the more recent Chevron tragedy – the ultimate protection of capital lies in local legal obstacles to enforcement of foreign judgments. These ensure against any (extracontractual) liability of the lead firm as decided by the courts of the place where the harmful industrial activities are conducted (usually, in the Global South). The laborious negotiation of the Hague Judgments Convention (Convention of 2 July 2019 on the Recognition and Enforcement of Foreign Judgments in Civil or Commercial Matters) would appear to confirm the difficulty of dislodging these national protective barriers: transatlantic disagreement over jurisdictional criteria was enough to kill the project of global free movement for judicial decisions. However, the irony of history lies in the miraculous rebirth of the same project in 2018, after

provide clear examples of the ways in which the structure of the value chain serves to protect the lead firm from the risk of liability in the courts of its 'home' country for 'harmful events' occurring downstream at the sites of production in the periphery (including structures of modern slave labour in the plantations).[143] The same can be said of the organisation of the textile industry and the screening-off of human disasters such as the Rana Plaza catastrophe (as seen above).[144] In all these cases, jurisdictional discontinuity is reinforced by the legal autonomy of the different contracts involved in the chain, each potentially governed by a different applicable law. Interestingly, the only means private law offers at present to break out of this enchainment is to reach as it were outside of itself and borrow tools from the sphere of economic regulation (such as competition law or antitrust), where the dynamics of power are more apparent.[145]

The second explanation for this bias of the international order (that is, in favour of unregulated capital) lies in the *modus operandi* of so-called social and environmental corporate responsibility. The latter comes in various forms: private 'codes' adopted under the label of corporate governance by multinational firms; industry-wide 'ESG' standards; or indeed international (public) principles of soft law (such as the UN Global Business Pact) that include the protection of human rights.[146] This assemblage of voluntary, self-regulatory or 'soft' undertakings constitutes an informal normative regime of uncertain legal status.[147] Promoted as filling an accountability gap in the

its spectacular diplomatic failure 20 years earlier and the (counterintuitively) proactive role of China in the success of this more recent venture. China's support for free cross-border movement of judgments can be put down to concern on its part regarding enabling the interoperability of decisions (including arbitral awards) relating to contractual disputes, all along the value chains of the planetary 'One Belt One Road'. This extraordinary geopolitical and economic initiative requires a series of jurisdictional institutions to guarantee the non-disruptive resolution of disputes along the way. In this respect, the convention will ensure the smooth flow of the awards of special courts of China downstream to the countries that have become entangled in the great new silk routes.

[143] Already encountered above, the case *Nestle USA, Inc v Doe et al* No.19-416, 593 US (2021) is one among many other examples. At an earlier stage in the long saga, the court of appeals for the ninth circuit had appeared ready to address the question of corporate power (766 F 3d 1013, 9th Cir 2014).

[144] Law's acceptance or even facilitation of deniability of specific forms of harm and of the erection of legally sanctioned knowledge blinders is resplendent in the Canadian *Das v Weston Rana Plaza* judgments, in terms of how self-circumscribed codes can structure what diligence is required, how use of intermediaries can be designed to eliminate direct knowledge, and how contractual terms of third-party auditors can define what needs to be looked at versus what can be ignored even if widely known (the possibility of building collapses in Bangladesh) *Das v George Weston Limited* 2017 ONSC 4129, www.canlii.org/en/on/onsc/doc/2017/2017onsc and *Das v George Weston Limited*, 2018 ONCA 1053 www.canlii.org/en/on/onca/doc/2018/2018onca.

[145] See again, in the same case (*Doe v Nestlé*) the (aborted) 'borrowing' of tools from the field of antitrust in order to address the use and abuse of market power in a situation governed by contract law.

[146] Either against states or their 'home' firms.

[147] They are shrouded in the same uncertainty as are (at least traditionally) unilateral commitments (without 'cause' or consideration) in domestic private law, or undertakings that claim specifically not to be legally binding (such as so-called 'gentlemen's agreements'). Classical legal thought required either formal agreement or some further 'cause' on the part of the debtor of an obligation in order that the latter be endowed with legal effect. However, comparative private law shows that voluntary understandings in the domestic sphere have been progressively held to account (through various devices such as reliance or estoppel, 'natural obligations', or indeed through legislative reform: see for example, the changes to the French Code Civil, by Ordonnance n° 2016-131 du 10 février 2016 portant réforme du droit des contrats, du régime général et de la preuve des obligations: 'Art 1100-1.Les actes juridiques sont des manifestations de volonté destinées à produire des effets de droit. Ils peuvent être conventionnels ou unilatéraux' (however,

international legal order, they are supposedly progressive and virtuous, and moreover occupy high moral ground[148] (whereas 'hard' legal accountability, dismissed as 'over-regulation', is unfriendly for business, as the infamous World Bank ratings and other 'valorimeters' suggest[149]). However, it is likely that such initiatives are largely designed to stave off binding 'public' (local or international) regulation, considered bad for business, rather than replace profit by other rationalities as the rule of the game.[150] Better a minimal (and widely advertised) voluntary undertaking than a structural change that might destroy existing immunisation.[151] Indeed, spontaneous concessions to virtue are certainly compatible with a neoliberal project, as long as their cost does not outweigh the gains involved in the protection against 'harder' duties to repair.[152]

It is notable in all events that attempts in courts to make such undertakings binding have been fought tooth and nail by the multinational corporate authors of such codes, who have all contested on various grounds (from the constitutional right of free speech[153] to the privity of contract, or lack of binding force of unilateral commitments for advertising purposes[154]) the transformation of their commercial promises, 'green' or purportedly ethical standards, or indeed internal vetting procedures, into legal obligations.[155] Moreover, when the level of corporate misconduct is such that it

the adjectival phrase 'destinées à produire des effets de droit' leaves open the question of the bindingness of private corporate codes).

[148] R Shamir, 'The age of responsibilization: On market-embedded morality' 37 (1) *Economy and society* 1–19. It is as difficult to fault an ethical commitment by a corporate actor to respect human and social rights or environmental standards along its value chains or on the sites of its industrial activities, as it is to challenge, whatever doubts one may harbour as to the means, the asserted end or concern for environmental protection or the reduction of global warming.

[149] See above 239. On 'valorimeters', see Latour, *Enquête*, 443.

[150] See Shamir, 'The age of responsibilization: On market-embedded morality'. The public vs private distinction resurfaces here in support of moves on a (somewhat lopsided) chequerboard, in which law is mobilised on one side to counter any gain achieved on the other.

[151] On immunisation, see Esposito, *Immunitas*. There are many further examples of the same ploy (examples are strategies of hold-out creditors in the collecting of sovereign debt, who have always successfully opposed a 'hard' international convention, see above 235; this is also the point made in respect of the relationship of Western (European) consumer markets in respect of the hidden world of extra-territorial production: see Mattei, 'Hard Code Now!

[152] These concessions can indeed provide 'liquidity for capital' (see above 236).

[153] See the extent of this argument, less familiar in European context, Supreme Court of California, *Mark Kasky v Nike, Inc*, 27 Cal 4th 939, 45 P 3d 243, 119 Cal Rptr 2d 296 (2002).

[154] These arguments are more usual in a European setting. See for instance, on the Total group's internal vetting procedure in the *Erika* pollution case, Court of Appeals of Paris, 30 March 2010, D 2010, 967, obs S Lavric, and 2238 obs L Neyret.

[155] Usually through devices of domestic consumer (contract), or tort law (see above 83, 233). Either (it is argued) the non-respect of a standard voluntarily undertaken is an element or evidence of negligent conduct, or it constitutes a violation of a duty of information owed to consumers (for examples, see: for the effect of Nike's code of conduct under consumer law see above 244; for the *Erika* pollution case involving the Total group and its self-regulating vetting procedure, see above n 154; for the effects, in terms of the debtor of a duty of care, resulting from managerial or advertising documents relating to the structure of a corporate group, see UKSC 2017/0185 *Vedanta*, cited above 47 et seq). There is of course significant discursive power in private codes and green standards and their integration into corporate communication and advertising strategies. It lies is the reinforcement of the idea (see the text above) that spontaneous private undertakings (soft law and self-regulation) are in some way 'better' (more efficient) than political action (hard law), that the economy is indeed self-propelling in a Hayekian way and the protection of the ecology as a mere cost to be set off by a (minimal) payment, or the (random) planting of a tree.

might potentially trigger positive obligations on the part of the state where the corporation is 'at home' (under a human rights treaty or constitutional provisions requiring 'state action' with subsequent invocability in 'horizontal' relationships with other private actors), we find that such obligations do not extend extra-territorially.[156] The linkage that might (easily) allow this very extension – the presence of an investment treaty by which the home state encourages its corporate citizens to conduct (possibly harmful) extractive activities abroad – is never or rarely mentioned. Very possibly, the new corporate 'duty of care' or 'vigilance' imposed on large corporate structures in respect of the interests affected by the foreign activities of a global value chain shows a way round this obstacle, since it creates a 'choke-point' at the very site of creation of value.[157]

However, at this stage, there is clearly a problem of collective action: the effectiveness of so-called 'ESG' commitments depends upon the extent to which firms are ready to disclose such risks under their reporting obligations, and none appear forthcoming.[158] This may explain the appearance of yet a new 'boundary struggle' over the legitimacy and veracity of expert scientific evidence. Thus recent changes in litigation strategy in the area of climate change see fossil fuel companies taken to court for suppressing internal climate research and publicly spreading doubt (rather than through the use tort law to address the present and future harms).[159] In return,

[156] On 'state action' and 'horizontal effect' as analogous requirements (in the idiom of United States constitutional law and European human rights law, respectively) in terms of the spatial 'reach' of rights (here, to touch the foreign conduct of corporations), see J Bomhoff, 'The Reach of Rights' (2008) 71 *Law and Contemporary Problems* 73.

[157] On the recent move towards a 'duty of vigilance', see above 233; on the ways in which value chains might be regulated at the 'choke points', see Ferrando, 'About capitalism and private international law'. Here it is interesting to recall (see above 211) the Supreme Court of Canada's 2020 *Araya v Nevsun* judgment: www.canlii.org/en/ca/scc. Abella J's majority decision recognises transnationalised substantive law under the guise of 'customary international law as applicable law' in 'private' law claims by forced labour victims in Eritrea against a Canadian company (on the 'in-between', a new-norm-forging decisional mode at work here, see above 211).

[158] This may explain why more recently, the focus of climate change activism has moved towards the obligations of states under treaties such the Paris Agreement, enforced against state parties by their own (administrative) courts. See for example, the path-breaking *Urgenda* case: *Urgenda Foundation v State of the Netherlands* [2015] HAZA C/09/00456689, in which a court in the Hague ordered the Dutch state to limit GHG emissions to 25 per cent below 1990 levels by 2020, finding the government's existing pledge to reduce emissions by 17 per cent insufficient to meet the state's fair contribution toward the UN goal of keeping global temperature increases within two degrees Celsius of pre-industrial conditions. In France, this was followed by a decision of 19 November 2020 by the Conseil d'Etat in favour of a local authority (the commune of Grande-Synthe), led by a group of associations (*l'Affaire du Siècle*), that enjoined the government to 'prendre toutes les mesures nécessaires' to put France back on track for reducing carbon emissions as it had committed to do under the Paris agreement. Another decision of the administrative court of Paris on 14 October 2021 ruled again in favour of *l'Affaire du Siècle*, acknowledging that the state (meaning successive governments) is bound by the commitments underwritten by France under the Paris agreement and must prove reparation for any environmental harm caused by its inaction, before the end of 2022. Such institutional moves are obviously to be welcomed, except that of course the weight of the fines applied to the government falls on the taxpayer, while the revenues of the private industries that have escaped government control do not necessarily come back to roost.

[159] As for the United States, 2017 saw a new wave of litigation against fossil fuel companies, this time brought by state attorneys general, targeting the industry's long-waged campaigns of disinformation and deception. These suits represent a shift in strategy. At least one seemed close to success – *Commonwealth of Massachusetts v Exxon Mobil Corp*, US District Court District of Massachusetts, No 19-12430-WGY, 28 May 2020 in which the complaint was that the oil company misled its investors about the threat that

however, quite extraordinary efforts have been invested in the discrediting of climate science.[160] By and large, viewing the various legal tools mobilised in such a context, it has been asked whether climate change litigation is actually 'fighting yesterday's battle'?[161] In legal terms, as long as liability is seen merely as a problem of costs to be factored into a business plan, or pollution redeemed by the (unverifiable) promise of planting forests 'in exchange' for their destruction, nothing is likely to change.[162]

Moreover, as long as legal notions of causation remain impervious to something equivalent to 'attribution science' (that deals in risks and probabilities rather than causal connections between individual emissions and events), then ecological destruction remains as if delinked from 'business as usual'.[163] Furthermore, there is a widespread idea, voiced by the courts themselves, according to which 'everyone has contributed to the problem of global warming and everyone will suffer the consequences'. In this judicial telling, climate change is simply the price we all must pay for the advantages of modern life.[164] That we are all 'in the same boat' in the face of

climate change poses to its business. However the federal court lacked jurisdiction. Nevertheless, it said that, 'in disclaiming federal jurisdiction over this case, the Court does not quarrel with [the] eloquent plea that "[i]f ever a problem cried out for a uniform and comprehensive solution, it is the geophysical problem of climate change"... Rather, the Court concludes that the "problem" at issue in this Case complaint is not geophysical but economic – namely, has ExxonMobil been sufficiently candid with its investors and customers in Massachusetts about the simmering calamity of global warming? That question is properly for the courts of the Commonwealth to decide'.

[160] See PN Edwards, 'Knowledge Infrastructures under Siege: Climate Data as Memory, Truce, and Target' in D Bigo, E Isin and E Ruppert (eds), *Data Politics: Worlds, Subjects, Rights* (New York, Routledge, 2019) 21–42. For an additional twist, on the dark side of (the concept of) Gaia, developed by James Lovelock in collaboration with Royal Dutch Shell, see L Aronowsky, 'Gas guzzling Gaia; or, a prehistory of climate change denialism' (2021) 47 *Critical Inquiry* 306–27, 327. As A Pottage ('Why Nature Has No Rights') explains: 'From the perspective of Shell, the theory that the biosphere generated its own conditions of existence through mechanisms of self-regulation which stabilized temperature and atmospheric chemistry was interesting because it allowed the company it to develop a particular strategy of climate denialism. If the Earth regulated its own atmosphere, then it seemed plausible to suggest that it could adapt to the effects of CO_2 emissions, and that pollution might itself be part of a "natural" cycle'.

[161] As a climate scientist observes, making industry pay for climate damages is 'just one small piece of the climate-justice puzzle. A successful lawsuit might win relief funds for a city after a hurricane, but will do nothing to hurt companies' "bottom lines"': see L Aronowsky, 'The Limits of Climate Change Litigation' NYRB, 3 November 2021 asking whether 'climate change is too big for court'.

[162] See above on the discursive value of codes, that entrench the idea that the economy is indeed self-propelling in a Hayekian way, so that the protection of the ecology as a mere cost to be set off by a (minimal) payment, or the (random) planting of a tree. Jaye Ellis ('Calculative Practices in International Environmental Governance') argues that political economy in the Anthropocene remains dominated by cognitive instruments and practices, such as standards and indicators which are conditioned on scientific input and mainly operate though managerial governance, rather than law.

[163] Aronowsky, 'The Limits of Climate Change Litigation'. See however, the debate on causation in the *Lliuya v RWE* case in Germany, in which a Peruvian farmer from Huaraz, Peru, filed claims for declaratory judgment and damages against RWE, Germany's largest electricity producer, for having knowingly contributed to climate change by emitting substantial volumes of greenhouse gases (GHGs), thereby contributing in some measure to the melting of mountain glaciers above his town. While the lower court (Essen District Court, 2016) judged that no 'linear causal chain' could be discerned amid the complex components of the causal relationship between particular greenhouse gas emissions and particular climate change impacts, this ruling was overturned on appeal. For a plea for a form of combinatory pragmatism in establishing causation, see F G'sell, 'Les théories contemporaines de la causalité. Droit et Philosophie', in S Ferey and F G'sell (eds), *Causalité, responsabilité et contribution à la dette* (Bruylant, 2018) 36, taking inspiration from J Dewey, 'What Does Pragmatism Mean by Practical' (1908) 5 *The Journal of Philosophy, Psychology and Scientific Methods* 85–99.

[164] Aronowsky, 'The Limits of Climate Change Litigation'.

the threat of Anthropocenic extinction is of course true, although it is equally likely that the degradation of our material lives will be starkly unequal according to our geographical, social and racial situation. Indeed, to the extent that it is used in this way, the idea of our shared, 'universal' responsibility is entirely drained of any ethical commitment on the shoulders of those who might still be in a position to bring about change. The pursuit of profit goes on regardless, and even economies that claim to be reducing their carbon consumption will continue to reap benefits from the externalised operation of the carbon industry elsewhere.[165] Moreover, efforts to lay blame on individual consumption with tools like the 'personal carbon footprint calculator'[166] softly displace blame and do nothing to unskew Gaia's great book of accounts.[167]

D. Development and the Capture of Time

The Capitalocene, writes political theorist Tim Mitchell, rests on a 'capture of the future'.[168] The colonial world fitted into this scheme in a specific way:

> It was imagined as the world of places that didn't properly have an economy; it was the world that had to be transformed, so it could have economies. This is the process that came to be called 'development'.[169]

As seen above, development is a crucial concept within the neoliberal political economy,[170] a political and economic model or ideal towards which the countries of the periphery must strive in order to be accepted within the global economic order. From a genealogical perspective, development is an avatar of the idea of civilisation that defined access to the concert of nations. Both include a powerful temporal element, suggesting an aspiration to progress through time – towards the very model that reinforces their state of dependency.

'Civilisation' evokes the exit of a population from a state of barbary or savagery through the abandonment over time of improper and unsophisticated practices and belief-systems in favour of the acquisition of 'culture', while 'development' suggests some sort of meritorious striving for 'progress' that similarly involves the

[165] In similar ways to the working of financial markets based in 'human collateral', seen above.

[166] Aronowsky, 'The Limits of Climate Change Litigation' pointing out that this perfectly neoliberal concept or device was introduced to the public by a British Petroleum marketing campaign in 2004.

[167] Latour, *Enquête*.

[168] T Mitchell, 'The Body Politic that Captured the Future', in Latour et al, *A Book of the Body Politic*, taking the example of infrastructure (railways) as a techno-political means of colonising the future.

[169] See above.

[170] As seen above, integration of 'developing' states within the international investment regime is part of the conditionality shaped and measured according to neoliberal economic objectives and ratings. It implies opening frontiers to foreign capital and all manner of infrastructural projects and extractive industries (mines, dams, land acquisition, monocultures) that provide production for exportation. A considerable amount of critical literature in the field of (international) law tracks the rise of the concept and its central role in neoliberal discourse on the international scene. It is central to the 'Washington consensus' reached by international economic institutions and part of the 'governance turn' that tended to substitute incentives, standards and indicators for hard law.

relinquishment of the primitive or the rustic in favour of the rational, the managerial and the efficient.[171] In both cases, the strong moral overtones of this temporality of progress are closely linked to an ideal in terms of economic status (and material prosperity). Describing the rise and deployment of an ideology of enclosure in eighteenth-century England, Susan Marks shows how the new order of expanding private property (in a domestic setting) and the correlative expropriation of the commons rested upon the discursive denigration of the past (and those who continue to be locked within it) as backwardness, drudgery, poverty.[172] Backwardness was ascribed to, or measured by, the economic. Unsurprisingly, a similar discourse applied in a colonial context to whole (primitive or savage) populations,[173] undergirded moreover by further fantasies linking the wild to the exotic.[174] Decadent, 'quasi-sovereign' China[175] and the 'veiled protectorate' of Egypt[176] found their way somewhere in-between, on the road towards assimilation. The backwardness of 'native peoples inhabiting an earlier stage of development' (in the words of JS Mill[177]) justified the visible helping hand of colonial power (or its agents).[178] Indeed, in 'the politics of civilisation', democracy could not apply to peoples that had not achieved a mature stage of collective development.[179]

At the high point of coloniality, law had largely integrated these temporal hierarchies, with help from the new co-productive disciplines of comparative law and colonial anthropology.[180] Private international law similarly contains multiple legal

[171] On the process of civilisation as involving the progressive separation of mind and body (or the suppression of the latter from view through self-control) see the opus of N Elias, *Über den Prozess der Zivilisation: soziogenetische und psychogenetische Untersuchungen*, vol I: *Wandlungen des Verhaltens in den weltlichen Oberschichten des Abendlandes*, vol II: *Wandlungen der Gesellschaft: Entwurf zu einer Theorie der Zivilisation* (Bâle, Haus zum Falken, 1939); trans French, *La Civilisation des mœurs* (1973) and *La Dynamique de l'Occident* (1975) ed Calmann-Lévy, collection 'Archives des sciences sociales'.

[172] Marks, *A False Tree of Liberty*.

[173] In 'Subjects of Sovereignty: Indigeneity, The Revenue Rule, and Juridics of Failed Consent' (2008) 71 *Law and Contemporary Problems* 191–216, Audra Simpson emphasises the ways in which 'indigeneity and sovereignty have been conflated with savagery, lawlessness, and "smuggling" in recent history', moreover with an example taken directly from the conflict of laws and the interpretation of the so-called 'revenue rule' (that prevents the application and enforcement of foreign public law).

[174] See Surkis, *Sex, Law, and Sovereignty in French Algeria*.

[175] Ruskola, *Legal Orientalism*.

[176] Under the entry for Evelyn Baring, the *Encyclopaedia Britannica* presents the 24-year rule of the 1st Earl of Cromer as Consul General of Egypt. There (and in view of the state of the country's finances), he 'instituted a form of government that came to be called the 'Veiled Protectorate', whereby he ruled the rulers of Egypt, with the assistance of a group of English administrators trained in India'.

[177] On the position of JS Mill in favour of the 'iron arm' of the East India Company, since the population was 'not ready' to receive direct rule, see Poole, *Reason of State, Law, Prerogative and Empire*, 185.

[178] The edifying account of Evelyn Baring in the *Encyclopaedia Britannica* (cited above) continues: 'Yet, in spite of his long stay in Egypt, he never attempted to learn Arabic and was never able to communicate either with the peasant whom he claimed to know so well or with the middle class that was to produce a new breed of nationalists. He had little liking for the Oriental mind, which he termed "slipshod", and even less understanding of it, despite his claims to the contrary. With age his aloofness increased, and he dismissed the young nationalist movement as unimportant. Instead he worked hard at effecting the Entente Cordiale of 1904 with France, which set the seal on the permanent occupation of Egypt'.

[179] On the more sinister version according to which the racialised humanity of colonised populations is disposable, or relegated to barren sacrificial zones, see Gonzalez and Mutua 'Mapping Racial Capitalism'.

[180] See DM Bonilla, *Legal Barbarians. Identity, Modern Comparative Law and the Global South* (Cambridge, Cambridge University Press, 2021); V Corcodel, Modern law and otherness: the dynamics

devices that have participated in the perverse temporal dynamics of the capitalist economy, reaping profits from the capture of the past. Its contribution is particularly significant because the spatial element of the economic order is so crucial. Enclosure is, as Susan Marks reminds us, 'a metonym for all the rest'. That the discipline contributed to the intellectual substratum of the colonial regime on this point is amply shown by various studies that illustrate similar patterns throughout comparative forms of colonialism, as will be seen below. Interestingly, private international legal technologies serve the colonial economic order through moves that involve not only property (enclosure of land) but its strict severance from family law.[181] The expropriation/expulsion[182] of local communities from their anchorage in land/place borrows from a combination of moves that connect the representation of territory as unoccupied with depictions of backwardness.[183]

For instance, in her study of jurisdictional aspects of British rule in New Zealand,[184] Nan Seuffert describes the ways in which the project of solidifying New Zealand as a white, Christian nation state was deployed through the drawing of jurisdictional boundaries in marriage cases that excluded Maori marriage laws and practices by associating them with the pre-modern, raced concepts of concubinage and polygamy. While consolidating an idea of nation, the Maori lands were simultaneously considered as unoccupied and subject therefore to the legal title of the new landowners. An analogous example comes from the legal history of French colonisation of Algeria. In a study drawing on the archive of the Court of Appeals of Algiers for the century that followed the declaration of French rule in 1830, as well as contemporary art,

of inclusion and exclusion in comparative legal thought (Cheltenham, Edward Elgar Publishing, 2019). Cf the observation by Rachel Seider, 'The Juridification of Politics', in M-C Foblets et al (eds), *The Oxford Handbook of Law and Anthropology* (Oxford, Oxford University Press, 2022), ch 38, that state law is judged by its ideals (progress) and indigenous law by ethnographic findings (static).

[181] On the separation of family and market, see below 295.

[182] S Sassen, *Expulsions: Brutality and Complexity in the Global Economy* (Cambridge MA, Harvard University Press, 2014).

[183] The patterns are similar around the colonised world (including the far north): see on 'Arctic-orientalism' S Hardt, 'By Gifts One Makes Slaves: Long-term Effects of Denmark's Colonization of Greenland' (2018) *Bard Digital Commons*: a key legal concept in Denmark's toolbox was the doctrine of *terra nullius*. While the indigenous peoples of Greenland had existed long before the Danish arrival, the Inuits' lack of western conceptualisation and vocabulary of sovereignty was enough to merit their non-existence in terms of autonomy over their land. *Cf* for Australia, Anti-Discrimination Commission, 'Aboriginal People in Queensland: A Brief Human Rights History,' 2017, http://hdl.handle.net/10462/pdf/10437, explaining that settlers claimed that Aboriginal peoples did not cultivate the land (no land management practices), and this was the (Lockeian) justification for colonial occupation. The Aboriginal Land Rights (Northern Territory) Act was passed by Commonwealth Parliament in 1976, providing for recognition of Aboriginal land ownership and granting land rights to 11,000 Aboriginal people (and enabling other Aboriginal people to lodge a claim for recognition of traditional ownership of their lands). In 1992, the High Court of Australia handed down its landmark decision in *Mabo v Queensland*, ruling that native title exists over particular kinds of lands – unalienated Crown Lands, national parks and reserves – and that Australia was never *terra nullius*, or empty land: www.abc.net.au/archives/80days/stories/2012/01/19/3412061.htm.

[184] N Seuffert, 'Jurisdiction and nation-building: Tall tales in nineteenth-century Aotearoa/New Zealand', in S McVeigh, *Jurisprudence of Jurisdiction* (New York, Routledge, 2007) 114–34; see too by N Seuffert, *Jurisprudence of National Identity. Kaleidoscopes of Imperialism and Globalisation from Aotearoa New Zealand* (Routledge, 2006), explaining further how territorial jurisdiction contributes to the construction of political subjectivity by tying individuals to the fixed boundaries of the modern nation state. Additional reading on the 'quiet genocide' of the 'stolen generation' of aboriginal children can be found (for example) at https://interactive.aljazeera.com/aje/2017/quite-genocide/index.html.

cartoons, political discourse and journalism, Judith Surkis paints an extraordinary picture of the imbrication between sex, law and sovereignty.[185] As far as the conflict of laws is concerned, she shows how the notion of indigenous 'personal status' was actually used to dissociate the local (or native) religious family law practices from the lands, that, indissociable under the latter, became subject to French civil law and massively transferred to the colonisers.

Some of the far-reaching structural consequences of such regimes, whose deleterious effects extended long into the future, are now acknowledged in contexts of transitional justice and memorial laws and enquiries in various places around the world.[186] Recognition of bygone wrongs is of course very important. However, its downside is emphasised by Fraser and Jaeggi: we are led to separate our present from the past as if we can compensate for historical injustice and turn the page. But these wrongs are ongoing;[187] the more they are denied, the more they are likely to resurface from our collective past.[188] In the same vein, feminist private international legal scholars Karen Knop and Annelise Riles have analysed 'the saga of the comfort women' (forced prostitution of Korean women by the Japanese army) as 'embodying' the return of repressed historical events.[189] One of the (many) significant points made by these scholars is that the simultaneous appearance of multiple statues of the 'comfort women' in many different sites is emblematic of the haunting presence of the past. Globalisation has undoubtedly enabled or accelerated the latter phenomenon, multiplying the places, times and shapes where conflicts arise and subverting earlier linear representations of universal temporality.[190] Indeed, the subconscious (whether individual or collective) knows no chronological time. The past is embroiled in the present as much as the latter captures the future. On this point, 'pluritopical' indigeneous epistemologies, encountered above, better account for the ways in which law creates

[185] Surkis, *Sex, Law, and Sovereignty in French Algeria*.

[186] For instance, in the case of Australia's 'stolen generation' of Aboriginal and Torres Strait Islander children, forcibly removed from their families between 1910 and 1970, Prime Minister Kevin Rudd offered a formal apology on 13 February 2008, on behalf of the Australian parliament. In France, in respect of the colonisation of Algeria, French President Emmanuel Macron (who had, before his election, qualified colonisation as a crime against humanity) proffered a formal apology on 20 September 2021 to Algerians who fought alongside French colonial forces in Algeria's war for independence, and were then massacred and ostracised as traitors.

[187] This point is made repeatedly in the context of structural inequalities affecting colonised indigenous populations, the stolen generation in Australia, the Inuits in Greenland or the descendants of the emancipated slave population of Haiti.

[188] Egregious historical wrongs – usually assessed as economic losses and thereby both measurable and commensurable are not behind us but, as Nancy Fraser points out, an ongoing mode of capitalist expansion (on the same dismal plane: slavery, land grab, apartheid, toxic products, genocide, ecological catastrophes).

[189] K Knop, A Riles, 'Space, Time and Historical Injustice: A Feminist Conflict-of-Laws Approach to the "Comfort Women" Agreement' (2017) 102 *Cornell Law Rev* 853. On collective subjectivities and the return of the repressed, see Mazurel, *L'inconscient ou l'oubli de l'histoire*.

[190] As Viveiros de Castro observes (*Ends of the World*, 114), one of the most significant contemporary debates revolves around the speed of history and its variation. It opposes the philosophical (metaphysical, political, aesthetic) current that proposes a political economy of acceleration and the partisans of a political ecology of deceleration (Stengers, *In Catastrophic Times*) which unfolds into a set of themes which she shares with B Latour: 'hesitation', 'attention', 'diplomacy', and the need for 'making room for others'. As seen above in Part II, the latter are importantly part of the shadow or alternative mode of existence of the conflict of laws.

its own fictional world of 'chronotopes'[191] rather than following its supposedly linear modern temporal trajectory.

II. DISEMBEDDING THE RULE OF LAW

At the core of the political economy, there is a still further form of capture, that of the rule of law itself, or the Enlightenment concepts of free will, reason and subjectivity that undergird it, at least according to its (notoriously elusive) definition in liberal democracies.[192] As observed by Norbert Elias in respect of the history of the latter, there is a paradoxical correlation between the increasing price conferred on individual autonomy as emancipation, and growing social atomisation and alienation.[193] Ultimately, neoliberal legality[194] has transformed the Enlightenment values into a

[191] M Valverde, *Chronotopes of Law: Jurisdiction, Scale and Governance* (Abingdon, Routledge, 2015).

[192] The rule of law is notoriously difficult to define (see the report by Paul Craig for the UK Parliament: https://publications.parliament.uk/pa/ld200607/ldselect/ldconst/151/15115.htm) and moreover loses itself in translation (*Etat de droit, Rechtstaat*). As Paul Craig explains, there is a first (classical legal) approach to the rule of law that is not concerned with the actual content of the law, in the sense of whether the law is just or unjust, provided that the formal precepts of the rule of law are met (clarity, generality, non-retrospectivity etc). The rationale for restricting the rule of law in this manner is that while we may all agree that laws should be just, that their content should be morally sound and that rights should be protected within society, the problem is to bring these issues within the rubric of the rule of law would rob this concept of an independent function. Laws would be condemned or upheld as being in conformity with, or contrary to, the rule of law when the condemnation or praise would simply be reflective of attachment to a particular conception of rights, democracy or the just society. A different view however is taken by those who believe that the rule of law is consubstantially linked to certain fundamental rights. But as Paul Craig further points out, this view requires some choice as to what are to count as fundamental rights, and the more particular meaning ascribed to such rights. In turn, it will reflect assumptions as to the importance of differing interests in society. Of course, any democracy will have some attachment to particular liberty and equality interests. However, significant differences of view exist even amongst those who subscribe to one version or another of liberal belief. In this respect, the issue remains as to how far social and economic interests ought to be protected, given that different visions of democracy, of a communitarian rather than liberal nature, interpret civil/political rights and social/economic rights differently. It is therefore neither fortuitous, nor surprising, that in even among various (common law) systems which possess constitutionally enshrined rights, such as the United States and Canada, there is considerable diversity of opinion as to whether this should be taken to mean some version of liberalism, a pluralist model, or a modified notion of republicanism. This point is equally true of ideas such as legality, rationality, participation, openness, proportionality, procedural fairness and the like, which can be interpreted differently depending upon the more general scheme into which they are to fit. Written from a public law or constitutionalist perspective, all these points apply in respect of the elusiveness of the concept of the rule of law in private law contexts, particularly within the conflict of laws. In the main, the latter is still however largely wedded to a proceduralist conception of the rule of law. Perhaps this is why the advent or 'migration' of fundamental rights in a private international law setting (see C Scott and R Wai, 'Transnational Governance of Corporate Conduct through the Migration of Human Rights Norms: The Potential Contribution of Transnational "Private" Litigation' in C Joerges, P Sand and G Teubner (eds), *Transnational Governance and Constitutionalism* (Oxford, Hart Publishing, 2004) 287–319) generates such strong doctrinal resistance (although as the above publication makes clear, the political economy of such resistance is a more obvious explanation).

[193] Elias, *Über den Prozess der Zivilisation*, 24.

[194] It is important here to distinguish (once more) between different liberalisms (hyper, embedded, political/economic, neoliberalism). Neoliberalism has become the dominant form and is often mistaken for a deregulatory hyper liberal project (in the sense that it would oppose state intervention). However, the neoliberal state is heavy-handed (which does not mean it is redistributive). Moreover, as seen above, it is perfectly compatible with democracy, to the extent that the world is 'made safe', and rights as long as they

form of instrumental rationality, amnesiac or indifferent to context.[195] This reversal goes far to explain the hegemony of economic calculus under the guise of an impartial, determinate, and humane rule of law.[196] Section II.A below attempts to track the ways in which law has accompanied, reinforced or even incentivised such a shift. A key point here is the emergence of the private legal depiction of contract – the meeting of two free wills – as the core organisational idea by virtue of which the contemporary forms of global capitalism are governed.[197]

Weighing in on the 'private' side of the law, the contractual form has facilitated the creation of free-floating systems (from global markets, to delocalised industries, to global value chains) in the name of individual autonomy. In other words, the public/private divide within the law has done much to protect informal power from external constraints or social pressures and to allow it to flourish, untrammelled. The 'private', in the international economic order – by which we are to understand, an ordering 'beyond the state', or beyond the pale of the jurisdiction of any particular state – is taken to signify the absence of any issue involving transnational political power.[198] As we have already seen above, one of the most enduring and significant effects of the public/private divide in liberal thought has been to divert attention away from the ways in which private law structures and justifies power. It does so to a large extent invisibly, as if its institutions were perfectly natural. As David Kennedy points out, it is usual to think of law as *regulating* the basic elements of global political and economic life, in providing 'the sinews of a constituted order' but not as involved in the very *creation* of markets, or money, or debt.[199] This of course has important implications for the content of our contemporary neoliberal 'common sense'.[200] The conviction that the economy is largely private or governed by an anonymous collective (non-human) entity known as 'the market' occludes the distributive issues and diffuses blame for deleterious economic consequences. Moreover, there is no such thing as an 'unregulated market'.[201]

reinforce individual entitlement and concern morals rather than economic reform). It can easily take on constitutional garb (see H Alviar Garcia, 'Neoliberalism as a Form of Authoritarian Constitutionalism' in H Alviar Garcia and G Frankenberg (eds), *Authoritarian Constitutionalism: Critique and Appraisal* (Cheltenham, Elgar, 2019) 37–56.

[195] One strong strand of critique consists in showing that the abstraction of laws from the specific social contexts in which they arise obscures their indeterminacy, their historical contingency, and the power relations underpinning them. For such a critique, see the various contributions to 'understanding the role of law in the neoliberal project' in Brabazon, *Neoliberal Legality*.

[196] Brabazon, *Neoliberal Legality*, 'Understanding neoliberal legality', 7.

[197] See Cutler, Dietz, *The Politics of Private Transnational Governance by Contract*.

[198] On the processes of depoliticisation of international space, see above.

[199] D Kennedy, *A World of Struggle – How Power, Law, and Expertise Shape Global Political Economy* (Princeton NJ, Princeton University Press, 2016).

[200] D Harvey, *A Brief History of Neoliberalism* (Oxford, Oxford University Press, 2005).

[201] In his discussion of the 'constitution of private law', Harm Shepel (*The Constitution of Private Governance* (Oxford, Hart Publishing, 2005) 406 observes that 'blaming the markets for the inadequacies of public – domestic and international – policies, as if the markets were "out there", skittish, autonomous, unshaped by law and policy, and subject to whims of their own invention – is more than suspect'. Markets are social – and therefore, legal constructs, so that the action of not plying discipline is, of course, in itself a form of regulation; *cf* L Pauly, 'Global Finance, Political Authority, and the Problem of Legitimation' in Hall and Biersteker (eds), *The Emergence of Private Authority in Global Governance Governance* (Cambridge, Cambridge University Press, 2002) 76, 77: 'markets have always obscured distributive issues and helped diffuse blame for negative economic consequences'.

In this context, private international law can be understood as the closest the law gets at present, to framing the global dimension (that is, again, 'beyond the state') of social and economic interaction in any systematic way. It has also been uniquely instrumental in promoting the libertarian idea of contract as untrammelled 'party autonomy', that migrated from the domestic to the international context at the turn of the twentieth century. The principle of 'party autonomy' is arguably the single most significant enabling factor in the contemporary transition from liberalism to neoliberalism,[202] which has seen sovereign states relinquish political control individually and collectively over the global economy. In order to better understand the involvement of private international law in this process, a short preliminary reflection is in order about the wider transformation of our legal commonsense, consciousness, or *episteme*. This is what Latour calls the 'U-turn' *(volte-face)* of Darwinism[203] (section II.A). The terrain will be prepared then to focus on the ways in which 'party autonomy' as an apparently enlightened, or Enlightenment value, became a licence to 'disembed', enabling the untrammelled growth of private economic power as if out of reach of, and above, the state (section II.B).

A. The Darwinian U-turn: A Brief but Giddy Detour

Freedom, in David Harvey's analysis, is the discursive key to the success of neoliberalism.[204] Yet in such a context, freedom exists only within the rules of the game and is therefore highly constrained.[205] A similar paradox affects the value of individual autonomy, that signifies not emancipation from but dependency upon the (transcendent or mysterious) market forces described above. Furthermore, by virtue of a series of analogous inversions, responsibility is trivialised in turn, supporting the notion that development is predicated upon individual entrepreneurial activity while social relations are encoded as market competition. Instead of subjects being responsible for their collective political choices, our Cartesian selves have become 'economised', atomised, self-alienated[206] and indifferent to the world we inhabit.[207]

[202] On the difference, see above, 253.

[203] B Latour & S Srum, 'Human social origins: Oh please, tell us another story' (1986) *J Social Biol Slrucr* 169–87; *cf* Descola, *Les formes du Visible* 349.

[204] Harvey, *Neoliberalism*.

[205] See too Brabazon, *Neoliberal Legality* 8, pointing out that the neoliberal project autonomises individuals *within* the game.

[206] As Pelluchon writes, on the question of alienation of self, our very subjectivity is part of the capture (*Les lumières à l'âge du vivant*, 98). What she calls the *Schema* (our collective world view including our legal consciousness) spreads its roots deep down in our archaic psyche, as in our social structures. But, however deeply rooted and enduring, there is nothing natural about the patterns, bifurcations, categories it engenders (see above 131 et s.) and nothing inevitable about the alienation. See too (for a far more critical view) on the links between atomisation, neoliberal experimentation and enlightened thought, N Klein, *The Shock Doctrine* (London, Penguin 2007) 118 et seq.

[207] These are all recurring leitmotifs in critical theory. As Poul Kjaer explains (*The Law of Political Economy* 119–23), the classical modernist narrative, as embodied in the advancements of the Atlantic revolutionary movements, in Europe, North and South America, from the 1770s to the 1820s, implied a focus on progress, emancipation and freedom, while the 'dark side', from Hegel onwards, has been consistently problematised through terms such as *alienation* (Marx), *anomie* (Durkheim), *colonialisation* (Habermas),

If our eyes are 'wide shut' to this distortion, it is because modern liberal democracy and its ideal of individual autonomy appeared in a very different context. The latter was the need to free populations from both divine right and the arbitrariness of terrestrial rulers.[208] While we must still ensure against the return of either,[209] nevertheless, today, 'nothing protects us from the divine right of capital' and attendant private power.[210]

This is of course not to suggest that earlier ages of modernity, including the very Enlightenment that produced individual autonomy, were historically golden. They involved a move away from (wild) nature into a sovereign order,[211] designed to guarantee the sanctity of local populations and later of property. However, for many, even in the world's colonial centre, the rise of democracy, political liberalism and private property was 'a false tree of liberty'.[212] In the colonial peripheries, moreover, it accompanied egregious expropriation and extraction, as seen above. There were clearly, then as now, deep collective blind-spots or cognitive dissonances in political, ethical and legal thought that made the supposed economic imperatives of enclosure and empire seem 'natural' (necessary or inevitable) and indeed compliant with the very values they undermined. The point here is to understand the ways in which, then and now, our specifically *legal* consciousness refracts a deeper (paralegal) register.[213]

de-differentiation (Luhmann), *disciplination* (Elias and Foucault), *existential fear* (Kierkegaard), *rationalisation* (Weber), *reification* (Adorno and Horkheimer), and *technification* (Heidegger). Kjaer analyses this as ultimately pointing in the direction of either a longing for, or at least serving as reflections on the consequences of a lost world understood and observed in holistic terms.

[208] The Atlantic revolutions in Western modernity (the Enlightenment) took place through processes of secularisation (as opposed to theological determinism), constitutional arrangements (ensuring the ultimate sovereignty of the people) and human rights (acknowledging individual dignity and freedom as protection against arbitrary intrusions of the institutionalised power). All these are important and deemed to be essential to democracy and the (elusive) rule of law.

[209] This book was written before the invasion of Ukraine. On the contemporary rise of authoritarianism in constitutional guise, see Alviar and Frankenberg, *Authoritarian Constitutionalism*.

[210] B Anderson, *Imagined Communities: Reflections on the Origin and Spread of Nationalism* (Verso, 2006).

[211] Latour (*Enquête*, 470) describes the encounter of the Moderns with other peoples 'strange enough' to not share their blindness towards the embroiled proliferation of everything that escapes the frames of economic apparatuses of calculation!

[212] Marks, *A False Tree of Liberty*. Etienne Balibar's radical critique of 'universals' (*Des Universels, Essais et conferences* (Galilée, 2016)) leaves little standing of these pillars of liberal thought. Far from putting an end to domination or asymmetry, institutions (family, state, church) are biased, and equality is a chimera as long as comparison is determined from an Archimedean point. Private property represented freedom from feudalism in the Enlightenment, revolutionary context, but then became dissociated from equality and exclusive of the commons, became enclosure. These historical and philosophical views are amply confirmed by the contemporary economic analysis of private property by T Piketty, *Capital and Ideology* (Cambridge MA, Harvard University Press, 2020); *cf* similarly, from a legal perspective, Pistor, *The Code of Capital*.

[213] See, borrowing from (social) consciousness studies the idea of a specifically legal consciousness, as the marker of an era and a means of historicising successive styles of law according to the dominant world view, D Kennedy, 'Three Globalizations of Law and Legal Thought: 1850–2000' in D Trubek and A Santos (eds), *The New Law and Economic Development* (Cambridge MA, Harvard University Press, 2010). As the text above suggests, 'consciousness' in this understanding is the reflection of a deeper psyche or moved by a collective subconscious. In the 'U-turn' as described by Bruno Latour, modernity came with its own psychic economy, an interiorised censure device. Transcendental concepts such as 'society' have separated us from our own materiality (or phenomenological bodies, as will be seen below). Economics claimed to be science. Nature itself became a mode of veridiction, naturalising what is precisely not 'natural', while blinding us to our entanglement with our surroundings as seen above.

In this respect, Fraser and Jaeggi describe the institution of capital as subject, 'as if it moves the whole mechanics',[214] depriving us of agency and cutting us off from a more ethical life, in which sociability is something other than the juxtaposition of rival existences.

One might say then that reason itself is captured in the process.[215] In the Enlightenment project, reason was a method (not a metaphysical assumption about the world[216]) for distinguishing the true from the false. It was the mark of the emancipation of the subject from the determinism of the transcendent forces that were so deeply embedded in the earlier *episteme*.[217] Authoritarianism and the teleology of history were replaced by political liberalism,[218] and the belief in divine forces by science. However, the emancipation was illusionary, or at any rate partial and short-lived. Notably, it did not prevent the great reversal that Latour describes as the *volte-face* of Darwinism.[219] Third world critique largely endorses this point on Darwinism from the perspective of racial capitalism (and its negation of alterity).[220] Within the new scheme, democracy through law was necessary, but only to the extent it was useful for capital (as in the example of property rights). Religion as superstition was expelled from the public sphere (into 'privacy'), but all too soon its place was invaded by 'the private'.[221] Classical legal theory was grounded on private law (property, contract), which progressively became disembedded from its social infrastructure.[222] This was

[214] Fraser and Jaeggi, *Capitalism. A Critical Conversation*, 27.

[215] *Cf* Pelluchon, *Les lumières à l'âge du vivant*, 27.

[216] Koskenniemi, 'International Law and raison d'état', 323.

[217] Foucault, *Des mots et des choses.*

[218] However, on the ambivalence of the 'fathers' of political liberalism (such as JS Mill) and the elusiveness (and double prong) of the rule of law, see above 248.

[219] Latour, *Enquête*, 441 et seq.

[220] S Santiago, in A Gazzola (ed) *The Space in-between: Essays on Latin American Culture, Latin America in translation* (Durham NC, Duke University Press, 2001) 17, writes on Darwin's evolutionary discovery, 'there is no doubt that the struggle for life works perfectly as a justification for the victory of the European from the great discoveries onward as a form of supremacy, including racial supremacy. Man is the wolf of man – this would be the proverbial form of the ethics of adventure when it is transformed into a standard of conduct on land'. On the same page he observes, 'The theories of the supremacy of the white race, established by the conscious or unconscious racism of the nineteenth century, do not discard the metaphorization of human relations by the relationships between men and animals. They do not discard the white man's position as a "hunter" (of animals, of women, and of nonwhite men)'.

[221] On our post-theological political economy, see E Santner, *The Weight of all Flesh: On the Subject-Matter of Political Economy* (New York, Oxford University Press, 2016). This account is well completed by that of S Zuboff, 'The Age of Surveillance Capitalism: The Fight for a Human Future at the New Frontier of Power' (2019) *Public Affairs*. As Corinne Pelluchon explains (*Les lumières à l'âge du vivant*), the problem is not that the frontier between public and private is fading, but that the private invades everything as public space is downgraded into a virtual one.

[222] On Polanyi's concept of 'disembeddeness', see above 224. Poul Kjaer (*The Law of Political Economy*) draws an interesting structural parallel between the respective works of Hayek and Polanyi. In 1944, they published *The Road to Serfdom* and *The Great Transformation* respectively and, in doing so, asked the same question: why had totalitarianism emerged and succeeded? The answers that they gave were, however, diametrically opposed to one another. Hayek's answer was that the economy had not been differentiated enough from the rest of society, ie, that society had become characterised by de-differentiation and a capture of the economy by politics. For Polanyi, on the other hand, the main problem was a society in which the economy had become 'too detached' and dis-embedded from the rest of society.

the shift from the modern liberal project to the late-modern neoliberal scheme, a further U-turn in the form of a complete dissociation of the economic order from social processes. Universalism embodied an aspiration to the common good but (as seen above, in the context of making the world 'safe' for investment) cast discredit on local politics, seen as parochial, corrupt or uninformed.

In what follows below, the particular focus will be the instrumentalisation, within this broader shift, of the idea of individual autonomy. The empowerment of the individual through the use of reason and the capacity to decide the forms of social (economic, technological) life was certainly not a project for the atomisation of our collective being-together, an alienation of self, or a state of anomy mirroring an analogous distancing and disregard for nature as for other parts (classes, races) of humanity.[223] And yet, within the neoliberal scheme, autonomy has become synonymous with individual utility (or profit-seeking), competition (for survival) and self-conservation (at the price of all other values); it is a deeply embedded efficiency-enhancing principle, emptied of all ethical content.[224] Once again, because this scheme reaches down into the deep layers of our (collective and individual) psyche, it is difficult to grasp that there is nothing natural about the patterns, bifurcations, categories it creates and nor indeed is there anything inevitable about the somatic effects it induces. In this last respect, our contemporary political economy is aptly depicted by Eric Santner as a somatic condition of our body politic, resulting from the transfer of the unbearable burden of sovereignty from the king (or his divine body) to the people (as body politic).[225]

The usefulness of exploring the role of private international law in the encoding[226] of this instrumental rationality lies in its ability to provide an emblematic illustration of the ways in which legality has participated in this long process. It has, as it were, set the tone and provided the infrastructure of the disembedded neoliberal

[223] Echoing Marx, Max Horkheimer argued that the history of (hu)man's efforts to subjugate nature is also the history of (hu)man's subjugation by (hu)man (*Théorie traditionnelle et théorie critique* (1937), trans C Maillard and S Muller (Paris, Gallimard, 1974)). In his *Economic and Philosophical Manuscripts* of 1844, Marx explained the worker's four-fold alienation under capitalist modernity (from nature, from the products of his labour, from other people, and from himself): the immediacy of nature is lost, and 'every self-estrangement of man from himself and nature is manifested in the relationship he sets up between other men and himself and nature.' (see A Schnaiberg, *The Environment: From Surplus to Scarcity* (Oxford, Oxford University Press, 1980).

[224] Meaning the freedom to think. See Pelluchon, *Les Lumières à l'âge du vivant*, 121, proposing an ethic that decolonises our imaginaries, allowing us to contest the dominant *Schema* and thereby escape from it. Neoliberalism produces, or depends upon, a 'heteronomous morality' that rests on dogma and custom. We labour under the illusion (Fraser and Jaeggi, *Capitalism. A Critical Conversation*, 128) that capital is the subject and we are its servants. This is of course the question of Gramscian hegemony: how do some ideas become so natural as to be part of our consciousness, blind us to cognitive dissonances, and indeed turn us into 'sleepwalkers', hurtling towards self-induced disaster? On the mysterious hegemony of law and its relationship to feelings, desires or effects of those who are subject to it, see H Carvalho et al, 'Concept Hegemony', *Critical Legal Pocketbook* (Counterpress, 2021) 72. See too S Ahmed, *The Cultural Politics of Emotion* (Edinburgh, Edinburgh University Press, 2004). On effects within the law and the emotional turn in human rights law and discourse, see A Katsiginis, 'The Affective Structures of International Human Rights', PhD dissertation, Sciences Po Law School, forthcoming.

[225] Santner, *The Royal Remains*. Thus we live our lives as frenetic 'busybodies' (*The Weight of All Flesh*).

[226] See again the coding metaphor used by Pistor, *The Code of Capital*.

order 'beyond the state' (that is, beyond the reach of local politics.[227] As Poul Kjaer forcefully points out, even as the Hegelian state triumphed in our political imaginaries, these were always underlain by baroque economic assemblages that straddled the public and the private, in legal form.[228] However, as seen above, this does not mean that states, through public international (financial) institutions, multilateral or bilateral (trade and investment) treaties or local market-supportive regulation, are absent; it merely signifies that neoliberal state intervention (including, importantly, the choice *not* to regulate[229]) unbridles market freedom rather than the reverse. The important point here is that the coding operations of private international law, particularly through the discursive use of contractual or party freedom, tend to keep the operation of power below the surface – that of a series of seemingly natural legal technologies.[230]

Among the consequences of this flattening effect, arbitrators are deciding governance issues, and sovereignty-free actors are designing their own normative space through the tools of contract law, with the approval of the courts. Illustrations of both of these trends are abundant and the cases well-known in private international law.[231] Thus the *Chevron* saga, in which an arbitration tribunal disqualified the judgment of the court of a sovereign state in respect of environmental and human damage resulting from oil extractive activities, with (more than) a little help from international

[227] It has been argued by H Dagan and A Dorfman, advocating a 'relational' private law that the normative DNA of the latter contains 'interpersonal human rights' ('Interpersonal Human Rights and Transnational Private Law' (2016), https://ssrn.com/abstract=2860275 or http://dx.doi.org/10.2139/ssrn.2860275. Far from the neoliberal (or indeed libertarian) ideal, 'this DNA is premised instead on a profound commitment to reciprocal respect to self-determination and substantive equality'. This conception is linked to private international law, recalling the approach advocated a century ago by the all but forgotten Jitta, as transnational private law as the 'private law of mankind' (see R Banu, *Nineteenth Century Perspectives on Private International Law* (Oxford, Oxford University Press, 2018). These ideas remind us that private law (like law in general) can lend itself to any number of readings. The political content of the law (Law I) crystallises according to the balance of forces involved, and the pressures brought to bear in various contexts. At any one time, this can become 'naturalised', so as to be perceived as inevitable and, to a large extent, pre-political. This is precisely what has happened to the principle of party autonomy, which carries neoliberal legality into the field of international contracting and dispute resolution.

[228] Kjaer, *The Law of Political Economy*; H Brunkhorst, *Critical Theory of Legal Revolutions: Evolutionary Perspectives* (London, Bloomsbury, 2014).

[229] See above. As we have seen, not plying regulation is a form of regulation, and an extremely powerful one.

[230] Some of the hidden power issues are the following: how did multinationals emerge as powerful economic actors with no correlative constraints from corporate, competition or ordinary tort law? How did 'private judicial services' become an industry in themselves, closing the loop around self-regulating sectors of the economy, such as insurance or finance? How did foreign investment gain a special immunity from local social and environmental regulation, on a world level? How did global value chains grow out of egregious violations of human rights, despite solemn and converging commitments on the part of states and private actors to eradicate slave labour? Why are structural or intergenerational forms of inequality not part of the quest for justice that is otherwise pursued by the courts? And why do various policies within domestic jurisdictions that seek (more or less successfully) to curb the excesses of individual profit-seeking – concern for weaker parties, protection of non-contracting stakeholders, considerations of the general interest – lose their relevance whenever economic flows take place beyond state boundaries? The 'judicial services' mentioned above cover several industries, of which commercial and investment arbitration, but now too various newly lucrative forms of mediation that are appearing in the world's free zones (see, flagging this development, the United Nations Convention on International Settlement Agreements Resulting from Mediation (New York, 2018) ('Singapore Convention on Mediation').

[231] See the cases assembled and analysed in H Muir Watt et al (eds), *Global Private International Law*, including the *Chevron* saga below (with analyses by D Fernandez Arroyo and L Caballo Pineiro).

investment law.[232] Another notorious example is Lloyd's of London successful overseas enforcement of judgments and awards in the United States against investors who had been deprived of the informational protection of the federal Securities Act through a highly sophisticated combination of private legislation, choice of law, and jurisdictional side-stepping.[233] Yet a further telling illustration in the area of financial markets can be found in the context of the legal aftermath of the financial collapse of Lehman Brothers.[234] These are all effects, in the legal field, of 'disembedded' liberalism, naturalised within our neoliberal legal commonsense. As will be seen, private international law actively provides the tools – governance through contract; the 'plug-in' network of international arbitration; the neutralisation of mandatory rules of local public policy; the free 'delocalised' movement of private awards – through which private actors have acceded to unshackle themselves from the constraints prevalent in the domestic sphere. At the core lies the (baroque) '*contrat sans loi*', or the principle of party autonomy in private international law, to which we shall now return.

B. Autonomy as a Licence to Disembed

The principle of party autonomy empowers private actors to soar – metaphorically and normatively – above domestic regulations and circumvent local court systems.

[232] An arbitrator acting under the aegis of the Permanent Court of Arbitration at the Hague ordered provisional measures to prevent the enforcement of the judgment of Ecuador, the sovereign party, to the extent that its award of damages to indigenous peoples dwelling at the site of the oil and gas extraction interfered with the protection of a private property right guaranteed under the bilateral agreement. See Permanent Court of Arbitration at the Hague, Interim Award of 9 February 2011. On 25 January 2012, the same tribunal asserted its jurisdiction to decide on the company's liability under an investment treaty. Then a global anti-suit injunction was ordered in favour of Chevron, only to be lifted a year later (see District Court, Southern District of New York, Orders of 6 February and 7 April 2011; Federal Court of Appeals for the Second Circuit, Judgment of 17 March 2011). On 26 January 2012, Judge Gerard Lynch of the US Court of Appeals for the Second Circuit said that such an injunction could only be sought 'defensively, in response to an attempted enforcement'. In the present case, the Ecuadorian plaintiffs 'made no effort to enforce their judgment in New York (nor indeed, in any other jurisdiction)'. The Ecuadorian judgment was handed down by the Court of Sucumbíos, Lago Agrio, Ecuador, on 14 February 2011. The arbitration under the BIT here was a United Nations Commission on International Trade Law (UNCITRAL) arbitration, but the legal devices used are those described in the text.

[233] See *Roby v Corporation of Lloyd's*, 996 F 2d 1353 (2d Cir 1993); *Bonny v Society of Lloyd's*, 3 F 3d 156 Cir (1993).

[234] See above 258. It was in the 'OTC' (over the counter) market that the disastrous credit swap agreements took place, at the heart of the legal saga. As explained by Hugh Collins, in 'Flipping Wreck', this market 'flourished internationally on the basis of a belief that the ISDA Master Agreement, together with its supplementary standardised documentation, constituted a form of *lex mercatoria*', providing a comprehensive system of self-regulation (on the artefactual and non-normative nature of the latter, see A Riles, 'A New Agenda for the Cultural Study of Law: Taking on the Technicalities' (2005) 53 *Buffalo LR* 973, observing that these standardised documents are usually and mistakenly read by lawyers as text, subject to the usual rules of legal hermeneutics). The master agreement was devised by all the major players – that is, the banks and their lawyers – with a view to providing an appropriate system of checks and balances between the parties to the transactions. The Lehman bankruptcy then gave rise to a conflict of laws case (see H Muir Watt et al (eds), *Global Private International Law*, 271 et seq) in which British and American courts, reaching utterly contradictory decisions, approached the legal issues in terms of their own national (and conflicting) insolvency laws, all the while ignoring the comprehensive system – as powerful as it is problematic – of self-regulation devised by the various financial players in the OTC market.

Now enshrined in national codes worldwide[235] and indeed still expanding as a central element of transnational soft law,[236] this principle gives parties to an international business agreement freedom to choose the law (that is, as will be seen below, the rules of any national legal system) governing their contract. Understood more broadly, the ability to choose extends to the forum competent to hear disputes arising under the contract, and this jurisdictional option in turn implies the possibility to contract out of state legal systems altogether, in favour of private arbitration. Checks on this freedom (in the form of 'regulatory touchdown',[237] exceptions, restrictions, controls or 'choke points') remain rare (in legislative or judicial practice, as in the specialised literature[238]). Yet although apparently technical – or 'natural', in a contractual setting – freedom of choice has become the foundation of a whole parallel world of private transnational ordering, complete with its own institutions and governing principles. Its role is rarely challenged by scholarship within the field of the conflict of laws,[239] any more than the various supporting fictions[240] which have worked to ensure its expansion. Such widespread and unquestioned acceptance points to its status as a foundational myth of private international economic law.[241]

[235] For an exhaustive depiction, see A Mills, *Party Autonomy in Private International Law* (Cambridge, Cambridge University Press, 2018).

[236] On its relationship to the *lex mercatoria*, see above 237.

[237] R Wai, 'Transnational Liftoff and Juridical Touchdown: The Regulatory Function of Private International Law in an Era of Globalization' (2002) 40 *Columbia Journal of Transnational Law* 209.

[238] The interests of the internal consumer market have however led the European Court of Justice to attempt a countermove to the extreme jurisdictional emancipation of arbitration in certain Member States (such as France), in a balancing act made acutely difficult because arbitration is excluded from the scope of European Union instruments and indeed its 'autonomy' is hotly defended by the arbitration industry (of which the sociology was depicted early on by Y Dezalay and B Garth, *Dealing in Virtue International Commercial Arbitration and the Construction of a Transnational Legal Order* (Chicago, Chicago University Press, 1996). For the moves to control awards, see the tone set by ECJ in Case C-126/97 *Eco Swiss China Time Ltd v Benetton International NV* of 1 June 1999 (on the jurisdiction of national courts to annul arbitration awards); on the battle engaged with the arbitration industry over the perceived intrusion of EU law, see H Muir Watt et al, *Le Tournant Global en Droit international privé* (Paris, Pédone, 2020), 'Quelle concurrence des juridictions privées? De Mitsubishi à Achmea', p. 149 et seq, with an analysis of the controversial *Achmea* case (Case C-284/16, ECJ 6 March 2018) by A Farhadi, p.169 et seq. Across the Atlantic, federal courts have been less inclined to give up a threshold control (see G Bermann and G Cordero-Moss, 'Free-wheeling judgments/awards: Mitsubishi Motors Corp. v. Soler Chrysler-Plymouth, Inc.', in H Muir Watt et al, *Global private international law*, Chapter 4), although, conversely, arbitration has spread to the consumer market.

[239] There are notable exceptions however: Wai, 'Transnational Liftoff and Juridical Touchdown'; Cutler, Dietz, *The Politics of Private Transnational Governance by Contract.* On the state of the art, see too, H Muir Watt, *Aspects économiques*, préc. However, the bulk of the scholarship reproduces conventional law and economics accounts of party autonomy as geared to individual justice (see M Lehmann, 'Liberating the Individual from Battles Between States: Justifying Party Autonomy in Conflict of Laws' (2008) 41 *Vand J Transnat'l L* 381, 413 or, of course, efficiency (see G Ruhl, 'Party Autonomy in the Private International Law of Contracts: Transatlantic Convergence and Economic Efficiency' (2007) *Comparative Research in Law & Political Economy*. Research Paper No 4/2007, http://digitalcommons.osgoode.yorku.ca/clpe/227, taking up from the link between party autonomy and regulatory competition, but, crucially, omitting the critical thrust), or indeed ancillary to wider projects in support of international arbitration (particularly in the many publications relating to the Hague principles promoting party choice of law in international contracts, cited above).

[240] One powerful fiction is the idea that the private arbitrator is the natural judge of the international legal order: see G Cuniberti, *Rethinking International Commercial Arbitration: Towards Default Arbitration* (Cheltenham, Edward Elgar, 2017).

[241] Indeed, its success has been unimpeded by the fact that significant issues as to its real ambit remain unsettled, as will be shown below. Nor does it seem to matter that despite its Kantian pedigree, its dominant

Excepting the (legendary) invention of party autonomy in connection with matrimonial property under the *Ancien régime* by Charles Dumoulin (or de Moliensis),[242] its first traceable use within the conflict of laws in an economic context seems to have been in early twentieth-century French judicial practice, to justify upholding the gold standard in international transactions.[243] In this context of growing international trade, consolidation of empire and monetary instability, it emerged as an early derogatory regime for cross-border contracts.[244] Thereafter, the idea of contractual autonomy prospered as a key methodological concept with profound (and certainly unforeseen) implications in terms of global governance, serving the progressive liberalisation of cross-border flows of capital, goods and services. As such, it fulfilled a significant governance function in creating an enabling environment for private sector activity in the context of a globally integrated economy. Moreover, it continues to provide crucial discursive support for the powerful imaginary – and legal fiction – of an autonomous (that is, disembedded) private transnational legal order, shedding discredit on local regulatory policies as parochial or protectionist. Above all, its operation enables regulatory arbitrage on a massive scale – the practice termed 'barrier-crossing' by economists, as seen above – transforming public regulation into private product. In this regard, then, it is key to the reversal of the relationship between law and market that is the very hallmark of neoliberalism.[245]

Such a reversal took place through an imperceptible change, a form of methodological slippage, in the original purport of contractual freedom in international contracting. In its early justifications, free party choice of law owes as much to conventional contract theory as it does to the Westphalian model of the public international legal order. The reasons for which any sovereign state would allow private actors to contract out of its own rules and substitute those of another were to be found both in the purported 'special needs' of cross-border private transactions[246]

justification is essentially utilitarian, linked to the needs of international trade. Moreover, neither the functionalist arguments drawn from governmental interests analysis, nor the potential democratic deficit resulting from the permission to contract out of local rules, nor indeed the uncertain economic rationality underlying the apparent indifference of states to free-riding by foreign parties on proven or novel regulatory models, detract from its remarkable success.

[242] Dumoulin, a lawyer practising at the bar of the (judicial) Parliament of Paris, was retained in 1525 by the heirs of the du Ganay family to sort out a conflict of laws as between the customs of Paris and Burgundy relating to marital property (common or separate). His argument (which triumphed), was that the custom of Paris applied (and the property was common) by reason of an implied choice of law (implied by the choice of the spouses' first marital domicile): See FK Juenger, 'Marital Property and the Conflict of Laws: A Tale of Two Countries' (1981) 81 *Columbia Law Review* 1061–79.

[243] *American Trading Co v Quebec Steamship Co.* (Cass civ, 5 déc 1910, Rev dr int, 1911. 395; JDI, 1912. 1156; S, 1991. 1. 129): '*La loi applicable aux contrats, soit en ce qui concerne leur formation, soit quant à leurs effets et conditions, est celle que les parties ont adoptée*'. France did not follow the gold standard at the time, so that such a reference was invalid under domestic contract law.

[244] For the context, see A Bloomfield, *Monetary Policy Under the Gold Standard, 1880 to 1914* (Federal Reserve Bank of New York, 1959).

[245] This shift from public to private is at the very core of the neoliberal project and as such, a key move in the 'self-immunisation' of the economic order: see above 244.

[246] The 'special needs of international commercial intercourse' is a recurrent discourse in the case law and scholarship all around the liberal world: see notably, in the United States, *The Bremen v Zapata Off-Shore Co*, 407 US 1 (1972) and the analysis in this respect by L Bizikova and A Brandão de Oliveira, in H Muir Watt et al (eds), *Global Private International Law*, 15 et seq. Like international commercial arbitration, whose growth followed on the generalisation of party autonomy as a foundational principle of choice of

and the dilution of the claim of any one polity to regulate such non-domestic transactions exclusively.[247] The private law perspective saw obvious economic advantage in allowing a free hand to the market, subject however to considerations of public policy; but such policy concerns were attenuated when the market was only partially domestic and therefore less likely to affect the local economy negatively. The public law view was that freedom to choose was a revocable concession by a presumptively like-minded community of sovereign states desirous above all of promoting the reciprocal benefits of international trade; there was certainly an underlying assumption of mutual trust among liberal regimes.

The important point here is that both these justifications implied that sovereign states were unconcerned, or their polities less affected, by agreements that did not directly involve their domestic economy; in a world where market was coextensive with territory, this idea translated methodologically into a presumption of territoriality of national regulation (as seen above). Social and economic policies were non-negotiable in homogenous cases which fell clearly within their regulatory ambit; conversely, such policies were not endangered by private contracting-out when the underlying economic exchange, bearing foreign (non-territorial) connections, was not perceived to 'belong' to the local economy. In such instances, once the threshold of the international crossed, the tone was that of an emancipation of the supra-local legal order from parochial concerns as embodied in the municipal or domestic law of any particular nation state, deemed maladjusted to the (indeterminate) needs of the brave new modern, post-parochial, world.[248] Briefly put, a consensual legal regime relating to free choice of law and forum was slowly aligning on the budding needs of what would become financialised global capitalism, through the invisible hand of the conflict of laws. This claim may seem extreme in the light of the broad contemporary consensus on the virtues of party choice (or, as David Harvey points out, the rallying virtues of individual freedom[249]). A short detour in further technical technique is called for at this point, therefore, before we sum up some of the conclusions to be drawn from its exploration in terms of the political economy.

At the early stages of this (great[250]) transformation, while free contractual choice of law was encouraged in the interests of cross-border commerce, its corollary was the assumption that the community of states – as represented in any given instance, by the state of which the legal system has been chosen, or the one which was sufficiently closely connected to the parties to justify the jurisdiction of its courts – would accommodate

law, the empowerment of private actors caters purportedly to the special needs of international economic intercourse.

[247] This element is important and explains why attempts to introduce the question of democratic deficit within the conflict of laws (how is it that parties can substitute their own choice of rules for democratically determined local laws?) have largely failed.

[248] There is a parallel 'special needs' discourse in the field of international arbitration. Interestingly, choice of (public or private) forum was allowed and encouraged in the United States before and to a greater extent than free choice of law, whereas, in European jurisdictions, the reverse was true and 'party autonomy' in respect of the selection of the governing law was established well before jurisdictional choice (see for the comparative historical evolution, H Muir Watt, 'Aspects économiques').

[249] See above 252.

[250] The context is that described by Polanyi, *The Great Transformation*, see above 224.

the requirements of the common good. Under either of the views described above, the power thus conceded to private actors to harness available state legislation to the needs of their cross-border transactions was therefore conditional on requirements ascribed to the rule of law. In this context, the latter was understood, in its procedural, private law version,[251] to encapsulate values of 'legal security' (closure, predictability, the upholding of bargains and insurance against the arbitrary intrusion of public authority, notably that of courts). Indeed, under the (early twentieth-century) paradigm of embedded liberalism, the relationship between state and market, law and territorial polity, signified that party autonomy in international contracting was destined to be exercised within a political framework that ensured the ultimate authority of public law. Party choice of law was a carefully monitored concession by the liberal sovereign. No unbridled '*contrat sans loi*', then, as its first opponents feared. Rather, a freedom to be subject to the sovereign legal order of one's choice, with the benevolent approval of all the others, in a form of mutual recognition of the substantive equivalence of all their market regulation.[252]

This explains the following three requirements or limitations on party choice. However, as will become apparent, none of these, in the contemporary legal context, fulfils the function of safeguarding the public interest for which it was initially designed. The first is the public (meaning, state-based or approved) origin of the chosen law, so as to prevent parties from cherry-picking or resorting to wholly 'private' rules.[253] The fear inspired by the concept of 'private legislation' may or may not be justified: it could be, at least as is frequently argued, that the content of the new law merchant (or *lex mercatoria*) has now developed sufficiently to present a coherent, reasonably complete and generally acceptable set of operative principles; it is also arguable that carefully thought out principles of substantive contract law drafted at an international level may be more valuable and adjusted to the needs of cross-border trade than many state laws which might be less progressive, less clear, more parochial, etc. In economic terms, it is often argued that the burden of over-regulation could be an evil greater than excessive freedom in the international sphere. Be all this as it may (or may not) be, although many legal systems allow parties to choose any law in the world, with no requirement as to geographical linkage to the state whose law is thus chosen and no condition as to the completeness, modernity or democratic legitimacy

[251] On the elusive content of the rule of law, even among liberal theories, see above. The 'new private law' scholarship today has abandoned the classic procedural terrain for a more human rights or 'relational' conception of the rule of law (see notably, H Dagan, *A Liberal Theory of Property* (Cambridge, Cambridge University Press, 2021)).

[252] Similar theoretical premises are also to be found, outside the field of contract, at the heart of the conflict of laws. The latter presupposes a certain commonality of normative preferences among like-minded (and pre-regulatory) sovereigns and the conflict itself is represented as the virtual availability of as many interchangeable sets of rules as there are connections between a given set of facts and different legal systems. Conversely, any given legal system is assumed to provide a set of rules (here, of contract law) that can suitably – that is, rationally – be applied in any geographical context. At least initially, such frameworks were indeed largely similar (because highly diluted), until the rise of public regulatory law in the United States, followed by various moves among the European economies, created acute policy clashes and sharpened judicial tools in transAtlantic conflicts.

[253] The 'rules of the game of monopoly' is the usual quip here.

of its legal system,[254] their freedom of choice nevertheless stops short of non-state norms.[255]

Underlying this enduring traditional restriction and the paradox of unlimited freedom of choice in relation to all the state-based legal systems of the world, is the idea that the contract law of all (liberal) states is presumptively interchangeable, because it is deemed to be based on a shared conception of societal needs (albeit largely facilitative and exclusive of specific regulatory interference), whereas norms of purely private facture cannot be supposed to implement similar conceptions. In other words, according to this vision, it is important that through this concession to (rational?) choice, the parties should not escape the network of state regulation. In order to ensure such a balance, the second condition for freedom of choice (in the terms outlined above) is the 'internationality' that triggers the principle of party autonomy: this is supposed to prevent wholly domestic contracts (or contracting parties) from circumventing local public policy. The exercise of free choice of law, then, is the exclusive prerogative of international contracts.[256] Such a condition presupposes a fine line separating the closely regulated world of the domestic (including regional, for instance, intra-European) economy, from the area of freedom where, beyond national (or again, internal market) frontiers, state policies relax their grip.

However, neither of these two requirements (choice of state law; internationality), makes sense in the light of the third condition: the requirement that public regulatory policies of connected states be safeguarded, at the latest at the recognition and enforcement stage.[257] This condition undoubtedly reflects the adjustment of private international law in the first part of the twentieth century to the 'age of the social'. This era was characterised by the appearance of public economic regulation affecting society (health, environmental, social protection) and the market (such as competition and securities law, consumer protection), as well as the rise of fundamental rights in fields previously considered to be immune from constitutionalisation.[258] At this time, then, the intensive expansion of the regulatory state in the domestic sphere transformed the nature and function of substantive private law (including contract law). In this changed normative, political and economic environment, private international law had to deal with the expansion of mandatory regulation of markets (such as antitrust or securities legislation) or foreign exchange, trade and investment (exchange controls). These new bodies of regulation came to be known as 'overriding provisions' or *lois de police*. They were deemed derogatory in that they sought

[254] This is the case, for instance, of the EU conflict of law rules contained in 'Rome I' Regulation (EC) No 593/2008 of the European Parliament and of the Council of 17 June 2008, on the law applicable to contractual obligations.

[255] These, according to recital 13 of the Rome regulation, may merely be 'incorporated by reference' into the contract, where they are necessarily subject to the contrary provisions of the governing law.

[256] Or rather, due to the extraordinary difficulty of defining this cardinal requirement, to contracts of which all the elements relevant to the situation at the time of the choice were not located within one state. The Rome I Regulation introduces, in addition, the idea that, for the purposes of European legislation, a domestic contract is one which is connected solely to Member States' territories as a whole (art 3(4)).

[257] That is, when the helping hand (public enforcement procedures) of the state of enforcement is required (and refused for a judgment or award that contravenes its public policies).

[258] Kennedy, 'Three Globalizations'.

to narrow the margin of private choice and moreover frequently claimed 'extra-territorial' scope.[259]

This meant that party choice could no longer be enforced systematically; courts had to 'give effect' to these external interferences (at least if they were those of the local sovereign, the state of the forum). It has also made it difficult to maintain the bright line between domestic and international spheres in terms of the respective intensity of state interests. In other words, the idea that sovereign regulatory concerns stop at national borders could not survive either the appearance of new forms of market regulation or the growing interconnectedness of local economies. The point here is that in the absence of a specific regulatory interest that would trump any other chosen rule anyway, neither the selection of a non-state law, nor the exercise of a choice of law in cases in which the (uncertain) threshold of the international is not crossed, endangers the public policies of potentially concerned states. Conversely, however, the protection of domestic social, environmental or economic regulation is not, or no longer, ensured by the sole requirement that the parties choose a state law, since the latter may quite obviously not pursue similar objectives.[260]

This might have been the end of the story (and is frequently presented as such within the field), but for the parallel moves in the direction of the emancipation of choice of forum (whether judicial or arbitral) agreements and the free movement of resulting judgments and awards.[261] A closer look that includes the latter developments shows that there has been a 'change of state': the reversal of the relationship between law and market, in perfect concordance with the neoliberal scheme, as seen above. In a nutshell, then, the principle of free choice reverses the relationship between public regulation and private choice and generates a competitive market for legal products and judicial services. Parties are emancipated from state authority, contributing thereby to the construction of a world of autonomous private ordering, and accrediting in turn the distinctiveness of the world of international transactions. Private actors are empowered to attain 'regulatory lift-off' because states have renounced – or have been constrained by competitive economic forces to give up – the means to ensure the primacy of public regulation over 'private legislation'. In other words, the former have acquired a licence to cross jurisdictional barriers unhindered. This happened incrementally, during the early years of neoliberalism. The mechanics of the reversal are the combined effect of choice of forum, choice of law and free movement of decisions or awards.

[259] On the difficulties surrounding this concept, see above 153.

[260] There is an additional methodological point here, in connection with the (much resisted) rise of 'interests analysis' (see above 82) in the conflict of laws: if the mandatory social and economic policies of connected states are implemented whenever it makes sense to do so in policy or 'functional' terms, then the quality of whatever non-state contract norms the parties may have chosen – in the (perhaps) unlikely event they have committed themselves to corrupt, incomplete, incoherent or non-progressive principles – hardly matters.

[261] See Regulation (EU) No 1215/2012 of the European Parliament and of the Council of 12 December 2012 on jurisdiction and the recognition and enforcement of judgments; the Hague Convention on Choice of Court Agreements 2005; and of course, the 'New York' Convention on the Recognition and Enforcement of Foreign Arbitral Awards, 1959.

The first element is the general acceptance of free choice of forum in cross-border litigation, in the name of party autonomy, along with the spectacular rise of arbitration. Such freedom is traditionally justified in terms of the promotion of international commerce by virtue of enhanced predictability, procedural economy and litigation risk-management. Reputedly more flexible, international commercial arbitration is seen to present all these advantages, with the added attraction of confidentiality; furthermore, when political stakes are high, such as in state investment contracts, arbitration offers an appearance of neutrality, its legitimacy being enhanced by its contemporary institutionalisation.[262] Increasingly commonplace in practice, forum agreements have thrived with the dwindling of initial doubts as to the desirability of allowing private actors either to appropriate access to private courts or to opt out of the public legal system in disputes engaging issues of public policy. Their generalisation, along with the parallel growth of international arbitration, is now understood (and promoted) as giving rise to a worldwide market in adjudication or dispute resolution. The important point here is that free choice of forum obviously impacts upon the applicability, and thereby the imperativity, of the mandatory rules of any state other than the chosen forum (which in the case of arbitration means practically none at all).[263] Allowing free choice of forum allows an opting out of regulatory regimes.

This is why the liberal scheme on which freedom of choice rests presupposes that any extension of the scope of party choice of court, or the enlargement of arbitrability, is compensated by the right to a 'second look' by the enforcing state over the judgments or awards issuing from the chosen forum. This implicit design is apparent in the Supreme Court of the United States' famous dictum in the *Mitsubishi* case (cited above), whereby 'in the event that choice-of-law forum and the choice-of-law clauses operated in tandem to as prospective waiver of a party's right to pursue statutory remedies … for antitrust violations, we would have little hesitation in condemning the agreement as against public policy'. However, it rapidly became clear that the 'second look' was, in many instances, either unrealistic (when no enforcement was required, the parties having settled, for instance), or problematic (when the supervising court is not better equipped than the arbitrator to make an assessment on the merits in economic terms), or indeed practically excluded through deference to the chosen forum (as in cases as notorious as the *Lloyd's* litigation, encountered above[264]). An additional, powerful economic incentive for states to renounce their 'second look' has been to provide a free zone for the arbitration industry. Moreover, the extreme liberalisation of arbitration law has come complete with various philosophical doctrines designed to legitimate the 'regulatory lift-off' thus achieved.[265]

[262] See on the myth of neutrality of international arbitration, Hassani, 'La neutralité de l'arbitrage international'.

[263] Such concerns hold true even when internationally mandatory provisions are at stake: there is no particular reason why courts should not be trusted mutually to uphold the interests of the members of a benign community of states and indeed, the Rome Convention (art 7-1) and Regulation (art 9-3) have gone a long way down this path.

[264] See above 258.

[265] For these justifications, see M Schinazi, *The Three Ages of International Commercial Arbitration* (Cambridge, Cambridge University Press, 2021).

The real problem with this evolution lies in the fact that when court access is thus privatised, there is a correlative absence of judicial (or arbitral) regulation of interests beyond those of the parties to the dispute. Enhancing global jurisdictional competition supposedly reaps benefits in terms of the improvement of the quality of courts worldwide. But it is instructive to turn to classic economic analysis – that can hardly be suspected of anti-libertarian bias – of possible ways to remedy the overload of the federal courts: privately designated judges lack both the legitimacy (conferred by public investiture) and the (private financial) incentive to take account of societal interests in their decision-making process.[266] This conclusion certainly plays out, for instance, in respect of the impact of human rights in investment arbitration, where contractual mandate and choice of law preempt much (or indeed any) consideration of wider public or third-party interests.[267] Although of course the public financing of the court system establishes both the legitimacy and the incentive which arbitration lacks in protecting societal interests beyond those of the parties to the litigation, the tendency of courts designated by choice of forum agreements to act 'as if they were arbitrators'[268] also detracts from this particular regulatory function. The faintness of the judicial 'second look' does the rest.

Thus, the centrality of private choice of law is so taken for granted, or at least, appears to be so solidly rooted in the history of Western private international law, that astonishingly little attention has been paid to the function it fulfils within the changing economic and political environment induced by globalisation. The cloak of tradition is reinforced by more recent law and economics doctrines, which tend to promote party autonomy as efficiency, in the form of predictability, reduced transaction costs, or facilitated risk-management. No doubt these virtues exist, at least for the party whose skills in contract negotiation and drafting are strongest. It is highly improbable however that the interests purportedly served by unbridled freedom of choice, whether cast as those of the market or of a purported community of merchants, are those of an adequate governance of the cross-border activities of private actors.[269] On the contrary, it has worked to transform national public regulation into a disposable private good in a deregulated economy. This holds true even after the various recent financial crises and the disastrous role played by self-regulation in subordinating wider public concerns to speculative interests, as seen above.

Despite its profound roots in our legal consciousness, this market or competitive (individual and interjurisdictional) model to which private international law has contributed in the often imperceptible ways investigated above, is anything but inevitable. Alternative scenarios exist, in which legal obligations are not premised

[266] See J Dammann and H Hansmann, 'Globalizing Commercial Litigation' (2008) 94(1) *Cornell Law Review* 1, building on W Landes and R Posner, 'Adjudication as a Private Good' (1979) 8 *Journal of Legal Studies* 235.

[267] There is a vast literature on this subject. For a (critical) overview of the situation as extended to the investment scene, see Perrone, 'Neoliberalism and economic sovereignty'.

[268] On this approach of the English courts to risk, see R Fentiman, *International Commercial Litigation*, 2nd edn (Oxford, Oxford University Press, 2015) p 8, 1.13 et seq.

[269] Once again, the (in)famous *Lloyd's* litigation (above) serves as a cautionary illustration of the cumulative effect of contract doctrine and private international law theory.

on a world of atomised subject; transfers of value are neither mercantile nor separate from the social relations in which they take place; the economy is not a site of generalised predation, but a moral register of fine-tuned solidarity; the pursuit of sustainable life replaces that of profit for its own sake. This is the cue to recall the indigenous ontologies encountered above, in which the sphere we think of as market entails entanglement rather than atomisation. In such a context, there is no room for individual autonomy as we have come to understand it in our late neoliberal modernity. In the place of our Darwinian economy of competition, as Marcel Mauss's study of gift famously demonstrates,[270] exchanges of goods and services are framed as gifts, from which springs an obligation to reciprocate involving ever further entanglement or interpersonal linkage, rather than the *quitus* that severs (or puts an end to relationships with others, or more generally, alterity).[271]

REVERSAL

The question for this book is whether the conflict of laws, having played the core role in the political economy as described above, is capable of embracing this contrasted approach. Once again, its shadow avatar will serve as a guide in the direction of an alternative form of legality, delving beneath the legal-economic subject to discover a 'relational' self, located moreover in an ontology of 'dwelling'. We have already encountered this 'dwelling perspective' in the exploration of alternative legal ontologies and the work of Walter Mignolo in Part II of this book. Now is the time to draw a further significant lesson in the present context of the relationship between the political economy and ethics. The thread that will be taken up here is the proposal by the anthropologist Tim Ingold of a notion of person-hood in which 'self is seen to inhere in the unfolding of relations set up by virtue of positioning in the environment'.[272] Ingold's insight in this respect is that our modes of relationship to the world and its inherent alterity are inseparable from the ways in which we value things and act morally.

The specific point here is that when Ingold designs an alternative ontological framework for what he imagines as an 'ethics of place' (with obvious echoes within the conflict of laws), he draws on the (recent) phenomenological tradition in Western thought.[273] In other words, when he suggests that ethical configuration of an ecological economy is vastly different, if not completely opposed, to one in

[270] M Mauss, *The Gift. The Form and Reason for Exchange in Archaic Societies* (Abingdon, Routledge, 2001); on the cosmic economy of sharing, see Descola, *Les formes du Visible*, 540. On the volumes of literature and reinterpretations to which the Maussian gift has given rise, see Pelluchon, *Les Lumières à l'âge du vivant*, 724.

[271] In what is hopefully faithful to Latourian terms, the economic accounting formula stays within its own sphere or mode of existence, allowing room for the beings of ethics to call us to account.

[272] T Ingold, *The Perception of the Environment: Essays on Livelihood, Dwelling and Skill* (London, Routledge, 2000) 261.

[273] His references are essentially Martin Heidegger and Maurice Merleau-Ponty. However, below, we shall turn more to Emmanuel Levinas (whose work is carefully explained, as a philosophy for the 'age of the living', by C Pelluchon, *Pour Comprendre Levinas* (Paris, Seuil, 2020)).

which self-contained individuals confront an external world,[274] he is pointing, paradoxically, to a reversal of which there are also seeds within the Western philosophical tradition itself. As we shall now see below, under the phenomenological approach of Emmanuel Lévinas, the most fearful threat to humanity (a threat far worse than death) is the 'depersonalisation' of self through the negation of the other.[275] This terrifying, totalitarian reduction of others to the status of things is linked in turn to the primacy of a political economy of give-and-take, or *donnant-donnant*.[276] It may well be, then, that the apparently 'exotic' elements to be found in non-modern cosmologies can be correlated to a residue, or minor jurisprudence, of modernity. Such a link is not designed to make indigenous thought in any way 'better', nor confer upon it a (entirely anachronistic) pedigree, but it may make the point being made here more communicable to the 'moderns'.

[274] See on this point, E. Nguyen-Vo: https://humansandnature.org/finding-ground-for-a-relational-ethic/.

[275] See Pelluchon, *Pour Comprendre Levinas*, 54: 'L'expérience totalitaire où les individus ne sont pas considérés comme des sujets mais comme des choses. Le pire n'est pas de mourir ou de ne pas avoir choisi l'existence, mais d'être nié, d'être recouvert par ce qu'*il y a* d'anonyme qui 'est la forme impersonnelle du verbe être … cette consommation impersonnelle'… C'est la disparition du Moi'.

[276] See again Pelluchon, *Pour Comprendre Levinas*, 39. A gift in this sense may entangle, but it does not expect a return.

6

An Ethic of Responsiveness: The Demands of Interalterity

A PRELIMINARY QUESTION is whether it makes any sense to submit our (neoliberal) political economy to an ethical critique. In their *Critical Conversation* on capitalism, Nancy Fraser and Rahel Jaeggi discuss this point, concluding affirmatively, to the extent however that ethics are not 'understood in a narrow sense' but as 'a form of life'.[277] Thus understood, an ecological ethic challenges the commodification of our world and the ensuing severances (encountered above) between ourselves and others, humanity and environment, economy and earth science. In this respect, the key to the 'deep' ecology[278] is our responsibility (answerability or accountability) for and before all the other forms of life that inhabit our common *demeure*[279] and upon which we depend.[280] The acknowledgement of such interdependence or entanglement contains an appeal, as Latour writes, emitted on ethical wave-lengths – if only we are ready to hear them – by all sorts of beings and objects that surround us and that call upon us to save ourselves.[281]

[277] Fraser and Jaeggi, *Capitalism. A Critical Conversation* 120 et seq. 'An ethically inspired critique … applies to capitalism in its entirety as a distorted mode of ethical life (*Sittlichkeit*)' (p 125).

[278] The notion (or movement) of 'deep' ecology (as opposed to a 'narrow' or shallow view of ecology as a branch of biology) is ascribed to the Norwegian philosopher, Arne Naess ('The Shallow and the Deep, Long-Range Ecology Movement' (1973) 16 *Inquiry* 95). It implies a new ecological, non-anthropocentric ethic, emphasising the inherent value of the natural world. It also has an evident aesthetic dimension – see T Lynch, 'Deep Ecology as an Aesthetic Movement' (1996) 5 *Environmental Values* 147–160, arguing that aesthetics (rather than morality) is the only way with which to confer philosophical consistency on this movement). Deep ecology is now seen to include other strands of ecological thought such as ecofeminism (see further below 293).

[279] The notion of '*demeure*' will appear repeatedly below, whether as the place from which the host can draw strength enough to welcome in the other (Levinas), or as the planet we (humans and non-humans alike) inhabit (Latour).

[280] On the acknowledgement of this dependence as a crucial part of an ecological ethic, see M Serres, *Le contrat naturel* (Flammarion Poche, 1990).

[281] The planet emits a Munchian cry, a 'dispatch from Gaia': see Latour, *Facing Gaia*. For a phenomenological approach to responsiveness, see Lindahl, 'Place-Holding the Future', particularly in the following passage about the call made by penguins to a human community: 'What is it for a legal order to *respond* to a demand for justice? To *represent* anew. Responsiveness is not a fortuitous feature of representation; representation is responsive representation. A collective's responsive representations never only 'follow' questions, in the twofold sense of coming 'after' and 'obeying.' Instead, responsive representations are *retroactive* in that the question to which they respond only becomes manifest in the responses themselves. The dynamic of question and answer unfolds a double asymmetry marked by the precedence of the question and the retroactivity of the response. The penguins' demand for justice confronts the inhabitants of (Manly) with the question, 'Who are we?' Regardless of how its representatives might respond to

But how exactly should we translate into legal idiom the ethical injunction to respond to the alterity that encompasses us (and, as we are beginning to suspect, is nested within our very selves)?[282] The claim in this chapter is that the same shadow version of the conflict of laws that resonates with the in-between on an ontological and aesthetic register[283] also provides an alternative ethical model for the relationship between self and other – a law that could be thought of as governing the encounter between interdependent life forms, each radically different, with their distinctive trajectories and modes of access to reality, and each intrinsically deserving of respect, protection and consideration in their own struggle for survival.[284] Abandoning the sense of ontological privilege (whether of self, humanity, or the forum), such responsiveness in legal form demands a de-centring of self, an extreme attentiveness to other forms of life[285] and the accommodation of otherness on its very own terms. This last point will unfold below as a crucial path to the very core of the conflict of laws and its shadow avatar (already encountered above).

The law of the other, then, embodies a horizon of alterity as a reaction against the great economisation of our world. In direct contrast to the neoliberal schema, it implies the primacy of responsibility over autonomy, of scruple over calculation.[286] In the place of market as a (pseudo) mode of existence, interactions with the 'beings of ethics' would be modelled upon the gift – a debt that can never be discharged (in the sense that it induces further relationality, not severance: *on n'est jamais quitte*[287]). The starting point can only be a radical ethical transformation of our *nomos*, that is our (modern, naturalist, neoliberal) ways of inhabiting our legal universe (as seen above). This is also the message carried by the current phenomenological turn in political and feminist ecology and philosophy; such a strand of thought is equally of crucial importance for our understandings of law, as we shall see. The exploration of the strictures and structures of neoliberal legality carried out above suggests the scale of the change required. Echoing Latour, we might say that this is not mere (macro) revolution but requires the minute investigation and perhaps overturning of every

this question, whether by enacting new rules or by leaving extant rules untouched, they propose a *self*-representation of the collective: the legal rules spell out what 'we', in hindsight, hold joint action to be about'. This passage also illustrates in powerful philosophical terms the critical potential of 'resequencing' as embodied juridically in private international law: see above 206.

[282] Of course, this is no way to suggest that positive law does not have an ethical other. Schiavone explains how two paradigms (*ius* and *nomos*; substantive justice and rigorous science) were always in Roman law's DNA, developing later in different directions (*Ius*, 404). On nesting, see above 104. On the alterity that is within ourselves (individually and collectively, see Mazurel, *L'inconscient ou l'oubli de l'histoire*).

[283] In the second part of this book, we saw that under the shadow version of the conflict of laws, legality can be seen on an ontological and aesthetic register as dwelling in the sphere of the in-between, as a readiness to act as go-between plural viewpoints.

[284] On this struggle for survival as the foundation of ethics, see Latour, *Facing Gaia* 441 et seq; *cf* making the same point and illustrating the contemporary revival of eco-phenomenology in ethical thought, Pelluchon, *Les lumières à l'âge du vivant*.

[285] Interpreting Gaia's ethical 'dispatch', it might be said, with Pelluchon, that it requires an 'Attention extrême aux vivants dans leurs milieux aux variations individuelles et au foisonnement de la vie, et à la manière dont elle s'invente sans cesse'.

[286] *Enquête*, 441 et seq; as will be seen below, Derrida makes the similar point that the law of hospitality excludes all calculation.

[287] Latour, *Facing Gaia* 464.

small component of every single one of our micro-legal ways of being, thinking and doing.

One specifically ethical strand of eco-phenomenology is inspired by the work of Emmanuel Levinas.[288] A compelling reason (among many) to return to phenomenology[289] in the shadow of Gaia's ire, is that it is a part of European philosophical thought[290] that not only survived but was arguably produced by, or enriched through, the (unspeakable) experience of the Holocaust. This point is crucial for scholarship in law and humanities that is currently attempting to imagine the place and shape of our legal, political and social world in the (philosophical and ecological) with a horizon of extinction.[291] In this respect, in a context that makes it so difficult to project our thoughts into times to come (or beyond time?), an eco-phenomenological ethic is already conjugated in the mode of a '*futur antérieur*'.[292] In other words, it is produced by a world in which extinction has taken place in our own past. This is also why it resonates with the indigenous cosmologies brought to Western attention by the ontological turn in anthropology (as seen above). Once again, extinction, or breakdown in Winnicott's psychoanalytical terms, has already taken place.[293] In the latter respect, it is remarkable that Winnicott's influential 'fear of breakdown' also has a powerful 'environmental' resonance.[294] It contrasts starkly with the Anthropocenic imaginary of a world of violence in which law in ethical form has lost all relevance.[295]

[288] Among Levinas's many books and publications, we refer in what follows to three in particular: *Totalité et Infini. Essai sur l'Extériorité*, (Paris, Le Livre de Poche, 1961, 1994); *Autrement qu'Etre ou Au-dela de l'essence* (Paris, Le Livre de Poche, 1974, 1994); *Altérité et Transcendance* (Paris, Le Livre de Poche, 1995, 2006). For a philosophical explanation of his difficult work, see Pelluchon, *Pour comprendre Levinas*, which must be read in conjunction with her *Les lumières à l'âge du vivant*.

[289] This return to phenomenology has been predicted by various thinkers of 'the era of the post', among whom S Bachir Diagne, *De langue à langue: L'hospitalité de la traduction* (Paris, Albin Michel, 2022) pointing to the thought of Maurice Merleau-Ponty, who understood the need to 'construire un universel de rencontres, de traductions'. On Diagne's philosophy of translation, see above.

[290] On the origins of phenomenology in the work of Husserl and Merleau-Ponty, see Pelluchon, *Pour Comprendre Levinas*. On the role of these authors in Ingold's anthropology of 'dwelling' and its resonance with indigenous cosmologies, see above 172.

[291] See, on law in 'panarchy', Janda, *Panarchy*.

[292] ibid.

[293] 'Fear of breakdown' is an unfinished article, published in *The Collected Works of DW Winnicott*: Vol 6, 1960–1963 (eds L Caldwell and H Taylor Robinson) (Oxford, Oxford University Press, 2016) 523 et seq: Winnicott contends that a fear of breakdown is an experience of a breakdown earlier in life which cannot be returned to without help. The experience is defended against because unthinkable anxieties or 'primitive agonies' prevail. What remains of (the patient's) life feels to him or her like an unlived life. See too T Ogden, 'Fear of Breakdown and the Unlived Life' (2014) 95 *Int J Psychoanalysis* 20. On the possible relationship (argued here) between the individual psyche and the historical subconscious of a collective, see Mazurel, *L'inconscient ou l'oubli de l'histoire*.

[294] Insofar as accounting for psychic Being (and its cracks) requires an overall understanding of the interaction between personal factors and those relating to the surrounding environment (nature and nurture).

[295] As seen above, law and enlightenment ethics were long associated with 'the humanities' in a world from which all humanity was eradicated. Corinne Pelluchon's project (in *Les Lumières à l'âge du vivant*) is to revisit the Enlightenment ethic of virtue and explore its potential as a contemporary eco-philosophy. Her point is that the values of the Enlightenment – modernity – are not to be rejected wholesale but must be untangled from the neoliberal Schema that (in the terms of the text above) captured them.

In this respect, the focus of Emmanuel Levinas' phenomenological approach is alterity:[296] he sees the 'face (or corporeality[297]) of the other' as a source of transcendence.[298] Alterity thus understood was the object in turn of a philosophical dialogue initiated by Jacques Derrida on the requirements of the law of hospitality as 'a universal law of singular and absolute difference'. Hospitality itself is a Kantian theme[299] revisited as relationship to alterity by both Emmanuel Levinas and Jacques Derrida.[300] According to their respective and largely complementary accounts, this law of hospitality is a universal law of 'singularity and absolute alterity'. It commands accommodation of 'the other's law, that was there before me'. Indeed, the acceptance of the other's law is the very condition for the encounter with being-as-other ('l'être en tant qu'autre').[301] This reference to the 'law of the other' is of obvious significance for the conflict of laws as a mode of approaching alterity in legal terms. The same is true, furthermore and equally importantly, for the more difficult statement according to which the law of the other is the law without which I am not *ipse*, myself. This paradox implies, as will be seen below, a reversal or 'substitution' as between host

[296] The most significant reference in twentieth-century Western philosophy to the figure of the Other is Emmanuel Levinas' *Totalité et Infini. Essai sur l'Extériorité* (Paris, Le Livre de Poche, 1961, 1994). This is of course not to say that alterity was not present previously, notably in the Kantian tradition. However, Levinas centred his own phenomenological thought on the Other (displacing Self). See S Moyn, *Origins of the Other. Emmanuel Levinas between Revelation and Ethics* (Ithaca NY, Cornell University Press, 2005). Some analyses of the Kantian tradition's approach to alterity are harsher, however: (E Viveiros de Castro, *Ends of the World*, 9): 'With Kant, in short, we lost the world and turned inwards, in what could be described as a veritable psychotic episode in the history of our metaphysics: the modern constitutive subject as narcissistic'.

[297] Levinas himself evolved on this point, substituting phenomenological corporeity for 'face': see Pelluchon, *Pour Comprendre Levinas*, 69 et seq.

[298] In *What is philosophy?* (Deleuze and Guattari 1991, 11-12), the Other appears as 'a condition of the field of perception'. Eduardo Viveiros de Castro explains this insight in the following terms: 'the existential possibility of those parts of the world that lie beyond actual perception is guaranteed by the virtual presence of an Other that perceives them; what is invisible to me subsists as real by being visible to an other … An Other is thus no one (neither subject nor object) but rather a structure or relation – the absolute relation that provides concrete actants with their relative positions as subjects or objects, as well as their alternation between the two positions: the Other refers (to) me to the other I and the other I to me. The Other is not an element within the field of perception; it is the principle that constitutes such a field, along with its content' (*The Relative Native: Essays on Indigenous Conceptual Worlds* (HAU, 2016)).

[299] On the Kantian heritage of hospitality, see Pelluchon, *Pour comprendre Levinas*.

[300] J Derrida, *Hospitalité*, vol 1, *Séminaire 1995–96* (Paris, Seuil, 2021); *De l'hospitalité* (dialogue with Anne Dufourmentelle) (Calmann-Levy, 1997); *Adieu to Emmanuel Levinas* (eds M Naas, PA Brault) (Palo Alto CA, Stanford University Press, 1999). Hospitality is a concept overladen with paradox. Its aporetic quality is visible in the (Derridean) concept of 'hostipitalité', in which enemy is indistinguishable from friend, host from guest. Hospitality is emblematically present in the Jewish tradition of *soukkot* (tent or camp) open to all strangers (who do not have to give their name and identity: this point is crucial, as will be seen below). Levinas himself did not want to be represented as a Jewish philosopher (Pelluchon, *Pour comprendre Levinas*, 248). However there is clearly a strand of Jewish thinkers (Arendt, Adorno, Horkheimer, Levinas) who attempt in this respect to 'humanise' responsibility. In this context, alterity differs radically from that, say of Sartre ('l'enfer c'est les autres') in that it is a struggle to make sense of the absurd and the void: Pelluchon, ibid, 219. However, emphasising the need to contextualise Levinas' Other not only in terms of a reaction to the Holocaust nor as a reversion to traditional Judaism but rather his own philosophically informed response to Heidegger's turn to nazism (in *Being and Time*), S Moyn, *Origins of the Other. Emmanuel Levinas between Revelation and Ethics* (Ithaca NY, Cornell University Press, 2005) 17, 23. In (very) short terms, the thesis of Levinas' *Totalité et Infini* is that Heidegger's secularised ethics and the social nature of the self, missed the encounter with the Other.

[301] Latour emphasises this point, *Enquête*, 452.

and guest. Now, such a substitution of foreign law for one's own is the very *modus operandi* of the conflict of laws.[302] However, understood as a radical imperative, hospitality as substitution certainly has an aporetic quality, meaning that it is unattainable as constantly subject to an internal 'conflict of laws' between an ideational norm and a contingent or positive legal framework.[303] Hence the concept of 'hostipitality' (hostis/hospis, host/hostage).

This very aporia serves as a cue for the reflection that follows, in fleshing out the demands of responsiveness towards the (foreign, strange, alien or absolute) other, as embodied in private international law. Firstly, it prods us to think (in the aptly ecological terms of feminist Ratna Kapur) 'beyond the fishbowl'.[304] The (difficult) point here is that reinforcing rights, recognition and tolerance – traditional values associated with the (schizophrenic) rule of law,[305] or democratic liberalism – are obviously not ethically 'wrong' per se. However, they cannot deliver on a radical promise of responsiveness in legal terms. This is because various (ethical and epistemological) traps or cunning ruses lie beneath the conventional assertions of equality and the correlative need to recognise difference (in respect of alien normative forms).[306] The encounter with foreign legal cultures or practices makes the conceits and contradictions of liberalism particularly visible in this respect. However, since objections linked to the wrongs of rights go against the grain of the usual ethical accounts of law, they are easily misunderstood and require a preliminary presentation of the difficulties of 'hearing the appeal of the other' (as both Derrida and Latour invite us to do, in different idioms) in (its arguably authentic) legal form (section I).

If liberal rights are 'not enough', then, the question is how to account more appropriately for alterity within the law, with its own tools, grammar and modes of veridiction. Here, the shadow version of the conflict of laws offers an intellectual model that comes remarkably close to the demands of (Levinassian/Derridean) hospitality in respect of

[302] Moreover, 'substitution' is a term of art within the latter, that refers more specifically to the various operations of adjustment required when an alien legal institution is called upon to function outside its initial environment.

[303] There is a literal aspect, then, to the reference to the 'conflict of laws' in Derrida's account of hospitality. The latter evokes a conflict of laws between two antinomic precepts. The conflict opposes law and justice, or the limited rights and obligations incumbent on states under the (positive) international law of hospitality and its natural law version, in which hospitality is absolute. In order to illustrate the latter, he refers to Plato's account of Socrates' appeal to the Athenians, in which Socrates argues that hospitality requires that he be allowed to speak his own language (not that of the 'tribunal') and all that language entails.

[304] R Kapur, *Gender, Alterity and Human Rights. Freedom in a Fishbowl* (Cheltenham, Edward Elgar, 2020). On eco-feminism, the gendered body and phenomenology, see below 293. For a critique of the pitfalls of the fishbowl metaphor itself from an anthropological perspective, see Viveiros de Castro, *The Relative Native*, 21, observing that its supposed neutrality 'demonstrates that the supposed opposition between naturalist universalism and culturalist relativism is, at least, very relative (and perfectly cultural), for it can be summed up as a matter of choosing the dimensions of the bowl, or the size of the cell where we are imprisoned: should it include all of humankind ecumenically, or should it be made to order for each culture? Or perhaps we might have one great "natural" prison with different cultural cell-blocks, some of them with slightly more spacious cells than others?'.

[305] See below 273.

[306] Elaborating a 'politics of difference' (I Young, *Justice and the Politics of Difference* (Princeton NJ, Princeton University Press, 2011)) implies deactivating an ethical and epistemological trap; *cf* a similar line of thought in Balibar, *Des Universels*.

the strange *nomos* of the other. It shows how difference may be accommodated on its own terms – not on those of the self or the host – to the point of effacement of self and substitution of the other. In this respect, we can trace clear echoes of this reversal of the relationship between host and guest in the ontologies and aesthetics of entanglement and border-dwelling encountered above, in which the 'gaze of the jaguar' is turned back, reflexively, on the observer, or self. In the same move, however, the shadow avatar of the conflict of laws allows for a dialectic at the very threshold of law's *demeure* between *hospis* and *hostis*, friend and foe, the foreign and the same, the general and the singular. In this respect, it contains the inklings of a response to the objection that the ideal of hospitality smooths over the violence that seems to be emerging today in every direction from the depths of our collective subconscious. Such may be the law's ethical response to 'the violence that is still to come' (section II).

I. THE APPEAL OF THE (LEGAL) OTHER

How to respond to the appeal of the other in legal form? The obvious difficulty of framing any such response in terms of hospitality is that modern communities[307] define themselves, in legal terms, as much by what they reject as what they have in common.[308] In this respect, the cunning of recognition[309] lies in the implicit exclusions necessarily or structurally involved in 'the promise of rights'[310] or more broadly, underlying the values of the rule of law.[311] The latter might seem to ensure the equal dignity of normative forms – whether embodied in specific institutions or more broadly in particular conceptions of legality – in all their extraordinary multiplicity and alterity. Yet, liberal rights operate within epistemological limits described as those of a 'fishbowl'.[312] The philosopher Corinne Pelluchon describes an analogous conundrum in her phenomenological project for the reinstatement of an 'ethic of values', as it were a renewed ecological reading of the principles of the Enlightenment.[313] As she points out, the latter, including human rights, are all intrinsically productive ideas, but they are 'not enough'[314] insofar as they continue to be interpreted through a distorted anthropocentric, ethnocentric or egocentric lens.[315] Such a lens also tends to

[307] As 'imagined' communities in B. Anderson's account, *op cit*.

[308] This exclusionary move is analogous to the psychic defences opposed by the somatic, atomised subject within the competitive political economy, as seen above.

[309] On misrecognition in private international law, see I Isailovic, '(Mis)recognition: essay on transnational law, identities and marginalization,' PhD Sciences Po, 2014.

[310] K Ciupa, 'The promise of rights: international indigenous rights in the neoliberal era', in Brabazon, *Neoliberal Legality*, 140.

[311] Brabazon (ibid) contends that this paradox is inherent in neoliberal legality.

[312] This is no doubt also the cost of the 'success story' of human rights, that have become the only available idiom (or the 'last utopia') through which to express the (human?) need for justice. In terms of political philosophy, an analogous critique has been forcefully addressed in respect of liberal institutions that purport to ensure equality (family, state, church) by Etienne Balibar (*Des Universels*).

[313] Pelluchon, *Les lumières à l'âge du vivant*.

[314] S Moyn, *Not Enough. Human Rights in an Unequal World* (Belknap Press, 2019).

[315] Janda (*Panarchy*, 67) makes a further interesting etymological point about the language of rights: 'It is specifically with regard to the idea of right(s) that the co-implication between law(s) as a legal system or code and the notion of "being (in the) right" emerges. But even in this context, rights are thought of

misconstrue various more contemporary doctrines analogously designed in one way or the other to pursue inclusiveness, such as relationality, the commons, fundamental rights, or recognition.

Perhaps more surprisingly, a similar assessment is equally valid for some of the concepts developed at the very heart of ecological discourse, such as the needs, interests and (legal) status of future generations.[316] In other words, these (legal and other) values, however emancipatory they are intended to be, tend to be reappropriated as further forms of 'liquidity' by neoliberalism (and its specific forms of legality). In all these cases, as in the idea (or advertising slogan) of 'green' capitalism,[317] the assertion of an ethical value turns against the very cause it purports to serve – unless it is preceded by a form of de-centring of self, understood not only as the individual psyche but also as 'humanity', 'culture' or collective consciousness. Part of the problem is that neoliberal legality is perfectly compatible with the assertion and indeed the effective protection of the rule of law, understood in various ways as formal equality.[318] As such, it shies away from correcting unequal economic distribution or indeed from considering the structural dimensions of (social or racial) capital.

In its approach to legal or normative difference, the conventional wisdom of private international law illustrates the (often unconscious, sometimes unwanted) exclusionary consequences of purportedly inclusive doctrines in several ways.

principally in juridical terms – that is, with regard to law (*ius*) – as the issue of entitlements, prerogatives, and dues, which have to do with liberties and freedom, as in the rights of individuals or birthright. At stake are primarily legal guarantees and protections of such rights, and less obviously a concern with being or obtaining as right. It seems, therefore, that the English name "law" needs to be deliberately and intentionally troubled or interrogated, for instance, juxtaposed with the etymological resonances of the word "rights", if one wants to raise the question of its relation to the idea of what is right … These terminological and etymological differences between languages signal that the linguistic framework in which such issues arise tends to influence, perhaps even orient and determine, the tenor and direction of deliberations'. For an alternative phenomenological approach to responsiveness to the concerns of future generations as a more-than-human collective, see Lindahl, 'Place-Holding the Future'.

[316] For such a critique, see S Humphreys, 'Against Future Generations', colloquium on *Planetary Responsibility*, December 2021 LSE/Sci po. Similarly, Derrida issues a warning that the duties of hospitality, that bind a 'lineage' (in favour of the descendants of the *xenos*) are 'pervertissables' (*Hospitalité*, vol 1, *Séminaire 1995–96* (Paris, Seuil, Bibliothèque Derrida, 2021) 120 and see below 297).

[317] We have already encountered the issue of 'responsible capitalism' above. An analogous analysis applies when capitalism claims to be 'green'. Today, as John Bellamy Foster and Brett Clark write, 'orthodox economics is reputedly being harnessed to an entirely new end: saving the planet from the ecological destruction wrought by capitalist expansion. It promises to accomplish this through the further expansion of capitalism itself, cleared of its excesses and excrescences. A growing army of self-styled 'sustainable developers' argues that there is no contradiction between the unlimited accumulation of capital – the credo of economic liberalism from Adam Smith to the present – and the preservation of the earth' However there is a fatal flaw that can be traced back to its conceptual foundations of classical economics: 'The rise of neoclassical economics in the late nineteenth and early twentieth centuries is commonly associated with the rejection of the labour theory of value of classical political economy and its replacement by notions of marginal utility/productivity. What is seldom recognized, however, is that another critical perspective was abandoned at the same time: the distinction between wealth and value (use value and exchange value). With this was lost the possibility of a broader ecological and social conception of wealth' (https://monthlyreview.org/2009/11/01/the-paradox-of-wealth-capitalism-and-ecological-destruction).

[318] See above. A similar reversal is apparent in the context of the hotly debated issues within the environmental sciences, the invocation of values such as transparency or scientific neutrality, that have been arraigned however to discredit scientific studies of climate change.

Because it remains ethno-centred (or Archimedean, in terms of perspective) as seen above, it stops short of the requirements of our ethical responsibility to acknowledge the intrinsic and incommensurable value of the law of all others (*les êtres-en-tant-qu'autres*). In Latour's terms, the 'law of the others' corresponds to all their own, equally legitimate, modes of veridiction.[319] This is not equality, because all these life forms are incommensurable. But each has its own intrinsic value in its distinctive trajectory. In other words, as we have already seen above, normative forms that are alien to modernity's (archaic?) obsession with the written word and dismissed as primitive, such as ceremonial rituals, oral traditions or 'mosaic' patterns[320] are equally a *nomos* that frames access to reality. Conflictuality in the encounter with the law of others is inevitable nevertheless. But denial and the will to assimilate always involve the institution of a hierarchical relationship between self and other – even in the mild form (demonstrated by the conflict of laws) of a preference for the legal classifications of the forum. This certainly does not mean that the host system has to accept definitively and without question whatever it might perceive as threatening to its stability or contrary to its values, as we shall see. However, under an ethical approach to alterity, the starting point for framing our relationship towards alterity cannot be a hermeneutic of suspicion (as produced within our legal consciousness by the political economy of late modernity).[321]

Just as the purported unity of a national community often rests on exclusionary factors, the rejection of difference in the name of individual identity also involves imaginaries that (consciously or not) appeal to exaggeration, fetishisation of symbols, the projection of heroic fantasies or the fear of collapse, and indeed generalised suspicion vis à vis all deviance from the norm. The developments below are underwritten by this parallel between the torments of the collective subconscious of our societies of late modernity and the struggles within the atomised individual psyche.[322] Three examples taken from the foundational axes of private international law will be used to demonstrate the counterproductive effect of purportedly inclusive values when they are not sufficiently detached from the 'centrisms' mentioned above in their encounter

[319] Again, Latour, *Enquête*, 452 emphasising this (pluriversal) point in response to the objection (Luc Ferry) that deep ecology is a form of eco-fascism. Each form of life is incommensurable and has intrinsic value on its own trajectory.

[320] A Mills, *The Lifeworlds of Law* and see above 195.

[321] On the hermeneutic of suspicion as characteristic of our legal consciousness, see D Kennedy, 'A Political Economy of Contemporary Legality' in P Kjaer (ed), *The Law of Political Economy*, 89–124.

[322] For this parallel, see Mazurel, *L'inconscient ou l'oubli de l'histoire*; in relation to Freud in particular, see D Herzog, *Cold war Freud. Psychoanalysis in an Age of Catastrophes* (Cambridge, Cambridge University Press, 2016); see too the following observation by M Rosenfeld, *A Pluralist Theory of Constitutional Justice*, (Oxford, Oxford University Press, 2022 forthcoming) 127: 'building, transforming, and maintaining any given constitutional identity entail interpretive undertakings that are analogous to those that Freud articulated in his engagement with the dynamic between the id, the ego, and the superego while psychoanalyzing dreams. The three most salient interpretive devices concerned include … negation, metaphor, and metonymy. All three of these bear upon key identitarian issues, or in other words, upon determinations along axes of identification and of differentiation'. This observation is placed in a chapter that recounts an encounter between Freud and Kelsen and explores the insights to be garnered therefrom in terms of understanding the relationship between law and justice.

with difference.[323] Thus, tolerance can produce rejection; purported equality of treatment, hierarchy; and rights, deprivation. The important point in each of these cases is to winkle out the stance of superiority and the lure of the instrumentalisation of the other, lurking under our liberal ideas of openness in respect of alterity, extraneity or foreignness.[324]

A. The Categories of Tolerance

As Isabelle Stengers writes in her appeal to 'do away with tolerance',[325] the latter slides easily into condescension and the establishment of a hierarchy between self and others. Moreover, as Emmanuel Lévinas emphasises, reification and depersonalisation are temptations that are inherent to the comparison of norms and laws, and to all those institutions that neutralise subjects in order to make them fit into categories and subject them to rules.[326] Both these reflections, well known in substance to (critical) comparative lawyers,[327] are significant to understanding private international law's traditional methodologies. The latter can be said to rest, on the one hand, on the idea of tolerance for difference embodied in foreign law,[328] and on the other, on the processing of the latter through a series of categories that reflect the structure and epistemology of the receiving legal system and serve as entry points or filters.[329] The cunning of tolerance lies, then, in a first epistemological and ethical trap, that is, the denial of alterity in the name of equality. Indeed, as will be seen below, the smoothing over of difference in an assimilationist mode contains an equally powerful (if less visible) value judgement on legal cultures other than one's own, just as much as the use of alterity to discriminate or disparage.[330]

[323] As seen above, there is scant critical thought in the conflict of laws, despite the fact that a central target of contemporary – post-structural, post-colonial, feminist – critique, common to comparative law, legal anthropology and public international law, is that various dominant paradigms or intellectual schemes of legal classification, clothed in scientific neutrality, transformed alterity into the basis for legitimising and constructing hierarchies between different world views, cultures, or moral economies, radicalising the differentiation between self and other.

[324] As will be made clear below, what follows is not a condemnation of the values discussed, but a plea for hyper-vigilance in their deployment. The field of 'environmental law' is an illustration of this need because it is paved with good intentions. This is the world of politics, or Law II, and requires constant, circular re-deliberation (on the requirements of POL as a mode of existence, distinct from asepticised governance and obviously incapable of being the object of a 'science', see Latour, *Enquête*, 327).

[325] I Stengers, *Pour en finir avec la tolérance* (ed Empêcheurs De Penser En Rond, 1997).

[326] We shall return to this point (and this text) below 292 et s. For Levinas, the transformation of persons into things (a feature of totalitarianism) is the worst thing that can happen to humanity (see C Pelluchon, *Pour Comprendre Levinas* (Paris, éd du Seuil, 2020) 191, observing the analogy with the temptation to manage humanity as 'human resources'. The latter vocabulary belongs of course to that of neoliberal governance).

[327] On commensurability (and the lack of it in respect of cultures, in and outside law), see in particular P Legrand (inter alia): 'Sur l'analyse différentielle des juriscultures' (1999) *Revue internationale de droit comparé* 1053.

[328] The idea that the conflict of laws embodies tolerance in respect of foreign law is a trope within the discipline.

[329] This process is called characterisation; it acts as an epistemological and ethical filter in respect of foreign laws.

[330] See above, 173 on the negation of alterity through the eminently modern 'narcissistic European gesture that aimed at seeing its own image repeated throughout the universe' (as observed by S Santiago, in A Gazzola (ed), *The Space in-between*).

In comparative legal studies, the heated debate over the premise of commonality (that is, the epistemological assumption of similarity between laws that underlies the dominant comparative method, 'functionalism') reveals that an implicit hierarchy between us and them can niche within an ostensibly neutral stance. As Pierre Legrand states, the quest for commonalities that commands dominant strands of comparative law signifies that 'I'll recognise you if and to the extent that you are like me.'[331] In other words, ironing out differences leaves little place for the acknowledgement and ethical attention due to alterity. Furthermore, any remaining discrepancy becomes an anomaly that leads to exclusion – when it does not lead to an occult or inverted rejection in the form of cultural exoticisation or legal orientalism.[332]

The conflict of laws provides many classical examples of the ways in which the use of juridical categories can lead to the exclusion or reduction of foreign institutions or practices that do not fit within the 'systematic structure' of the host legal system, that is, that do not comply with its underlying cultural world view.[333] Contemporaneously with the institution of comparative law as a discipline, the discovery of difference in the morphology of legal systems[334] led, paradoxically, to the dominance of a methodological approach that required the flattening of difference. Conflicting conceptions of legal institutions – varying interpretations of Roman law within the civilian world (the 'poor widow's quarter'[335]), unfamiliar imports to the latter from the common law (trusts[336]), strong vestiges of canon law from the Byzantine empire (is a Greek orthodox religious marriage ceremony a legal form or an issue of substance?[337])

[331] Legrand, 'Sur l'analyse différentielle des jurisultures'.

[332] See Ruskola, *Legal Orientalism*, tracing back to Montesquieu and then to the traders of the British empire, the idea that the East is despotic or illiberal, as opposed to the West's concern for the rule of law (noting however that prejudices, in the neutral sense used by Gadamer, can only be managed, not eliminated: ibid, 51). Similarly, in his study of 'Black Gaius', questioning the supposed cultural 'purity' of the Roman legal tradition, Monateri shows how comparative legal thought in the twentieth century ran along lines already traced by linguistic theory. The cultural (racialised) purity of language was echoed in a genealogical narrative that recounted the Roman Christian origins of the continental legal system as (imagined) legal community (P-G Monateri, 'Black Gaius: A Quest for the Multicultural Origins of the "Western Legal Tradition" (2000) 51 *Hastings LJ* 479). On colonial legal imagery such as the 'veiled protectorate', or other sexual fantasies of the coloniser, see above 248.

[333] The doctrinal justification for such exclusions is the 'theory of characterisation'. Characterisation applies to the dispute or to specific legal issues. It consists in selecting the appropriate legal category that should house the claim according to the viewpoint of the court (the forum).

[334] Including among those in the close cultural proximity shared by the concert of nations and Savigny's community of laws.

[335] See the case of the 'poor widow's quarter', claimed before the French colonial court under the Code Rohan in force in Malta: Court of Appeals of Algiers, 24 Dec 1889, *Bartholo*, B. Ancel & Y Lequette, *Grands arrêts de la jurisprudence de droit international privé*, 5th edn, n° 9.

[336] This was a classic difficulty in comparative conflict of laws: see, attempting a solution, the Hague Convention on the Law Applicable to Trusts and on their Recognition, 1985.

[337] A classical example concerns the ways in which secular courts tend to treat foreign religious forms, with multiple ripple effects thereafter. Thus, a ceremony that carries a crucial significance, say, for the celebration of a marriage under a foreign law, will tend to be considered as a mere formality in a secular court. This means that a civil form accomplished in the country of the latter will suffice to wed two people whose personal laws prescribe a religious celebration as a condition of validity of their marriage. The latter is not taken seriously on its own terms, but made to fit into the category 'form' of the secular forum. Conversely, having accomplished only the religious celebration without the civil form, they will be considered unmarried. Here, the religious form is merely tolerated, in the name of religious freedom, but given no civil effect (this is value pluralism and not legal pluralism, as seen above). See for a concrete illustration of the ways in which exclusion takes place in the name of the systematic structure of the forum legal system, the French *Caraslanis* case (Cour de cassation, Civ 1 février 1955, n° de pourvoi: 55-02.067).

and progressively, the arrival before the courts of the metropolis of citizens from the periphery bearing the legacy of colonial cultures[338] – led both to the affirmation of the forum as the sole, or Archimedean, reference point and to the need to make foreign law 'fit' into the structure of the host legal system. The problem has in no way disappeared by the apparent smoothing of legal differences.[339] A significant illustration can be found in the (more recent) case of the Hopi masks, in which 70 Katsinam shamanic masks, sacred to an Indian tribe of Arizona, had found their way to a French private collection and were put up for auction in France.[340] In their pursuit of provisional measures before a French court to prevent the dispersal of the collection, the Hopis were denied legal title (and therefore, legal standing) on various grounds, including the unenforceability of foreign law at the provisional stage and the unfamiliarity of collective tribal cultural property under French civilian legal categories.

As seen above, a series of ingenious devices (created by the courts or imagined by jurists) ensures that the management and processing of legal misfits form an overarching perspective.[341] However, once repressed, differences come back to roost in one way or another. The polygamous (French/Algerian) citizen, the incestuous (Swiss/Russian) uncle and niece, or the limping statusless child (Italy/Ukraine), are all the warped figures[342] produced by the denial of alterity. Less perceptible moreover are the underlying fantasies and imaginaries that are relayed through the apparently technical structure of the legal system and its categories. Judith Surkis' study of the nineteenth-century colonial construction of personal status in Algeria (that is, beyond the familiar European 'community of laws'), presented above, shows how orientalist colonial imaginaries were projected onto local indigenous customs and religious institutions, distorting their very meaning and internal balance.[343] Today,

[338] Hence the famous imbroglio of the polygamous (formerly Tunisian) French citizen in the *Chemouni* saga (see Cour de Cassation, Chambre civile 28 Jan 1958, Bull 1958, I, n°60, p 48; and 19 février 1963 n° 60-11.930).

[339] On the reasons for the remanence of the problem of misfit in the 'era of the post', see M Xifaras, 'The Global Turn in Legal Theory' (2016) XXIX *Canadian Journal of Law & Jurisprudence* 215–43.

[340] See M Cornu, 'About Sacred Cultural Property: the Hopi masks case' (2013) 20 *International Journal of Cultural Property* 451–66. The application for provisional measures was heard and refused by the Paris Court of first instance (TGI Paris, interim orders of 12 April 2013, RG n°13/25880; 6 December 2013, RG n°13/59110; 27 June 2014, RG n°14/55733). The Hopi masks are worn by dancers who personify the Katsinam dolls, spirits that incarnate in turn diverse aspects of the Hopi cosmos: see Descola, *Les formes du Visible* 348 et seq.

[341] 'Characterisation' was soon to be followed by other devices, such as renvoi, preliminary questions and all sorts of (obsessional) apparatuses that serve to veil the morphology of difference, in the very name of tolerance.

[342] These are all classical tropes of private international law, to be found in most textbooks. They are also the spectral figures of law's hauntology (see below 301).

[343] The fantasies projected onto the Muslim family and its law did not wait for the formalisation in Savigny's opus of the 'normative communion of Christian-Roman laws' to materialise in very similar forms around the colonial world, as Judith Surkis' exploration of the judicial archive of the Court of Algiers under French rule so tellingly demonstrates. Notably, family matters remained within the orbit of indigenous personal law (often largely reimagined as allowing extraordinary sexual licence), while being separated however from the land regime: the latter became subject to the (French) civil, secular and codified law of property (and ensured a massive transfer of title to the colonisers). This example was replicated around the colonial world – in the British colonisation of India, or in New Zealand, as shown by Nan Suffert's study (also presented above).

similar neocolonialist imaginaries continue to project fantasies – of rejection and fascination, relating to sexuality (polygamy) or punishment (stoning) – on Muslim communities, whether foreign or domestic.[344] Moreover, the supposed lawlessness of more distant 'archaic' cultures is still considered a feature of underdevelopment or indeed more mystifying queerness. As the question of the status of the Muslim veil shows, legal orientalism takes on many varied, contemporary forms.[345]

Within the conflict of laws, then, the question of our relationship to alterity appears as a central but deflected debate about the proper shape of legal categories.[346] Diversity can indeed be hosted, but only (at least in the conventional account) on the terms (that is, within the categories) designed by the host legal system.[347] This warrants a brief reminder[348] in the form of a short detour via recent political-theoretical debate as to the respective implications of liberalism and pluralism in the context of our contemporary, postcolonial, multicultural societies.[349] The difficulties

[344] On the 'Shariah law row' triggered in the United Kingdom by the Archbishop of Canterbury, Rowan Williams' plea for greater legal pluralism, see www.independent.co.uk/news/uk/home-news/archbishop-ignites-sharia-law-row-779505.html. For egregious 'anti-foreign law' measures in the United States around the same time, see www.splcenter.org/hatewatch/2018/02/05/anti-sharia-law-bills-united-states, relating that since 2010, 201 anti-Sharia law bills had been introduced in 43 states. In 2017 alone, 14 states introduced anti-Sharia law bills, with Texas and Arkansas enacting the legislation.

[345] On legal orientalism, see Ruskola, *Legal Orientalism;* and on its current forms in the veil debate, see G Frankenberg, *Comparative Law as Critique* (Cheltenham, Elgar, 2016) 113 et seq.

[346] Deflected here means that it hides something else. This can be seen in the debates about characterisation, seen above. The forum's classificatory scheme is distanced discursively from legal 'substance', or the concrete stakes in dispute between litigants (along with their political and geopolitical implications). It meant that the unruly interference of claims framed in terms of foreign laws are perceived as risks that called for order in order to protect the cohesion of the host legal system: an allocatory method designed to avoid a messy form of legal pluralism lacking direction and in which, potentially, 'anything goes'.

[347] On hospitality within the shadow avatar, see below 301.

[348] The opposition between monism and pluralism has already been encountered above in Parts I and II of this book as a matter of methodology, epistemology, aesthetics and ontology.

[349] Concretely, this debate came to occupy the public space in England, when the Archbishop of Canterbury argued, in 2008 (see above), that multicultural societies need something more than liberalism if various religious communities with their diverse world views and lifestyles are to live together in harmony within the same territory. The ensuing controversy, which degenerated very quickly into the 'Shariah law row', is particularly interesting from the perspective of private international law, because it concerns the modes of coexistence of different normativities. How best, asked the Archbishop, to allow Muslim communities to live in Britain according to the 'principle of recognition'? The liberal response – that is, the traditional response in Western secular, liberal democracies – is one of conditional tolerance towards the other (who is not necessarily a foreigner in a technical sense but who claims a cultural lifestyle which is not shared by the majority of the political community). This means that different religious convictions are tolerated in the name of the freedom of expression. Various legal devices have allowed liberal democracies to accommodate, by and large, various changes in social morality. The debate in political theory then asks to what extent legal pluralism can really improve on liberal tolerance? What can pluralism bring that liberalism does not already allow? And, more importantly, what of the risk of communitarianism, cultural relativism, laxism, the lack of solutions to conflicts, or the collapse of order into 'dissociative' perspectivism' (so termed by Pierre Schlag), that are all bound to ensue if liberalism's frontier control, or vigilant door-keeping, disappears? One familiar (and often feminist) objection to the pluralist idea is that it imprisons the members of the community in its own rules, without any possibility of escape from what might be felt as a rigid frame. Communitarianism means isolation for the group and estrangement for its individual members. This would be particularly problematic, for instance, for Muslim women, who may have no desire to live by the norms of an inegalitarian society. However, according to the Archbishop's text, a member of the community may always claim the benefit of the law of the land if so desired, and access the state courts to do so. Moreover, it is also the case that once recognised as living law, the law of the community is likely to evolve in its interactions with its environment. Private international law endorses both these points.

are linked, on the one hand, to 'global legal pluralism' (the multiplication of non-state normativities as an alternative to state-centred monism), and on the other, to the status of religious or ethnic communitarianism in a secular, egalitarian state. As seen above, pluralism has different meanings when it is used respectively as a political or as a legal concept. In the first sense (value pluralism), largely coterminous with political liberalism, it signifies that a polity acknowledges multiple values that may be given expression under the *archè* of only one, unitary, form and source of legality. Protection of privacy or freedom of expression are typically the 'rights-based' tools that provide this space, but other forms of legal reasoning (such as creating reasonable exceptions, or balancing out opposing interests) also contribute to protect multiple beliefs and practices in a democratic society.[350] And of course, historically, these legal forms were all an important victory against the arbitrariness of divine right, royal privilege, or the autocratic Leviathan.

However, under a second meaning, (legal) pluralism accepts that multiple legal norms coexist on an equal footing (including within one territorial space). It is this recognition of law's plurality that enters into conflict with the liberal scheme of legal monism (as seen above) and its injunction of formal equality of all before the law, since it rejects the prior requirement, embedded in monism, of conformity to a model fashioned in the likeness of self. Merely creating spaces of (sub-legal) protected privacy (for other beliefs) or allowing for exceptions to the norm (for different cultural practices) – both characteristic of liberalism and value pluralism – are no longer enough: pluralism means acknowledging that a given community[351] may choose under which norms it wishes to live, as long as this choice does not subtract from or threaten the broader common good. In terms of the conflict of laws, this means changing the location of legal authority.[352] The liberal model of value pluralism is analogous to the multilateralist methodology described above: the latter retains control over the conditions of reception of foreign law; it tolerates alterity conditionally, according to predefined criteria that it draws up in its own likeness. When applied to foreign law, these terms refer, as we know, to the shape of legal categories and the scope of the law as defined by choice of law rules. As long as different cultures were marginal within a dominantly homogeneous society, liberalism was (arguably) adequate to ensure peaceful coexistence of different cultural forms. However, dealing with difference as exception in a multicultural society is obviously inappropriate, and liable to generate the sort of political tensions which are tragically apparent in Western communities today. The response, then, has to be *more not less* acceptance of alterity.[353]

[350] See the formulation used by the ECtHR in *Refah Partisi (the Welfare Party) and Others v Turkey* App nos 41340/98, 41342/98, 41343/98 et al. Judgment 13.2.2003 [GC].

[351] The definition of community beyond (outside, across or below) the state raises obvious problems that are closely linked, in circular fashion, to those that attend non state legality. To the extent that the two are inextricably linked, our choice here is to stay with the latter, and keep to the idea that law is whatever claims to be such, as long as it accepts to enter the concert of communities by means of integrated coordinatory device (see on this point, R Michaels, 'Law and Recognition – Towards a Relational Concept of Law', in N Roughan and A Halpin (eds), *In Pursuit of Pluralist Jurisprudence* (Cambridge, Cambridge University Press, 2019), and above 207).

[352] See on this point, D Boden, 'Le pluralisme juridique en droit international privé' (2005) 49 *Archives Philo Droit* 275–316.

[353] So while nativism, originalism, protectionism and other legal forms of intolerance are apparently gaining ground in political discourse in Western societies (not to mention the eruption of warfare, invasion,

B. The Social Construction of Acceptability (*Ordre Public*)

The notoriously disorderly 'exception' known as '*ordre public*' (lost in translation as 'public policy', or 'public order') in the conflict of laws, covers a variety of values, principles, or mandatory policies. These are 'exceptional' both procedurally (because they ground arguments that are raised in defence to a claim based on the legal rule), and substantively (because they authorise a derogation from the rule of law). These are often ascribed to some sort of transcendent order (such as natural law, 'universal principles of justice' or fundamental rights). However, at the same time, *ordre public* has obvious family links with other politically potent and equally elusive concepts that evoke police power, such as 'reason of state' or 'state of necessity', that also legitimate the reversal of rule of law and exception.

In respect of its specific avatar in the conflict of laws, the need for an exception is framed traditionally as the necessary counterpart of the purported neutrality, impartiality or blindness of the choice of law rule: its 'leap into the unknown' undeniably requires a safety net. However, the exceptional, defensive function of *ordre public* (to which we shall return below) has shifted, so that it has become a filter in respect of alternative or alien (non-modern, non-secular) legal forms or categories. Such a filter involves only too often a negative (or condescending) value judgement.[354] Various institutions of foreign family law in particular (polygamy, divorce of all kinds, paternity suits, same-sex marriage, adoption, surrogacy etc) have, from time to time, been subject to a civilisational gut reaction of this kind. Indeed, just like the requirement of compliance with the shape of legal categories evoked above, this particular form of epistemological firewall developed in the context of colonial encounters with alterity, embodies, as Silviano Santiago writes of tolerance in such a context:

> above all the lack of respect (and not mere intellectual curiosity) in relation to the Other; it is intolerance with the values of the Other. It is the main effect of the narcissistic European gesture that aimed at seeing its own image repeated throughout the universe. In full glory, the so-called universal history begins with European expansionism. The New World is only the occasion for another mirror, and the native is the clay to mould a double, similar figure – and add more violence and destruction.[355]

Drawing on contemporary findings in anthropology, as seen above, theories of early twentieth-century comparative law divided the world's cultures into 'families',

repression and corruption), it is important to remember that there is nothing either natural, or inevitable, nor even invincible, about them. This will be the cue to bring in legal pluralism, of which the analogue is statutism, the shadow version of the conflict of laws. As seen above, it accepts that authority is vested in the other, who decides for herself and on an equal footing on what terms she will enter. It is in this form that both pluralism and hospitality have always been present within the law as alternative attitudes to foreignness or otherness.

[354] See above how the temporal element of 'development' contains a value judgement as to the state of being locked in primitive thought and poverty. Indians were deemed to possess human reason, and thus be capable of being held to a universal code based on Spanish rules. However, on the other hand, they were deemed to be different due to their specific social and cultural practices (T Anghie, 'Francisco De Vitoria and the Colonial Origins of International Law' (1996) 5 *Social & Legal Studies*, 325, 327). By deeming Indians capable of adhering to universal norms, yet at the same time at variance with them, this scheme created a system of norms that was inevitably violated by the Indians, which justified endless Spanish incursion into their society (ibid, 326, 329–31).

[355] Gazzola (ed) *The Space in-between*, 13.

classified according to the intensity of their proximity with the heritage of the (Roman Christian) West. 'Legal barbarians',[356] that is, those whose 'primitive' modes of access to reality did not fit with a universalised[357] ideal of civilisation, were relegated to the periphery (and similarly disqualified by international law from the concert of nations) In this respect, the exception of public policy or *ordre public* similarly represents a ploy of 'imagined community'.[358] The dual ideas of universality and non-derogability of certain values serve both as the amplifiers of difference and the parameters of exclusion. However, the threshold is uncertain and the triggering factors are the subject of endless debate (individual injustice assessed *in concreto*, intolerable norms envisaged *in abstracto*, additional parameters of proximity, or again, expectations rooted in past histories, situations or practices etc).[359] Above all, these uncertainties provide a niche for rationalities of exclusion or rejection of alterity.

Beyond the variability of our own social institutions, there are always – as seen above in respect of the shape of our legal categories – further assumptions or fantasies underlying our own cultural construction of moral acceptability. The temptation (into which courts and others regularly fall) is to relegate practices that are endowed with entirely diverse meanings in their own cosmological context, to the realm of the 'undeveloped', or, in the mode of an anathema, to the primitive or the savage.[360] Three examples taken from anthropological or culturalist approaches to the comparative moral economies of law (successively from the work of Philippe Descola, Louis Asser-Andieu and Pierre Legrand) can serve to show that what we perceive to be the most abhorrent of 'foreign' practices – cannibalism, incest, excision[361] – may well have a symbolic significance in context that does not justify their relegation to 'barbarian' status (even if we do not accept them).[362] The following observation on Lévis-Strauss'

[356] DM Bonilla, *Legal Barbarians*.

[357] Meaning imposed upon the universe, conceived as one. On pluriversality, see above.

[358] B Anderson *op cit* and see above 143.

[359] Thus, there is a widely shared principle according to which the requirements of public policy – or the limits of the intolerable – must be assessed on the day the court sits. Such a principle only serves to emphasise their inconstancy and relativity, in time and space. The various family law institutions cited above, rejected yesterday and promoted today (or the reverse), are archetypical sites of such axiological variations within Western legal cultures. The assumption here (familiar to constitutional jurisprudence), is that the judiciary has an inherent legitimacy to decide upon the social-legal acceptability of given practices or *mores* (and moreover an innate or intuitive receptivity to the trends of public opinion, that dispense with empirical research or indeed technical expertise). Secondly, once the appropriate standard of acceptability (or in earlier versions, 'civilisation') is established, a delicate modulation ensues as to the intensity of its requirements according to the spatial distance and specific temporality of individual situations (this is the 'principle of proximity', traced by Lagarde, 'Le principe de proximité dans le droit international privé contemporain' (1986) 196 *Rec Cours Académie de droit international de La Haye*. When the values are enclosed in human, fundamental or constitutional rights, the assessment of the threshold of intolerability takes on the different form of balancing, or again proportionality, but does not change in substance.

[360] On the underlying assumptions of 'development' as a chronological concept, see above Part II.

[361] See respectively, Descola, *Les formes du Visible*, cannibalism as 'le moyen paradoxal d'incorporer l'altérité au plus profond, tout en restant fidèles à eux-mêmes', p 544; L Asser-Andrieu, 'Le crépuscule des cultures. L'affaire Pitcairn et l'idéologie des droits humains' (2012) 3 *Droit et société* 763–87; P Legrand, 'Foreign Law. Understanding Understanding' 6(2) *Journ Comp Law* 67 referring (fn 388) to RA Shweder, '"What About Female Genital Mutilation?" and Why Understanding Culture Matters in the First Place' in RA Shweder, M Minow and HR Markus (eds), *Engaging Cultural Differences* (New York, Sage, 2002) 216–15.

[362] On 'legal barbarians', see again Bonilla, *Legal Barbarians*. This is the point made by Legrand; indeed, we know from longstanding debates over 'cultural relativism' that any attempt to resist the universalism of the Western belief-system is likely to be resisted in binary terms.

account of the Indian colonial encounter in *Tristes Tropiques* by Silviano Santiago merits reflection:

> the Indians of Puerto Rico devoted themselves to capturing whites in order to drown them. Afterward, they stood guard over the ocean, watching out for corpses for weeks on end in order to determine whether they were subject to the laws of putrefaction. Not without irony, Lévi-Strauss concludes: 'The whites would invoke the social sciences while the Indians placed more trust in the natural sciences; whereas the whites proclaimed that the Indians were beasts, the latter were happy to take the former as gods. While both were equally ignorant, the latter belief was at least worthier of men.' Violence is always practised by the Indians for religious purposes. Faced with the whites, who considered themselves to be the bearers of God's word, each and every one a prophet, the reaction of the Indian is to test to what extent the words of the Europeans translate into transparent truth.[363]

It is important to dissipate any misinterpretation that the provocative examples cited above are likely to induce. The point here is in no way to claim that these practices are in any way 'good' in the moral terms of (our) cultural codes, nor, more importantly, that 'we' should accept them within the bounds of our communities.[364] However, the argument here is that alien cultural practices, perceived as primitive (or condemned as savage), may entertain a far more respectful vision of otherness than our Western/naturalist/modernist own.[365] Philippe Descola's classification of the various relationships that collectives entertain with alterity brings home the fact that non-modern visions (animism, totemism, analogism) are more attentive than their modern counterparts to the extraordinary interdependence of all forms of beings (sentient and non-sentient, visible and invisible, past and future). We should be aware that many of our own practices appear wasteful and cruel in the eyes of non-modern or non-naturalist communities.[366] Our grabbing of land and natural resources, our cruelty and neglect of other species, and our colonisation of the rest of humanity, all appear entwined and equally devastating from the perspective of the jaguar.[367]

Indeed, 'naturalism' supports the belief that there are various traits that are a-historical and a-contextual, that is, inherent to human nature and therefore universal (in a world that is unitary and not pluriversal, as seen above). Here however, the interdisciplinary cross-fertilisation of critical anthropology (the 'thick' description of culture[368]), ethno-psychoanalysis (the integration of ethnography and social history in the formation of the psyche[369]) and history (repairing its omission of the collective psyche in the explanation of historical events or social attitudes[370]) suggests a

[363] Gazzola (ed) *The Space in-between*, 27. On this example, see already above, 282.

[364] On the 'we' in community (and law), see Lindahl, 'Place-Holding the Future'.

[365] This point is highlighted with particular clarity by Descola *(Les formes du Visible)* in respect of cannibalism as a mode of 'devenir-autre' (p 438).

[366] Indeed as Anthony Angie points out, in *Imperialism, Sovereignty and the Making of International Law* (Cambridge, Cambridge University Press, 2005), the West forgets its own history.

[367] On the 'gaze of the jaguar', see above Part II.

[368] C Geertz, *The Interpretation of Cultures* (New York, Basic Books, 1973).

[369] Mazurel, *L'inconscient ou l'oubli de l'histoire.*

[370] Ibid. The idea in this book is that anthropology should be (or is, in its critical forms) attentive to the cultural fashioning of psychic economies, while psychoanalysis should (or is, in rare cases) sensitive to cultural history and language, beyond individual biographies.

very different take. This tension is patent in attitudes towards war and aggression, sexuality and family, shame and honour, crime and punishment. Anthropological descriptions of the practices, social institutions and belief-systems of diverse communities (and comparative legal studies in their wake) emphasise the extraordinarily varied range of censorship devices (across different communities, in space and time) that divide the acceptable from the inconceivable, the sacred from the profane, desire from rejection.[371]

To return, then, to the conflict of laws, we can see how the exception of public policy highlights these tensions and contradictions within the cultural 'construction of the intolerable'.[372] It points to the extreme variability of values that are proclaimed at any point as universal or inderogable. What is interesting too, however, is that it also suggests ways to address these inevitable paradoxes that attend the encounter between embedded belief systems and the ever-changing individual needs of equity in individual cases. In this respect, on the other (tails) side of the (heads) coin of public policy or reason of state, the message is that an ethical stance towards alterity does not enjoin one culture to adopt institutions that are abhorrent to it, or, what is more to the point here, even to admit them in the form of a foreign law or judgement. However, it does require that these other schemes are acknowledged as alternative modes of access to reality, endowed with equal dignity to our own. Here then is a (further) invitation to unravel the stance of moral superiority that rejection of alterity in the name of apparently liberal value judgements tends to occlude.

C. Wrongs of Rights

The two preceding paragraphs show how the cunning of difference has always been to enfold exclusion within an assertion of equality. If this ruse extends to liberal rights, then there may also be reasons to be wary of the contemporary trend to confer rights on nature.[373] The question here then is whether the

[371] Given the centrality of sexuality and gender in the understanding of cultural difference, a good example is the 'invention' of sexuality in the Western seventeenth century, as analysed by Michel Foucault: this obviously does not mean that sexuality did not exist before modernity (nor that it does not exist outside the West!), but that the latter induced a novel way of thinking about human life, health and intimacy – so that sexuality was not repressed but actually 'produced' by new forms of (bio-)power, themselves in turn indissociable from emerging medical science and technologies and above all the new (biopolitical) functions of state in respect of its population.

[372] D Fassin, 'L'ordre moral du monde Essai d'anthropologie de l'intolérable', in D Fassin & P Bourdelais (eds), *Les Constructions de l'intolérable. Études d'anthropologie et d'histoire sur les frontières de l'espace moral* (Paris, La Découverte, 2005)

[373] As Ratna Kapur suggests (*Gender, Alterity and Human Rights*). On the idea of natural personhood or Nature as subject of rights, the available legal and philosophical literature is now very abundant. For some forerunners, see M Serres, *Le contrat naturel* (Flammarion Poche, 1990, 2020), making a plea for a new pact enacting a vital symbiosis and involving the duties of humanity towards Nature; MA Hermitte, 'La Nature, sujet de droit ?' (2011) 66 *Annales Histoire, Sciences Sociales*; on the deep ecological renewal of Spinoza's relational subject, see Naess, 'The Shallow and the Deep'. For a very critical view of natural personhood from an indigenous, feminist perspective: V Marshall, 'Removing the veil from the "Rights of Nature": The dichotomy between First Nations customary rights and environmental legal personhood' (2019) 45 *Australian Feminist Law Journal* 233–48. On the dark sides of the rights of Nature, see A Pottage, 'Why Nature has no Rights' in AA Nakagawa & C Douzinas (eds), *Non-Human Rights. Critical Perspectives*

latter – in the holistic constitutional and gendered form of Mother Earth, or perhaps in the terrifying guise of Latour/Lovelock's Gaia, or as embodied in individualised trees, animals or rivers – has legal (fundamental or 'human') rights in the eyes of modern legal systems, and correlatively, standing in court so as to be able to invoke them.[374] The strategy is of course to find legal grounds for instituting correlative duties to protect on the part of humanity and hard liability on those (individuals or collectives) that cause damage to the planetary commons.[375] In the path of recent anthropological moves (encountered in Part II above) to 'think like a mountain',[376] several legal systems of the global South have ventured down this path in various ways.[377] Spectacularly, Pachamama has been given legal (constitutional) status and considered 'a living being, a subject entitled to rights' in Ecuador and Bolivia.[378] More frequently, specific rivers or lakes have been endowed with personhood.[379] These moves accompany the slow recognition of indigenous 'property rights' over land inhabited by spiritual beings.[380] Just as this book goes to press,

(Cheltenham, Elgar, 2023, forthcoming), arguing (p 2) that 'the effect of recognizing "Nature" as a person is not to protect it from corporate globalization. On the contrary, the function of the signifier "Nature" is at once to intensify and obfuscate the subjection of natural entities to those forces. The sense of vitality that allows the signifier to perform this function is generated by the *episteme* of twentieth-century fossil capital, which, ironically, turns out to be genealogically associated with the theoretical impulse that generates images of a possible posthuman Earthly legality' (and, more anecdotally, pointing to the fact that Lovelock's Gaia actually originated in a study commissioned by Royal Dutch Shell). For a radical critique of rights discourse from the perspective of critical legal studies, as a form of alienation of existential feelings or aspirations that requires their transformation into a (legal) framework which participates in turn in the very consciousness that such discourse is designed to challenge, P Gabel and D Kennedy, 'Roll Over Beethoven', *Stanford Law Review* (1984) 36 *Critical Legal Studies Symposium* 1–55, 27.

[374] On the legal standing of natural entities, the pioneer is C Stone. 'Should Trees Have Standing? Towards Legal Rights for Natural Objects' (1972) 45 *Southern California Law Review* 450–501. For a recent and severe critique of the way in which the 'rights of nature' have served, on the contrary, the cause of epistemic extractivism, see Pottage, 'Why nature has no rights'. Contrary to what is often claimed, conferring rights on animals and future generations is not a new idea, at least in the civilian legal tradition: see JP Marguénaud, 'L'animal sujet de droit ou la modernité d'une vieille idée de René Demogue' (2021) *Revue trimestrielle de droit civil* 591.

[375] The legal and philosophical literature on the global commons is at least as abundant as on nature's personhood and usually goes together.

[376] See above 193.

[377] These are countries with large indigenous populations or multi-religious communities that have nevertheless in the course of 'development' and their integration in the concert of nations adopted a court system following the Western institutional model.

[378] See A Escobar, 'Transition Discourses and the Politics of relationality. Towards Designs for the Pluriverse' in B Reiter (ed), *Constructing the Pluriverse, The Geopolitics of Knowledge* (Durham NC, Duke University Press, 2018) 63, 71 on *buen vivir* and the rights of nature. For an example, see Corte Constitucional Del Ecuador, Sentencia *Camaronera Reserva Cayapas*, no 166-15-SEP- CC, 20 May 2015, pp 9–10. Judge Wendy Molina Andrade points to the change of paradigm under which Nature, as a living being, is considered a subject 'entitled to rights … as opposed to the classic anthropocentric conception in which Nature is considered as a mere supplier of resources.' However, the figure of Pachamama is not perceived in the same way among the different indigenous peoples present in these countries.

[379] See on the rights of the Colombian River Atrata, S Revet, 'Les droits du fleuve – Polyphonie autour du fleuve Atrato en Colombie et de ses gardiens' (2020) September-December *Revue européenne d'analyse des sociétés politiques, Sociétés politiques comparées*, 52.

[380] See Inter-American Court of Human Rights, *Mayagna (Sumo) Awas Tingni Community v Nicaragua* (2001), the first ruling to protect the traditional occupation of lands by indigenous peoples (against a concession to log within the Community's traditional lands; see L Alvarado, 'Prospects and Challenges in the Implementation of Indigenous Peoples' Human Rights in International Law: Lessons from the Case of Awas Tingni v. Nicaragua' (2007) 24 *Arizona Journal of International and Comparative Law* 609–44.

the UN Human Rights Committee has ruled that the islanders of Torres Straits must receive reparation from the Australian government for its failure to implement adaptation measures to protect their homes, private lives and families as well as their ability to maintain their traditional way of life, and to pass on their culture and traditions to future generations.[381]

While still rare today, these examples of ecological judicial activism bear witness to highly creative legal strategies. Indubitably, beyond the rights of indigenous peoples, the 'rights of nature' are a powerful discourse, a striking imagery with visible political-ecological effects.[382] They have put the spotlight on the plight of various species or biosystems, underlined the links between traditional cultural practices and environmental husbandry, and signalled a space of struggle to the attention of civil society worldwide (alias the 'international community') under the new climate regime.[383] For instance, conferring legal personhood on a river from which communities draw their livelihood is a means to ensure a rallying point for political resistance to the terrible destruction of biocultural diversity or the needless suffering inflicted on non-human lives. At first sight, then, conferring rights and legal standing on beings devoid of (human) agency may be the best means that modern law can provide in order to make audible the call (indeed, legally, the appeal) of the other. Furthermore, interesting precedents in the field of cultural property might seem to make transnational litigation the most propitious starting point from which to diffuse such ideas in Western legal systems. There are some (rare) instances of 'cultural' entities appearing in court in conflict of laws cases and requiring their own restitution to their homeland. Thus in a case before the English courts involving the fate of a *Sivalingam*, or sacred statue, that had been looted from an Indian temple, the legal issue was 'whether a foreign legal person, which would not be recognised as such under English law and which has an essentially inanimate content, can sue in the English courts'.[384] That the court

This change in modern conceptions of title to (immovable) property has – in cases of 'cultural objects' – also affected 'movables', so as to account in legal terms for the quasi-agency of sacred artefacts, although the movement is very slow (see on the legal saga of the Hopi masks, M Cornu, 'About Sacred Cultural Property: The Hopi Masks Case' (2013) 20 *International Journal of Cultural Property* 451–66).

[381] For a full account: www.nature.com/articles/d41586-022-03186-6.

[382] To the extent that the project has become the rights of nature project and has evolved into what is described as no less than 'an intersectionalist politics of plurinational communities, interdisciplinary actors and interspecies agents, forged in centuries of dispossession and struggles for justice, and directed currently against corporate globalization and its ongoing colonization of nature': TJ Demos, 'Rights of nature: the art and politics of Earth jurisprudence' (2015), https://cpb-us-e1.wpmucdn.com/sites.ucsc.edu/dist/0/196/files/2015/10/Demos-Rights-of-Nature-2015.compressed.pdf.

[383] On the possible new political assemblages, D Matthews, 'From Global To Anthropocenic Assemblages: Re-Thinking Territory, Authority And Rights In The New Climatic Regime' (2019) 82 *The Modern Law Review* 4.

[384] See *Bumper Development Corp Ltd v Commissioner of Police of the Metropolis* [1991] 4 All ER 638, in which the court held that the sculpture *Natar aja* belonged to the god Shiva himself as 'localised' in a stone emblem at the site of a ruined temple in India, and had to be returned. The court had to consider the legal capacity in India of a temple and/or Sivalingam to hold title to property and pursue an action in the UK. It found that the temple had a valid title to the Nataraja superior to that enjoyed by the private buyer/developer. More broadly, then, the conflict of laws hypothesis arises when an entity endowed with legal personhood, agency or standing in its country of origin claims to act before a Western court that does not recognise these forms of subjectivities in its own domestic system. The difficulty is not new: historically it arose with the rise of the corporate form and continues today in the case of class actions, groups acting in the name of future generations etc. From the perspective of a conflict of laws analysis, there is a delicate distribution to operate between the law of the forum governing the procedural aspects of legal

ordered the deity to be returned shows that the concept of a legal person or subject endowed with rights can be enlarged to accommodate new figures, with particularly promising elasticity in international settings that raise conflicts of laws.[385] And after all, if purely fictitious persons (corporations, classes, future generations) are endowed with legal agency, there does not seem to be any reason why other nonhuman entities should not. Such beings seem to be an emblematic illustration of Latour's 'quasi-subjects' in the terms of the law.[386]

However, the attribution of rights can also be a more ambivalent move, and one that requires a singular vigilance towards an epistemological pitfall analogous to the cunning of difference described above.[387] First of all, rights beget counter-rights.[388] Then, the broader danger is that the repertoire of rights exposes such advances to a reappropriation by the rationalities of neoliberal legality. This is also valid for related (and increasingly popular) legal concepts such as the idea of 'stewardship' or 'trust' in respect of natural entities:[389] they all come with a more or less perceptible risk of

standing (who or what is qualified to act? say, corporations) and the law governing the legal personhood or constitution of the agent (that 'fills up' the legal categories allowed by the forum, say, by determining what a corporation is under its own rules). In *Bumper*, the court referred to the title of the temple under Hindu law – judging too that the state of Tamil Nadu would have title to the Nataraja under the provisions of Indian law, including the Indian Treasure Trove Act of 1878. This overture contrasts however with many cases in which a similar move is stifled by devices of uniformisation: on the Hopi mask case, for instance, see above 287.

[385] Or conflicts of cosmologies: see S Brachotte, 'The Conflict of Laws and Non-Secular Worldviews: A Proposal for Inclusion', PhD Dissertation, Sciences Po, Law School, 2022.

[386] Latour, *Enquête*, 357 et seq. Quasi-subjects and quasi-objects are (non-) categories that show up the artificiality of modernity's distinction between subject and object.

[387] See Marshall, 'Removing the veil', characterising natural personhood as a 'veil' in respect of indigenous epistemologies. See too on the operation of the fiction of legal personhood as a means not just of masking (nature) but of hard-wiring the underlying reality of life beneath the mask, Pottage, 'Why Nature Has No Rights'. As seen above, the emergence of human rights (under diverse names and in various geopolitical settings) as a contemporary avatar of natural law – the 'last utopia' (Moyn, *Not Enough*), to which we cling in the absence of alternative ideological (political, religious) horizons – has given rise to the controversial claim that they are actually 'part of the problem' (Kennedy, 'A Political Economy of Contemporary Legality'). This claim acknowledges that it is difficult to be against human rights as such, just as it is hard to be against equality, justice, autonomy, freedom or other liberal ideals embodied in the rule of law. These values played an important emancipatory role in the history of Western modernity at various points, sparking revolutionary change. Undoubtedly, many conquests in terms of the place of minorities in society, or the visibility of marginal groups within the formal world order, are indebted to litigation strategies or activist movements that appeal in one way or the other to human rights. Arguably, these still constitute the most disruptive common repertoire currently in effective use within legal systems with which to challenge existing structures and institutions. They continue to give legal form – that is, to help formulate – aspirations for the pursuit of social justice. However, as H Brabazon points out (*Neoliberal Legality*), rights (their content, binding force, scope, etc) remain 'contested territory' and may actively distract from any more radical critique of the modes of operation of the neoliberal economy and its associated schemes of thought. On the one hand, the multiplication of autonomous individuals (including emancipated slaves, colonised populations, women) as economic actors is a factor of capitalist expansion. On the other, contrary to what is widely believed, rights do not represent a radical critique of existing structural injustice, but are enrolled by neoliberal legality in order to exclude its further destabilisation.

[388] Notoriously, in the form of intellectual property, for instance; see, with immediate ecological implications, *Monsanto Canada Inc v Schmeiser* [2004] 1 SCR 902, 2004 SCC 34 a Supreme Court of Canada case on patent rights for biotechnology. Monsanto (successfully) sued a farmer for patent infringement (for the 'use' of patented genetically modified plant cells), that the latter claimed had strayed accidentally into his fields.

[389] Although these are of course legal concepts, they are usually used in a managerial setting, often associated with (the intrinsically laudable) call for 'sustainable development', to mean making humanity or

misrecognition, depoliticisation and abstraction.[390] There is hardly any need to recall (as seen above) that social corporate responsibility, now including an environmental component, has actually done little to save the planet through 'green' trade, investment and finance (or 'ESG' standards). What Fraser and Jaeggi have termed a 'tragedy-cum-farce' points to the reasons for which it is certainly more interesting to understand the constitutional status of Pachamama as a mandatory blind against the deleterious effects of neoliberalism, rather than as the institution of yet a new bearer of rights.[391]

As there are no concrete examples (as yet) of transnational moves by natural entities to gain standing and claim rights in foreign domestic courts, two analogies may be helpful. A first example concerns the space conceded to alien cosmologies through rights conferred on indigenous groups in international law or within (multicultural) Western legal systems. Such collective cultural rights, granted as compensatory measures to disadvantaged minority groups, have undoubtedly led (albeit unevenly) to an acknowledgement within the international community that indigenous people were exploited, discriminated against and assimilated during the colonial era, and in some cases, have given rise to state-funded reparations and governmental apologies for past injustices. This means that the emancipation of indigenous people is framed as a moral project. However, the problem of framing emancipation as a moral issue is that the underlying moral philosophy is 'too thin'. This is a point made by Fraser and Jaeggi in their 'conversation' on the definition of critical theory and what distinguishes it from moral philosophy: if moral wrongs are merely accidental, then it makes sense to pursue reforms to correct them. But if they are systemic, that is, arising from the deep structures of society, structural change is needed (or an epistemology 'beyond the fishbowl'); morality merely 'blackboxes' the processes.[392] Here, it may well be that very recent eruptions of alternative grammars (new utopias or more radical forms of critique) such as the political ecology, various radical eco-feminisms,[393] or the

different nation-states or communities trustees or stewards of nature, as a way of overcoming the lack of legal agency of the latter. See for an overview, J Bennett et al, 'Environmental Stewardship: A Conceptual Review and Analytical Framework' (2018) 61 *Environmental Management* 597–614.

[390] Or indeed displacement, in Hans Lindahl's terms: see on the example of 'penguins' rights', his 'Place-Holding the Future': 'It is tempting to assume that justice is done to the penguins' claim when they are granted a place and time of their own within the Australian legal order. But would these really be their own place and time? Have "we" not already taken possession of the penguins by recognizing that they "belong to 'us'"? Has not a certain assimilation already come about – an unjust appropriation of place – when referring to the *Manly* (the name of a place in Australia) colony of penguins?'

[391] Her constitutional status ensures the primacy of the protection of the natural commons over concessions, sales and other moves by the state in favour of private investment that would destroy the forests and pollute the rivers. The need for such a move is amply illustrated within the ambit of private international law by the *Chevron* saga in Ecuador (above, 258).

[392] There is of course a long and important tradition of criticism of the morality of rights, of which the *locus classicus* is Marx's 'On the Jewish Question' ([1843] 1975). As Nancy Fraser points out, in Fraser and Jaeggi, *Capitalism. A Critical Conversation* 122, beyond these moral dilemmas, critical theory must problematise the very processes (structural mechanisms and institutional arrangements) that produce them. It must eschew the 'black box' approach that underpins the freestanding moral critique preferred by egalitarian liberalism. On a similar rejection of the 'blackboxing' (by standard sociology) of the processes that lead to the outcomes observed, see B Latour, *Reassembling the Social. An introduction to actor-network-theory* (Oxford, Oxford University Press, 2005); *cf* too in law, K McGee, 'On Devices and Logics of Legal Sense: Towards Socio-technical Analysis' in McGee (ed), *Latour and the Passage of Law*, 61.

[393] The term ecofeminism was coined by French feminist Françoise d'Eaubonne in 1974 (see C Goldblum, *Françoise d'Eaubonne & l'écoféminisme* (Paris, ed Passager clandestin, 2019). Today, its most prominent

recentering of focus on bare, or phenomenological, life (that 'matters'),[394] announces new lawfare – a new boundary struggle – at the structural limits of neoliberal legality. In that case, the creation of new non-human subjectivities would reinforce this move.[395]

Conversely, it is also conceivable that instead of serving as instruments of emancipation, indigenous rights can coexist in a perfectly symbiotic relationship with the rationalities of the neoliberal order.[396] On the one hand, such rights are shaped by the latter, on the other, they serve to perpetuate its influence. Thus they are often seen from within indigenous communities as symbiotic with economic moves and expectations of authenticity that are as likely as not to reproduce familiar forms of coloniality along with their underlying imaginaries and projections.[397] As observed by Kristin Ciupa in her critique of the 'promise of rights' in this context, 'rights bearers are assimilated into the repertoire of the neoliberal order, and the latter in turn tends to produce new subjectivities that are entirely compatible with the latter, in the sense that they will be incentivised to accept the channels and tools that it makes available'.[398] This will do nothing to improve the structural conditions of indigenous people, blackboxed in such an analysis. In a similar way, Arturo Escobar warns of the colonisation of indigenous life forms through the apparently favourable concept of *buen vivir*, as a ruse of development discourse.[399] To go back to the idiom of jurisdictional jurisprudence, the latter maintains the 'peculiar' status of native peoples in a

representative is Donna Haraway, on whose contribution in the context of the return of the (gendered) body in ecological politics, see below 294.

[394] 'Black lives matter'.

[395] They tend to be the repertoires of social movements or critical scholarship, rather than aspirations to obtain enforceable rights in courts in respect of racial violence or the failure to rescue endangered migrants.

[396] The issue of liberal 'autonomy' will be picked up further below. However, here, it is apt to recall that "The mansion of modern freedoms stands on an ever-expanding base of fossil-fuel use' (D Chakrabarty, 'The Climate of History: Four Theses' (2009) 35 *Critical Inquiry*) of which the most essential was the right to property (Pottage, 'Why Nature Has No Rights', adding that even before the advent of the steam engine, possessive individualism externalised its material engagements with the earth by pretending that the value of land was produced by the rational industry of European men rather than by the plantation economy of the colonial period and by the slaves and resources that were treated as 'cheap nature' within that racialised economy).

[397] On legal orientalism, see above 280. A further critique is that international indigenous rights instruments circumscribe the category of indigeneity, incorporating only certain forms of indigeneity that are manageable within the dominant political economy. See C Kuipa, 'The Promise of Rights: International Indigenous Rights in the Neoliberal Era', in H Brabazon *Neoliberal Legality*, 140–66. These rights come with the risk of essentialisation, that is, of expectation of authenticity and performance. See too, in an effort to conceptualise differences in the ways in which indigenous claims (to cultural property) are shaped and legitimated, VT Hafstein, M Skrydstrup, 'Heritage vs. property. Contrasting regimes and rationalities in the patrimonial field', *The Routledge Companion to Cultural Property* (Routledge, 2017) 38–53: the argument is that distinct technologies of governmentality (property, heritage) produce distinct set of claims.

[398] Kuipa, 'The Promise of Rights'. The term 'neoliberal multiculturalism' to refer to the complementary role that cultural rights play in integrating culturally divergent groups into the neoliberal system (C Hale, 'Neoliberal Multiculturalism: The Remaking of Cultural Rights and Racial Dominance in Central America' (2005) *Political and Legal Anthropology Review* 10–28.

[399] Escobar, 'Transition Discourses and the Politics of relationality'.

state of exception, stopping far short of the recognition of sovereignty to determine a lifeworld.[400]

A second, glaring example also intimately related to political ecology is that of animal rights. Abuse of animal life on a massive scale (through intensive farming, slaughterhouses, pharmaceutical and other scientific experiments etc) has undoubtedly given rise to various intellectual (anti-species) protest movements, new dietary trends in the West (in its richer societies), and more diffuse (often schizophrenic) empathy. The latter does not exclude either the lures of consumerism, or the tricks of financialisation (as seen above). In his account of rights and deep ecology, Tim Benton analyses the ruse of assimilation in the 'deontological approach' that extends the basic principle of equality of consideration as applied to the rest of humanity, to members of other species.[401] As seen above in respect of other human groups, condemning discrimination (or multiplying rights-holders) is unlikely to be radical enough to dislodge neoliberal rationalities, which can quite easily conciliate 'thin' moral concerns with the reduction of other forms of life to the status of commodities (amusements, or disposable resources). This brings us back, then to a more radical critique of a rights-based approach to the protection of non-human nature and the issue of anomic desire.[402] As Tim Benton writes, the question is why we appeal to the (modern invention of) rights in the first place. Rights, as he points out, are only needed to protect individuals from their neighbours because something has gone deeply wrong in society. Here, in other words, is the 'Darwinian U-turn' described by Latour.[403] Competitive, egoistic individuals, acting under conditions of scarcity, are impelled to invade one another's basic interests unless restrained by a firmly enforced framework of rights. Warped ethics, notes Benton (to which we might add, warped

[400] M Rifkin, 'Indigenizing Agamben: Rethinking Sovereignty in Light of the "Peculiar" Status of Native Peoples' (2009) 73 *Cultural Critique* 88–124. We can add here Alain Pottage's critique ('Why Nature Has No Rights') of the rights of nature movement 'an epistemic community deeply imbricated with juridical authority' and fashioned or composed in such a way as to naturalise a Euro-American vision of nature as a community of interdependent entities. And this vision is hypothecated to a representation of indigenous peoples as the guardians of this community, a vision that retrenches a production of otherness that was one of the prime effects of colonialism, and which thereby sustains the ideology of property that the rights of nature movement purports to overcome. The charge is that 'nature becomes something identifiably "natural" by becoming more like colonial conceptions of the human, whose existence can only be legitimized by legal personhood'. The citations in the passage above are to A Rawson & B Mansfield, 'Producing juridical knowledge: "Rights of Nature" or the naturalization of rights?' (2018) 1 *Environment and Planning E: Nature and Space* 99–119, 100.

[401] As Tim Benton observed in 'Rights and justice on a shared planet: More rights or new relations?' (1998) 2 *Theoretical Criminology* 149–75, 158, 'it is rather taken for granted by the advocates of animal rights that the key to giving practical protection to the interests of non-human animals is to get them recognized as rights-holders. That this assumption seems uncontroversial is a testimony to the current moral authority of the discourse of human rights, from which the argument for animal rights draws.' Under this (thin moral/deontological) approach, our attitudes to members of other species are a form of prejudice no less objectionable than prejudice about a person's race or sex.

[402] The radical ethical case also draws attention to the difficulty – familiar to law, as seen above 289 – that the effects we see can rarely if ever be assigned to any particular individual agency, so they stand outside the scope of rights as they are generally understood in the liberal tradition.

[403] Far from being 'natural' or inherent in the human condition, rights (as shown by Marx in 'The Jewish Question') are the consequences of a historically specific type of civilisation – characterised by capitalism and the nuclear family (*cf* Balibar, *Des Universels*).

accounting) undermines all the traditional forms of normative regulation of desire, sweeping away local or status-bound notions of sufficiency and appropriateness in consumption. Such anomic desire knows no limits. Competitive performance is the incessant demand at work, whilst status seeking and the competitive pursuit of 'positional goods' (or social capital) increasingly shapes and constrains consumption and the use of leisure time. Eric Santner's description of the somatic effects on society of the neoliberal political economy – the incessant agitation of busybodies – serves once again as a cautionary tale.

A more radical turn – beyond the (epistemological) 'fishbowl' of lists of liberal rights – is required, then, if we are to respond adequately, in legal form, to the appeal of the other – including the diminishing voices of the birds, animals, insects, or micro-organisms that sustain the inhabitability of the earth. Such calls, as Bruno Latour observes, are appeals 'to save ourselves'; they are audible on ethical frequencies emitted by everything (every being and every thing) that surrounds us, depends on us and upon which we depend in turn.[404] These emissions are increasingly acute. We need, in other words, an ethos in the terms of the law that draws from the Maussian analysis of the gift that entangles, a legal version of the entwinements and bonds depicted above, in ways that counter the great economisation driven by neoliberal legality. But what would the move from 'thin' ethics to 'deep' ecology look like, in legal form? How might law enact the primacy of responsibility over autonomy; the foundational nature of gift, not market, and hence the exclusion of all calculation; a debt that can never be discharged (*n'est jamais quitte*); a non-competitive hospitable relationship to the other: the deactivation of all the centrisms (ethno, anthropo, ego) evoked above? The contention here is that the shadow avatar of the conflict of laws has the potential, once more, to respond in legal terms to the appeal of alterity. The key lies in the mirror effect between the welcome it extends to foreign law and the Levinassian/Derridean imperative to make way for the 'law of the other'.

II. THE LAW OF THE OTHER

Eco-phenomenology – that is, a philosophical move that draws on the resources of phenomenology to express our deepening concern for the natural world – is emerging currently as an antidote to the senselessness of our ways of inhabiting the earth. As seen above, our modern, jurisdictional and neoliberal schemes have severed subjects (our subjectivities) from their past and their surroundings, reinforced hierarchies within humanity, emptied space and instrumental time, and rendered other forms of life invisible. We have denied alterity, neglected the face of the other.[405] Initially

[404] Latour, *Enquête*, 454.

[405] Levinas' phenomenological account of the face-to-face relation that entails an inescapable and infinite responsibility for the other (*Totalité et infini*, 1961) (or *Totality and Infinity*, 1969), then *Autrement qu'être* (1974) (or *Otherwise than Being*, 1981). See R Bernasconi, 'Levinas, Emmanuel (1906–95)' *Routledge Encyclopedia of Philosophy* (1998), www.rep.routledge.com/articles/biographical/levinas-emmanuel-1906-95/v-1; 'Dialogue with Emmanuel Levinas', in RA Cohen (ed), *Face to Face with Levinas* (State University of New York Press); C Pelluchon, *Pour comprendre Levinas. Un philosophe pour notre temps* (Le Seuil, 2020). For the purposes of this book, it is significant that, as Bernasconi notes 'in analyses

a salutary reaction against religious obscurantism or teleological determinism, the cartesian scission of mind and body (and the avatars of the same pair: society and environment, subject and object), was gradually co-opted into the economised worldview of the 'Capitalocene'.[406] This is why, as explained in the previous section, modernity's model of legality – the liberal rule of law, along with rights, tolerance and even new subjects – is 'not enough' to counteract the forces of obscurantism that distort the very values of planetary responsibility and the various pacified forms of *vivre-ensemble*, or *buen vivir* in which many of us earth-dwellers[407] think we believe.

A possible avenue, then is to open our legal consciousness to the alternative possibilities of terrestrial being (corporeity) and inhabiting (dwelling-place or *demeure*) offered under the *archè* of the Western tradition itself, by the return of phenomenology as an ecological ethic.[408] This means seeing our common phenomenological experience of being on earth as the seat of an equally shared solidarity with all other forms of life, similarly struggling for survival on our planet's thin crust, the biosphere or 'crisis zone'.[409] Once again, the (legally elusive) body – gendered, finite, somatic, bare[410] – is a cardinal motor of this move.[411] *Habeas corpus*![412] Eco-phenomenology, then, expresses in philosophical terms a resistance to the economisation of the world. It resonates potently within contemporary feminist theory as 'eco-feminism'.[413] An analogous turn is visible throughout an array of disciplines, including the

that stretch phenomenology to its limits and beyond', Levinas finds 'alterity within the self'. The extreme version of this neglect of alterity (of which colonisation and various forms of servitude are the expressions, as seen above) is the fascist denial of the other in the form of a belief in the organic communion of (faceless) individuals: on the shadow cast by Hitlerian biologism on Levinas' thought and the difference between such doctrine and a phenomenology that sees the body as the site on alterity, intersubjectivity and therefore of ethics, see Pelluchon, *Pour comprendre Lévinas*, 163.

[406] JW Moore, *Anthropocene or Capitalocene? Nature, History, and the Crisis of Capitalism* (Oakland CA, PM Press, 2016).

[407] Or 'terriens' (Latour, *Où Atterrir?*).

[408] We owe it to Husserl's phenomenology to have replaced the conventional idea of truth by that of horizon (Pelluchon, *Pour comprendre Lévinas*, 37). It postulates that reality is not an object (or an environment) external to the subject, but is perceived or experienced through consciousness. In revisiting the process through which a phenomenon is given to our consciousness, the project of phenomenology is to make visible a horizon of meaning that is generally obstructed by our habits of thought, preconceptions and prejudices.

[409] Latour, *Enquête*, recalling that our planetary biosphere is a thin crust where the struggle for life takes place.

[410] And the subject of sovereignty, *homo sacer* (see above 164).

[411] The current turn to phenomenology accompanies or signals a return of vulnerable bodies or corporeality and their place on earth. Levinas relies precisely on this phenomenological insight in his reflection on alterity and transcendence, but with the further twist that the other is never (completely) accessible to my consciousness.

[412] On *Habeas corpus* as a legal defence of bare life (of aliens detained as enemy combatants outside US territory) see *Boumediene v Bush*, 553 US 723 (2008), deciding on a bare majority that Guantanamo Bay detainees were entitled to the writ of *Habeas corpus* (protected in Art I, s 9 of the US Constitution).

[413] The return to the body is a feature of (eco-)feminist thought, that brings together both the political economy and political ecology at various junctures. At risk of oversimplification or reductiveness, we can recall several of these entwined strands, already mentioned above, that bring back the body into legal consciousness at the same time as an increased attention to the ecology. Firstly, then, various strands of feminist theory revisit the body in legal terms, tracking the ways in which social and legal imaginaries take 'shape' (see above 194). In feminist (post-)colonial legal studies, a further focus of various contemporary

'earth sciences', where our bodily existence is emphatically 'terrestrial'[414] and non-dissociable from its 'holobiont' or the myriad forms of life that are both inside and outside of us. Paradoxically, the recent revival of 'the humanities' (political, legal, digital etc)[415] attempts in a (non-anthropocentric) vein to retrieve what is left of 'humanity' not only as an ethical virtue, but also as a broader vision of our 'body politics'.[416]

Legality, as we know, was historically instrumental in the very foundation of the category of modern personhood as opposed to that of things (subject to property). This led, as we have also seen, to modernity's forgetfulness of the body or materiality,[417] and, in respect of the ecology, to the ever-widening gap between self and environment. Moreover, law's abstract assumptions about personhood claimed a universal validity, to the detriment of the world's non-modern (minor, residual, primitive) epistemologies.[418] One sign however that such assumptions are being shaken – whether by the development of new technologies (enhanced humanity), the decline of soul-based religion, biopolitics, feminism or racial politics etc – is that the body is re-emerging and reclaiming its legal place between persons and things, subject and object, self and environment.[419]

This return of the repressed body[420] within the law is singularly visible on its private international front, where conflicts arise from diverse and ever moving cultural understandings of the body and its parts, reproduction, parenthood, the definition of

strains is the solidarity between the social reproductive order, the political order of empire and the economic order of extractive capital. In more specifically eco-feminist varieties, Donna Haraway's reflection on the (female) body as cyborg is apt to describe ('modern') slavery in global value chains (see above 252). Indeed, innumerable other examples, of which the most obvious is international networks of prostitution, support Haraway's contention that the disregard for human – and particularly subaltern – life goes hand in hand with environmental devastation. We are reminded once more of the necessary parallelism of our attitudes to self, humanity and other forms of non-sentient nature, that can and have all been subject to coloniality in different ways.

[414] On terrestriality, see in addition to Latour (*Où atterrir*), Lindahl, 'Place-Holding the Future', 28 et seq.

[415] From the perspective of law, Judith Surkis's study of the sexualised imaginaries underlying French colonial sovereignty (encountered above) is an excellent illustration of this new focus of the new 'political and juridical' humanities. The key here lies in the metaphysics of metaphor. It is supplied, as we have seen above, by Eric Santner, observing the somatic effects of the migration of sovereignty from the Christic incarnation in the royal body to the body politic of the people. See Santner, *The Royal Remains*. Legality is affected by this body politics (Latour, *Où atterrir*), the bodily transformation of the sovereign.

[416] Latour et al, *The Body Politic*.

[417] See above, the works of Elias, Mazurel, Agamben. The bodily dimension of life was long excluded from the domain of knowledge (especially legal and philosophical, or metaphysical) that has formed our modern consciousness. This did not prevent (bio)politics from revolving (invisibly) around the control of bodies.

[418] On the modern conceit of universality, see below.

[419] See above 137 and Esposito, *Immunitas*, observing that the body has long oscillated between person and thing without finding a place. However, at the same time, technological objects appear as a form of (subjective) life, and not merely a servile function.

[420] 'Le retour de ce qui a été refoulé constitue l'histoire souterraine et taboue de la civilisation et l'exploration de cette histoire ne révèle pas seulement le secret de l'individu mais aussi de la civilisation.' (H Marcuse, *Éros et Civilisation* (Paris, Seuil 1971 23.). As seen above, Santner (*The Royal Remains*) has explored the theme of the somatic return of the repressed in the individual and collective psyche, in particular in respect of the sublime royal or imperial body coming back to haunt the (somatic) body politic of the sovereign people or (see Monateri, 'Black Gaius') the elusive corporate bodies of contemporary capitalism. On the somatic effects of the order of linear time, as created by the jurists, see K Pomian, *L'ordre du temps* (Paris, Gallimard, 1984).

life and the meaning of death.[421] Reproduction and surrogacy, marriage and sexuality, migration and corpses, burials and religious rites, all give rise to very variable divides between the sacred and the profane, taboos and socially accepted customs, shame and dignity, the visible and the invisible, and the very distinction between life and death. In other words, even if these questions surface before the courts in very technical guises,[422] it is here that the encounter with absolute alterity takes place in legal form. Moreover, once again, we must keep in mind that there is a necessary solidarity between the body of the human other and the organisms that compose it and contribute to its life and survival (holobiont); between humanity and nature; between individual psyche and collective consciousness; between self and other.

The question is how to revisit and draw from these experiences of legal 'body conflicts'? Here then is the cue to turn to Emmanuel Levinas' phenomenological approach to the 'face of the other'.[423] The 'face' of the other is to be understood, in phenomenological terms, as the other's singular, vulnerable corporeity. Importantly, this phenomenological apprehension of the other (or 'others', *autrui* rather than *autre*) is ethical and not cognitive. Here, the essential point is that our encounter with alterity thus understood opens a horizon from which flows our ethical responsibility, our obligation to respond. Levinas describes this horizon, made visible by the presence of the other, as 'split' because the other is beyond representation.[424] The argument developed below is that this depthless vista opened by alterity resonates powerfully, in legal terms, within the shadow ethos of the conflict of laws. In this respect, according to Levinas and in dialogue with Jacques Derrida's own account of hospitality (to which we shall also return[425]), our responsibility is to welcome in the other in on their own terms, or 'in their own language and all that it entails'.[426] The latter reference undoubtedly includes the 'law of the other', foreign law.[427] Clearly, the injunction to defer to the law of the other entails a radical de-centring, a full reversal of the traditional relationship between host and guest. In this substitution resides the deep meaning of private international law's residual jurisprudence.

[421] The conflicted body politics of the conflict of laws caused by international surrogacy agreements (often associated with same-sex parenthood) is one clear illustration of gender trouble (J Butler) and the links between sovereignty and sexuality (Surkis, *Sex, Law, and Sovereignty in French Algeria*), evoked above.

[422] This is of course too wide an area to be able to provide concrete examples. But the latter occupy a large amount of space in standard text books and casebooks on private international law (usually in chapters that separate persons, property family and markets, according to the pattern described above 137).

[423] This is an important break with Husserl. See Pelluchon, *Pour comprendre Lévinas*, 162 on the important point that the face or phenomenality of the other is to be understood on an ethical register (the other is in excess of representation) and most emphatically not riveted to the (modern) biological body, meaning blood, race or heredity.

[424] 'L'horizon se fissure parce que autrui est en excès sur sa manifestation' (Pelluchon, *Pour comprendre Lévinas* 39).

[425] For the references on hospitality used here, see above 272.

[426] Bachir Souleymane Diagne was Derrida's pupil. His important work on language as hospitality (*De langue à langue: L'hospitalité de la traduction*), part of his vast intellectual project to decolonise Western philosophy, is discussed above in relation to the conflict of laws as lingua franca.

[427] Indeed, Derrida evokes, literally, the existence of a 'conflict of laws' (between natural and positive law) at the very core of hospitality as seen above.

As suggested above, moreover, there is a powerful ecological potential in this understanding of our 'split horizon'. The responsibility that flows from the encounter with alterity extends potentially beyond the sole human other to englobe animal life and indeed the entire natural world in all its vulnerable corporeality on Earth's fragile crust. As Corinne Pelluchon has suggested, there is ample room in Levinas' thought for an eco-phenomenological reading of the encounter with radically other forms of life.[428] In terms of the law, the ethical idea of responsibility obviously resonates strongly with various (public and private, comparative) legal incarnations of duties of care, obligations towards others, and sanctions of neglect. However, the shadow version of the conflict of laws is a far more promising place to look for more significant echoes of Levinassian responsibility. As we shall now see, it displays deeper traces of the aporetic incommensurability of alterity (section II.A) and its correlative ethical imperative to make way for the law of the other (section II.B).

A. Responsibility and the Experience of Incommensurability

In Levinas' phenomenological approach, 'facing' the other (like 'facing Gaia'[429]) is an experience of radical incommensurability.[430] Alterity – considered here as the human other – is thus defined as the incommensurable being-as-other (*'l'être en tant qu'autre'*). At this stage, it is interesting to emphasise once more that while the idiom here is clearly that of Western (Judeo-Christian) ethics and the (historical) horizon that of the endo-European devastation of humanity in the Holocaust, there are some striking analogies with indigenous cosmologies encountered above in the context of a similar '*futur antérieur*' of both colonial and ecological extinction. Alterity is constitutive, writes Viveiros de Castro,[431] a trace of the other's gaze that I carry as part of myself.[432] Its rejection, echoes Western social critique, is *thanatos*, barbary disguised as enlightenment, a culture of death.[433]

[428] Pelluchon, *Pour comprendre Lévinas* 95 et seq.

[429] Latour, *Enquête*.

[430] An extremely important point for what follows below is that (as explained by Pelluchon, *Pour comprendre Lévinas*, 84) phenomenology is intrinsically attentive to differences or singularity, and the heterogeneity of modes of access (including law) to reality, contrary to 'objectivation' that orders (unitary) reality by sorting and fitting other beings into pre-existing categories (as does 'monism': see above).

[431] *Le regard du jaguar*; Descola, *Les formes du Visible*, 438, 439.

[432] In the radically different idiom of the Western modern (paradoxically unmodern and largely theological) philosophical tradition, we might say that the phenomenological experience of absolute alterity is a source of transcendence. It must therefore be understood on an ethical (not a cognitive) register. It connects up corporeality with a plane that might be called spiritual in that it implies the experience of the incommensurable (Pelluchon, *Pour comprendre Lévinas*, 37). This is a far cry from the tepid form of tolerance to difference induced by or compliant with the regime of rights, as seen above. It also goes against the grain of a long tradition of modern thought that relies on the one hand on an anthropology of the human as wolf (Hobbes), or later on, as rational calculator, pursuer of self-preservation or abstract subject of rights and on another, on the formal equality of all individuals (human) and indeed the ontological privilege of (hu) man over Nature.

[433] T Adorno & M Horkheimer, *Dialectique de la Raison* (Paris, Gallimard, 1974); H Byung-Chul, *Thanatocapitalisme* (Paris, PUF, 2021).

Once more, as Levinas writes, the face of the other in all their singularity is the source of our ethical responsibility towards them. The encounter with the other as vulnerability, precarity and nudity, calls on our ability to respond – to be responsible, accountable or answerable. Latour uses a similar language, with the important difference (to which we return below) that his vision of alterity encompasses all the equally vulnerable beings and things whose survival depends upon us, and ours on theirs. In either case, the intrinsic asymmetry in my relationship with the other constitutes the exclusive source of all my responsibility – meaning that my responsibility is not commanded by any external (positive or transcendent) norm but by the sole presence or encounter with the other.[434]

The face of the other as the foundation of our ethical responsibility according to Levinas gave rise, in turn, to a philosophical dialogue with Jacques Derrida, and his own (aporetic) concept of 'hostipitality'.[435] In this (posthumous) exchange, the commands of hospitality are seen to be exceptionally demanding: hospitality requires accepting to be subject to 'the other's law, that was there before me'. Remarkably, Derrida specifically evokes the possible inclusion of non-human life forms in the category of the 'other'. His later book *L'animal que donc je suis*[436] ('The animal that therefore I am') addresses the question of our relationship to non-human species. As Corinne Pelluchon suggests, nothing precludes the extension of the (Levinassian) idea of alterity to all these animal others.[437] Indeed, if we accept de-centring of our own epistemè, then, when viewed through the 'gaze of the jaguar', these others may further include all sorts of (invisible) entities whose trajectories cross our own.

The law – that of the other – is evidently very present in this account. It appears too in the Levinassian imperative to relinquish my own sovereignty, as compelled by the vulnerability of the other. The resonance is strong here within the shadow version of the conflict of laws, to the extent that the latter commands us to listen to the foreigner-stranger in their own language and under their own law. This brings us back to the law of the other as experience of legal incommensurability. As seen above, the hallmark of the shadow, statutist version of the conflict of laws is that it allows in foreign law on its own terms, refusing to reduce foreign forms to the measure of the legal categories of the forum. In other words, foreign law crosses the threshold on the terms of its own underlying world vision or cosmology. This shadow methodology, then, has the acknowledgement and respect for the other's singularity and dignity at its ethical core. Through the obligation to give effect to foreign law, the host forum must accommodate unfamiliar, heterogenous institutions, including practices and worldviews that correspond to alien modes of access to reality.

[434] See Pelluchon, *Pour comprendre Levinas*, 71.

[435] As seen above. This compound of *hostis* and *hospis* is designed to show up the dialectic of self-contradiction within hospitality, an attitude that always remains poised 'sur le seuil d'elle-même, un carrefour aporétique' (similar to the aporia that affects law as justice, conflicted between two different logics). On the importance of the threshold, see below.

[436] *Op cit*. The book is about the status of the animal in modern and contemporary philosophy (Descartes, Kant, Levinas, Lacan et Heidegger). Derrida is the first philosopher to evoke the idea of animal genocide (as in the massive animal mistreatment in slaughterhouses, to which public opinion (and Law I) is increasingly sensitive). Today, concern for the disappearance of species has broadened to the accelerated impoverishment of biodiversity.

[437] At p 95 et seq.

At the same time, as can be seen in the very unexceptional 'private law' cases it deals with, it shows up the uncanny ordinariness, the quotidianity of the encounter with the strange, that upsets (or splits) our settled horizon of (natural-seeming) legal categories. Available illustrations of this point in comparative case law on the conflict of laws are largely counter-examples, since conventional approaches, as already seen above, tend precisely not to respect the terms of the other. For instance, land is rarely understood (as it might be under an indigenous cosmology) as peopled with sacred beings;[438] nor do modern, secular courts usually pay attention to a sartorial code that sees dignity as embodied in certain forms of dress;[439] nor is it frequent for a sacred object to be heard in its request for its own return from the temple from which it has been looted.[440] And although moves to give standing to rivers or other natural entities might well entail as yet unpredictable changes in our understanding of legal subjectivities, as seen above, we have yet to see any such entities or indeed Pachamama herself establish their legal standing in a foreign court.

However, an interesting and aptly ecological example from our own Western past – a conflict of laws in time – will serve to illustrate how the experience of incommensurability might take place in the courtroom.[441] Emphasising (once again) the

[438] There are attempts however to come to term at least with different conceptions of collective property: see above. For one (not necessarily successful) effort of the Canadian Supreme Court to integrate the idea that land is inhabited by the spirit of the grizzly bear, see *Ktunaxa Nation v British Columbia (Forests, Lands and Natural Resource Operations)* 2017 SCC 54, Report [2017] 2 SCR 386 and Brachotte, 'The Conflict of Laws and Non-Secular Worldviews'.

[439] For an analysis of the various assumptions underlying the prohibition of the Muslim burka in Western legal systems (and more broadly, the complex normative matrix of dress), see Frankenberg, *Comparative Law as Critique*, 113 et seq.

[440] See above 287.

[441] This was a century before Hobbes' (modern) comment on the exclusion from the body politic of the Commonwealth of non-human living creatures, 'such as Bees, and Ants, [that] live sociably one with another, (which are therefore by Aristotle numbred amongst Politicall creatures) and yet have no other direction, than their particular judgements and appetites; nor speech, whereby one of them can signifie to another, what he thinks expedient for the common benefit: and therefore some man may perhaps desire to know, why Man-kind cannot do the same. To which I answer, First, that men are continually in competition for Honour and Dignity, which these creatures are not; and consequently amongst men there ariseth on that ground, Envy and Hatred, and finally Warre; but amongst these not so … Secondly, that amongst these creatures, the Common good differeth not from the Private; and being by nature enclined to their private, they procure thereby the common benefit. But man, whose Joy consisteth in comparing himselfe with other men, can relish nothing but what is eminent. Thirdly, that these creatures, having not (as man) the use of reason, do not see, nor think they see any fault, in the administration of their common businesse: whereas amongst men, there are very many, that thinke themselves wiser, and abler to govern the Publique, better than the rest; and these strive to reforme and innovate, one this way, another that way; and thereby bring it into Distraction and Civill warre. Fourthly, that these creatures, though they have some use of voice, in making knowne to one another their desires, and other affections; yet they want that art of words, by which some men can- represent to others, that which is Good, in the likenesse of Evill; and Evill, in the likenesse of Good; and augment, or diminish the apparent greatnesse of Good and Evill; discontenting men, and troubling their Peace at their pleasure. Fifthly, irrationall creatures cannot distinguish betweene Injury, and Dammage; and therefore as long as they be at ease, they are not offended with their fellowes: whereas Man is then most troublesome, when he is most at ease: for then it is that he loves to shew his Wisdome, and controule the Actions of them that governe the Common-wealth. Lastly, the agreement of these creatures is Naturall; that of men, is by Covenant only, which is Artificiall: and therefore it is no wonder if there be somewhat else required (besides Covenant) to make their Agreement constant and lasting; which is a Common Power, to keep them in awe, and to direct their actions to the Common Benefit' (*Leviathan*, 1651, 'of Commonwealth', ch XVII).

extent to which we moderns tend to forget our own recent history, law's alternative ecological horizon is visible through the example of the (now largely forgotten) animal trials of the Renaissance – judicial proceedings against all manner of creatures that took place all around Europe for several centuries, starting at the threshold of modernity. These premodern trials (used as examples both in comparative law[442] and then in legal theory[443]) illustrate the ways in which legality might accommodate the law of the other, or hear the appeal of radical forms of alterity.

Thus, in the trial of the rats of Autun in 1522,[444] hordes of crop-eating rats were victorious (after several episodes of hearings held *in absentia*) in their defence, because their summons to court had not respected their need for due notice, adequate time to assemble, and equal protection (from the farmers' cats) before the law. But is this not just a way of extending liberal rights to rats, in the tepid if not anthropocentric form described above? A further instance involving swarms of grape-devouring snout-beatles serves however to dispel any remaining impression of legal familiarity. A double episode of devastation of grape harvests and ensuing protestation from the wine producers of St Julien (still a well-known claret), led the court to consider that since God ordained that the produce of the earth was to be shared between all living creatures, the insects, while excluded from the vineyards, were to be given a perpetual and exclusive easement over a plot of land outside the village in which to sojourn, properly supplied in the fruit necessary for their survival. If the insects had not actually won their case, their needs were nevertheless taken entirely seriously, on their own terms, and balanced fairly against those of their human adversaries.

This causes William Ewald, in an attempt to answer the fascinating anthropological question: 'What was it like to try a rat?', to write of the rat's great advocate, Chassenet, that:

> we need to find our way into his cosmos, to excavate the pattern of beliefs and sentiments that was characteristic of his age. We need to imagine what it would be like to shudder at heresy, and to regard torture as a normal punishment; to believe the old metaphysics, and to participate, with full seriousness, in a legal proceeding like the trial of the rats of Autun. What would one have to believe, and how would it feel? All this assumes that there was

[442] W Ewald, 'Comparative Jurisprudence(I): What Was it Like to Try a Rat?' (1995) 143 *U Pa L Rev* 1889; P Schiff Berman, 'Rats, Pigs, and Statues on Trial: The Creation of Cultural Narratives in the Prosecution of Animals and Inanimate Objects' (1994) 69 *NYUL Rev* 288. Legality itself was of course undergoing paradigmatic change at the time in continental Europe and the sentencing of pigs, sows (and piglets), swarms of locusts or rats, was grounded on a mixture of morality, religion, emerging substantive rules or principles, and procedural equity. Trials were ecclesiastical or secular according to complex jurisdictional parameters and the accused were collectives or individuals. Sentencing was sometimes followed by extraordinarily cruel forms of punishment: animals dressed up as humans were sent to the stake, buried alive, or sent to Siberia. The lucky ones got off lightly, and were sent to prison for a year. In the common law world, Blackstone had a hard job in making sense of the early case law based on the institution of *Deodand* (forfeited to God) in respect of non-sentient objects, including orchards, knives and cartwheels that had, innocently or not, caused harm.

[443] See G Teubner, 'Rights of Non-Humans? Electronic Agents and Animals as New Actors in Politics and Law' (2006) 33 *Journal of Law and Society* 497–521.

[444] An accessible historical source is WW Hyde, 'The Prosecution and Punishment of Animals and Lifeless Things in the Middle Ages and Modern Times' (1916) 64 *U Pa L Rev* 696. Records of the trial of the rats of Autin (see the text below) have survived (many others were rat-eaten …), proceedings that attracted attention by reason of the prestige of the advocate of the accused rats, the theologian, Chassignat.

> some range of conscious experience that Chassenet underwent as he thought about his arguments and addressed them to the court: something it was like to be Chassenet, something the experience was like for him. And my suggestion is that it is ultimately that range of experience we must recapture if we are to make sense of the animal trials.

It is remarkable that Chassenet (a theologian who authored a treatise in Latin on what might be described as the excommunication of insects), when later appointed as judge in an ecclesiastical trial of (human) heretics, set to elaborating a jurisprudence of dignity and mercy by referring to the arguments previously deployed in favour of the rats, whose case therefore provided a precedent or analogical model for human rights, and not the reverse. 'Think from the animal as starting point', writes Derrida, in *L'animal que donc je suis*: the gaze of the animal contains the appeal, audible or silent, that calls us outside of ourselves.[445]

Acknowledging (here, in respect of the medieval, largely theological, *nomos*) both the extent of the alterity of the law of the other and the uncanny strangeness of one's own (when viewed through the gaze of the jaguar, or that of the learned excommunicator of insects, or indeed the snout-beetle itself), is certainly a cardinal step towards the formulation, in legal terms, of our responsiveness – responsibility towards the planet and its multiple, dependent and vulnerable forms of life. Certainly, the unfamiliarity of such trials in our (modern) eyes is reinforced by the extraordinary contrast, emphasised by Ewald, between the 'humanity' of the judgments in these cases and the quite extraordinary cruelty of the punishments, in the form of torture, meted out to various animals that were found guilty in other instances.[446] But, as Ewald also points out, a lawyer (or citizen) of the Renaissance would just as certainly have been at least as shocked had they witnessed the wanton devastation of the planet and its creatures, under later conditions of modernity.[447] From the perspective of other contemporary non-modern cosmologies, our own daily indifference (tolerance?) towards the bodily existence of foreign migrants or the homeless, would be at least as shocking.

At this point, we can return to the philosophical dialogue between Derrida and Levinas and the question of whether radical alterity (envisaged in human shape by Levinas) can extend to the animal *that therefore I am* and more widely to all other beings, sentient or not, that inhabit our world in all their alien singularity. The other here is what I – the sovereign self – am not. Suggesting that the Levinassian experience of incommensurability might even begin with the non-human other, Derrida, in his

[445] Derrida, *L'animal que donc je suis*, 156: 'Car une pensée de l'autre, de l'infiniment autre qui me regarde, devrait au contraire privilégier la question et la demande de l'animal, ne pas la faire passer avant celle de l'homme mais penser celle de l'homme, du frère, du prochain à partir de la, possibilité d'une question et d'une demande animales, d'un appel, audible ou silencieux, qui appelle en nous hors de nous, du plus loin, avant nous après nous, nous précédant et nous poursuivant, de manière inéluctable, tellement inéluctable qu'il laisse la trace de tant de symptômes et de blessures, de stigmates de dénégation dans le discours de celui qui voudrait se rendre sourd à cet appel'.

[446] Clearly, ideas of causation differed radically from our own, as well as of redress (is this why the sow was dressed in human clothes before hanging?) and punishment. The point here is that this opens a range of other possible approaches (not all desirable). Radical transformation in legal ideas of causation is precisely what is called for by scientists in the struggle against climate change.

[447] A similar point is made by both Latour and Descola in their 'asymmetrical' anthropology.

work on *The Specters of Marx*,[448] also evokes all the other marginal beings that haunt the periphery of our lives ('hauntology'). In the light of the above, these figures can be understood in various, non-anthropocentric ways so as to include animals, vegetables and minerals, but also the metaphysical, invisible or spiritual beings that inhabit the belief systems of other cosmologies. Indeed, in his last published work, *Alterity and Transcendance*, Levinas himself defines the (human) other phenomenologically, as 'in excess of all possibility of representation'.[449] This excess beyond representation and beyond words (the ineffable) has been analysed as the aesthetic hallmark of the theological[450] and political sublime that continues to shadow our lives.[451] As the void of sovereignty that cannot be represented (as seen above). The point here is that the radical other not only constitutes my horizon of meaning, but points beyond my (phenomenological) horizon. The latter is thereby 'split'. In this respect, as Peter Sloterdijk writes in respect of our ecological responsibility, we have to be 'torn' by something that transcends us in order to think.[452] This might also mean that the more we make room for the law of all others, the more the risk is great to find ourselves torn between radically conflicting injunctions. What then does it mean to be hospitable in such a context, and furthermore in legal terms? Once again, the shadow version of the conflict of laws provides a possible avenue towards legal inter-alterity.

B. Hospitality and the De-centring of Self

In *Totality and Infinity*, Levinas devotes a chapter to 'Interiority and Economy'. Through this interesting association of concepts (the *oikos* as *psyche*), he draws attention to the phenomenological importance of our terrestrial[453] habitation. For Levinas, our phenomenological abode (*demeure*) is actually co-constitutive of self or identity – with the crucial qualification that it is open to the stranger, as hospitality requires. The notion of *demeure* obviously resonates within the conflict of laws with domicile, localisation,[454] territory, or refuge, in which (mobile or migrant)

[448] Derrida, *Specters of Marx: The State of the Debt, the Work of Mourning and the New International (Spectres de Marx: L'Etat de la dette, le travail du deuil et la nouvelle Internationale* (Paris, ed Galileé, 1993)).

[449] Hans Lindahl provides a powerful illustration by means of the example of the recognition of the penguins' call for recognition in his text 'Place-Holding the future', cited above: 'the "more" of more-than-human collectives is not merely shorthand for a collective composed of humans and nonhumans. It concerns the *excessiveness* of the penguins' demand for justice, and this in a twofold sense. For the one, their claim evokes what might be called a recognitive excess, ie, what cannot be said and done within a given legal ordering of such a collective, however inclusive: the unordered and unorderable for a given legal order. For the other, and more radically, the precedence of the question calls forth what might be called an excess beyond recognition.'

[450] On the (complex) place of religion (Judaism) in Levinassian ethics, see above 272. On the other as 'epiphany' in Levinas' thought, see Pelluchon, *Pour comprendre Lévinas* 258 et seq.

[451] See Monateri, *Dominus Mundi*.

[452] P Sloterdijk, *You Must Change Your Life. On Anthropotechnics* (Cambridge, Polity, 2014) 268.

[453] Evoking Husserl's *La terre ne se meut pas* (Paris, Minuit, '1934, 1989). This also evokes terrestriality (Lindahl, 'Place-Holding the Future'), Latour's 'terrions', or earth dwellers (T Ingold), as seen above.

[454] On phenomenological location, see Pelluchon, *Pour comprendre Lévinas* 141, associating 'gravity' (*pesanteur*) and place.

individuals, communities in search of recognition, or even metaphysical entities such as corporations, are 'at home'.[455] And indeed, for Levinas, the *demeure* is the terrestrial refuge[456] in which we need on occasion to retreat in order to think – in other words, to encounter ourselves. Home (or privacy or community) is not only a place of refuge, where one feels in one's place, but it is home that actually constitutes self.[457] However, importantly here, it is also a threshold over which to welcome the foreigner – the multifarious, alien and dependent forms of life that coexist alongside us on our earth.[458] I cannot be myself nor encounter the other unless I have my place, my base and my refuge. But it is precisely because I have my place that I can stand at the threshold and open it to the other.[459]

Thus, Levainassian hospitality sees our responsibility towards the other in terms of a dialectic between inside and outside.[460] Each in their home (community, conscience) is simultaneously within and without.[461] This works very precisely against the exclusionary nature of frontiers and thresholds and emphasises the scandal of allowing the alien others to lose their lives (at sea) or to lack a place (domicile or territory) to which to belong.[462] But how then to avoid the risk of dissociation and dissolution that dogs the steps of hospitality (and in legal form, pluralism and the conflict of laws) at every turn? There is an evident risk of dislocation that comes with the shock of absolute strangeness at the threshold. The encounter with the alien gives rise to an obvious need for some kind of negotiation, diplomacy and an ultimate defence, so as to avoid the dual risk of invasion or colonisation, and of a state of chaos in which 'anything goes'. The unconditional welcome extended to the other is always at risk of reversing into fear and rejection. Here, Levinas' account takes us to an ultimate horizon at the aporetic core of hospitality. In order to see how this aporia can be approached in

[455] For corporations, see above 241.

[456] Perhaps, in Latour's terms (*Enquête*, 34), this *demeure* is needed to provide a habitat for the moderns, wandering lost between economy and ecology, the former being uninhabitable and the latter as yet unready.

[457] Also a place within our consciousness where one can retire or seek refuge in order to be quiet and escape the pressure of dominant ways of life (ideologies): ibid, 145.

[458] And we should add, within our own biological make-up as holobiont and within our own psychic being that incorporates alterity, reflected in our split horizon.

[459] A camp with the barest of privacy, food and water is hardly such a place, that can only be inhabited by the haunting figure of *homo sacer*.

[460] Pelluchon, *Pour comprendre Lévinas*, 143.

[461] Ibid, 145. On dwelling in the threshold of the in-between, see above 189 et seq.

[462] In *Totality and Infinity*, Levinas points in the direction of law as a means of framing society as fraternity. This is where he introduces the notion of 'extraterritoriality' (as seen above, a cardinal concept in jurisdictional jurisprudence) meaning here that the imperative of fraternity reaches beyond the sole political community. The latter is inclusive not exclusionary. The ideal of fraternity has tragically, at least for the time being, a very marginal impact on the evolution of our legal political responsibility towards the rest of humanity, even when the latter appears not as an abstraction but in the concrete form of suffering, starving or drowning bodies. The terrible irony of *Habeas corpus* in such a context shows up in a cartography of migrant mortality at the frontiers of more powerful, prosperous, or formerly colonial states today. There are however, from time to time, attempts to give legal teeth to the idea of fraternity within the jurisprudence of cross-border migration. See for example, the recent judicial saga in France over the incrimination of complicity in illegal migration and the requirements of fraternity, see G Tusseau, 'Le Conseil constitutionnel et le délit de solidarité. De la consécration activiste d'une norme constitutionnelle sous-appliquée à la révélation d'une stratégie contrainte de communication juridictionnelle (Cons const. 6 juill. 2018, n° 2018-717/718 QPC M. Cédric H. et autre)' (2019) 1 *Revue critique de droit international privé* 35–64.

legal terms, we need to go back to the meaning of the de-centring of self required by Levinas' account of hospitality, and the ensuing negotiation at the threshold. In both respects, the resonance within the shadow avatar of the conflict of laws is striking. The latter offers the model both for a radical substitution of self and other, and a diplomatic dialectic at the frontier, between the singular and the general, the ethical and the particular, or between law and equity.

Firstly, then, the idea of substitution. In *Autrement qu'être*, Levinas writes that 'I must be the hostage of the other before I can be myself.'[463] Prolonging the dialogue in *Hospitalité*, Derrida emphasises that the injunction of the law of 'absolute' hospitality[464] is demanding to the point of unattainability, because it requires the very substitution of the law of the other for my own. It dispossesses me of my sovereignty, imposing limits because the other emits an appeal to which I much respond, obliging me to come out of my solipsism.[465] This responsibility has nothing to do with a religion or a moral philosophy that sacralises life, but can be understood as a charge incumbent on the one who hears the call of the other. Furthermore, it goes beyond the legal idea of obligation as bond, because it exceeds all subjectivity.[466] Above all, it affects the (normative) terms on which the other must be welcomed by the host. There is no real (or absolute) hospitality unless the other is allowed in on their own terms, or 'in their own language and all that it entails'.[467] This assuredly includes the *nomos* of the other, foreign law.

Absolute hospitality, then (for Levinas as for Derrida), is an unconditional invitation to enter (*viens!*) without question, that is without asking for the name of the other at the threshold (or exercising an identity control at the frontier), nor requiring the other to speak the language of the host. The imperative of hospitality mandates a response to and for the other.[468] In this respect, it means stepping aside, de-centring the self, lowering the various (invisible) cultural and psychic barriers to a true encounter with the other in all their singularity.[469] The host relinquishes the sovereign frontier

[463] At p 116. However, the meaning of this reversal is often misunderstood and dismissed as hyperbolic. It is helpful here to refer to the reflection devoted by Levinas on the importance of the threshold of home, community or conscience (above).

[464] As opposed to its (relative) positive version in international and municipal laws of asylum and immigration.

[465] For a rare formulation of such an appeal in legal scholarship, engaging with the question of unalienated relationality in social-phenomenological terms, see P Gabel, *The Desire for Mutual Recognition, Social Movements and the Dissolution of the False Self* (Abingdon, Routledge, 2018) and Gabel & Kennedy, 'Roll over Beethoven'. The argument is that the legacy of social alienation inherited from prior generations envelops us in a milieu of a 'fear of the other'.

[466] Similarly, while hospitality can be understood as structurally 'relational', in that it is a relationship to the other, it is far more radical than what is ordinarily thought of as 'relational' in law. Its requirements are both existential and imperative: it is not an affair of mere courtesy, is not conditioned by reciprocity, nor is it measurable (or proportionate) as a reparation for fault. Nor indeed is it reducible to charity, pardon, or care. See Pelluchon, *Pour comprendre Lévinas*. It evokes, rather, relational forms in indigenous thought (see A Escobar, *Pluriversal Politics: The Real and the Possible* (Durham NC, Duke University Press, 2020) as seen above 172 et seq.).

[467] See above 187, on the inclusion of law in these implications of language.

[468] 'Répondre à' and 'répondre de'. A point taken up, as we have seen, by Latour.

[469] Pelluchon, *Pour comprendre Lévinas*, 113: 'la substitution s'oppose au primat du *je*. Les autres *d'emblée* me concernent.'

control that has come to be synonymous with the threshold of (home) territory or (personal) privacy.[470] Whether the other is foreign or enemy, a wandering guest or a part of psychic or cultural being, the de-centring of self that is required by hospitality stretches to the point of the substitution of guest for host, other for self.

But here we see the aporia of hospitality. If its ultimate ethical requirement is a radical reversal between self and other, it means harbouring simultaneously under the same roof *hospis* and *hostis*, friend and enemy, host and guest; it folds over again as an identicality of host and hostage. The ethical injunction to make room for alterity at the very core of my own existence means, then, my readiness to let the other stand in my place.[471] The reversal between host and hostage breaks with the primacy of subjectivity or identity as defined by autonomy (as seen above), pushing the relinquishment of self to the point of assuming responsibility for the other. In this respect, it is a highly 'dangerous' method insofar as it upsets the separations so carefully crafted around the liberal subject, its identity and autonomy, its *quitus* or '*être quitte*'. Indeed, the self as governed by the law of hospitality differs in shape from the subject crafted by all the liberal philosophies that mandate the respect of common rules designed to protect the dignity of individual subjects and ensure the conditions for their peaceful but competitive coexistence.[472]

Thus, according to Levinas, the presence of alterity disturbs or 'splits' my established horizon of meaning, in the sense that that alterity also bears the trace of the infinite, thereby opening a metaphysical vista 'in excess of phenomenality'; as seen above, it is this trace that is the source of our ethical responsibility. But there is a further, important point. This split horizon is not the site of a merely private, bilateral encounter (as the 'face of the other' might suggest), but the plane on which, through the gaze of all others, all forms of alterity make their ethical call upon us. In this sense, our responsibility is 'universal'.[473] Therefore, my intersubjective encounter with a singular other also carries a political significance, because through the eyes of the singular other there is also this gaze of all others. While this point recalls more familiar legal definitions of justice in the Western Judeo-Christian tradition as requiring the (spectral[474]) presence of an impartial third party, it raises the question evoked at the beginning of this Chapter, of the relationship between ethics and politics. Levinas' unambiguous answer is the primacy of the ethical. The reason he gives provides us with the very transition we need to move back from ethics to law.

[470] Today, surveillance capitalism crosses the frontiers of privacy (as seen above: see Zuboff, 'The Age of Surveillance Capitalism'). The injunction to open the frontier needs reinterpreting in this context.

[471] The host-subject is hostage to the guest (and these very chains, writes Levinas in a difficult passage of *Autrement qu'être*, 228, are freedom).

[472] Levinas' conception of alterity, surmises Pelluchon (*Pour comprendre Lévinas*, 58), is a philosophical and political revolution in respect of the subject and subjectivity, as momentous as the (Foucauldian) 'discovery' of man or sexuality in preceding centuries.

[473] Levinas seeks to show thereby that my ethical obligation towards the other, revealed in, or imposed upon me by the existence of the singular other, independently of any form of reciprocity (prior debt or culpability) or external norm, is the condition of possibility of a universal, political responsibility. This means an obligation to respond towards all others on their terms, and not the reverse mode practised by coloniality, that is, the imposition on all others of one's own terms.

[474] See G Bensussan, *Éthique et expérience. Lévinas politique* (Paris, La Phocide, 2008); Pelluchon, *Pour comprendre Lévinas*, 191.

In sum, for Levinas, the temptation to de-personalise the other (or reduce them to the status of commodity or bio-resource to be managed) is inherent in the comparison and measurement involved in all norms, laws and institutions that neutralise subjects in order to make them fit within categories and subject them to rules.[475]

Returning at this point to the conflict of laws, it is hardly necessary to underline the significance of this critique in respect of its conventional methodological model. It recalls the recurring jurisprudential debate between monism and pluralism already encountered many times above. However, beyond this negative dimension, it is equally evident that 'hospitality', 'substitution' and the emblematically legal injunction to hear the appeal of the other in their own language all resonate powerfully in the shadow avatar of this discipline, including through the chinks in the dominant scheme. When allowing foreign law to self-define its categories and scope, this minor avatar provides – as it were, existentially – a process of reversal between self and other, host and guest, required by hospitality and the ethical imperative to respond to alterity: it gives effect to the law of the other (foreign law) on the latter's own terms. To take a familiar example, when (Muslim) foreign law institutes the *kafalah* as a custodian type of intra-family adult-child care relationship for religious-educational purposes,[476] (Western) domestic law (through the voice of the court that is called upon to give it effect in respect of a child resident in its own jurisdiction), has various options, which correspond to as many distinct modes of understanding the operation of cultural translation (go-between) that has to take place. It may decide to force the institution to fit among its own legal concepts (the *kafalah* is an adoption); it may decide to accept the latter as such (refusing the legal effects attached to adoption) without any regard to its meaning in a novel context (the child will live under a status that singles her out as alien); or it may seek to understand the terms of the other from the other's own standpoint.

This third avenue is 'substitution', a term of art within the discipline that points to the intricate labour of adjustment sometimes required in order to allow a foreign institution to preserve its meaning in an alien context.[477] Beyond the technical aspects (which belong to the classical toolbox of private international law[478]), the fact that

[475] See on this point Pelluchon, *Pour comprendre Lévinas*, 191.

[476] This example concerns intercountry adoption. To what extent can a *kafalah* (an Islamic family law institution according to which a child may be entrusted to a guardian with a view to his or her education and religious upbringing) be considered as equivalent to a Western-style adoption (entailing full or partial transfer of legal parentality to the adoptive parents)? The case law in Western courts involving conflicts of laws on the principle of an assimilation between the two diverse models and, if accepted, their effects, was very abundant before the rise of cross border surrogacy (see, for example, a rare conflict of laws case before the ECtHR, *Harroudj c France* (requête n°43631/09) 4 October 2012.

[477] For instance, the articulation of complex bodies of substantive law such as succession or insolvency give rise to a whole series of assessments on the part of the court as to the equivalence or substitutability of one concept for another (completed by the challenge of 'transposing' a given category into another context). The canon on all these operations (adaptation, substitution, transposition) is G Cansacchi's lecture at the Hague Academy, 'Le choix et l'adaptation de la règle étrangère dans le conflit de lois' (1953) 83 *Recueil des Cours de l'Académie de Droit international*. For an in-depth study of these intricate intellectual operations in the field of succession where English and French models use very different techniques, see S Godechot, *L'articulation du trust et du droit des successions* (Paris, Éditions Panthéon Assas Thèses, 2004).

[478] For the intricate technical aspects, see Cansacchi, 'Le choix et l'adaptation de la règle étrangère dans le conflit de lois'.

there is actually a device within this discipline called 'substitution' is significant, in the light of the phenomenological mode of description that is designed to bring to (day)light meanings or connections that routines of thought and practice usually hide from our sight. Furthermore, the whole discipline of the conflict of laws may be seen to be grounded not only on a recognition of plurality but on also the premise of the substitutability of one law for another. In the broader sense retained by Levinas, 'substitution' also means not only that we must de-centre our standpoint in order to allow in the law of the other in ways that are meaningful for the latter, but that we must accept, as a general rule, our own substitutability (that of self) by the other. In this respect, the difference between the major and minor keys of the partition played by the conflict of laws (between the conventional model and its shadow avatar) is that, under the second, as the above example illustrates, the substitution (of the foreign for self) takes place by a proper enquiry into the terms of the foreign law, that define the conditions on which its institutions may maintain their meaning within the legal ordering of the host system. This means that the host forum must set aside its own categories and preconceptions in order to make way – including through concessions, adaptations and tweaking of its own categories – for a possibly incommensurable conception of personality or family, persons or things, or life or death, accompanied by radically different parameters of the tolerable and the intolerable, taboo and licence, etc.

Of course the obvious risk (and usual objection) is the upsetting of the (necessarily fragile) equilibrium composed of all the multiple arbitrages and beliefs on which the host legal system rests. To return to an ethical register, Levinas' ideal of reversal between self and other is sometimes rejected as hyperbolic, and indeed its implications misunderstood.[479] The whole idea of substitution goes very clearly against the grain of 'jurisdictional thinking' and the exclusionary effect of the frontier (or privacy), as seen above.[480] And indeed, Levinassian phenomenology is far more radical in its approach to alterity than various doctrines (with ramifications in law) such as 'relationality' or 'care', insofar as it requires complete effacement of the sovereign self.[481] However, the objections linked to the hyperbolism or indeed paradoxical nature of this reversal tend to overlook Levinas' equally important view that this

[479] On the key to the critique of hyperbolism, see Pelluchon, *Pour comprendre Lévinas*, 116: 'Le renversement hyperbolique que Levinas opère le conduit à se démarquer radicalement de toute la tradition qui définit l'identité par la liberté'. In other words, it corresponds to a resistance drawn from a deformed concept of autonomy, as seen above. Its implications are also often misunderstood. Indeed the whole of idea of substitution goes very clearly against the grain of 'jurisdictional thinking' and the exclusionary effect of the frontier (or privacy), as seen above. The idea of care for the other (or self-respect as the foundation of one's own obligation to respect others), is preferred (for instance by Ricoeur) or considered politically more acceptable.

[480] The aporia of hospitality, as Derrida points out, is an internal opposition between the contingencies of positive law (of asylum or immigration policies) and our radical responsibility towards alterity. A concrete illustration that is close to private international law concerns forced (political or economic) migration, to which Derrida's reflection on hospitality was already turned. There are many illustrations within the ambit of the conflict of laws: see for instance on the Manus island (an immigration camp set up by Australia) class action case, H Muir Watt (ed), *Global Private International Law*, 548, with analyses by S Corneloup and J Verhellen; for cases involving the frontiers of the EU and the 'Dublin' regulations, see H Muir Watt, *Discours sur les méthodes*.

[481] On these doctrines of private law, see above 94.

aporetic relationship between self and other is not purely bilateral (nor subjective, nor arbitrary, nor casuistic, nor whimsical): as we have seen, the face of the other contains the gaze of *all* others. This subtle philosophical sequence finds an exact echo in the shadow avatar of the conflict of laws, once again. Indeed, the latter suggests that there is a further, indispensable process nested within law's ontological oscillation,[482] an ultimate dialectic on the threshold (of home) or the frontier (of community) at the moment of encounter with the law of the other.

This is precisely the point at which the elusive figure of *ordre public*, largely placeless within the conventional account of the conflict of laws, comes home to roost.[483] Revisited in the context of the shadow avatar of the discipline, it takes on particular significance, and a more complex function and meaning. As we know, the host forum has to set aside its own legal view in order to allow a situation created (or a right vested) under a foreign law to fulfil its course. It is poised as it were on the threshold of the legal order and stands aside to welcome in the law of the other, on their own terms. In this sense it is 'hostage' to foreign law, its legal other. At the same time – and this is where we come back to *ordre public* – it is clearly not true to say that by allowing such reversal, 'anything goes'. Once the foreign law has been heard on its own terms, a diplomatic negotiation can take place. The forum can deploy the 'supreme art of compromise'.[484] Thus, it can be seen as a negotiation that takes place at the threshold of home or community. In this respect, it institutes a dialectic between inside and outside, friend and foe, self and other, the singular and the plural. It involves, in phenomenological terms, a moment of 'suspension of judgement' in which we must put aside all we think we know in order to apprehend the radical strangeness of the other's very alterity.[485] Furthermore, it reserves the possibility of an ultimate decision to exclude, framed nevertheless by the gaze of all others.

The deployment of the exception of public policy in the conflict of laws provides multiple examples of this dialectic: the 'passage of law'[486] goes back and forth, between multiple registers (concrete and abstract, general and individual), at the threshold of the host legal system. Thus, varying degrees of personal and geographical proximity are factored in; duration and social expectations have to be accounted for; likewise, ripple effects in the forum state, or the diverging interests of various

[482] See above, Part II.

[483] On the placelessness of ordre public, see above 170. As an 'exception' it is very generally described as unruly, elusive, indeterminate, etc, as is sovereignty itself, described as placeless or void. The idea of the return of the repressed is once again to be found in Monateri's depiction of the spectre of the *Dominus mundi*, that rules us from the grave (Monateri, *Dominus Mundi*, 172).

[484] Latour, *Enquête*. To be clear: compromise does not mean that anything goes, nor that it is always appropriate. For instance, Isabelle Stengers argues that there is no sense in compromising with capitalism: there is only fighting it. Against Gaia, on the other hand – an indifferent material assemblage rather than a malign spiritual power – there is no sense in fighting, but only compromising, composing with, because its intrusive transcendence has from now on rendered ridiculous all epic or historical versions of human history, forcing us to think this situation, unheard of in modernity, which is the absence of choice (*In Catastrophic Times: Resisting the Coming Barbarism* (Open Humanities Press/Meson Press) 58).

[485] As seen above, the Husserlian phenomenological reduction is cognitive and applies to the essence of things (see Pelluchon, *Pour comprendre Lévinas*, 41) whereas Levinas' version is ethical: the other (alterity) is in excess of representation. This is why the Levinassian concept of alterity can be seen as a philosophical revolution (ibid, 44). An exciting point for the conflict of laws!

[486] Latour, *Enquête*.

active and passive parties to an action are likely to enter into the balance. This process has the potential either to dispose of the conflict, or to whittle it down to its most irreductible form.[487] There is a point however at which diplomacy may have reached its limits and there comes the time of reckoning. This, then, is the second mode of *ordre public*, the process that Annelise Riles names as the indispensable and ultimate 'ethical moment'.[488]

Back now to hospitality in legal terms. As we know, the aporetic nature of hospitality ('hostipitality') means two things. Firstly, that the law of the other must not be treated with suspicion at the outset, but welcomed in through substitution as a matter of principle. Secondly, however, once the reception of foreign law is envisaged, on 'as-if' mode, any identified risk to oneself and others has to be taken entirely seriously.[489] But how then to guard against the surreptitious return of ethnocentrism, bias or stance of superiority that creeps back all too easily into any such ethical judgement? Importantly, as we have seen, in Levinassian terms, this necessary ethical assessment takes place in the name ('in the gaze') of all the others. Where does this lead, if it is only to reformulate the traditional requirement of the impartial third party (as seen above), or to recast the inherently liberal idea that the court must act in the general interest, or for the common good, or in the name of universal values? We know, as seen above, that the mere formal proclamation of the latter does not prevent their egregious violation on the ground. The depredation and devastation of human and natural resources in the Capitalocene is in large part due to the cunning of universalism, disguised as absolute and therefore exclusionary value.[490]

We have come back then, full circle, to the question of plurality in the conflict of laws. The idea to be drawn from the close scrutiny of *ordre public* replaced in the context of its diplomatic and ethical mission at law's very last frontier is precisely not that the values of the host community have to be imposed *urbi et orbi*. At the law's ultimate frontier, they are instantiated not as the triumphant or colonising rule of law, but as mere exception, framed by the concrete contingencies of an individual case and immediately dissolved. Moreover, this does not mean that such values, intervening on occasion, have to be exclusionary, as a matter of ethical, or indeed epistemological or ontological principle. There is no reason they should impede the acknowledgement of other universes with their own equally cherished and possibly antagonistic

[487] Because these are arguments about policy and values, it is unsurprising that neo-statutist 'interests analysis' follows this process as normal practice (in the sense of not the exception). On the idea (developed in the American functionalist 'revolution', see above 92) of revisiting the potentially interested state's real interests before concluding that there is a 'true' conflict, with similar results under impartial interest weighing (B Currie), California's 'comparative impairment' method, or Louise Weinberg's 'consequentialism', see S Symeonides, 'The Choice-of-Law Revolution. Fifty Years after Currie: An End and a Beginning' (2015) 2 *University of Illinois Law Review*.

[488] Riles, 'A New Agenda for the Cultural Study of Law', describing this as a contribution of feminist thought to the conflict of laws.

[489] On the pride of place of as-if reasoning in the conflict of laws, see above 58.

[490] As recalled immediately below, with reference to an observation by Descola, all cultures practise a certain form of universalism, in the sense that they take their own world view as the only or the best one possible for the foundation of their own political community, but not all impose this world view on others, and many accept that there are many worlds, or a pluriverse, with which they cohabit.

worldviews. Indeed, to the contrary, as seen above, they should accommodate, to the greatest extent possible, the gaze of all the alien others. As Philippe Descola points out, all cultures have values that are foundational for themselves and that they believe to be universal.[491] This plurality is law's split ecological horizon, the 'plane of encounter', on which all the various schemes of identity and relationality in the world, all manner of alien beliefs and practices, plural visions and modes of access to reality, can co-inhabit the same earth; a form of 'pluriversality'.[492] In legal form, this implies an ideal of mutual hospitality as between different laws or *nomos*, each acknowledging both the strangeness of itself and the coexistence of alien worlds. At law's ultimate frontier, in the shadow of extinction, the shadow version of the conflict of laws provides for such a model of legal 'inter-alterity'.

COALESCENCE

Law's ultimate frontier is the site of the ever-moving boundary struggle within our *oikos*. On the one hand, this frontier is constantly drawn and redrawn in the light of the encroaching demands of neoliberal legality and its ideals of competition, calculation and individualism, its emptying of space and time, and its severance between humanity and environment. On the other hand, there is a countervailing move, an urgent call to find a legal form for our ethical responsibility towards the world and the multiple forms of biological and cultural life that we have reduced to the status of expendable and external resources. In all these respects, the conflict of laws, taken in its shadow avatar, provides the intellectual model for an alternative jurisprudence. It embodies the *nomos* of law's threshold, coalescing[493] the in-between of different worlds and providing the grammar in which communication can be established among them.

At this point, we can return once more to Latour's 'passage of law' and the question of law's exclusionary effect.[494] Commenting on 'plasma', or the residues of all the beings that disappear into the void without trace,[495] Laurent de Sutter writes that law is more generous than it might be thought: its 'peculiar metaphysics' (explored above) can account for all the remains (the intentions, emotions, ideas, attachments etc) that affect us.[496] This is emblematically true for the conflict of laws. It suggests a

[491] Descola, *Les formes du Visible*, 348.

[492] Above 137, and Descola, *Les formes du Visible*, 666.

[493] Coalescence (used across the board in phonetics or historical linguistics, microbial ecology or genetics) is the process of coming or growing together (of phonemes) to form one thing, segment, sound or system.

[494] See above, 111.

[495] Traces, residues and attachments are all part of law's 'peculiar metaphysics', and resonate particularly powerfully within the conflict of laws, as we have seen throughout his book. As Janda observes (*Panarchy)* there is always a residue at the threshold (suggesting indeed that the word law and its relationship to layer and threshold derives from the Old Norse for the latter, *lagu*).

[496] L de Sutter, 'Plasma! Notes in Bruno Latour's Metaphysics of Law', in McGee (ed), *Latour and the Passage of Law*, 196, 205. If truth is authentic only insofar as it leaves a trace its artificiality then (he reasons) law embodies the truth of the world. But what about the massive exclusion of the beings without trace, that is, without the trace of law's attachments, to which Latour gives insufficient attention?

model of law that reattaches and repairs broken bonds, weaving fragile threads that would otherwise be lost, between all manner of different worldviews and their own idiosyncratic institutions. It outlines a *demeure* that is a refuge and an opening to the foreign and the strange; a place of inward reflection on self and encounter with alterity; a site of recentering and de-centring.[497] In all this, its lode star is the ethical injunction of absolute hospitality towards the alien forms of life upon which we depend for our very existence. These include all the foreign forms of life-in-the-law to which an ecological jurisprudence must give its full and immediate attention.

[497] Derrida, *De l'hospitalité*. This signifies, once again, that the 'law of the other' is welcomed in, on its own terms, along with its language and 'all that language implies'. This, as Descola further emphasises, is the most demanding of ontological and ethical commitments (*Les formes du Visible*, 689).

7

Residue

Law's Last Judgment: The Threshold of Our Responsibility

'L'anthropologie … conjointement avec l'histoire, nous offre le témoignage que d'autres façons d'être au monde sont possibles, radicalement différentes de celles que la modernité a inventées. Si l'on se débarrasse de l'illusion évolutionniste, à savoir que les Indiens d'Amazonie, les Inuits ou les tribus des hautes terres de Birmanie représentent notre passé, si l'on admet plutôt qu'ils représentent des alternatives originales à ce que nous sommes devenus, alors ces autres manières de vivre la condition humaine représentent non des modèles immédiatement transposables, mais des tremplins pour imaginer des futurs différents'.[1]

'Au fond, c'est bien de cela qu'il s'agit: Peut-on instituer les Modernes dans des habitats, sinon stables, du moins durables et raisonnables? Plus simplement et plus radicalement: peut-on leur offrir enfin une demeure? Après toutes ces années d'errance dans le désert, ont-ils l'espoir d'atteindre non pas la Terre promise, mais la Terre, tout simplement, la seule qu'ils aient à la fois sous les pieds et autour d'eux, Gaïa la bien nommée'.[2]

THE 'LAST FRONTIER' evokes a horizon of extinction. The only place to start thinking about our world, as Latour observes, is the end.[3] That is, he explains, 'from a reflection on various ontological issues involving collapse

[1] Descola, P, 'La ZAD, expérience cosmopolitique Inédite'. Interview by Nicolas Truong, *Le Monde*, 27 September 2022. Unofficial translation: 'Anthropology, alongside history, provides us with the testimony that other ways of being in the world are possible. If we get rid of the evolutionist illusion that sees the Indians of Amazonia, the Inuits or the tribes of the high planes of Burma as a remnant of our past and if we accept that these are, rather, original alternatives to what we (moderns) have become, then these other ways of inhabiting the human condition represent, not immediately transposable models, but springboards for imagining different futures.'

[2] Latour, *Enquête sur les modes d'existence*, 35. Unofficial translation: 'In fact, that is what it is all about: Can we establish the Moderns in habitats that are, if not stable, at least durable and reasonable?

If not stable, at least sustainable and reasonable? More simply and more radically:

Can we finally offer them a home? After all these years of wandering around in the desert, do they have any hope of reaching a home?

Do they have any hope of reaching not the Promised Land, but the Land, quite simply, the only one they have at the same time?

After all these years of wandering in the desert, do they have any hope of reaching not the Promised Land, but the Land, simply, the only one they have both under their feet and around them, the aptly named Gaia'.

[3] See his Preface to Danowski and Viveiros de Castro, *The Ends of the World* (perspective).

of modern time, the alteration of our relationship towards alterity'.[4] To the extent that ongoing ecological disaster is the result of accumulated collective policies and individual decisions,[5] and its effects unevenly distributed along geopolitical lines and among human, animal and vegetal constituencies, our inevitable meeting with Gaia makes loud and urgent calls upon our sense of responsibility and justice. But it also challenges in radical ways both our modes of production of knowledge about reality and our relationship to alterity.

This book has attempted to show that modern legality is as profoundly entangled within all these epistemological, ontological, aesthetic issues as it is instrumental in shaping our moral consciousness and our political economy.[6]

In terms of jurisprudence, the question arises both as to the prospects of law's own survival as a mode of existence in the global turn, and to its place at the threshold of the ultimate transitions of material and metaphysical life on earth. What can we retrieve from the enlightened remnants of Western legality, that in our 'catastrophic times'[7] appears so tragically out of time, out of step, and out of joint? Is law able in any way to prevent our planet's fragile crust from becoming a generalised 'sacrifice zone', an inhabitable place where only the wandering hauntological figure of 'bare life' remains? The latter – of which the cases currently processed through positive private international law offer increasing evidence – is constantly spreading to the multiple universes that struggle for survival beyond the devastation wrought by the combined effects of global capitalism in all its guises (whether colonial, racial, financialised, gendered or algorithmic), and the concomitant 'ontological privilege of humanity' (in respect of other species), modernity (in respect of other cultural modes of access to reality) and the West (in respect of the rest of the world).

Undergirding secular statehood, territorial enclosure and expansion of empire, law has undoubtedly played a constitutive role in all these processes, formalising life and detaching our world from its materiality. Drawing on the resources of Roman legality, this 'great bifurcation' involved the severance of mind from body, persons from things, self from other, nature from culture, humans from animals. By late modernity, in the international order, it had redrawn the respective spheres of the intimate and the public, imposed development on the primitive, and prised away the economy from the reach of politics. As the nested pair of its public counterpart, private international law, in particular, has contributed emblematically to the global commodification of everything. Our responsibility – our answerability, our ability to respond to the call

[4] It is here that we meet Gaia (that is, the end of the anthropological separation of morality and geophysics) as the mother of all time: see Danowski and Viveiros de Castro, *The Ends of the World* 112, on Pachamama, the 'Mother of World-Time'.

[5] For a good example see https://euobserver.com/green-economy/155930.

[6] To dispel any lingering doubt on this point, see G Samuel, commenting on the 'rather startling paradox', according to which 'the foundations of modern historical scholarship were laid down by French jurists during the sixteenth century. The philological methods employed by these jurists 'created the most basic attitudes which have gone into the making of historicism'. Yet, as Samuel further notes, 'law as a discipline has succeeded in banishing history; in the 17th century mathematics (*mos mathematicus*) became the new logos … and lawyers, like other scientists, had no need for history': Samuel, *Rethinking Historical Jurisprudence* (Cheltenham, Edward Elgar, 2022) 34.

[7] Stengers, *In Catastrophic Times*.

of all the other forms of life that depend upon us – has disappeared into a vortex of ontological indetermination between law and fact.

The argument that weaves through this book is that there is a possible counter-move to be made, a means of reversing gear in terms of legality's own political ecology. It is an attempt to explore the residual, interstitial normative forms that might still emerge, in the threatening shadow of Gaia, in order to acknowledge 'nature's splendid alterity'. In this respect, the first, liminal finding is that of the extraordinary complexity – *com plessis* – of law's own trajectories. The traces of 'law's passage', like those of language, speak of fragility, vacillation and duality. *Ius* and *lex*, *loi* et *droit*, *langue* and parole. Sovereignty itself is nested, while legality weaves endlessly in and out of a 'thousand plateaux'. We must refuse the aesthetic temptation of simplification, the need for linearity and closure conventionally associated with law's forms and methods. The 'rush for order' that drove the constitution of empire is not the solution, but part of the problem. On this point, the heuristic use of the conflict of laws shows that there is indeed an alternative, shadow legal mode of reception of alterity that is open to the foreign – the law of the other – on its own terms.

A second idea is that such 'minor jurisprudence' (or abyssal legal form) emerges in the legal imaginaries of those who have already faced extinction, whether in the form of colonial or genocidal extermination, or the destruction of their natural habitat, like those of other species in the biosphere. History is the blind-spot of the modern Western collective psyche; the fear of breakdown, like that of disappearance and void, is a deep echo of our own forgotten past, our own '*futur antérieur*'. This loss of meaning explains why the West looks increasingly towards the indigenous cosmologies of the global South and their forms of ecological knowledge previously consigned to the realm of the epistemologically archaic and the economically inefficient. These alternative ways of perceiving and doing teach us the virtues of 'dwelling in the border', of seeing legality as a primary form of translation and diplomacy shuttling back and forth between different ontological worlds. Once again, resisting the Archimedean perspective and hierarchical categorisations (whether cultural, racial, or gendered), the conflict of laws provides a pattern that resonates with shamanic forms of interlegality.

The third and last lesson that emerges from the go-between function and in-between ontology of private international law, in the constant labour of reattachment that it pursues in the shadow of its more visible support for the neoliberal global order, is the link that exists between all forms of denial or repression of alterity. If legal enclosure (the rush to expropriate and appropriate through the twin legal forms of *dominium* and *imperium*) is a 'metonym for all the rest', then the same can be said for the separations and classifications put in place by modern legality and reinforced through law's own political economy. In other words, refusal or neglect of difference constantly replicates itself in biological, cultural, social or psychic terms. Capitalism is racial, just as it drives our modes of (ac)counting; difference is at the very core of self, exactly as it runs through nature and culture; power produces subjectivities in the same way as it controls our phenomenological bodies; ecological disaster is an effect of the law as much as the result of practices of mineral extraction.

Gaia, or the earth itself, stands in judgement of our modern failure to hear the appeal of all the forms of life that depend upon us for survival. But it is here that our planetary responsibility can begin, on the terms of the law. *Quod omnes tangit*.[8] Leaving behind our economy of severance and atomisation, we need a global ecology of attachments among all the beings that inhabit the biosphere, an oikos of ligatures governed by the law of the other. The shadow avatar of the conflict of laws provides the pattern for hospitality towards the other at the threshold of law's *demeure*, a (split) ethical horizon within earth's 'crisis zone'. It has unseen roots that link it to indigenous cosmologies hitherto excluded from 'our' very notion of legality. Is there anything wrong, then, with slowing down or going backwards (to being indigenous)? As Eduardo Viveiros de Castro observes in 'Ends of the World', a curiously recurrent topos in discourses on the environmental crisis is that 'history does not move backward', that 'we cannot go back to the Stone Age' (or to the Amish, the Middle Ages, or the Garden of Eden …):

> Just as we once abhorred the vacuum, today we find repugnant the very idea of deceleration, regression, retreat, limitation, degrowth, applying brakes, descent … Anything that brings to mind any of these movements toward an intensive sufficiency of world (instead of an epic overcoming of the 'limits' separating us from a hyperworld) is immediately accused of naive localism, primitivism, irrationalism, bad conscience, guilt, or even just fascistic tendencies.[9]

Indeed, as Bruno Latour observes in turn, the moral high ground is 'occupied by people who give lessons to the others from no other authority than having dismally failed to change anything'.[10]

However, Viveiros de Castro further contends that Amerindian collectives, with their comparatively modest populations, their relatively simple technologies that are nonetheless open to high-intensity syncretic assemblages, are a 'figuration of the future', not a remnant of the past. Masters of 'techno-primitivist bricolage and politico-metaphysical metamorphosis', they are one of the possible chances, in fact, of a subsistence of the future. Ironically, as noted at the beginning of this book, law's last frontier is the very threshold at which the frontiers that conferred such apparent invulnerability to the purveyors of modernity, must disappear. Now at the end of our reflection, a further cruel paradox emerges: as the ice at the poles of our planet dissolves into the sea, intellectual icebergs made of dogma and closure multiply and expand, accelerating the former through various forms of denial or indifference. This is precisely why, as argued by de Sousa Santos, it is imperative to recover and valorise the epistemological diversity of the world and make way a new kind of bottom-up

[8] Quod omnes tangit ab omnibus tractari debet: on this Roman legal precept, see G Teubner, 'Quod Omnes Tangit: Transnational Constitutions without Democracy?', in (2018) 45(1) *Journal of Law and Society* 5–29.

[9] Danowski, D and Viveiros de Castro, E, *Ends of the World* (Cambridge, Polity Press, 2017), 14, 15, 19, 120. It is true too that the representation of the past as a golden (Edenic) age is equally flawed and has probably gone far to enable the classic climate-denial argument according to which ecological action is driven by a (supposedly ridiculous) desire to return to an age of candles and caves.

[10] Latour, 'Affects of Capitalism'.

cosmopolitanism, in which conviviality, solidarity and life triumph against the logic of market-ridden greed and individualism.[11] 'Justice against epistemicide!'[12]

Law (in alternative mode) is implicated in this battle as much as (symmetrical) anthropology, political-economic theories (of racial capitalism) or (non-cognitivist) art forms.[13] In this respect, the shadow version of the conflict of laws points towards alternative ways of understanding the cohabitation of multiple nomos and narratives on our planet. The book that ends here is thus an attempt to reverse, in counterfactual terms,[14] the legal divisions and expropriations that have devastated the infinite and subtle diversity of the diverse worlds with which 'we' coexist and whose very alterity sustains life itself. From the brink of the Western tradition,[15] it suggests the chinks through which the latter can still be acknowledged and welcomed, at the very last frontier of our law.

[11] De Sousa Santos, *Epistemologies of the South*.

[12] The phrase figures in the full title of de Sousa Santos' aforementioned book. This reinvestment of legality by justice is the opportunity to return to a significant etymological question raised by Janda in *Panarchy*, p 65: 'The conceptual distinction between "Law" and "Right" in English brings into view the crucial question of law's relation to what is right and/or rightful, not only in the sense of having a lawful or legitimate claim but also being just, equitable, fitting. Yet this distinction appears to be subsumed, if not set aside, in the very term "law", which refers both to the idea of law and to specific, legislated rule, statute, ordinance, or regulation.'

[13] All of these approaches have been discussed in the course of this book. See in particular, for an alternative cosmovision that draws its epistemological foundations from the world of plants, E Valdenebro, 'Le principe métanthropique: Faire lieu à partir d'une épistémè végétale possible', PhD Thesis, Univ Paris 8, 2022. See above 133.

[14] On the use of counterfactuals as a means of making alternatives visible, see R Wenzlhuemer, 'Counterfactual Thinking as a Scientific Method'/'Kontrafaktisches Denken als wissenschaftliche Methode' (2009) 34 *Historical Social Research/Historische Sozialforschung* 27–54.

[15] 'World on the brink': see E Viveiros de Castro, *The Ends of the World*.

Bibliography

BOOKS

Adorno, T and Horkheimer, M, *Dialectique de la Raison* (Paris, Gallimard, 1974).

Agamben, G, *Homo Sacer: Sovereign Power and Bare Life, Meridian: Crossing Aesthetics* (Palo Alto CA, Stanford University Press, 1998).

Agamben, G, *Open: Man and Animal* (Palo Alto CA, Stanford University Press, 2002).

Agamben, G, *The Signature of All Things: On Method* (New York, Zone Books, 2008).

Agamben, G, *Homo Sacer 22. The Kingdom and the Glory, For a Theological Genealogy of Economy and Government* (Palo Alto CA, Stanford University Press, 2011).

Ahmed, S, *The Cultural Politics of Emotion* (Edinburgh, Edinburgh University Press, 2004).

Alviar Garcia, H, 'Neoliberalism as a Form of Authoritarian Constitutionalism', in Alviar Garcia, H, and Frankenberg, G (eds), *Authoritarian Constitutionalism: Critique and Appraisal* (Cheltenham, Elgar, 2019).

Ancel, B, 'Destinées de l'articles 3 du Code civil', in *Le droit international privé: esprit et méthodes – Mélanges en l'honneur de Paul Lagarde* (Paris (Paris, Dalloz, 2005).

Ancel, B and Lequette, Y, *Grands arrêts de la jurisprudence de droit international privé* (Paris (Paris, Dalloz, 2005).

Anghie, A, *Imperialism, Sovereignty and International Law* (Cambridge, Cambridge University Press, 2005).

Antunes Madeira da Silva, F, 'The Conquest of the Devil's Paradise: International law, Frontier-making and Capitalist power', PhD dissertation, Sciences Po Law School, November 2022.

Audren, F and Barbou des Places, S, *Qu'est-ce qu'une discipline juridique?* (Paris, LGDJ Lextenso, 2018).

Austin, JL, *How to Do Things with Words*, 2nd edn (Cambridge MA, Harvard University Press, 1975).

Bachir Diagne, S, *De langue à langue: L'hospitalité de la traduction* (Paris, Albin Michel, 2022).

Bachir Diagne, S and Amselle, JL, *En quête d'Afrique(s)* (Paris, Albin Michel, 2019).

Bakhtin, M, 'Discourse in the Novel' in Michael Holquist (ed), *The Dialogic Imagination* (Austin TX, University of Texas Press, 1981).

Balibar, E, *Des Universels, Essais et conférences* (Galilée, 2016).

Bandopadhyay, S, *All Is Well: Catastrophe and the Making of the Normal State* (New York, Oxford Academic 2022; online edn).

Banu, R, *Nineteenth Century Perspectives on Private International Law* (Oxford, Oxford University Press, 2018).

Bartelson, J, *Sovereignty as Symbolic Form Critical Issues in Global Politics* (Abingdon, Routledge, 2014).

Barthes, R, (2010) *Camera Lucida: Reflections on photography*, R Howard, trans (New York, Hill and Wang, 1980).

Bartin, E, *Etudes de droit international privé* (Paris, 1899).

Batiffol, H, *Aspects philosophiques du droit international privé* (Paris, Dalloz, 1956).

Baumann, Z, *Liquid Modernity and Beyond* (Cambridge, Polity, 2000).

Baxi, U, *International Natural Resources Law, Investment and Sustainability* (Abingdon, Routledge, 2017).

Beck, U, *Qu'est-ce que le cosmopolitisme?* (Paris, ed Aubier, Alto, 2006).

Becker Lorca, A, *Mestizo International Law: A Global Intellectual History 1842–1933* (Cambridge, Cambridge University Press, 2016).

Belaïdi, N, 'Gérer la diversité culturelle pour gérer la diversité biologique Droits des peuples autochtones et souveraineté des Etats sur la biodiversité' in *Le protocole de Nagoya en dialogue Biodiversité et sociétés* (Paris, Museum national d'histoire naturelle et IRD, 2020).

Benjamin, J, *Shadow of the Other Intersubjectivity and Gender in Psychoanalysis* (Abingdon, Routledge, 1998).

Benoistel, A, 'Le concept de renvoi mobile: une théorie de la reconnaissance entre le droit international privé et les libertés de circulation européenne,' PhD dissertation, Univ Paris I, 2018.

Benslama, F, *La psychanalyse à l'épreuve de l'Islam* (Paris, Flammarion, 2002).

Bensussan, G, *Éthique et expérience Lévinas politique* (Paris, La Phocide, 2008).

Bentham, J, 'Principles of International Law', in J Bowring (ed), *The Works of Jeremy Bentham*, vol II (Edinburgh, 1838–1843).

Benton, L *Law and Colonial Cultures, Legal regimes in World History 1400–1900* (Cambridge, Cambridge University Press, 2009).

Benton, L, *A Search for Sovereignty Law and Geography in European Empires 1400–1900* (Cambridge, Cambridge University Press, 2010).

Benton, L, 'Possessing Empire Iberian Claims and Interpolity Law', in S Belmessous (ed), *Native Claims Indigenous Law against Empire, 1500–1920* (Oxford, Oxford University Press, 2012).

Benton, L and L Ford, *Rage for Order The British Empire and the Origins of International Law 1800–1850* (Cambridge MA, Harvard University Press, 2017).

Benton, L and N Perl-Rosenthal (eds), *A World at Sea Maritime Practices and Global History The Early Modern Americas* (Philadelphia PA, University of Pennsylvania Press, 2021).

Berman, H, *Law and Revolution The formation of the Western Legal Tradition* (Cambridge MA, Harvard University Press, 1983).

Berman, PS, *Global Legal Pluralism: A Jurisprudence of Law Beyond Borders* (New York, Cambridge University Press, 2012).

Bermann, G and Cordero-Moss, G, 'Free-wheeling judgments/awards: Mitsubishi Motors Corp v Soler Chrysler-Plymouth, Inc', in H Muir Watt et al, *Global Private International Law* (Cheltenham, Edward Elgar, 2019).

Bernasconi, R, 'Levinas, Emmanuel (1906–95)', in *Routledge Encyclopedia of Philosophy* (Abingdon, Routledge, 1998).

Birla, R, *Stages of Capital: Law, Culture and Market Governance in Late Colonial India* (Durham NC, Duke University Press, 2009).

Birrell, K and Dehm, J, 'International law and the humanities in the Anthropocene,' in Chalmers, S and Pahuja, S (eds) *Routledge Handbook of International Law and the Humanities* (London, Routledge, 2021).

Black, CF, *A Mosaic of Indigenous Legal Thought Legendary Tales and Other Writings* (Abingdon, Routledge, 2018).

Bloomfield, A, *Monetary Policy Under the Gold Standard, 1880 to 1914* (New York, Federal Reserve Bank of New York, 1959).

Boden, D, 'L'ordre public: limite et condition de la tolérance: recherches sur le pluralisme juridique', Doctoral dissertation, Paris I, 2002.

Bollée, S, *Global Private International Law* (Cheltenham, Elgar, 2018).

Bollée, S, *Le Droit international privé et le tournant global* (Paris, Pédone, 2020).

Bomhoff, J, 'The constitution of the conflict of laws' in Muir Watt, H and Fernandez Arroyo, D (eds), *Private International Law and Global Governance* (Oxford, Oxford University Press, 2014).

Bomhoff, J, D Dyzenhaus, T Poole (eds), *The Double-Facing Constitution* (Cambridge, Cambridge University Press, 2020).

Bonneuil, C and Fressoz, J-B, *L'événement Anthropocène* (Paris, ed du Seuil, 2016).

Borrows, J, (Kegedonce), *Drawing Out Law: A Spirit's Guide* (Toronto, University of Toronto Press, 2010)

Borrows, J, *Canada's Indigenous Constitution* (Toronto, University of Toronto Press, 2010).

Boureau, A, *L'errance des normes: Elements d'éthique scholastique (1220–1320) La Raison Scholastique,* (Paris, ed Les Belles Lettres, 2016).

Bouriau, C, *Le 'comme si': Kant, Vaihinger et le fictionalisme* (Paris, Les Éditions du Cerf, 2013).

Brabazon, H (ed), *Neoliberal Legality: Understanding the Role of Law in the Neoliberal Project* (New York, Routledge, 2016).

Brachotte, S, 'The Conflict of Laws and Non-Secular Worldviews: A Proposal for Inclusion', Doctoral Dissertation, Sciences Po, Law School, 2022.

Brett, A, *Changes of State: Nature and the Limits of the City in Early Modern Natural Law* (Princeton NJ, Princeton University Press, 2011).

Brunkhorst, H, *Critical Theory of Legal Revolutions: Evolutionary Perspectives* (London, Bloomsbury Press, 2014).

Bryant, LR, *The Democracy of Objects* (Open Humanities Press, 2011).

Buffon, GL (Le Clerc de), *Les Epoques de la Nature* (1780).

Bureau, D and Muir Watt, H, *Droit international privé*, 5th edn (Paris, PUF, 2021).

Butler, J, *Bodies that Matter: On the Discursive Limits of Sex* (Abingdon, Routledge, 1993).

Butler, J, *Gender Trouble: Feminism and the Subversion of Identity* (Abingdon, Taylor and Francis, 1999).

Byung-Chul, H, *Thanatocapitalisme* (Paris, PUF, 2021).

Callies, GP and Zumbansen, P, *Rough Consensus and Running Code: A Theory of Transnational Private Law* (Oxford, Hart, 2010).

Capra, F and Mattei, U, *The Ecology of Law Toward a Legal System in Tune with Nature and Community* (San Francisco CA, Berrett-Kohler Publishers, 2015).

Carlson, A, 'Environmental Aesthetics', in *Stanford Encyclopedia of Philosophy* (Palo Alto CA, Stanford University Press).

Carvalho, H et al, 'Concept Hegemony', in *Critical Legal Pocketbook* (Counterpress, 2021).

Castoriadis, C, *L'institution imaginaire de la société* (Paris, ed Seuil, 1999).

Chakrabarty, D, *Provincializing Europe: Postcolonial Thought and Historical Difference* (Princeton NJ, Princeton University Press, 2007).

Charbonnier, P, *Abondance et liberté Une histoire environnementale des idées politiques* (Paris, La Découverte, 2022).

Chen, L, *Chinese Law in Imperial Eyes: Sovereignty, Justice and Transcultural Politics* (New York, Columbia University Press, 2016).

Ciupa, K, 'The promise of rights: international indigenous rights in the neoliberal era', in Brabazon, H (ed), *Neoliberal Legality: Understanding the Role of Law in the Neoliberal Project* (New York, Routledge, 2016).

Claire Cutler, A and Dietz, T, *The Politics of Private Transnational Governance by Contract* (Abingdon, Routledge, 2017).

Clastres, P, *La Société contre l'État Recherches d'anthropologie politique* (Paris, Éditions de Minuit, 1974).

Clastres, P, *Mythologie des Indiens Chulupi* (Louvain, Peeters, 1992).

Cohen, RA, 'Dialogue with Emmanuel Levinas,' in *Face to Face with Levinas* (New York, State University of New York Press).

Collins, H, 'Flipping Wreck: *Lex Mercatoria* on the Shoals of *Ius Cogens*' in Grundmann, S, Moeslein, F, Riesenhuber, K (eds), *Contract Governance – Dimensions in Law and Interdisciplinary Research* (Oxford, Oxford University Press, 2015).

Connell, K, 'Objects in Human Drag: The Queerness of Object-Oriented Ontologies', MA Thesis, Contemporary Art, Design and New Media Art Histories, OCAD University, Canada, 2016.

Cooren, F, 'In the name of the law: Ventriloquism and Juridical Matters', in K McGee (ed), *Latour and the Passage of Law* (Edinburgh, Edinburgh University Press, 2015).

Corcodel, V, *Modern law and otherness: the dynamics of inclusion and exclusion in comparative legal thought* (Cheltenham, Edward Elgar, 2019).

Corneloup, S, and Verhellen, J, 'Privatisation of international migration flows' in H Muir Watt et al, *Global Private International Law* (Cheltenham, Edward Elgar, 2019).

Cotterrell, R, and del Mar, M (eds), *Authority in Transnational Legal Theory. Theorising Across Disciplines* (Cheltenham, Edward Elgar, 2016).

Culver, K and Giudice, M, *Legality's Borders: An Essay in General Jurisprudence* (New York, Oxford University Press, 2010).

Culver K and Giudice, M, *The Unsteady State: General Jurisprudence for Dynamic Social Phenomena* (Cambridge, Cambridge University Press, 2017).

Cuniberti, G, *Rethinking International Commercial Arbitration: Towards Default Arbitration* (Cheltenham, Edward Elgar, 2017).

Currie, B, *Selected Essays on the Conflict of Laws* (Durham NC, Duke University Press, 1963).

d'Aspremont, J, *After Meaning The Sovereignty of Forms in International Law* (Cheltenham, Edward Elgar, 2021).

d'Azevedo, J, *Tribunal Theologicum, et Juridicum contra subdolos Confessarios in Sacramto: Penitentie ad venerum solicitantes ereptun* (Mich Rodrigz, 1726).
Dagan, H, *A Liberal Theory of Property* (Cambridge, Cambridge University Press, 2021).
Dagan, H, *Reconstructing American legal realism and rethinking private law theory* (Oxford, Oxford University Press, 2013).
Dakhlia, J, *Lingua franca. Histoire d'une langue métisse en Méditerranée,* (Actes Sud, 2008).
Danowski, D and Viveiros de Castro, E, *Ends of the World* (Cambridge, Polity Press, 2017).
de Sousa Santos, B, *Demodiversity: Toward Post-Abyssal Democracies* (Abingdon, Routledge, 2020).
de Sousa Santos, B, *Epistemologies of the South Justice against Epistemicide* (New York, Routledge, 2014).
de Sousa Santos, B, *Toward A New Legal Common Sense* (London, Butterworths, 2002).
de Sutter, L, 'Plasma! Notes on Latour's metaphysics of Law', in K McGee (ed), *Latour and the Passage of Law* (Edinburgh, Edinburgh University Press, 2015).
de Toledo, C, *Le fleuve qui voulait écrire (Les auditions du parlement de Loire Audition de Bruno Latour)* (Paris, Les liens qui libèrent, 2021).
Deleuze, G and Guattari, F, *Capitalisme et Schizophrénie II, Mille Plateaux* (Paris, ed de Minuit, 1980).
Deleuze, G and Guattari, F, *Capitalism and Schizophrenia* Vol 2, *A Thousand Plateaus*, Trans Brian Massumi (London and New York: Continuum, 2004).
Demos, TJ, 'Rights of nature: the art and politics of Earth jurisprudence' (2015), https://cpb-us-e1.wpmucdn.com/sites.ucsc.edu/dist/0/196/files/2015/10/Demos-Rights-of-Nature-2015.compressed.pdf.
Derrida, J, *De la grammatologie,* (Paris, ed Minuit, 1967).
Derrida J, *La mythologie blanche, Marges de la philosophie* (Paris, Minuit, 1972).
Derrida, J, *Specters of Marx: The State of the Debt, the Work of Mourning and the New International* (*Spectres de Marx: L'Etat de la dette, le travail du deuil et la nouvelle Internationale* (ed Galileé, 1993).
Derrida, J, *De l'hospitalité*, dialogue with Anne Dufourmentelle (Paris, Calmann-Levy, 1997).
Derrida, J, *Adieu to Emmanuel Levinas* (eds M Naas, PA Brault) (Palo Alto CA, Stanford University Press, 1999).
Derrida, J, *L'animal que donc je suis* (éd Galilée, 2006).
Derrida, J, *Psyche: Inventions of the Other* (Palo Alto CA, Stanford University Press, 2007).
Derrida, J, *Hospitalité*, vol 1, *Séminaire 1995–96* (Paris, Seuil, 2021).
Descola, P, *Par delà nature et culture* (Paris, Gallimard, 2005).
Descola, P, *Les formes du visible* (Paris, éd du Seuil, 2021).
Dezalay, Y and Garth, B, *Dealing in Virtue International Commercial Arbitration and the Construction of a Transnational Legal Order* (Chicago, Chicago University Press, 1996).
Dicey, AV and Bassett Moore, J, *A Digest of the Law of England with Reference to the Conflict of Laws* (London, Sweet & Maxwell, 1896).
Dicey, Morris and Collins, *The Conflict of Laws*, 15th edn (London, Sweet & Maxwell, 2012).
Douzinas, C, 'Postmodern Jurisprudence: The Law of Text in the Texts of Law', in S McVeigh (ed) *Jurisprudence of Jurisdiction* (New York, Routledge, 2007).
Drakopoulou, M, 'Of the Founding of Law's Jurisdiction and the Politics of Sexual Difference: the case of Roman law', in S McVeigh (ed) *Jurisprudence of Jurisdiction* (New York, Routledge, 2007).
Edwards, PN, 'Knowledge Infrastructures under Siege: Climate Data as Memory, Truce and Target' in D Bigo, E Isin and E Ruppert (eds), *Data Politics: Worlds, Subjects, Rights* (New York, Routledge, 2019).
Eitel, K, and Meurer, M, *Exploring Multifarious Worlds and the Political Within the Ontological Turn(s)* (Berliner Blätter, 2021).
Elias, N *Über den Prozess der Zivilisation: soziogenetische und psychogenetische Untersuchungen*, Vol I: *Wandlungen des Verhaltens in den weltlichen Oberschichten des Abendlandes*, Vol II: *Wandlungen der Gesellschaft: Entwurf zu einer Theorie der Zivilisation* (Bâle, Haus zum Falken, 1939).
Elias, N, *La Civilisation des mœurs* (Paris, Pocket, coll 'Évolution', 1973).
Elias, N, *La Dynamique de l'Occident* (Paris, ed Calmann-Lévy 1975).
Engels, F, 'Socialism: Utopian and Scientific', in *Marx and Engels: Collected Works*, Vol 24 *(1874–1883)* (New York, International Publishers, 1989).
Escobar, A, 'Transition Discourses and the Politics of relationality Towards Designs for the Pluriverse', in Reitner, B (ed), *Constructing the Pluriverse, The Geopolitics of Knowledge* (Durham NC, Duke University Press, 2018).
Escobar, A, *Pluriversal Politics: The Real and the Possible* (Durham, NC, Duke University Press, 2020).

Esposito, R, *Communitas: Origine e destino della comunità?* (Torino, Einaudi, 1998).
Esposito, R, *Persons and Things: From the Body's Point of View (Theory Redux)* (Cambridge, Polity Press, 2015).
Fabbri, P, *La svolta semiotica* (Rome, G Laterza, 2001).
Fabian, J, *Le temps et les autres Comment l'anthropologie construit son objet* (Toulouse, Anacharsis, 2006).
Fabra-Zamora, J, (ed) *Jurisprudence in a Globalized World* (Cheltenham, Edward Elgar, 2020).
Fanon, F, *Peau noire, masques blancs* (Paris, Le Seuil, 1952).
Fassin, D, 'L'ordre moral du monde Essai d'anthropologie de l'intolérable', in Fassin, D and Bourdelais, P (eds), *Les Constructions de l'intolérable Études d'anthropologie et d'histoire sur les frontières de l'espace moral* (Paris, La Découverte, 2005).
Fassin, E *La vie, Mode d'Emploi critique* (Paris, Le Seuil, 2018).
Feichtner, I, 'Law of Natural Resource Extraction and Money as Key to Understanding Global Political Economy and Potential for Its Transformation', in P Kjaer (ed), *Law's Political Economy* (Cambridge, Cambridge University Press, 2020).
Fentiman, R, *International Commercial Litigation*, 2nd edn (Oxford, Oxford University Press, 2015).
Fentiman, R, 'Foreign Law as Local Law: a Case of Mistaken Identity?', *Liber Amicorum Monika Pauknerová* (Wolters Kluwer, 2021).
Ferguson, K, *Williams James: Politics in the Pluriverse* (Parlux, 2005).
Fernandez Arroyo, D, and Caballo Pineiro, L, in Muir Watt, H et al, *Global Private International Law* (Cheltenham, Edward Elgar, 2019).
Ferrando, T, 'About capitalism and private international law', in Muir Watt, H et al, *Global Private International Law* (Cheltenham, Edward Elgar, 2019).
Fitzpatrick, P, *The Mythology of Modem Law* (London, Routledge, Chapman & Hall, 1992).
Forsythe, DE, *Studying Those Who Study Us: An Anthropologist in the World of Artificial Intelligence* (Palo Alto CA, Stanford Univ Press, 2001).
Foucault, M, *L'archéologie du savoir* (Paris, Gallimard, 1969).
Foucault, M, *Les Mots et Les Choses Une archéologie des sciences humaines* (Paris, Gallimard, 1990) (trans: *The Order of Things: An Archaeology of the Human Sciences*, Vintage, 1994).
Foucault, M, *Naissance de la biopolitique*, ed M Senellart (Paris, Gallimard-Seuil, 2004).
Fournier, M, 'Comparative Law gets entitled', Thesis, University of Victoria, 2018.
Fox Keller, E, *The Mirage of a Space Between Nature and Nurture* (Durham NC, Duke University Press, 2010).
Francescakis, P, *La Théorie du renvoi* (Paris, Dalloz, 1958).
Frankenberg, G, *Political Technology and the Erosion of the Rule of Law Normalizing the State of Exception,* (Cheltenham, Edward Elgar, 2015).
Frankenberg, G, *Comparative Law as Critique* (Cheltenham, Edward Elgar, 2019).
Fraser, N, and Jaeggi, R, *Capitalism, A Conversation in Critical Theory* (Cambridge, Polity Press, 2018).
Friedman, L, *A History of American Law*, 4th edn (Oxford, Oxford University Press, 2019).
G'sell, F, 'Les théories contemporaines de la causalité Droit et Philosophie', in S Ferey and F G'sell (eds), *Causalité, responsabilité et contribution à la dette* (Bruylant, 2018).
Gabel, P, *The Desire for Mutual Recognition, Social Movements and the Dissolution of the False Self* (Abingdon, Routledge, 2018).
Garapon, A, and Lassègue, J, *Justice digitale Révolution graphique et rupture anthropologique* (Paris, PUF, 2018).
Garapon, A, and Lassègue, J, *Le numérique contre le politique* (Paris, PUF, 2021).
Geertz, C, *The Interpretation of Cultures* (New York, Basic Books, 1973).
Gilli, P, 'Comment cesser d'être étranger Citoyens et non-citoyens dans la pensée juridique italienne de la fin du Moyen Âge', in *Actes des congrès de la Société des historiens médiévistes de l'enseignement supérieur public*, 30e congrès, *L'étranger au Moyen Âge* (Göttingen, 1999).
Ginzburg, C, *Mythes, Emblèmes, Traces Morphologie et histoire* (Paris, Verdier, 1986, 2010).
Godechot, S, *L'articulation du trust et du droit des successions* (Paris, Éditions Panthéon, 2004).
Goldblum, C, *Françoise d'Eaubonne and l'écoféminisme* (ed Passager clandestin, 2019).
Golder, B, and McLoughlin, D, *The Politics of Legality in a Neoliberal Age* (Abingdon, Routledge, 2018).
Goodrich, P, *Law in the Courts of Love: Literature and Other Minor Jurisprudences* (Abingdon, Routledge, 1996).

Gothot, P, 'Simples réflexions à propos de la saga du conflit des lois', in *Le droit international privé: esprit et méthodes, Mélanges en l'honneur de Paul Lagarde* (Paris, Dalloz, 2005).
Graddy-Lovelace, G, *The Power of Seeds and the Politics of Agricultural Biodiversity* (Boston MA, MIT Press, 2019).
Graeber, G, *Debt: The First 5,000 Years* (Melville House, 2011).
Grotius (or de Groot), H, *De jure belli ac pacis* (1625).
Gurtwirth, S, 'Providing the Missing Link: Law after Latour's Passage', in K McGee (ed), *Latour and the Passage of Law* (Edinburgh, Edinburgh University Press, 2015).
Gutmann, D, *Le sentiment d'identité, étude de droit des personnes et de la famille* (LGDJ, 2000).
Hafstein, T and Skrydstrup, M, 'Heritage vs property Contrasting regimes and rationalities in the patrimonial field', *The Routledge Companion to Cultural Property* (Abingdon, Routledge, 2017).
Haggenmacher, P, *Grotius et la doctrine de la guerre juste* (Paris, Presses Universitaires de France, 1983).
Halpérin, JL, *Entre nationalisme juridique et communauté de droit* (Paris, PUF, 1999).
Hamilton, C, Bonneuil, C and Gemenne, F (eds), *The Anthropocene and the Global Environmental Crisis Rethinking Modernity in a New Epoch* (Abingdon, Routledge, 2015).
Haraway, D, *Simians, Cyborgs and Women: The Reinvention of Nature* (Abingdon, Routledge, 1991, republished 2015).
Haraway, D, *Staying with the Trouble: Making Kin in the Chthulucene* (Durham NC, Duke University Press, 2016.
Hardt, M and Negri, A, *Empire* (Cambridge MA, Harvard University Press, 2000)).
Harman, G, 'Politics and Law as Latourian Modes of Existence', in K McGee (ed), *Latour and the Passage of Law* (Edinburgh, Edinburgh University Press, 2015).
Harms, L, *Faith in Courts* (Oxford, Hart, 2022, forthcoming).
Harvey, D, *A Brief History of Neoliberalism* (Oxford, Oxford University Press, 2005).
Hassani, A, 'La neutralité de l'arbitrage international: essai de déconstruction d'un mythe', PhD Thesis, Law School of Sciences Po Paris, 2021.
Hatzimihail, N, *Preclassical Conflict of Laws* (Cambridge, Cambridge University Press, 2021).
Henkin, L; Pugh, RC; Schachter, O; Smit, H, *International Law: Cases and Materials* (St Paul MN, West Publishing Co, 1980).
Hermitte, M-A, 'Artificialisation de la nature et droit(s) du vivant' in P Descola (ed), *Les Natures en question* (Paris, Odile Jacob/Collège de France, 2018).
Herzog, D, *Cold war Freud. Psychoanalysis in an Age of Catastrophes* (Cambridge, Cambridge University Press, 2016).
Hobbes, T, *Leviathan* (1651).
Hochstrasser, T, *Natural Law Theories in the Early Enlightenment* (Cambridge, Cambridge University Press, 2000).
Holmes, OW, *The Common Law* (1900; published by the Gutenberg project in e-book form).
Horkheimer, M, *Théorie traditionnelle et théorie critique*, trans C Maillard and S Muller (Paris, Gallimard, 1974).
Howes, D, *The Sensory Studies Manifesto: Tracking the Sensorial Revolution in the Arts and Human Sciences* (University of Toronto Press, 2022).
Huber U, 'De Conflictu Legum Diversarum in Diversis Imperiis', in *Praelectiones Juris Romani Et Hodierni* (1689).
Husserl, E, *Ideas Pertaining to a Pure Phenomenology and to a Phenomenological Philosophy: Studies in the Phenomenology of Constitution,* (1912–1928) (Dordrecht/Boston, Kluwer, 1989).
Husserl, E, *The Crisis of European Sciences and Transcendental Phenomenology: An Introduction to Phenomenological Philosophy* (1936) (Northwestern University Studies in Phenomenology and Existential Philosophy, 1970).
Ingold, T, *The Perception of the Environment Essays in Livelihood, Dwelling and Skill* (Abingdon, Routledge, 2000).
Ireland, P, 'Property, Private Government and the Myth of Deregulation' in S Worthington (ed), *The Law of Political Economy: Transformation in the Function of Law* (Cambridge, Cambridge University Press, 2020).
Isailovic, I, '(Mis)recognition: essay on transnational law, identities and marginalization', PhD Thesis, Sciences Po, 2014.

James W 'A New Name for Some Old Ways of Thinking (1906/07) reprinted in *The Project Gutenberg EBook of Pragmatism*, 2004).
Janda, R and Lehun, R, 'The Conflict of Human and Nonhuman Laws' in I Braverman (ed), *Animals, Biopolitics, Law: Lively Legalities* (Abingdon, Routledge, 2017).
Jasanoff, S (ed), *States of Knowledge: The Co-Production of Science and Social Order* (London, Routledge, 2004).
Jasanoff, S, *Designs on Nature: Science and Democracy in Europe and the United States* (Princeton NJ, Princeton University Press, 2010).
Jasanoff, S, *Can Sciences Make Sense of Life?* (Cambridge, Polity, 2018).
Jessup, P, *Transnational Law* (Boston MA, Yale University Press, 1956).
Joerges, C and Fal, J (eds), *Karl Polanyi, Globalisation and the Potential of Law in Transnational Markets* (Oxford, Hart, 2011).
Jouanjan, O, *L'esprit de l'école historique du droit* (Presses Univ Strasbourg, 2004).
Jouanjan, O, *Justifier l'injustifiable. L'ordre du discours juridique nazi* (Paris, PUF, 2017).
Juenger, F, *Selected Essays on the Conflict of Laws* (Brill, 2001).
Jung, CG, *L'Energétique psychique* (Genève, Georg, 1973).
Kantorowicz, E, *The King's Two Bodies: A Study in Mediaeval Political Theology* (Princeton NJ, Princeton University Press, 1957.
Kapur, R, *Gender, Alterity and Human Rights Freedom in a Fishbowl* (Cheltenham, Edward Elgar, 2020).
Karayanni, M, *Conflicts in a Conflict A Conflict of Laws Case Study on Israel and the Palestinian Territories* (Oxford, Oxford University Press, 2014).
Katsiginis, A, 'The Affective Structures of International Human Rights', PhD Dissertation, forthcoming, Sciences po Law School.
Kennedy, D, *A Critique of Adjudication: Fin de Siècle* (Cambridge MA, Harvard University Press, 1997).
Kennedy, D 'Law-and-economics from the perspective of critical legal studies', in Newman, P (ed), *The New Palgrave Dictionary of Economics and the Law* (Basingstoke, Macmillan, 1998).
Kennedy, D, *The Rise and Fall of Classical Legal Thought* (Beard, 2006).
Kennedy, D, 'A Left Phenomenological Alternative to the Hart/Kelsen Theory of Legal Interpretation' in *Legal Reasoning, Collected Essays* (Aurora CO, The Davies Book Publisher, 2008).
Kennedy, D, 'Three Globalizations of Law and Legal Thought: 1850–2000' in Trubek, D and Santos, A (eds) *The New Law and Economic Development* (Cambridge MA, Harvard University Press, 2010).
Kennedy, D, *A World of Struggle – How Power, Law and Expertise Shape Global Political Economy* (Princeton NJ, Princeton University Press, 2016).
Kennedy, D, 'A Political Economy of Contemporary Legality', in P Kjaer (ed), *Law's Political Economy* (Cambridge, Cambridge University Press, 2020).
Kerr, J, *A Most Dangerous Method* (Vintage Books, 1994).
Klein, N, *The Shock Doctrine* (London, Penguin 2007).
Kohn, E, *How forests think Toward an anthropology beyond the human* (Berkeley CA, University of California Press, 2013).
Koskenniemi, M, *The Gentle Civilizer of Nations The Rise and Fall of International Law 1870–1960* (Cambridge, Cambridge University Press, 2001).
Koskenniemi, M, *From Apology to Utopia* (Cambridge, Cambridge University Press, 2005).
Koskenniemi, M, 'International Law and Raison d'Etat: Rethinking the Prehistory of International Law', in Kingsbury, B and Straumann, B (eds), *The Roman Foundations of the Law of Nations* (Oxford, Oxford University Press, 2010).
Koskenniemi, M, *The politics of international law* (Oxford, Hart, 2011).
Koskenniemi, M, 'Carl Schmitt and International Law', in J Meierhenrich and O Simons (eds), *The Oxford Handbook of Carl Schmitt* (Oxford, Oxford University Press, 2017).
Koskenniemi, M, *To the Uttermost Parts of the Earth: Legal Imagination and International Power 1300–1870* (Cambridge, Cambridge University Press, 2021).
Lagarde, P, 'Approche critique de la *lex mercatoria*' in *Le droit des relations économiques internationales, Etudes offertes à B Goldman* (Litec, 1982).
Laplantine, F, and Nouss, A, *Etudes des métissages, des hybrides et des circulations* (Flammarion, 2007).

Latour, B, 'Love your monsters: Why We Must Care for Our Technologies As We Do Our Children' in M Shellenberger (ed), *Love Your Monsters: Postenvironmentalism and the Anthropocene* (Breakthrough Institute, 2011).
Latour, B *Politics of Nature* (Cambridge MA, Harvard University Press, 2004).
Latour, B *Enquête sur les modes d'existence. Une anthropologie des modernes* (Paris, La Découverte, 2012).
Latour, B, *La Fabrique du Droit* (Paris, La Découverte, 2002).
Latour, B, *Reassembling the Social: An Introduction to Actor-Network Theory* (Oxford, Oxford University Press, 2005).
Latour, B, 'Facing Gaia: Six lectures on the political theology of nature', *The Gifford Lectures on Natural Religion*, Edinburgh, 2013.
Latour, B, 'The Strange Entanglement of Jurimorphs', in K McGee (ed), *Latour and the Passage of Law* (Edinburgh, Edinburgh University Press, 2015).
Latour, B, 'Composing the New Body Politic from Bits and Pieces', in B Latour, S Schaffer, P Gagliardi (eds), *A Book of the Body Politic. Connecting Biology, Politics and Social Theory*, San Giorgio Dialogue (ed Cini Fondazione, 2017).
Latour, B, *Facing Gaia: Eight Lectures on the New Climatic Regime*, Polity Press, 2017).
Latour, B, *Où suis-je ? Leçons du confinement à l'usage des terrestres* (Paris, La Découverte, 2021).
Latour, B, Simon Schaffer, Pasquale Gagliardi (ed), *A Book of the Body Politic. Connecting Biology, Politics and Social Theory,* San Giorgio Dialogue 2017 (ed Cini Fondazione)).
Lauterpacht, H, *Private Law Sources and Analogies of International Law With Special Reference To International Arbitration* (1927).
Leclerc, O, Encinas de Munagorri, R, Hennette-Vauchez, S, Herrera, CM, *L'analyse juridique de (x) Le droit parmi les sciences sociales* (Paris, Kimé, 2016).
Lefort, C, *Essais sur le politique (XIXe-XXe siecles)* (Paris, ed Seuil, 1986).
Legrand, P, 'The Same and the Different', in P Legrand and R Munday (eds), *Comparative Legal Studies: Traditions and Transitions* (Cambridge, Cambridge University Press, 2003).
Leiter-Bockley, A, 'Making the World Safe for Investment: the Protection of Foreign Property 1922–1959', PhD Thesis, Melbourne Law School/Vienna Law School, 2019.
Leopold, A, *Think Like a Mountain* (London, Penguin Classics, republished 2021).
Leshem, D, *The Origins of Neoliberalism Modelling the Economy from Jesus to Foucault* (Columbia University Press, 2016).
Levinas, E, *Totalité et Infini Essai sur l'Extériorité* (1961) (Paris, Le Livre de Poche, 1994).
Levinas, E, *Autrement qu'Etre ou Au-dela de l'essence* (1974) (Paris, Le Livre de Poche, 1994).
Levinas, E, *Altérité et Transcendance* (1995) (Paris, Poche, 2006).
Levi-Strauss, C, 'The Structural Study of Myth', in *Structural Anthropology* (NewYork, Basic Books, 1963).
Lévi-Strauss, C, *Anthropologie structurelle II* (Paris, Plon, 1973).
Lévi-Strauss, C, *La Pensée sauvage* (1962).
Lindahl, H, *Authority and the Globalisation of Inclusion and Exclusion* (Cambridge, Cambridge University Press, 2018).
Lovelock, J, *The Revenge of Gaia, Why the Earth is Fighting Back and How We Can Still Save Humanity* (London, Allen Lane, 2006).
Lovelock, J, *Novacene, The Coming Age of Hyper Intelligence* (Boston MA, MIT Press, 2019).
Ludueña Romandini, F, *La comunidad de los espectros I Antropotecnia* (Buenos Aires, ed Miño y Dávila, 2010).
Lynch, M, 'Circumscribing Expertise: Membership categories in courtroom testimony' in S Jasanoff (ed), *States of Knowledge* (Abingdon, Routledge, 2006).
Lyotard, JF, *La Condition postmoderne: rapport sur le savoir* (Paris, Minuit, 1979).
Maier, CS, *Once within Borders: Territories of Power, Wealth and Belonging since 1500* (Cambridge MA, Belknap Press of Harvard University Press, 2016).
Maine, H, *Ancient Law: In Connection with the Early History of Society and its Relation to Modern Ideas* (London 1863).
Maldonado Bonilla, D, *Legal Barbarians. Identity, Modern Comparative Law and the Global South* (Cambridge, Cambridge University Press, 2021).
Mangabeira Unger, R, *The Universal History of Legal Thought* (Deep Freedom Books, 2021).

Marcuse, H, *Éros et Civilisation* (Paris, Seuil, 1971 [1955]).
Margolies, D, Ozsu, U, Pal, M, Tzouvala, N (eds), *The extraterritoriality of law: history, theory, politics* (Abingdon, Routledge, 2019).
Margulis, L, *Symbiotic Planet: A New Look at Evolution* (New York, Basic Books, 1998).
Marks, S, *A False Tree of Liberty, Human Rights in Radical Thought* (Oxford, Oxford University Press, 2019).
Marx, K, *Economic and Philosophical Manuscripts* (1844).
Marx, K and Engels, F, *Collected Works*, Vol 52 (NewYork, International Publishers, 1987).
Mattei, U and Nader, L, *Plunder: When the Rule of Law is Illegal* (Wiley-Blackwell, 2008).
Mauss, M, *The Gift: Forms and Functions of Exchange in Archaic Societies* (London, Cohen and West, 1966 (reprinted in Paperback, 2011)); in French: 'Essai sur le don Forme et raison de l'échange dans les sociétés archaïques' (1923–1924) *Année Sociologique,* (republished in *Sociologie et anthropologie* (Paris, PUF, 1968)).
Mayer, P, 'Le mythe de l'ordre juridique de base ou *Grundlegung*' in *Etudes offertes à Berthold Goldman* (Paris, Litec, 1983).
Mazurel, H, *L'inconscient ou l'oubli de l'histoire – Profondeurs, métamorphoses et révolutions de la vie affective* (Paris, La Découverte, 2021).
Mbembe, A, *De la Postcolonie Essai sur l'imagination politique dans l'Afrique contemporaine* (ed Karthala, 2000).
McGee, K, 'For a juridical ecology of ligatures', in Latour, B, Schaffer, S, Gagliardi, P (eds) *A Book of the Body Politic, Connecting Biology, Politics and Social Theory* (Giorgio Cine, 2017).
McGee, K (ed), *Latour and the Passage of Law* (Edinburgh, Edinburgh University Press, 2015).
McGee, K (ed), 'Introduction', in *Bruno Latour and the Passage of Law* (Edinburgh, Edinburgh University Press, 2015).
McGee, K, 'On Devices and Logics of Legal Sense: Toward Socio-technical Legal Analysis', in K McGee (ed), *Latour and the Passage of Law* (Edinburgh, Edinburgh University Press, 2015).
McGee, K, *Heathen Earth: Trumpism and Political Ecology* (Punctum Books, 2017).
McLachlan, C, *Foreign Relations Law* (Cambridge, Cambridge University Press, 2017).
McVeigh, S, *Jurisprudence of Jurisdiction* (New York, Routledge, 2007).
Methta, V, 'Anekantavada: The Jaina Epistemology', in Reitner, B (ed), *Constructing the Pluriverse The Geopolitics of Knowledge* (Durham NC, Duke University Press, 2018).
Michaels, R, 'Globalizing Savigny? The State in Savigny's Private International Law and the Challenge of Europeanization and Globalization', in M Stolleis and W Streeck (eds), *Dezentralisierung Aktuelle Fragen politischer und rechtlicher Steuerung Im Kontext der Globalisierung* (Baden-Baden, Nomos, 2007).
Michaels, R, 'Globalization and Law: Law Beyond the State', in *Law and Society Theory* (Banakar and Travers, 2013).
Michaels, R, 'Law and Recognition: Towards a Relational Concept of Law,' in N Roughan and A Halpin, *In Pursuit of Pluralist Jurisprudence* (Cambridge, Cambridge University Press, 2019).
Michaels, R, 'The Functional method in comparative law', in M Reimann and R Zimmermann (eds), *The Oxford Handbook of Comparative Law* (Oxford, Oxford University Press, 2019).
Mignolo, W, *Local Histories/Global Designs: Coloniality, Subaltern Knowledges and Border Thinking* (Princeton NJ, Princeton University Press, 2000).
Mignolo, W, *Darker Sides of the Renaissance: Literacy, Territoriality, and Colonization* (University of Michigan Press, 2003).
Mignolo, W, 'On Pluriversality and Multipolarity', in Reitner, B (ed), *Constructing the Pluriverse The Geopolitics of Knowledge* (Durham NC, Duke University Press, 2018).
Miles, K, *The Origins of International Investment Law: Empire, Environment and the Safeguarding of Capital* (Cambridge, Cambridge University Press, 2013).
Mills, A, *Party Autonomy in Private International Law* (Cambridge, Cambridge University Press, 2018).
Mitchell, T, *Carbon Democracy: Political Power in the Age of Oil* (Verso, 2013).
Mitchell, T, 'The Body Politic that Captured the Future', in B Latour et al (eds), *A Book of the Body Politic. Connecting Biology, Politics and Social Theory*, San Giorgio Dialogue 2017 (ed Cini Fondazione).
Monateri, P-G, *Geopolitica del diritto: genesi, governo e dissoluzione dei corpi politici* (Rome/Bari, Laterza and Figli, 2013).

Monateri, P-G, *Dominus Mundi, Political Sublime and the World Order* (Oxford, Hart, 2018).
Monateri, P-G, 'Early Roman Law and the West', in H Pihlajamäki, M Dubber and M Godfrey (eds), *The Oxford Handbook of European Legal History* (Oxford, Oxford University Press, 2018).
Monateri, P-G, *Advanced Introduction to Comparative Legal Methods* (Cheltenham, Edward Elgar, 2021).
Moore, JW, *Capitalism in the Web of Life* (London/New York, Verso, 2015).
Moore, JW, *Anthropocene or Capitalocene? Nature, History and the Crisis of Capitalism* (Oakland CA, PM Press, 2016).
Morizot, J-B, and Mengual, EZ, *Esthétique de la rencontre* (Paris, Seuil, 2018).
Morizot, J-B, *Wild Diplomacy Cohabiting with the Others Among Us* (New York, State University of New York Press, 2019).
Moyn S, *Origins of the Other Emmanuel Levinas between Revelation and Ethics* (Ithaca NY, Cornell University Press, 2005).
Moyn S, *The Last Utopia Human Rights in History* (Cambridge MA, Harvard University Press, 2012).
Moyn S, *Not Enough Human Rights in an Unequal World* (Boston MA, Belknap Press, 2019).
Muir Watt H, *Private International Law and Public Law* (Cheltenham, Edward Elgar, 2017).
Muir Watt, H, *Discours sur les méthodes du droit international privé: pour un droit de l'inter-altérité* (Brill/Nijhoff, 2019).
Muir Watt, H, Bizikova, L, Brandao de Oliveira, A, Fernandez Arroyo, D (eds) *Global Private International Law* (Cheltenham, Edward Elgar, 2019).
Muir Watt, H, Bizikova, L, Brandao de Oliveira, A, Ma, M, Fernandez Arroyo, D (eds), *Le Tournant Global en Droit international privé* (Paris, Pédone, 2020).
Murphy, T, 'Legal fabrications and the case of "cultural property"', in A Pottage and M Mundy (eds), *Law, Anthropology and the Constitution of the Social* (Cambridge, Cambridge University Press, 2004).
Nancy, J-L, Preface in Fallen, C, *L'anomalie créatrice* (ed Kime, 2012).
Neidhart, A-H, 'The Transformation of European Private International Law A Genealogy', PhD Dissertation, European University Institute, 2018.
Neyret, L, 'Construire la responsabilité écologique,' in A Supiot and M Delmas-Marty (eds), *Prendre la responsabilité au sérieux* (Paris, Presses Universitaires de France, 2015).
Orford, A, 'A Jurisprudence of the Limit', in *International Law and its Others* (Cambridge, Cambridge University Press, 2006).
Orford, A, *International Authority and the Responsibility to Protect* (Cambridge, Cambridge University Press, 2011).
Ost, F, *La nature hors la loi: l'écologie à l'épreuve du droit* (Paris, La Découverte, 2002).
Osterhammel, J, *The Transformation of the World A Global History of the Nineteenth Century* (Princeton NJ, Princeton University Press, 2014).
Ouattara, I, 'The Griots of West Africa, Oral Tradition and Shared Knowledge', in Reitner, B (ed), *Constructing the Pluriverse, The Geopolitics of Knowledge* (Durham NC, Duke University Press, 2018).
Pahuja, S, *Decolonising International Law Development, Economic Growth and the Politics of Universality* (Cambridge, Cambridge University Press, 2013).
Pajuha, S, 'Conserving the World's Resources?' in Crawford, J and Koskenniemi, M (eds), Cambridge Companion to International Law (Cambridge, Cambridge University Press, 2012).
Patterson, D, *Legality's Borders: An Essay in General Jurisprudence* (Oxford, Oxford University Press, 2010).
Pauly, L, 'Global Finance, Political Authority and the Problem of Legitimation' in Hall and Biersteker (eds), *The Emergence of Private Authority in Global Governance* (Cambridge, Cambridge University Press, 2002).
Pavel, C, *Law Beyond the State* (Oxford, Oxford University Press, 2021).
Pelluchon, C, *Pour comprendre Levinas* (Paris, Seuil 2020).
Pelluchon, C, *Les Lumières à l'Age du Vivant* (Paris, Seuil, 2021).
Perrone, N, 'Neoliberalism and economic sovereignty: property, contracts and foreign investment relations', in H Brabazon (ed), *Neoliberal Legality: Understanding the Role of Law in the Neoliberal Project* (New York, Routledge, 2016).
Piketty, T, *Capital and Ideology* (Cambridge MA, Harvard University Press, 2020).
Pillet, A, *Principes de droit international privé* (Paris Pédone 1903).
Pistor, K, *Code of Capital: How the Law Creates Wealth and Inequality* (Princeton NJ, Princeton University Press, 2020).

Polanyi, K, *The Great Transformation: The Political and Economic Origins of Our Time* (New York, Farrar & Rinehart, 1944)).
Pollock, D, 'Shamanism' *Oxford Bibliographies* (Oxford, Oxford University Press, 2018).
Pomian, K *L'ordre du temps* (Paris, Gallimard, 1984).
Poole, T, *Reason of State, Law, Prerogative and Empire* (Cambridge, Cambridge University Press, 2015).
Pottage, A, 'Introduction, The Fabrication of Persons and Things', in M Mundy and A Pottage (eds), *Law, Anthropology* and *the Constitution of the Social: Making Persons and Things* (Cambridge, Cambridge University Press, 2004).
Pottage, A, 'Why Nature Has No Rights' in AA Nakagawa and C Douzinas, *Non-Human Rights Critical Perspectives* (Cheltenham, Edward Elgar, 2023, forthcoming).
Pottage, A, and Mundy, M (eds), *Law, Anthropology and the Constitution of the Social: Making Persons and Things* (Cambridge, Cambridge University Press, 2004).
Pufendorf, S, *De jure naturae et gentium* (ed Frank Böhling, 1688) (English trans CH Oldfather and WA Oldfather, in *De jure naturae et gentium libri octo*, vol 2 (Oxford, Clarendon Press, 1934).
Rasulov, A, 'New approaches to international law: images of a genealogy', in JM Beneyto and D Kennedy (eds), *New Approaches to International Law: The European and the American Experiences* (TMC Asser-Springer, 2012).
Ratner, S, *The Thin Justice of International Law A Moral Reckoning of the Law of Nations* (Oxford, Oxford University Press, 2015).
Reitner, B (ed), *Constructing the Pluriverse, The Geopolitics of Knowledge* (Durham NC, Duke University Press, 2018).
Ricoeur, P, *L'idéologie et l'utopie* (Paris, Seuil, 2005).
Roberts, A, *Is International law really international?* (Oxford, Oxford University Press, 2018).
Rochfeld, J, Cornu, M and Orsi, F (eds), *Dictionnaire des biens communs* (Paris, PUF, 2017).
Rogge, M, 'Nevsun puts Canada's Corporate Decision Makers in the Human Rights Zone', Working Paper n° 70 (Corporate responsibility Initiative, Harvard Kennedy School, 2020).
Rosenfeld, M, *A Pluralist Theory of Constitutional Justice* (Oxford, Oxford University Press, 2022).
Roughan, N and Halpin, A, *In Pursuit of Pluralist Jurisprudence* (Cambridge, Cambridge University Press, 2017).
Ruskola, T, *Legal Orientalism China, the United States and Modern Law* (Cambridge MA, Harvard University Press, 2013).
Ryngaert, C, *Jurisdiction in International Law* (Oxford, Oxford University Press, 2008).
Saïd, EW, *Orientalism*, (Penguin Classics, 2003).
Samuel, GH, 'Is Law a Fiction?', in M Del Mar, W Twining (eds), *Legal Fictions in Theory and Practice* (Springer, 2015).
Samuel, GH, *Epistemology and Method in Law* (Aldershot, Ashgate, 2003).
Samuel, GH, 'Epistemology and Comparative Law: Contributions from the Sciences and Social Sciences', in M Van Hoecke (ed), *Epistemology and Methodology of Comparative Law* (Oxford, Hart, 2004).
Samuel, GH, 'Imitation of Life: Resonances Between Law and Fact and Fact and Law', in S Taekema, B van Klink and W de Been (eds), *Facts and Norms in Law* (Cheltenham, Edward Elgar, 2016).
Samuel, GH, *Rethinking Legal Reasoning* (Cheltenham, Edward Elgar, 2018).
Samuel, GH, *Rethinking Historical Jurisprudence* (Cheltenham, Edward Elgar, 2018).
Santiago, S, *The Space in-between: Essays on Latin American Culture, Latin America in translation* (Durham NC, Duke University Press, 2001).
Santner, E, *The Royal Remains – the people's two bodies and the endgames of sovereignty* (Chicago, Chicago University Press, 2011).
Santner, E, *The Weight of All Flesh: On the Subject-Matter of Political Economy* (New York, Oxford University Press, 2016).
Santos, FJA, Baldus C and Dedek H (eds), 'Classification of contracts: A view from a common lawyer' *Vertragstypen in Europa: Historische Entwicklung und europäische Perspektiven* (Berlin/Boston, Otto Schmidt/De Gruyter, 2011).
Sassen, S, *Losing Control? Sovereignty in the Age of Globalization* (Columbia University Press, 2015).
Saunders, D, 'From the Conseil d'Etat to Gaia: Bruno Latour in Surfaces and Depths', in K McGee (ed), *Latour and the Passage of Law* (Edinburgh, Edinburgh University Press, 2015).

Sbriccoli, M, *L'interpretazione dello statuto Contributo alla storia della funzione di giuristi nell'età comunale* (Milano, 1969).

Scelle, G, *Précis du droit des gens* (1933).

Schiavone, A, *Ius L'invenzione del diritto in Occidente* (Turin, Einaudi, 2005).

Schinazi, M, *The Three Ages of International Commercial Arbitration* (Cambridge, Cambridge University Press, 2021).

Schmitt, C, *The nomos of the Earth in the International law of the Jus Publicum Europaeum* (New York, Telos Press, 2006) (English translation of *Der Nomos der Erde im Volkerrecht des Jus Publicum Europaeum* (Berlin, Duncker and Humblot, 1950).

Schnaiberg, A, *The Environment: From Surplus to Scarcity* (Oxford, Oxford University Press, 1980).

Schofield, P, *Utility and Democracy: The Political Thought of Jeremy Bentham* (Oxford, Oxford University Press, 2006).

Schroder, P, *Trust in Early Modern International Political Thought, 1598–1713* (Cambridge, Cambridge University Press, 2017).

Scott C (ed), *Torture as Tort: Comparative Perspectives on the Development of Transnational Human Rights Litigation* (Oxford, Hart Publishing, 2001).

Scott, C and Wai, R, 'Transnational Governance of Corporate Conduct through the Migration of Human Rights Norms: The Potential Contribution of Transnational "Private" Litigation' in Joerges, C, Sand, P and Teubner, G (eds), *Transnational Governance and Constitutionalism* (Oxford, Hart Publishing, 2004).

Sedgwick, EK, *Epistemology of the Closet* (Berkeley CA, University of California Press, 1990).

Sedgwick, EK, *Touching Feeling: Affect, Pedagogy, Performativity* (Durham NC, Duke University Press, 2003)).

Serres, M, *La Traduction Hermès III* (Paris, ed Minuit, 1974).

Serres, M, *Le contrat naturel* (Flammarion Poche, 1990, 2020).

Seuffert, N, *Jurisprudence of National Identity Kaleidoscopes of Imperialism and Globalisation from Aotearoa New Zealand* (Abingdon, Routledge, 2006).

Seuffert, N, 'Jurisdiction and nation-building: Tall tales in nineteenth-century Aotearoa/New Zealand', in S McVeigh (ed) *Jurisprudence of Jurisdiction* (New York, Routledge, 2007).

Shahar, I, *Legal Pluralism in the Holy City* (Abingdon, Routledge, 2015).

Shepel, H, *The Constitution of Private Governance* (Oxford, Hart Publishing, 2005).

Shiva, V, *Ecofeminism* (New Delhi, Kali for Women/Zed Books, UK, 1993).

Shweder, RA, 'What About Female Genital Mutilation?' in Shweder, RA, Minow, M and Markus, HR (eds) *Engaging Cultural Differences* (New York, Sage, 2002).

Shweder, RA, 'Why Understanding Culture Matters in the First Place' in Shweder, RA, Minow, M and Markus, HR (eds) *Engaging Cultural Differences* (New York, Sage, 2002).

Sieder, R, 'The Juridification of Politics' in M-C Foblets et al (eds), *The Oxford Handbook of Law and Anthropology* (Oxford, Oxford University Press, 2022), ch 38.

Simenel, R, *L'origine est aux frontières*, (CNRS, Éditions de la Maison des Sciences de l'homme, 2013).

Simpson, A, *Mohawk Interruptus Political Life Across the Borders of Settler States* (Durham NC, Duke University Press, 2014).

Slaughter, M-A, *A New World Order* (Princeton NJ, Princeton University Press, 2009).

Sloterdijk, P, *You Must Change Your Life On Anthropotechnics* (Cambridge, Polity Press, 2014).

Smith, M *An Ethics of Place: Radical Ecology, Postmodernity,and Social Theory* (New York, SUNI, 2001).

Somek, A, *The Legal Relation Legal Theory After Positivism* (Cambridge, Cambridge University Press, 2017).

Sornarajah, M, *The International Law on Foreign Investment* (Cambridge, Cambridge University Press, 2010)).

Souriau, E, *Les différents modes d'existence* (Paris, Presses Universitaires de France, 1943; republished 2009, introduction by Isabelle Stengers and Bruno Latour).

Stein, P, *Roman Law in European History* (Cambridge, Cambridge University Press, 1999).

Stein, P, *A History of Roman Law* (Cambridge, Cambridge University Press, 2005).

Stengers, I, 'The Cultivation of Ways of Overlapping: a Matter of Reclaiming', in Latour et al, *Body Politics* (Cini Foundation, 2017).

Stengers, *Pour en finir avec la tolérance, Cosmopolitiques VII* (Paris, ed La Découverte, 1997).

Stengers, I, *Cosmopolitiques I* (Paris, ed La Découverte, 2003).
Stengers, I, *In Catastrophic Times: Resisting the Coming Barbarism*, (Open Humanities Press/Meson Press, 2015).
Stoczkowski, W, *Anthropologies rédemptrices: le monde selon Lévi-Strauss* (ed Hermann, 2008).
Story, J, *Commentaries on the Conflict of Laws, Foreign and Domestic* (1834).
Straumann, B, 'The *Corpus iuris* as a Source of Law Between Sovereigns in Alberico Gentili's Thought' in Kingsbury, B and Straumann, B (eds), *The Roman Foundations of the Law of Nations* (Oxford, Oxford University Press, 2010).
Surkis, J, *Sex, Law and Sovereignty in French Algeria, 1830–1930* (Ithaca NY, Cornell University Press, 2019).
Symeonides, S, 'Material Justice and Conflicts Justice in Choice of Law', in P Borchers, J Zekoll (eds), *International Conflict Of Laws For The Third Millennium: Essays In Honor Of Friedrich K Juenger* (Transnational Publishers, 2001).
Symeonides, S, 'Codification and Flexibility in Private International Law' in Brown, KB and Snyder, DV (eds), *General Reports Of The XVIIIth Congress Of The International Academy Of Comparative Law* (Springer, 2011).
Symeonides, S, *Codifying Choice of Law Around the World: An International Comparative Analysis* (Oxford, Oxford University Press, 2014).
Tang, C, *The Geographic Imagination of Modernity Geography, Literature and Philosophy in German Romanticism* (Palo Alto CA, Stanford University Press, 2008).
Taylor, C, 'On the Diversity of Goods' in *Philosophical Papers, Philosophy and the Human Sciences* Vol 2 (Cambridge, Cambridge University Press, 2012).
Tesson, S, *Les chemins noirs* (Paris, Gallimard, 2015).
Teubner, G, *Law as an Autopoietic System* (Oxford/Cambridge, Blackwell Publishers, 1993).
Teubner, G, *Constitutional Fragments: Societal Constitutionalism and Globalization* (Oxford, Oxford University Press, 2012).
Tsing, A, *The Mushroom at the End of the World. On the Possibility of Life in Capitalist Ruins* (Princeton NJ, Princeton University Press, 2015).
Tzouvala, N, *Capitalism As Civilisation: A History of International Law* (Cambridge, Cambridge University Press, 2020).
Vahinger, H, *The Philosophy of 'As If'* (Fakenham, Cox and Wyman, 1968).
Valdenebro, E, 'Le principe métanthropique: Faire lieu à partir d'une épistémè végétale possible', PhD Thesis, Univ Paris 8, 2022.
Valverde, M, *Chronotopes of Law: Jurisdiction, Scale and Governance* (Abingdon, Routledge, 2015).
Valverde, M and Weaver, A, '"The Crown wears many hats": Canadian Aboriginal Law and the Black-boxing of Empire', in K McGee (ed), *Latour and the Passage of Law* (Edinburgh, Edinburgh University Press, 2015).
van Dijk, N, 'The Life and Deaths of a Dispute: An Inquiry into Matters of Law', in K McGee (ed), *Latour and the Passage of Law* (Edinburgh, Edinburgh University Press, 2015).
Veyne, P, *Les Grecs ont-ils cru à leurs mythes? Essai sur l'imagination constituante* (Paris, Christian Jacob, 1985).
Viveiros de Castro, E, *Métaphysiques cannibales* (Paris, PUF, 2009).
Viveiros de Castro, E, *The Relative Native: Essays on Indigenous Conceptual Worlds* (HAU, 2016).
Viveiros de Castro, E, *Le regard du jaguar Introduction au perspectivisme amérindien*, trans Pierre Delgado (Éditions la Tempête, 2021).
von Busekist, A, 'Idealism or pragmatism? Ad hoc multilingualism and Open English', in PA Kraus and F Grin (eds)*The Politics of Multilingualism: Europeanisation, globalisation and linguistic governance* (Amsterdam, John Benjamins, 2018).
von Clausewitz, C, *Vom Kriege* (Berlin, 1832).
von Savigny, FC, *Vom Beruf unserer Zeit für Gesetzgebung und Rechtswissenschaft* (1814, revd 1828).
von Savigny, FC, *System des heutigen römischen Recht*, 8 vols (1840–1849); French translation: *Traité de droit romain*, 8 vols (Paris, Firmin Didot Frères, 1855–1859; English translation of Vol 8: *Private International Law A Treatise on the Conflict of Laws* (London, T and T Clark, 1869).
Walker, N, *Intimations of Global Law* (Cambridge, Cambridge University Press, 2015).
Walzer, M, *Spheres of Justice: A Defense of Pluralism and Equality* (New York, Basic Books, 1983).

Wasserstein Fassberg, C, 'The Public in Private International Law', in Y Emerich, L Saint-Pierre Harvey (eds), *Le public en droit privé* (Yvon Blais, 2019).
Watson A, *Joseph Story and the Comity of Errors: A Case Study in Conflict of Laws* (University of Georgia Press, 1992).
Weil, P, 'Droit international et contrats d'Etat', in *Mélanges Reuter* (Pedone, 1981).
Wendt, A, *Quantum Mind and Social Science, Unifying Physical and Social Ontology* (Cambridge, Cambridge University Press, 2015).
Williams, E, *Capitalism and Slavery* (1944, republished with a New Introduction by CA Palmer, University of North Carolina Press, 1994).
Winnicott, D, 'Fear of Breakdown' in DW Winnicott, C Winnicott, R Shepherd, M Davis (eds), *Psycho-Analytic Explorations* (Abingdon, Routledge, 1989).
Winnicott, DW, *The Collected Works of DW Winnicott*: Vol 6, 1960–1963, eds L Caldwell and H Taylor Robinson (Oxford, Oxford University Press, 2016).
Wittgenstein, L, *Philosophical Investigations* (Macmillan Publishing Company, 1953).
Woll, C, *Economic Lawfare: The Geopolitics of Corporate Justice* (Cambridge MA, Harvard University Press, 2021).
Younes, C, 'Le droit et la différence', Thèse de doctorat en Droit privé (dir Étienne Le Roy) Univ Paris 1, 2004.
Young, I, *Justice and the Politics of Difference* (Princeton NJ, Princeton University Press, 2011).
Zierler, D, *The Invention of Ecocide: Agent Orange, Vietnam and the Scientists Who Changed the Way We Think About the Environment* (University of Georgia Press, 2011).
Zimmermann, R, Reid, K, Visser, D (eds), *Mixed Legal Systems in Comparative Perspective: Property and Obligations in Scotland and South Africa* (Oxford, Oxford University Press, 2005).
Zuboff, S, *The Age of Surveillance Capitalism: The Fight for a Human Future at the New Frontier of Power* (Public Affairs, 2019).
Zumbansen, P (ed), *The Oxford Handbook of Transnational Law* (Oxford, Oxford University Press, 2021).

ARTICLES

Agostini, E, 'Le mécanisme du renvoi' (2013) *Revue critique de droit international privé* 545.
Alvarado, L, 'Prospects and Challenges in the Implementation of Indigenous Peoples' Human Rights in International Law: Lessons from the Case of Awas Tingni v Nicaragua' (2007) 24 *Arizona Journal of International and Comparative Law* 609–44.
Appadurai, A, 'The Past as a Scarce Resource' (1981) 16 *Man*.
Aronowsky, L, 'Gas guzzling Gaia; or, a prehistory of climate change denialism' (2021) 47 *Critical Inquiry* 306–27.
Aronowsky, L, 'The Limits of Climate Change Litigation', *New York Review of Books*, 3 November 2021.
Asser-Andrieu, L, 'Le crépuscule des cultures L'affaire Pitcairn et l'idéologie des droits humains' (2012) 3 *Droit et société*.
Audit, B, 'Le caractère fonctionnel de la règle de conflit (Sur la crise des conflits de lois)' (1984) 186 *Recueil des course l'Académie de Droit international* (RCADI).
Balkin, J, 'Nested Oppositions' (1990) 99 *Yale LJ* 1669.
Barbisan L, 'Eccentric Bodies From Phenomenology to Marxism – Walter Benjamin's Reflections on Embodiment' (2017) I *Anthropology and Materialism*, Special issue, 'Discontinuous Infinities'.
Bartin, E, 'Une conception nouvelle de l'empire de la loi locale par opposition à la loi personnelle et à la loi territoriale' (1935) 52 *Recueil des Cours de l'Académie de Droit international* (RCADI).
Baskin, J, 'The Unbearable: Toward an Antifascist Aesthetic', *New York Review of Books*, 2020.
Batiffol, H, 'Réflexions sur la coordination des systèmes nationaux', (1967) 120 *Recueil des Cours de l'Académie de Droit international* (RCADI).
Baxi, U, 'Mass torts, multinational enterprise liability and private international law' (1999) 276 *Collected Courses of the Hague Academy of International Law*.
Beauvois, F, 'L'indemnité de Saint-Domingue: "Dette d'indépendance" ou "rançon de l'esclavage"?' (2009) 110 *French Colonial History*.

Belleau, C 'Les juristes inquiets : classicisme juridique et critique du droit au début du XXème en France' (1999) 40 *Les Cahiers du droit* 507–44.

Bennett J, et al, 'Environmental Stewardship: A Conceptual Review and Analytical Framework' (2018) 61 *Environmental Management* 597–614.

Benton, L, 'Legal Spaces of Empire: Piracy and the Origins of Ocean Regionalism' (2005) 47 *Comparative Studies in Society and History*.

Benton, T, 'Rights and justice on a shared planet: More rights or new relations?' 2(2)*Theoretical Criminology* 149–75.

Benton, L and Clulow, A, 'Empires and Protection: Making Interpolity Law in the Early Modern World' (2017) 12 *Journal of Global History* 74.

Berman, PS, 'Rats, Pigs and Statues on Trial: The Creation of Cultural Narratives in the Prosecution of Animals and Inanimate Objects' (1994) 69 *NYU L Rev* 288.

Blackman J and Mukhi, R, 'The Evolution of Modern Sovereign Debt Litigation: Vultures, Alter Egos and Other Legal Fauna' (2010) 73 *Law and Contemporary Problems* 47, 49.

Boden, D, 'Le pluralisme juridique en droit international privé' (2005) 49 *Archives Philo Droit* 275–316

Boden, D, 'Erga-': Contribution sémantique et lexicale à une étude unifiée des relations entre ordres juridiques' (2021) *Revue critique de droit international privé*.

Bomhoff, J, 'The Reach of Rights: "The Foreign" and "The Private" in Conflict-of-Laws, State-Action and Fundamental-Rights Cases with Foreign Elements' (2008) 71 *Law and Contemporary Problems* 39–72.

Bonito Oliva, R, and Campbell, T, 'From the Immune Community to the Communitarian Immunity: On the Recent Reflections of Roberto Esposito' (2006) 36 *Diacritics*.

Brilmayer, L, and Listwa, DB, 'Continuity and Change in the Draft Restatement (Third) of Conflict of Laws: One Step Forward and Two Steps Back?' (2018) 128 *The Yale Law Journal*.

Brown, SD, 'Science, Translation and the Logic of the Parasite' (2002) 19 *Theory, Culture and Society*.

Bucher, A 'L'ordre public et le but social des lois en droit international privé' (1993) 239 *Recueil des Cours de l'Académie de Droit international* (RCADI).

Bucher, A, 'Vers l'adoption de la méthode des intérêts ? Réflexions à la lumière des codifications récentes' (1996) 12 *Trav Comité fr droit international privé* 209–37.

Bussani, M, 'Current Trends in European Comparative Law: The Common Core Approach' (1998) 21 *Hastings Int'l and Comp L Rev*.

Campbell, P, 'The Sea as a Hyperobject: Moving beyond Maritime Cultural Landscapes' (2020) 8 *Journal of Eastern Mediterranean Archaeology and Heritage Studies*.

Campbell, T, 'Bios, Immunity, Life: The Thought of Roberto Esposito' (2006) 36 *Diacritics*.

Cansacchi, G, 'Le choix et l'adaptation de la règle étrangère dans le conflit de lois' (1953) 83 *Recueil des Cours de l'Académie de Droit international* (RCADI).

Carman, HJ, 'England and the Egyptian Problem' (1921) 36 *Political Science Quarterly*.

Cavers, D, 'A Critique of the Choice of Law Problem' (1933) 47 *Harvard Law Review* 173.

Cavers, D et al, 'Comments On Babcock v Jackson, A Recent Development In Conflict Of Laws' (1963) 63 *Columbia Law Review* 1212.

Chakrabarty, D, 'The Climate of History: Four Theses' (2009) 35 *Critical Inquiry*.

Chazal, JP, 'Le propriétaire souverain: archéologie d'une idole doctrinale' (2020) 1 *Revue trimestrielle de droit civil*.

Chen, H, 'E Levinas' Ethics of Responsibility-for-the-other and its Implications for Ecological Thinking', PESA Conference 2002, https://pesaorgau/images/papers/2012-papers-English/E18pdf.

Christiaens, T, 'Agamben's Theories of the State of Exception: From Political to Economic Theology' (2021) 110 *Cultural Critique*.

Churchwell, S, 'The Lehman Trilogy and Wall Street's Debt to Slavery' *New York Review of Books*, 11 June 2019.

Clastre, P, 'Échange et pouvoir: philosophie de la chefferie indienne' (1962) *L'Homme*.

Coelho, F, 'Improvisations of a Tropical Cartesianism', Critical Studies in Improvisation (2011) 7 *Brazilian Improvisations/Improvisações Brasileiras*.

Cornu, M, 'About Sacred Cultural Property: the Hopi masks case', (2013) 20 *International Journal of Cultural Property*.

Cover, R, 'Foreword: *Nomos* and Narrative' (1983) 87 *Harvard Law Review*.

Dagan, H and Dorfman, A, 'Interpersonal Human Rights and Transnational Private Law' (2016) 51 *Cornell International Law Journal*.

Dammann J, and Hansmann, H, 'Globalizing Commercial Litigation' (2008) 94 *Cornell Law Review* 1.

de la Vega, X, 'Jean-François Lyotard (1924–1998) – La fin des grands récits' (2007) 6 *Sciences Humaines*.

de Sousa Santos, B, 'Law: A Map of Misreading Toward a Postmodern Conception of Law' (1987) 14 *Journal of Law and Society*.

Derrida J, 'La Différance' (1968) juillet-septembre *Le Bulletin de la société française de philosophie*.

Dewey, J, 'What Does Pragmatism Mean by Practical?' (1908) 5 *The Journal of philosophy, psychology and scientific methods* 85–99.

Dodge, WS, 'Breaking the Public Law Taboo', (2002) 43 *Harvard International Law Journal* 161.

Domke M 'Basic Questions of Conflict of Laws before the French Cour de Cassation, 1938–1941' (1943) 5 *The University of Toronto Law Journal* 95–112.

Eller, KH and Salminen, J, 'Reimagining Contract in a World of Global Value Chains' (2020) *European Review of Contract Law*.

Ellis, J, 'Calculative Practices in International Environmental Governance: In (Partial) Defence of Indicators' (2020) 9 *Transnational Environmental Law* 297–321.

Erb, C, 'A Spiritual Blockbuster: Avatar, Environmentalism and the New Religions' (2014) 66 *Journal of Film and Video*.

Esquirol, J, 'Making the Critical Moves: A Top Ten in Progressive Legal Scholarship' (2021) 92 *University of Colorado Law Review*.

Ewald, W, 'Comparative Jurisprudence(I): What Was it Like to Try a Rat?' (1995) 143 *University of Pennsylvania Law Review* 1889.

Fischer, M, 'The lightness of existence and the origami of "French" anthropology: Latour, Descola, Viveiros de Castro, Meillassoux and their so-called ontological turn' (2014) 4 *HAU: Journal of Ethnographic Theory* 331–55.

Fitzpatrick, P, 'Marxism and Legal Pluralism' (1983) 46 *Australian Journal of Law and Society*.

Foessel, M, 'Néolibéralisme versus libéralisme?' (2008) Nov *Revue Esprit, L'Etat entre néolibéralisme et régulation*.

Ford, R, 'Law's Territory (A History of Jurisdiction)' (1998–99) 97 *Michigan Law Review* 889.

Foussard, D 'Le droit international privé de Foelix ou l'art périlleux de la transition (1840–1847)' (2020) *Rev crit droit international privé*.

Frankenberg, G, 'Critical Comparisons: Re-thinking Comparative Law' [1985] 26 *Harvard International Law Journal*, 411.

Gabel, J, 'Effets pervers et fausse conscience' (1987) Juillet-Décembre *Cahiers Internationaux de Sociologie* 339–54.

Gabel, P, and Kennedy, D, 'Roll over Beethoven' (1984) 36 *Stanford Law Review,* Critical Legal Studies Symposium.

Galán, A, and Patterson, D, 'The Limits of Normative Legal Pluralism: Review of Paul Schiff Berman, Global Legal Pluralism: A Jurisprudence of Law Beyond Borders' (2001) 3 *International Journal of Constitutional Law*.

Geulen, E, 'Pour une généalogie du genre dans l'œuvre de Walter Benjamin' (2004) *Tumultes* 161–88.

Gilbert, S, Sapp, J, Tauber, A, 'A Symbiotic View of Life: We Have Never Been Individuals' (2012) 87 *Quarterly Review of Biology*.

Gillespie, MA, 'Temporality and History in the Thought of Martin Heidegger' 43(168) *Revue Internationale de Philosophie*.

Goldman, B, 'Frontières du droit et lex mercatoria' (1964) *Archives de Philosophie du Droit* 177.

Gonzalez, C and Mutua, A, 'Mapping Racial Capitalism: Implications for Law' (2022) 2 *Journal of Law and Political Economy* 127.

Gordon-Walker, C, 'Beyond Inclusion: Canadian and Indigenous Sovereignty in Mainstream Museums' (2018) 199 *British Columbian Quarterly* 129–49.

Gordon-Walker C, and Black, M, 'Introduction, Indigeneities and Museums: Ongoing Conversations' (2018) 199 *British Columbian Quarterly*.

Goren, J, 'State-to-State Debts: Sovereign Immunity and the 'Vulture' Hunt' (2010) 41 *George Washington International Law Review* 681, 689.

Gothot, P, 'Le renouveau de la méthode unilatéraliste' (1971) 1 *Rev crit DIP*.

Gros, F, Lorenzini, D, Revel, A, Sforzini, A, 'Introduction' (2013) 4 *Raisons politiques* 5.
Gruenbaum, D, 'From Statehood to Effectiveness: The Law of Unrecognised States in Private International Law' (2022) 86 *Rabels Zeitschrift für ausländisches und internationales Privatrecht*.
Guerra Medici, MT, 'The Mother of International Law: Christine de Pisan' (1999) 19 *Parliaments, Estates and Representation*.
Hale, R, 'Coercion and Distribution in a Supposedly Noncoercive State' (1923) 38 *Political Science Quarterly* 470 (republished in *The Canon of American Legal Thought* (Princeton NJ, Princeton University Press, 2007).
Haraway, D, 'A Manifesto for Cyborgs: Science, Technology and Socialist Feminism in the 1980s' (1985) 80 *Socialist Review*.
Haraway, D, and Gane, N, 'When We Have Never Been Human, What Is to Be Done? An Interview with Donna Haraway' (2006) 23 *Theory, Culture, Society*.
Hardt, SS, 'By Gifts One Makes Slaves: Long-term Effects of Denmark's Colonization of Greenland' (2018) *Bard Ditgital Commons*.
Hermitte, M-A, 'La Nature, sujet de droit ?' (2011) 66 *Annales Histoire, Sciences Sociales*.
Hesselink, M, 'Anything Goes in Private Law Theory? On the Epistemic and Ontological Commitments of Private Law Multi-pluralism' (online paper EUI, 14 January 2022).
Hohfeld, WN, 'Fundamental Legal Conceptions as Applied in Judicial Reasoning' 26 *Yale Law Journal* 710.
Howes, D, 'Response to Tim Ingold' (2022) 27 *Journal of Material Culture* 340–44.
Hyde, WW, 'The Prosecution and Punishment of Animals and Lifeless Things in the Middle Ages and Modern Times' (1916) 64 *University of Pennsylvania Law Review* 696.
Ingold T, *The Temporality of Landscape* (1993) 25 *World Archaeology*.
Ireland, P, 'Financialization and Corporate Governance', Corporate Governance and Globalisation Colloquium, September 2008.
Janis, M, 'Jeremy Bentham and the Fashioning of 'International Law' (2014) 78 *American Journal of International Law* 405–18.
Jansen, N, and Michaels, R, 'Private Law Beyond the State? Europeanization, Globalization, Privatization' (2008) 54 *American Journal of Comparative Law* 843.
Juenger FK, 'Marital Property and the Conflict of Laws: A Tale of Two Countries' (1981) 81 *Columbia Law Review* 1061–79.
Kanter, D et al, 'Gaps and opportunities in nitrogen pollution policies around the world' 3 (11) *Nature Sustainability* 956–63.
Karayanni, M, 'Choice of Law under Occupation: How Israeli Law Came to Serve Palestinian Plaintiffs' (2009) 5 *Journal of Private International Law* 1.
Kaushal, A, 'The Politics of Jurisdiction' (2015) 78 *The Modern Law Review*.
Kegel G, 'The Crisis of Conflict of Laws' (1964) 112 *Collected Courses of the Hague Academy of International Law*.
Kegel G, 'Story and Savigny' (1989) 37 *American Journal of Comparative Law*.
Kennedy, D, 'Form and Substance in Private Law Adjudication' (1976) 89 *Harvard Law Review* 1685–1778.
Kennedy, D, Towards an Historical Understanding of Legal Consciousness: The Case of Classical Legal Thought' (1980) 3 *Res In Law and Society* 3–24.
Kennedy, D, 'Stages of the Decline of the Public/Private Distinction' (1982) 130 *University of Pennsylvania Law Review* 1349.
Kennedy, D, 'A Semiotics of Legal Argument' (1991) 42 *Syracuse Law Review* 75.
Kennedy, D 'The Political Stakes in "Merely Technical" Issues of Contract Law' (2001) 19 *European Review of Private Law* 14, 25.
Kennedy, D 'The Hermeneutic of Suspicion in Contemporary American Legal Thought' (2014) 25 *Law Critique* 91–139.
Kjaer, P, 'Constitutionalizing Connectivity: The Constitutional Grid of World Society' (2018) 45 *Journal of Law and Society*.
Kjaer, P, 'L'idée sociologique de connectivité et le droit international privé' (2019) *Rev crit DIP* 929.
Kleinheisterkamp, J, 'Lord Mustill and the Courts of Tennis – Dallah v Pakistan in England, France and Utopia' (2012) 75 *The Modern Law Review*.
Knop, K, 'Citizenship, Public and Private' 71 *Law and Contemporary Problems* 309–342.

Knop, K and Riles, A, 'Space, Time and Historical Injustice: A Feminist Conflict-of-Laws Approach to the "Comfort Women" Agreement' (2017) 102 *Cornell Law Review* 853.

Koskenniemi, M, 'Lauterpacht: the Victorian Tradition in International Law' (1997) 8 *European Journal of International Law* 215.

Koskenniemi, M, 'Empire and International Law: The Real Spanish Contribution' (2011) 61 *University of Toronto Law Journal*.

Koskenniemi, M, 'Expanding Histories of International Law' (2016) 56 *American Journal of Legal History* 104–12.

Koskenniemi, M, 'Sovereignty, Property and Empire: Early Modern English Contexts' (2017) 18 *Theoretical Inquiries in Law* 355.

Lagarde, P, 'Le Principe de proximité dans le droit international privé contemporain' (1986) 196 *Rec Cours Académie de droit international de La Haye*.

Landes, W and Posner, R, 'Adjudication as a Private Good' (1979) 8 *Journal of Legal Studies* 235.

Latour, B 'Biography of an inquiry: On a book about modes of existence' (2013) 43 *Social Studies of Science*.

Latour, B, 'How to remain human in the wrong space? A comment on a dialogue by Carl Schmitt' (2021) 47 *Critical Inquiry* 699–718.

Latour B and Srum, S, 'Human social origins: Oh please, tell us another story' (1986) 9 *Journal of Social and Biological Structures* 169–87.

Lazar, M, 'Du populisme à gauche: les cas français et italien' (1997) 56 *Vingtième Siècle Revue d'Histoire* 121–31.

Legrand P, 'Sur l'analyse différentielle des juriscultures' (1999) 10 *Revue internationale de droit comparé* 53.

Legrand, P, '*On the Singularity of Law*' (2006) 47 *Harvard International Law Journal* 517–30.

Legrand, P, 'Foreign Law Understanding Understanding' 6(2) *Journal of Comparative Law*.

Legrand, P, 'Negative Comparative Law and its Theses' (2021) 16 *Journal of Comparative Law* 647.

Lehmann, M, 'Liberating the Individual from Battles Between States: Justifying Party Autonomy in Conflict of Laws' 41 *Vanderbilt Journal of Transnational Law* 381, 413 (2008).

Len, L, 'Hermeneutical Injustice, Contract Law and Global Value Chains' (2020) *European Review of Contract Law*.

Levin, DM, 'The Body Politic: Political Economy and the Human Body' (1985) 8 *Human Studies* 235–78.

Lewontin, R, 'It's Even Less in Your Genes', *New York Review of Books*, 26 May 2011.

Lindahl, H, 'Place-Holding the Future: Legal Ordering and Intergenerational Justice for More-Than-Human Collectives' (2021) 10 *Journal of Legal Philosophy* 313–30.

Lippert, J, 'Vulture Funds: The Reason Why Congolese Debt May Force a Revision of the Foreign Sovereign Immunities Act' (2008) 21 *New York International Law Review*.

Lipstein, K, 'Proof of Foreign Law: Scrutiny of its Constitutionality and Validity' (1965) 42 *British Yearbook of International Law* 265.

Lipstein, K, 'Inherent Limitations in Statutes and the Conflict of Laws' (1977) 26 *International & Comparative Law Quarterly* 884.

Lissitzyn, O, 'Territorial Entities Other than Independent States in the Law of Treaties' (1968) 125 *Recueil des Cours de l'Académie de Droit international* (RCADI).

Lorek-Jezińska, E and Więckowska, K, 'Applied Hauntologies: Spectral Crossings and Interdisciplinary Deconstructions' (2017) 8 *AVANT The Journal of the Philosophical-Interdisciplinary Vanguard* 15–23.

Lorenzen, E, 'Huber's *De Conflictu Legum*' (1919) 13 *Illinois Law Review* 375.

Lorenzen, E, 'Story's Commentaries on the Conflict of Laws – One Hundred Years After' (1934–35) 48 *Harvard Law Review* 15.

Ludington, S et al, 'Applied Legal History: Demystifying the Doctrine of Odious Debts' (2010) 11 *Theoretical Inquiries* L 247, 253.

Lynch, T, 'Deep Ecology as an Aesthetic Movement' (1996) 5 *Environmental Values*.

Macfarlane, R, 'The Landscapes Inside Us', *New York Review of Books*, 1 July 2021.

Maier, CS, 'Consigning the Twentieth Century to History: Alternative Narratives for the Modern Era' (2000) 105 *American Historical Review* 807–31.

Manderson, D, 'Modernism, Polarity and the Rule of Law' (2012) 24 *Yale Journal of Law and the Humanities* 475.

Mann, FA, 'The doctrine of jurisdiction in international law' (1964) 111 *Collected Courses of the Hague Academy of International Law*.
Mann, FA, 'The Doctrine of International Jurisdiction Revisited after Twenty Years' (1984) 186 *Collected Courses of the Hague Academy of International Law*.
Marguénaud, JP, 'L'animal sujet de droit ou la modernité d'une vieille idée de René Demogue' (2021) *Revue trimestrielle de droit civil*.
Marshall, V, 'Removing the veil from the "Rights of Nature": The dichotomy between First Nations customary rights and environmental legal personhood' (2019) 452 *Australian Feminist Law Journal* 233–48.
Mattei, U, 'Hard Code Now!' (2002) 2 *Global Jurist Frontiers* Art 1.
Matthews, D, 'From Global To Anthropocenic Assemblages: Re-Thinking Territory, Authority And Rights In The New Climatic Regime' (2019) 82 *The Modern Law Review*.
Maury, J, 'Règles générales des conflits de lois' (1936) 57 *Recueil des Cours de l'Académie de Droit international*.
Mayer, P, 'La neutralisation du pouvoir normatif de l'Etat en matière de contrats d'Etat' (1986) 113 *Journal du Droit International*.
Meijers, E, 'La question du renvoi' (1938) 38 *Bull Inst Int* 191.
Mélice, A, 'Un concept lévi-straussien déconstruit: le "bricolage"' (2009) 5 *Les Temps Modernes*.
Metallic, N, 'Deference and Legal Frameworks Not Designed By, For or With Us', www.administrativelawmatterscom/blog/2018/02/27/deference-and-legal-frameworks-not-designed-by-for-or-with-us-naiomi-metallic/.
Mills, A, 'Renvoi and the Proof of Foreign Law in Australia' (2006) 25 *The Cambridge Law Journal*.
Mills, A, 'The Lifeworlds of Law: On Revitalizing Indigenous Legal Orders Today' (2016) 61 *McGill Law Journal* 847.
Monateri, P-G, 'Black Gaius: A Quest for the Multicultural Origins of the "Western Legal Tradition"' (2000) 51 *Hastings Law Journal* 479.
Moore, JW, 'Madeira, Sugar, and the Conquest of Nature in the "First" Sixteenth Century: Part I: From "Island of Timber" to Sugar Revolution, 1420–1506' (2009) 32 *Review (Fernand Braudel Center)* 345–90.
Moore, JW, 'The Capitalocene, Part I: On the Nature and Origins of Our Ecological Crisis' (2017) 44 *The Journal of Peasant Studies* 594–630.
Morris, J 'The Proper Law of a Tort' (1952) 64 *Harvard Law Review* 881–95.
Muir Watt, H, 'Aspects économiques du droit international privé' (2005) 307 *Recueil des Cours de l'Académie de Droit international*.
Muir Watt, H, 'Dette souveraine et main visible du marché: de nouveaux enjeux du droit international privé des contrats' (2015) *Rev crit droit international privé*.
Muir Watt, H, 'Conflicts of laws unbounded: the case for a legal-pluralist revival' (2016) 7 *Transnational Legal Theory*.
Muir Watt, H, 'Le droit international privé au service de la géopolitique: Les enjeux de la nouvelle Convention de la Haye du 2 juillet 2019 sur la reconnaissance et l'exécution des jugements étrangers en matière civile ou commerciale' (2020) *Rev crit droit international privé* 427.
Naess, A, 'The Shallow and the Deep, Long-Range Ecology Movement' (1973) 16 *Inquiry* 95.
Negri, T, 'Postface to the Complete Text of the Journal Futur Antérieur' *Multitudes*, www.multitudesnet/postface-to-the-complete-text-of/.
Neuhaus, P, 'Savigny und die Rechtsfindung aus der Natur der Sache' (1949/50) IS RabelsZ 364, 366.
Nordstrom, RJ, 'Ohio's Borrowing Statute of Limitations – A Quaking Quagmire in a Dismal Swamp' (1955) 16 *Ohio State Law Journal* 183.
Ogden, T, 'Fear of Breakdown and the Unlived Life' (2014) *International Journal of Psychoanalysis*.
Ogus, A, 'Competition Between National Legal Systems: A Contribution of Economic Analysis To Comparative Law' (2008) 48 *International and Comparative Law Quarterly* 409.
Oppetit, B, Droit et économie (1992) *Archives de philosophie du droit*.
Oppetit, B, 'Le droit international privé, droit savant' (1992) 234 *Recueil des Cours de l'Académie de Droit international*.
Paul, JR, 'The Isolation of Private International Law' (1988) 7 *Wisconsin International Law Journal* 149.
Paul, JR, Comity in International Law (1991) 32 *Harvard International Law Journal* 1.

Pecastaing, S, 'Poe et Baudelaire: pour une hantologie du texte', 2014, https://telarchives-ouvertesfr/tel-00997440.

Pelluchon, C, 'L'éthique des vertus: une condition pour opérer la transition environnementale' (2017) 1 *La pensée écologique,* Les transitions écologiques (dossier).

Phillips, J, 'A Successor to the Moguls: The Nawab of the Carnatic and the East India Company, 1763–1785' (1985) 7 *The International History Review* 364–89.

Picone, P, 'La méthode de la référence à l'ordre juridique compétent en droit international privé' 197 *Recueil des Cours de l'Académie de Droit international.*

Rawson, A, and Mansfield, B, 'Producing juridical knowledge: "Rights of Nature" or the naturalization of rights?' (2018) 1 *Environment and Planning E: Nature and Space* 99–119.

Reed, S and Goodrich, HF, 'Forward Directive or Dialectic?' (1953) 6 *Vanderbilt Law Review* 441.

Reimann, M, 'The Historical School Against Codification: Savigny, Carter and the Defeat of the New York Civil Code' (1989) 37 *American Journal of Comparative Law* 97–98.

Revet, S, 'Les droits du fleuve – Polyphonie autour du fleuve Atrato en Colombie et de ses gardiens' (2020) *Revue européenne d'analyse des sociétés politiques, Sociétés politiques comparées* 52.

Rifkin, M, 'Indigenizing Agamben: Rethinking Sovereignty in Light of the "Peculiar" Status of Native Peoples' (2009) *Cultural Critique.*

Riles, A, 'A New Agenda for the Cultural Study of Law: Taking on the Technicalities' (2005) 53 *Buffalo Law Review* 973.

Riles, A, 'Anthropology, Human Rights and Legal Knowledge: Culture in the Iron Cage' (2006) 108 *American Anthropologist.*

Riles, A, 'Cultural Conflicts' in Knop, K, Michaels, R and Riles, A, 'Transdisciplinary Conflict of Laws' (2008) 71 *Law and Contemporary Problems.*

Rittich, K, and Halley, J, 'Critical Directions in Comparative Family Law: Genealogies and Contemporary Studies of Family Law Exceptionalism' (2010) 58 *American Journal of Comparative Law* 753.

Roosevelt III, K, 'The Myth of Choice of Law: Rethinking Conflicts' (1999) *Faculty Scholarship at Penn Law* 1340.

Ruhl G, 'Party Autonomy in the Private International Law of Contracts: Transatlantic Convergence and Economic Efficiency' (2007) Comparative Research in Law and Political Economy Research Paper No 4/2007.

Ruskola, T, 'Raping Like a State' (2010) 57 *University of California Law Review.*

Samuel, G, 'Comparative Law and Jurisprudence' (1998) 47 *International and Comparative Law Quarterly* 817–36.

Samuel, GH 'Taking Method Seriously' (2007) 2 *Journal of Comparative Law* 94 and 2104.

Samuel, GH, 'Is Law Really a Social Science? A View from Comparative Law' (2008) 67 *Cambridge Law Journal* 288–321.

Schachter, O, 'International Law In Theory And Practice General Course in Public International Law' 178 *Collected Courses of the Hague Academy of International Law.*

Schlag, P, 'The Aesthetics of American Law' 115 *Harvard Law Review* (2002) 1047, 1055.

Schlag, P, 'Normativity and the Politics of Form' (1991) 139 *University of Pennsylvania Law Review* 801.

Scott, C, 'Dialogical Sovereignty: Preliminary Metaphorical Musings' (1992), https://digitalcommonsos goodeyorkuca/all_papers/191.

Scott, C, 'Indigenous Self-Determination and Decolonization of the International Imagination' (1996) 18 *Human Rights Quarterly* 814–20.

Shamir, R, 'Capitalism, Governance and Authority: The Case of Corporate Social Responsibility' (2010) 6 *Annual Review of Law and Social Science.*

Shamir, R, 'The age of responsibilization: On market-embedded morality' 37 (1) *Economy and Society* 1–19.

Sheikh, D, 'Staging repair' (2021) 25 *Law Text Culture* 144–77.

Sieder, R, '"To Speak The Law": Contested Jurisdictions, Legal Legibility and Sovereignty In Guatemala' (2020) 43 *PoLAR – Political and Legal Anthropology Review.*

Simpson, A, 'Subjects of Sovereignty: Indigeneity, The Revenue Rule and Juridics of Failed Consent' (2008) 71 *Law and Contemporary Problems* 191–216.

Slattery, B, 'The Grounds of Human Rights' (2021), https://ssrncom/abstract=3846427 or http://dxdoiorg/102139/ssrn3846427.

Stone, C, 'Should Trees Have Standing?–Towards Legal Rights for Natural Objects' (1972) 45 *Southern California Law Review* 450–501.

Symeonides, S, 'The American Revolution and the European Evolution in Choice of Law: Reciprocal Lessons' (2008) 82 *Tul Law Review* 1741.

Symeonides, S, 'Rome II and Tort Conflicts: A Missed Opportunity' (2008) 56 *American Journal of Comparative Law* 173–222.

Symeonides, S, 'The Choice-of-Law Revolution Fifty Years after Currie: An End and a Beginning' *University of Illinois Law Review,* Issue 2 (2015).

Taylor, A-C 'Pierre Clastres et la dérision du pouvoir chez les Indiens: un commentaire' (2013) *Terrain, Anthropologie et Sciences humaines* 114–21.

Teubner, G, 'Rights of Non-Humans? Electronic Agents and Animals as New Actors in Politics and Law' (2006) 33 *Journal of Law and Society.*

Teubner, G, 'Legal Irritants: Good Faith in British Law' (1998) 61 *Modern Law Review.*

Teubner G, 'Quod Omnes Tangit: Transnational Constitutions without Democracy?', in (2018) 45(1) *Journal of Law and Society* 5–29.

Thomas, Y, 'Les artifices de la vérité en droit commun médiéval' (2005) *L'Homme* 175–76.

Thomas, Y, '*Fictio legis*: L'empire de la fiction romaine et ses limites médiévales' (1995) 21 *Droits* 17.

Torre-Schwab, M, 'La justice rappelle les Etats à leurs obligations' (2021) 567 *La Recherche.*

Twining, W, 'Diffusion and Globalization Discourse' (2006) 47 *Harvard International Law Journal.*

Tusseau, G, 'Le Conseil constitutionnel et le 'délit de solidarité' (2019) 1 *Revue critique de droit international privé.*

Valverde, M, 'The Crown in a Multicultural Age: The Changing Epistemology of (Post)colonial Sovereignty' (2012) 21 *Social Legal Studies.*

Vanuxem, S, 'Du droit de déambuler Le paysage comme lieu de passages' (2021) 19 *Les Cahiers de l'Ecole de Blois* 10–19.

Véronique, D, 'Créole, créoles français et théories de la créolisation' (2000) 85 *L'information grammaticale.*

Viveiros de Castro, E, 'Exchanging Perspectives: The Transformation of Objects into Subjects in Amerindian ontologies' 10(3) *Common Knowledge.*

Viveiros de Castro, E, 'The Relative Native: Essays on Indigenous Conceptual Worlds' (2015) 3 *HAU: Journal of Ethnographic Theory.* Translation of M Holbraad, 'O nativo relativo' 8 (1) *Mana* 113–48.

von Mehren, AT, 'Choice of Law and the Problem of Justice' (1977) 41 *Law and Contemporary Problems.*

Wai, R, 'Transnational Liftoff and Juridical Touchdown: The Regulatory Function of Private International Law in an Era of Globalization' (2002) 40 *Columbia Journal of Transnational Law* 209.

Wai, R 'The Interlegality of Transnational Private Law' (2008) 71 *Law And Contemporary Problems* 107.

Watson, A, 'The Importance of Nutshells' (1994) 42 *American Journal of Comparative Law* 3.

Wengler, W, 'Die Vorfrage im Kollisionsrecht' (1934) 8 *RabelsZ* 149.

Wengrow, D and Appiah, KA, 'The Roots of Inequality: An Exchange' *New York Review of Books* 13 January 2022.

Wildcat M, and De Leon, J, 'Creative Sovereignty: The In-Between Space: Indigenous Sovereignties in Creative and Comparative Perspective' (2021) 19 *Borderlands Journal* 1–28.

Wilson, JD, 'Baldus de Ubaldis' (1902) 12 *Yale Law Journal.*

Winnicott, D, 'Fear of Breakdown' (1974) l *International Review of Psycho-Analysis* l03.

Xifaras, M, 'The Global Turn in Legal Theory' (2016) XXIX *Canadian Journal of Law and Jurisprudence* 215–43.

Yntema, H, 'The Comity Doctrine' (1966) 65 *Michigan Law Review* 9.

Zalamea, P, 'En diálogo con un mundo antiguo: las pinturas de las casas coloniales de Tunja en el marco de un Renacimiento global' (2019) 36 *Revista Historia y Sociedad.*

Zeno-Zencovich, V, 'The Mediterranean and Legal Pluralism' (2021) 12 *Comparative Law Review.*

Zimmermann, 'L'héritage de Savigny Histoire du droit, droit comparé, et émergence d'une science juridique européenne' (2013) XXVI *Revue internationale de droit économique.*

CASE NOTES

(1939) *Revue critique de Droit international privé* 472, note Niboyet.
(1939) S, 1942173, note Niboyet.
(1948) II JCP 4422, note Lerebours-Pigeonière.
(1949) *Revue critique de Droit international privé* 89, note Batiffol.
(1955) *Revue critique de Droit international privé* 723, note Batiffol.
(1995) *Revue critique de Droit international privé* 308, note Lequette.

REPORTS, COLLOQUIA, LECTURES, EXHIBITIONS, OBITUARIES

Colomonos, A, 'The aesthetics of knowledge' Seminar Recitals, Sciences po Paris, 6 October 2022.

Descola, P, *Le Monde*, idees, 3 November 2022, www.lemonde.fr/idees/article/2022/11/03/a-bruno-latour-ta-pensee-audacieuse-est-devenue-la-pensee-du-temps-present_6148386_3232.html.

Forray, V, 'Le nouveau droit naturel' Faculty Seminar, Sciences po, October 2021 (on file with author).

Humphreys, 'Against Future Generations' Colloquium on Planetary Responsibility, December 2021, LSE/Sci po.

Janda, R, Globinar, Paris, May 2022.

Kisukidi, NY, 'Décoloniser l'universel' *La vie des idées*, Collège de France 2 May 2019, https://laviedesideesfr/Decoloniser-l-universelhtml.

Kundnani, A, https://www.kundnaniorg/what-is-racial-capitalism/.

Latour, B, 'On some of the Affects of Capitalism', Lecture given at the Royal Academy, Copenhagen, 26 February 2014.

Martinez, J-L, ('Paris-Athènes Naissance de la Grèce moderne (1675–1919)', Le Louvre Paris, exhibition, October 2021.

Monateri, P-G, Globinar, Sciencespo, Autumn 2021, noting the structural similarity between the belief in autonomous markets and *Dominus mundi*.

Pottage, A, Globinar, Sciences po, May 2022.

Report of the EU Parliament, www.europarleuropaeu/RegData/etudes/BRIE/2018/625116/EPRS_BRI(2018)625116_ENpdf.

Vanuxem, S, 'Du droit de déambuler Repenser la liberté d'aller et venir à l'âge de l'anthropocène' Conference, Sciences po, Faculty Seminar, Spring 2022.

Index

The references below are to page numbers. Footnotes figure explicitly cited for case citations only. Proper names (without initials) are in italics (please refer to the bibliography for the full references). Terms consubstantially related to the topic of the book are indicated as *passim*.

www.ingramcontent.com/pod-product-compliance
Ingram Content Group UK Ltd.
Pitfield, Milton Keynes, MK11 3LW, UK
UKHW020219041026
15470UKWH00012B/544

9 781509 940103